Borneo

Sabah • Brunei • Sarawak

the Bradt Travel Guide

Tamara Thiessen

www.bradtguides.com

Bradt Trave
The Globe P

edition
2

BRUNEI

Sabah

MALAYSIA

Sarawak

INDONESIA

N

Bradt

SOUTH CHINA

SEA

Gunung Kinabalu National Park: this ancient, sacred park is home to Mount Kinabalu, the island's highest peak at 4,095m
page 192

Bandar Seri Begawan: exotic Islamic traditions intermingle with impressive modern architecture and spicy food in Brunei's capital
page 137

Niah Caves: once occupied by prehistoric hunter-gatherers, these UNESCO-classified caves are archaeological treasure chests
page 293

Bako National Park: this spellbinding, diverse national park contains 16 well-marked trails — perfect for spotting the proboscis monkey
page 267

Semenggoh Nature Reserve: an ideal day trip from Kuching, the Semenggoh wildlife rehabilitation centre is home to semi-wild orang-utans
page 272

Miri

Lambir Hills National Park

Maruc

Niah Caves

Niah National Park

Bintulu

MALAYSIA

Long Lan

Mukah

Belaga

Selangu

Sarawak

Sibu

K Rajang

Sarikei

Kapit

Santubong

Bako National Park

KUCHING

Semenggoh Nature Reserve

Bandar Sri Aman

INDONESIA

0 50km
0 50 miles

SOUTH CHINA SEA

P Layang-Layang

P Banggi

Limbuak

P Malawali

Kudat

P Jambongan

Jambongan

Mt Kinabalu
4095m

Gunung Kinabalu
National Park

Teluk Labuk

P Kanawi

Tunku Abdul
Rahman Park

KOTA KINABALU

Ranau

Sandakan

P Tiga Park

Tambunan

Crocker Range
National Park

Sabah

Beaufort

LABUAN

Keningau

Maliau
Basin

Victoria

Lahat Datu

BANDAR SERI
BEGAWAN

Tenom

Danum
Valley

P Sakar

P Tabawan

Lawas

P Timbun Mata

Limbang

Ilu Temburong
National Park

Long
Pa Sia

P Gaya

UNEI

Tawau

Semporna

Long
Semado

G Murud
2423m

P Sipadan

P Sebatik

ng Mulu
nal Park
2377m

Long
Seridan

Bareo

Danum Valley: flying frogs, pygmy elephants and over 340 species bring the wildlife-rich rainforests of the Danum Valley alive
page 239

Maliau Basin: for a true wilderness experience, intrepid explorers can endure tents, rugged terrains and loads of leeches in Borneo's 'lost world'
page 231

Coral Triangle: immerse in Sabah's marine paradise with a day dive at Sipadan or resort stay on Mabul or Kapalai islands
page 234

Ulu Temburong National Park: longboats carry passengers through wide bays and tangled mangrove forests to reach the 'green jewel' of Brunei
page 154

CELEBES SEA

BORNEO

Gunung Mulu National Park: a northern Sarawak wonder world of rainforests, limestone caves and exotic tropical bugs, from birdwing butterflies to leaf insects
page 302

KEY

■ Capital city
● Main town
○ Other town
✈ Airport
✈ Airstrip
— Road
—·— International boundary
----- National park/reserve

Borneo Don't miss...

Discover pristine coral reefs
Large fan corals are a common sight on the reefs at Sipadan Island, eastern Sabah
(SB) page 44

Explore Brunei's capital – Bandar Seri Begawan
The night market is an exciting place to try local cuisine at a fraction of the price of the restaurants
(HL/A) page 137

Take to the trees on a canopy walk for a birds' eye view of your surroundings
Here the canopy walkway in the Danum Valley
(SB) page 239

Visit the Sepilok Orang-utan Sanctuary
An orang-utan-viewing hotspot in Sabah
(CM/FLPA) page 220

Climb amidst the limestone pinnacles of Gunung Mulu National Park, Sarawak
Trekking, caving and longboat safaris are all options in this national park
(RD/TIPS) page 302

left   Sarawak State Legislative
        Assembly building, Kuching
        (DA) page 243

below   Sandakan, a city on stilts, is
        Sabah's second-largest town
        (GAR/TIPS) page 211

bottom The Sultan Omar Ali Saifuddien
        Mosque in Bandar Seri Begawan
        was built in 1958
        (TT) page 150

right An unusual sculpture adorns a traffic island in central Kota Kinabalu, Sabah (DA) page 163

below Fresh Malay food served at the Gadong *pasar malam* (night market) in Bandar Seri Begawan (TT) page 147

middle Detail from the Tua Pek Kong Temple in Lundu, Sarawak (DA) page 271

bottom A river float parade on the Sarawak River in Kuching (DA) page 243

above   A stall on Kuching's waterfront selling typical fruit-flavoured drinks (TT) page 259

left   Kek Lapis Sarawak is a traditional layer cake, colourful with intricate patterns (DA) page 107

below   Kuching Sunday Market on Jalan Satok (TT) page 257

AUTHOR

Tamara Thiessen is a freelance journalist and photographer from Australia, working on newspapers, magazines, guidebooks and illustrated book titles on four continents. After two decades working in news, current affairs and programme production for the Australian Broadcasting Corporation, SBS World News, Deutsche Welle Radio and European Parliament Radio Reports, she now spends most of her time travelling and writing about foreign places, lifestyle and culture. As a France-based correspondent, she has written for

newspapers including the *Toronto Globe & Mail*, *Montreal Gazette*, *Sydney Morning Herald*, *Melbourne Age*, *Sunday Business Post* (Ireland), *South China Morning Post* and *Singapore Straits Times*. Amid constant globetrotting, her travel-inspired reports and photographs have been published in many magazines, including *National Geographic Traveller* (UK), *Business Traveller*, *Condé Nast Traveller*, *Islands Magazine*, *Monocole*, *Sport Diver*, *Hotel News Now*, and the in-flight publications of Qantas, US Airways, Delta Airlines, Air Emirates, SN Brussels, Jet Star, easyJet, LAN Airlines and Air Jordan. A contributing writer and photographer to the Eyewitness Travel Guides to Australia, France and Italy, and *Style City Europe*, she is author and photographer of *Café Life Sydney*, *Café Life Vienna* (due in late 2012) and *Museyon Guides Chronicles of Rome* (2012). Tamara has fully updated and re-edited this second edition of her guidebook.

AUTHOR'S STORY

I was born in Tasmania, so remote and wild islands are an intrinsic part of my genetic make-up. Drawn inexorably to isolated places and the searing sense of other-worldliness they often bring, in the mid-1990s my childhood dreams of Borneo – fanned by forays into *National Geographic* magazine – were rekindled.

Asking a native Malaysian about beautiful places to visit in his country, he sketched Sabah and Sarawak on a paper napkin, and told me how extraordinary but threatened Borneo's rainforests and animals were. Clutching that scrap of paper, the desire to visit Borneo simmered away for another couple of years. When I got there, the island was just as it had been described – a place of unforgettable wildlife and people, facing a serious challenge to its environment.

One of the most unbearable, heart-rending tragedies of the world today, I believe, is the irreversible destruction of the beauty and uniqueness of places like Borneo. Whilst some changes to the natural environment and traditional ways of life may be inevitable, even necessary, others certainly are not. As West Malaysia is consumed by a speedy, hyper-modern lifestyle, Borneo's singularity – its natural beauty, cultural richness and traditional village lifestyles – stands out even more. Those lucky enough to visit the island, whether travelling from London, New York or Sydney, will hopefully be inspired to help protect this extraordinary island of forested fantasies.

PUBLISHER'S FOREWORD   *Hilary Bradt*

The first Bradt travel guide was written in 1974 by George and Hilary Bradt on a river barge floating down a tributary of the Amazon. It was followed by *Backpacker's Africa*, published in 1979. In the 1980s and '90s, the focus shifted away from hiking to broader-based guides to new destinations – usually the first to be published on those places. In the 21st century, Bradt continues to publish these ground-breaking guides, along with guides to established holiday destinations, incorporating in-depth information on culture and natural history alongside the nuts and bolts of where to stay and what to see.

Bradt authors support responsible travel, with advice not only on minimum impact but also on how to give something back through local charities. Thus a true synergy is achieved between the traveller and local communities.

Second edition published May 2012   First published 2008

Bradt Travel Guides Ltd, IDC House, The Vale, Chalfont St Peter, Bucks SL9 9RZ, England   www.bradtguides.com
Published in the USA by The Globe Pequot Press Inc, PO Box 480, Guilford, Connecticut 06437-0480

Text copyright © 2012 Tamara
Maps copyright © 2012 Bradt Travel Guides Ltd
Photographs copyright © 201   Individual photographers (see below)
Contributing editor to 2008 e   Tamara Moses
Project Managers: Elspeth Be   Anna Moores

The author and publisher hav   the accuracy of the information   this book at the time of going to p   accept any responsibility for any l , injury or inconvenience resulting fr   in this guide. All rig   rved.
No part of this publication m   mitted   any form or by any means, electr   otherwise without   the prior consent of the publishe   to Bradt Travel uides Ltd in the UK or to the Glob   quot Press Inc in North and South America.

ISBN: 978 1 84162 390 0
British Library Cataloguing in Publication Data
A catalogue record for this book is available from the British Library

Acknowledgements

My immeasurable appreciation goes to Tourism Malaysia, and the Sabah and Sarawak tourism boards for their assistance with travels to and in Malaysia; to local tour operators, particularly Borneo Eco Tours and TYK Adventure Tours in Sabah, and Sarawak-based Borneo Adventure, for their generous on-the-ground support, fantastic guides and local knowledge; and to the innumerable hotels, resorts and guesthouses who offered me Bornean hospitality par excellence during my travels.

Alongside the local cultural organisations who assisted me with information, I would like to express my utmost gratitude to the several notable Borneo experts who freely gave of their time and knowledge to make invaluable contributions to the guidebook: archaeologist Peter Bellwood for clarifying the complex and sometimes very confusing Bornean prehistory; Dr Glen Reynolds and Sir Peter Crane for their insights into Borneo's natural history and conservation; anthropologist Victor King; archaeologist Huw Barton; and Heidi Munan for her insights into Sarawak craft.

I would also like to thank the Commissioning Editor at Bradt, Rachel Fielding, for her invaluable co-operation in bringing together this edition as well as Project Editor, Elspeth Beidas, Managing Editor, Anna Moores and copy editor, Jen Haddington. Finally, thanks to everyone I have encountered on my travels in Malaysian Borneo and Brunei; to the people of the island whose culture, spirit and warmth – along with the heavenly natural world – make it the most memorable place in my arguably short, but highly privileged, history of world travels.

Contents

LIST OF MAPS

UPDATES WEBSITE AND FEEDBACK REQUEST

If you have any comments, queries, grumbles, insights, news or other feedback please contact us on ✆ 01753 893444 or ✉ info@bradtguides.com. We will forward your comments to the author who may include updates in a 'one-off update' on the Bradt website at www.bradtguides.com/guidebook-updates.html.

Introduction

Borneo – the very name conjures up an image of sultry island mystery, maritime escapade and swampy, steamy jungle adventure. Situated at the junction of four seas in the heart of southeast Asia, its history is one of fierce headhunters and pirates, long-haul migrations and seafaring invasions. The name 'Borneo' ostensibly comes from a European transformation of Bruni, a once-powerful Muslim trading post on the west coast of the island, known today as Brunei.

The third-biggest island in the world after Greenland and New Guinea, Borneo is home to three nations: Brunei, Malaysia and Indonesia. Throughout its rich and colourful history, the island has been regarded as remote and mysterious – an aura fuelled over time by talk of pirate-ridden seas, savage natives, inhospitable landscapes and turbulent politics. Even today, it takes at least an extra two hours to reach Borneo from West Malaysia. Far from a turn-off, that remoteness, along with its rich tribal vestiges and exotic flora and fauna, is making Borneo a prime destination for those seeking cultural and natural authenticity

With over 200 indigenous tribes and large Chinese and Malay populations, Borneo represents a fascinating chapter in the world's ethnographic history. The two Malaysian states of Sabah and Sarawak, and the self-ruled Sultanate of Brunei – the areas this guide covers – each have their own stories to tell, but are inextricably linked to each other by history. All three came under British influence at some stage, which has left lasting impressions, and were the site for significant human migrations.

Borneo's natural wonders are undoubtedly its greatest and most famous asset. As a 'biodiversity hotspot', its variety and richness of life is unparalleled. Just 10ha of Bornean rainforest can support 700 species of tree – as many as are found across the whole of North America! The island is home to as many bird species as Europe and as many mammals as Australia, including Asia's only great ape, the orang-utan. Over 5,000 of Borneo's plant species are not found anywhere else in the world, and 500 animal species are unique to the island.

Like many paradises, however, the very thing that makes Borneo so unique is under threat. The island's bountiful natural endowment and traditional cultures have been seriously eroded over the last half-century, with up to half of its tropical forests lost, and much of its extraordinary flora and fauna pushed towards extinction.

The urgency for conservation has not waned over the past three decades. Local organisations, international scientists, media and tourists have all helped to turn up the heat on the threats to Borneo's forests, assisting natives who have long been fighting to save their island. As the world slowly awakes to the consequences of environmental destruction, and the conservation of tropical forests and biodiversity become increasingly prominent on the world's agenda, hopefully Borneo's remaining natural treasures will be preserved for future generations.

Part One

GENERAL INFORMATION

I

Background Information

GEOGRAPHY

Straddling the Equator between 4–7°N and 4°S, Borneo is three times the size of Great Britain – a total of 743,294km². Sabah, Sarawak and Brunei between them account for less than a quarter of the island, with the Indonesian region of Kalimantan occupying the rest (NB Indonesian Borneo is not covered in this guide).

Surrounded by several straits and four oceans, Borneo is a generous blob among dozens of island spots and specks in the humid, tropical zone of southeast Asia. The South China Sea lies to the northwest, the Sulu Sea to the north, the Celebes Sea to the east and the Java Sea to the south. The island is located east of Semananjung Malaysia – Peninsular Malaysia – where the Malaysian capital Kuala Lumpur is situated; the two Malaysian states on Borneo – Sarawak and Sabah – are often referred to as 'East Malaysia'.

The shape of Borneo resembles that of a dog: its ears point upwards towards the Philippines; a paw extends across the Makassar Strait to Sulawesi; the tail juts westward towards Singapore and feet dip down towards Jakarta. Often considered to be extremely mountainous, over half of Borneo is actually covered by swampy, waterlogged coastal areas of less than 150m elevation. Only 5% of the island lies above 3,000m (approximately 9,000ft) and most mountain peaks are around 2,000m (approximately 6,000ft). Many of these lie near Borneo's rooftop, Gunung (Mount) Kinabalu, the 4,095m mountain in the northwestern tip of Sabah. The tallest peak in southeast Asia between the Himalayas and Papua New Guinea, Mount Kinabalu towers high over Sabah. The presence of this colossal granite eruption qualifies Borneo as the 'sixth-highest island in the world'.

MALAYSIAN BORNEO Malaysian Borneo is composed of two states: Sabah and Sarawak.

Sabah Sabah occupies the northern chunk of Borneo, forming the head of the 'dog'. Many rivers spring from Sabah's mountainous interior, and the surrounding hills are criss-crossed by an extensive network of river valleys. Nearer the coastal plains are lower-lying swampy hills. Sabah's chant *'negeri di bawah bayu'* ('land below the wind') comes from its location – just south of the typhoon belt that occasionally blights the Philippines, in the equatorial doldrums.

Sarawak Sarawak is a land of rivers. Rivers narrow and wide run through the countryside and cities in an incredible navigable network of 3,300km. The state's 55 rivers provide a vital link between the coast and remote interior, and are still the only means of transport to some places today.

3

BRUNEI A small enclave of a nation squashed between Sabah and Sarawak's frontiers, the 5,765km² of Brunei account for less than 1% of the total land area of Borneo. A mini-Borneo even within such physical constraints, it combines wide coastal plains of mangrove, *nipa* and peat swamp, rainforest and hilly terrains. In comparison with the 720km and 1,600km coastlines of Sarawak and Sabah respectively, Brunei extends just 161km along the South China Sea (the Laut China Selatan).

POPULATION DENSITY AND DISTRIBUTION Northern Borneo is very sparsely populated by Asian standards, with on average 17 people per square kilometre, compared with 74 on Peninsular Malaysia. A third of the island's 16 million people live in Sabah, Sarawak and Brunei. Historically, the population was divided between coastal and inland dwellers – most early human settlements were concentrated along the coast and on riverbanks. Until the late 19th century, the hinterland was relatively uninhabited, whilst the coast and floodplains of major rivers were densely populated. Though these patterns still exist today, the distinction has faded with soaring urbanisation. In the mid-1970s, about 15% of Sarawak's population lived in towns and cities – today that figure is 50% and rising. Much the same can be said for Sabah, where today about half of the population live in urban areas, compared with 20% in 1970. This rapid evolution is having major repercussions on the environment, through urban waste problems and coastal and river pollution.

CLIMATE

The climate of Borneo is equatorial-tropical, and distinguished by marked wet and dry seasons: the wet season (or 'northeast monsoon') generally runs from November to March, the dry season (or 'southwest monsoon') from May to October. Official start and end points vary though, and there is a variable period of transition between seasons. In the wet season, there is usually some rainfall every day and there can also be violent storms, monsoon winds, flooding, landslides and torrential rains.

Half of the annual rainfall on Sarawak's greater west coast falls between December and March, and the hilly slopes of the Kelabit Highlands (inland Sarawak) receive the highest annual rainfall – more than 5,000mm. The wettest months tend to be January and February, which are then directly followed by the driest – March and April.

In Sarawak, which is closest to the Equator, there is little variation in day length throughout the year. There is only a seven-minute difference between the shortest and longest days.

The sun rises and sets at around the same time every day between 06.00 and 18.00. Sunshine is bountiful, but a typical day will usually have some cloudy periods as well. The climatic exception is Mount Kinabalu, which has varying alpine microclimates, and can be quite chilly at the top.

Also see page 69 in *Practical information* for more information on when to visit.

BORNEO'S CLIMATE AT A GLANCE

Temperature Lowlands 23–33°C; Highlands 13–27°C. Steady throughout the year, varying by less than 2°C

Humidity 75–85% – can be uncomfortable; rainforest average 80%, up to 100% at night

Annual rainfall 2,500–4,000mm, usually 150mm minimum in most months

HISTORY

The following sections are a brief summary of the island's history. For more information see the titles listed in *Further information, Appendix 2*, page 315.

RAINFOREST TREASURES – EARLY TRADE WITH INDIA AND CHINA There is evidence to suggest that India was trading with southeast Asia from as early as 290BC, with Chinese traders joining the continental market around AD1000. During this period of internationalisation, Borneo's tribes were gradually drawn into networks of trade in spices, camphor, precious woods and other exotic forest products.

The 11th to 13th centuries saw an explosion of trade between China and the Indo-Malaysian archipelago in forest products, metals, gemstones and spices. A whole gamut of exotic export products came from the Bornean rainforests: beeswax for ointments, aromatic woods for incense, rubber, resin and rattan.

Some of the Chinese merchants settled in Borneo's ports. Excavations in the Sarawak River delta (south of Kuching) show evidence of a sizeable Chinese settlement, dated to the 10th–13th centuries. Other excavations in Brunei and Sabah suggest the Chinese were trading ceramics for spices even earlier than this.

Borneo polities remained independent of each other until recent times, but important Islamic sultanates were established from the 14th and 15th centuries onwards in Brunei and the Sulu Archipelago (southern Philippines). The Hindu and Buddhist kingdoms of western Indonesia during the first millennium had little influence in Malaysian Borneo.

MALAY CULTURE AND EARLY EMPIRES Malay culture was embedded into Borneo from the 7th to 13th centuries, propagated by trading empires. During this period, the maritime empire of Srivijaya ruled supreme, controlling international sea trade across the Malay Archipelago. Originating in Sumatra, the influence extended through Borneo, with many Sumatran Malays said to have settled on the island during this time.

In the 14th century, Srivijaya ceded to the Java-based Hindu empire Majapahit. Borneo absorbed some Hindu influences, traces of which remain today. The Majapahit Empire started to topple at the end of the 15th century.

ENTER ISLAM It was around this time that Islam got a foothold in Borneo, though its presence had been felt since the 13th century. Muslim trading states had become established in Sumatra, Java, Malacca and the Moluccas (the spice islands of Ternate and Tidore).

Malay language and culture, and Islam, proceeded to flourish along the coasts of what are today Sabah and Sarawak, as vessels from Malaya and Sumatra anchored in port. Traders, teachers and missionaries all played a hand in the implantation of Islamic culture and civilisation in the region. Islam spread to Brunei under the influence of trade, and the sultanate came to act as a centre of Islamisation for other parts of Borneo. Smaller Muslim-Malay states gradually emerged all over the island during the 17th century, some converting purely for strategic and mercenary reasons, as they had done earlier to Hinduism and Buddhism. The Sultanate of Brunei ruled over much of northern Borneo until the 19th century, through some significant territorial tugs of war.

Throughout this period, Borneo's economic influence was still marginal on a regional scale. The southern Philippines area of the Sulu Islands emerged as a powerful late 18th-century sultanate, and attempted to wrench parts of northern Borneo under its control. The Sultan of Brunei is said to have failed to honour an agreement to cede Sabah to Sulu, and the effects of these chronic territorial tensions are still felt today.

WHITE RAJAHS AND RANEES – EUROPEANS IN BORNEO The Portuguese were the first Europeans to set foot in Borneo, and the Spanish attacked Brunei in 1578, briefly occupying the port. However, no external power gained total control over the country, despite continual tugs of war. Instead it was the Sultanate of Brunei that ruled over much of what is today Sabah and Sarawak for over two centuries, through a court of noble envoys, *raja* (princes) and locally appointed Malay chiefs.

However, the sultans' methods were met with resistance. Under the weight of rebellion and piracy, Brunei's control over the region waned and colonial forces expanded to fill the vacuum created by the receding empire. The British saw power in Borneo as a way of protecting British shipping routes to China, and got a footing in northern Borneo through a series of naval coups to protect the weakened sultanate. From the mid 19th century, Borneo was carved up territorially between European powers: the British in the north, and the Dutch in the south. Despite having a reputation as being a haunt for pirates, home to headhunters and rife with tropical diseases, competition was fierce for the last piece of available land in the area – what is today Sabah.

The foundations of Sabah

Sabah at that stage did not exist – it fell within the Sultan of Brunei's territories. However, the sinking sultanate was forced to hand over several parts of its empire that it could no longer control, and in the mid-1860s a ten-year lease of Sabah was agreed with the American consul to Brunei, Claude Lee Moses. Sadly he did nothing more than run off to Hong Kong with the cession fees! British trading arrangements had far more lasting repercussions.

The birth of the BNBC

In 1875, Gustavus Baron Von Overbeck, the Austrian consul in Hong Kong, won the deeds to the American Trading Company. Austria wasn't interested in a colonial acquisition and Overbeck turned to a London-based merchants' firm run by Alfred Dent. Backed by Dent's money, they gained leases from the Sultan of Brunei for some 50,000km² of northern Borneo territory. A deal with the Sultan of Sulu won them another chunk of land, and the foundations of the British North Borneo Company (BNBC) were laid. Overbeck sold out to Dent and the company was officially baptised with a Royal Charter in 1881.

The BNBC had the freedom to administer as it saw fit, but heavy taxes on everything from rice to boats and birds' nests evoked resentment and resistance from Sabahans. However, none were successful (despite some credible efforts), and the BNBC administered the region of British North Borneo – known today as Sabah – until it became a British protectorate in 1888.

Meanwhile, in Sarawak...

Brunei's need to seek outside support for protection was also the key to the beginning of a decisive era in Sarawak's history. In 1839, James Brooke – a Bengal-born, former British army officer and gentleman adventurer – sailed up the Sarawak River on his schooner *The Royalist*.

Here he encountered Raja Muda Hassim, a consort of the sultan who was sent to suppress an uprising of exploited Malay and Dayak against the sultanate. The coastal and river dwellers had been hit with taxes, their men forced into working in the antimony mines, their women and children into slavery. With the situation spiralling out of Brunei's control, the junior prince begged Brooke to help him regain order. He was rewarded with land and the title of *rajah* – ruler – of Sarawak in 1841. Thus began a somewhat unlikely chapter in Sarawak's history, which was to leave a lasting impression. For nearly a century, three generations of the Brooke family – hailed as the 'White Rajahs' – reigned over the state.

The Brooke empire spreads The Sultan of Brunei grew to be reliant on the British, and on Brooke, to help protect his sultanate. Brooke successfully suppressed the pirates who frequently wreaked havoc in coastal and river areas, enabling him to secure more land under his control as he worked his way up the coast. Some pirate-quashing missions were excessively brutal, sparking disapproval from Britain and even resulting in a commission of inquiry, though he was later acquitted. The Anglo–Brunei Treaty, signed in 1848, guaranteed British control of trade along the northwest coast, free trade and access to Brunei ports. It also prevented the sultan ceding territory to any other nation without British consent – giving the British a tight grip on authority in the region.

And spreads... From its origins as a small riverside settlement, by the 1890s the White Raj had expanded through much of Sarawak, devouring territories from Kuching south to the Indonesian border and all the way north to Limbang. Even the BNBC ceded land to the Brookes. A lot of this expansion was driven by James Brooke's nephew, Charles, who succeeded him in 1868. As well as significantly extending the territory, no-nonsense Charles formed the Council Negari (State Council), boosted the economy and straightened out unruly tribes.

Charles Brooke was in turn succeeded by his son, Charles Vyner Brooke in 1917. Unlike family members before him, Vyner Brooke felt the Brooke dominion in Sarawak was something of an anachronism and chose to work in co-operation with a Supreme Council, diminishing the family's autocratic power. This decision was bitterly resented by the next in line, Anthony Brooke, who saw inheritance of his uncle's legacy as his birthright. Anthony stormed off to Singapore. The Brooke dynasty continued in Sarawak for over a century, until Japanese invasion on Christmas Day 1941.

THE LAST GENERATION

In the *Daily Telegraph*, in June 2007, author Philip Eade wrote of the third *rajah*, Charles Vyner Brooke: 'Vyner's career was encapsulated in one of the more impressive entries in *Who's Who*: "Has led several expeditions into the far interior [of Borneo] to punish headhunters; understands the management of natives; rules over a population of 500,000 souls and a country 40,000 square miles in extent."'

For better and for worse, the European presence had a major impact on tribal and Malay societies in Borneo. Most historians agree that the biggest effect of colonial rule was the eradication of headhunting, bloody inter-tribal feuding, piracy and slavery. Over the first half of the 20th century, British rulers in Sabah and Sarawak promoted economic development, improved public welfare, and introduced infrastructure, bringing transport, health care, education and industry. Government and society were transformed, with Western taxation and law systems and territorial borders established.

WORLD WAR II IN BORNEO The Japanese invaded Borneo on Christmas Day 1941, and occupied several areas of Sabah and Sarawak until liberation by Australian forces in 1945. Hundreds of British, Australian, Chinese and other Allied troops died a brutal death at the hands of the invaders. According to the Sandakan Memorial Park, 'The POWs under the Japanese suffered appalling living conditions, hard labour and death.'

Rebellion against the Japanese, led by the Chinese, showed some initial success, but the Japanese won with brute strength – guerrillas on the ground were no match for Japanese bombs. Headhunting was quickly resumed during the occupation. Some 1,500 Japanese heads were collected, *paranged* (a *parang* is a steel sword) with glee – prized by the Dayaks (natives) for being 'nice round heads with good hair and gold teeth'. Though the Brooke regime had actively extinguished this barbaric tradition, it was actually encouraged by Tom Harrisson (future curator of the Sarawak Museum) who famously parachuted into the jungle and recruited 1,000 Kelabit tribesmen to fiercely attack the Japanese.

There are many recorded instances of bravery and humanity towards the Allied troops by Sabah's and Sarawak's indigenous populations. They built shelter for escapees, provided them with medical supplies and helped them across enemy lines.

The aftermath of war The towns and economies of northern Borneo were badly hit by the war, as was the tenability of both Chartered Company rule in North Borneo and Brooke administration in Sarawak. The BNBC did not have the resources to rebuild after the devastation of the war, which had levelled Sandakan and Jesselton (now Kota Kinabalu). It sold its assets to the British government and in 1946 the British Protectorate of North Borneo became a Crown Colony. Political parties sprang up, squabbled, then joined forces, resulting in the Sabah Alliance. Sabah actually became an independent country for 16 days before joining the Federation of Malaysia.

When the Japanese surrendered, Sarawak was placed under Australian military administration and Charles Vyner and Sylvia Brooke took exile in Australia. In return for a large pension, claimed one account, he retired to England. In 1946, upon his urging, the State Council voted to cede Sarawak to Britain and the old Raj became a British Crown Colony, remaining so until the formation of Malaysia in September 1963.

MERDEKA! Malaysia had gained independence from Britain in 1957. Tunku Abdul Rahman, the prime minister of the freshly independent federation of Malayan states, was pushing for a wider alliance – to include Sarawak, North Borneo, Singapore and Brunei. Though Brunei snubbed the federation, the others signed up for the expanded federation in 1963, allowing Sabah and Sarawak their rightful *merdeka* (independence) from foreign rule. Singapore subsequently quit the federation in 1965, but the others remained.

Brunei's decision to opt out of the federation meant that not only was it the only Muslim dynasty to re-establish itself after independence, it was also the only one to remain a British protectorate in the post-war years and not become a British Crown Colony. Brunei turned to partial self-rule from 1959 until 1984, when it regained its independence and returned to sovereign rule.

GOVERNMENT AND POLITICS

SABAH AND SARAWAK Sabah and Sarawak are among the 13 states which, together with three federal territories (the capital Kuala Lumpur, Labuan Island and Putrajaya), make up the Federation of Malaysia. Malaysia is a constitutional

THE FALL OF AN EMPIRE

In his book *Sylvia, Queen of the Headhunters: An Outrageous Englishwoman and Her Lost Kingdom* Philip Eade attributes the downfall of the Brooke dynasty in part to Ranee Sylvia, Vyner Brooke's wife. 'She did nothing to dispel the impression that Sarawak was populated by headhunters and lotus eaters, and saw to it that her position as Ranee remained enshrouded in myth. Her peculiar status and activities were endlessly celebrated by the press, but the Colonial Office had long regarded her as "a dangerous woman".'

Drawing in part on Sylvia Brooke's autobiography written in the 1940s, Eade's book is full of fascinating insights into some of the real machinations of the Brooke–Borneo people's relationship, including their last night spent in a longhouse among rows of smoked Japanese heads, and their departure, when the Ranee wrote: 'hundreds of little boats lined the river banks, and behind the boats the crowds were so dense they looked like a forest of dazzling flowers with their golden sarongs and little coloured coats... I would have felt further from tears if some of them had denounced us and called down curses on our heads instead of invoking this gracious and merciful benediction, this unanimous affection.'

After the Brookes returned to London, and the Privy Council, according to Eade, 'ordered the annexation of Sarawak to the British Crown' in July 1946, Sylvia wrote that: 'shorn of our glory ... [they were] faced with adjusting to a world in which we were no longer emperors but merely two ordinary, ageing people, two misfits'.

monarchy, with two chambers of democratic parliament – the *Dewan Negara* (State Council) and the *Dewan Rakyat* (People's Council). The East Malaysian states of Sabah and Sarawak elect their own state legislative assembly to decide on state affairs, but fall under national jurisdiction for all federal matters, and share the same king.

Monarchy The king, or *yang di-pertuan agong* (paramount ruler), of Malaysia acts as leader of the Islamic faith and official head of state. The latter role is largely symbolic, and in reality the king has little legislative control – similar to the British monarch. His powers include a say in appointing the prime minister and granting parliamentary dissolution, acting on the advice of the legislature. The *yang di-pertuan agong* is selected every five years by the nine hereditary sultans of Malaysia. The states without a hereditary sultan appoint their own state figureheads – Sabah and Sarawak both have a *yang di-pertua negeri* (head of state), appointed by the king, on the advice of the federal government. Those governors join the other states in the 'Conference of Rulers' to elect the *yang di-pertuan agong*.

Government Loosely based on the British system, Malaysia has three levels of government – federal, state and local. In the federal sphere, executive power is vested in a prime minister who, along with (the two houses of) parliament, is elected every five years. The Senate-like *Dewan Negara* (State Council), is partly elected by the king, partly by the state parliaments, whilst the House of Representatives-style *Dewan Rakyat* (People's Council) is chosen by a national vote.

Legislative power is divided between federal and state governments. While the majority of political matters are decided at a federal level, Sabah and Sarawak (like the other 11 Malaysian states) have exclusive jurisdiction over matters of local government, land, forestry and agriculture. Sabah and Sarawak also enjoy special autonomy from the federal government, akin to the special position of Northern Ireland in the United Kingdom's set-up. As well as its own head of state, each state also has its own constitution and elected assembly. The state assembly is led by a chief minister (*menteri besar*) and cabinet, and legislates on matters outside the federal parliament sphere.

Local government At a local government level, the many levels of administration are befitting of an English-inspired system of government. In Sarawak, the 13 state divisions are administered by district officers, and are further divided and administered by Sarawak administrative officers. Beyond that, at the level of *kampungs* (villages), local affairs are taken in charge by the *ketua kampung* (village chief), also known as the *penghulu*.

BORNEO'S GOVERNMENT AND POLITICS AT A GLANCE

Malaysia's prime minister (Dato' Sri) Najib Razak
Malaysia's king Sultan Mizan Zainal Abidin
Sabah's chief minister (Datuk Seri) Musa Haji Aman
Sabah's head of state (Tun Datuk Seri) Juhar Mahiruddin
Sarawak's chief minister (Sri) Abdul Taib Mahmud
Sarawak's head of state (Tun) Abang Muhammad Salahuddin Abang Barieng
Brunei's sultan and prime minister Hassanal Bolkiah

MERDEKA! MERDEKA! MERDEKA!

It features in the name of shopping plazas, football fields, hotels, hairdressers and banks throughout Sabah and Sarawak. *Merdeka*, meaning independence, was the cry echoing through what is now the Merdeka Stadium in Kuala Lumpur on 31 August 1957, when independence was proclaimed and the Malaysian flag raised. The bid for independence was led by Tunku Abdul Rahman Putra Al-Haj, who headed the delegation of Malaysian ministers that negotiated the deal through to completion.

While the relationship of Sabah and Sarawak with the federal government may be generally ambivalent, public enthusiasm for Malaysian independence and for the concept of nation seems very strong if the *merdeka*-count can be taken as an indication. A similar thing could be said for the frequency of crests, coats of arms, flags and other patriotic displays.

Immigration When Sabah and Sarawak surrendered self-government to become part of Malaysia, one thing they both kept hold of was absolute power over their immigration laws. This means that even Malaysians from the peninsula have to produce passports and fill out immigration forms when entering Sabah and Sarawak. This small bureaucratic hiccup is a shred of nominal autonomy in Malaysian Borneo. The trail-blazing prime minister of the 1990s, Dr Mahathir Mohamad, described it as being totally out of step with the idea of a single nation, and his contention over the immigration issue was just one of many thorns in the often prickly state–federal relationship between east and West Malaysia.

Political parties Malaysia is governed by a coalition of 14 political parties, the Barisan Nasional (National Front), led by the predominant United Malays National Organisation (UMNO). The UMNO has held power since Malaysia's independence

FLAGS AHOY!

THE MALAYSIAN FLAG The 14 red and white horizontal stripes on the flag represent the 13 Malaysian states, plus the federal entity. The flag is known as Jalur Gemilang (Stripes of Glory). The blue rectangle to the upper left is meant to unify these different states and people. Within it there is a yellow star and moon crescent. The 14 points of the star again represent the federation; the crescent symbolises Islam; and the yellow is the dab of royalty and rulers.

THE FLAGS OF SABAH AND SARAWAK Since 1988 Sabah has had its own flag with the state symbolised by a black silhouette of Mount Kinabalu and its five divisions by the five colours: red, white, royal blue, zircon blue and icicle blue. Sarawak's flag, the Bendera negeri Sarawak, was also adopted by the state parliament in 1988. It uses the same colours as that of the Brooke Rajah flag – red, yellow and black – minus the Christian and monarchist symbols of a cross and a crown. The yellow star in the middle of the flag has nine points standing for the number of administrative divisions at the time, though today there are 11. The Sarawak flag was first raised at the National Day parade in Kuching in 1988. The unveiling of the flags probably marked a refreshed sense of state nationalism after 25 years of being parts of Malaysia.

in 1957 – currently holding two-thirds of the parliamentary seats – and the Prime Minister of Malaysia has always been from this major Malayan group. All other parties in the coalition represent a different ethnic group. Two other prominent parties are the MCA – the Malaysian Chinese Association – and the MIC – the Malaysian Indian Congress. The MCA is the largest of several Chinese parties, each of them representing factions of the large and diverse Chinese community. It has been riddled for years by bitter squabbles.

BRUNEI With the sultan as self-elected, supreme executive authority, Brunei is an independent 'constitutional' sovereignty. Sultan Haji Hassanal Bolkiah is not only sovereign ruler, but also prime minister, defence minister, finance minister and head of the Islamic faith. Under the country's 1959 constitution he was invested with full executive authority, later amended to include full emergency powers. His brother, Prince Jefri Bolkiah, was finance minister until he caused a financial and personal scandal, squandering millions on a line-up of playboy acquisitions – his super-yacht was called *Tits*, complete with two tenders, *Nipple I* and *Nipple II*!

The sultan's son – the crown prince and would-be 30th sultan – Haji Al-Muhtadee Billah – is the senior minister at the prime minister's office, while another of the sultan's brothers holds the foreign affairs portfolio. The other ministerial posts are shared among a close group of allies, personally hand-picked by His Majesty. There are no elections. The sultan is advised on national policy by several councils, which he appoints – a Council of Cabinet Ministers, Religious Council, Privy Council, a Council of Succession and a Legislative Council.

Political parties Ever since a 1962 coup aimed at gaining political democracy, Brunei has been ruled by strict decree of the sultan, with zero tolerance of political parties – countenanced for a few years in the mid-1980s, but outlawed again in 1988.

The Brunei Solidarity National Party (PPKB) first registered in 1985 but has been largely inactive since; the Brunei People's Party (PRB) has been banned since 1962; and the Brunei National Democratic Party lost its government registration in 1988. The sultan is said to be making efforts to allow for democracy and public participation in political processes, in recognition that the country has to opt for less isolationism and better global relations for economic and political survival. So far there has been no major public call for dissident political parties to come forth and make themselves heard.

JUDICIARY AND LAW

SABAH AND SARAWAK In judicial affairs, both Sabah and Sarawak have a High Court that comes under the supreme jurisdiction of the Malaysian Federal Court and Court of Appeal. All these courts took a page out of the British judicial system. In Sarawak, James Brooke established a Court of Justice in 1841, and Charles Brooke established a more developed court system in 1870, adding a Supreme Court, Magistrates' Court and Native Court.

Today, both states have special laws dealing with indigenous affairs, dealt with by the Native Courts. Various ordinances deal with Native Customary Rights (NCR) and claims of native communities to ancestral land. State governments have introduced many new laws to seriously curb (or 'tighten their claws' as one critic put it) Native Customary Rights. Well before the British set up courts, or the Malaysian Constitution was born, the indigenous communities had their own complex body of customary law called *adat*, which governed their daily lives and socio-economic dealings. This was only recognised in a very limited manner by the NCR.

BRUNEI Brunei has a dual legal system, combining elements of English common law and court structure with Islamic sharia law – known in Malay as *syariah*. The majority of cases are handled by the Supreme Courts system, which includes a Magistrates' Court, High Court, Intermediate Court and Court of Appeals. The final court of appeal for civil cases can be made only through the Judicial Committee of the Privy Council, which sits in London. The Syariah Courts co-exist with the Supreme Courts and deal particularly with family law matters such as Muslim divorces, and questions of Malay-Muslim custom.

ECONOMY

SABAH AND SARAWAK Historians have said that Borneo was somewhat neglected during European presence. In Sarawak, the White Rajah did nothing to encourage large-scale private enterprise or capitalist investment, and the British government were not keen on investment. Sarawak and Sabah entered the Federation of Malaysia as disadvantaged, politically undeveloped and marginal territories. Since then they have become something of an 'offsite production centre' for Malaysian primary industry, producing timber, petroleum, palm oil, rubber and other raw materials for export.

Since the 1980s, Malaysia has transformed itself into a major industrial force and southeast Asia's third-richest country. Sabah and Sarawak are developing at a much slower rate. Unlike Peninsular Malaysia, there is very little secondary industry, though there are signs of a small Silicon Valley developing in the greater Kuching area.

The differences of standards of living and earnings between Malaysian Borneo and the peninsula have lessened since the 1990s, when one-third of Sabah's residents lived in poverty, though 2009 saw Sabah ranked among Malaysia's poorest states. Despite a wealth of natural resources, economic growth and per capita GDP in Sabah (US$4,500) is still well lower than the Malaysian average (US$7,800), and over eight times less that of neighbouring Brunei (US$27,000) (based on 2009 figures). Sarawak, on the other hand, was cited as the richest state in Malaysia by various economic reports in 2010, with a per capita GDP of about US$9,500. While the Sabah government says its per capita income doubled in two decades from around US$1,300, to US$2,650 in 2010, some put the mean monthly income as low as US$1,900, and poverty rates in 2009 at 19.7% (compared with the national rate of 3.8%), citing a subsidy-development economy as one of the problems. The gap seems to be widening between poor states such as Sabah and wealthier states, with the Malaysian government aiming at a per capita income of over US$15,000 by 2020. Based on the current situation, Sarawak seems well in line to reach that goal, but not Sabah, although the state government seems to be pinning great hopes on the palm oil sector, oil and gas industry and biotechnology for economic miracles.

The wealth generated from agriculture and forestry is said to largely bypass the chronically poor, particularly indigenous communities in rural areas.

Agriculture, forestry and fishing have underpinned Sabah's and Sarawak's economies for decades. However, since the early 2000s, tourism has been the fastest-growing sector of Sabah's economy, and the fourth foreign revenue earner after palm oil, crude petroleum and plywood. Tourism in Sarawak is also catching up.

In Sabah, agriculture provides about one-third of the state's GDP, a third of the jobs and a third of the state's export earnings. Palm oil, cocoa and rubber are the three biggest agricultural industries. The state is Malaysia's biggest crude cocoa producer, providing 70% of the national crop, and rubber is the third most important commercial crop. Both rubber and cocoa beans are sent to Peninsular Malaysia for downstream processing into high value-added products.

For now, and the foreseeable future, the timber industry is the backbone of Sarawak's economy. The annual value of Sarawak's wood products export was about 7.4 billion MYR in 2011, and the government announced it would be targeting 54 billion MYR of export value for the wood-based industry by 2020.

The timber industry is also a major employer in the state – in 2007 it provided jobs to 40% of people employed there. Sarawak also grows 95% of Malaysia's black pepper, which sees the country ranked as the world's fifth-largest pepper producer with an annual yield of around 20,000 tonnes.

Palm oil In the last 15 years palm oil has overtaken forestry as the biggest export (and environmental issue) in Sabah (see *Monoculture* box, *Chapter 7*, page 213). Sabah produces over a quarter of Malaysia's palm oil and the controversial crop is the state's biggest earner, contributing over 40% or 4 billion MYR of the state's revenue.

In recent years increasing numbers of farmers have converted their land over to oil palm cash crops, with the promise of high yields and quick returns. The plantation expansion boom (and deforestation) was further fanned by the promise of biofuel. Yet the much vaunted development of a thriving biofuel industry in Sabah, using palm oil as a potential renewable energy source, has been thwarted. The setbacks began in 2008, with drops in crude oil prices set against higher costs of palm oil supplies, and in 2010 biodiesel production in Malaysia dropped by 60%.

In Sarawak, as indigenous tribes were encouraged to convert their forested land into oil palm, plantations increased by 9.5% within one year (2010) and the state now has 0.9 million hectares of the crop compared with Sabah's 1.4 million hectares.

BRUNEI In September 2010, the *Brunei Times* reported that the country's GDP had been listed as the fifth highest in the world by US business publication *Global Finance*. Following on the heels of Qatar, Luxembourg, Norway and Singapore, Brunei notched up per capita earnings of US$48,714. The Asian Development Bank (ADB) forecast economic growth of 1.7 to 1.8% in Brunei between 2011 and 2012 due to global economic recovery and higher oil prices.

A small nation with an intensively resource-based economy, Brunei's primary economic and social fuel is in its extensive oil and gas fields. Brunei's oil-rich economy, says its government, affords its population high living standards 'resulting in positive social indicators such as high literacy rates, longer life expectancy, and low unemployment and crime rates. The government provides for all medical services and subsidizes rice and housing.' However, with life expectancies of the oil and natural gas resources as low as 25 and 40 years respectively, Brunei is under increasing pressure to find oil alternatives.

In its Asian Development Outlook report in 2011, the Asian Development Bank said Brunei urgently needed to diversify its economy away from a dependency on the oil and gas sectors, which account for 88% of the nation's exports and 40% of GDP (down from 75% in the 1970s). The government's 'economic diversification program' is targeting international finance, tourism, transport, logistics and ICT as potential growth areas. Clearly it has a long way to go in assuring Brunei's future generations as high a standard of living as those of the oil-cushioned past. In a speech in 2010, leading Brunei businessman and acting chairman of the Brunei Economic Development Board, Timothy Ong, said: 'In terms of HDI, which measures quality of life taking into account income per capita, mortality and education, Brunei is 30th in the world. The fact that we are behind three countries in Asia that have no natural resources ... reminds us that we must make the transition from being just a resource-rich economy towards (also) being a knowledge-based economy.'

PEOPLE

ORIGINS AND PREHISTORY As the midpoint between China, the Indonesian Archipelago and the Pacific region, Borneo is an age-old sea crossroads of southeast Asia; southerly migrations through the island are known to have taken place tens of thousands of years ago. The thoroughfare left its footprints on the population of Borneo to become what it is today: a human rainbow of racial intensity and multi-hued traditions.

The racial mosaics of Sabah and Sarawak are quite different in their intricacies. However, the people of Borneo are believed to originate from a common ancestral stock, along with the people of Sumatra, Java, Bali, Sulawesi Island, the Philippines and the Malay Peninsula. Scant information is available about the precise period of arrival of the ancestors of today's indigenous people to Malaysian Borneo, though it is believed to have started around the 15th century. Some earlier tribes were wiped out through clan warfare or simply moved on to other places.

Early hunter-gatherers There is evidence of human presence in Borneo as far back as 45,000 years ago; one of the most important archaeological finds of the 20th century was near the west coast of Sarawak. A 40,000-year-old human skull, along with stone tools, animal bones and human burials, was unearthed at the mouth of the Niah Caves. The immense cave has been described as the most important archaeological site in Asia. The discovery, made by Tom Harrisson in 1958, confirmed the presence of prehistoric hunter-gatherers in Borneo. Similar remains have also been found in caves in southeastern Sabah. Since 1958, the area surrounding the caves has been granted national park status (see *Chapter 12, Northern Sarawak*, page 294).

Austronesian migrations Despite the evidence of such early *Homo sapiens* in Borneo, the linguistic ancestors of today's native populations are believed to have settled more recently. Austronesians migrating through Taiwan and the Philippines from around 2500BC are believed to have settled in Borneo, the Philippines and Indonesia. People with closely related Austronesian languages also settled the Malay Peninsula, other parts of the Malay Archipelago and the Pacific Islands, to as far as Hawaii, New Zealand and Easter Island.

The early Austronesian-speaking migrants who moved to the Philippines and Borneo from Taiwan around 2000BC took with them knowledge of 'weaving, bark-cloth making, pottery, pigs, dogs, rice, and finely polished stone tools', says Professor Peter Bellwood from the Australian National University School of Archaeology and Anthropology. People originally settled in lowland coastal areas, with shifting agriculture and rice production becoming ingrained in their culture. Only with the advent of metal use, iron in particular, were tribes able to penetrate the forests further inland.

The story of the Austronesian-speakers tells of one of the most remarkable migrations in human history, from which people in the area of southern China 4,000–5,000 years ago set out and settled vast parts of southeast Asia. Today, an estimated 300 million people speak Austronesian languages, populating a large chunk of the planet from Madagascar through to New Zealand and Hawaii. These people 'share over 1,000 related languages that derive from a common linguistic homeland in Taiwan', Professor Bellwood says in his 1997 book *Prehistory of the Indo-Malaysian Archipelago*. 'Before Christopher Columbus and the explosive expansions of Hispanic languages and English, the Austronesian language family was by far the most widespread in the world.'

Today There are now over two dozen major ethnic groups living in Malaysian Borneo, and a handful of such groups in Brunei. Between them, they speak over 80 different dialects. Like Malaysia as a whole, Sabah and Sarawak have large contingents of Malay, Chinese and Indian populations, but stand out for their much wider variety of other ethnic groups. Brunei on the other hand has a big Malay majority.

ETHNIC GROUPS Borneo's ethnic make-up is colourful and multi-layered, having been touched by various influences over the centuries. For every different type of landscape – highland, lowland, coast and interior – there are different indigenous tribes and dozens of sub-tribes. There are around 70 different ethnic communities between Sabah and Sarawak alone. Brunei is predominantly Malay but also has Chinese, Indian and indigenous populations such as the Iban and Murut.

Indigenous peoples

Sarawak Sarawak's population comprises 27 different ethnic communities, speaking 45 different languages and dialects. Around 50% of the population are indigenous races, 28% are Chinese and 21% Malay (*Melayu*).

Iban The major ethnic group of Sarawak are the Iban, who migrated en masse from deep within the Kalimantan hinterland from the 16th century through to the 19th. A nomadic yet territorial group, they successively annexed large parts of Sarawak, from the southern border region right up through the centre of the state, eventually reaching the coast. Around 30% of the Sarawak population today is Iban – a much smaller number also migrated to Brunei. The Iban were erroneously referred to by 19th-century Europeans as 'sea Dayak' (sea natives) when in fact they were inland, river-dwelling people. The term most likely arises from their superior boating skills, acquired from other tribes during years of commandeering the coast, and their dabblings in piracy.

THE 'DAYAKS' OF SARAWAK

In Sarawak, the collective name Dayak is given to all the indigenous tribes (and is also sometimes used to refer to all indigenous people of Borneo). Its origin is debatable but it has been widely used to denote inland-dwelling people as opposed to the Malay coastal populations. The word Dayak is not considered derogatory and is commonly used to refer to indigenous issues and events. Settled agriculturalists and forest nomads use it themselves to affirm their indigenousness both politically and culturally, and to differentiate themselves from the rest of the population

The closest equivalent in Sabah is the Kadazandusun, an umbrella term for the largest native population, which includes many ethnic subgroups and represents about a fifth of the population.

The name Iban was synonymous with headhunting and hunter-gathering; various tattoos portrayed the success of an Iban man at these traditional activities. As shifting cultivators, Ibans originally built their homes near navigable rivers; they were designed to last as long as their exploitation of rice farming in the area, before they moved on to new pastures. The first Iban settlements in Sarawak were at Lubok Antu, south of Kuching towards the Indonesian border. Many still live in and around this area, sometimes on several hours' boat journey from the nearest town. While some of today's longhouses sport modern luxuries such as televisions and fridges, afforded by employment in local timber and oil industries, many aspects of Iban life, from foraging for food to domestic structure, remain strongly traditional. Larger communities count up to 20 families subsisting primarily on rice, fish, jungle food and a good dose of *tuak*, or rice wine. One thing is certain, from all of Borneo's diverse tribes, the upriver dwelling 'sea Dayaks' stand out for being as water-savvy as ever.

Bidayuh The Bidayuh, meaning 'people of the interior', live in the hinterland regions of southwest Sarawak, pushed back from the coast by Iban invasions and pirate attacks; the Europeans dubbed them the 'land Dayaks'. However, their gentle-mannered and timid nature belies their warrior past – in their circular community houses or *baruk*, which rose over a metre off the ground, skulls of their enemies were displayed as headhunted trophies. Their (living) guests traditionally slept out in the *baruk*, with the severed heads in place of paintings on the walls! These houses are thus sometimes simplistically translated as 'head houses'. The trophy heads followed retaliation attacks: peace-loving people, the Bidayuh attacked when provoked rather than out of sheer bloodthirstiness.

The Bidayuh people are masters of building with bamboo, expertly fashioning the dried stalks of the plant into a huge range of implements, from farming tools and cooking utensils to musical instruments, not to mention utilising its properties for their ingenious water system. This gravity-based plumbing system not only provides water for the longhouses but also waters the fields of rice and vegetables in times of little rain. Existing in just a small slither in the Samarahan District, the Bidayuh number 135,000 – about 8% of the population.

Orang Ulu The remainder of the population consists of various tribes, including the coastal **Melanau**, the **Kelabit** people who live in the highlands of northeast Sarawak near the Indonesian border and several ethnic minorities who live in the interior. Collectively these upriver races are known as the **Orang Ulu**, literally 'people of the headwaters'. They number about 100,000 and account for 6% of Sarawak's population. The name 'Orang Ulu' was originally attributed to the larger **Kayan** and **Kenyah** tribes who live in the Upper Rejang and Upper Baram river areas, but included smaller contiguous groups including the Kajang, Kejaman, Punan, Penan and Ukit. The term now embraces other mid- and lower-river people such as the Berawan and Murut, the Lun Bawang, Lun Dayeh and the Kelabits.

Kayan Another headhunting group who migrated from Kalimantan into Sarawak, the Kayan gradually moved, or were forced by other tribes, way up north. Some among the population of 15,000 still live in longhouses along the 400km Sungai Baram and its tributaries, and the lower Sungai Tubau in the Kapit Division. Kayan women have tattoos on their hands and legs – the men wear leopards' teeth in their ears. Though it is becoming increasingly rare to see, they once all had earlobes hanging down towards their shoulders extended with the help of brass and other metal weights. Like other tribes, their greatest skills grew from their lifestyle and many of those in Sarawak were

17

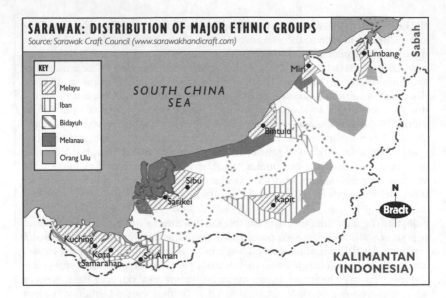

SARAWAK: DISTRIBUTION OF MAJOR ETHNIC GROUPS
Source: Sarawak Craft Council (www.sarawakhandicraft.com)

KEY
- Melayu
- Iban
- Bidayuh
- Melanau
- Orang Ulu

SOUTH CHINA SEA

Limbang
Miri
Bintulu
Sibu
Sarikei
Kapit
Kuching
Kota Samarahan
Sri Aman

Sabah

KALIMANTAN (INDONESIA)

buoyed along by rivers. The Kayan traditionally carved their boats from a single block of *belian* (ironwood) – the strongest tropical hardwood.

Kenyah The Kenyah people are closely related to their Kayan neighbours, and brutally rivalled the Ibans together as age-old allies. For centuries, both have also practised shifting cultivation of dry rice in the upper parts of the Baram River. It's believed they could be the first of the aboriginal groups in Sarawak, preceding the Iban, after migrating from the Sungai Kayan (Kayan River) area of East Kalimantan where many of their cousins still live.

Sabah In Sabah about 39 different indigenous groups account for 50% of the population.

Kadazandusun This is the largest group, encompassing several distinct sub-tribes including the **Rungus** and the **Dusuns** of Tuaran, Ranau and Tambunan, all of whom speak very closely related dialects. With varying degrees of Chinese physical similarities, they most likely migrated from southern China thousands of years ago. Formerly known as Duson, meaning village or orchard people, this was construed as an uncomplimentary name given by Malay coastal dwellers, and was changed to Kadazan in the 1970s. Once farming people – and fierce headhunters – the Kadazandusun communities are concentrated mainly along the west coast and in the hinterland areas of Penampang, Ranau, Tambunan and Keningau through to the Sarawak border. As Sabah's population rises, so the Kadazandusun's shrinks – in the 1970s they were a large majority at over 30% of the population. That has since fallen to around 19% of Sabah's three million-plus people.

Politically, the group refers to itself as Kadazandusun – sometimes written as Kadazan-Dusun – though some official population counts still separate them as the Kadazan and the Dusun. Many of the individual races would never identify with anything but their proper tribal name: **Dusun**, **Rungus**, **Lotud**, **Minokok**, **Tambanuo**, **Tindal** and **Orang Sungai** ('river people'), and it's far more courteous to do the same.

Bajau This is the second-biggest ethnic group in Sabah, representing 13% of the state population. Like Kadazandusun, Bajau is a collective term for several ethnic groups, all of them originating from the Philippines and the Sulawesi coast of Indonesia: the **Bajau**, the **Illanun**, **Suluk**, **Obian** and **Binadan**. With a history of seafaring migrations, and partly of piracy, they are still largely a coastal-dwelling people, with large communities on both the east and west coasts of Sabah.

Murut The Murut people represent the third-largest indigenous group – about 50,000 live in the hinterland of Sabah's west coast and in the Kinabatangan river area. There are also tribes of Murut in Sarawak and Brunei. Dressed in black and sporting multi-coloured beads, they are longhouse dwellers and many still live traditionally, their houses close to rivers and with high levels of community co-operation. A good illustration of Borneo's kaleidoscopic culture is that even as such a relatively small slice of the population, the Murut are broken down into 14 sub-ethnic groups speaking 12 dialects, some of whom do not understand each other. Living in and alongside forests, the Murut are great botanical healers: each community has its own herbalist, a *mongugusap*, wiser old men or women who use plants – roots, barks and leaves – and animals to cure a variety of ailments. From diarrhoea to diabetes and high blood pressure, it seems that when you have an intimate knowledge of the forest, there's a natural cure for everything.

Brunei Only 12% of Brunei's population is made up of indigenous tribes, though the 'Malay' majority (73%) are actually Melanaus and Kedayan – people indigenous to northern Borneo. **Muruts**, **Ibans**, **Dayaks** and **Dusuns** form the tiny slice of Brunei's indigenous population.

Major non-indigenous populations
Melayu (Malay) Originating from Yunnan, China, the Malay people first reached the Malaysian Peninsula around 2000BC. Due to many influences from the neighbouring areas like Java, Sumatra, the Indian subcontinent, China, the Middle

TATTOOING TRADITIONS

The Kayans, Ibans, Kenyah and Kelabits all have strong tattoo traditions. The Kayans are portrayed as being the creative force behind most tattoo designs. Kayan men carved highly stylised designs of animals – hornbills, dogs, scorpions – onto wooden blocks that could be easily transferred onto skin and shared between villages. Tattoos were collected like passport stamps, as proof and souvenirs of journeys. It was the Kayan women, however, that traditionally applied the tattoos. These were usually made from soot or charcoal, and occasionally impregnated with special materials believed to make the tattoo more powerful, such as a piece of meteorite or animal bone. Kayan women would be adorned with their first tattoo as they passed into adulthood, although the most intricate designs were reserved for those of higher class and greater wealth. A design unique to the Kayan is the talisman (*lukut*) on the wrists, which is believed to prevent the soul from escaping the body. In Iban society, men apply the tattoos, often after a successful headhunting expedition. Indeed, tattoos in all Dayak societies often have more than a mere decorative purpose – they can be symbols of status, success and wealth.

East and the West, the cultures of the Malaysian Peninsula have been shaped and reshaped. This is probably due to the strategic position for trade, consequently influencing its custom and social identity.

The Malays are the largest ethnic group in Bornean Malaysia, accounting for more than 50% of the population. In Sabah and Sarawak however, that figure is closer to 25%. The Malay population in Brunei is highest, at 73%. Malays started arriving in Borneo from the 1400s, from trading kingdoms in Sumatra (Indonesia). Nearly all of them settled on Borneo's shores and subsisted as fishermen. Today the Malay *kampung* (villages) still cling largely to the coast. Some of those *kampung* in the Kuching area are named after Javanese towns from where the locals sprang. The Malays are known for their gentle mannerisms and rich arts heritage.

'The main defining characteristic of "Malayness" is the Islamic religion,' writes Victor T King in *The Peoples of Borneo*, adding 'one of the most important distinctions in Borneo is between those who are Muslims and those who are not'.

Not all Muslims, however, are Malay. Some major ethnic groups, such as the Bajau in Sabah and the Melanau in Sarawak, have converted to Islam but many still maintain their own cultural identity. Their Malay conversion from Hinduism and Theravada Buddhism to Islam began in the 1400s, largely influenced by the decision of the royal court of Malacca.

The Federal Constitution of Malaysia defines a Malay as someone who practises Islam and Malay customs, speaks the Malay language and is the child of at least one parent who was born within the Federation of Malaysia before independence on 31 August 1957.

The question of 'Malayness' is quite a paradox, especially when it appears that the origins of many 'Malay' people in Borneo lay with the island's indigenous

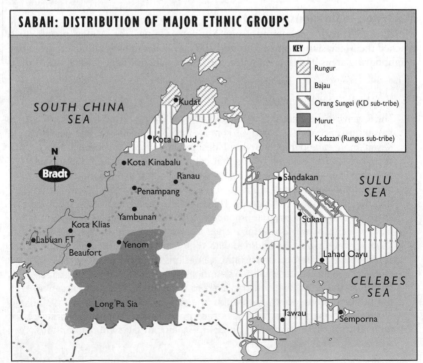

SABAH: DISTRIBUTION OF MAJOR ETHNIC GROUPS

KEY
- Rungur
- Bajau
- Orang Sungei (KD sub-tribe)
- Murut
- Kadazan (Rungus sub-tribe)

SOUTH CHINA SEA

Kudat

Kota Delud

Kota Kinabalu

Ranau

Penampang

Yambunan

Kota Klias

Labuan FT

Beaufort

Yenom

Long Pa Sia

Sandakan

SULU SEA

Sukau

Lahad Oayu

CELEBES SEA

Tawau

Semporna

Bradt

N

The Penan tribe have been making international headlines since the 1980s, when the consciousness of the devastation of Borneo's forests and indigenous traditions first started to break through island barriers. Many Penan were among those arrested for protesting against logging; despite being inherently shy people, having had little contact with the world beyond the forest until recent years, their determination to do something about the all-out war on their forest homes made them go public.

The Penan are among the only hunter-gatherers remaining in southeast Asia, and the last tribe in Borneo still living this traditional lifestyle. They live in groups of 20–30 in the upper Rejang river area and along the Sungai Baram in central Sarawak, and around Sungai Limbang in northern Sarawak. The Penan use blowpipes to kill deer and wild boar, moving to new areas when their supply of wild sago flour starch (which they make from sago palms) runs out; they supplement their diet with wild fruits, jungle roots and plants. Their shyness of the world outside the forest, and of sunlight, shows in the paler shades of their skin in comparison with other tribes. There is common confusion between them and the less numerous, dialectally distinct Punan.

Prince Charles of Great Britain caused outrage in Malaysia when he accused the country of collective genocide over the Penan. The Malaysian government maintained that it simply wanted the Penan to integrate with society for their own sake, attempting (unsuccessfully) to lure the hunter-gatherers to settle in luxurious longhouses; meanwhile, the logging continued.

The dispute continues, with Penan leaders maintaining that without the forests they 'become poor and lose our homes, with no hope of good jobs. Our children are robbed of their future and their heritage. We have the right to live in the lands of our ancestors, just as you do.'

According to Malaysian and international law, the Penan have clear land rights and have to be consulted before any logging can proceed, but these rights are often openly violated.

Background Information PEOPLE

tribes. Large numbers of the island's Malay population are believed to descend from Dayak tribes who converted to Islam from the 16th century onwards. Such a switch is called *maskuk Melayu* – to convert to Malay.

Chinese In Sabah, Sarawak and Brunei, the diverse Chinese communities represent the second-largest race of people and the largest non-indigenous group – 30% in Sabah and Sarawak and 15% in Brunei. Although evidence of Chinese settlements dating to the 10th and 11th centuries has been found, most of the ancestors of today's Chinese population came as settlers in the 18th century, during the early years of the British North Borneo Chartered Company in Sabah and the White Rajah's reign in Sarawak (see *History*, page 5). Most of them were Hakka Christian farmers, and this is still the biggest Chinese race in Sabah. There are also populations of Cantonese, Mandarin, Teochew, Hokkien, Hainanese and Henghua, each with their own dialects.

From Sabah's east coast to Sarawak's west coast, the Chinese colour Malaysian Borneo's and Brunei's towns red with their festivities, urban mentality and businesses. In Sabah, many Chinese have intermarried with other races, in particular with the large Kadazandusun population; there are prevalent Sino-

Kadazan and Sino-Dusun subcultures in Sabah, with people who practise both Kadazandusun and Chinese customs. Today, with typical industriousness, the Chinese are strongly represented in the services and retail sectors and have turned small shops into multi-million-dollar businesses. Thousands of others operate coffee shops and restaurants.

LANGUAGE

The language map of Borneo is as much of a mosaic as the ethnic one. Throughout Malaysian Borneo and Brunei, there are around 100 different regional and tribal dialects spoken. *Bahasa* is Malay for language, so English is *Bahasa Inggeris*, French *Bahasa Perancis*, etc.

The official national language of Malaysia is Malay – *Bahasa Melayu*. Another slightly different version is *Bahasa Malaysia*. Although mutually understandable, they are not entirely the same. There are also some state variations of Malay – *Bahasa Sarawak* is Sarawakian Malay, spoken like a dialect with only a sprinkling of different words, but enough to surprise visitors from the peninsula. *Bahasa Malaysia* and *Bahasa Melayu* are similar to *Bahasa Indonesia* and can pretty much be understood from Sumatra to the Philippines.

While Malay may be the national language of Malaysia, it is far from being the true *lingua franca* in Malaysian Borneo. In Sabah, for example, only a quarter of the population are Malay and the state harbours more than half of Malaysia's indigenous languages – the estimated 39 ethnic communities speak some 55 different languages in 80 dialects. There are four major linguistic families: Dusunic, Murutic, Paitanic and Sama-Bajau.

TRIBAL LANGUAGES Many tribal languages, as throughout Borneo, are thought to descend from the Austronesian and Malayo-Polynesian language family trees, due to the Austronesian settlement of the island around the third millennium BC. Even in one minority group such as the Bidayuh in Sarawak, there are a dozen dialects, and some do not even understand each other. Sabah's largest linguistic group, the Dusunic, is splintered into 14 dialects including Dusun, Rungus and Bisaya. Due to imperial influence, English is spoken fluently by more Kadazans in Sabah than any other ethnic group. A similar situation occurs with the Iban in Sarawak. With the decline of the Kadazan language and other tribal vernaculars, the Sabah state government introduced policies to try and counter their extinction, including encouraging public schools to start teaching indigenous dialects. The **Kadazandusun Cultural Association** (*www.kdca.org*) and the **Kadazandusun**

LINGUISTIC DIVERSITY IN NORTHERN BORNEO   *with Peter Martin*

Like the biodiversity in northern Borneo, the linguistic diversity is wonderfully rich. Malay, in one form or another, is used along the coastal strip and in the towns. There are distinct varieties of Malay in Brunei, Sabah and Sarawak and English is spoken in major urban areas. But beneath the surface of Malay and English, there is an abundance of linguistic diversity, which encompasses major languages such as Iban (Sarawak and Brunei), Bidayuh (Sarawak), Kadazandusun (Sabah), Tutong (Brunei) and several varieties of Chinese. Many of the languages of the three northern Borneo states have not been described in detail, and remain unwritten. There is also considerable evidence that there is a shift away from some of these languages to a form of Malay.

Peter Martin is Professor of Linguistics and Education, University of East London, and has written widely on language issues in Brunei and Sarawak. He is editor of Shifting Patterns of Language Use in Borneo, *and co-editor of* Language Use and Language Change in Brunei Darussalam.

Language Foundation (*www.klf.com.my*) are both very involved in language issues, and their offices and websites are useful reference points for many other cultural links.

CONSERVING LANGUAGE AND CULTURE A study conducted in the mid-1980s showed that mass media, urbanisation, the education system, intermarriage and language prestige were all having their effect on the decline of indigenous languages in Sabah. Since then things have deteriorated, but the cultural vigilance has gained ground, as echoed in the following verse. It is written in Dusun dialect and kindly translated into English by Dr Benedict Topin from the Kadazandusun Cultural Association (KDCA).

Atagak o boros, atagak o koubasanan	Lose our language and we will lose our culture
Atagak o koubasanan, atagak o kointutunan	Lose our culture and we will lose our identity
Atagak o boros, atagak o pirotian	Lose our language and we will lose our understanding
Atagak o pirotian, atagak o puinungan, pisohudungan om pibabasan	Lose our understanding and we will lose our harmony, co-operation and peace
Atagak o pibabasan, atagak o piobpinaian	Lose peace and we will lose our brotherhood and sisterhood
Atagak o piobpinaian kopitongkiad o rikoton do rusodon.	Lose our brotherhood and sisterhood and we will be dispersed in our journey towards common destiny.

RELIGION AND SPIRITUALITY

Over the centuries Borneo has been visited by many different traditional faiths and spiritual beliefs, just as it has by ethnic tribes, traders, explorers, migrations and missionaries. All these influences have brewed a rich religious life, which plays an integral part in culture and society. Under the official seal of Islam there are other mainstream religions and many fascinating, though fading, rituals of tribal devotion to extensive spirit worlds.

RELIGIOUS HISTORY

Islam The religion came to the trading states controlled by Brunei's rulers from the late 13th century. Within a couple of centuries, the people were converting en masse to the religion of powerful Muslim merchants. Prior to that Buddhism and Hinduism were widely practised, as well as indigenous spiritual rituals.

In the 18th and 19th centuries, Islamic faith spread like wildfire into the hinterland areas of present-day Sabah and Sarawak, and many indigenous people converted. Religion reinforced the divisions between state-based and tribal society.

Christianity With the arrival of Europeans came the pressure of conversion to Christianity for Islam to compete with. This had profound effects on indigenous cultures. Thousands of Iban and Orang Ulu people including the Kelabits and Kayan turned to various denominations of Christianity and many of these former headhunters now celebrate Christmas Day.

Even the most remote ethnic communities were taken under the wings of Christianity. The same thing happened with Sabah's Kadazandusun peoples. In the process, some indigenous religions became extinct. Religious conversion was not just God-driven; it was used to improve law and order, to erode the power base of Muslim sultanates, reduce slavery and headhunting, and socialise people who were used to living in warring factions. As odd as it may seem today, headhunting was very central to the spiritual beliefs of all those tribes who engaged in it.

RELIGION TODAY Islam is the official religion of Malaysia, enshrined in the Constitution. Buddhism and Christianity are also prevalent along with Hinduism, Taoism and tribal religions. Important dates on the Muslim, Buddhist and Christian calendars are nationally observed with public holidays, as are major spiritual celebrations of indigenous peoples. In Malaysian Borneo, Islam is less widespread due to the greater imprint of Christianity. Sabah and Sarawak are the only two Malaysian states to celebrate Easter – about a quarter of their populations are Christian, compared with just 2% of the population in western Malaysia; one-third are of Islamic faith and over 17% are Buddhists and Taoists. Mosques, Buddhist temples, Catholic and Anglican churches are seen in cities and countryside. Large numbers of indigenous peoples including the Kadazandusun in Sabah and Iban in Sarawak have converted to Christianity, and the Bajau in Sabah and Melanau in Sarawak to Islam. Many maintain their animistic and other traditional belief systems as well, not only in private but as a key part of public celebrations. Death rituals, harvest festivals, effigies for healing and tattoos all play a part.

Islam in Borneo In Muslim-dominated cities and towns, the chants of Islamic prayer resonate through streets at dawn, and seep eloquently into skies at dusk. In Brunei, Islam is far more predominant – two-thirds of the population are practising Muslims. If you see the sign *KUDAT* in hotels, on the ceiling or table or in a bedside drawer, the arrow alongside it is not pointing out an emergency exit, but the direction of Mecca. One of the five pillars of Islam is that Muslims must make a pilgrimage – a *hajj* – to Mecca, the birthplace of Islam, once in their lifetime. By doing so, men are bestowed with the title *Hajji* and women *Hajja*. Such trips to Saudi Arabia are only possible for a relatively privileged few in poorer southeast Asian Muslim countries. In Brunei there are many *hajji* and *hajja*. Among them is the sultan, with *Hajji* just one of the words in his seemingly endless title.

Religious harmony As freedom of religion heats up as a pointed social and political issue in Muslim-dominated western Malaysia, the situation in East Malaysia (ie: Malaysian Borneo) seems to have progressed through its inherent greater religious diversity. In general, the religious atmosphere is one of tolerance and inter-religious respect. The different cultures and religions are relatively harmonious and it is common for people, in public and in private, to celebrate with those of different faiths. Often different religious beliefs coexist among different generations of one family, spiritual occasions are celebrated together by different indigenous groups and some of them, such as the Kadazandusun Tadau Ka'amatan (harvest festival) in Sabah and the Gawai Dayak (the Iban harvest festival in Sarawak), are highly communal. It's hard not to be touched by this peaceful coexistence; Sabah is one of the few places left on earth where many faiths live together in harmony.

TRIBAL BELIEFS

Iban The Iban's spirituality is believed to be something of a fusion of animism, Hinduism and Buddhism, brewed centuries back. Though hundreds of Iban converted to Christianity, the public signs of their traditional beliefs are still very potent through their festivals – the Gawai Dayak harvest festival, Gawai Kenyalang hornbill festival and Gawai Antu festival of the dead. The Iban dances – highly intuitive narratives – are punctuated by an array of mythical figures depicting relationships between the natural, spirit and human worlds. The *kenyalang*, or hornbill, is sacred to the Iban because the hornbill's nest, *tansang kenyalang*, is the abode of their supreme god of war Aki Lang Sengalang Burong – also known as 'the earth tremor which trembles and causes the full moon to fall'. In his earthly form, the Iban god takes the form of the eagle-like bird of prey, the Brahminy kite (*Haliastur Indus*).

Orang Ulu The Kayan, the Penan and the Kenyah wear cloaks of Christianity of varying denominations, but their animist beliefs live on in the supreme Bungan cult – an adaptation of their spirit-dominated worlds – and Bungan celebrations.

Melanau Old rituals remain very vividly in the minds and practices of many indigenous folk. The Melanau in Sarawak are a good example – two-thirds of them at least have converted to Islam, yet they still take part in some very feisty displays of animistic worship, and use carved wooden figurines to heal people. Journalist Diana Rose, who was born in the Melanau heartland of Mukah on Sarawak's west

ANIMISM

Many indigenous spiritual beliefs fall within the world of animism, where souls and spirits are attributed to animals, plants and various objects. Some academics have rejected the term animism, as with paganism, accusing it of depreciating traditional belief systems as simplistic and illiterate, especially when applied to Africa. There does not seem to be the same aversity to the term in Borneo and people use both animism and paganism to describe some very complex belief systems and ceremonies hinging on spirits and souls, magic and myth, spells and charms, and powerfully symbolic rites linked with birth, harvest and death. Indeed, animism is said to be more developed, elaborated and intellectualised among the Ibans and related tribes of Borneo than anywhere else in the world. The beliefs are so varied they actually defy a one-word definition. (See *Tribal beliefs*, above, for some brief descriptions.)

A common practice among the indigenous tribes of Borneo, until the first decades of the 20th century, was headhunting; bands of young men would venture out to surrounding villages to collect the heads of enemies or other tribes. The freshly collected heads would be skinned and dried, smoked over a fire or boiled, and then hung up for all to see in the longhouse. The dried skulls were believed to possess powerful spiritual properties, providing vital transfusions of energy for villages. Heads were thought to be able to ward off evil spirits, disease and misfortune, whilst offering protection, fruitful crops and favourable weather. An unhappy head was capable of bringing terrible woes such as plagues, fires and droughts, so they were well looked after with offerings of food and blessings. Heads were the focus of much ritual, symbolising the procreative power of nature: the Kayan and Kenyah tribes in central-north Borneo regularly held large festivals to honour the heads.

Heads were believed to lose their potency over time, so fresh heads were always required to replenish a village's spiritual energies. Although the practice has been all but eradicated, there are still the occasional reports of headhunting. Nowadays however, young male Dayaks are more expected to do a *bajalai*, or journey, to prove their worth rather than accomplish a successful headhunting mission. Many tribes still embrace and celebrate their headhunting histories however, using replica heads made out of coconut shells.

coast, says this: 'The original religion of the Melanau people was Liko, meaning "people of the river". In the Liko religion, life and the environment are one. Followers worship the spiritual world including the superior *tou* spirits and the lesser *belum* spirits that cause sickness. The pagan Melanau use effigies of sickness spirits when practising healing. Many Melanau today are Christian and Muslim, though they still celebrate traditional festivals, most notably Kaul.' (See *Chapter 11, Central Sarawak*, page 285, for more.)

Kadazandusun Among the major ethnic groups of Sabah, the spirit world has reigned supreme. The best illustrations of this are the rituals of **Tadau Ka'amatan**, the rice harvest festival. The Kadazandusun believe that rice has a spirit, called Bambarayon or Bambaazon, which rejuvenates and ensures the bounty of next year's harvest. The thanksgiving festival is held to welcome the rice spirit back, to restore spirits that were lost in careless harvesting, to nourish the rice spirit with offerings of food, and for merrymaking and friendship. The whole thing is underscored by a legend and the need to fight off famine through worship.

Rituals carried out during and around the festival include the *bobohizan* (priestess) selecting seven stalks of the best rice from the paddy before the festival begins. These are then presented to the owner of the rice field after the harvest, and symbolise the homecoming of the rice spirit. The most important part of the festival, however, is the Magavau ceremony, which takes place in the paddy under the first full moon after the harvest. Magavau involves a hunt for lost or strayed rice spirits who have been disturbed by mishandling of the crop or by pests. A sword-wielding male *bobohizan* leads the ceremony followed by a chain of female *bobohizans* who chant ritual verses to summon home the missing spirits. Triumphant, piercing cries peel out over the paddy when a spirit is recovered. See *Public holidays and festivals*, page 112, for more on Tadau Ka'amatan.

CULTURE

Forget the opera, theatre and grand literary occasions. The performing arts of Malaysian Borneo and Brunei are found (often free of charge) in the streets and in the people. The costumes, crafts, dance and music are steeped in tradition. Far from museum pieces, the traditional customs of music, dance and rhythm are alive and kicking. Of course, there are organised indoor (and outdoor) performances, shows, festivals and orchestras, but they lack some of the verve of the raw performances.

MUSIC, SONG AND DANCE Everywhere you go in Borneo, each different culture sings out its own unique rhythm. Between all the various ethnic cultures – indigenous, Chinese and Malay – there is a rich tradition of instrumental music, song and dance performances. Music and dance most often go together; many dances are deeply symbolic and in some cases tied strongly to spiritual worlds and ceremonies.

Gongs and other instruments Gongs are a big feature of cultural performance and music ensembles in Malaysia, in both indigenous and Malay music. There are many different types of gong.

Bruneians introduced the *kulintangan* into Sabah, which is played among ethnic groups of the Kadazandusun peoples on the west coast and the Muslim Bajau on the

INSTRUMENTAL BORNEO

The students from Seri Insan Secondary School in Kota Kinabalu provided these insights into Sabah's musical landscape – they live up to being 'bright human beings' as the school's name proclaims. According to them, four main groups of instruments feature in Sabah's traditional musical culture: *membranophones* (drums), *idiophones* (bronze or brass gongs), *aerophones* (flutes) and *chordophones* (string instruments).

Like many other cultures, there are many types of vocal music including love songs, battle songs, epic tales and ritual chanting. Instrumental music is as rich and complex as vocal music, with a variety of solos and ensembles. Instruments may be played by either men or women.

Most gong ensembles have a drum to emphasise the main rhythmic patterns. Drums from the interior region around Tambunan are called *karatung*. Also known as *gandang* or *gondang*, these are usually cylindrical in shape with a single head of cowhide or goatskin bound to the body. The most common types of *idiophones* are bronze or brass gongs. Every gong has a name denoting its sound or the rhythm it plays. A gong ensemble consists of seven to eight gongs, depending on the community. One such ensemble is the *sopogandangan*, which is played as an accompaniment to *magarang* dancing in Tambunan, or *sumazau* in Penampang.

Sabah has a wide variety of traditional *aerophones*, including short bamboo end-blown mouth flutes called *suling*; longer nose flutes known as *turali*; jaw's harps named *turiding*; and *sompoton*, or mouth organs.

One of the *chordophones* used in Sabah is the *tonkungon*, a tube made either from a node or large *poring* bamboo. A large hole is cut in the back or in the top to enhance resonance and thin strips incised in the surface to form strings or chords.

east coast. It looks like a series of brass casseroles lined up – eight small, knobbed gongs in xylophone-form which several players gong-chime away in turn.

In Brunei a stringed lute, the *gambus,* is played to the beat of Malay dances such as *joget* and *zapin*. Its hollow body is made from *nangka*, which is covered with lizard or goat skin and the neck coated with a thin wooden veneer. Three pairs of brass or gut strings are traditionally plucked with the claw of an anteater. There's a Pesta Gambus festival held every year on Sabah's west coast among the Brunei-Malay community and there are *pesta* gongs all over the place.

Song and dance in sickness and health
Music and dance are central to Malay festivities. The *joget* is most common, a dance of lively tempo with lots of hand and leg movement, performed by couples in brilliantly coloured traditional silk dress. Its origins lie in Portuguese folk dance, having infiltrated Malay culture during the Malacca spice era. The dance is just as heated, but graceful as well, and there are several regional variations and adaptations.

The Bajau of Sabah perform dance rituals such as the *magamboh* to offer thanksgiving, though this is now an extremely rare dance performance. Dance may also be used to heal a sick member of the community, sometimes accompanied by an elaborate bath, visits to the graves of ancestors and prayers for the sick person and their family. The community as a whole takes note of the issue at hand, coming together at times of hardship and worry. After offering thanks and seeking blessing from the gods, the gong is struck and its resonant chime heralds the beginning of the dance.

Keeping the music alive
While Western influences have had an altering effect (not all negative) on Dayak music and dance in Sarawak, efforts are under way to conserve traditional art forms. A big effort is being made to revive Bajau dance traditions among young people after it was realised that most of them could perform rap and hip hop, but not the traditional *tambawan* (performed by women only), the *lellang* (by men only) and the graceful *limbaian*.

Shamans and storytelling in dance and music
Music is an important medium in many spiritualist ceremonies. The *kulintangan* is still used in some rituals presided over by the Kadazandusun *bobohizan* (or *bobolian,* depending on the tribe). Music and crafts are threaded together too, as are music and storytelling. The traditional Iban women's dance – *ngajat indu* – is performed with costumes of woven *pua kumbu* cloths. Iban music and dance tells many stories of their past as virile combatants. In the *ngajat lesong* dance, the protagonist warrior displays his might by picking up a 20kg block of wood with his mouth, then dances round with it posed on his chin. The *ngajat pahlawan* is a dance to welcome the victorious warrior home after a successful week of headhunting.

Dances celebrate death, life and birth. The *datun julud*, an Orang Ulu dance, tells of the happiness of a prince when he was blessed with a grandson. From this grew a tradition; the Kenyah tribe, whose village consists of just one longhouse, perform it to welcome guests. The dancing is accompanied by the sounds of the *sape*, and much clapping and singing. 'A common aspect of the Kayan and Kenyah tribes is the singing of the *parap*, a folklore song relating expressions of love, happiness, loneliness and anger, while singing praises for the beauty of nature and all living things,' says the Sarawak Tourism Board.

Other tribes dance to appease spirits, to ask them for harvest blessings and for spiritual healing. Others pass legend and folklore through generations. In

THE LEGEND OF HUMINODUN

The legend of Tadau Ka'amatan is that of Huminodun. Huminodun was the only daughter of the god Kinoingan, who sacrificed her (by cutting her up into many pieces) to end a great famine. It's her flesh and blood that are attributed to bountiful crops today – not only rice crops, but coconuts, maize and yams.

Malaysia's leading online newspaper *Malaysiakini.com*, Sim Kwang Yang wrote of Iban storytelling: 'They have a whole legion of folklore and myths ... a myth of creation, and legends of heroes and titans which bear some resemblance to the ancient Greek myths. Since the Ibans have no written language, their myths and legends are handed down from generation to generation by word of mouth. The telling and retelling of stories, sometimes through the lyrical form of the *Sampi* recitals that go on for hours at a time, make the Ibans great orators.... To call them merely animists is a little unfair. They certainly have a sort of pantheistic idea, in which the jungle and the land are alive with spirits.'

CRAFTS The cultural landscapes of Sabah, Sarawak and Brunei are woven in beads, fibres, fabrics and plants of many colours, shapes and forms. Every tribe has its distinctive craft and skills. The Kadazandusun are known for their hand-woven rattan baskets and bamboo musical instruments; the Rungus and Kelabits for their beadwork; the Murut for their blowpipes; and the Bajau for their colourful woven mats and food covers, *tudung dulang*. Indigenous crafts often wear a very strong mark of local flora – like part of a geo-cultural identity. Whether they have been made from forest woods or wickers, or the leaves or hard shells of tropical fruits, many of these things could not be truly replicated anywhere else.

With the vegetative world as intensely varied as it is in Borneo, there has always been quite a range of construction and crafting materials – different woods are used for boats, houses, musical instruments, hunting objects and tools; rattan was woven into rope, baskets, bird cages, mats and crates; *nipa* palm fronds used for thatched roofs; bamboo for musical instruments. Many of these 'functional' objects can appear to be quite simple – yet their often ingenious and attractive design qualifies them as traditional art, as much as the more intricate and embellished items made from precious materials.

Weaving Much of traditional life endures in Borneo; arriving in Melanau heartland in the region of Mukah, coastal Sarawak, you may see women sitting near the river weaving all kinds of basketry and traditional *terendak* sun hats from the fronds of sago palm – an economic staple and a cultural filament too.

Baskets are made by every tribe, using rattan, bamboo, *nipa* leaves and pandanus. Pandanus (screw pines) fruits are crafted into foodstuffs while their sheaths and fibre go into many household items: *tikar pandan* (pandan mats) are made by the Kadazans of Papar on Sabah's west coast. The patterns on these, having once probably been more sober, are being turned out in many colourful patterns, woven into dining and drink mats to sell to tourists, but that doesn't mean they lose their inborn crafted quality and authenticity. The Kadazandusun people also weave many rattan baskets, and purses covered in beads. The woven wonders of Borneo are not only sold to visiting foreigners however – Malaysia provides 30% of the world's rattan.

Background Information **CULTURE**

29

Fabrics Different cloths (*kain*) form the basis of diverse woven handicraft traditions. The Iranun, an ethnic minority originally from the southern Philippines who live in small pockets on the east and west coasts of Sabah, traditionally used *kain dastar* as headgear during festive celebrations. Now they use the heavily motifed fabrics to make *dastar* purses, sashes and more. The Iranun community in Kota Belud, two hours north of Kota Kinabalu, are said to have gone further – combining the *dastar* tradition with that of *songket*, which uses gold coloured threads, to create *sampin songket dastar*, an amazing fusion of the gold-coloured threads and motifs. *Songket* originated among the Malayans of Brunei. There are lots of woven fabrics and cloth in Brunei; only here you may encounter real gold thread so make sure you have your purse with you. *Kain songket* ('cloth of gold') sarongs feature a woven cloth common to Malay cultures in Brunei, Sabah and Sarawak, which originates from the days when the Sultanate ruled over all these territories. The three-quarter or full-length sarongs featuring geometric or floral patterns are part of common daily dress for many Malay people. Equally intricate and richly symbolic are the *pua kumbu* 'blankets' of Sarawak's Iban, whose abstract designs and motifs of plants and animals have a sacred link to important life passages, from birth to marriage and death.

COSTUMES The striking black velvet elegance of the Kadazandusun people attending a festival with their elaborate trimmings and embroidery stand out

BEAD CULTURE IN BORNEO

with Heidi Munan, cultural researcher and Honourable Curator of Beads at the Sarawak Museum. She has lived in Kuching for over 30 years.

The Dayaks of Borneo have long had a vibrant beadwork culture. Beads were held to impart their two salient properties – physical strength and brilliance – to the wearer. Small glass beads were brought by traders from distant lands, which added to their mystical value. The manufacture and use of bead-worked garments and ornaments was traditionally linked to a person's status within society. This applies particularly to the people of Central Borneo, where the most potent designs were restricted to the aristocracy. Beadwork itself was gender-defined in that only women threaded the beads, but men designed the patterns. Today, many old taboos and restraints have become obsolete. Not so the craft of beadwork – beadwork is produced for sale in the coastal towns; some young designers incorporate traditional design in their fashion creations. Much beadwork is still done for home use and at regional festivals the young women are covered in more beads than their grandmothers ever dreamt of owning! The skills are passed from mother to daughter and materials are readily available. In sum, beadwork is flourishing in Borneo.

Bead culture is strong in Sarawak's Kayan, Kenyah, Bidayuh and highland Kelabit communities, and among Sabah's Rungus population. In her book, *Beads of Borneo,* Heidi Munan explains that, excluding beads made from bone, teeth, seed and stone, many beads used in tribal crafts have long been imported. From as early as the 6th to the 12th century, trade with China and India brought beautiful, exotic beads. An ancient Kelabit headhunting song says that 'strangers came to buy pork and sell beads'. Later, Dutch and English explorers brought Venetian and Bohemian beads.

among the many beautiful costumes that go with ceremony, dance and music all over Sabah, Sarawak and Brunei.

According to the Kadazandusun Cultural Association, the men's jacket and trousers bear some Chinese influence. 'There are three different styles of blouses for the women. One is a blouse with short sleeves – *sinuangga* – worn by young ladies. Another is a blouse with three-quarter-length sleeves – *sinompukung* – worn by middle-aged ladies for daily or casual use. The third one – *kihongon* – is worn by elderly women and female ritual specialists or priestesses during ceremonies.' The blouses are worn over a long cylindrical black skirt – *tapi*. Traditionally it was plain black cotton but rather striking renditions are trimmed with gold *siring*. The outfit is usually in silk and velvet for ceremonial occasions and cotton for day wear. Mass-made versions are appearing to sell to tourists. Likewise the men's long-sleeved shirt, *gaung*, and black trousers, *souva*, have been dollied up with gold buttons, and trimming.

The men wear some very fancy headgear: the *siga* is a conical hat made out of hand-woven cloth, *kain dastar*, which is then folded or twisted in a number of distinctive ways including *hinopung* – python form – and *kinahu* – pot-holder style.

Like many cultures, the Kadazandusun top off their couture with lots of accessories: brass and silver spiral bracelets (*tiningkokos*); hairpins (*titimbak*) to decorate and fasten the hair bun of women's often very long dark hair; necklaces (*hamai*), earrings (*simbong*) and brooches made with gold coins (*paun*). The

Beads of varying value were used to mark out social status between the indigenous aristocrats, and the middle and lower classes within tribes. Among the Kelabits for example, lower classes were rarely allowed to wear beads or bear traditional motifs, says Heidi. 'Aristocrats would buy or exchange slaves with different families, using beads as a form of payment. If you were captured during tribal war, your family may have used beads as ransom payment.' With so much power accorded to these little gems, beads were also used in a spiritual sense – for example during agricultural rites to bless planting and harvesting of crops.

The Kelabits, both men and women, still live out the bead tradition and are busy handing it on to younger generations. Women regularly wear bead necklaces and belts made from peppercorn beads; on special occasions such as weddings, they don the bead caps called *pata* made from the noble *ba'o rawir* – drinking straw beads. Men sport *kabo* – red seed bead bobble – with their Sunday suits or *batik* shirts.

Beaded creations have become popular among tourists with a couple of major downsides – rising prices, fake productions and the loss of antique beads to far off lands. 'Short of breaking the beads,' says Heidi, 'it's hard to tell the difference.' The proliferation of fakes is getting to a point that the Kelabits were even reported to be looking at a certification system, with the authenticity of bead creations authorised by the Pemanca or high chief of the Kelabit community.

Personally I don't care if the beads I buy are not old – I would rather those artefacts be kept among those who made them. However, I do not want cheap, machine-made replicas. A traditionally made creation hanging close to you is something to treasure.

New *pata* caps sell for around 1,000MYR while an antique one can fetch well over 20,000MYR. Individual antique beads can cost from 300–1,000MYR. Heirloom beads are priceless.

more *himpogot* or silver 'dollar belts' a person is wearing, anything from one to three around the waist and hips, the more wealthy they are. Men wear a black, or sometimes coloured, waist sash (*kaking*). As for the *bobohizan* priestess, her outfit is one of total feathered splendour. If you love costumes get hold of *An Introduction to the Traditional Costumes of Sabah*; see page 316.

The costumes of Borneo's tribes reflect their ethnic diversity: the noble formality of Malay outfits; the simple black sarongs and bodices of the Rungus, emblazoned in multi-hued black beads; and the strikingly beautiful, pom-pom-strung poncho and silver-feathered headdress of the Iban.

2

Natural History

Life on Earth is not evenly spread around our planet. Borneo – the world's third largest island – is one of its richest treasure-houses, full of an immense variety of wild animals and plants, all living in a magnificent tropical forest.

Sir David Attenborough, backing the WWF's Heart of Borneo project in 2007

BIODIVERSITY

Despite extensive destruction of its natural environment through forestry and agriculture, large areas of Borneo remain a paradise of tropical forests filled with a staggering array of plants and animals. The world's 'biodiversity hotspots' cover less than 1% of the earth's surface but are home to over half of all the world's plant and animal species. Borneo is one of these hotspots, bringing it on a par with the Amazon and equatorial Africa for species diversity.

Many of these are endemic – not found anywhere else – and it's estimated there are over 5,000 flowering plants unique to Borneo, as well as some 500 mammals, birds, reptiles and fish. Indeed the island is just one of two places where the orang-utan, Asia's only great ape, has survived. The island's flora is also rich and varied. Just 10ha of Bornean rainforest can contain up to 700 tree species – more than are found in the whole of North America. The total flora count of up to 15,000 plant species includes 6,000 endemics, more than 3,000 different trees and 2,000 orchids. The WWF says Borneo may have the highest plant diversity of any region on earth: since the mid-1980s, 422 new species have been discovered.

As for animal species, scientific research in the decade up to 2004 alone upturned 260 new insects, 30 freshwater fish, seven frogs, five crabs, two snakes and one toad, to name a few. Now those finds seem to represent just the tip of the iceberg. In April 2010, three years after researchers began to probe the forests at the centre of the island, known as the 'Heart of Borneo' (HoB; see page 63), the WWF said 123 new species had been identified.

The research followed a conservation deal which was struck between the governments of Malaysia, Brunei and Indonesia to protect the 220,000km^2 rainforest zone. The new species discovered include a frog with no lungs, a 'ninja' slug which fires 'love darts' at its mates, the world's longest insect (the 57cm-long Chan's megastick), a bird called the spectacled flowerpecker and a snake whose neck blazes bright orange colours to ward off predators.

The WWF's 2010 report, *Borneo's New World: Newly Discovered Species in the Heart of Borneo*, says the Heart of Borneo is an 'island within an island', home to ten species of primate, more than 350 birds, 150 reptiles and amphibians and a staggering 10,000 plants that are found nowhere else in the world. Adam Tomasek, leader of the Heart of Borneo initiative, said the discovery of three new species a month since the

While travelling around the Malay Archipelago from 1854 to 1862, pioneering explorer and naturalist Alfred Russel Wallace made two important discoveries central to biological science.

After completing his travels around the Amazon Basin, Wallace set sail for southeast Asia, documenting his travels and collecting species he found along the way. In the eight years he spent travelling around the region he collected a staggering 125,660 specimens, 1,000 of which were new to science. Through his observations of the region's flora and fauna, Wallace formulated ground-breaking theories about the environment and the evolution of species, similar to those of Charles Darwin. However, unlike Darwin, Wallace failed to elaborate on his ideas and did not work out a mechanism as to how evolution might occur. As a result, Darwin received much more credit and fame for his work and is often quoted in history books as the sole author of the revolutionary theory.

This was not the only breakthrough that Wallace made during his time in the Malay Archipelago. Whilst travelling around the islands, he noticed a striking pattern of distribution of animals across the archipelago and identified a distinct line that separated two groups of fauna with different origins. On one side they showed similarities to species found in southeast Asia, whilst on the other side species were clearly affiliated to Australasian fauna. Wallace had discovered the fault-line boundary separating two vast continental plates that had drifted together over time effectively to bring two significantly different stocks of wildlife into close proximity. 'Wallace's Line' was consequently named in his honour.

agreement, was 'ample justification' for protecting the region. 'As the past three years of independent scientific discovery have proven, new forms of life are constantly being discovered in the Heart of Borneo. If this stretch of irreplaceable rainforest can be conserved for our children, the promise of more discoveries must be a tantalising one for the next generation of researchers to contemplate.'

GEOLOGY

Like all other islands, Borneo owes its isolation to tectonic plate movement and rising sea levels. Along with the Peninsular Malay and the islands of Java and Sumatra, the island is part of the Sunda Shelf, a stable continental shelf that runs below the shallow South China and Java seas, as an extension of mainland Asia. Youthful on a geological scale, Borneo's foundations were set in place with the buckling of the earth's crusts around 15 million years ago. Over the next three million years, these underwater landmasses were forced above sea level by tectonic plate movement. When sea levels rose at the end of the last Ice Age, 12,000 years ago, Borneo was separated from Sundaland and the other territories with which it shares much common fauna.

Even today, most of Borneo's landmass lies at less than 150m above sea level and a marshy coastal belt – composed partly of rich alluvial (deposited by water) soils washed down from the mountains – girths much of the island, and extends inland towards some hills and valleys. The centre of the island, however, is dominated by significant mountain ranges. These are concentrated in the north of Sabah, but extend southwest and northeast, with a few isolated peaks of 1,500–2,000m standing tall along the Sabah–Sarawak and Sarawak–Kalimantan borders.

SABAH Separating the low-lying coast from the rest of Sabah is the 100km-long Crocker Range, formed 35 million years ago as ocean sediments were compressed into sandstone and shale and later brought to the surface by geological uplift. Most of the range lies 500–900m above the sea, though it does feature southeast Asia's highest mountain, Mount Kinabalu (4,100m) and Malaysia's second-highest peak, Gunung Trus Madi (2,643m). Several rivers rise from this mountainous core, including Sungai Kinabatangan, Malaysia's second-longest river, which flows east to the Sulu Sea.

Rearing high over the Crocker Range, Mount Kinabalu is Borneo's highest point – and, in fact, the highest point between the Himalayas and New Guinea. The mountain was formed from a ball of molten granite beneath the earth's surface 10–15 million years ago, later hardening to form a granite mound (known as a 'pluton'). This mound was then forced upwards, bursting through the Crocker Range relatively recently – one million years ago – making it one of the earth's youngest non-volcanic mountains. These forces are still at work, and Mount Kinabalu continues to grow by more than half a centimetre each year. Glaciers from recent ice ages have shorn the sandstone and shale that once covered the granite core and carved the summit into the stunning form of sharp peaks, vertical cliffs and valleys seen today.

Another geomorphologic wonder of Sabah is Maliau Basin, a spectacular crater-like hollow with a diameter of over 20km and rugged rims reaching up to 2km in height. Formation of the basin began around 15–20 million years ago, when much of Sabah was still submerged. Through a series of deposition and deformation events, Maliau and other basins were formed, further shaped through progressive elevation and buckling of the earth's crust.

SARAWAK Inland Sarawak hosts a spectacular array of limestone features, including pinnacles, protrusions and record-breaking caves. The world's largest cave chamber and cave passage, and southeast Asia's longest cave, are all found within Gunung Mulu National Park. Sculpted by the corrosive action of water flowing through limestone and sandstone mountains, the immense subterranean system is continually being reformed; dripping water creates new features and rock is worn away by underground rivers.

BRUNEI Much of Brunei is low-lying coastal plains of alluvial soils, marked by mangrove-fringed river estuaries. The interior is dominated by hills composed of sandstone and shale that form, along with clay and mudstone, most of Brunei and west Sarawak's bedrock. The Temburong District in eastern Brunei is more mountainous, with Bukit Pagon peaking at 1,843m. Brunei Bay, which is shared with Sabah and Sarawak, is heavily indented and features marine terraces cut by waves of the South China Sea.

ECOSYSTEMS AND FLORA

Though Borneo is often perceived as the archetypal jungle-covered island, it actually hosts a variety of other equally important habitats. Though definitions differ, major ecosystem types can be divided into the following categories: tropical rainforest, montane forest, limestone forest, sub-alpine and summit forest, heath forest, coastal forests and wetlands.

2

TROPICAL RAINFOREST Tropical rainforest covers 3% of the earth's surface and lies exclusively between the tropics, in a belt around the Equator. At one time as much as 90% of Borneo was under forest cover, but today that figure is much smaller – 50–60% in Malaysian Borneo. Much of this has been logged or left to regenerate as secondary forest and only pockets of primary 'old growth' rainforest remain. In Sabah, these can be found in the central Danum Valley and Imbak Canyon region, Sepilok Forest and Tabin wildlife reserves on the east coast, and lower elevations of Mount Gunung Kinabalu National Park. In Sarawak, there is primary rainforest in some of the national parks in the south – Kubah, Bako and Tanjung Datu – and on the central and north coast, Similajau, Niah and Lambir Hills parks.

Life in the forest's layers Despite the apparent chaos of growth, tropical rainforest is actually organised into at least three overlapping vertical layers.

Emergent (or overstorey) layer These forest giants tower over the canopy layer, projecting through at heights of up to 90m. The towering slivery-grey Menggaris (*koompassia excelsa*) is one such species with trunks that grow up to 3m in diameter. The commonly named 'honeybee trees' are crowned by a mesh of horizontal branches where the giant bees (*apis dorsata*) make their nests, safely out of reach of the honey-loving sun bear.

Canopy layer Most of the productivity in a tropical rainforest occurs in the canopy. At a height of 25–45m, sunlight and rain are most available for exploitation by trees and plants.

Dipterocarp forest Trees from the Dipterocarpaceae family dominate Borneo's rainforest canopy. The country is home to some 267 species – more than anywhere else in southeast Asia – and at the latest count 155 of those were endemic. Together these species account for up to 80% of tree species in Bornean forests. Sadly, they are also subject to the highest level of commercial logging activity: 80% of Borneo was once covered in lowland dipterocarp forest, but this has now been seriously whittled away.

Understorey and lower layers Below the canopy, the understorey contains younger trees patiently waiting for a gap to appear in the canopy. When this happens, they suddenly burst into rapid growth to claim the prized position in the canopy. Smaller trees and flowering bushes are also found here, and in Borneo the understorey features many species of the Euphorbiaceae and Rubiaceae families as well as Dipterocarpaceae. Euphorbiaceae is the second most common floral family in Borneo, with over 150 species from shrubs to creepers and wild fruiting plants. In some places such as the Danum Valley, Euphorbiaceae and Rubiaceae species dominate the understorey. Other common families are Lauraceae (laurels), Ericaceae (heaths and heathers) and Annonaceae (custard apple).

Lauraceae Borneo 'ironwood' (*Eusideroxylon zwageri*), locally known as *belian*, is a species of laurel that has been used by indigenous people for centuries to make roofs and a whole range of other things. Belian trees can reach heights of up to 40m and live for several hundred years (and take almost as long to decay). They are a common (non-dipterocarp) species in undisturbed forest canopies, though they have become less prevalent in many areas due to over-exploitation for their high commercial value. Belian timber is extremely durable, and is in great demand for heavy construction, roofing, agriculture and other uses.

As is sadly the case with many tree species, *belian* is more threatened in Indonesian Borneo – the species is now considered endangered in Kalimantan. When traditional agriculture became more industrial, larger trees began to disappear at a faster rate. When farmers started using *belian* as support stakes in pepper crops in the 1970s, numbers began to decline at very high rate indeed.

Fruit trees and palms Hundreds of tree species with edible fruit and nuts are found in the rainforest and have provided indigenous people with a bountiful and varied diet for centuries. Commonly used species include durian (Bombacaceae), mango (Anacardiaceae) and pawpaw. Several fruiting trees belong to the Moraceae

READY FOR TAKE-OFF

Dipterocarp trunks emerging from their huge buttress roots 'look like rockets on the launch pad'. This fitting description was made in *Natural History* magazine in 1999. 'Their spreading limbs provide platforms and runways more than a hundred feet in the air, enabling many kinds of animals to eat, sleep, and give birth without ever descending to the ground.'

The name 'dipterocarp' comes from the Greek, meaning 'two-winged seed' and describes the helicopter-style method with which the seeds are dispersed. The cyclical, sporadic and sudden flowering of Dipterocarpaceae trees, known as masting, determines the reproductive rhythm of the entire forest. Species from orang-utans and gibbons to hornbills and bats are entirely dependent on this flowering and subsequent fruiting and the manner in which dipterocarps 'dictate bounty and scarcity in the rainforest'. 'Dipterocarps do not depend on animals or the wind to disperse their seeds. Flanked by two winglike sepals, the seeds are heavy and gyrate to the ground close to the parent tree. Mature trees may not reproduce for three to ten years and then suddenly blanket the forest floor with their pea- to walnut-sized seeds. Masting is not unique to dipterocarps, but nothing compares with what takes place here: a long hiatus in reproduction throughout the forest canopy, followed by a sudden and simultaneous fructifying.'

'Flowering of the Forest – Dipterocarp trees of Borneo', by Art Blundell was published in Natural History *magazine (US) in July 1999*

KING OF THE FOREST

Alfred Russel Wallace greatly admired wild durian (*Durio testudinarum*), dubbing the fruit 'the king of the forest' and the orange as queen. These large green fruits are common in the rainforest. Their noxious-smelling flowers and fruits are produced directly from their trunks, a phenomenon known as cauliflory. In a letter to the then director of Kew Royal Gardens, Sir William Jackson Hooker, Wallace wrote:

> The Durian grows on a large and lofty forest-tree, something resembling an Elm in character, but with a more smooth and scaly bark. The fruit is round or slightly oval, about the size of a small melon, of a green colour, and covered with strong spines, the bases of which touch each other, and are consequently somewhat hexagonal, while the points are very strong and sharp. It is so completely armed that if the stalk is broken off it is a difficult matter to lift one from the ground. The outer rind is so thick and tough that from whatever height it may fall it is never broken. As a tree ripens the fruit falls daily and almost hourly, and accidents not infrequently happen to persons walking or working under them. When a Durian strikes a man in its fall it produces a fearful wound, the strong spines tearing open the flesh, while the blow itself is very heavy; but from this very circumstance death rarely ensues.

Printed in volume 8 of Hooker's Journal of Botany *in 1856*

family including the jack-fruit-like *tarap* (*Artocarpus odoratissimus*), figs (*Ficus* sp) and many lesser-known fruits such as *peruput* (*Artocarpus rigidus*) and *timakon* (*Artocarpus lanceifolia*). One custard apple variety is used in a green, tangy drink called *sour sop*. Sago palms (*Eugeissona* sp) are a source of starchy energy, notably for the nomadic Penan who extract its fibrous pulp and turn it into flour.

Creepers and climbers The understorey is a dense, delightful world bedecked with rich entangles of lianas, lichens, orchids and epiphytic plants. The last are among the shade-tolerant species that thrive in the rainforest understorey, having developed ingenious ways of surviving. **Epiphytes** grow on the surface of other plants without needing to embed their roots in the ground and include many kinds of lichens, liverworts, orchids, mosses and ferns. **Lianas**, woody climbers, are organic ladders – they start on the forest floor but use trees, and one another, to climb towards the forest-canopy light to reproduce.

MONTANE FOREST Montane forest occurs at altitudes above 900m. This is sometimes further divided into lower montane forest (900–1,500m) and upper montane forest (1,500–3,300m).

Lower montane forest In lower montane forest the density of trees thins out, forest canopies drop as low as 20m, and oak-chestnut trees (Fagaceae) gradually take precedence over rainforest trees. Many orchids, both epiphytic and terrestrial varieties, flourish in these cooler conditions, as well as climbers such as rattan palm. In Sabah, lower montane environments exist in the Crocker Range, the Tawau Hills Park and lower elevations of Gunung Kinabalu National Park around the park headquarters. There are over 1,000 orchid species on Mount Kinabalu – 40% of all orchid species found on Borneo.

Upper montane forest In upper montane or **cloudforest** the spread of oak-chestnut trees is replaced by mossy forests rich in conifers, tea trees and pitcher plants. As altitudes rise, the vegetation becomes shrubbier in appearance and more stunted, the soils are thin and the canopy drops to 10m or less. Frequent cloud cover brings cool mists which shower the understorey and propagate luxurious undergrowths of numerous species of lichens, mosses, ferns and orchids. Colourful rhododendrons thrive particularly well in the upper reaches (3,300m).

Within Sabah, this upper montane habitat type is restricted to Mount Kinabalu and the Trus Madi mountains and the unique habitat supports many rare and restricted-range species. Studies of floristic diversity in the area have shown Mount Kinabalu's species density is greatest at altitudes of 2,500–3,000m rather than at lower elevations, as may be expected. Nine species of pitcher plant dwell on Mount Kinabalu, in the crossover of lower and upper montane forest and in the rare **ultramafic forest**, where the dark, metallic soils are rich in nutrients thanks to the presence of mineral-rich ultramafic rocks.

LIMESTONE FOREST Composed of mostly small trees and shrubs, this type of forest can be found growing on limestone hills and formations, including the Gomantong and Madai caves in Sabah, and Niah and Mulu caves in Sarawak.

SUB-ALPINE AND SUMMIT FOREST Once you rise above 3,200m on Mount Kinabalu, the upper montane forest is replaced with scrubby sub-alpine vegetation made up of gnarled, stunted, wind-blown and bare trees. These trees and small shrubs rarely grow more than 50cm and are often confined to rock crevices that contain small patches of soil and protect them from the elements. These plant species are often referred to as granite boulder flora.

HEATH ('*KERANGAS*') FOREST Though relatively rare today, heath forest consists of small, poorly nourished trees growing in highly leached (nutrients washed away by rainwater) sandy soils. Found at the same altitude as lowland rainforest, they are concentrated around Sabah's and Sarawak's coastal and inland areas. In estuarine areas of Sarawak the Iban call it *padang kerangas* ('land where padi cannot be grown'), because rainwater cannot be retained to flood the land for planting rice paddy fields. Rain falling on the open vegetation and poor soils encourages the growth of acid-loving plants such as rhododendron and the tropical she-oak *Gymnostoma*. Heath forest is low in diversity but rich in endemic plants adapted to nutrient-poor soils such as pitcher plants, climbing epiphytes and, in the Bako National Park, ant plants (*Clerodendrum*). *Kerangas* forest is also found in the Lambir Hills and Similajau national parks on northern Sarawak's coast.

COASTAL FORESTS AND WETLANDS Sarawak, Sabah and Brunei contain a variety of wetland habitats. Wide coastal plains and marshy areas almost completely surround the island, stretching for up to 70km inland along the river system. Sabah's Wildlife Department groups beach vegetation and mangroves, freshwater swamp forest and riparian riverine forest all under the umbrella of 'coastal forest'. These types of habitat are found 0–30m above sea level.

Beach forests Commonly consisting of coarse **casuarinas** coastal grass and *Pandanus* (a genus of tropical palm trees), beach forest accounts for just a few per cent of total vegetation. Due to coastal development schemes, these habitats are dwindling, now often seen as a 'decorative remnant in developed areas'. Casuarinas

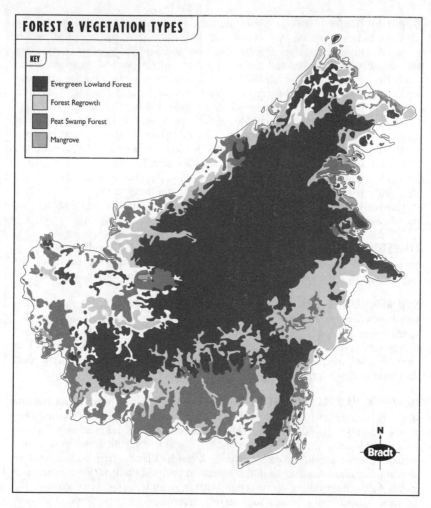

FOREST & VEGETATION TYPES

KEY

Evergreen Lowland Forest

Forest Regrowth

Peat Swamp Forest

Mangrove

N

Bradt

are colonising species seen in strips along the coast in certain areas. *Casuarina equisetifolia* is the most common variety, seen swaying in the wind at heights of 30–60m. They are joined by other, mostly herbaceous, plants and shrubs with waterborne seeds.

Only plant species that can cope with the harsh saline environment survive, and as a result plant diversity in beach forest is relatively low. Some species – known as 'strand flora' – have moved back from the water line and occur behind a casuarinas fringe and a thin strip of mangroves. One such species is seashore screw pine (*Pandanus odoratissimus*), which is regularly sighted by the coast and features in many Sabah food dishes – the flesh of its huge fruits is used to make green cakes, green coconut paste (*kaya*) and even green bread.

Mangrove forests At the frontier where the worlds of sea and land meet, mangrove trees dominate. Their success in such a hostile environment is attributed to special adaptations to cope with the high salt and low oxygen levels. As the tide subsides, the trees' secrets are revealed – arching, tangled roots protrude above the surface, allowing the trees to absorb oxygen from the air when exposed and nutrients from the water when submerged.

Mangroves form important barriers from the sea, protecting coastal lands from the erosive actions of the tides and holding together unstable sandy soils. Many species of wildlife depend on mangroves for nesting and breeding grounds, exploiting the sheltered, tangled root system to lay eggs and raise young. In Sabah, Sarawak and Brunei mangroves are important breeding grounds for leaf monkeys, crocodiles, fish, large colonies of flying foxes, and wetland birds such as herons and egrets.

Mangroves usually grow in pure stands, and can often be found adjacent to lowland rainforest and coastal heath – a prime example is the Bako National Park in Sarawak. Mangrove forests were once widespread in low-lying coastal regions and along saline river estuaries, but now account for a tiny per cent of the state. Having been harvested for firewood, building and crafts for centuries by tribal peoples, the real damage was done with extensive clearing of mangrove-covered state land for industrial and urban developments, as well as for the mangrove timbers and the woodchip industry. More mangroves are under threat with growing urbanisation. Already a big belt of Kota Kinabalu city lies on what were once mangroves, and more are set to be swallowed up with the construction of shopping malls, apartment complexes and hotels. Though large-scale harvesting of mangroves for export has now been all but phased out, they are still used locally for firewood and other uses.

Brunei has slightly more remaining, with around 4% of its territory containing intact mangrove forest. Brunei Bay has one of southeast Asia's largest (relatively) undisturbed tracts of mangrove forest.

Nipah forests Nibong (*Oncosperma*) and nipah (*Nypa fructitans*) palms are found mingling with mangroves; the former in the dryer parts of mangrove forest, the latter in tidal reaches of rivers, such as along the Kinabatangan Estuary. Nipah palms are less salt tolerant than mangroves and often occur in pure stands of 'nipah forest'. Nipah leaves are used by coastal communities – Malay, Bajau and Melenau – for roofing known as *atap*, and for basketry and other crafts. Nipah sap was once used as a form of fuel. Certain areas in Sandakan were once known as 'energy plantations' because of the large tracts of nipah forest. Many of those areas are now planted with palm oil, used (controversially) as an alternative 'green' energy source. Brunei's riverbanks and estuaries are a good place to see nipah and nibong forest.

Transitional forest The crossover area between mangrove, nipah or swamp wetlands and dry land is sometimes referred to as 'transitional forest'. This belt of vegetation is characterised by thorny nibong palms, rattan (Palmae) and brown-reddish tinged merbau trees (*Intsia palembanica*), a durable hardwood.

Swamp forest According to the Sabah Forestry Department, swamp forest can be broadly separated into freshwater swamp and peat swamp. Freshwater swamps receive their water supply from streams and rivers, while peat swamps receive moisture solely from rainfall.

Freshwater swamp forests (riparian riverine forests) When lowland rainforest is intersected by rivers, with an absence of tidal influences, specific riverine species of trees and plants flourish along the light-filled, water-lapped riverbanks: shrubs, creepers and climbing plants such as rattan, bamboo, begonias, ginger and bright yellow simpoh (*Dillenia excelsa*) grow in the fertile alluvial

2

Rafflesias, orchids, pitcher plants and other unusual blooms have come to symbolise the extraordinary beauty of Borneo's forests and the botanical wonders which exist in them. Some feature on the endangered species list, but one hopes the awe and attention they attract as 'power flowers' will help to save them.

RAFFLESIA With its cabbage-shaped, riotous ruby-coloured blooms, the rafflesia isn't just an icon in Malaysian Borneo, it's an obsession. Also known as the 'corpse flower' for the rotting-flesh smell it emits when in bloom, the foul odour of this lowland rainforest and hill forest species has done little to dampen its popularity. Indeed, challenging smells in the botanical world (durian fruits are just as malodorous) seem to heighten interest. In 1928 Swedish entomologist Eric Georg Mjöberg described the smell as 'a penetrating odour more repulsive than any buffalo carcass in an advanced stage of decomposition'. The carcass smell attracts carrion flies in what has been described as 'pollination by deception'. Far from being a carnivore, the rafflesia is a parasitic plant that embeds and spreads its roots among Tetrastigma vines. The largest species in the rafflesia family is *Rafflesia arnoldii* (also known as the corpse lily in the US), which can produce flowers up to 90cm wide and weighing over 7kg – it is the largest known flower on the planet.

The first European to report it was surgeon and lay-naturalist Joseph Arnold, who discovered it during an expedition to the depths of Sumatra in 1818 with Sir Stamford Raffles. 'To tell you the truth, had I been alone with no witnesses I should have been fearful of mentioning the dimensions of this flower,' wrote Arnold. The giant flowers had long been admired by indigenous people, who reportedly use it for labour pains and post-natal fatigue, and as an aphrodisiac and fertility charm. Anglicised in Raffles's honour, the Rafflesiaceae family consists of 17 species, five of which are found in Malaysian Borneo: *R. keithii* and *R. tengku-adlinii* are only found in Sabah, while *R. arnoldii*, *R. pricei* and *R. tuan-mudae* can be seen in both Sabah and Sarawak. The rafflesia's strongholds in Sabah include the Crocker Range, Gunung Kinabalu National Park and Maliau Basin; and Gunung Gading National Park in Sarawak. Known collectively as *Bunga pakma*, they generally grow in hill rainforest but also lower montane forests at elevations between 400–1,300m.

The rafflesia bud – a darkish brown lump the size of a large grapefruit – lies on the host vine for around nine months as it slowly swells in size. Upon its sudden opening, the giant flower heads have no leaves and virtually no stem, but five mammoth petals. Blossoming occurs over several days; during this time alerts are issued by national parks, wildlife departments and tourism offices, prompting a mad rush to see the flowers. They are at their most beautiful during their first day or two of blossoming. They then become covered in brown blemishes, and the flesh darkens and rots, to reveal a 15cm-wide fruit full of thousands of tiny, hard-coated seeds. It still isn't known whether elephants, ants, squirrels or other animals disperse the seeds – a theory hypothesised by Arnold – or why the flowers are so large.

The need for protection of the rare rafflesia is high; the flowers are threatened by spreading urbanisation, trampling by animals and people, and damage caused by egg-laying wasps. As many as nine out of every ten buds never open, apparently shrivelling and dying for inexplicable reasons.

With no specific breeding season, rafflesia can appear at any time, though blooms tend to be slightly more frequent between November and January. There are a number of hotlines you can call to check on the rafflesia status of the area you are in – check with national park or tourism offices, though you may be as likely to smell the blooms before you hear about them!

For more information see the illustrated *Rafflesia of the World* (Natural History Publications, Malaysia, 2001) by Dr Jamili Nais, Assistant Director of Research and Education for Sabah Parks.

PITCHER PLANTS Few plants capture the imagination more than the carnivorous pitcher plants (genus: *Nepenthes*). With an incredible diversity of designs, these jug-shaped, open-mouthed pitchers are modified petioles (stalks) that grow along herbaceous vines and specialise in luring, trapping and devouring insects and small animals. The insects are attracted to the anthocyanin pigments (the colourful cups are often flushed with maroon and pink) or lures of nectar around the rim. But when they venture inside the trap, they slip on the mucus-lined walls and fall into the pool of liquid at the bottom, where they are dissolved by bacteria or enzymes secreted by the plant. Because the meat-eating plants derive their nutrients in this unlikely manner, they can survive in very poor soil.

Of the 30 species of *Nepenthes* found in Borneo, around half occur in Malaysian territory. The huge *Nepenthes rajah* is the largest of the genus, and is found only in Gunung Kinabalu National Park and near Gunung Tambuyukon. The largest-ever pitcher recorded contained a staggering four litres of liquid and a half-digested rat! Other species are endemic to the upper reaches of Mount Kinabalu, including *N. burbidgeae*, *N. villosa* and *N. edwarsiana*. Also known as 'monkey cups', the pitchers are used by some tribes to cook rice or carry water.

Prime pitcher-plant locations include the Gunung Kinabalu National Park and Maliau Basin in Sabah, and Bako, Gunung Mulu and Lampir Hill national parks in Sarawak. They are far less elusive than Rafflesia, though you often have to climb to see them – most occur at 1,500–2,600m. Tham Yau Kong (e *thamyaukong@ thamyaukong.com; www.thamyaukong.com*) runs one-day to two-week *Nepenthes*-spotting tours in Sabah.

ORCHIDS Exquisitely delicate and intensely colourful, Borneo is said to house around one tenth of the world's orchid species: that's 2,500 out of a documented 25,000 species in the Orchidaceae family. About 1,200 of these (including several endemic species) are found in Gunung Kinabalu National Park. The Rothschild's slipper (*Paphiopedilum rothschildianum*) exists only on Mount Kinabalu and is so rare that its specific location on the mountain was for many years kept secret because of repeated attempts of smuggling. Now protected by law, its close relatives include four other 'slipper orchid' species, one of which (*P. dayanum*) is also classed as endangered.

Other orchid treasures, says Dr Jamili Nais of Sabah Parks, include 'an amazing gigantic elephant-ear orchid (*Phalaneopsis gigantean*); peculiar species like the snake orchid (*Paraphalaneopsis labukensis*), which has rounded, cylindrical leaves looking like a snake; and the giant or tiger orchid (*Grammatophyllum speciosum*). About 120 Bornean orchids are on the IUCN's Red List– at least 70 of which are listed as critically endangered.

RHODODENDRONS Adding resplendent colour to rainforest and mountain environments, Borneo's 50 or so species of rhododendron range from ground-
continued overleaf

hugging shrubs to hanging epiphytes, with pink and red tubular flowers. Around 30 are found in Sabah, including 12 endemic species. Gunung Kinabalu National Park is a good place to see them.

LIPSTICK FLOWERS Various species of extravagant, multi-coloured 'lipstick flowers' (genus: *Aeschynanthus*, family: Gesneriaceae) are found in both Sabah and Sarawak. These Old World epiphytes flourish in temperate, montane forest environments such as Mount Kinabalu. According to Anthony Lamb, British botanist and author of *The Lipstick Flowers of Sabah* and *The Lipstick Flowers of Sabah and Sarawak* (Singapore Botanic Gardens, 2003/2005) the name was originally applied to *Aeschynanthus pulcher* from Java, because the flower buds emerging from the cylindrical calyx tube look like ladies' lipsticks. Former director of Sabah's Agricultural Park, Lamb has catalogued some of the most rare and unusual species including *A. magnificus*, *A. speciosus*, *A. tricolour* and *A. siphananthus*. Sabah has over 25 types alone, ten of which are found on Mount Kinabalu.

soils. Riverine forest plays an important role in absorbing floodwaters, protecting riverbanks and reducing soil erosion from hill slopes into rivers.

Peat swamp forests Mostly seen in Sarawak, peat swamp forests lie further inland from the mangroves and nipah, woven within river deltas. Acidic peat swamp forms as deposits of organic matter build up behind the mangroves and rivers drain towards the coast. These mires – the likes of which exist in the Maludam National Park in southern Sarawak – are habitats for proboscis monkeys and langurs; Sarawak's rare reptile, the false gharial; and aquatic species, including numerous wetland birds some of which will be on long continental migrations. Peat swamp forest covers 15,000km^2 of Sarawak's coastline, but the forests have been so extensively exploited to feed Sarawak's sawmills that they are almost depleted of timber trees.

MARINE ECOSYSTEMS Coral reefs and seagrass beds are the two most important marine ecosystems around Borneo. The latter are important grazing grounds for dugongs (sea cows) and sea turtles, and provide vital nurseries for many species of fish. Coral reefs are equally vibrant ecosystems. Indeed, much of Sabah's east coast and surrounding islands touch on an area dubbed the 'Coral Triangle', which encompasses the Sulu and Sulawesi seas. Over 1,800 species of fish have been recorded here, including 400 species of algae, five of the world's eight species of sea turtle, 22 marine mammal species and over 450 types of coral.

However, the reefs also face several challenges: the large rivers of Sarawak deposit sediment around the coast hindering coral formation and many of Sabah's reefs have been damaged by the practice of dynamite fishing – using explosives to surface dead fish en masse – as well as coral bleaching, sedimentation, coastal development and over-fishing. Serious conservation issues are being faced in the border-crossing area shared by Malaysia, the Philippines and Indonesia. Soaring populations and subsequent urban waste and pressure on resources, poaching and fishing piracy are all stressing the fragile ecosystem.

Enormous efforts are being made by Malaysian grassroots organisations and international NGOs to work with local communities and help them protect the seas around Borneo. WWF Malaysia has several conservation programmes in the region, and many efforts are under way to expand the protected marine zones. The Marine Conservation Society has been working with Sabah Parks on the Semporna Islands project since 1988 to protect the marine biodiversity of the area and ensure a better future for the people who depend on its islands and reefs. The first milestone was the establishment in 2004 of the Semporna Islands Park (also known as the Tun Sakaran Marine Park) – Malaysia's largest marine park. Situated off the southeast coast of Sabah, it covers 340km^2 of sea and coral reefs, 10km^2 of land and eight islands. Since 2005, the UK-based Darwin Initiative, which helps countries safeguard their biodiversity by funding collaborative projects, has been backing conservation strategies in the park. Current activities are focused on raising awareness of marine biodiversity as well as working with local communities to promote alternative livelihoods that will alleviate pressure on reef resources.

FAUNA

MAMMALS Logging activities have shrunk Bornean forests, and the habitat of an estimated 222 mammals, to half their original size. Displaced animals include elephants, rhinos and wildcats, and 44 endemic mammals, from iconic species such as the orang-utan and proboscis monkey to lesser-known wonders including banded langurs, tree-climbing sun bears, giant squirrels and the Borneo clouded leopard. Smaller mammals to be found include otters (hairy-nosed, oriental and small-clawed), porcupines, tree shrews, rats, bats and scaly pangolins. Nocturnal creatures include the 'flying lemur' or *colugo* (see box, page 55), bearded pig, the sambar deer and the world's smallest hoofed mammal – the lesser mouse deer.

The total mammal count rises sporadically with exciting new discoveries and new 'mystery mammals' that baffle scientists. However, the depletion of Borneo's forests does not bode well for the survival of its mammals, especially endangered species like the Sumatran rhinoceros and pygmy elephant, which are only sighted occasionally.

Primates Some of the world's most interesting primate species are found on Borneo, and are relatively easy to see in the island's 'open' forests. Primates are characterised by their grasping hands with fingers rather than paws; fingernails rather than claws; and eyes on the front of the face, enabling stereoscopic colour vision.

Borneo is home to two types of ape – not including humans – orang-utans and gibbons; eight Old World monkeys (family: Cercopithecidae), including macaques, langurs (leaf monkeys) and the peculiar proboscis monkey; the slow loris, and the extraordinary tarsier, a primate so strange that taxonomists still cannot agree on which group it should be classified in. The prosimian (suborder that most closely represents ancestral primates) lorises and tarsiers are strictly nocturnal, but Borneo's monkeys and apes are active mostly during the day.

Apes
Orang-utans (*Pongo pygmaeus*) With its innate magnetism and undeniable appeal, the 'man of the forest' – from the Malay *orang* for 'person' and *hutan* for 'forest' – has become a mascot of Borneo, which is home to 90% of the world's orang-utans. The other 10% of the 'real ape' population exists in the tropical forests of neighbouring Sumatra. Asia's only great ape exists exclusively in the tropical rainforest of the islands of Borneo and neighbouring Sumatra. Actually of African origin, they are thought to have dispersed to Asia during the Miocene period.

Orang-utans are almost entirely arboreal, spending more time in the trees than any of the other great apes. Males may reach up to 100kg, making them the largest arboreal animal on the planet, though the largest males may descend to the ground to cross gaps in the trees, travelling on all fours on the forest floor. Due to their large size, orang-utans use a form of locomotion known as quadrumanual climbing rather than the brachiating technique used by many other primates (see *Gibbons*, pages 48–9). This involves clambering through the trees grasping firmly with both hands and feet. They are surprisingly agile considering their size, aided by their extremely long arms, which may reach up to 2m long in males. As they do not swing or jump, 'orangs' will rock branches back and forth until they reach the other side.

Females may be up to 50% smaller than males; sexual dimorphism is so extreme it led early European explorers to believe they were entirely different species. Dominant males grow huge pads on their cheeks, and exhibit their superior rank by 'long calling', a booming grunt that can be heard up to 2km away and may be accompanied by violent branch shaking. Unlike other apes, orang-utans are largely solitary, spending much of their time travelling alone looking for food. A mother will be accompanied by her offspring until it becomes independent at around eight to ten years. Orangs have a long childhood, and may be suckled for up to six years. During this time they will watch their mother closely, learning which foods are good to eat and how to process them. Wild orang-utans enjoy a long life, some living up to an estimated age of 70 years.

Orang-utans will eat a diet of 100% fruit when it is available, but more usually this constitutes 60% of their dietary intake. They move around the forest based on the availability of fruits, building a mental map of the forest to remember where and when trees are fruiting. A variety of other foods are eaten, including leaves, fungi, eggs, honey termites and small vertebrates. Orang-utans have a predilection for figs, and will stay in a laden tree for days on end, gorging themselves on the sweet fruits. They are the only species other than elephants that can crack open the sugar-rich durian fruit. As such, they are important dispersers of seeds through the forest.

Orang-utans are mostly active during the day. Each evening, an individual will construct a sophisticated nest high in the trees, weaving thin branches together to make a flat sleeping platform complete with a 'roof' to provide shelter from the rain. As well as being a flagship species, orang-utans are also an 'indicator species' – barometers for the well-being of the forest. If orang-utan populations are declining, it is a sign that the forest and all that live within it are in trouble too.

WHY ARE ORANG-UTANS ORANGE?

The long, shaggy, bright orange body hair of the orang-utan is immediately striking and unmistakable. Variation between individuals is great and may change with age, from bright orange in infants to auburn and deep burgundy in adults. But why is the 'red ape' so vividly coloured?

Whilst the fiery colours blaze in the sunlight, they virtually disappear in the shadows of the forest canopy. The dark skin underneath absorbs the light so it is this you see rather than the hair on top, making the ape functionally black and virtually invisible. This 'trick of the light' may help orang-utans to blend into their scenery, whilst enabling them to be seen by other members of the species – another explanation for their bright colouring is to announce their presence to other orang-utans.

USELESS, DIRTY AND DUMB OR DIGNIFIED AND INTELLIGENT?

Adorable and endangered, orang-utans tug at many people's heart strings for the plight they have endured and they have become a flagship for Malaysian tourism – but it hasn't always been that way. Orang-utans were once depicted as useless, dirty and dumb by 19th-century explorers and scientists, write Gisela Kaplan and Lesely J Rogers in *The Orang-utans* (Allen and Unwin, Australia 1999).

Stories were told of orang-utan males who abducted fragile English ladies and raped them in trees. The orang-utan was said to grow too large and strong for a pet, and to be of only limited use as a domestic helper. The ape was said to compare poorly in entertainment value to the chimpanzee and, overall, was not perceived as having any immediate medical or research value. It was further alleged that the orang-utan was difficult to observe, boring to watch because of its 'sluggish' behaviour and difficult to keep confined.

Based on their experiences with orang-utans in Sabah, the authors saw just how far from dumb these animals were, particularly in the extent to which they are adapted to their rainforest environment.

The fact that the orang-utan's habitat is shrinking seems all the more cruel when we understand how resourceful and flexible orang-utans are. In everything they do they are master generalists, just as humans are said to be. They are perhaps the fastest of the great apes in problem solving, have excellent memories and are superb imitators. They are also very skilled trapeze artists – as the largest mammal in the canopy, negotiating this habitat requires developed cognitive abilities.

Orang-utans are accomplished and innovative tool users, using leaves as hats or umbrellas when it rains, or as gloves to climb spiky-trunked trees. Sumatran orang-utans craft termite-capturing 'fishing rods' from twigs, poking them into termite nests to collect the insects as chimpanzees do. This intelligence goes beyond the confines of life in the rainforest. Orang-utans fall within a cognitive circle which was once thought to only include humans: they can make fires, learn to play a guitar, wash clothes, use tools and imitate whatever they see humans do, by simply observing rather than by being taught. 'In some areas a five-year-old orang-utan may perform at about the same level as a four-year-old human child.' They are in fact 97% genetically similar to us, sharing a common ancestor 10–12 million years ago.

Orang-utans are gentle, intelligent, complex and contemplative, often sitting for hours just gazing. As Willie Smits told *The Age* newspaper in 2004, 'The world would be a better place if humans were a bit more like orang-utans.'

Orang-utan conservation The orang-utan's dependence on trees for food and shelter, its slow breeding rate and need for large amounts of space, make it extremely vulnerable to hunting and habitat loss. Females may not breed until they reach 17 years of age, and with an inter-birth period of eight to nine years – the longest of any mammal – populations struggle to recover from losses. Around 40,000–50,000 wild orang-utans are thought to be left today – a figure half what it was 20 years ago – and the remaining population is suffering dramatic declines greater than ever before. At current rates, the orang-utan could be the first great ape to be made extinct in modern times.

The two habitat countries of the orang-utan, Malaysia and Indonesia, established protection for the species over 30 years ago, at a time when the 'red ape' and its plight was relatively unknown; they endured capturing, poaching and trade for pets and other markets. Things seemed to be looking hopeful as hunting and trading began to let up, national parks were established and laws began to be enforced. The first orang-utan rehabilitation centre was opened in Sarawak in 1961 by pioneering Barbara Harrison, and killing the apes was forbidden by law two years later in Sabah.

However, things changed as Indonesia and Malaysia entered the global economy in the 1980s and '90s. Indiscriminate logging and the conversion of forests to plantations for cash crops such as palm oil soon superseded any previous willingness to protect the species. Fires raged in Kalimantan as companies cleared forests to make way for crops, releasing huge amounts of carbon dioxide into the atmosphere, contributing to global climate change and increasing the El Niño effect of drought in the tropics – fuelling further fires and destroying more of the orang-utan's habitat. Around 80% of orang-utan habitat has been radically degraded or totally destroyed, and orang-utans without rainforest are like fish without a sea.

The 1990s saw numerous campaigns and documentaries, bringing the orang-utan into the spotlight as they captured the hearts of the world. Reports of cruelty and illegal transportation of orang-utan babies made international headlines. One famous case was that of the 'Bangkok Six' in 1990. Six orang-utans were transported from Borneo to Bangkok in wooden crates, one of which was upside down for the whole trip, without food and water. Photos of the frightened, exhausted babies shocked and saddened readers worldwide. Though things have improved, the occasional case crops up that makes me question whether things have really changed at all. In July 2007, I opened a local newspaper in Sabah to read headlines of attempted smuggling of dozens of orang-utans, including babies. They were found packed into a cage ready to be taken to the Netherlands for scientific tests, excreting on each other and even cannibalising each other. The sheer unconcerned cruelty was simply heartbreaking.

Illegal logging, conversion of the forest to plantations and the illegal pet trade are the main continuing threats. In some previously densely forested regions of Sabah and Sarawak that have been given over to large plantations, the orang-utan is considered to be a complete pest, one that must be disposed of to save crops. The fact that hunting orang-utans is illegal has not eliminated the practice.

What can be done to help? Increasing foreign investment will allow Malaysia and Indonesia to rely less on their raw natural resources and manage them more efficiently. Introducing certification of ethically sourced (sustainable) palm oil and labelling of products on supermarket shelves, will allow consumers to avoid palm oil that has not been produced from sustainable sources. The Malaysian government needs to ensure that laws are enforced and the orang-utans – and the forests on which they depend – are protected.

Gibbons Gibbons are the smallest of the ape family (indeed they are often referred to as 'lesser apes') and Borneo is home to two species – the **Bornean** or **Mueller's gibbon** (*Hylobates muelleri*), whose distribution extends throughout much of the island, and the **agile gibbon** (*Hylobates agilis*), found only in Indonesian Borneo. Both species inhabit dipterocarp forests, swinging with admirable ease through the high canopy using a form of locomotion known as 'brachiation'. This involves the gibbon hooking its long fingers over a branch and using a hand-over-hand, under-branch motion to effortlessly and gracefully swing through the trees at high speed like arboreal acrobats.

Gibbons live in family units consisting of two monogamous adults and two to three offspring. These pairs were thought to be faithful until studies revealed that mating with neighbours was common during inter-group encounters and some pairs will allow an extra adult to join them for short periods! Pairs do still mate for life though, and sing powerful duets at dawn to both strengthen the bond between them and announce their presence to the neighbours. The whooping song of the gibbon is one of the most evocative sounds of the forest, and can be heard up to 2km away.

Old World monkeys These fall into two distinct groups: the generalist Cercopithecinae sub-family, and the specialist Colobinae sub-family. The Cercopithecinae, or 'cheek-pouch monkeys', have evolved pockets in their mouths, which they fill with food and then retire to a safer place to eat. They also have 'ischial callosities', fleshy pads on their rear ends that act as built-in cushions. The only Cercopithecines outside of Africa are the macaques, of which Borneo is home to two species. In contrast, the Colobinae are selective in what they eat, choosing only leaves. These are digested in bacteria-inhabited, sacculated stomachs which process the toxins found in the leaves. Borneo's five langur species (also known as 'leaf monkeys') and the bizarre proboscis monkey are all members of the Colobinae.

Langurs Langurs, or leaf monkeys, are nimble primate lightweights at just 5–7kg in weight and 200–600cm in length. 'Langur' means 'long tail', and they certainly live up to their name – their tails are often longer than their bodies. Langurs are a diverse group found across Asia, and Borneo is home to five species.

The most widespread is the **maroon langur** (*Presbytis rubicunda*). Also known as the red langur, its fur is actually a fiery orange, with a ghostly blue-tinged face. Maroon langurs can be seen in lowland rainforest in Sabah and Sarawak, and in hill and mountain forests including those in the Kelabit Highlands. **Hose's langurs** (*Presbytis hosei*) are found in the northwest of the island, and have a grey upper and cream lower body with black hands and feet. Their pale pink faces have distinct black bands across the cheeks and a prominent black crest on top of the head. Hose's langurs (also known as gray langurs) live in the canopy of lowland and hill forests.

THE PROBOSCIS MONKEY

The peculiar proboscis monkey (*Nasalis larvatus*) is an endemic species to Borneo and a few small islands very close to its shores. Its most distinguishing feature is its nose, huge and fleshy in males, and upturned and pixie-like in females. The male's pendulous nasal feature grows continuously and may reach a quarter of the length of his body! The function of this strange facial appendage remains to be determined, though it is thought to act as both an 'organ of resonance', amplifying the male's strange *kee-honk* vocalisation, and a thermoregulatory device. Females also seem to prefer males with larger noses.

Together with their pot belly and swaggering gait, the proboscis monkey's large nose led locals to nickname them *kera belanda* ('Dutch monkeys') – a rather unkind reference to the Dutch plantation owners of colonial times. The pot belly contains bacteria that help to digest the monkey's diet of toxin-containing leaves. The spindly legs that dangle from beneath these strange-looking primates as they rest also once earned them the description of looking like they are wearing 'a bomber jacket over ballet tights'.

Proboscis monkeys live near the waterways and coasts of Borneo, in mangrove, nipah, peat swamp and riverine forests. They can be seen catapulting themselves across expanses of water by swaying branches back and forth to gain momentum or, when a gap is too large, diving into the water and swimming across single file. With partially webbed feet, proboscis monkeys are accomplished swimmers. On land they will sometimes walk bipedally, swaggering and swaying from side to side on their hind legs.

Proboscis monkeys are threatened by habitat loss and fragmentation – the monkeys cannot cross plantations, which effectively isolate remaining populations.

Some of the best places to observe proboscis monkeys include Brunei's mangrove forests and riverbanks, Sarawak's Bako and Kuching Wetlands national parks, and Sabah's Kinabatangan river area and the Klias Wetlands. Proboscis monkeys are now rivalling orang-utans as the most popular primates to see in Borneo – it seems their striking appearance may help to save them from extinction. If they continue to draw in economy-boosting tourists, they may prove to be a viable alternative to cash crops.

Found exclusively in Sarawak, the inky **banded langur** (*Presbytis melalophos*) is so called due to its distinctive black cheek bands. Colouring varies between black and white, black, red and white, and (in *Presbytis melalophos cruciger* – one of several recently identified types) burgundy with black markings. Adult males make a distinctive, loud *ke-ke-ke* call. Banded langurs live in lowland and hill forest including those in the Tanjung Datu and Maludam national parks. The **silvered langur** (*Presbytis cristata*) bears a physical resemblance to the banded variety, but it lacks the bands on its face – instead it is entirely charcoal coloured. The extremely rare **Miller's grizzled langur** is found only in some forests of East Kalimanton.

Macaques Macaques are one of the most successful primate genera, with a wider geographical range than any other primate except *Homo*. Unlike most other monkeys, macaques spend a lot of their time on the forest floor and lower canopy levels, where they feed on a variety of foods from fruit, leaves and seeds to insects, eggs, lizards and other small invertebrates. The **pig-tailed macaques** (*Macaca nemestrina*) of Borneo have a short tail that is carried half-erect, resembling that of a pig – hence the name. They are mostly olive-brown in colour, with whitish underparts and brunette patches on the head and neck. Males can reach up to 9kg and measure 500cm and can be quite intimidating with their stocky stature and bold nature.

Long-tailed macaques (*Macaca fascicularis*) are varying shades of grey and reddish-grey with fairer hair underneath. Many have prominent cheek whiskers and facial hair. Travelling in large troops of 20–30, they can cover up to 1.5km between dawn and dusk and can be very noisy.

Both of Borneo's macaque species live in lowland rainforest and hill forest as high as 1,300m; the long-tailed macaque is also found on coastal wetlands, small islands, mangroves and beach forest. Macaques will raid plantations and sometimes tourist lodges, so beware! I have had my fair share of run-ins, including one in the forest while pointing a camera lens too close at a pig-tailed macaque – not advisable. In my experience, the pig-tailed variety is more menacing.

Prosimians These are the forerunners of the monkeys and apes, 'prosimian' literally meaning 'before monkeys'. Of the two sub-orders of primates, prosimians make up the Strepshirhini, or wet-nosed primates. Primates within this sub-order, which include the lemurs of Madagascar, bushbabies of Africa and lorises of Asia, rely more heavily on olfactory (smell) communication and possess several anatomical differences from the other, more visually oriented Haplorhini primates which include monkeys, apes and humans.

Slow lorises (*Nycticebus menagensis*) In contrast to the other fast-moving agile primates of Borneo, the nocturnal slow loris takes things at a much slower pace, creeping and clambering through the forests at night with slow, deliberate movements. Lorises can cling to branches for hours on end with their powerful grip, and communicate through the forest using olfactory and auditory – including ultrasonic – communication. Grey-brown to reddish brown in colour, with a dark strip down the spine towards the base of the short tail, lorises are among the least-studied of all primates. Their diet consists of slow-moving, often toxic invertebrates. Lorises produce toxic secretions themselves, exuded from their underarms, which they lick to numb prey when biting into them. These prosimians can reach up to 28cm in length and weigh around 2kg. Protected under Sabah's 1963 Fauna Conservation Ordinance, these endangered primates are threatened with habitat destruction and hunting.

Western tarsiers (*Tarsius bancanus*) Tarsiers are something of a bone of contention in primate taxonomy (and they take their name from their extended tarsus leg bone). Scientists cannot agree on which of the two primate sub-orders they should belong to, with compelling evidence for their inclusion in either group. This bizarre-looking nocturnal primate looks like it could be an extra from *The Lord of the Rings*; its extraordinarily large eyes are the biggest of any mammal in relation to body size, with each eyeball weighing more than its brain! Their long, powerful hind legs fold thrice into a zigzag at rest but spring into action as the diminutive creature makes spectacular leaps of up to 40 times its body length between the trees. Tarsiers live in lowland rainforests across Borneo, though they are rarely seen. Nocturnal species are often located by shining torches into the darkness and looking for the reflected torchlight from the animals' eyes. However, tarsiers lack such reflective eyes, enabling them to remain elusive in the dark forests at night. More often they are heard, making distinctive high-pitched shrieks. Tarsiers are among the smallest primates in the world, 70–150cm in length and weighing around 1kg. Their diet is entirely carnivorous, consisting of large insects and lizards, and even bats and birds. The best place to see them in Borneo is the Danum Valley in Sabah.

Large mammals

Borneo pygmy elephants Despite being known as a 'pygmy' species, the Borneo pygmy elephant is still among the largest land mammals in Asia, with males reaching over 2m in height. However, they are still much smaller than their mainland Asian counterparts, who can stand at over 3m tall, whilst their African cousins are even larger. Their compactness gives them an endearing charisma, and their tolerant nature allows onlookers to get up fairly close to them. The herbivorous pachyderms are an important part of the forest ecosystem, trimming vegetation and dispersing seeds throughout the forests. They are also lovers of durian, swallowing the fruits whole – spikes and all.

Recent genetic and archaeological evidence appears to have solved the riddle of the Borneo pygmy elephant's origins. Thought for many years to have been introduced from mainland southeast Asia or Sumatra, genetic evidence recently revealed the species to be genetically distinct from other southeast Asian elephants, strengthening the case for their protection as a distinct species. Whilst some scientists immediately heralded Borneo's elephants as an endemic species (*Elephas maximus borneensis*), more recent research has shown that there is no archaeological evidence of a long-term elephant presence on Borneo. So where *did* they come from? It appears that the 'Borneo' pygmy elephant is in fact the last vestiges of a subspecies that has long been extinct on its native island – Java. The last of the Javan elephants disappeared shortly after Europeans arrived in southeast Asia, and the 1,500 or so remaining in Borneo are most likely the descendants of two individuals introduced to Borneo 300 years ago as a gift from the Sultan of Sulu (present-day Philippines). These findings make it even more crucial to protect them from the habitat destruction, poaching and persecution that threaten them today.

Many of the elephants' traditional migratory routes have been converted to plantations, bringing them into conflict with humans when they continue to travel through them.

Elephants can cause considerable damage as they walk through, and forage in, farmers' crops. Their range is fairly small, restricted to lowland rainforest of eastern and central Sabah (Danum Valley and surrounding areas), and into Kalimantan. This range is being further eaten into by conversion of forests to plantations, bringing the elephants into more conflict with people.

Sumatran (Asian two-horned) rhinoceros (*Dicerorhinus sumatrensis*) The Sumatran rhinoceros, also known as the Asian two-horned or hairy rhinoceros, is the smallest of the five extant species of rhino today – at around 2.5m long, just over 1m tall and weighing around 800kg. The Sumatran rhino is a tropical forest ungulate (hoofed, grazing animal), classified along with horses, zebras and tapirs as 'perissodactyls' – odd-toed ungulates – as they have three toes.

There are two subspecies, only one of which (*Dicerorhinus sumatrensis harrissoni*) is found on Borneo. The other (*Dicerorhinus sumatrensis sumatrensis*) is native to Sumatra and Peninsular Malaysia. Their reddish-brown hide has patches of stiff, dark hair which keeps mud caked to the body, helping to cool the animal and protect it from insects. Regular mud-wallowing keeps the protective layer intact. Despite their thick skin, Sumatran rhinos are teetering on the edge of extinction after years of heavy poaching and habitat destruction.

'Rhinoceros' means *nose-horn*, and the animals have been hunted for decades for their keratin-rich horns, which are used in Asian medicine. The creation of forestry access roads deep into the forest home of the rhino led to an influx of poachers who target rhinos, especially in the Tabin Wildlife Reserve and several

RHINO AND ELEPHANT CONSERVATION

The WWF considers the three Asian rhino species as 'flagships' – 'charismatic representatives of the biodiversity of the complex ecosystems they inhabit'. By protecting them and their habitat, many other species benefit. WWF teams have been working on rhino conservation for decades. In 1998 WWF created the Asian Rhino and Elephant Action Strategy (AREAS), aimed at not only protecting specific areas but at reviewing land-use practices, strengthening anti-poaching efforts, monitoring trade of rhino horns and raising public awareness. The Sumatran rhino – *Badak Sumatra* in Malay – is a protected species within Sabah's national parks and reserves. According to the WWF, only two areas in Sabah – Tabin and the Ulu Segama-Kuamut area – contain rhino populations with prospects of long-term survival, 'if adequate protection and management is allowed'.

Amid serious forest loss, the Sabah government moved to protect the Tabin rhino population in 1984, with the establishment of the 1,225km^2 Tabin Wildlife Reserve.

The rhinoceros of the Ulu Segama-Kuamut area, says the WWF, are scattered through a vast area of several contiguous forest reserves, 'probably centred within an area of less than 4,000km^2 in the catchment areas of the upper Segama and upper Kuamut Rivers'. The latter area includes the Danum Valley and Maliau Basin Conservation areas in the Sabah Foundation's 100-year logging concession.

In 2003, WWF and Columbia University researchers proved that Borneo's elephants are genetically distinct from other Asian elephants. Together with Sabah's Wildlife Department, surveys have been carried out on elephant populations, tracking them with satellite radio collars. Despite being endangered, they are not a protected species in Sabah and are very vulnerable to being hunted, shot at or electrocuted for 'trespassing' on oil palm plantations. The WWF calls them 'the least-understood elephants in the world'. What is known is that they rely on having large open areas to live in – but their habitat is increasingly shrinking.

areas adjacent to the Danum Valley Forest Reserve,' says the WWF. It is in these areas that conservation efforts are being focused.

The Sumatran rhino is classified as 'Critically Endangered' on the IUCN Red List, though the WWF worryingly claim it to be 'possibly extinct' in Sarawak and Kalimantan, with 'fewer than 25 surviving in Sabah' (the IUCN on the other hand believe there could be up to 50). Once widespread throughout Borneo, numbers have plummeted in recent times, dropping by half in the last 15 years. The original threats of poaching and deforestation, are now joined by the palm oil industry as more and more forest is converted to plantations (see page 60).

Bornean clouded leopard (*Neofelis nebulosa diardi*) In 2007, Borneo's largest predator was recognised as a unique subspecies. Based on DNA research, scientists at the US National Cancer Institute concluded that the 1m-long wildcat – one of Asia's largest – differed from mainland species it had previously been lumped with, to a similar extent that other large cat species such as leopards and snow leopards differ. The species diverged around 1.4 million years ago, around the time Borneo separated from the mainland.

Separate studies of fur patterns also provided a key. Mainland leopards have large cloud-like markings on their skin – swirls of black around big tawny patches; their Bornean cousins are the inverse: thin tawny cloud-linings, around many more speckled dark clouds and with much more black overall. The clouded spots provide effective camouflage, allowing the leopard to hide from its prey in the forest, pouncing on unsuspecting deer, wild pigs and monkeys. Their presence is an indication of forest health – the fact that they are rarely sighted today shows not only the effects that habitat loss and over-hunting have had on their populations, but also how degraded the forests themselves have become.

Civets Of the several kinds of cat-like civets, the largely tree-dwelling, usually nocturnal binturong (*Arctictis binturong*) is perhaps the most fascinating, known as the 'bear-cat' because its stocky, dark-furred body gives it a bear-like appearance.

CLOUDED CONSERVATION

The clouded leopard, or *harimau dahan* in Malay, is a 'totally protected species' in Sarawak, and protected in Sabah's parks and reserves. It is listed as endangered by CITES and vulnerable by the IUCN. The WWF maintains an extensive leopard conservation operation, and puts Borneo's clouded leopard population at somewhere between 5,000 and 11,000. Their 'last great forest home' is the Heart of Borneo, in both Sabah and Kalimantan.

Extensive conservation and research work on this species is being carried out by the American Clouded Leopard Project, which provides this insight on the leopard's behaviour:

Clouded leopards are one of the best climbers in the cat family. They are able to climb upside down underneath tree branches and hang from branches with their hind feet. Several adaptations allow the leopards to achieve these amazing arboreal skills: their legs are short and stout, providing excellent leverage and a low centre of gravity while climbing; large paws with sharp claws allow them to gain a good grip on tree branches; and the tail is extremely long – up to three feet, the same length as its body – and is extremely important as a balancing aid.

The 'flying lemur' is a double misnomer, for it is neither a lemur nor does it truly fly. Though it is not a primate like a lemur, recent research suggests that it may be the closest living relative of the primate group. Previous studies had indicated it was more closely related to the Scandentia group, which includes tree shrews.

Flying lemurs (also known locally as *colugos* or *kubungs)* belong to the Dermoptera group. Dermoptera literally means 'skin wings' and refers to the patagium, a flap of skin between its limbs and tail, which is used to glide (rather than fly) between the trees of Borneo's forests. The strange squirrel-like animal can reach distances of up to 70m using its 'wings', though is much less adept at climbing trees. During the daytime, *colugos* hang upside down much like bats, or cling to tree trunks. They come out at dusk and feed throughout the night on leaves, flowers and sap, which they scrape from tree trunks using a 'comb' formed by the fusion of lower teeth.

Other civets include the masked palm civet (*Paguma larvata*) and common palm civet (*Paradoxurus hermaphroditus*), Malay civet (*Viverra tangalunga*) and Sunda otter-civet (*Cynogale bennettii*).

Sun bear (*Helarctos malayanus*) Averaging 1m in length, the sun bear, or honey bear as it is also known, is the world's smallest bear species. Endemic to Borneo, the sun bear is largely arboreal and primarily nocturnal, feeding on insects in the rainforests at night. As their alternative name suggests, they also have a taste for honey, using their long, sharp claws to reach beehives at the top of tall trees. Their dark fur makes them difficult to spot in the dark, though the V-shaped patch of lighter fur on its chest is a giveaway. Its intimidating 'bark' and hoarse grunts drive off potential threats – Sarawak Forestry classifies it, along with the pygmy elephant, as one of the few potentially dangerous animals on the island, because of the 'unpredictability of its behaviour'. The *beurang*, as it is known in Malay, is threatened by habitat loss and poaching, both for meat and medicinal purposes, and is listed by the IUCN as endangered.

Giant squirrel (*Ratufa affinis*) This dark-furred squirrel with a white underbelly and luxurious brush tail is one of the world's largest tree-dwelling rodents, growing up to 50cm in length to the tip of the tail, and weighing up to 1.5kg. It feeds on leaves, shoots, birds' eggs, bark and insects during the day when it is most active and can make leaps of up to 6m between trees. It is fiercely territorial, defending its home patch with raspy chattering sounds.

Bearded pig (*Sus barbatus*) This surprisingly large creature, looking much like a wild boar but with far more facial hair, can be rather formidable in appearance but is actually quite shy by nature. Their long, oversized heads are covered with a coarse beard of bristles all the way along the lower jaw, made even more ungainly by upward-pointing incisors that protrude from either side. Though they are primarily nocturnal, I have sighted them during the day lolling around muddy environs of the Bako National Park in Sarawak, foraging for earthworms, fallen fruits and seeds. The bearded pig's thick skin and lightly fuzzy coat colouration varies from grey to reddish brown, depending on how much wallowing it has been doing.

Natural History FAUNA

2

The females make large nests on higher flood-free ground, out of piles of torn-off shrubs, saplings and plants.

BIRDS Borneo's forests are alive with birdsong. Of the island's 620 listed birds, 420 are known to breed there and 51 are endemic; the rest are found throughout the Malay Archipelago. The Bornean endemics include large birds such as eagles, falcons, pheasants and partridges, through to much smaller wren-babblers, flycatchers, flowerpeckers and thrushes. Two-thirds of Borneo's endemic birds live only in montane areas, which makes Sabah in particular a birdwatcher's paradise.

The wonderfully named chestnut-crested yuhina, chestnut-hooded laughing thrush, Bornean treepie and Bornean whistler all occur above 1,000m, and are must-sees for ardent birdwatchers. 'Other mountain endemics are the Bornean stubtail, the Everett's thrush, the friendly bush warbler, the mountain blackeye, the eye-browed jungle-flycatcher, the Whitehead's trogon, the broadbill and the spiderhunter,' says Bornean bird specialist and guide C K Leong. 'Some lowland endemics of particular interest are the Bornean-banded pitta, the white-crowned shama, the white-fronted falconet, the yellow-rumped flowerpecker, the black and crimson pitta, the blue-banded pitta and the Bornean bristlehead (the only species in its family).'

Buwler's pheasant (*Lophura bulweri*) The male Buwler's pheasant is, as Sarawak National Parks puts it, 'spectacularly handsome, with splendid blue facial wattles and a long, spreading, curved white tail'. Bulwer's pheasant is only found in tropical hill forests of central and northern Borneo, where it nests and forages on the ground and roosts in trees. It is a poor flier but a fast and nimble runner, using a combination of darting runs and flurried bursts of flight to avoid predators. During the mating season the male produces a shrill, piercing cry and performs a tail-spreading, wattle-raising dance for females. Though widespread in central Borneo, it has a low population density and is threatened by illegal hunting and habitat loss.

Hornbills Sarawak's list of 'totally protected species' contains 26 birds, including various egrets, eagles, pigeons and terns. However, the most coveted are the hornbills, which earn their name from the large horn-like casques that crown their colourful beaks. There are eight species of hornbill, all of them protected and all with delightful names, from the white-crowned to the bushy-crested, wreathed, wrinkled and oriental pied varieties, to the two largest species: the helmeted hornbill (*Buceros vigil*) and the rhinoceros hornbill (*B. rhinoceros*).

Though not endemic to Borneo, the rhinoceros hornbill is the symbol of Sarawak, believed by the Iban people, who call them *kenyalang*, to be messengers from the spirit world. Their huge wings, which have a span of over 1m, make a distinctive whooshing sound overhead as they fly past. Like most hornbills, the female builds her nest in the cavities of large trees and seals up the hole with mud, leaving just enough room for the male to pass fruit through as she broods. When the young hatch, the female leaves the nest and feeds her offspring through the hole with her partner, with whom she will mate for life. The hornbill is dependent on large trees for nesting places, but selective logging practices have limited their options. Sabah's diverse forests support an extraordinarily varied avifauna, and have been a magnet for ornithologists for over a century. A comprehensive reference guide is *The Birds of Borneo* by B E Smythies, but a more up-to-date and manageable field guide is the *Pocket Guide to the Birds of Borneo* compiled by Charles M Francis (see Appendix 2, page 317).

Top birdwatching spots To see the various Asian and Bornean riverine, lowland or montane birds, top birdwatching areas are **Gunung Kinabalu National Park** (see page 192), **Danum Valley** (see page 239) and the **Kinabatangan river** area (see page 221). The 200 species in the Kinabatangan floodplain include all eight species of hornbills.

AMPHIBIANS AND REPTILES There are some 150 known endemic frog and reptile species across Borneo, but new discoveries happen regularly. Prominent reptiles include several rainforest and mangrove snakes, the bizarre-looking monitor lizard (*Varanus salvator*), geckos, giant turtles, painted terrapins, and a couple of crocodiles.

Frogs According to WWF figures, Borneo is home to 150 known frog species. Within the past decade or so, at least seven frogs and a giant river toad have been discovered. A *Field Guide to the Frogs of Borneo* (see *Appendix 2*, page 317) is available, describing such gems as the Bornean horned frog, green paddy frog, jade tree frog, blue-spotted tree frog, greater swamp frog and Mjoberg's dwarf litter frog.

Snakes Borneo's snakes number more than 150, of which a few are venomous. Among the several pythons is the reticulated python with its diagonal beadwork-like decoration in black, white and mustard. Others include the king cobra, common cobra and black spitting cobra, the Sarawak water snake and mangrove snakes. At Bako National Park in Sarawak, the only dangerous snake in Borneo is found: the triangular-headed Wagler's pit viper.

Crocodiles Saltwater crocodiles (*Crocodylus porosus*), which live in the coastal swamps and rivers of Sarawak, are nicknamed *bujang senang* ('happy bachelor') after one infamous 6m individual that went on a killing rampage in the Sungai Batang Lupar River in southeast Sarawak in 1993, before being shot dead. A lot more can be learnt about this bloodthirsty bachelor at **Jong's Crocodile Farm** near Kuching, where his skull is on display in a museum.

Care should be taken when visiting areas where there are crocodiles. You would be very ill-advised to swim in the rivers where they dwell. The warning from Sarawak Forestry says: 'Adult crocodiles have a largely fishy diet, though sometimes develop a taste for dead or dying prey. Prey are taken alive and, unless they are very small, are generally left to rot before being eaten. They tend to be aggressive during mating season or when guarding nesting areas. They are territorial and will attack if you come on to their territory.'

Malayan false gharial crocodile (*Tomistoma schlegelli*) These crocodiles have long, narrow noses tipped by a bulbous form. They are residents of Sarawak's rivers, peat swamps and mangroves, normally nesting by the riverbank. Despite being described by the state as a 'taxonomically unique and harmless crocodilian species', human parts were found in the stomach of a 3m female in the 1990s. They feed primarily on fish, but it is thought that this particular croc might have enjoyed some of the happy bachelor's leftovers.

Monitor lizards (*Varanus salvator*) Monitor lizards are decidedly antediluvian and reptilian in appearance. They live in all sorts of water habitats – even urban puddles – and can be seen lurking in tropical forests, mangroves, swamps, farmland and towns. Predatory and unfussy, monitor lizards will eat anything: young monkeys, snakes, lizards, birds, crabs, domestic chickens, carrion, human faeces and food waste. One species, the earless monitor lizard known as *cicak purba*, is a particularly bizarre, ancient-looking lizard.

FRESHWATER FISH Some of the most important recent discoveries have been freshwater fish, **catfish** in particular, which display amazing adaptations to their environment. The WWF recently announced the discovery of a 'forest-walking catfish' in Borneo, so called because it can travel short distances over land. They are also named labyrinth catfishes after the 'labyrinth organ', a specialist gill adaptation that allows a special suborder of fish to take in oxygen from the air. Another species of catfish secretes poisonous mucus that causes instant death to other fish in the vicinity.

Since the mid-1990s, 30 new freshwater fish have been identified in Borneo, but one of the most fascinating has been known for a while. The green arowana, or **dragon fish** (*Scleropages formosus*), is a primitive 'living fossil' of a fish, representing an ancient lineage of fish species. Known locally as *kelesa*, it is a large freshwater fish found in Sarawak's rivers and lakes, preying on smaller fish, insects, worms, spiders, small lizards, small snakes and frogs.

INVERTEBRATES

Insects Lowland tropical rainforest harbours the greatest diversity of insect life on the planet, and the Bornean rainforest teems with insect life. There are over 100,000 species of beetles, hundreds of butterflies, stick and leaf insects, cicadas, cockroaches, dragonflies, termites, ants and mosquitoes. At Gunung Kinabalu National Park, insects are said to represent 'the bulk of the fauna' with thousands of different species. Like much of Borneo's natural history, insects are understudied, but Sabah Parks has been collaborating with the German Society for Tropical Ecology to increase understanding of the insect world. Gunung Kinabalu National Park has some 300 **butterflies**, mostly around the lowland rainforest and foothills areas but also on lower montane slopes. Over 50 are endemic to Sabah – the stunning Rajah Brooke's birdwing (*Trogonoptera brookiana*) wears a cloak of black with a jagged frill of metallic emerald green triangles all along its wings. It was first catalogued by Alfred Russel Wallace in 1854, who collected hundreds of insect specimens in Borneo – he named it after Rajah James Brooke who presented him with the specimen. Many butterfly specimens are contained in the 'Borneensis' collection, which is housed within the University Malaysia in Sabah.

The website of the ASEAN Review of Biodiversity and Environmental Conservation (ARBEC) (*www.arbec.com.my*) provides good links to studies and findings in entomology and other areas. One such link is to Dr J Holloway's *Moths of Borneo* (*www.mothsofborneo.com*), an 18-volume work documenting the larger **moths** of Borneo – currently estimated at some 4,500 species, and all of which are illustrated in colour. The Universiti Sarawak Malaysia, the Natural History Museum in London and ARBEC are responsible for making the entire work available online.

Crustaceans There is a great variety of freshwater crustaceans in Borneo such as lobsters, giant river prawns (*udang*) and crabs, all of which are important food sources to *orang sungai* (river-dwelling populations). Mangroves especially have many interesting clawed critters, such as hermit crabs and fiddler crabs, which burrow into the mudflats among the mangroves. Male fiddlers are equipped with one overgrown, vividly coloured claw, which serves to attract females during the mating season and ward off male competitors trespassing on his mudpatch territory.

The claw – called a *cheliped* – grows so big it can constitute 65% of his total body weight. The horseshoe crab, known in Sarawak as the *belangkas,* is not actually a crab but a descendant of an extinct marine arthropod lineage, the trilobites.

MARINE LIFE The coral reefs on the west and east coasts, particularly around the east coast's islands, support a huge variety of extravagantly coloured fish: lion fish with their 'mane' of chocolate brown and white frills, giant frogfish, hump head parrotfish, red and white clown fish, mandarin fish, snake eels and garden eels and many kinds of small colourful sand-dwelling gobies. There are also many molluscs, crustaceans and echinoderms including crabs, shrimps, giant clams, squid, blue-ringed octopus, cuttlefish, sea urchins, sea cucumbers and sea horses.

One of the fish to watch out for when diving is the clown triggerfish; it can bite, charge at you or chase you to the top of the water in mating season.

Corals Used as a barometer of marine biodiversity and coral health, the reefs of Sabah and Sarawak are home to hundreds of species of bright-banded and flecked butterfly fish. The corals themselves are kaleidoscopic in colour and variety – fern, stag horn, mushroom, cabbage and brain varieties are all common. All hard and soft corals are protected species in Sarawak, but sadly many reefs are suffering from the effects of dynamite fishing.

Sharks There are quite a few sharks in Borneo's waters, though no deadly ones. It is common to see white-tip reef sharks when diving. In mid-2007 the Borneo shark (*Carcharhinus borneensis*) – a species of which no sightings were reported for over a century, and was thought to be extinct – was declared 'rediscovered' by Universiti Malaysia Sabah researchers. The shark can reach up to 20m in length and is brown on top with a white underside. The university's Borneo Marine Research Institute warned at the time that sharks could soon be extinct in Sabah because of the over-harvesting of fins.

Dolphins All dolphins, porpoises and whales are protected in Sarawak and sightings of several species are commonplace especially between March and September: the Irrawaddy, bottlenose, Indopacific humpback, finless porpoise and pantropic spotted dolphin.

Sea turtles I have been lucky enough to experience the wonder of swimming among sea turtles – *penyu* – several times in Borneo, in the aquamarine waters off Sabah's east coast. They seem such solid, wise creatures, but several species are seriously threatened due to poaching (of both adults and eggs), habitat loss, pollution and accidental catch in fishing nets. Even without these extra pressures, life as a turtle is tough, with low reproduction rates and slim chances of survival of babies. Witnessing the plight of the youngsters trying to make their first journey to the sea (see *Chapter 7, Northeast Sabah*, page 218) can be heartbreaking.

The Turtle Islands in Sabah have the world's largest remaining populations of **hawksbill turtles** (*Eretmochelys imbricata*). The species is critically endangered, partly due to the enduring market for tortoiseshell jewellery and curios – the black and brown shell with splashes of yellow is unfortunately very popular. The name comes from their narrow pointed beak, reminiscent of a bird of prey, though locals know them as *penyu sisik* – 'scaled turtle', which refers to their attractive shells.

Larger **green turtles** (*Chelonia mydas*) are a protected species in Sabah and Sarawak, though Sarawak's population of green turtles has halved since the 1970s.

They are still one of the most widely seen and the biggest of the marine turtles, reaching over 1m in length. Despite weighing over 150kg they can swim at speeds of 15–20 km/h. Their name comes not from their carapace – this is olive or darker grey with swirled motifs – but from the colour of their meat. Like all marine turtles, they are a traditional food source for local people.

Whether indigenous people have the right to continue traditional practices of eating species now at risk of extinction is a controversial issue. Suluk people and the Bajau Laut ('sea gypsies') eat marine algae, sea grass and large fish including barracuda, grouper and red carp of deeper waters. Some also eat dolphins and **dugong**. This tusked 'sea-cow' is a protected species and ocean heavyweight, reaching lengths of over 3m and touching on 600kg.

Ocean dangers This warning is issued to visitors of the Tanjung Datu National Park in western Sarawak, but applies to many other coral reefs around Borneo:

> The reefs are home to several venomous creatures, including sea snakes, coral snakes, stonefish and cone shells. Marine snakes are generally harmless if undisturbed. Stonefish may conceal themselves in mud or sand around coral, especially at low tide, so do not walk or swim barefoot around coral reefs. Cone shells are highly venomous and should not be handled under any circumstances.

DEFORESTATION

Just a few centuries ago, over 90% of Borneo was carpeted in thick, luscious forests. Since the age of discovery and exploration, humans have voraciously spread across the island exploiting natural resources. In the mid-1980s, 75% of the natural forest cover remained, but by the early 1990s, Sabah had only 66% of its original forest left and today, only 50% of Borneo's natural forest remains – a mere 7% of which is virgin lowland forest. The situation is most grave in Kalimantan (Indonesian Borneo), but Sabah and Sarawak too have been seriously affected by excessive forest exploitation.

Since the 1960s half of Sabah's and Sarawak's primary forest has been logged, either selectively or intensively. Massive destruction was wreaked in the two Malaysian states for three decades, reaching a crescendo in the 1980s when an unrestrained timber industry raged, producing large-scale tropical hardwood exports, and exploitation of the forest for agriculture was rife and unchecked. Between 1963 and 1985, 2.8 million hectares of primary forest was logged in Sarawak alone, and deforestation rates doubled from 1980 to 1990. Things have slowed somewhat today, but 850,000ha are still estimated to be lost each year.

Decades of intensive logging for timber products, and the later extensive conversion of forests to rubber, palm oil and cocoa plantations, have been accompanied by huge losses of biodiversity and indigenous people's homes. Many timber licences issued by the Sarawak government cover the traditional lands of natives. Since early 1987, native people have been protesting about this encroachment, putting up blockades across timber roads in a desperate attempt to stop logging activities. Logging in dipterocarp forest has been shown to be excessive, with poor management of water catchments and poorly controlled logging operations.

THE SAWMILLS OF MALAYSIA Sabah and Sarawak have been described as the 'sawmills of Malaysia'. More than 70% of Malaysia's plywood mills are in the two states, and they produce nearly all of the country's exported timber. Almost all

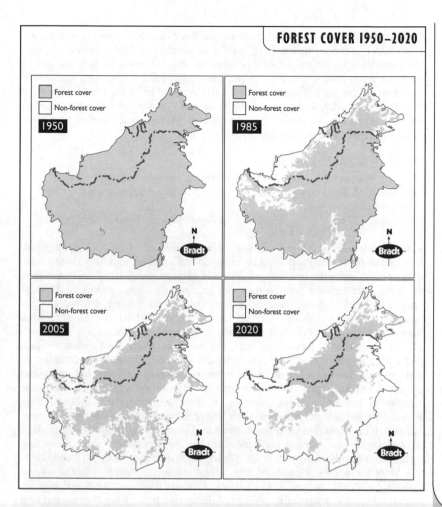

Forest cover
Non-forest cover
1950

Forest cover
Non-forest cover
1985

Forest cover
Non-forest cover
2005

Forest cover
Non-forest cover
2020

trees felled are for export. Forestry underpins the economy and provides thousands of jobs – 40% of people in Sarawak are employed in the timber industry. The dipterocarp forests are the sites of most hardwood exploitation. Dipterocarp timber is not of very high quality though, and most is used to produce plywood and sawn timber for construction – door and window frames, flooring, decking and other such uses.

Ninety per cent of logging licences ('forest concessions') were supposedly terminated in Sabah in 2000. The industry says cutting forests has been reduced to a trickle, but many logging operations are still carried out in government reserves, on large concessions that are still valid for decades to come. The woodchip industry in Malaysia apparently stopped in 1995, but hardwood exploitation has not ceased.

Critics say that palm oil has simply taken up where logging left off, wreaking just as much, if not more, environmental damage in its path. The industry took over as Sabah's biggest employer in the 1990s, and is now its biggest exporter, reaping 40% of total revenue – over a quarter of Malaysia's palm oil.

Forestry remains the biggest industry in Sarawak, though palm oil is hot on its heels. The round-the-clock forestry practices that were rife in Sarawak in the

1990s have apparently eased, but there are still large timber-harvesting operations. Amid international criticism from NGOs of continuing bad forestry practice, misinformation in the local media is common. News reports in Sarawak talk of the state's 'green gold' – lush tropical rainforest cover of 70% – with no mention of the extent of logging and losses. Such reports are used to let the forestry industry justify their activities, while turning the blame onto traditional shifting cultivation practices: 'As soon as we open a forestry road the natives come running in to clear the land', one timber company said in a report in 2007.

FACING UP TO THE CONSEQUENCES

If the forests become too fragmented, their ability to function efficiently is compromised. Half a rainforest does not contain half the number of original species. It contains far fewer.

Wild Borneo, Nick Garbutt and Cede Prudente

As forest cover drops below 20%, many species are lost or become endangered. Scientific studies have shown logging in Sabah and Sarawak to have serious effects on the extent and intensity of reproduction of plant species, including dipterocarp trees. An international symposium on biodiversity conservation in tropical rainforests, held in Japan in 2006, heard that the continuing deforestation in Malaysian Borneo was threatening 200 orchid species, 35 bird species, all rafflesia flowers and over 80% of primate species to the point of extinction.

In 2007, UNESCO joined the battle for Borneo's forests, saying that through illegal logging, the island's rainforests would soon be decimated. According to Conservation International, with the extensive logging in protected areas and current deforestation levels, lowland forests in Kalimantan may soon disappear completely: 'Recent estimates show that Kalimantan's protected lowland forests declined by 56 percent between 1985 and 2001, primarily from logging, and that less than 33 percent of lowland forest and peat swamp remains across all of Indonesian Borneo.' Current predictions on the life expectancy of the remaining lowland forests – the most biologically diverse habitat – range from 2012 until 2018.

A lot of the deforestation stems from illegal industry. In a report in the *Jakarta Globe* in April 2011, the Indonesian Forestry Ministry itself said that illegal logging, land clearance, forest fires and mining had devastated Indonesian Borneo and cost the country US$36.4 billion. Additionally, Maria Monica Wihardja from Jakarta's Centre for Strategic and International Studies says that illegal deforestation (resulting from crop plantations and mining activities) in East Kalimantan alone costs the government US$100 million in loss of revenue.

CONSERVATION

The riches of Borneo's forests were one of the first things to attract outside interest to the island. As early as the 10th century, Borneo's Asian neighbours wanted a share in its natural bounties. The Chinese traded ceramic jars in exchange for Borneo's jungle treasures. 'Luxury goods' were produced for the Asian market, using Borneo's turtles, birds, bark and wood.

The magnitude of Borneo's natural riches is not yet reflected in sufficient levels of protection. However, things are changing. Recent reinforcement of of Malaysia's (1972) Protection of Wildlife Act aims to enable a more solid legal framework to safeguard flora and fauna at a national level. In 2003, the Sarawak Forestry Corporation was created to manage the forests and national parks of the state. The concept of sustainable forest management was virtually non-existent until the late 1990s. The Corporation has adopted the International Union for the Conservation of Nature (IUCN) recommended action that at least 10% of its land area should be in totally protected areas.

SARAWAK One area in which Sarawak appears to be setting a precedent, at least relatively, is the legal protection of its wildlife and flora. Commercial sale and capture of wildlife is outlawed under its 1998 Wildlife Protection Ordinance, which imposes severe penalties – 50,000MYR and imprisonment is the going rate for killing a rhino. Hunting, however, was not banned, as 'it was recognised that rural communities depend on wild meat'. The ordinance safeguards 52 of Sarawak's rare and endangered mammals, birds and reptiles as 'Totally Protected Species' and another 40 as 'Protected Animals'. Only two plants are 'Totally Protected' – the various rafflesia species and the dipterocarp tree species *D. obloglofolius*. Another 46 plants, including many other dipterocarps and other tree species, are simply 'Protected'.

These latest moves are the first signs of Sarawak moving towards adhering to international conventions in forest policy. The Protected Areas and Biodiversity Conservation Unit, a section of the Sarawak Forestry Corporation, is the 'custodian of Sarawak's national parks', responsible for environmental protection and conservation activities throughout the state. Its vision is to be 'globally recognized as a leader in management of totally protected areas'.

SABAH In some ways, Sabah is lagging behind in the modernity of its approach and extent of its parks, though it does have a dedicated Wildlife Department in which its conservation goals and strategies are vested. However, this department falls within the Ministry for Tourism Development, Environment, Science and Technology – not exactly a major government portfolio.

Only 13 mammals, reptiles and plants make it onto Sabah's 'Totally Protected Species' list and, under the state's 1963 Fauna Conservation Ordinance, species are only protected if they are within a national park or other protected area. Since the late 1990s, the state has been showing a more concerted effort to implement CITES and other international agreements on biodiversity. The Sabah Wildlife Conservation Enactment of 1997 was the first to seriously set aside and manage protected areas, and regulate wildlife exploitation.

THE FUTURE FOR BORNEO Since it hit world headlines and the US supplied major funding, there's been a lot of talk of the 'Heart of Borneo' conservation project agreement between the island's three nations. But even this large core of remaining rainforest is threatened says the WWF: 'Logging, land-clearing and conversion activities are considered to be the greatest threats. Today the conversion to oil palm plantations can be considered one of the biggest threats for the remaining rainforests in Borneo and the species that inhabit them.'

With such an apparently bleak outlook, can things be turned around? Experts in forest rehabilitation say the effects of selective logging on biodiversity are not necessarily irreversible. Dr Glen Reynolds, senior scientist at the Danum Valley Field Centre, says 'even lowland rainforests which have been selectively logged still support the highest levels of biodiversity ... It is the conversion of forests to plantations – particularly oil palm – that has the really disastrous impacts on biodiversity.'

THE HEART OF BORNEO – NOW OR NEVER As the forests of Borneo rapidly disappear, it is becoming apparent that the current fragmented network of protected

The rainforest of Borneo has been high on the international conservation agenda for decades. The reason is simple – Borneo is one of the world's most important centres of biological diversity and there is still time to make a difference. Over the past decade, significant help for conservation in the Borneo rainforest has come from many national and international initiatives, including the Darwin Initiative of the UK government. A key aim has been to help countries that are rich in biodiversity but relatively poor financially and in human resources, to develop innovative approaches to conservation and sustainability through international partnerships. An encouraging sign has been the 'Heart of Borneo' initiative that is supported by the governments of Brunei, Indonesia and Malaysia.

A primary target of national and international efforts in Borneo has been the conservation and sustainable management of the forests in Sabah, which has involved improving means to assess and manage plant diversity. A key partner in Borneo is Yayasan Sabah ('The Sabah Foundation'), a charitable foundation set up in the mid 1960s with the aim of improving education, health, welfare and other social services for the people of Sabah. Yayasan Sabah's income derives mainly from managing around a million hectares of tropical forest, of which about 15% is already devoted to primary forest reserves. These include the Danum Valley and Maliau Basin conservation areas, which are of global conservation importance.

The **Danum Valley Conservation Area** preserves some of the last remaining lowland rainforest in the whole island of Borneo. It is a pristine and more or less intact ecosystem of almost 450km², dominated by giant dipterocarp trees, legumes and other trees. It is also home to globally significant populations of large mammals, such as the Bornean pygmy elephant, the binturong (a type of arboreal civet), the sun bear and the Sumatran rhino. Danum and surrounding areas also support more than 4,000 orang-utans – the largest population of this primate in the world. First set aside by Yayasan Sabah, Danum is now designated as a Class I Protection Forest Reserve by the Sabah state government. As a result of a long-term partnership with the UK's Royal Society, it is well monitored from one of the most active of all research stations in southeast Asia.

areas does not have long-term viability. For forests to survive they must be within a connected network to prevent isolated pockets of forest being doomed to failure.

Expanses of pristine rainforest teeming with life still exist in Borneo's hilly interior, but only parts are protected. As logging companies and plantation owners set their sights on the next lucrative schemes, in 2007 WWF stepped in with an ambitious project to save what is left.

The 'Heart of Borneo' (see *Biodiversity*, page 33) refers to a region the size of the United Kingdom – 220,000km² – in the central northern region of the island, encompassing parts of Malaysian, Bruneian and Indonesian Borneo. The conservation zone is of undeniable biological importance, harbouring up to 6% of the world's biodiversity, a figure expected to rise with the discovery of new species.

According to Adam Tomasek, leader of the Heart of Borneo initiative, the threats to the Heart of Borneo – one of only two places where elephants, orang-utans, rhinoceros and clouded leopards share the same territory – are enormous. 'Past experience shows us that the natural capital harbored within the Heart of Borneo is of great commercial interest ... By the 1980s major commercial operations were

In contrast to Danum, the **Maliau Basin Conservation Area** contains relatively little lowland rainforest, but it is nevertheless of great conservation importance. Covering nearly 600km², it is a remarkable block of tropical forest – virtually the entire catchment of the Maliau River – almost encircled by a dramatic escarpment that rises to over 1,600m in places. The basin includes spectacular waterfalls and vast tracts of forest. Again, this area was originally set aside by Yayasan Sabah and then formally upgraded to a Class I Reserve.

Then in 2003, an exciting development for conservation came when Yayasan Sabah designated the **Imbak Canyon** as a new conservation area.

Exploratory expeditions, which included scientists from the UK and other countries, together with partners from Sabah and elsewhere in Malaysia, confirmed its truly exceptional conservation value. It is the last remaining significant area of unprotected lowland dipterocarp rainforest in Sabah and a crucial link between Danum to the southeast and Maliau to the southwest.

The conservation reserves at Danum Valley, the Maliau Basin and now the Imbak Canyon are a testament to the foresight of Yayasan Sabah in preserving large tracts of forest – for the people of Sabah, and also for the unique animals and plants that these areas sustain. It would be all too easy to harvest the timber and clear the land for oil palm plantations. Instead, watersheds are protected and key parts of the unique natural heritage of one of the world's most remarkable tropical islands have been secured for the future. The challenge now is how to manage the forest matrix in which the reserves are embedded in the best possible way. Well-developed buffer zones, and forest management systems that encourage the free movement of plants and animals among the three protected areas, will be crucial. If implemented effectively they will ensure that the outstanding conservation values of Maliau, Imbak and Danum are secure, and that the global significance of these remarkable places will continue to increase – rather than diminish – for many, many years into the future.

Sir Peter Crane, evolutionary biologist, is a former Director of the Royal Botanic Gardens, Kew, England. Since 2009, he has been dean of the Yale School of Forestry and Environmental Studies.

eating away at the once untouchable and impenetrable forests of Borneo. The last 20 years of the century saw more timber cut and traded from Borneo than from the entirety of the Amazon and Congo regions. Timber companies, palm oil plantations, mining operations, hydropower and other infrastructure developments are all key players within the Heart of Borneo landscape.'

The WWF has attempted to identify areas where such developments would have the least devastating environmental effects. Its tactic, said Tomasek, is to work co-operatively with the private sector, to try and heed off threats: 'Our experience has shown that far greater results can be realised and sustained when business, government and civil society work toward a common goal.'

PROTECTED AREAS
Sarawak Sarawak claims to have one of the most extensive sweep of protected-areas in Malaysia, encompassing 18 national parks, four wildlife sanctuaries and five nature reserves, a total area of 512,387ha. Of the 18 national parks, only those open to the public are listed below. The wildlife sanctuaries are all

closed to visitors – they exist to 'preserve and conserve vulnerable ecosystems or endangered wildlife'.

In a state nearly the size of England, reserved areas constitute less than 5% of the land. Nearly half of the state is 'Permanent Forest Estate', apparently for 'sustainable forestry', though critics would say this is simply logging.

Of the total 300,000ha of national park the following are open to visitors:

Name	Area (ha)	Division	Date gazetted
Bako	2,727	Kuching	4 May 1957
Gunung Gading	4,196	Kuching	3 May 1988
Kubah	2,230	Kuching	11 May 1989
Tanjung Datu	1,379	Kuching	19 May 1994
Talang Satang	19,414	Kuching	4 November 1999
Kuching Wetland	6,610	Kuching	10 October 2002
Batang Ai	24,040	Sri Aman	11 May 1989
Similajau	7,064	Bintulu	20 April 1978
(Similajau Extension	1,932	Bintulu	2 June 2000)
Gunung Mulu	52,865	Miri	3 October 1974
Niah	3,138	Miri	2 January 1975
Lambir Hills	6,949	Miri	26 June 1975
Loagan Bunut	10,736	Miri	29 August 1991
Rajang Mangroves	9,373	Sibu	3 August 2000

The five **nature reserves** are:

Name	Area (ha)	Division	Date gazetted
Wind Cave	6.16	Kuching	4 November 1999
Sama Jaya	37.92	Kuching	23 March 2000
Semenggoh	653	Kuching	20 April 2000
Bukit Hitam	147	Limbang	22 June 2000
Bukit Sembiling	101	Limbang	22 June 2000

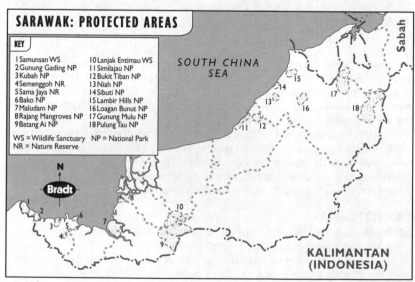

SARAWAK: PROTECTED AREAS

KEY

1 Samunsan WS
2 Gunung Gading NP
3 Kubah NP
4 Semenggoh NR
5 Sama Jaya NR
6 Bako NP
7 Maludam NP
8 Rajang Mangroves NP
9 Batang Ai NP
10 Lanjak Entimau WS
11 Similajau NP
12 Bukit Tiban NP
13 Niah NP
14 Sibuti NP
15 Lambir Hills NP
16 Loagan Bunut NP
17 Gunung Mulu NP
18 Pulung Tau NP

WS = Wildlife Sanctuary   NP = National Park
NR = Nature Reserve

SOUTH CHINA SEA

Sabah

KALIMANTAN (INDONESIA)

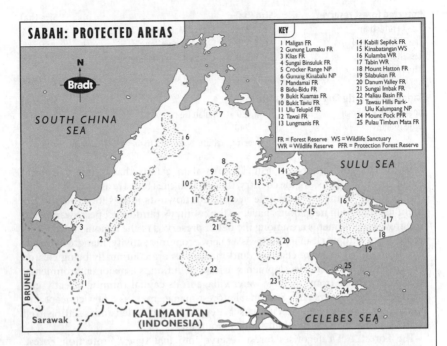

KEY
1 Maligan FR
2 Gunung Lumaku FR
3 Klias FR
4 Sungai Binsuluk FR
5 Crocker Range NP
6 Gunung Kinabalu NP
7 Mandamai FR
8 Bidu-Bidu FR
9 Bukit Kuamas FR
10 Bukit Taviu FR
11 Ulu Telupid FR
12 Tawai FR
13 Lungmanis FR
14 Kabili Sepilok FR
15 Kinabatangan WS
16 Kulamba WR
17 Tabin WR
18 Mount Hatton FR
19 Silabukan FR
20 Danum Valley FR
21 Sungai Imbak FR
22 Maliau Basin FR
23 Tawau Hills Park–
Ulu Kalumpang NP
24 Mount Pock PFR
25 Pulau Timbun Mata FR

FR = Forest Reserve   WS = Wildlife Sanctuary
WR = Wildlife Reserve   PFR = Protection Forest Reserve

Sabah Things are very different in Sabah, where there are just six national parks, gazetted under the 1984 Parks Enactment and managed by Sabah Parks. Three of these are terrestrial parks: Mount Kinabalu, the Crocker Range and Tawau Hills; and three are marine parks: Turtle Island, Tunku Abdul Rahman and Pulau Tiga. In total, this approximates 266,000ha.

Under the 1968 Forest Enactment (revised in 1984) there are seven classes of 'Protected Forest Reserves' ranging from 'Class I Protection Forest Reserve' to 'Class VI Virgin Jungle Reserve' and 'Class VII Wildlife Reserve'. Class II forest – commercial forest – is not listed on Sabah Forestry's website and amounts for the bulk of these reserves – 2,685,199ha.

According to *Discovering Sabah* (Natural History Publications, Borneo), of the seven classifications, only four may be regarded as protected areas. The main function of Class I Protection Forests is to safeguard water supplies, soil fertility and environmental quality. Danum Valley and Maliau Basin are two such reserves. Class VI Virgin Jungle Reserves comprise some 50 relatively small areas intended to provide undisturbed forest for research and the preservation of gene pools. The fourth conservation class is Class VII Wildlife Reserves, which are for the protection of wildlife. The core of the large Tabin Wildlife Reserve today falls under Forest Class VII. In 1997 the Wildlife Conservation Enactment enabled the creation of more protected areas. There are projects in the pipelines for gazetting more areas.

Terrestrial & marine parks	Size (ha)		Size (ha)
Lower Kinabatangan	27,800	Lankayan Billean Tegapil Marine	
Sipadan	12	Conservation Area	30,000
Kota Belud	12,200	Kinabalu	75,370
Mantanani Kecil	61	Tawau Hills	27,927
Kota Kinabalu	24	Crocker Range	139,919

Protected forest reserve	Size (ha)		Size (ha)
Class I Protection	342,216	Class V Mangrove	316,024
Class II Commercial	2,685,119	Class VI Virgin Jungle	90,386
Class III Domestic	7,350	Class VII Wildlife Reserve	132,653
Class IV Amenity	20,767		

Marine parks (including coral reef)	Size (ha)		Size (ha)
Tungku Abdul Rahman	4,020	Pulau Tiga	15,864
Turtle Islands	1,740		

Source: Discovering Sabah, *Natural History Publications, Borneo*

BRUNEI The government of Brunei Darussalam claims that 'primary tropical jungle' covers about 75% of the country, though also cites forestry as a major activity. Thanks to oil, Brunei has had little need to cut down its forests for export to the extent its Malaysian neighbours have, so the country's rainforests, peat swamp and mangrove environments are among the better preserved in the region. However, its record is not entirely clean – forestry is a major economic activity; mangrove woods have been culled to make charcoal, and mangroves are continually being cleared for urban and industrial developments. Urban pollution is a major environmental issue, with sewage from the huge water village in its capital running directly into the river and its ecosystems. Sustainable forest management is a new concept, but the country is aware of the need to preserve everything it has left and is setting itself up to be a beacon of sustainability and ecotourism.

The Forest Act categorises forest reserve into five types: Protection Forest, Conservation Area, Recreational Area, Production Forest and National Park. There is just one national park, the 50,000ha **Ulu Temburong National Park**, created in 1988 within a huge forestry reserve. A further 32,000ha of reserves are classified for conservation purposes, and there are many urban and rural recreational areas. A respectable 15% of Brunei's total land area is fully protected. The Forestry Department manages the reserves and has started to carry out some early day greening activities, such as rehabilitating degraded lands and raising public awareness. There has been talk of bolstering the Wildlife Protection Act, established in 1978, to give it more scope to create national parks and sanctuaries.

3

Practical Information

WHEN TO VISIT

WEATHER There are frequent mentions of wet and dry monsoons (and which to avoid) but there is not a clear-cut best period to visit Borneo. Each season has its advantages and drawbacks, and none are so critical that they necessitate planning an entire trip around them. The dry season (southwest monsoon) generally occurs from May to October, though huge downpours and floods can occur in June and July. The wet season (northeast monsoon) is generally from November to April, and whilst monsoon rains can make life difficult and uncomfortable, they can quickly clear to blue skies in December. Unfortunately, as almost everywhere across the globe, climate change and seasonal unpredictability is becoming a reality.

Particularly for active and adventure holidays, the time the weather is most likely to hinder your travel plans is the wet season. Heavy rains and general bad weather may cause flights into remote regions to be cancelled and travel by boats may be affected. Those who plan to do a lot of trekking should be prepared for short bursts of wet weather at any time of the year. During the northeast monsoon, seas can be extremely rough; in January 2007, a tour company boat capsized off the north coast of Sabah because of a sudden change in weather conditions. Conversely, if there is not enough rain, travel upriver by boat is impeded. In the hotter periods with lower rainfall, river trips may be partly self-propelled, as travellers are called on to get out of the longboats and push upstream.

CROWDS As far as crowds go, it is best to avoid school holiday periods and major festive celebrations. The busyness of these periods can not only make it hard to find accommodation, but may also make the hotels very noisy. The main school holidays are usually the last week of May to the last week of June, and six weeks from mid-November through to the end of December. There are also one-week holidays around mid-March and late August.

WHAT KIND OF HOLIDAY?

Whether you are travelling solo, with a group, as a family, on a package holiday or independently, the variety that Borneo offers means almost everyone can find what they are looking for in a holiday. The high standard of hotels, health and safety and relative ease of transport by air, road and river enable a trouble-free holiday to be had by all. The highlands, remote river areas and challenging peaks also offer scope for the more adventurous traveller. For those who prefer beach and sun, Borneo is a perfect beach-filled package-holiday destination, with the added attractions of diverse culture and wildlife. A handful of tour operators offer high-end tailor-made tours combining the best of Sabah, Sarawak and Brunei. The cost of travelling between these places is relatively cheap. Nevertheless, a consideration if you are on a budget and/or time-restricted is to only visit one Malaysian state. Both Sabah and Sarawak offer enough variety of wildlife, scenery, social life and activities to form a holiday on their own. If I had to generalise, I would probably recommend Sabah for those looking for a culturally enhanced beach holiday with islands, diving and mountains, and Sarawak for remote river and highland experiences and greater cultural colour in cities and towns.

If you are lucky enough to have more time and money then you can afford to branch out (but avoid making the common mistake of trying to see too much), whether you organise the transfers yourself or pay a tour company to do the work for you. If you have a special interest, be it diving, trekking or birdwatching, it is a good idea to opt for a tailor-made tour or design your own trip using specialist local operators. For details, see *Sports and other activities*, page 114–19.

HIGHLIGHTS

FAUNA AND FLORA The flora and fauna hotspots of Borneo are so numerous and varied that it is impossible to categorise them, but below is a brief key to some major attractions and lesser-known wonders.

Ulu Temburong National Park, Brunei Whether done as a day trip or with an overnight stay, the journey to the Temburong National Park, which begins on the riverbanks of Brunei's capital, forms half the wonder of the trip. Meandering through a network of waterways, mangrove and tropical rainforest, you will enjoy a cultural immersion as you pass through the town of Bangar and witness the incredible boating skills of the Iban people. The walk to the suspension bridge in the park will put you at dizzying heights with views over Brunei and Malaysian Borneo.

Gunung Kinabalu National Park, Sabah The steamy alpine world in which Borneo's Gunung (Mount) Kinabalu sits can be enjoyed whether you climb to the peak or not. The complexity of vegetation in the 75,370ha World Heritage park is apparent even on a shorter trek – through its rainforest and lower montane areas, around park headquarters, and other parts such as Poring Hot Springs. The butterfly- and bloom-filled park has been designated as a Centre of Plant Diversity for Southeast Asia by UNESCO, and is exceptionally rich in species.

Bako National Park, Sarawak A wonderland mix of mangroves, peat swamp, heath and lowland rainforest, with epic coastal rock formations. On the fauna front, highlights include bright green snakes, bearded pigs and the proboscis monkey. About 150 of the pendulous-nosed, pot-bellied creatures live here (see *Chapter 3, Natural History*, page 50). The trails are excellent (as long as a tree doesn't fall on you, which is what happened to me when I visited!). It's on the back doorstep of Kuching, about 40km away.

Danum Valley The closest you will get to the 'Heart of Borneo' (see *Natural History*, pages 63–5) without heading deep into the Maliau Basin. Here you may see gibbon, orang-utan, long-tailed macaque, bearded pig, sambar deer, rhinoceros hornbill, maroon langur, western tarsier, clouded leopard, red leaf monkey and a diversity of birds – though you may need to stay for a few days to catch a glimpse of such a wide variety of wildlife, rather than just doing a one-hour safari on the back of a (rather noisy) truck.

Orang-utan encounters The huge appeal of this charismatic primate attracts many people to Borneo; seeing one is often at the top of their agenda. Orang-utan rehabilitation centres and sanctuaries (Sepilok in Sabah, and Semenggoh in Sarawak) are an easy option for quick sightings. Other wild places to see them (and vast amounts of other wildlife) include the Tabin Wildlife Reserve on Sabah's east coast, the floodplain of the Lower Kinabatangan River and the Danum Valley Conservation Area.

Proboscis monkeys The proboscis monkey comes in a close second as the most popular primate to see in Borneo. They can be seen in mangrove and peat swamp forests such as the Lower Kinabatangan and Klias Wetlands in Sabah, along Brunei's waterways and in the Bako National Park in Sarawak.

River safaris The boat journey along the Sungai Kinabatangan, Sabah's longest river, is awe-inspiring with its remoteness, natural richness and other-worldly beauty. For wildlife and birdwatching it is one of Borneo's most intense experiences, and the various lodges along the river (in their varying degrees of rustic) leave you with a bolstering feeling of being in deep jungle for a night or two. Late-afternoon boat trips lead up tributaries of the river to see shy proboscis monkeys and macaques. The world-scale preciousness of the area has unfortunately not protected it from forestry and palm oil invasion, but conservation and community development work is taking place. You can stay with river-living (*orang sungai*) communities, which boosts local economy.

Journeys along Sarawak's rivers are journeys into ethnography rather than nature. You can travel through the Taman Negara Batang Ai in the southeast, and the Sungai Rendang in central Sarawak, and up through central Sarawak to Kapit and Belaga.

ISLANDS AND BEACHES If you are looking for coasts, beaches and diving then without doubt Sabah is the place to head, especially the islands off its north and east coast.

CITIES AND CULTURE With its intensely Islamic faith, river tranquillity, royal riches, mosque silhouettes and Malay culture and cuisine, Bandar Seri Begawan, Brunei's capital, offers a snapshot of Borneo's history and ethnic colour. Kuching, Sarawak's main city, is mesmerising in its oriental and antiquated airs, yet neighbourly and friendly. The Sungai Sarawak runs through the centre and the indigenous Iban and Bidayuh cultures are woven through its watery fabric. Kota Kinabalu, Sabah's capital, is more the modern resort, a Côte d'Azur of Borneo where people party late into the night. Sandakan, Sabah's original capital, is dilapidated on stilts and cloaked in lush hills. An ocean crossroads of migrants, it exudes maritime charm.

Cultural shows The dance performance at the **Sarawak Cultural Village** remains an absolute highlight: a joyous insight into a cross-section of Malay, Chinese and indigenous dance. It is a mainstream tourist attraction, but there are many small, singular shows. For an all-in-one cultural taste, this is well delivered and high quality.

SCENIC DRIVES
East coast, Sabah Often referred to as 'cowboy towns', the settlements on the coastal stretch from Tawau to Lahad Datu and Semporna are not only the springboard to some incredible islands and to the Danum Valley inland, they are in themselves an offbeat and vivid cultural experience, taking you from thriving Chinese-dominated

3

port cities, businesses and restaurants to Muslim-operated outdoor markets and exotic flavours. The seafood on the east coast is the best in Borneo.

Kudat Peninsula, Sabah Without doubt, the whole region north of Kota Kinabalu offers one of the most leisurely opportunities for driving over several days in Borneo. Culminating in the Kudat Peninsula and the so-called 'Tip of Borneo', the ride takes in markets and towns, coast and countryside. More difficult, but not impossible, is to do the journey by bus: regional buses connect the towns.

Pan-Borneo A stretch that is more off the beaten track of tourist operators is that between Kuching and Brunei. If you are in a car, take the Pan-Borneo Highway, heading north to Miri. You can also take a mix of coaches, buses and boats to do the trip. Highlights along the way are the Chinese city of Sibu, the Melanau people's stronghold of Mukah, the Niah Caves, and the best sago and fish salads in the world. See *Chapter 11, Central Sarawak*.

SUGGESTED ITINERARIES

Decide what you most want to see in Borneo in the available time: culture and ethnic groups, jungle and wildlife, beaches and coast, highlands and islands, or a varied mix of all. This will help determine where you should visit, either following the suggestions below or tweaking them to better suit your main interests. Given the ease and frequency of air travel, it is common for tour operators to propose week-long itineraries that cherry-pick from the best of Borneo, but I would always emphasise quality over quantity.

ONE WEEK If you only have a week, stick to just one Malaysian state. You could start with a one-day, one-night stopover in **Brunei**, visiting Temburong National Park, the water village and mosques on a packaged tour. Next, head to Sabah and spend a day wallowing in the watery charm of **Kota Kinabalu**. Don't miss the dawn to dusk markets – fish market, craft market and evening *pasar malam* food market – held along the waterfront stretch of Jalan Tun Fuad Stephens. For the best view of the city climb to the top of Signal Hill; if your visit coincides, visit the Sunday market on Jalan Gaya, and eat seafood at the open-air Sri Selera food court. The next day, head off to **Gunung Kinabalu National Park** – the winding journey takes about two hours by car and passes vegetable markets, food stalls and craft stalls in villages such as Kampung Nabalu. You can also take a taxi or bus to the park entrance from the Merdeka Field station. The 17km-return Summit Trail to the top of Mount Kinabalu requires an overnight stay, permits and a guide, and you need to book well ahead for that and accommodation in the park on your return. From one of the park lodges, you can also spend two days soaking up the mountain scenery on unguided walks – first head to park HQ for a *Mount Kinabalu Park Trails* map – and visit the farmers' markets and the World War II war memorial at nearby Kundasang. Many climbers end their walk with a night at Poring Hot Springs, part of the Gunung Kinabalu National Park, where rangers will post alerts on any Rafflesia flowers in bloom.

Return to Kota Kinabalu for a flight to the coast city of **Sandakan**: the views are ethereally beautiful over the rickety water village, and the harbour full of old-world fishing vessels facing the Philippines and Sulu Sea. Head off to the afternoon feeding session at the **Sepilok Orang-utan Rehabilitation Centre**, half an hour from town, then later explore the sights of Sandakan by foot.

The next day, head off with a local operator along the 560km-long **Sungai Kinabatangan** river – the trip into the mighty yet blighted (by forestry and oil palm plantations) jungled interior of Malaysia's second-longest waterway comes close to being the most magical river journey in Borneo. Many of the tour operators, from budget to upmarket, offer packages including lodging, food and transport. In the mangrove and freshwater swamp environments of the Lower Kinabatangan Sanctuary, you will come in close contact with orang-utans, proboscis monkeys, Bornean gibbons, pygmy elephants, Sumatran rhinoceros and pit vipers. Over 200 bird species are found here, with eight types of hornbill alone, including the rare wrinkled hornbill.

Head south to **Lahad Datu**, a gateway to some of the largest remaining areas of 'old growth' virgin rainforest, including the Tabin Wildlife Reserve, the Danum Valley Conservation Area, Maliau Basin and Imbak Canyon. Spend at least two entire days taking in the flora and fauna. Danum and the surrounding forests are home to 4,000 orang-utans – the world's largest population of the primate – yet there are serious concerns about the $438km^2$ reserve being encroached on by a logging 'concession' area and oil palm plantations.

If you are a diver, you might want to exchange or shorten the jungle experience to cap off your visit with a couple of days' diving. The east coast's Bajau sea gypsy territory of **Semporna**, is the springboard to Sabah's dive and snorkel islands, Pulau Sipadan, Mabul, Kapalai and Mataking. Purchase an all-inclusive stay on an island resort or stay in town, and use a budget operator for day trips.

TWO WEEKS In two weeks, you can spend time travelling between Sabah and Sarawak, via Brunei, and see some highlights in each. Your main consideration will be how much time to allot to different activities: do you want to tackle the mega-mountain (Mount Kinabalu), jungle and river trip, accompanied by some smaller cultural bites, or alternatively, get a big taste of Borneo's people, cities, countryside and villages with a smaller glimpse of nature?

Start a two-week tour with the week-long itinerary outlined above, taking in the best of Brunei and Sabah. If you are travelling independently, however, you may want to travel by ferry from Brunei to Kota Kinabalu via the island of **Labuan**. You could also include in the Sabah itinerary a day or overnight trip north to the **Tip of Borneo** (*Tanjung Simpang Mengayau*), passing through the longhouse settlements, *tamu* (farmers' markets) and coconut plantations of the Kudat Peninsula.

Following the week in Brunei and Sabah, head to Sarawak for a mix of upriver adventure and rich ethnic immersion. With its airs of an old Chinese trading town, **Kuching**'s beauty emanates from the banks of the Sungai Sarawak River. Spend two days here and use the *tambang* (covered wooden boats) to cross over and eat in the restaurants of the Malay *kampung* by night, or charter one for an hour and float down the river past the Masjid Mosque, a perfect piece of Arabia on the Kuching skyline.

Allow time to see the museums and colonial buildings and shop for handicrafts along the waterfront Jalan Bazaar. One of Borneo's best places to see 'semi-wild' orang-utan is the **Semenggoh Wildlife Rehabilitation Centre**, 20km south of the city. North of Kuching and accessed by speedboat are the mangroves, amphibians and proboscis monkeys of **Taman Bako National Park**, which is worth a day trip at least (or stay overnight in basic park chalets after tackling one of the 16 walking trails). A more comfortable option is to head to a resort at **Damai Beach**, on the neighbouring Santubong Peninsula.

The next day head to the **Sri Aman District**, which skirts the Indonesian border and is the heartland of Sarawak's most populous tribe, the Iban. Along the way, if you are self-driving, stop at **Serian**. The small market town is distinguished by its 'Big Durian' – the king of local fruits – and undercover *tamu,* whose stalls sell fruit and snacks such as *pisang goring* (fried banana).

Some 194km from Kuching, **Bandar Sri Aman**, on the Batang Lupar River, is a trading and transport hub, and gateway to the Batang Ai National Park. More traditional longhouse communities in the Batang Ai National Park can only be reached by boat, which leave from the jetty at the Batang Ai hydro-electric dam. The best thing is to book a trip with a Kuching-based operator, which includes a two-night stay in either the Hilton Batang Ai or a longhouse of varying standards.

Tweak this itinerary accordingly if you want to hone in on one particular activity, such as diving, birding or trekking. Clearly if you want to spend four days diving on Sabah's east coast islands, or flora fondling in Gunung Kinabalu's richly flowered environs, then something will have to go from this suggested schedule.

ONE MONTH A whole month's stay in Borneo will enable you to taste the best of Brunei, Sabah and Sarawak – as outlined in the two-week journey above – and will also allow you some major dabbling in specialised activities of your choice. For example, you could enjoy a whole week of diving, birding or mountaineering (all of these are best done in Sabah). It also allows you to pad out some of the visits, starting, for example, with an extra night's stay in Brunei's capital.

For a serious, yet pricey, side adventure in Sabah, head off to the **Maliau Basin** – the so-called 'Lost World' – and endure tents, rugged terrains and loads of leeches. The trips range from several days to a fortnight.

If you want the wildlife minus the hard adventure, spend more time in Sabah's or Sarawak's national parks and reserves – the Kinabatangan River, Tabin and Danum, in the former, and Bako National Park in the latter.

Linger an extra couple of nights among the primates and birds of the Kinabatangan River and an extra day among Sandakan's dilapidated, colourful stilted villages before heading further south to the **Danum Valley**.

This is the closest you will get to the 'Heart of Borneo' (see *Natural History*, page 33) without venturing deep into the Maliau Basin. A two- to three-day stay in Danum increases chances of an impressive inventory of possible sightings: gibbon, orang-utan, long-tailed macaque, bearded pig, sambar deer, rhinoceros hornbill, maroon langur, western tarsier, clouded leopard, red leaf monkey and a wondrous diversity of birds. (Though nearby Tabin is probably even better in this regard.)

Down in Sarawak, **Bako** has a wonderland mix of mangroves, peat swamp, heath and lowland rainforest, with epic coastal rock formations. On the fauna front, highlights include bright green snakes, bearded pigs and the proboscis monkey. About 150 of the pendulous-nosed, pot-bellied creatures live here (see box, page 50). Though the lodgings are exceptionally basic, true nature (and back-to-nature) lovers, will be happy to spend at least two nights here, exploring the excellent trails to hidden beaches and coves. At either end of a Bako visit, also spend more time in fascinating Kuching.

Rather than doing the standard overnight trip to Batang Ai and its longhouse communities, east of Kuching, opt for a real river adventure. Borneo Adventure organises up to 11-day treks on the arduous **Red Ape Trail,** which has been endorsed by the Orang-utan Foundation and mapped out with the local Iban communities. Budget outfitters also touch on the region.

For an off-the-beaten-track adventure, drive, or take a bus, from Batang Ai towards Central Sarawak, whose lifeblood is the 760km-long Batang Rejang, Malaysia's longest river.

On the way to the regional capital Sibu, you may wish to break the journey in the town of **Sarikei**, in whose acidic soils pineapples, pomelo (large citrus fruits) and avocado thrive.

At the confluence of the Rejang and Igan rivers, 130km from the South China Sea, **Sibu** is a transport hub for the whole Rejang Basin. Explore its huge harbour, Chinese temples and gardens. With its population of Chinese, Melanau, Iban and Orang Ulu, Sibu has some of the best quality and value food in Borneo: spend at least a day and night at the markets and coffee shops, sampling dishes such as *mee udang* (river prawns in a bowl of spicy broth) and *mee sua* (longevity noodles).

Stay in Sibu another night and visit a longhouse settlement on the Rejang, or take an express boat north to the coastal region of **Mukah** and experience the seafaring Melanau people's culture and signature dish *umai* (a spicy salad of raw shredded fish marinated with lime, ginger and chilli). River enthusiasts might want to consider a boat cruise along the Rejang. If not, wind up the trip by heading further north along the Pan Borneo Highway to Miri, stopping for a few hours along the way to see the caves at **Niah National Park**. In this oil town turned resort town, you can go diving or take a plane journey into the **Gunung Mulu National Park**, whose UNESCO-classified caves are archaeological treasure chests.

TOURIST INFORMATION

SABAH AND SARAWAK The worldwide offices of **Tourism Malaysia** are invaluable for general travel information, while the websites of the Sabah and Sarawak tourism boards provide the most comprehensive, up-to-date information and are a good direct point of enquiry and feedback.

Sabah Tourism Board 51 Jln Gaya, KK; ✆6088 212121; e info@sabahtourism.com; www.sabahtourism.com. Precise & highly visual information on attractions, events, tour operators, lodgings & other practicalities.

Sarawak Tourism Board 6th & 7th Floors, Bangunan Yayasan, Jln Masjid Kuching; ✆+6 082 423600; e stb@sarawaktourism.com; www.sarawaktourism.com. A fresh white & green appearance but the website is a little busy, & lacks strong visual content & aesthetic structure.

Tourism Malaysia (*www.tourism.gov.my*) The new website offers limited information but super slideshows of Borneo's top destinations. The 'contact us' link to overseas offices of the Malaysia Tourism Promotion Board has been obscured by the high-tech digital presentation. Some of the major overseas offices are listed below.

Australia 355 Exhibition St, Melbourne; ✆03 96543177; Ground Floor, MAS Bldg, 56 William St, Perth, ✆08 94810400, e mtpb. perth@tourism.gov.my; Level 2, 171 Clarence St, Sydney, ✆02 92994441/2, e malaysia@ malaysiatourism.com.au

Canada 1590–1111 West Georgia St, Vancouver; ✆604 6898899; e info@ tourismmalaysia.ca; www.tourismmalaysia.ca **France** 29 Rue des Pyramides, Paris; ✆01 42974171; e mtpb.paris@tourism.gov.my

> **KK AND BSB**
>
> Kota Kinabulu, the capital of Sabah, is locally abbreviated to KK, while Bandar Seri Begawan, the capital of Brunei, is locally abbreviated to BSB. Please note that throughout this book, certain addresses use these abbreviated names.

Germany Weissfrauenstrasse 12–16, Frankfurt am Main; ☎69 460923420; e info@tourismmalaysia.de; www.tourismmalaysia.de **UK** 57 Trafalgar Sq, London WC2N 5DU; ☎020 7930 7932; e mtpb.london@tourism.gov.my or info@tourism-malaysia.co.uk

USA 818 West Seventh St, Suite 970, Los Angeles, ☎213 6899702, e mtpb.la@tourism.gov.my, www.tourismmalaysiausa.com; 120 East, 56th St, Suite 810, New York, ☎212 7541113, e mtpb@aol.com

BRUNEI Information about travel in Brunei is best obtained through the central Brunei Tourism office in Brunei itself. Overseas, Royal Brunei Airlines offices (*www.bruneiair.com*) and Brunei high commissions and embassies (listed under *Red tape*, pages 80–2) are useful sources of information.

Brunei Tourism Jln Menteri Besar, BSB, Brunei Darussalam; ☎673 2382822/2382832; e info@tourismbrunei.com; www.tourismbrunei.com. A stunning website with gorgeous visuals & excellent content design.

Royal Brunei Airlines 49 Cromwell Rd, London SW7 2ED; ☎020 7584 6660; e lonrba@rba.com.bn **Royal Brunei Airlines** Level 14, BT Tower, 1 Market St, Sydney; ☎02 82675300; e rbasyd@rba.com.bn

TOUR OPERATORS

There are advantages to using local tour operators: first and foremost, they provide in-depth local knowledge and add a strong personal touch; second, employing local people and companies helps the local economy, creates jobs and is far more energy efficient than a business run offshore. Familiarise yourself with local operators in the areas you plan to visit – they can help organise special interest tours for independent travellers or take the entire weight off your shoulders by providing a start-to-finish itinerary. What an international company might gain on sleekness, they can lose on authenticity and depth. Some international travel companies, indicated below, work with home-grown agencies, employing local guides rather than running the whole show themselves. Both the Sabah and Sarawak tourism board websites (*www.sabahtourism.com; www.sarawaktourism.com*) include directories of tour operators. Company details can also be found in the members' directory of the Malaysia Association of Tours and Travel Agents (MATTA) (*www.matta.org.my*).

INTERNATIONAL

Birding Worldwide ☎+61 412 943593; e enquiries@birdingworldwide.com.au; www.birdingworldwide.com.au. An Australia-based bird tour group with 20 years of Asian touring experience, directed by *Birds of Borneo* author Susan Myers. Borneo & Peninsular Malaysia birding is a major highlight. They also offer tailor-made tours.

Intrepid Travel ☎UK +44 (0)1373 826611/+44 0800 7811660; US & Canada +18 668 478 192; Australia +13 00 364 512; New Zealand +09 5 200 972; e info@intrepidtravel.com; www.intrepidtravel.com. For environmentally conscious, independent travellers who want to travel in a group or on a budget. Intrepid offers several tours of Borneo;

all are outlined on their website with itineraries, prices, trip notes & more. Based in Australia, with sales offices in New Zealand, UK, Ireland, US & Canada. Integrity of green image boosted with several responsible travel awards, & by achieving the goal of becoming carbon neutral by 2010. Women make up about two-thirds of its clientele. **Victor Emanuel Nature Tours** ☎+1 512 328 5221; f +1 512 328 2919; e info@ventbird.com; www.ventbird.com. America's largest specialist bird (& natural history) tour company. **World Expeditions** ☎UK +44 20 8545 9030; Australia (Sydney office) +61 2 8270 8400; US + 1 613 241 2700; Canada +1 613 241 2700; www.worldexpeditions.com. Adventure & outdoor travel with offices in the UK, US, Canada, Australia & New Zealand. Offer a 9-day 'Borneo

Flora & Fauna' trip, plus Mt Kinabalu climbs & Red Ape trail adventures in Sarawak.

AUSTRALIA

Borneo Tour Specialists ☏+61 7 3221 5777; e travel@borneo.com.au; www.borneo.com.au. Pre-set & tailor-made trips with several detailed itineraries & extensive country information on its website. Reservations office based in Brisbane.

Gecko's Adventures (Peregrine Adventures) 380 Lonsdale St, Melbourne; ☏+61 3 8601 4444; e websales@peregrine.net.au; www. geckosadventures.com. Treks & safaris operated by the 'groovy young thing' part of Peregrine Adventures.Small groups, good prices & local guides.

CANADA

50plus Expeditions 760 Lawrence Av, Toronto; ☏+1 866 318 5050; e office@50plusexpeditions. com; www.50plusexpeditions.com. Specialise in adventure travel for people over 50. Comprehensive 15-day trip of Borneo including Sabah, Sarawak & Brunei. Their website could do with a sophisticated overhaul.

Deep Discoveries PO Box 73, Mulhurst Bay, Alberta; ☏+1 780 389 3658; e info@ deepdiscoveries.com; www.deepdiscoveries.com. Dedicated dive & adventure travel specialist.

UK & IRELAND

Adventure Alternative ☏+44 (0)28708 31258, (Ireland) ☏04870 831258; www. adventurealternative.com. For mountain adventure, this Northern Ireland-based company has a 14-day 'Roof of Borneo Adventure' that goes way off the over-beaten Mount Kinabalu climb to take in the Eastern Plateau & the North Ridge. This is only for the seriously mountain-at-heart – 12 days are spent climbing & camping, with highly experienced expedition leaders. They also do a 3-week 'Borneo Trilogy' adventure with trekking in the Kelabit Highlands in Sarawak. Aptly described as 'non-technical trekking' – to distinguish it from the more demanding Mount Kinabalu Climb & whitewater rafting in Sabah.

Audley Travel New Mill, New Mill Lane, Witney, Oxon; ☏+44 (0)1993 838100; www.audleytravel. com. The award-winning agency offers 'tailor-made journeys for the discerning traveller', run by specialists. Itineraries include the 15-day Borneo Headhunters adventure & 18-day 'Borneo

Uncovered', taking in the best of Sabah & Sarawak. The stunningly visual & eco-sensitive website includes a slide-show & interactive wildlife map.

Borneo Travel UK arm of Borneo-based TYK Adventure Tours (see page 79), whose international operations are directed by Bob Jones: ☏+44 (0)844 840 7777; e bob@travel-trading.demon.co.uk; www.borneo-travel.com. If you're looking for an adventure & outdoor holiday, this award-winning venture has survival, mountain-biking & trekking tours plus tailor-made tours for activities such as birdwatching, rock climbing & rafting.

Chaka Travel 98 University St, Belfast; ☏028 90 232112; e mark@chakatravel.com; www.chakatravel.com. Golfing holidays in Sabah.

Exodus Holidays Grange Mills, Weir Rd, London SW12 0NE; ☏+44 (0)845 863 9600; e sales@ exodus.co.uk; www.exodus.co.uk. Family-friendly adventure holidays with small-to-medium groups under tour leaders & local guides. 14-day 'Trails of Borneo' tour requires good fitness, includes 3 days of walking, & a mix of hotels, lodges, camping & mountain huts.

Nature Trek Cheriton Mill, Cheriton, Alresford, Hants; ☏+44 (0)1962 733051; e info@ naturetrek.co.uk; www.naturetrek.co.uk. Wildlife tour specialist with 2 Borneo itineraries, focusing on orang-utans, birds & the rainforest. Their 21-day tour, which they describe as a 'birdwatching extravaganza', takes in top birdwatching sites in Sabah: Kinabatangan, Mount Kinabalu & Danum Valley. There are very good reviews of the trip. All their tours are guided by specialists trained as naturalists, environmental scientists & ecologists.

Saga Holidays ☏+44 (0)800 096 0078; e reservations@saga.co.uk; www.saga.co.uk. Cushy package group holidays for the over-50s. Offer a 14-day Borneo rainforest adventure with a tour 'manager'. Save with online bookings.

The Travel Collection Kuoni Hse, Dorking, Surrey; ☏+44 (0)1306 744311 (sales), +44 (0)1306 744319 (helpdesk); e tours@ travelcollection.co.uk; www.travelcollection. co.uk. Part of the Kuoni Travel group, itineraries include 8-night 'Wildlife of Borneo' holiday staying in high-end hotels.

World Primate Safaris ☏UK +44 (0)1273 691642, US 1866 357 6569; e sales@ worldprimatesafaris.com; www. worldprimatesafaris.com. Tailor-made trips to see orang-utans & more.

USA

Dive Borneo ☎+1 618 529 8033; e info@ diveborneo.com; www.diveborneo.com. Linked to www.emalaysiatravel.com, a service destination travel specialist with lots of information on Malaysia.

Go Borneo ☎+1 888 359 8655; e info@ goborneo.com; www.goborneo.com. With extensive Borneo knowledge, & using local guides, the group offers adventure & family packages, & day tours.

World Of Diving & Adventure Vacations 301 Main St, El Segundo, California; ☎+11800 GO DIVING/1800 46 34846; e mail@worldofdiving. com; www.worldofadventure.com. Specialises in diving trips to Sabah's east coast islands with 7-day round trips from Los Angeles to Tawau all inclusive.

BORNEO
Sabah and Sarawak

Borneo Adventure 55 Main Bazaar, Kuching; ☎+60 082 245175; e info@borneoadventure. com; www.borneoadventure.com. Upmarket ethical, this Sarawak-based company has wildlife-, adventure- & culture-focused tours in Sarawak & in Sabah as well as custom-made trips. It says it is 'dedicated to providing our clients with ethical tourism products that are sustainable', & steps this way with an ethnically diverse group of very professional guides, its own eco-lodges & practical & in-touch information on its website.

Borneo Birds e ckleong@borneobirds.com; www.borneobirds.com. The website of resident Bornean bird specialist C K Leong, provides a brilliant, photographic inventory of Bornean birds, from barbets & bee-eaters to whistlers & woodpeckers. In conjunction with TYK Adventure Tours, CK tailor-makes 1-day to 2-week birding trips, including a 12-day around Sabah tour taking in Manukan Island, Tabin Wildlife Reserve, the Kinabatangan River & Gunung Kinabalu National Park.

Borneo Divers 9th Floor, Menara Jubili, 53 Jln Gaya, KK; ☎+60 088 222226; e info@ borneodivers.info; www.borneodivers.info. Longest-operating & extremely reputable operator with a training institute in Kota Kinabalu offering courses at all levels. Those who enrol for the PADI course reportedly get generous discounts on Mabul Island dive packages (dives, accommodation, etc).

Borneo Eco Tours Lot 1, Pusat Perindustrian, Kolombong Jaya; Mile 5.5, Jln Kolombong, KK; ☎+60 088 438300; e info@borneoecotours.com; www.borneoecotours.com. Launched in 1991 by well-known eco-author Albert Teo, the group has 40 excellent guides/specialists, 15 AC vehicles, speedboats, riverboats & rafting equipment. Many awards to its name for its conservation & responsible tourism efforts. Vast choice of nature & cultural tours, treks & activities, all well outlined & easily booked on its site. Value packages & a budget corner. Operates the Sukau Rainforest Lodge & Borneo Backpackers in Kota Kinabalu.

Borneo Nature Tours Blk D, Lot 10, Ground Floor, Sadong Jaya Complex, KK; ☎+60 088 267637; www.borneonaturetours.com. Adventure & nature tours with the operator of the Borneo Rainforest Lodge in the Danum Valley Conservation Area. Heading out from there, they organise adventure treks into the Maliau Basin Conservation Area, deemed the 'lost world' of Sabah.

Borneo Ultimate Sports Adventure Tours (BUSAT) Lot G29, Ground Floor, Wisma Shopping Centre, KK; ☎+60 088 225188/225199; e borneoultimate@hotmail.com; www. borneoultimate.com.my. Another Sabah-based operator big on bike adventures & bike/rafting day trips & packages. 'Kinabalu Mountain & Rafflesia & Waterfall' day-biking trips, at easy & intermediate levels, as well as 2–4-day tours of all kinds – some involving biking, rafting & camping. Dedicated & locally tuned.

Intra Travel Service ☎+60 088 261558; e enquiry@intra-travel.com.my; www.intra-travel. com.my. Upmarket Sabah-based company aimed at incentive travel sector. Member of the International Eco Tourism Society & American Express Travel Service Network, & PATA (Pacific Asia Travel Association). Its activities focus on jungle activities within the Tabin Wildlife Reserve in northwest Sabah, nature & adventure programmes, theme parties, team-building exercises, aerial sightseeing, special interest eco-adventures, golf tours, diving tours, hotel & transportation bookings.

Outdoor Treks ☎+60 82 36 3344; m +6012 8886460; e best@bikcloud.com; www.bikcloud. com. The kind of youthful, enthusiastic & down-to-earth company that draws in the film production crews & adventure travel programmes. They are familiar with a whole lot of mountain-bike trails within 1–100km from Kuching's central business district, as well as kayaking, guided nature treks, rock climbing & caving. Sarawak based.

Pulau Sipadan Resort & Tours 484 Bandar Sabindo, PO Box 61120, Tawau 91021; ☎+60 897 65200; e kapalai@tm.net.my; www.dive-malaysia.com; www.sipadan-resort.com, www.lankayan-island.com. Packages based around their dive resorts on Lankayan & Kapalai islands, as well as their Sepilok Nature Resort. Very professional set-up, popular with families for their child-friendliness & fun. Confusing number of websites!

SI Tours 10th Floor, Wisma Khoo Siak Chiew, Sandakan Town; ☎+60 089 673502/03; e info@sitoursborneo.com; www.sitoursborneo.com. Local company specialising in adventure, wildlife & cultural tours. Package itineraries & custom tours to Kinabatangan, Gomantong Caves & Turtle Islands National Park. Guides are passionately local & mostly well informed. The company is deeply committed to the environment & indigenous communities – & creating jobs for them.

Traverse Tours Lot 227–229, 2nd Floor, Wisma Sabah Jalan Tun Fuad Stephen; ☎+60 88260501/2; e sales@traversetours.com; www.traversetours.com. This 'indigenous' tour group has really accelerated its offerings in recent times, from its traditional territory of whitewater rafting & river tours with its Riverbug affiliate (*www.riverbug.asia*), to its new cultural centre near Kota Kinablau, Mari Mari (& under the same name, a backpacker diver's accommodation on & day tours to Mantanani Island). They are professional & highly enthusiastic.

TYK Adventure Tours Lot 48–2F, 2nd Floor, Beverly Hill Plaza, Jln Bundusan, Penampang; ☎+60 088 720826/727825; e tykadto@tm.net.my; www.tykadventuretours.com. Small operators with responsible travel written all over them. Based in west coast Sabah – Kota Kinabalu, Mt Kinabalu, Crocker Range – but do nature & adventure trips all over Sabah including the Sandakan Death March walking tour & North

Borneo Mountain Biking. The multi-ethnic team from the director down is hands-on involved in tours, each with their own particular forte. Cycling & rafting trips, survival camps, village & longhouse stays & extended trekking. Also have a group of associated experts (eg: historians) increasing their local knowledge. Organise the Miki Survival Camp in the foothills of Mount Kinabalu (see page 202).

Wildlife Expeditions ☎+60 089 219616 (Sandakan), +60 088 246000 (KK); e enquiry@wildlife-expeditions.com; www.wildlife-expeditions.com. Sabah-based operator with a large range of reasonably priced half/full-day & overnight excursions from Kota Kinabalu, Sandakan, Brunei, Kuching & Miri to all the best places of interest. Pretty big-scale, established operator, they work with Brunei Tourism & mid-market package-holiday operator Kuoni (*www.kuoni.co.uk*), upmarket Saga (see above under UK operators) & Go See Touring (see Australian operators). 7-day wildlife tour of Borneo plus shorter itineraries. They have a Kinabatangan River lodge.

Brunei

Freme Travel Services ☎2234280; e fremeinb@brunet.bn; www.freme.com.or www.brunei-tours.freme.com. An established company with its head office in Kuala Belait, an office in the capital & a firm foothold nationwide. The company has its own fleet of premium coaches & has a lot of experience with British visitors.

Sunshine Borneo Tours & Travel No 2 Simpang 146, Jln Kiarong, Kampung. Kiulap, Bandar Seri Begawan, Brunei; ☎+673 2446812/3; e sales@exploreborneo.com; www.exploreborneo.com. The local partner for Royal Brunei Airlines, sold overseas as Golden Touch Holidays through RBA offices (e goldentouch@rba.com.bn; www.bruneiair.com). A very Bruneian, highly conscientious, concerned & punctual operator, do day trips & excursions within Brunei. Also have a branch in the lobby arcade of the Empire Hotel & Country Club in Jerudong (☎+673 2610578).

RED TAPE

VISAS AND ENTRY REQUIREMENTS

Malaysian Borneo If you have already passed through Malaysian customs in Kuala Lumpur, it is surprising to face passport control again on arrival in Sabah or Sarawak, but keeping control of their own immigration checks was one of the conditions for them joining the Federation of Malaysia in 1963. It's all just a formality, particularly for citizens of the UK, Australia, Ireland, the USA, Brazil, Canada, France, Italy, Germany, the UAE, South Korea, Japan, South Africa, Tunisia and a host of other western European, South American and Middle Eastern countries who do not need a visa to enter Malaysia for a visit of up to three months. It is mandatory, however, to be holding a passport which is valid for at least six months on arrival, as well as a return or onward ticket. An extension of up to two months is possible. Passport holders from countries which require a visa will be issued with a 30-day stay on arrival, which can in principle be extended for another 60 days at the Immigration Department in Kota Kinabalu. Citizens of countries including Costa Rica, Mexico, Lithuania and the Ukraine require a visa for a stay exceeding one month. For more information on visa requirements for all countries go to the website of the Malaysian Immigration Department: www.imi.gov.my.

Brunei No visa is required for residents of the USA (90-day entry), the UK, Ireland, Germany, Austria, New Zealand, Singapore, Malaysia, the United Arab Emirates, Oman and Korea (30-day entry), and residents of Belgium, France, Italy, Spain, the Netherlands, Luxembourg, Denmark, Norway, Sweden, Poland, Canada, Peru, Japan, the Philippines, Indonesia and Thailand (14-day entry). Australians are granted visas on arrival (30-day entry). A single-entry visa costs US$20 and lasts for ten days; a multi-entry visa lasts for 30 days and costs US$30; a 72-hour transit visa costs US$5.

If you require a visa and arrive into Brunei by road from Sabah or Sarawak, be aware that you must have Brunei dollars on you (which can be withdrawn from a bank in Malaysia) to pay the visa fee. There are no ATM machines at the immigration checks, and they do not take credit card payments.

CUSTOMS The Malaysian customs department has enforced the green and red lane system for visitor arrivals nationwide. The green lane means nothing to declare; you will face hefty penalties if you are found carrying undeclared dutiable goods and should be in the red lane. Duty-free allowances per traveller include one litre of wine or spirits, 225g of tobacco, gifts and souvenirs valued at up to 400MYR (excluding goods from duty-free islands Langkawi and Labuan which must not exceed 500MYR). Customs duty on non-exempt items equals 30% of the overall value. See the customs department website for full details: www.customs.gov.my.

Brunei customs laws include particular rules relating to alcohol, which you cannot buy anywhere in the country. Non-Muslims over 17 years of age can bring in two bottles of liquor (about two litres) and 12 cans of beer, which has to be declared to customs upon arrival. Passengers over 17 can carry in 200 cigarettes, 60g of tobacco, 60ml of perfume and 250ml eau de toilette.

The trafficking of drugs in Brunei carries the death sentence.

EMBASSIES AND CONSULATES

ABROAD Embassy opening hours vary greatly and are generally from 08.00–16.30 Monday–Friday but it is always best to ring ahead and check.

Malaysian diplomatic missions
Ⓔ Australia Malaysian High Commission Canberra, 7 Perth Av, Yarralumla; ✆+61 2 6273 1543; e malcanberra@netspeed.com.au

Ⓔ Canada Consulate General of Malaysia, Suite 1805, Terasen Centre, No 1111, West Georgia St, Vancouver; ✆+1 604 685 9550; e mwvcouvr@ axion.net; www.kln.gov.my

E Ireland Embassy of Malaysia, Level 3A-5A, Shelbourne Hse, Shelbourne Rd, Ballsbridge, Dublin; ☎ +353 1 6677280; e mwdublin@mwdublin.ie

E New Zealand High Commission of Malaysia; 10 Washington Av, Brooklyn, Wellington; ☎ +64 4 3852439/+64 4 8015659; e mwwelton@xtra.co.nz

E UK Malaysian High Commission, 45 Belgrave Sq, London SW1X 8QT; ☎ +44 20 7235 8033; e ruzaidi@btconnect.com; www.jimlondon.net

E USA Embassy of Malaysia, 3516 International Court NW, Washington, DC 20008; ☎ +1 202 572 9700; e malwashdc@kln.gov.my. Consulate General in New York: 313 East 43 St; ☎ + 1 212 490 2722; e malnycg@kln.gov.my. There is also a Consulate General in Los Angeles.

Brunei's diplomatic missions

E Australia High Commission of Brunei Darussalam, 10 Beale Cr, Deakin, ACT; ☎ +61 2 6285 4500/02 6285 4501; e consular@brunei.org.au; www.brunei.org.au

E Canada High Commission of Brunei Darussalam, 395 Laurier Av East, Ottawa, Ontario; ☎ +1 613 2345 6560

E UK High Commission of Brunei Darussalam, 19–20 Belgrave Sq, London SW1X 8PG; ☎ +44 20 7581 0521; e bruhighcomlondon@hotmail.com; http://ukinbrunei.fco.gov.uk

E USA Embassy of Brunei Darussalam, 3520 International Court NW, Washington, DC; ☎ +1 202 2371 838; e info@bruneiembassy.org, washington.usa@mfa.gov.bn; www.bruneiembassy.org

IN MALAYSIA Foreign embassies are in Kuala Lumpur (see *www.kln.gov.my*). The British Council is on the ground floor of the Api-Api Centre in Kota Kinabalu.

E Australia Australian High Commission, 6 Jln Yap Kwan Seng; ☎ +60 3 2465555

E Austria Austrian Embassy, 7th Floor, MUI Plaza Bldg, Jln P Ramlee; ☎ +60 3 2484277

E Belgium Belgian Embassy, 8A Jln Ampang Hilir; ☎ +60 3 2625733

E Canada Canadian High Commission, 7th Floor, OFK Plaza, 172 Jln Ampang; ☎ +60 3 2612000

E China Chinese Embassy, 229 Jln Ampang; ☎ +60 3 2428495

E Denmark Danish Embassy, 22nd Floor, Wisma Angkasa Raya, 123 Jln Ampang; ☎ +60 3 2416088

E France French Embassy, 192–196 Jln Ampang; ☎ +60 3 2484122

E Germany German Embassy, 3 Jln U Thant; ☎ +60 3 2429666

E Italy Italian Embassy, 99 Jln U Thant; ☎ +60 3 4565122

E Japan Japanese Embassy, 11 Persiaran Stonor, Off Jln Tun Razak; ☎ +60 3 2427044

E The Netherlands Dutch Embassy, 4 Jln Mesra, off Jln Damai; ☎ +60 3 2485151

E New Zealand New Zealand High Commission, 193 Jln Tun Razak; ☎ +60 3 2382533

E Singapore Singapore High Commission, 209 Jln Tun Perak; ☎ +60 3 2616277

E Sweden Swedish Embassy, 6th Floor, Wisma Angkasa Raya; ☎ +60 3 2485433

E Switzerland Swiss Embassy, 6 Persiaran Madge; ☎ +60 3 2480622

E UK British High Commission, 185 Jln Ampang; ☎ +60 3 2482122

E USA US Embassy, 376 Jln Tun Razak; ☎ +60 3 2489011

The UK also has **Honorary British Consuls** in Sabah (Kota Kinabalu) and in Sarawak (Kuching).

E Sabah Mr Peter Mole; ☎ +60 88 253 333; m +60 (0)19 882 3978; e peter.mole@pekah.com

E Sarawak Mrs Valerie Mashman; Kuching; ☎ +60 82 250 950

IN BRUNEI All the following embassies are along the riverfront area of Bandar Seri Begawan city centre (☉ *09.00–17.00 Mon–Fri*).

E Australia Australian High Commission, Level 6, Dar Takaful IBB Utama Bldg, Jln Pemancha; ☎ +673 2229435; e austhicom.brunei@dfat.gov.au; www.bruneidarussalam.embassy.gov.au

e Canada Canadian High Commission, 5th Floor, Mc Arthur Building, No 1 Jln McArthur; ✆+673 2220043; e hicomcda@ppl.brunet.bn; www.brunei.gc.ca

e New Zealand The New Zealand High Commission in Kuala Lumpur is accredited to Brunei, Level 21, Menara IMC, 8 Jln Sultan Ismail; ✆+673 32078; e nzhckl@streamyx.com; www.nzembassy.com

e UK British High Commission, 2nd Floor, Block D, Kompleks Yayasan Sultan Haji Hassanal Bolkiah, Jln Pretty, Bandar Seri Begawan; ✆+673 2222231; e brithc@brunet.bn; www.britishhighcommission.gov.uk/brunei

e USA Embassy of the United States of America, 3rd Floor, Teck Guan Plaza, Jln Sultan (corner of Jln McArthur); ✆+673 2220384; e amembassy_bsb@state.gov, http://bandar.usembassy.gov

GETTING THERE AND AWAY

BY AIR The main international airports in Borneo are in Bandar Seri Begawan (the capital of Brunei, commonly known as BSB), Kota Kinabalu (the capital of Sabah, commonly known as KK) and Kuching (the capital of Sarawak), so your choice of airline will clearly be determined by your proposed itinerary. Sabah Tourism (*www.sabahtourism.com*) provides an excellent summary and map of all international flights to Kota Kinabalu under its 'Getting to Sabah' section.

Flights from the UK, US, Europe, Australia, New Zealand and Middle East

AirAsia (*www.airasia.com*) Emblazoned in its dynamic, trademark red, Asia's leading low-cost airline is gradually stepping further afield, with flights from London and Paris into increasing numbers of Asian destinations, including Kuala Lumpur, but also through to Australia. All flights from London and Paris connect smoothly with continuing flights on to several Bornean destinations, while there are direct international flights to Kota Kinabalu from Singapore, Taiwan, China, Hong Kong, the Philippines and Indonesia. With London–Kuala Lumpur one-way economy flights priced as low as €157/£128 (though subject to big last-minute swings), compared with double that and over for most mainstream carriers, the skies are being seriously shaken up.

Royal Brunei Airlines (*www.bruneiair.com*) The only non-stop long-haul flights to Borneo are provided by Royal Brunei Airlines (RBA). The airline operates direct flights to Bandar Seri Begawan from the UK, Australia, New Zealand and the Middle East. It has significantly upgraded its planes for long-haul routes – the new Boeing 777s include 30 business-class seats that transform to full-length flat beds and 255 reclining economy-class seats.

From London, direct flights to Bandar Seri Begawan operate four times weekly from Heathrow's Terminal 4, as well as three flights via Dubai.

Four-times weekly direct flights between London and Melbourne via Bandar Seri Begawan were introduced in 2011, expanding the Australian connections to Brunei, which already include direct flights from Brisbane and Perth. There are four flights weekly from Auckland, New Zealand.

Malaysia Airlines (*www.malaysiaairlines.com*) Malaysia Airlines (MAS) operates twice-weekly direct flights from both Sydney and Perth to Kuching.

Relatively seamless routes from many worldwide destinations transit the Malaysian capital Kuala Lumpur. Malaysia Airlines operates non-stop international flights to Kuala Lumpur from London, Amsterdam, Paris, Rome, Zurich, Frankfurt, Stockholm, New York, Los Angeles, Buenos Aires, Sydney, Perth, Adelaide, Brisbane, Melbourne, Auckland, Dubai, Cape Town and Johannesburg. Sometimes an overnight stay in

Kuala Lumpur is necessary, ahead of follow-on flights to Bandar Seri Begawan, Kota Kinabalu, Labuan Island, Kuching and Sibu (Sarawak's second city).

From Kota Kinabalu, Malaysia Airlines connects to Tawau, Lahad Datu and Sandakan in Sabah, and Kuching, Miri, Mulu, Limbang, and Sibu in Sarawak.

Singapore Airlines (*www.singaporeair.com*) For quality and a seamless trip, this airline is a very good option for reaching Borneo. Planes fly non-stop to Singapore from London, Manchester, New York, Los Angeles, San Francisco, Moscow, Rome, Milan, Copenhagen, Paris, Frankfurt, Zurich, Athens, Brisbane, Sydney, Melbourne, Perth, Adelaide, Auckland, Christchurch, Dubai, Abu Dhabi, Johannesburg, Cape Town, Tokyo and Beijing. After as little as a one-hour transit, there are connecting flights to Kota Kinabalu, Kuching and Brunei with Singapore Airlines subsidiary, Silk Air (*www.silkair.com*), or on code share with Malaysia Airlines.

Singapore Airlines also has flights in the UK from Aberdeen, Newcastle, Belfast, Glasgow, Edinburgh, Leeds/Bradford and Teesside passing-by London.

Jetstar (*www.jetstar.com*) Australia's low-cost airline Jetstar operates direct flights in both economy and business class between Kuala Lumpur and Melbourne, Kuala Lumpur and Auckland (New Zealand), and indirect flights from Kuala Lumpur to Sydney, Hobart, Launceston, Adelaide and the Gold Coast (via Melbourne). Direct Kuala Lumpur to Perth flights are operated by Jetstar Asia.

Other carriers Flying from the US to Hong Kong, Cathay Pacific passengers could then link with the one-a-day direct flight to Kota Kinabalu, operated by the Hong Kong-based **Dragon Air** (*www.dragonair.com*), part of the Cathay Pacific group. If you fly **Delta Airlines** (*www.delta.com*) they have non-stop flights to Taipei, in Taiwan, then on to Kota Kinabalu with Malaysia Airlines.

Flights from Asia

Royal Brunei Airlines Regionally, Royal Brunei Airlines operates daily services from Bandar Seri Begawan to Singapore, Shanghai, Bangkok, Kuala Lumpur, Manila, Jeddah, Jakarta, Surabaya, Ho Chi Minh City and Hong Kong.

There are 17 weekly flights from Bandar Seri Begawan to Kota Kinabalu, and five flights to Kuching, assuring smooth regional connections throughout Borneo.

Malaysia Airlines Stepping up direct regional connections, Malaysia Airlines introduced several flights to Kuching from Japan (Tokyo and Osaka) and Korea (Incheon) in 2011, adding to its existing direct services to Kota Kinabalu from Japan, China (Hong Kong), South Korea (Seoul) and Taiwan (Taipei).

Malaysia Airlines also has flights to Sabah and Sarawak from other Asian ports, including Hong Kong.

AirAsia Air Asia has revolutionised the Asian skies in the past few years, opening up travel almost for all. Its highly competitive prices, fun presentation and snappy service mentality frequently see it nominated as Asia's top low-cost airline. The airline has many direct connections from Kuala Lumpur to Kota Kinabalu, Sandakan and Kuching. It also has direct flights to Kota Kinabalu from Bangkok (allowing connections with Thai Airways, Qantas or British Airways flights among others).

If you fly into Hong Kong from London with British Airways or from the US, as mentioned above, or with Qantas, you can then fly with Dragonair (*www.dragonair. com*) on their once-daily flights to Kota Kinabalu.

Firefly (*www.fireflyz.com.my*) Regional Asian low-cost Firefly connects Kuala Lumpur with several Malaysian Borneo cities, including Kota Kinabalu, Kuching, Sandakan and Sibu, and Johor Bahru in southern Malaysia with Kota Kinabalu and Kuching.

Which airline?
If sheer quality and comfort of service are your priorities, for long-haul trips it is hard to beat the track records of Singapore Airlines and Malaysia Airlines (with a special star for the price–quality rapport of economy long-haul). For price, Malaysia Airlines is very competitive. Upgrades to Royal Brunei Airlines' fleet from mid-2010 should add another notch of comfort to their overall ratings with larger planes, a new in-flight entertainment system and angled (as opposed to completely lie-flat) beds in business class. The cheapest flights on Just the Flight (*www.justtheflight.co.uk*) often turn up Malaysian Airlines, Air Emirates (via Dubai) and Qatar Airways (via Doha), so if you are not fussed about taking a direct flight – or are looking to enjoy an exotic stopover – the latter two could be entertained. Transit flights can also be taken via Bangkok (Thai Airways), Hong Kong (Cathay Pacific), Taipei, Kaoshiung, Manila, Cebu, Seoul, Singapore and Tokyo. These trips can be very tiring, involving two transfers, unless you use the trip to stop over in a couple of interesting places.

For checking general flight prices and availability, good sites include www.expedia.com, www.justtheflight.co.uk, www.webjet.com.au, www.travelocity.com and www.travelocity.co.uk. For online travel agents, try www.trailfinders.com, www.statravel.com, www.flightcentre.au and www.flightcentre.com. For airline quality checks and star rankings in all brackets, from first class to budget airlines, see Skytrax (*www.airlinequality.com*).

The airline you choose should also tie in with your itinerary and where you want to start your trip. Royal Brunei Airlines makes it easy for an in-and-out of Brunei if coming from the UK or Australia. From there, internal flights are readily available to Sabah and Sarawak's capital cities.

HEALTH with Felicity Nicholson

PREPARATIONS Preparations to ensure a healthy trip to Borneo require checks on your immunisation status: it is wise to be up to date on tetanus, polio and diphtheria (now given as an all-in-one vaccine, Revaxis, that lasts for ten years) and hepatitis A. Immunisations against typhoid, hepatitis B, rabies and Japanese encephalitis may also be recommended. Hepatitis A vaccine (Havrix Monodose or Avaxim) comprises two injections given about a year apart. The course costs about £100, but may be available on the NHS; it protects for 25 years and can be administered even close to the time of departure. Hepatitis B vaccination should be considered for longer trips (two months or more) or for those working with children or in situations where contact with blood is likely. Three injections are needed for the best protection and can be given over a three-week period if time is short for those aged 18 or over (though it can be used off licence for those aged 16 or older). Longer schedules give more sustained protection and are therefore preferred if time allows. Hepatitis A vaccine can also be given as a combination with hepatitis B as 'Twinrix', though two doses are needed at least seven days apart to be effective for the hepatitis A component, and three doses are needed for the hepatitis B. This is only available for those aged 18 or over.

The newer injectable typhoid vaccines (eg: Typhim Vi) last for three years and are about 85% effective. Oral capsules (Vivotif) may also be available for those aged six and over; three capsules over five days lasts for approximately three years, but may be less effective than the injectable forms. Vaccination against typhoid should be encouraged unless the traveller is leaving within a few days for a trip of a week or less, when the vaccine would not be effective in time.

Vaccinations for rabies should be offered to everyone, time allowing, but are even more important for travellers visiting remote areas, especially if you are more than 24 hours from medical help and always if you will be working with animals (see *Rabies*, page 88).

Ideally you should visit your own doctor or a specialist travel clinic to discuss your requirements if possible at least six weeks before you plan to travel.

Good starting points for general health and safety advice are foreign embassies. See the travel advice on the British Foreign and Commonwealth Office website (*www.fco.gov.uk*). The International Society of Travel Medicine (*www.istm.org*), emedecine.com (*www.emedecine.com*) and The Travel Doctor (*www.traveldoctor. co.uk*) are also useful for medical and health information. Fit for Travel (*www. fitfortravel.scot.nhs.uk*) is another excellent website which uses the same information as the professional website Travax.

FIRST-AID KIT
- A good drying antiseptic, eg: iodine or Savlon Dry Antiseptic (don't take antiseptic cream)
- A few small dressings (Band-Aids)
- Suncream
- Insect repellent and bite treatment
- Aspirin or paracetamol
- Antifungal cream (eg: Canesten)
- Anti-diarrhoea tablets such as Imodium
- Rehydration sachets
- Ciprofloxacin or norfloxacin, for diarrhoea
- Tinidazole for giardia or amoebic dysentery (see below for regime)
- Antibiotic eye drops, for sore, 'gritty', stuck-together eyes (conjunctivitis)
- Alcohol-based hand rub or bar of soap in plastic box
- Condoms or femidoms

TROPICAL DISEASES
Malaria This is a serious and potentially fatal disease transmitted by mosquitoes, for which there is no vaccine. There are hugely differing estimates of the prevalence of malaria in Borneo, ranging from 'successfully eliminated' to 'widespread'. Most sources agree that the risk is greater in more remote areas and fairly low in urban and coastal regions.

Current recommendations for prophylaxis are Malarone, or doxycycline for those travelling to rural areas of Borneo and unless neither of these tablets are suitable for you then you would be advised to take them. (Lariam is no longer considered to be effective for rural Borneo.) Seek medical advice as to which is the most appropriate for you and follow the regime recommended carefully. That said, no malaria tablets are 100% effective and so you should always take precautions against mosquito bites. This includes wearing trousers and long-sleeved shirts particularly between dusk and dawn. Apply insect repellents containing around 50–55% DEET to exposed skin at the recommended intervals, and when necessary sleep under a permethrin-impregnated bed net. These may not be provided, so it is wise to take your own, especially if you are visiting remote areas.

Early diagnosis of malaria is essential for effective treatment, so if you suspect you or a companion has contracted the disease then seek medical help as soon as possible. Symptoms are flu-like and may include fevers, chills, muscle and joint aches, headache, tiredness, nausea, vomiting, and occasionally diarrhoea. The only consistent feature is a high temperature of 38°C or more and that alone should also make you suspect malaria. It can develop from as early as six to seven days after exposure, to up to as much as one year, so continue to be vigilant upon your return and seek medical advice if you develop flu-like symptoms.

For further advice and malaria information see www.fitfortravel.nhs.uk/destinations/malaysia.htm, www.preventingmalaria.info and www.traveldoctor.co.uk/ malaria.htm.

Other diseases There are occasional outbreaks of **hand, foot and mouth disease** (HFMD) across Malaysia. The most recent large-scale outbreaks were in Sarawak in

LONG-HAUL FLIGHTS, CLOTS AND DVT

Any prolonged immobility, including travel by land or air, can result in deep vein thrombosis (DVT) with the risk of embolus to the lungs. Certain factors can increase the risk and these include:

- Previous clot or close relative with a history
- People over 40, but greater risk over 80 years
- Recent major operation or varicose veins surgery
- Cancer
- Stroke
- Heart disease
- Obesity
- Pregnancy
- Hormone therapy
- Heavy smoking
- Severe varicose veins
- Being very tall (over 6ft/1.8m) or short (under 5ft/1.5m)

A deep vein thrombosis (DVT) causes painful swelling and redness of the calf or sometimes the thigh. It is only dangerous if a clot travels to the lungs (pulmonary embolus). Symptoms of a pulmonary embolus (PE) include chest pain, shortness of breath, and sometimes coughing up small amounts of blood and commonly start three to ten days after a long flight. Anyone who thinks that they might have a DVT needs to see a doctor immediately.

PREVENTION OF DVT
- Keep mobile before and during the flight; move around every couple of hours
- Drink plenty of fluids during the flight
- Avoid taking sleeping pills and excessive tea, coffee and alcohol
- Consider wearing flight socks or support stockings (see www.legshealth.com)

If you think you are at increased risk of a clot, ask your doctor if it is safe to travel.

July 2006. However, this viral infection occurs worldwide, particularly during the late summer and early autumn. It most commonly affects young children and in the main is not a serious infection. The risk of HFMD can be reduced by taking good personal hygiene precautions.

- Wash hands frequently, especially before eating, after using the toilet, and after nappy changes.
- Ensure contaminated surfaces are cleaned with disinfectant.
- Ensure contaminated tissues and other materials are disposed of appropriately.

There are periodic outbreaks of **dengue fever** (for which there is no vaccination). This viral infection is spread by day-biting mosquitoes. It causes a feverish illness with headache and muscle pains like a bad, prolonged, attack of influenza. There may be a rash.

Japanese encephalitis is another viral disease transmitted by infected mosquitoes. Vaccination is recommended for those likely to be frequently exposed to bites during long stays, repeated visits or if staying in rural infected areas. The newer vaccine Ixiaro (two doses given ideally 28 days apart; if time is short then the second dose may be given 21 days after the first dose of vaccine) has none of the more serious side effects of the older vaccines and therefore should be recommended for all rural travel if time and budget allow. (This vaccine is currently only licensed in the UK for those aged 16 or over. For those under 16 the older Green Cross vaccine can be used, which consists of three doses of vaccine over a minimum of 21 days.) The disease is endemic, with small numbers of cases occurring year-round in East Malaysia (Sabah and Sarawak), but in addition epidemics occur following the start of the rainy season in Peninsular Malaysia (April to October) when mosquitoes are most active.

WATER In Malaysia water is treated, but it is still best to avoid drinking tap water. You would also be advised to clean your teeth with bottled water and to avoid ice in drinks.

AIR QUALITY Malaysia, and in particular Sarawak, periodically suffers from smoke haze pollution. Hazardous air-quality levels are reached due to extensive burning of forests in neighbouring Indonesia. The Malaysian Department of Environment (*www.doe.gov.my*) offers more information on this.

FOOD There are strict laws and health standards for food preparation, though this doesn't necessarily equate to high standards of cleanliness in coffee shops. Establishments with a grade A or B (see *Cleanliness*, page 110) are usually of a good standard; anything of grade C or lower may be less than satisfactory.

TRAVELLERS' DIARRHOEA There is always a risk of getting a dose of travellers' diarrhoea; perhaps half of all visitors will suffer and the newer you are to exotic travel, the more likely that will be. By taking precautions against travellers' diarrhoea you will also avoid typhoid, paratyphoid, hepatitis, dysentery, worms, etc. Travellers' diarrhoea and the other faecal-oral diseases come from getting other peoples' faeces in your mouth. This most often happens from cooks not washing their hands after a trip to the toilet, but even if the restaurant cook does not understand basic hygiene you will be safe if your food has been properly cooked and arrives piping hot. The most important prevention strategy is to wash your hands before eating anything.

TREATING TRAVELLERS' DIARRHOEA *Dr Jane Wilson-Howarth*

It is dehydration that makes you feel awful during a bout of diarrhoea and the most important part of treatment is drinking lots of clear fluids. Sachets of oral rehydration salts give the perfect biochemical mix to replace all that is pouring out of your bottom but other recipes taste nicer. Any dilute mixture of sugar and salt in water will do you good: try Coke or orange squash with a three-finger pinch of salt added to each glass (if you are salt-depleted you won't taste the salt). Otherwise make a solution of a four-finger scoop of sugar with a three-finger pinch of salt in a 500 ml glass. Or add eight level teaspoons of sugar (18g) and one level teaspoon of salt (3g) to one litre (five cups) of safe water. A squeeze of lemon or orange juice improves the taste and adds potassium, which is also lost in diarrhoea. Drink two large glasses after every bowel action, and more if you are thirsty. These solutions are still absorbed well if you are vomiting, but you will need to take sips at a time. If you are not eating you need to drink three litres a day plus whatever is pouring into the toilet. If you feel like eating, take a bland, high carbohydrate diet. Heavy greasy foods will probably give you cramps.

If the diarrhoea is bad, or you are passing blood or slime, or you have a fever, you will probably need antibiotics in addition to fluid replacement. A dose of norfloxacin or ciprofloxacin repeated twice a day until better may be appropriate (if you are planning to take an antibiotic with you, note that both norfloxacin and ciprofloxacin are available only on prescription in the UK). If the diarrhoea is greasy and bulky and is accompanied by sulphurous (eggy) burps, one likely cause is giardia. This is best treated with tinidazole (four x 500mg in one dose, repeated seven days later if symptoms persist).

You can pick up salmonella and shigella from toilet door handles and possibly bank notes. The maxim to remind you what you can safely eat is:

PEEL IT, BOIL IT, COOK IT OR FORGET IT

This means that fruit you have washed and peeled yourself, and hot foods, should be safe, but raw foods, cold cooked foods, salads, fruit salads that have been prepared by others, ice cream and ice are all risky, and foods kept lukewarm in hotel buffets are often dangerous. That said, plenty of travellers enjoy fruit and vegetables, so do keep a sense of perspective. If you are struck, see box above for treatment.

Shellfish, crabs and some larger fish can be affected by 'red tide' – an algal bloom that produces harmful toxins. These can become incorporated into other sea creatures and may be harmful if consumed by humans. The Health Ministry issues warnings when this occurs, and restaurants follow their advice. Larger seafood restaurants in Borneo with their own tanks still trade during these periods.

RABIES Rabies is potentially carried by all warm-blooded mammals and is passed on to man through a bite, scratch or a lick of an open wound. More rarely it can be contracted by saliva getting into your eyes, nose or mouth. You must always assume any animal is rabid, even if it looks well, as there is a ten-day period where the animal is infectious but looks perfectly well. Scrub the wound with soap under a running tap or while pouring water from a jug for a good 10–15 minutes. Find a reasonably clear-looking source of water (but at this stage the quality of the water is not important), then pour on a strong iodine or alcohol solution of gin, whisky or rum. This helps stop the rabies virus entering the body and will guard against wound infections, including tetanus. Then get to medical help as soon as possible.

Pre-exposure vaccination for rabies is ideally advised for everyone, but is particularly important if you intend to have contact with animals and/or are likely to be more than 24 hours away from medical help. Ideally three doses should be taken over 28 days, though if time is short then 21 days will suffice. Contrary to popular belief these vaccinations are relatively painless. The main reason for having pre-exposure vaccine is to avoid the need for Rabies Immunoglobulin (RIG), which is a pre-formed antibody made from human (HRIG) or equine (ERIG) blood. It is hard to come by in a lot of countries and it is doubtful that Borneo would have any, meaning that you would have to evacuate to Kuala Lumpur or Singapore. Five doses of a cell-derived vaccine (HDCV, PEP or Verorab) are also needed on days 0, 3, 7, 14 and 28. If you have had the pre-exposure course of three doses of vaccine then the RIG is no longer needed and only two doses of vaccine are given three days apart. This is often easier to find locally and most often would not require evacuation.

If you are bitten, scratched or licked over an open wound by a sick animal, then post-exposure prophylaxis should be given as soon as possible, though it is never too late to seek help, as the incubation period for rabies can be very long. Tell the doctor if you have had pre-exposure vaccine, as this should change the treatment you receive. And remember that, if you do contract rabies, mortality is 100% and death from rabies is probably one of the worst ways to go.

DOCTORS There are two medical systems in Malaysia. Both public and private health care are widely available and of a high standard. Private health care is very inexpensive. You can arrange to see a doctor easily at a medical centre or surgery, or ask your hotel to organise a doctor to visit you there. It is more expensive than public health care, but you are guaranteed a high level of service, and English-speaking staff. Medical staff administer most medication on the spot, so you shouldn't need to go to a pharmacy as well. Health centres and hospitals are listed in the relevant guide chapters. For a full list of hospitals and district health officers in Sabah and Sarawak, see the Malaysian government portal (*www.moh.gov.my/ MohPortal/govhospPublic.jsp*).

BRUNEI Brunei is relatively free from malaria and other tropical diseases. It is outside the typhoon belt, has no active volcanoes and is not prone to earthquakes or other major natural disasters.

TRAVEL CLINICS AND HEALTH INFORMATION A full list of current travel clinic websites worldwide is available on www.istm.org/. For other journey preparation information, consult www.nathnac.org/ds/map_world.aspx. Information about various medications may be found on www.netdoctor.co.uk/travel.

UK
✚ **Berkeley Travel Clinic** 32 Berkeley St, London W1J 8EL (near Green Park tube station); ☎020 7629 6233; ⏰ 10.00–18.00 Mon–Fri, 10.00–15.00 Sat
✚ **Edinburgh Travel Health Clinic** 14 East Preston St, Newington, Edinburgh EH8 9QA; ☎0131 667 1030; www.

edinburghtravelhealthclinic.co.uk; ⏰ 09.00– 19.00 Mon–Wed, 09.00–18.00 Thu & Fri. Travel vaccinations & advice on all aspects of malaria prevention. All current UK prescribed anti-malaria tablets in stock.
✚ **Fleet Street Travel Clinic** 29 Fleet St, London EC4Y 1AA; ☎020 7353 5678; e info@ fleetstreetclinic.com; www.fleetstreetclinic.com.

com; ⊕ 08.45–17.30 Mon–Fri. Injections, travel products & latest advice.

✚ **Hospital for Tropical Diseases Travel Clinic** Mortimer Market Bldg, Capper St (off Tottenham Ct Rd), London WC1E 6AU; ☎ 020 7387 4411; www.thehtd.org; ⊕ 13.00–17.00 Wed & 09.00–13.00 Fri. Consultations are by appointment only & are only offered to those with more complex problems. Check the website for inclusions. Runs a Travellers' Healthline Advisory Service (☎ 020 7950 7799) for country-specific information & health hazards. Also stocks nets, water purification equipment & personal protection measures. Travellers who have returned from the tropics & are unwell, with fever or bloody diarrhoea, can attend the walk-in emergency clinic at the hospital without an appointment.

✚ **InterHealth Travel Clinic** 111 Westminster Bridge Rd, London SE1 7HR; ☎ 020 7902 9000; e info@interhealth.org.uk; www.interhealth. org.uk; ⊕ 08.30–17.30 Mon–Fri. Competitively priced, one-stop travel health service by appointment only.

✚ **MASTA** (Medical Advisory Service for Travellers Abroad) At the London School of Hygiene & Tropical Medicine, Keppel St, London WC1E 7HT; ☎ 09068 224100 (premium-line number, charged at 60p/minute); e enquiries@ masta.org ; www.masta-travel-health.com. For a fee, they will provide an individually tailored health brief, with up-to-date information on how to stay healthy, inoculations & what to take.

✚ **MASTA pre-travel clinics** ☎ 01276 685040; www.masta-travel-health.com/travel-clinic. aspx. Call or check the website for the nearest; there are currently 50 in Britain. They also sell malaria prophylaxis, memory cards, treatment kits, bed nets, net treatment kits, etc.

✚ **NHS travel websites** www.fitfortravel. nhs.uk or www.fitfortravel.scot.nhs.uk . Provide country-by-country advice on immunisation & malaria prevention, plus details of recent developments, & a list of relevant health organisations.

✚ **Nomad Travel Clinics** Flagship store: 3–4 Wellington Terrace, Turnpike Lane, London N8 0PX; ☎ 020 8889 7014; e turnpike@nomadtravel. co.uk; www.nomadtravel.co.uk; walk in or appointments ⊕ 09.15–17.00 daily, late night Thu. See website for clinics in west & central London, Bristol, Southampton & Manchester. As

well as dispensing health advice, Nomad stocks mosquito nets & other anti-bug devices, & an excellent range of adventure travel gear. Runs a Travel Health Advice line on ☎ 09068 633414.

✚ **The Travel Clinic Ltd, Cambridge** 41 Hills Rd, Cambridge CB2 1NT; ☎ 01223 367362; e enquiries@travelclinic.ltd.uk; www. travelcliniccambridge.co.uk; ⊕ 10.00–16.00 Mon, Tue & Sat, 12.00–19.00 Wed & Thu, 11.00–18.00 Fri

✚ **The Travel Clinic Ltd, Ipswich** Gilmour Piper, 10 Fonnereau Rd, Ipswich IP1 3JP; ☎ 01223 367362; ⊕ 09.00–19.00 Wed, 09.00–13.00 Sat

Trailfinders Immunisation Centre 194 Kensington High St, London W8 7RG; ☎ 020 7938 3999; www.trailfinders.com/travelessentials/ travelclinic.htm; ⊕ 09.00–17.00 Mon, Tue, Wed & Fri, 09.00–18.00 Thu, 10.00–17.15 Sat. No appointment necessary.

✚ **Travelpharm** www.travelpharm.com. The Travelpharm website offers up-to-date guidance on travel-related health & has a range of medications available through their online mini-pharmacy.

Irish Republic

✚ **Tropical Medical Bureau** 54 Grafton St, Dublin 2; ☎ 01 2715200; e graftonstreet@tmb. ie; www.tmb.ie; ⊕ until 20.00 Mon–Fri & Sat mornings. For other clinic locations, & useful information specific to tropical destinations, check their website.

USA

✚ **Centers for Disease Control** 1600 Clifton Rd, Atlanta, GA 30333; ☎ 800 232 4636, (800) 232 6348; e cdcinfo@cdc.gov; www.cdc.gov/travel. The central source of travel information in the USA. Each summer they publish the invaluable *Health Information for International Travel*.

✚ **IAMAT** (International Association for Medical Assistance to Travelers) 1623 Military Rd #279, Niagara Falls, NY 14304-1745; ☎ 716 754 4883; e info@iamat.org; www.iamat.org. A non-profit organisation with free membership that provides lists of English-speaking doctors abroad.

Canada

✚ **IAMAT** Suite 10, 1287 St Clair Street West, Toronto, Ontario M6E 1B8; ☎ 416 652 0137; www. iamat.org

+ TMVC Suite 314, 1030 W Georgia St, Vancouver, BC V6E 2Y3; ☎604 681 5656; e vancouver@tmvc.com; www.tmvc.com. One-stop medical clinic for all your international travel health & vaccination needs.

Australia and New Zealand
+ TMVC (Travel Doctors Group) ☎1300 65 88 44; www.tmvc.com.au. 30 clinics in Australia & New Zealand, including: *Auckland* Canterbury Arcade, 174 Queen St, Auckland 1010, New Zealand; ☎(09) 373 3531; e auckland@traveldoctor.co.nz; *Brisbane* 75a Astor Terrace, Spring Hill, Brisbane QLD 4000, Australia; ☎07 3815 6900; e brisbane@traveldoctor.com.au; *Melbourne* 393 Little Bourke St, Melbourne, Vic

3000, Australia; ☎(03) 9935 8100; e melbourne@traveldoctor.com.au; *Sydney* 428 George St, Sydney, NSW 2000, Australia; ☎(02) 9221 7133; e sydney@traveldoctor.com.au
+ IAMAT 206 Papanui Rd, Christchurch 5, New Zealand; www.iamat.org

South Africa
+ SAA-Netcare Travel Clinics ☎011 802 0059; e travelinfo@netcare.co.za; www.travelclinic.co.za. 11 clinics throughout South Africa.
+ TMVC NHC Health Centre, corner Beyers Naude & Waugh Northcliff; ☎0861 300 911; e info@traveldoctor.co.za; www.traveldoctor.co.za. Consult the website for clinic locations.

SAFETY

British, US and Australian authorities issue warnings against travelling around the coast of East Malaysia, particularly the islands off the east coast of Sabah. These islands have been the site of political tensions and volatility as territorial disputes between Indonesia and Malaysia bubble (see *Diving in Borneo* box, page 117). Tourists have been the target of kidnappers in the past. Accommodation on some islands has been closed and the area is under constant military surveillance.

URBAN SAFETY AND CRIME There is a relatively low risk of being mugged or robbed, but be sensible in keeping personal belongings close to you, and be on the lookout for pickpockets in markets. Be warned that some streets and roads, even in the state capitals, are very unkempt – keep an eye out for large cracks and holes. The low crime rate of Brunei comes in large part from government stability and economic prosperity.

ANIMALS There are several poisonous snakes on Borneo, both terrestrial and marine (see *Chapter 2 Natural History*, page 57). Caution must be taken at certain beaches. There are no deadly mammals, but jungle walks should be attempted with guides rather than alone.

WOMEN TRAVELLERS

After many years as a solo woman globetrotter, Malaysia stands out as probably the safest country in which I have travelled in terms of personal security, general public friendliness and political stability. In September 2010, the Oxford Business Group identified the high levels of overall safety in Malaysia as one of the main reasons for it having 'strengthened its position as south-East Asia's top tourism destination'. Malaysia rated second only to China in Asia for its political and social stability. I cannot recall ever hearing about horrendous crimes against women in the daily news, with the exception of one very high-profile murder case.

The sense of general personal security as a woman traveller is even greater in Borneo, because of its island friendliness and relatively low urban density. In my frequent and extended travels in Brunei, Sabah and Sarawak, I have not once felt

3

personally threatened by men. In larger cities such as Kota Kinabalu, Kuching and Miri I always feel very safe walking around freely in key public areas, though poorly lit backstreets and more remote urban zones are best avoided at night. The fact that Malaysia is such a street-living society, with a density of people in key public areas, adds to the overall feeling of safety.

In Brunei, the huge esteem shown for women makes it one of the safest countries in the world in which a woman can travel on her own. The incidence of crime is virtually nil – no doubt due largely to the serious punishments for criminal offences – while assaults against women are unheard of (though may perhaps go unreported).

I certainly feel that the respect shown towards me, and my personal feelings of comfort, are boosted by my respect for Malaysian Muslim customs and subsequent dress sense (longer skirts, blouses, no miniskirts or bare shoulders).

Muslim women in Brunei and Malaysia wear a *tudong*, a veil or scarf, on their head. While there is no expectation for foreigners to do the same, it is advisable to carry a light scarf in your bag to don at appropriate moments (for example when visiting religious sites). While skimpier garments are becoming more common amongst the clubbing classes of Kuala Lumpur, Borneo remains more conservative.

See also *Cultural etiquette*, pages 123–4.

DISABLED TRAVELLERS

After contacting a couple of major UK and US associations that deal with disabled travel and being told they did not have Borneo covered, it appears that up until now there has not been a lot of call for them to do so. This is likely to change as Borneo receives more tourists. For the time being, travelling on public transport, especially small town buses, would not be easy. Most four–five-star hotels claim to have facilities for the disabled including wheelchair access and 'adapted' rooms. The lack of dedicated disabled-friendly tours to Borneo doesn't mean your chosen tour company will not do the job for you and create an itinerary. If you are travelling independently the best thing is to contact the Sabah and Sarawak tourism offices for assistance and recommendations once you have a basic itinerary planned. They can also answer specific questions and contact hotels and other businesses directly. Use the various associations (see below) as your advocates so that they know there is a demand for such information. For further information see Mobility International USA (*www.miusa.org/ncde/intlopportunities/malaysia*) as well as www.canbedone. co.uk; www.disabledtravelers.com and www.able-travel.com.

FAMILIES

On the whole, Malaysian Borneo is safe, sunny and friendly and makes an inexpensive, educational, adventurous and exotic family holiday.

It's not a destination to just soak up some sun – there is so much more on offer. A volunteer family holiday, living and helping out in one of the villages, would be a fantastic experience.

Many city hostels – especially the 'lodge' kind – have family rooms from 115MYR with breakfast included. With their lounges, sun decks and other travellers for company, these may provide a more fun atmosphere than the small room, square-wall environment of a shoestring hotel which have family rooms from 100–150MYR. If you have more to spend, and want more privacy, then there are family rooms in most of the hotels. Another good option is serviced apartments.

Beyond the cities, there are beach resorts that have self-contained family rooms (or just pay for two or three rooms for your brood, they can be so cheap), mountain resorts with chalet accommodation (sometimes self-contained), longhouse rentals or family-friendly homestays.

SINGLE TRAVELLERS

Many of the advantages and disadvantages of travelling alone in Borneo are not very different from doing so in other places. I found, particularly in luxury hotels, the staff grilled me as to whether it was 'just *one* for breakfast?' – 'I'm not hiding anyone' is my usual reply. If you are seeking peace and quiet take a book or a newspaper.

Practically speaking, single travellers are heavily penalised in Malaysian and Bruneian hotels. There are virtually no single rates – either there is no difference in price between a single and double, or the difference is negligible. A better choice is to stay in the places where being single does pay – homestays, bed and breakfasts, hostels, budget to mid-range beach resorts, and the occasional hotel suite or apartment which offer a single rate suitably priced for the 'flash packer'. Even if you have more to spend, these are generally more friendly places, and many offer the chance to upgrade to a bigger or more comfortable room. All that said, if you do want a hotel environment, shoestring to budget hotel rooms start at between 60MYR and 120MYR and you will have a lot of space. Just make sure that if you're paying for a double room you're getting one. The same price bracket in some country hotels may get you anything from a superior room to a suite.

GAY AND LESBIAN TRAVELLERS

One of the most highly regarded gay and lesbian associations active in Borneo is **Utopia Asia** (*www.utopia-asia.com*). Its general advice for travellers in Malaysia is: 'Gay life in Malaysia as in other Asian countries is blossoming, despite conservative religion-based discrimination and outdated colonial era laws.'

Former deputy prime minister, Anwar Ibrahim, was famously removed from office by a trumped-up sodomy conviction that was reversed by Malaysia's High Court in 2004. Muslims, both local and visitors, are also subject to religious law which may (though rarely does) punish gay or lesbian sexual activity with flogging, and male transvestism with imprisonment. Even though religious law does not apply to non-Muslims, Islam is the state religion under Malaysia's constitution and thus homosexual citizens face official discrimination. Police may arrest any person (Muslim or not) for having sex in a public place (such as cruise spots). Visitors are well advised to respect Malaysian law and customs while they are guests in the country. Having said that, police generally have not detained foreigners during raids on local gay businesses, focusing instead on ethnic Malay customers, almost 100% of whom, by law, are considered Muslim at birth.

See Utopia Asia's *Utopia Guide to Malaysia,* which has listings for the gay and lesbian scene in 17 cities including Kota Kinabalu and Kuching. The guide can be ordered online (*www.utopia-asia.com/utopiaguide/utopiaguides.htm*) and includes gay scene city maps and listings of organisations, bars, discos, spas, accommodation and restaurants, with a special section highlighting venues that are particularly welcoming to women.

Kota Kinabalu is definitely Borneo's capital of camp. Whilst there are no overtly gay hotels, there are some that are discreetly so and others which are gay-friendly. There are some well-known gay and lesbian bars and nightclubs in Kota Kinabalu.

Kuching is far more conservative. Brunei is unfortunately much less tolerant of homosexuality, and the gay community is mostly 'undercover'. The nearest place where public displays of affection can be shown without the fear of being arrested is Miri in Sarawak.

WHAT TO TAKE

What you take is dependent on what kind of holiday you are planning as much as personal tastes. Rather than provide an exhaustive list of what to take, I have listed a few things you may not want to do without.

MAPS Whilst basic tourist maps of towns are available in Borneo, it is best to bring your own for the rest of your trip. They should be as detailed as is relevant for what you want to do – see *Getting your bearings*, page 101. This is especially important if you are travelling independently on trekking trips and going to places such as Gunung Kinabalu National Park – maps available at the park are not very good on scale and legend. **Periplus Publishing** (*www.peripluspublishinggroup.com*) produce travel maps of Sarawak and Sabah at a scale of 1:1,000,000, including Kota Kinabalu, Kuching and Bintulu city plans. Periplus also do good language books – various Behasa, Melayu-Behasa and Inggeris dictionaries including a good pocket one.

CLOTHES Leave your jeans at home! No matter how addicted to your denim you are, it weighs a tonne, dries slowly and is uncomfortable in humid climates. My packing skills (and suitcase weight) have improved dramatically during recent trips to Borneo. The tropics are the best minimising agent – for a start, you will not want to have too many clothes on, and those that you do should be light, sleek and airy. My travel wardrobe includes one pair of smart cotton trousers, one fast-dry, high-tech pair of walking trousers (or sportswear skirt if you prefer), two casual cotton skirts or dresses or shorts, depending on your style, one evening skirt or dress and one pair of slinky night trousers. Next, to mix-and-match with all of the above, I take two or three casual tops and two dressy ones, including a long-sleeved shirt for general wear or over bathers, plus a light cardigan to survive the sometimes polar temperatures in planes, buses and restaurants. This also comes in handy for cooler-climate trips, such as to Gunung Kinabalu National Park – the only place mentioned in the book where temperatures drop to 15°C. Finally, I pack a flimsy jogging outfit – unfortunately jogging shoes always add bulk, which is why ideally you will also use them for hiking (with the exclusion perhaps of heavy-duty trails). My wardrobe is intended as a guideline only – what you take will obviously depend on the nature of your holiday, whether predominantly sightseeing or serious adventure. Anyone planning to do hiking- or boating-related activities needs a light waterproof jacket.

Aim exclusively for pure cotton, linen and silk clothing, or cotton-silk and cotton-nylon mixes. Avoid scratchy materials such as viscose and rayon or heavy, humid viscose-elastane combinations.

If you are planning an ascent of Mount Kinabalu or other peaks, you will need to take some thermal and waterproof clothing fit for near-zero temperatures (see *Chapter 6, West Coast Sabah*, page 192).

Both sexes should try to keep the shoe count to a maximum of four pairs, including walking or jogging shoes, flip-flops/thongs, practical sightseeing shoes and possibly a more chic pair of day/night shoes. Avoid confined or tight footwear as your feet will feel clammy and may swell up. Good walking shoes or sandals in breathable leather are great for walking around cities in the heat. Quality leather flip-flops are ideal for walking around cities, or on the beach, in comfort; higher heeled versions double up for a tropical day and night, casual-chic look.

See also *Women travellers*, pages 91–2.

MONEY

EAST MALAYSIA

Currency The currency of Sabah and Sarawak is the Malaysian ringgit (MYR). Notes come in denominations of 1, 5, 10, 50 and 100RM. One ringgit comprises 100 sen. Coins come in 5, 10, 20 and 50 sen denominations. The exchange rate in December 2011 was US$1 = 3.2MYR, €1 = 4.2MYR, £1 = 4.9MYR. Check exchange rates with the Malaysian newspaper, The Star Online (*www.biz.thestar. com.my/business/exchange.asp*).

Exchanging and spending Foreign currencies and travellers' cheques can be readily exchanged at banks and at licensed money exchanges in larger cities, as well as at hotels and some department stores. Credit cards (Visa, MasterCard, American Express and Diners Club) are widely accepted in hotels and bigger restaurants and businesses, but not in small local shops. Payment by cheque is not accepted. Payment by credit card becomes more difficult the further from major cities you go, as does the possibility of exchanging money and cashing travellers' cheques. ATM machines are scarce outside of cities and medium-sized towns.

Major national Malaysian banks with branches in Sabah and Sarawak include Bumiputera Commerce and RHB Bank. Bank hours are generally 09.30–16.00.

Until 2005, the Malaysian ringgit was equal in value to the US dollar (in response to the Asian financial crash). People still commonly quote in dollars in marketplaces and shops, so if you are quoted an unreasonably high price this could be the explanation. The difference between 1MYR and US$1 is more than three-fold. Ask if you are unsure.

BRUNEI The Brunei dollar (BND) is equal in value to the Singapore dollar, which is also legal tender in Brunei. The dollar comes in 1, 5, 10, 50, 100, 500 and 1,000 denominations; coins come in 1, 5, 10, 20 and 50 cents. All major credit cards are accepted throughout the country. Most Bruneian banks are government sanctioned to handle travellers' cheques and currency exchange.

CARRYING CASH In both Malaysia and Brunei, it is advisable to always carry some cash, especially when travelling in the countryside. ATMs can be hard to come by and unreliable, even at airports.

BUDGETING

Borneo caters pretty well for all budgets, and is particularly good value for those with less money to spend. Other parts of southeast Asia may be cheaper, but often they will also have a greater choice of 'high-end' products and services. Borneo has a wide range of budget accommodation and food. It is possible to live inexpensively whatever your budget. The hotels, car hire, tours and trips are likely to be your biggest expenditures. There are so many good hotel deals, and much inter-bleeding of categories between budget/mid range and mid range/upmarket, you can easily upgrade a notch or two for some hotel nights.

Some typical daily items and their costs are:

Loaf of bread	1.60–2MYR	1.5 litre bottle of water	1.50–2MYR
Street snack	1–3MYR	1 litre of milk	4–5MYR
Postcard	approx 70 sens	1 litre of soft drink	2.50MYR
International postage up to		1 litre of petrol	1.90MYR
20gm	1.40–1.50MYR	Local bus fare	1–2MYR
T-shirt	10–15MYR		

UPMARKET Hotels which are truly five-star on an international par generally charge 1,000–1,200MYR for premium, suite-like rooms, with standard rooms available for 700–900MYR. These rates can drop by 30–40% for long-term stays booked via the internet. In December 2011, for example, the Shangri-La Rasa Ria Resor was offering 14-day stays for 575MYR a night.

Generally, four-star hotels – and even some five-star properties – will offer prices well below these rates. Certain hotel booking sites price standard rooms at the Hyatt Regency in Kota Kinablu at 360MYR, double rooms at 460MYR and club rooms at 560MYR. For this price you can enjoy 46m² rooms, and for 100MYR more, possibly business lounge access and other privileges that come with top-end accommodation. The food in coffee shops and markets counts among the most authentic available; however, if you prefer to dine in air-conditioned restaurants there are plenty to choose from. A daily spend of US$130–180 will allow for upmarket hotels with extras, top-range food and tours and car hire.

MID RANGE In the mid-range category there are some very good deals to be had on two- to three-star hotels, especially with online promotions. Many hotels offer deals, such as a superior double room with breakfast, for two people over two nights for 300MYR; this works out to just 75MYR (around US$20/£10) per person per night for bed and breakfast. The relatively new hotel, Novotel 1 Borneo, has been offering standard rooms at budget prices (150–350MYR) and executive suites for mid-range to upmarket prices (360–620MYR).

With some day tours using local operators and dining in hotel restaurants, an average daily budget might be US$60–80 (around £30–40/€40–50).

Remarkable upgrades into luxury accommodation brackets can be had when travelling on a mid-range budget, especially if you plan ahead and book hotels independently online. Even five-star city hotels have been known to offer special rates of 350–500MYR for a double room. Add occasional car hire to this, and a daily budget may be in the region of US$80–100 a day per person.

SHOESTRING/BUDGET If you are on a tight budget, the best option is to stay in hostels, homestays and no-star hotels; eat street food from stalls and markets and dine at coffee shops; take buses and ferries, and flights with AirAsia, and wing it on your own when visiting local places rather than take guided tours. The food available at markets for 1–3MYR is delicious, and in coffee shops you won't need to pay any more than 10MYR for a good meal including soft drinks. In Brunei, prices are around double. In either country, you can eat very well for US$5 at the markets.

If you are on a restricted budget but can go that extra bit further, budget hotels may be an option. A single/double room will cost 50–60MYR. You will be able to eat at a few more coffee shops than markets, and choose a (budget) tour company for the occasional half- or full-day excursion. Budget options are outlined in each guide chapter.

It's feasible to live comfortably enough off 110–150MYR a day (approximately US$32–45/£20–25/€25–30).

GETTING AROUND

BY AIR Though travelling distances within each Bornean state are not especially long, many people rely on air travel for longer journeys (such as west- to east-coast cities). This is partly because it is there – flights to the major cities and towns are abundant and cheap – and partly because of the state of most of the roads. Why spend six hours travelling in a car when you can fly in 40 minutes? With many remote inland areas and a 1,000km western coastline marked by four major cities (Kuching, Sibu, Bintulu and Miri), flights are even more common in Sarawak. If speed and convenience are what you are looking for, then flying is a good option. If you are concerned about the environmental effects of air travel, or want to take in the scenery between towns (and brave the roads), then see below for other options.

Established or no frills? With the slogan 'Now Everyone Can Fly' plastered all over their bright red aircraft, AirAsia (*www.airasia.com*) are loved for liberating the skies and contributing to aviation democracy with their affordable prices. However, they are also loathed for the frustrations they create through chronic delays, and a rather blasé attitude towards customers – though not without typical Asian politeness. With increasingly competitive prices being offered by Malaysian Airlines, it's hardly worthwhile enduring the relative discomfort and disarray of AirAsia to save a few pennies. However, as with all low-cost airlines, the prices do make it very attractive and AirAsia are more friendly, professional and comfortable than Ryanair, for example – more on a par with easyJet or German Wings. Malaysian Airlines are far more reliable, if a little more expensive. Their safety record and policy are unwavering; they allow 20kg for domestic flights (compared with AirAsia's 15kg); they have on-board refreshments and assigned seats; and they allow ticket changes. If AirAsia cancels a flight on the other hand, you have the option of either taking another flight later that day or losing your ticket. If you arrive at the AirAsia check-in desk any later than 30 minutes ahead of departure they are uncompromising, but if they keep *you* waiting for an hour, no apologies are offered. All that said, many people swear by them, rather than at them – and they fly frequently and cheaply. Just be prepared for the delays! Overall, the choice provided by the two is fantastic.

Fares Fares for **Malaysian Airlines** can be as low as 159MYR from Kuala Lumpur to Kuching, Sibu, Bintulu and Miri (all in Sarawak), Kota Kinabalu and Labuan; 30MYR from Kota Kinabalu to Miri, Labuan, Tawau and Sandakan; and 21MYR from Kuching to Sibu. However, do not expect to see these prices if booking online the day ahead of travel or during peak travel periods. Having said this, it can be possible to benefit from last-minute deals, depending on where you are heading and how bookings are looking for that destination. There are massive price variations in quoted internet fares from one day to another, so it pays to have flying flexibility and to book ahead. The same 159MYR fare for Kuala Lumpur to Kuching may triple if you need to buy at short notice.

AirAsia fares tend to be even lower, though MAS have been catching up with them under the heat of huge competition. AirAsia offer a fast and inexpensive means of getting around Sabah and Sarawak, if you time your bookings right. The airline offers journeys as low as 20MYR for Sandakan–Kota Kinabalu, 60MYR for

3

Kuching–Kota Kinabalu and 53MYR for Kota Kinabalu–Tawau. The last journey in an express coach will take eight hours and cost 70MYR, so the company has helped revolutionise travel to and in Borneo.

Rural air services (RAS) All rural air services (RAS) in Sabah, Sarawak and Labuan are operated by MASWings, a subsidiary of Malaysia Airlines. Under their former operator – FlyAsianXpress (FAX), a subsidiary of AirAsia – scheduled flights were renowned for being cancelled or delayed, because of repairs, breakdowns or bad weather. As one guide commented 'some people say that FAX Airlines stands for Flight Always Cancelled!' Today, however, the number of MASWings fans is skyrocketing with their successful management of the new service. In November 2011, the *Borneo Post* reported the vital role the airline was playing for its 1.2 million passengers a year: flight frequency had more than doubled from 450 to 950 flights a week since 2007, and the old fleet of Fokker 50s had been replaced with sophisticated aircraft such as the ATR 72-500. MASWings' rural network covers some 21 destinations in Sabah and Sarawak; it also assures several weekly flights between remote regional centres in the two states. In 2012, its expanding rural network will reach out towards Indonesia and the Philippines.

BY CAR The cost of car rental is similar to Western prices: around 100–150MYR a day. Perhaps with the exception of the longest trips (from west to east in Sabah, or north to south in Sarawak), trips by car offer a good mix of independence, ease and maximum viewing along the way. Car journeys are particularly economical in Brunei, where petrol costs 50 cents a litre, about 20BND to fill a tank. Prices are double that in Sabah and Sarawak, where petrol costs around 1.9MYR a litre, or 90MYR a tank. (Just about everything else works in the opposite sense – double the price in Brunei.) Most national driving licences (UK, US, Australian) can be used in Malaysia for three months, beyond which you require either a Malaysian driving licence or an annually renewable International Driving Permit.

Roads All major roads are dual carriageways; there are no multi-lane expressways. The speed limit is 100km/h on open roads. Distances are now metric, but there are still vestiges of the former imperial system as far as the location of some places goes (see *Getting your bearings*, page 101). The major routes are all of decent (and improving) quality. Minor roads can vary enormously, and if you're driving around a lot you'll encounter some bumpy roads and unsealed sections as you travel between towns or through plantations and rural areas. Most routes leading into developing towns or rising tourist attractions are either undergoing roadworks or are earmarked for improvement.

Rules In Malaysia you drive on the left-hand side of the road and the cars are right-hand drive. Road signs are not brilliant – in their regularity or clarity, in cities or on highways. Things are better in Sarawak, where the British influence is more noticeable, and international signage is far more common on major routes, especially on the west coast Pan-Borneo Highway. Two road signs you will see a lot are *AWAS* (slow) and *Dilarang Masuk* (private – no entry).

With the low population density it is easy to manoeuvre on the open road, though it is more difficult in cities – streets are small and quite congested. Due to strict licence conditions and enforcement, road safety standards seem very high and the quality of driving is impressive. All licences have to be renewed annually and public service vehicles require a special licence. Expect police checks and road blocks, especially in southeast Sabah towards the Indonesian border, where they are checking for illegal trafficking of people and general contraband.

Inter-state travel Travelling between states by car is possible; it depends on your itinerary, how much time you have, and whether you want to make the road trip part of your journey and get a feel for the landscape. The Pan-Borneo Highway, Lebuh raya Pan Borneo (also referred to as the Trans Borneo Highway), links Sabah to Brunei and to Sarawak.

Although long road trips can be enjoyable, it is worth bearing in mind the practicalities of travelling between states, described here by a friend who tried it: 'It takes eight to ten hours to drive from Kota Kinabalu to Brunei town, which involves between three and five river crossings using a ferry – adding to the time and cost of the journey. And there is always the risk of having your passport taken at one of the numerous checkpoints.' If you are heading for Sarawak, you have to take this same route and travel through Brunei, as there is no direct road once you reach Lawas through to Miri, which makes it a convoluted journey. Kota Kinabalu to Miri is a 12-hour drive; continuing south to Kuching would make at least a 20-hour journey.

Immigration checkpoints Between Sabah, Sarawak and Brunei, these are found at Sindumin in Sabah to Merapok in Sarawak; Tedungan in Sarawak to Kuala Lurah in Brunei; and Sungai Tujoh in Brunei to Sungai Tujuh Miri in Sarawak. The Tedungan to Kuala Lurah is one of the busiest, with waits of up to an hour. Sungai Tujoh (being the only place where holders of Frequent Traveller Cards can pass between Brunei and Sarawak) can also involve nightmarish waits as Bruneians head to the border for a weekend in Miri. Avoid it on long weekends when up to 1,500 cars will pass in a day. The Bruneian checkpoints in particular are not well staffed. There also checks involved in the ferry crossing from Lawas in Sarawak to Labu in Brunei and from Puni in Brunei to Limbang in Sarawak.

Further road information, key distances and estimated driving times are included in the relevant chapters of this guide. Sabah Tourism also has an interactive distance chart online (*www.sabahtourism.com/distancechart/distancechart.html*).

BY BUS While buses provide a cheap, comfortable form of transport that can be both fun and effective, the urban bus system in both Sabah and Sarawak is a bit of a shambles. Problems include too many bus companies, no central bus terminal and confusion (at least for the outsider) of where to take each type of bus from. The situation is improving in the capital cities as the infrastructure evolves, but in smaller towns buses are not the best option.

Town buses *Bas mini* (minibuses) ply city and suburban areas but also do some longer inter-city journeys. The vehicles are generally numbered rather than named, with a route diagram at key bus stops. Different bus companies usually operate particular patches, serving specific towns and surrounding areas.

Long-distance buses Air-conditioned 'express buses' for long-distance trips leave from a different terminal from town buses. In bigger cities these are usually located in the suburbs and referred to as the long-distance bus station. Several coach and express bus operators vie for longer journeys, both intra- and inter-state. All these choices don't necessarily mean travelling by bus is easy though. Long-distance bus stations (even in smaller towns) can be very inconveniently located, meaning you also have to take a minibus to the city or town centre. Tour operators use comfortable, 8–12-seat, air-conditioned recreational buses, for which they must have a licence.

Long-distance buses can be a very cost-effective (though not necessarily time-effective) way of travelling. For example, to cross Sabah from Kota Kinabalu to the east coast city of Tawau (roughly 12 hours) costs 50MYR, including a meal. Inter-state travel by bus is more complicated – for example, travelling between Miri (Sarawak) and Bandar Seri Begawan (Brunei) involves changing buses four times and crossing two rivers by ferry. More details of all these journeys are given in the relevant chapters.

My advice would be to limit bus journeys to four or five hours. Air fares of less than 50MYR between Kota Kinabalu and Kuching make anything more than this feasibly avoidable on a budget. Another option would be to stop off at places along the way and break the bus journey up. This is a great way to see smaller places you would otherwise miss, but depends on whether you have the time.

BY BOAT

Ferries Ferries are an efficient and interesting way of travelling in Borneo. Some of the main links are Brunei to Sabah (via Labuan Island), Brunei to Limbang in Sarawak, Kota Kinabalu to Brunei (via Labuan), and Labuan to Menumbok in Sabah. Various operators, including passenger and car ferries, ply these routes. **Labuan Tourism**'s homepage (*www.labuantourism.com.my*) is a good place to check timetables and prices; Labuan is a thoroughfare of ferry passage between Sabah and Brunei.

The journey between Brunei's and Sabah's capitals can be done in about four hours. All ferries go via Labuan Island; there are no direct passages. Have your passport on hand for clearing immigration. If heading to Brunei, ensure you have the necessary money for the visa. There are several daily departures and the fare from Kota Kinabalu through to Brunei will cost between 60 and 80MYR, depending on which ferry and ticket class you take. Child transport generally costs between 30–40% less.

There are also regular ferries between Labuan and Limbang and Lawas in Sarawak, and Sipitang in southern Sabah. Ferries leave Brunei for Limbang – a half-hour journey – with the option of continuing by road (bus or car) north to Sabah or south through Sarawak.

River transport Boats are an integral part of the public transport system, especially in Sarawak, with its 55 rivers. They are used for crossing rivers and bays, and for travelling into jungles and to remote villages. What's more, boat journeys, especially those in Iban longboats (*temuai*), are often a hugely enjoyable part of the trip.

Small fibreglass vessels, twin-engine motorboats and speedboats are used for river excursions and transfers, while large, high-tech express boats are used for longer river trips, especially into central Sarawak. They are also the primary public transport between towns along Sarawak's west coast and in parts of Brunei.

As air travel replaces the absolute need for extensive longboat trips, especially to reach hinterland areas of Sarawak, such journeys are really only within reach of the independent traveller with enough cash to pay for the wonder of doing a six- to ten-hour river trip or an overnight custom-made adventure. Two-hour trips are a common feature of packaged river safaris and tours for both budget and upmarket travellers. If you are travelling independently, do everything you can to suss out the local public boat services to reach nearby towns, villages and islands. These are not always well publicised; information can be found at the public jetties.

GETTING YOUR BEARINGS

MAPS For some reason, maps in Sabah and Sarawak are of poor quality and very difficult to get hold of. The owner of one award-winning tour company in Sabah told me of his joy when he visited London in the 1990s and found the best maps of Sabah he had ever seen! Things have no doubt improved since then, but if the quality and availability of tourism maps – especially in Sabah – are any indication, then you are well advised to bring your own maps. If you are just visiting the cities then the tourist maps will probably be sufficient, but if you want more detail or have a special interest – mountaineering, general touring, self-drive, nature-spotting – bring maps with sufficient details to suit your needs.

Apparently 'due to many requests', Sabah Tourism will soon be issuing a tourist map of the state for visitors. The Kota Kinabalu city map they provide is reasonably useful, but Sabah Tourism has, until recently, been unable to provide town and city maps for other destinations. Sarawak Tourism (again) does a much better job. Their large fold-out map of the state does not give topographic detail fit for hiking, but does show rivers, mountains and small towns. On the reverse side there is an excellent Kuching city map, city/town maps of Sibu, Miri, Bintulu, Kapit and Sarikei, and maps of the Damai Beach area and Gunung Mulu National Park. Brunei is only afforded basic detail on the map. Pick one up from tourist offices in any of the towns mentioned above.

See also, *What to take*, page 94.

DIRECTIONS Road signs are as elusive in Borneo as street names. In Kota Kinabalu and its coastal surrounds, there are hardly any signs along major roads, and if you ask people (including local tour guides) which road or street you are on, they usually shrug their shoulders. The same is found in small towns; you might find that one street in the town has a name, but no-one ever uses it. Locals generally orient themselves in relation to a landmark – the name of a bank, a shopping centre, or a business of some kind. So if you need directions, ask where a certain place is, rather than which street it is in.

TOWN, VILLAGE AND ROAD NAMES A village (such as Kundasang, just south of Gunung Kinabalu National Park) is a *kampung*, sometimes spelt *kampong*. A small town (such as Ranau, a few kilometres from Kundasang) is known as a *pecan*. A medium-sized town is a *bandar*, and a big city is a *bandarayar*. A village on water is a *kampung ayer* (pronounced 'eye-er'). Roads are mostly called *jalan* (abbreviated to *jln*). Lanes and pathways are *lorong* and avenues are *lebuh*. Long *jalan* can change name three times along one city strip. Confusingly, tourism offices (and sometimes locals) switch between referring to streets in Malaysian and English. Jalan Bazaar in Kuching varies rather erratically between its real name and the anglicised version 'Main Bazaar' on maps.

TOWN LAYOUT AND ADDRESSES Sabah's, Sarawak's and Brunei's town centres have been traditionally built into 'shop-lots'. Shops, bazaars, coffee shops and all kinds of other traders occupy these wall-to-wall blocks of shops. Shopping centres too are composed of shop-lots. Addresses for hotels, restaurants and offices will often take the confusing format of 'Ground Floor, Block 3, Lot BG, 38 Kompleks Kuwasa, Jalan Karamunsing'.

Kompleks are commercial centres, usually with a mix of businesses and shops. Shopping centres and some department stores are called *wisma* (eg: Wisma Merdeka).

Despite kilometres now being the accepted measure of distance, addresses for places outside of town are often given in terms of miles from the nearest city or town centre. So 'Mile 8' means eight miles from, for example, Sandakan. However, you will also see 'Km 8' (etc) as a point of reference; it depends on the locality.

ACCOMMODATION

HOTELS The Malaysian Tourism Minister, Datuk Seri Tengku Adnan Tengku Mansor, has started toughening up criteria for national hotel ratings, because the department had received many complaints from locals and tourists saying that Malaysian hotels were not up to standard. It's difficult to make blanket statements about hotel standards. However, if the tourism minister says there is a problem with Malaysian hotel standards on a national level, these problems are even more acute in Malaysian Borneo.

The 'Hotel Monitoring Team' of the Ministry of Culture, Arts and Tourism (MOCAT) keep an eye on the 992 registered hotels and more than 2,200 tourist accommodation premises nationwide. To receive any kind of rating, hotels must be MOCAT registered. MOCAT also has another grading system, the **Orchid** classification, for all lodgings that don't qualify for star ratings. This applies to budget hotels, family-owned 'resorts', homestays, bed and breakfasts, hostels and inns. You can expect a three-Orchid resort to be very comfortable and clean, perhaps with a pool, Wi-Fi and other facilities. For a full list of star- and Orchid-rated hotels in Sabah and Sarawak, see www.etourz.com.

The **Malaysian Association of Hotels** (*www.hotels.org.my*) issues hotel star ratings. Some budget hotels have a no-star rating; you can check to see if they are registered or have any other classification – the **Malaysian Budget Hotels Association** (MBHA) has a new website (*www.malaysiabudgethotels.com*) with an online booking system for all of its registered members. There is a Sabah branch of the MBHA in Papar, southeast of Kota Kinabalu (✆ *088 915273;* e *versus@pc.jaring. my*).

In Brunei, the **Brunei Association of Hotels** (*www.hotelsofbrunei.com*) issues star ratings to registered hotels, and its website has descriptions of (and links to) its members, including everything from budget to luxury establishments.

In reality Accommodation choices and standards in Borneo are generally inadequate. The tourism industry in Sabah, Sarawak and Brunei openly admits to the lack of a truly high-end product – even the capital cities have only a handful of top-class hotels. In all categories, there are shortfalls in both facilities and service compared with international standards: a 'five-star' hotel for example, often matches a three- or four-star establishment in a sophisticated market.

Outside of the capitals of Bandar Seri Begawan, Kota Kinabalu and Kuching tourism development is still in its infant stage. This is the case even in medium-sized business cities such as Sibu and Miri, which have just a couple of truly noteworthy hotels.

Hotel choices in smaller towns or lesser-known places can be extremely limited. Day trips from the nearest big city are a good option in this case. If, on the other hand, you are happy with authenticity, no-star hotels, rustic resorts and homestays in the forest and countryside will provide just that.

In spite of the divergence in service standards, travellers in Borneo benefit from Asia's hallmark hospitality, amplified by the island friendliness.. Harnessed to the tourism industry growth are continual upgrades in hotel quality.

Rates Standards may be lower than those in many Asian capitals, but prices generally are too. Many hotel bargains are to be had, particularly in the well-supplied two- to three-star bracket, so you can shop around for the best deal. Rates quoted are usually inclusive of a standard 10% service charge and 5–10% government service tax. Good hotels will make this clear on their website; if not it pays to ask. Some hotels quote a 'weekend rate' of up to 30% less than going rates, especially business hotels in smaller towns where they most need the weekend leisure clientele.

Booking The best deals are found on the internet, especially for independently run city hotels. Many of these offer promotional deals such as 30–40% cuts on published rates, or extra nights and services. If you are organising your own travels, it is advisable to book ahead, especially during the peak foreign visitor months (June–September), as well as

HOTEL PRICE CODES

Accommodation listings are laid out in decreasing price order, under the following categories: Luxury, Upmarket, Mid range, Budget and Shoestring. Serviced apartments, hostels and homestays are grouped together and also listed in decreasing price order. The following key (also on the inside front cover) gives a further indication of prices. See *Budget* on pages 95–6 for advice on choosing accommodation categories to suit your pocket.

$$$$$	600MYR +
$$$$	450–600MYR
$$$	300–450MYR
$$	150–300MYR
$	<150MYR

Malaysian school holiday periods (see *When to visit*, page 69). A couple of good domestic booking sites include the **Hotels Association** (*www.hotels.org.my*), though it tends to favour three- to five-star hotels and exaggerate some of the ratings. A good general Malaysian travel site with a reservations system is **CUTI** (*www.cuti.com.my*), endorsed by Tourism Malaysia.

Check-out In hotels, check-out time is generally 12.00. Be aware that if you are on a tour and have transfers by plane, boat and bus or excursions, local tour operators often start days very early, with check-out sometimes as early as 06.00 or 07.00. Check-in at hotels is generally from 14.00.

Payment Four- and five-star hotels, and some two- and three-stars, accept a wide variety of credit cards (American Express, Visa, MasterCard, Diners Club, etc). Expect to pay by cash or cheque for most jungle lodges, homestays and family-owned resorts.

Entertainment and internet For all hotels, a major new criterion being imposed by the MOCAT is Wi-Fi access on all floors of a hotel building and this requirement is increasingly being met in Sabah and Sarawak. Most four- and five-star hotels will have a high-speed internet connection in rooms, and Wi-Fi in the lobby and public areas. Many top-notch hotels continue to impose a charge for the service whereas for hostels up to four-star hotels it is largely free of charge. Modern budget hotels, two- to three-star business hotels and backpackers' hostels/lodges are more likely to be connected than conservative, small-town hotels. Only high-end hotels, a handful of mid-range and exceptional one- to two-star establishments will have 'Astro' (satellite) television. Even when there is a large choice of channels,

Practical Information ACCOMMODATION 3

access to the BBC may be excluded – the best have CNN, BBC, Discovery Channel, Disney and Cinemax Movies.

Room service Room service in Malaysia is generally very affordable if you are happy to eat like a local. You are likely to find several good-quality main course Chinese and Malay dishes for 7–10MYR in a three-star hotel, or 15–20MYR in a four- or five-star establishment. Western food is much more expensive – pork chops or fish and chips may cost around 30–40MYR in a mid-range hotel, whereas you can feast on rice, noodles and satay delicacies for half the price. Family hotels will invariably have a kids' menu.

Breakfast can often be disappointing in budget to mid-range hotels, with a 'spread' reduced to packaged white bread, an over-cooked noodle dish and under-ripe fruit. While three-star hotels and up usually do a better Western-style breakfast, quality breads and cereals can still be sorely absent. A small number of luxury hotels offer little more than bread, cake and cereal on the breakfast buffet; the most reputable provide multi-ethnic smorgasbords of Asian and Western foods, homemade breads and cakes, on-the-spot cooked noodles, Indian staples, sushi, fruits and sweets.

Smoking in hotels As smoking rates in much of the rest of the world decline, in Malaysia they are forever on the rise, particularly amongst young people. Statistics show 50% of male adults and 30% of 12- to 18-year-old boys smoke. Malaysia has lagged behind on introducing and enforcing wide-reaching smoking bans and the hotel industry has been affected by this, with smoking permitted in many hotel lobbies and restaurants. In June 2010 however, the Malaysian government announced it would extend existing smoking bans to the private sector, which includes hotel lobbies as well as centralised air-conditioned offices.

With regards to rooms, most four- to five-star hotels have dedicated non-smoking floors, but there is a slow trend by part of the industry towards 100% non-smoking hotels.

Sports facilities Gyms in hotels with less than a luxury rating are few and far between, so make the most of them when you get the chance if you are trying to keep fit whilst travelling. The heat makes it tough to run outdoors. Three- to five-star hotels, better homestays and beach lodges may have swimming pools. Other noteworthy fitness centres are included where relevant later in the guide.

NATURE LODGES AND ISLAND RESORTS Most major tour operators specialising in nature and/or diving tourism also manage their own lodgings in key locations, or are affiliated with particular lodges or resorts. This creates something of a monopoly – the accommodation on offer will be controlled by the same people running the tours. This is not necessarily a bad thing, except when the only accommodation on offer is not of an acceptable standard. The standard of lodgings on river and jungle trips is fairly rustic, ranging from basic forest camp to clean and comfortable dwellings. Most lodgings have generator-powered electricity. There is no luxury option, but the basic living conditions are part of the experience.

Coastal and island resorts are less basic than river and forest lodges, with better food, services and accommodation. There are some luxury island resorts.

National parks Accommodation in national parks tends to be very basic. In Sabah and Sarawak there are often no cooking facilities, which is very limiting as it means you have to drive to a nearby town for food.

LONGHOUSE STAYS It is possible to stay as a guest in the longhouses of several tribes, most commonly Sabah's Rungus and Sarawak's Ibans. In Sarawak, you can stay in quiet remote areas to experience local life. Some longhouse accommodation is purpose-built for those wanting the traditional feel without living among a family. Most longhouse accommodation in Sarawak is in the Skrang, Lemanak, Batang Ai and Rejang river areas. Longhouses can be booked directly or through a tourist office. Many organised tours, such as hiking, river safaris and cultural trips include a longhouse stay.

Longhouse facilities are usually basic. A two-person room will usually include pillows, mattresses, mosquito nets, bed sheets, towels, blankets and slippers. A modern communal bathroom or traditional bathing facilities are provided for guests. Food will often be fresh fish and vegetables, which may have been gathered from the jungle. Activities may include hunting, fishing, making jewellery and cooking. The threat of malaria is greatest in the most remote upriver areas. The Health Department carries out regular checks; if malaria is detected then tourism authorities are alerted and visits to affected areas are suspended.

HOMESTAYS It is also possible to stay with a family in their home as part of the 'homestay' programme. This is a very up close and personal way of experiencing the lifestyle of local people and you may not have much privacy. Similar in principle to a bed and breakfast, homestay programmes may be run by an individual family or by a whole *kampong* (village) and can be booked through tourist offices. A homestay directory can be found at http://travelmalaysiaguide.com/homestay.

BED AND BREAKFASTS 'True' bed and breakfasts are rare in Borneo, as homestays offer a similar equivalent. A few are listed on www.insite.com. They can be as cheap as a hostel but offer more services than a budget hotel, such as a pool and out-of-city calm.

EATING AND DRINKING

FOOD Borneo's mixture of cultures creates a fragrant broth of cuisines. I hope this chapter will help you to avoid the tongue-tied moments I have experienced trying to order food, not knowing with any certainty what I am about to eat!

Malaysians and Bruneians are nations of eaters. Whilst there are distinct food cultures, it is impossible to separate them. For example, rice (*nasi*) and noodles (*mee*) are staples of both Malay and Chinese cuisines and are almost impossible to avoid. Both Chinese and Malay dishes use noodles heavily, in *laksa* and other soups, or in main-meal noodle dishes. Freshly made *mee* comes in various forms: large white or yellow ribbon wheat noodles, spaghetti thin noodles and clear vermicelli noodles. In some coffee shops you can choose the ones you want from the masses hanging at a noodle stall at the entrance. Then you have to decide on the style you want them cooked – the big differences being 'wet' (with sauce) or 'dry' (without); fried (*goreng*) or not fried; spicy or mild. Increasingly, dried noodles are being used, so when you get the chance to taste the real thing then do so. *Sedap dimakan!* (Bon appetit!)

Malay food Malay cooking is spicy, salty and thick with flavour, in keeping with all the cultural influences that have infused it over the centuries. Sambal and satay are two staples of Malaysian and Bruneian cuisine. Satay is marinated and barbecued chicken, beef or lamb skewered on bamboo sticks – typical 'fast' Malay food, eaten from street stalls and markets. Usually it's served with salad and a peanut sauce. Sambal puts the spice in Malay food; all kinds of ground chilli pastes are used to flavour dishes or are served as a condiment. Sambals can be sweet (*sambal manis*) or hot (*sambal olek*) or fishy (*sambal belacan*, shrimp) and are flavoured with the gamut of typical Malay spices.

Rice (nasi) The most typical breakfast fare is *nasi lemak* – literally fat, or tasty rice, though it isn't as fatty as it sounds. The rice is steamed, aromatised with coconut milk and pandan leaves, and garnished with spicy fried anchovies, sliced cucumber, peanuts and hard-boiled egg. At markets and roadside stalls, it is often sold wrapped traditionally in a banana leaf. There are several other ubiquitous *nasi* dishes: *nasi kuning* (yellow rice with egg, coconut and cucumber); *nasi goring* (fried rice); *nasi ayam* (rice with slithers of steamed or roasted chicken); *nasi campur* (mixed rice); and if you are vegetarian ask for *nasi dengan sayur* (rice with vegetables).

Noodles Popular Malay noodle dishes are *mee goreng* (spicy fried thick noodles); *mee mamak* (spicy-hot fried yellow noodles); and *mee rebus* (thick blanched noodles in a gooey, sweet and spicy sauce, served with hard-boiled eggs and green chillies).

Curry Typical fish, chicken and vegetable curries are *kari ikan, kari ayam, kari sayur*, respectively. These are gently spiced and cooked with a light dose of coconut.

Meat Beef and chicken appear often. The first is the basis of the famous tangy coconut *beef rendang*, served with turmeric rice (*nasi kunyit*), while red cooked chicken, *ayam masak merah*, is a casserole of chicken pieces in tomato.

Seafood Prawns (*udang*) and fish come in many forms. Whole grilled, fresh fish is known as *ikan panggang*. The best places to eat seafood are small coastal restaurants where you order and eat barbecued fish, prawns and squid – *sontong panggang* – by the weight, often for as little as 2MYR per 100g in very small seafood towns on the coast. Prawns from the sea, or giant river prawns, are served whole and spicy in *sambal udang*, with lashings of shrimp and tamarind paste, chilli, garlic and shallots.

Vegetables There are many vegetable dishes in a Malay spread: *sayur campur* (mixed vegetables) includes carrot, cabbage, broccoli, cauliflower and beans cooked in a light oyster sauce. The same vegetables but stewed in coconut is *sayur lodeh*. Individual dishes of 'local vegetable', which may mean roots collected from the jungle that morning, feature on many rural and urban tables. These may include *midin*, dark green fern tops called *pucuk paku*. Shoots of all kinds are served up – cucumber, yam and *pucuk rajah* (emperor shoots).

Fusion One of the most widespread fusions is Indian-Muslim *mamak* (uncle's) cuisine. The dishes are mostly served up at food stalls and small Indian-Muslim eateries or 'Islamic restaurants'. They serve up *mamak* specials such as tandoori chicken and fish-head curry, often round the clock. The fast-food varieties are *roti canai* (after its area of origin, Chennai in India) – famous, flaky, oily unleavened bread, cooked on an open grill. *Roti canai* (pronounced *chan-eye*) is often served with a side dish of curry for dipping the bread in – vegetarians can have it with *dhal* (split pulses). The *roti canai* translates into various other forms including *roti telur*

– egg roti filled with egg and onion – again served with curry or *dhal*. *Murtabak* is wrapped *roti canai*, filled with minced meat, egg and onion.

A fusion of Malay and Chinese food is *nyonya* (grandma's) cuisine. It combines the spices of Malay food with marinated, sour Chinese flavours and results in dishes like the tangy and fishy *assam laksa*.

Chinese food With such a large and diverse Chinese population, many cities in Borneo have restaurants specialising in different kinds of Chinese food – Cantonese, spicy Szechuan, Teochew and Hakka. At traditional coffee shops and street stalls, meat dumplings, steamed sweet or savoury buns (*pau*) and rice porridge (*moi*) are often served for breakfast, with dim sum popular for lunch. One of the most delicious staple Chinese noodle dishes is *char kway teow*, flat rice noodles with beansprouts, egg, chilli and shrimp (or chicken). Monosodium glutamate is widely used; to ask for your food without MSG, look to the *Survival glossary* on page 109.

Soup Noodle soups are popular at lunch. *Wantan mee* is a noodle soup, with floating stuffed envelopes of prawn or pork; *mee suah* has fish balls or pork in it; and *tom yam* is a spicy shrimp noodle soup. A famous Hokkien herbal soup is *bak kut teh* – literally 'pork bone tea'. *Laksas* of many kinds are common at Chinese coffee shops, and are served with prawn, chicken or egg. Fish and chicken clay pots with noodles are also a popular choice.

Vegetarian There are many soybean-, soybean curd- and tofu- (*tau foo*) based dishes in soups, noodle dishes, clay pots and curries.

Fish/seafood Chinese do great fresh seafood from small stalls, coffee shops and restaurants, serving up dishes such as sweet and sour fish, deep-fried fish with mango sauce, butter prawns, black pepper crab and oyster fried with egg.

Sweet stuff Look out for cake shops (*kedai kek*) making their own Chinese baked goods such as *siew pao* (baked bun with chicken), yam pastry buns, egg custard tarts, steamed red bean cakes, lotus and red bean yeast buns and *hakka* soybean cakes.

Indigenous foods Every ethnic group has its traditional cuisine tied closely to their way of living, whether this is inland or by the sea. Coastal cuisine features many sago and coconut dishes and marinated seafood salads, whilst people living inland eat much rice and freshwater fish. Wild fruits and vegetables are used as much as home-grown crops. You may get to taste traditional dishes of indigenous people when visiting smaller towns and *tamu* markets and if staying in homes and longhouses. Wonderful and weird specialities abound, such as the bamboo-shoot pickle – *bosou hobang* – of the Murut in Sabah. Kadazandusun love their tangy pickles from mango and other fruits. And let's not forget fermented rice wine – called *tuak* by the Iban in Sarawak but also *lihing* among the Kadazandusun in Sabah. You will need to eat well to offset the effects of this!

Fruit The fruit bowl is always full with bananas (*pisang*) of many kinds (also try the *pisang goreng*, fried bananas at the market); rambutan; jackfruit; jungle fruits such as the sweet, pulpy and aromatic *tarap* (*artocarpus odoratissimus*) and *cempedak* – a cousin to the jackfruit; both are big, with thick husks full of pod-shaped fruits.

Vegetarian food The huge variety and wide availability of vegetable dishes in Malay, Indian and Chinese eateries means that vegetarians will rarely encounter problems. Even in coffee shops where only meat and fish dishes appear on the menu as main courses, there are always vegetable side dishes which can be eaten as mains, with rice or noodles. Only extremely rarely (if at all) will coffee shops feature a dedicated vegetarian selection. This you will find in some international diners only.

DRINK
Coffee-shop drinks The typical coffee shop *harga minuman* (drinks list) may look something like this, with prices ranging from 1 to 2MYR in most places.

Kopi o	black coffee with sugar
Kopi o kosong	black coffee no sugar
Kopi c susu	coffee with condensed milk
Kopi-si	coffee with unsweetened (Carnation) milk
The o	black tea with sugar
Ping so kopi o ping	black sweetened iced coffee
Kopi o kosong ping	black iced coffee unsweetened
Kopi-si ping	iced coffee with unsweetened milk
Air limau	lemon water drink
Teh tarik	'pulled' tea: very strong and sweet, brewed black tea with condensed milk

Alcoholic drinks With over 60% of the population of Malaysian Borneo being Muslim, alcohol is not served in Malay-run cafés and restaurants, or at outdoor food stalls and open-air diners. The majority of Chinese-run *kopitiam* are also restricted to food only, though a handful may serve beer. The main places serving alcoholic drinks are licensed bars and international restaurants. Wine in particular – given it is all imported – tends to be expensive, as are spirits, while a pint of beer generally costs as much as it does in London's poshest pubs. Take the prices at The Loft in Kota Kinabalu as a gauge: a whisky is 14MYR, a pint of beer 19MYR, a bottle of wine 69MYR and a glass of wine 14MYR.

Brunei rhymes with dry – bring your own alcohol into the country according to regulations (see *Customs*, page 80, for more detail). The sale and consumption of alcohol are prohibited in public places, though foreigners can carry in alcohol for their private consumption.

EATING OUT Food is readily available, often of exceptional quality (in both freshness and flavour) and very cheap. Market food can easily outstrip restaurants and is available at night markets, food courts or *taman seleras* – parks full of open-air restaurants. Any formal or fine dining takes places in Western and international restaurants. The best advice is to eat local and eat fresh.

Coffee shops Lively, open-air coffee shops are highly characteristic of Malaysian culture. Most of them started

RESTAURANT PRICE CODES

Restaurant listings are laid out in decreasing price order, under the following categories: Upmarket, Mid range, Budget and Shoestring. Prices are based on the cost of a main meal per person.

$$$$	60MYR+
$$$	20–60MYR
$$	10–20MYR
$	<10MYR

Tanpa perasa	no monosodium glutamate
Tanpa garam	without salt
Tambah	add
Sedikit	less or a little
Kurang	less (eg: *kurang manis* – less sweet)
Minyak	oil/fat
Tidak	no

If you don't want sugar in anything, just add *kosong* – empty.

out serving coffee with morning dumplings and noodles. Today the *kedai kopi*, as they are called in Malay, also serve a long list of typical dishes and drinks. These open-fronted food and drink stores – officially *kedai makanan dan minuman* – line city streets. Menus include various noodle, rice and curry dishes.

Chinese coffee shops – conversely known as *kopi tiam* – serve dumplings and soups, including *laksa* specialities cooked on the spot. On the whole, coffee shops provide good, cheap food and an authentic atmosphere. The best ones are full of locals, huddled around plastic chairs and linoleum tables. In the middle of the tables there is usually a jar of homemade *lada* – a fiery soy, salt and chilli mix ready for piling on your food.

Hotel coffee shops are more often than not enclosed and air conditioned. Many of those in three- and four-star establishments have a strong local clientele, and serve Malay and Chinese specialities; international luxury brands have a stronger Western touch.

Food courts Nutritious, tasty food to go is available from shopping-centre food courts, usually on the top floor – where there may be one or two dozen shops preparing all kinds of food. It's either cooked on the spot, in the case of noodles and in most Chinese places, or is pre-prepared and kept warm in bains-marie (especially with Malay and Indo-Malay kitchens) full of chicken, fish, pork and vegetable curries and stews; roasted meats; and steamed greens with chilli and prawn paste. The storekeeper will ladle dishes of your choice onto a plate of rice, or you can choose your own in a food court. All of this can be eaten there or as a take-away (*bungkus*).

Restaurants Restaurants can be small, simple diners serving Malay, Indonesian, *mamak* or Chinese food, not much different from a *kedai*, through to air-conditioned fancier places. Hotels have several dining choices, from coffee shops to restaurants, offering both Western and local food. In bigger hotels, there will be several diners catering to local and Western tastes, or both. Chinese restaurants are often large clamouring places, but they can also be some of the best seafood restaurants. Any trendy, obviously international establishment will be a restaurant rather than a coffee shop, unless it is a café or bistro, though this is very avant-garde in Borneo. Fine dining places tend to be very dated; think 1970s–80s.

Smoking in restaurants Generally, there are no non-smoking rules or set-aside spaces, other than in shopping centres. Some individual restaurants may have a non-smoking policy, especially more Western or international places. Coffee shops tend to

Practical Information EATING AND DRINKING

3

have more smoke-free air as they are open-fronted. Although smoking rates among Malaysia's youth are increasing, most restaurants don't actually have many smokers.

Western fast food
Look out for the familiar logos – they won't be far away in main cities.

Halal
There are hundreds of halal eateries in Malaysia, from street stalls to coffee shops and restaurants. No non-halal products will be served in these restaurants – this includes pork, any pork by-products (such as lard), and (if they are fully halal) alcohol. All the food should, in theory, have been produced in accordance with Islamic law, including all vegetables, spices and meats.

Street food
Gerai makan (food stalls) are all over the place, in the streets and markets, along roadsides and highways, by day and night. They sell many noodle and rice dishes cooked on the spot, as well as pre-prepared packages of *nasi lemak* and other rice dishes: *murtabak, roti canai*, satays, etc – most have their speciality. There are large open-air or covered public spaces full of *gerai makan* stalls, and semi-permanent food kitchens set up every day in some towns. Sometimes known as *taman selera* ('appetite parks'), these are somewhere between a stall and makeshift coffee shop.

Similar to the night markets, you will often find a whole lot of small food shops – *kedai* – cooking up food around an open area with tables and chairs, usually with some kind of nice outlook. Roadside *gerai* sell smoked meats, grilled corn on the cob, *puding kelapa* (a gelatinised coconut dessert), prawn crackers, nuts, bananas and drinks.

Markets (*pasar*)
The main food markets by night are the *pasar malam*, evening markets that have many *gerai makan*. There are also wet markets, dry markets, central markets, night markets, *tamu* and Ramadan markets. Wherever there is a market there is food in multitude forms: fresh, dried, raw, cooked, aromatic, wild, exotic; a huge array of produce for preparing food at home; fruits and nuts; Chinese pastries and buns. Usually a market will have some *gerai makan* food stalls pretty close by, if not under the same roof.

Eating-out practicalities

Cleanliness
Local councils grade places as 'A', 'B' or 'C' class. The lowest-grade coffee shops and small restaurants are usually fine, though more 'fancy' restaurants with a C grade are best avoided. C-rated coffee shops can have filthy toilets but great food. Others pride themselves on having the cleanest loos in town. The *gerai makan* stalls are all subject to food hygiene laws and regulation, as far as the preparation, utensils and ingredients go.

Service
As long as you can convey what you want simply, most Malay and Chinese will understand. Things are generally cooked as you watch – this is helpful if you are vegetarian or have allergies or special diet needs.

Tipping
Service charges are included in bills and tipping is not customary.

Prices
Meal prices range from 2–3MYR at a market stall, double that in a coffee shop, to 20–40MYR for a main course in a restaurant. The more you dine in five-star international-style hotels, the more the prices increase.

PUBLIC HOLIDAYS AND FESTIVALS

Public holidays in East Malaysia generally fall into two categories, national and state, both of which embrace religious celebrations, cultural festivals and dates of major national importance. Brunei also has public holidays to mark significant state dates such as political independence, the sultan's birthday and religious occasions. Probably more important than the state occasions, and celebrated in a far more personal way, are the religious and ethnic celebrations – though these differ between East Malaysia and Brunei. The sultan is 'our Sultan' in Brunei – he is part of the people's daily lives, so his birthday is a big event. The same can't be said of the Malaysian king, who has less of an impact in Sabah and Sarawak than on the peninsula. Major state-wide celebrations mark important dates on the spiritual calendars of indigenous people, and of the Chinese, Malay and Indian populations, who observe Buddhist, Muslim, Hindu and Christian traditions. Festive rituals often combine a high level of spirituality and prayer, with colour, joy and feasting – but that doesn't exclude commercialism. The general racial harmony that exists throughout Borneo leaks through to the festivals. People of different faiths celebrate with their friends on major holy days and in Sabah and Sarawak there are some specific inter-cultural celebrations heartily enjoyed by all.

There are some seven major religious and cultural celebrations across East Malaysia and Brunei that are marked by a public holiday. They are listed below, along with other public holidays to mark state occasions. Public holidays rarely cause business to come to a standstill, at least not shops. Banks and government offices close, but shopping centres will remain open for at least half the day, varying from place to place. The advantage of Borneo being so multi-faith is that only those who are truly celebrating the day for their culture or religion will stop completely. The shopping 'temples' are open all hours.

PUBLIC HOLIDAYS IN SABAH, SARAWAK AND BRUNEI There is huge regional and national variation between Sabah, Sarawak and Brunei for public holidays; even for the celebration of the same events holiday dates can vary between one region and another, never mind the common variable dates from year to year for different ethnic festivals. The following are an indication only, for the shifting holidays.

1 January	New Year's Day
January/February (variable date)	Chinese New Year (two-day event held in the last week of January or first week of February)
23 February	National Day Brunei
February	Prophet Muhammad's birthday
Good Friday	(Sabah & Sarawak only)
1 May	Labour Day
May (variable date)	Wesak Day (height of Buddhist calendar)
30–31 May	Tadau Ka'amatan (Harvest Festival) Thanksgiving to the rice spirits of the Kadazandusun (Sabah & Labuan only)
1–2 June	Pesta Gawai, Sarawak Gawai Festival (Sarawak only)
2 June	Birthday of Yang di-Pertuan Agong, Malaysian king
15 July	His Majesty the Sultan of Brunei's birthday
August (variable date)	Hari Raya Aidilfitri or Hari Raya Puasa (the day of breaking the fast) (two days in late August)
31 August	Hari Kebangsaan (National Day). Celebration of Malaysian independence, Merdeka, 1957

3

9 September	Birthday of Yang di-Pertua Negeri Sarawak's head of state (Sarawak only)
16 September	Birthday of Yang di-Pertua Negeri Sabah's head of state (Sabah only)
5 November	Ramadan end of Muslim fasting (Brunei)
November (variable date)	Deepavali Hindu light festival (one day in the first half of the month)
November (variable date)	Awal Muharram (Ma'al Hijrah), the 'Muslim New Year' and first day of Muslim calendar (held in the second half of the month)
20 December	Hari Raya Qurban
25 December	Christmas Day

CHINESE LUNAR NEW YEAR The Chinese New Year is full of festivity and friendship, thanksgiving and hopes of prosperity – and cries of *Kong Hee Fatt Choy*! (Happy New Year!). After a month of preparation, in which homes are loudly decorated with lanterns, firecrackers and calligraphy, guests laden with gifts of mandarins and oranges visit, ready for much feasting and games of *mah-jong*. Celebrations also take place in the Chinese temples, making this an ideal time to visit one. The dates vary from year to year according to the lunar calendar, beginning on the first day of the full moon and lasting for a fortnight. Like other Chinese festivals celebrated in Sabah, Sarawak and Brunei, the New Year festival is strong on symbolism and folklore, dance and colour – especially red. The highlight of the public festivities is the 'lion dance' – troupes of dragon-like figures prance through the streets to the beats of drums, warding off evil spirits, ushering in fortune and frightening the mythical lion away.

WESAK DAY This is the most important date on the Buddhist calendar, marking the birth, death and enlightenment of Buddha. It is marked by prayers, offerings and chanting; and the release of doves and tortoises at Buddhist temples. Another magical time to head to a temple.

TADAU KA'AMATAN (Harvest Festival) Each district of Sabah holds its own various festivities for this big event, the height of the indigenous calendar in Sabah. The celebrations can go on for the entire month of May culminating during the Grand Finale on 30 and 31 May at the Kadazandusun Cultural Association Hall (KDCA) in Penampang, just south of Kota Kinabalu. Tadau Ka'amatan, in indigenous tongue, sometimes translates to Pesta Kaamatan in Malay. It is celebrated by the Kadazandusun and Murut communities in Sabah.

DEEPAVALI The Hindu Festival of Light, a triumph of good over evil, is held on the seventh month of the Hindu calendar. Houses are decorated with lights, old debts settled, sweets sent to friends, new clothes purchased, and all the Sikh temples (*Gurdwaras*) conduct prayer services and serve vegetarian food.

HARI RAYA AIDILFITRI Also called Hari Raya Puasa, this is a day of celebration held at the end of the month-long Muslim fast of Ramadan. The fasting ends on the first sighting of the new moon, in the tenth month of the Muslim calendar, *Syawal*.

HARI KEBANGSAAN The Malaysian National Day marks Malaysian independence in 1957, when the Union Jack was lowered and the Malaysian flag hoisted to mark the end of colonial rule. It is marked by street parades in the capital cities, though celebrated less flagrantly than on Peninsula Malaysia.

SHOPPING

By far the most wonderful places to shop, for anything, are the markets (*pasar*). A visit to a marketplace is possibly one of the most authentic cultural experiences you can have – experiencing the sights, sounds and smells of true local culture and an amazing range of produce, from fresh fruit and fish, jungle vegetables and speciality foods, to clothes and handicrafts.

Every region, city and town will have several markets: the *pasar besar* is the main market, often held daily in cities and in towns, and once a week in some country districts. The *pasar besar* in cities and large towns is often held undercover, and increasingly in new two- to three-storey buildings, incorporating several different traditional markets, such as the 'wet market' (*pasar basah*), which sells fish and meats, and other food, regional produce and handicraft markets. The *pasar malam* is a night market – some are food-only, others offer a mix of produce. Some towns also have specific craft markets – *pasar pertukangan*. Larger ones in the cities are flooded with Filipino and Indonesian produce, though as always the best things are those found close to the source. You can always bargain in the marketplace.

You are more likely to find a priceless memento of your travels in more rural markets. Some of the most beautiful and authentic items you can buy are woven textiles, bamboo and rattan baskets, beaded jewellery from shell, glass and plant seeds, pottery, carved wooden bowls and batik. In Brunei you will find more brass, gold and silver than beads and bamboo. See *Chapter 1, Culture*, pages 29–32, for more on traditional handicrafts and markets. Local shopping tips can be found in the guide chapters.

TAMU A rural market, the weekly *tamu* was apparently introduced by the British North Borneo Company to create a communal meeting place and ease ethnic tensions through trade. Both the name and the custom have spread to Brunei and to Sarawak, but *tamu* are still most common in Sabah where they are held on a varying day of the week from place to place. A growers' market, crafts market and commercial bazaar all in one, each one is unique, shaped by the cultural and agricultural environment. Farmers and fishermen bring their produce (including water buffalo). Traders pile their stalls high with an exotic array of strangely shaped and wonderfully coloured produce: kitchen and clothing wares; bric-a-brac; home-grown, homemade and jungle-reaped produce. The *tamu* remain a vital part of social and trading life rather than a tourist attraction – though some have become more tourist oriented – and the best ones are often those with the fewest tourists. My best memories include those of Ranau, Kudat, Tuaran in Sabah; Sibu, Serian and Miri in Sarawak; and Brunei's *tamu*. There is also a *tamu besar* – a major *tamu* – held once a year in the *tamu*'s town of origin, Kota Belud.

GENERAL SHOPPING There are shopping plazas, supermarkets, electronic stores and pharmacies all over the cities and towns. City and town shops (*kedai*) – food and retail stores, electronics and clothes shops – are often clustered into large blocks of 'shop-lots', sometimes around a public square in smaller towns, but also in multi-storey shopping centres. New plazas, malls and commercial centres (*kompleks*) are popping up in the capital cities and coastal towns. Between the dozens of city shop-lots and older shopping centres packed with shop-lots, you will find just about everything you need. However, neither Malaysian Borneo nor Brunei has the exciting department-store shopping or the modern emporiums that exist in Singapore, Hong Kong, Bangkok and Kuala Lumpur. There is little in the way of local or imported quality couture or food items, and department stores lack any major pizzazz, though things are clearly changing. Some of the malls (especially the older ones) are more like massive shop-lots – cluttered and not very attractive. Nonetheless, items are relatively cheap. There are once-yearly major sales, but every day is a sale with the 'Buy One Free One' slogan applied to clothing, jewellery and food things.

Tax-free shopping Labuan is a duty-free shopping and tax haven, and duty-free shops at airports are very good. Brunei is tax-free too, but you won't find duty-free spirits and wine on the shelves there.

ARTS AND ENTERTAINMENT

The karaoke craze has not escaped Borneo, though it is now declining in favour of trendy, international **bars and clubs** in Sabah and Sarawak. These hip hangouts are also eroding the tradition of a hotel-based nightlife in Kota Kinabalu and Kuching. The **live music** scene is thriving, though music is a bit behind the international times. Traditional dance and music performances are one of the most heartening forms of entertainment. Brunei, being alcohol-free, has a quieter night scene, but there is evening fun to be had at markets.

For anyone interested in the real cultures of Borneo, the best forms of art-based entertainment are the **festivals**, and the dance and music performances. These are very regional – Sabah, Sarawak and Brunei organised – but also very local in their nature. Each town and ethnicity will have cultural performances and *pesta* (festivals) celebrating dates and events dear to them. The local tourism offices are the best place to check for a list of upcoming events. Sabah and Sarawak tourism also have online events listings.

Museums in general are open seven days a week, but hours can vary from 09.00–16.30/17.00 to 10.00–18.00. Admissions also vary greatly – some, including the Sarawak Museum, are free; others such as the Sabah State Museum cost a hefty 15MYR with no reductions for students or children. For more information on arts, see *Culture* in the *Background Information* chapter, pages 29–32.

SPORTS AND OTHER ACTIVITIES

Borneo is better known for its wildlife than extreme outdoor sports, but there is still plenty of adventure to be had, often alongside nature experiences. Boasting Malaysia's three highest mountains, Sabah attracts mountaineers from near and far, though the Malaysian massifs are less of a challenge for climbers. Adventures encompassing natural wonders can be experienced through diving, whitewater rafting, rugged jungle treks and off-the-beaten-path mountain climbing. Good locations include Sabah's Gunung Kinabalu National Park and Maliau Basin, and the Kelabit Highlands of Sarawak. A few local Sabah and Sarawak companies specialise in a mix of light to medium intensity outdoor adventure, such as mountain-biking, rafting, trekking and rock-climbing excursions.

TREKKING Due to Borneo's highly bureaucratic national parks and reserves, arduously humid climate, dangers of walking alone and advantages of local knowledge, it may well be better to use a tour organiser for well-established treks. Permits, insurance and guides are obligatory in Gunung Mulu National Park in Sarawak and Gunung Kinabalu National Park in Sabah. Unfortunately for those who prefer to be independent and unrestricted, you can't just turn up and trek because of the need to book trekker's accommodation and a guide in advance. Gunung Mulu and Gunung Kinabalu National Park do not have extensive trail networks; instead there are one or two major routes and a few shorter walks around park headquarters, though these are usually fairly limited. This is common throughout the national parks and reserves of Borneo, unlike those in Europe, North America and Australia that often have a system of well-marked trails that can be followed independently. Outside of national parks, however, in areas like the Danum Valley conservation area, walks tend to be of the 'well-marked nature trail' kind. A serious 'wilderness' adventure is the Maliau Basin, with rugged terrain, sleeping in tents and lots of leeches, though it is quite expensive as this is only available as an organised trip (See *Chapter 8, Southeast Sabah*, page 231). Another relatively little-known area just north of here is the Imbak Canyon.

There are plenty of other, more relaxed places for trekking around Borneo. The Kelabit Highlands provide an opportunity to trek through a highland landscape and rich culture, permit- and guide-free. This is an established tourist route. Other areas include the Penrissen Highlands south of Kuching and the Crocker Range. It is possible to organise your own trek around these areas. For details of where to obtain topographic maps, see *What to take*, pages 94–5.

Day hiking There are many other parks and reserves with easy- to medium-grade trails where you can experience a good mix of lowland and hill rainforest. These make pleasant half/full-day walks. Good areas include the Tawau Hills Park, Tabin Wildlife Reserve and Sepilok Forest Reserve on the east coast of Sabah; and the Bako, Lambir Hills and Similajau parks in Sarawak. Nearly all of Sarawak's 18 parks (most of which are around Kuching) have at least a couple of decent tracks, and Bako and Lambir Hills have 10–12, though few exceed three or four hours. Sarawak provides more for day hikers than Sabah; its many national parks are well set up, with good park information, maps, trails and rangers. The national parks website (*www.forestry.sarawak.gov.my/forweb/homepage.htm*) is also very user-friendly with details of every park and reserve, conservation and wildlife information and information on upcoming events.

There are also areas that are just enjoyable to walk around. The Santubong Peninsula just north of Kuching is one – there are a few trails over the mountain, including the Mount Santubong Summit Trek (see *Chapter 10, Southern Sarawak*, page 266). Be aware that this walk is quite challenging and requires good fitness levels. Some of the most pleasant walks through mountain scenery can be taken along country roads, through *kampungs* alongside national parks. In Sabah especially, there are plenty of interesting paths to follow that are off the usual tourist routes. Always take safety into consideration whilst walking; it is not advisable to walk alone and some wildlife can be dangerous.

Jungle adventure treks Organised jungle adventures range from youth-oriented survivor-camp trips (which combine hiking with edgy survival activities such as eating snakes) to straightforward treks. Highlights include the Headhunter's Trail in northern Sarawak, the Salt Trek in the Crocker Range, parts of the Sandakan-Ranau death-march trail and (more costly) trips into the heart of Borneo and remote places such as the Maliau Basin. All local tour groups involved in outdoor adventure organise such trips.

MOUNTAIN ADVENTURE For more serious mountain adventures, see some of the tour operators listed on pages 76–9. A good website to search for adventure-based tours is www.adventuresportsholidays.com. For keen climbers and mountaineers another interesting site to visit is www.borneoclimbing.com, maintained by Wilfred Tok Beng Cheong – a key member of the **Mountaineering Society of Singapore** and a regular guide on Mount Kinabalu. His **Adventure Factors Mountaineering Centre** (AFMC) (*Sabah;* e *info@adventurefactors.com*) provides technical climbing courses, mountain treks and adventures, including rock climbing and abseiling. The centre also runs programmes for light, intermediate and serious trekkers on the summits and slopes of Mount Kinabalu.

For really off-the-beaten-track Kinabalu climbs, hardcore climbers head to the Eastern Plateau, via Bowen's Route or Kotal's Route. Both were apparently pioneered during the Royal Society expeditions on the mountain in the mid-1960s. Some of the adventure tour operators organise these routes.

Rock climbing and abseiling The granite peaks of Mount Kinabalu are the main attraction for rock-climbing enthusiasts in Sabah; in Sarawak, the limestone crags and sandstone environs of the Mulu Caves in the north, and the Fairy Caves near the town of Bau (40 minutes from Kuching) are popular for caving and climbing. The official Malaysian tourism portal, www.virtualmalaysia.com, states: 'Routes here [Mount Kinabalu] are generally conventional, although there are a handful of lines with fixed gear. Most of the routes in Malaysia are bolted sport climbs on limestone crags, with some exceptions on granite walls.' Climbing is possible throughout the year.

A website of interest to climbing enthusiasts is www.borneoclimb.com, the personal page of veteran outdoor adventurer, Basil Lung. Kota Kinabalu-based Basil is an associate guide of TYK Adventure Tours (see page 79). For youth adventure activities and camps, contact **Outward Bound Sabah** (*Locked Bag 181, 88745 KK, Sabah, Malaysia;* \ *088 750311;* e *obsabah@outward.po.my*). According to their award-winning adventure tour guide, Tham Yau Kong, rock climbing is still a relatively new pastime in Sabah, and most of the facilities that exist are for beginners and training. He says, 'Until recently, Mount Kinabalu seemed to be the only place for rock climbing. Now Singaporean rock climber Wilfred Tok has set up a programme to assist foreign climbers and encourage local people to try it too. Located in Inanam, the challenge begins with a trek from Kampung Kirrongu. The path leads to a natural rock face where participants are trained in the basics of rock climbing, from dressing correctly to scaling the heights. The night is spent camping by a stream. The next day is spent climbing and abseiling. The thrill is incomparable!'

Wilfred Tok and his professional rock climbing team at **Mountain Torq** (*Unit 3-36, Asia City Complex, 3rd Floor, Jalan Asia City, 88000 Kota Kinabalu, Sabah, Malaysia;* \ *88 268126;* e *enquiry@mountaintorq.com; www.mountaintorq.com*) operate the Via Ferrata on Mount Kinabalu. Borrowing from the Italian expression for a high alpine path customarily set-up with cables and ladders (it literally means 'iron road'), the Kinabalu pathway is the highest in the world. They claim both novices and pros can join in on the adventure, as long as they have no fear of heights.

CYCLING AND MOUNTAIN BIKES Neither Sabah nor Sarawak is easy for road cycling – there are no dedicated cycle routes on main roads, neither in the main cities nor the countryside. There are, however, some great off-road mountain-bike adventures to be had. 'The Crocker Range is quite a challenge, and Kota Kinabalu to

DIVING IN BORNEO

The following overview is intended to help you choose the dive location best suited to your level and interests; more details on marine environments, dive operators and lodgings are found in relevant destination chapters.

DIVE DESTINATIONS In Sarawak, you can dive off the coast around Miri, and further north in Brunei. It is Sabah, however, that tops the list of Borneo's best dive destinations. Good dive spots are found between the west coast islands of Labuan and Layang Layang, Lankayan off the north coast and Sipadan, Mabul and Kapalai off the east coast. According to China-based writer, William Moss, the diving attractions in Sabah include reefs, atolls and lagoons; shore diving and drift diving; and lots of pelagic life. 'The area off of Tawau and Semporna is particularly rich, featuring the islands of Mabul, Kapalai, and Sipadan. Any diver planning a trip to the area should divide their time between these locations – a week of dives will yield an amazing diversity of marine life of all sizes and shapes.'

The east coast islands in the Sulawesi and Celebes seas have brought both fame and infamy to Bornean diving. Lying in territorial waters between Indonesia and Malaysia, the area is considered by some to be dangerous, and foreigners are often advised against visiting and diving in the area (see *Safety*, page 91). In April 2000, Sipadan made world headlines when an extremist Filipino Muslim group kidnapped a group of European tourists from the Borneo Diver's Resort. All accommodation on Sipadan has since closed, on both security and environmental grounds, and Sipadan is under constant military surveillance. Most diving accommodation is now found on other islands, but Sipadan remains a marine-lovers magnet.

DIVING SEASON Rough weather during the northeast monsoon season may affect diving conditions and ease of travel by boat. William Moss maintains that diving can be enjoyed all year round, though some inhabitants may be seasonal visitors, such as Layang Layang's hammerheads. Some say that April to July is the best time to dive.

DIVING CONDITIONS Surface water temperatures range from 24–31°C. A 3mm suit is sufficient for most diving conditions, though many people dive in skin-suits. Visibility averages around 20m but varies considerably, from 6–10m inshore to 15–30m-plus at offshore locations.

ACCOMMODATION Lodgings on the islands are usually closely linked with particular dive operators. Staying overnight on one of the islands is a memorable experience. The difference in price between staying on an island or choosing to stay on the mainland and make dive trips each day depends in part on the package you negotiate with an operator. If you pre-book your whole trip through an international dive operator, try and negotiate a price that includes all diving, equipment, accommodation, transfers and meals. Most of the local dive operators with island-based accommodation will offer this in any case. One of the best general information websites to help make a selection is www.divetheworldmalaysia.com. It details dive sites, accommodation listings and more.

Practical Information SPORTS AND OTHER ACTIVITIES

3

the east coast of Sabah makes a good one-week trip,' says Tham Yau Kong. 'People think Sabah is easy for cycling, but don't underestimate how hard the humidity and heat can make it.'

As the adventurer-founder of TYK Adventure Tours, Tham is well known, and a good point of call for cycling enthusiasts (e *thamyaukong@thamyaukong.com; www.thamyaukong.com*). In the late 1990s he created the eco-friendly cycling business 'Eco Tourism on Pedals', and was one of the founders of the Mount Kinabalu International Mountain Bike Race and other cycling challenges. Along with his cycling associates, he claims to have entered the *Malaysia Book of Records* for being the first group to mountain-bike-circumvent Mount Kinabalu, and believes mountain biking as a sports tourism activity will become big in Borneo.

In Sarawak the area around Kuching in particular is excellent for mountain-bike adventure, as are the parks and rainforest reserves west towards Sematan and north towards the Santubong Peninsula and Damai Beach. This is where the Rainforest Cup mountain-bike event is held each year, and there is a Battle of Borneo event at Mulu. Brunei has several reserves with mountain-biking trails, starting right in the city.

RAFTING The two main rivers for rafting in Sabah are the Sungai Padas and Sungai Kiulu rivers in the hinterland of the west coast. According to operators, both are certified as Grade III and Grade II respectively in the international whitewater rafting grading system. Indigenous people, with their amazing water navigation skills, quickly caught on to whitewater rafting in the 1980s. The dry season is the best time for novices. Rivers can swell to Grade IIII during the wet season, more suited to more experienced rafters. Outside of the wet season, the Sungai Kiulu is too low for rafting so the Padas gets most of the crowds during other times of the year. Kiulu rapids include 'Headhunter', 'Adrenaline Flow' and 'Merry Go Round'. Make sure you go with a licensed operator, some of which are listed on pages 78–9. The standard Padas excursion is a day trip, but longer trips can be arranged with accommodation at the Padas River Lodge in Rayoh. The basic trip provides a safety and technical briefing and life jackets. Experienced rafters can arrange for a custom-made trip. In Sabah, operators will arrange transport from Kota Kinabalu through the Padas Gorge. Bring a change of clothes, warm layers, a waterproof jacket and well-fitting shoes or diving boots. Spectacle wearers should bring something with which to anchor glasses, whilst contact-lens wearers are advised to wear spectacles to avoid lens contamination.

BIRDWATCHING Susan Myers runs **Birding Worldwide** (see *International tour operators* on page 76), and is the author of *Birds of Borneo* and *Field Guide to the Birds of Borneo*. Susan generously shares her trip reports online (*http://users. wired.net.au/susan*) to help independent birders organise their trip. She says that in Sabah, 'The birding is out of this world.' During a 17-day trip to five key sites, she once recorded 230 species. 'This included some highly sought-after species, such as the giant pita, storm's stork, Bornean bristlehead and Whitehead's trogon.' Local Bornean bird specialists offer one- to 12-day trips. There are several bird sanctuaries (run by the Wildlife Department) in Sabah, three or four on the west coast and in Kota Kinabalu itself.

GOLF Sabah's long, indented west coast is marked by several world-class golf resorts set spectacularly between Mount Kinabalu and the South China Sea. Sutera Harbour's Golf and Country Club in Kota Kinabalu has won awards as Malaysia's top course; to the north are the Dalit Bay Golf and Country Club in Tuaran, Nexus Golf Resort Karambunai and Kudat Peninsula's Golf & Marina Resort. At 1,500m altitude, the Mount Kinabalu Golf Club is the highest in Sabah, while the Borneo Highlands Resort in Sarawak has received the most accolades as a cool-climate, ecologically minded golfing set-up. Brunei's top courses are the Royal Brunei Golf & Club, and the Empire Country Club course by Jack Nicklaus. Online UK magazine *Golf Today* (*www.golftoday.co.uk*) includes comprehensive details of these resorts on its world golf course guide.

CULTURAL HISTORY If archaeology, ethnography and anthropology are your main interests, then you should visit the Niah Caves in northern Sarawak, the Sarawak and Sabah state museums, the Islamic museums of civilisation and art and the mosques and museums of Brunei. The whole of northern Borneo is one incredible outdoor ethnographic museum, with living cultural displays everywhere. There are also several brilliant local indigenous cultural associations mentioned in the guide worth making contact with.

PHOTOGRAPHY

Taking photographs of **people** in Borneo, as anywhere else, is a deeply personal thing – different people react differently, and it's up to the photographer to perceive individual wishes in this regard, and react accordingly. On the whole, I find I am greeted by spontaneous and willing subjects in both children and adults. People tend to interact with you as you take photos – it's a great joy, and a great privilege. There are exceptions to the rule though; members of some ethnic groups are more timid than others – the Kadazan Dusun are often more extroverted and urban-wise, as are the Bajau, whereas the Rungus tend to be more shy and rural. It is best to ask permission before taking shots of individuals from close range, and this is a good general rule of respect. In rural areas you yourself are more likely to be the source of fascination, not only as a tourist, but as photographer with a fancy camera. For street photography, and shots of crowds and groups, you can comfortably take photos without prior permission and without fearing adverse reactions. While some Muslim people clearly do not warm to being photographed, the situation is very different, for example, than in a country such as Morocco where people can react angrily to being photographed, even as part of a crowd. Out and about in crowds amongst predominantly Muslim populations in Brunei and Malaysian Borneo, I have never felt constrained at being able to snap away to my heart's content.

Buildings are another thing altogether. Government buildings, even shopping centres and other public or retail spaces, often have no-photo policies, though they are generally enforced politely and discreetly. For **art galleries** and **museums**, it's a case-by-case affair; state museums may allow you to take photos outside, but none within.

MEDIA AND COMMUNICATIONS

NEWSPAPERS Sabah, Sarawak and Brunei have their own newspapers. There seems to be little demand for international newspapers. Even in four- and five-star hotels in the capital cities it is standard practice to hang a regional paper such as the *Sabah Times*, the *Daily Express*, the *Borneo Post* or the *Sarawak Tribune* on your door – it is very rare to be offered international papers. If you love your

3

daily newspapers you may find the *International Herald Tribune* in mixed bazaars of some towns, and a couple more choices in good English-language bookstores in the capitals, though these are likely to be back copies. Local newspapers are quite British-tabloid in look and thin on content, especially foreign coverage. The *Daily Express* is considered to be the best newspaper in Sabah. The most prevalent English-language newspaper in Sarawak is the *Borneo Post*, which also has a section in Behasa Melayu, and by far the best foreign coverage. The weekend version is the *Sunday Post*. The Malaysian national English-language newspaper *New Straits Times* also circulates. In Brunei there are three daily newspapers: the Malay-language *Media Permata* and English-language *Brunei Times* and *Borneo Bulletin*, this being the best. A punchy, political online Malaysia-wide newspaper is Malaysia Now (*www.Malaysiakini.com*). The state-run Malaysian news agency is Bernama (*www.bernama.com*). An interesting Brunei blog is the Weekly Brunei Resources (*http://bruneiresources.blogspot.com*).

RADIO Radio stations in Sarawak seem to reflect the cultural diversity far better than television, with day-long or half-day services in Bahasa Malaysia, Mandarin, Hakka, Hokkien, English, Iban and Bidayuh and half-day broadcasts in Kayan and Kenyah. Some of these are broadcast by WaiFM, others by the local radio station of Radio Television Malaysia (RTM). Sarawak FM has 24-hour Malay broadcasts. Sabah also has RTM radio and some English content on its FM stations – Hitz, Era and Mix FM. Radio Television Brunei (RTB) operates three radio stations – two in Malay, one switching between English, Mandarin and Hindustani programming. Commercial radio station Kristal FM is bilingual English–Malay and also operates cable television, Kristal Astro.

TELEVISION Malaysian Borneo receives two government-run (RTM) Malay television channels, TV1 and TV2, and privately owned stations such as TV3, NTV7 (these are very common in hotels), 8TV and TV9. Satellite Astro TV is very popular and provides channels such as CNN, BBC, Star World Movies, Cinemax Movies, Vision 4 (movies), Star Sport, and Japanese and Chinese channels, but even in hotels that provide this service the choice of available channels varies and can be extremely minimal in two- and three-star hotels. Radio Television Brunei has one television station with largely Malay-language broadcasts.

TELECOMMUNICATIONS
Telephone dialling codes All local dialling codes in Sabah and Sarawak start with three digits, such as 088 for Kota Kinabalu. The Malaysian dialling code (covering Sabah and Sarawak) is +60. If calling from overseas, drop the first zero of local numbers (eg: +6 088 334567). When in Malaysia, dial the whole number if calling from outside that town or region. Drop the local prefix only when in the town or city itself. The dialling code for Brunei is +673.

Public phones Malaysia's national telephone company is Telekom Malaysia Berhad (TM). Together with private-owned Citiphone it provides payphone booths in the city and countryside. You can use either coins or pre-paid phonecards with these. Calling cards, which function by code, are widely available from phone shops but also street stores, in 5MYR, 10MYR and 20MYR denominations.

Mobile phones Called 'hand phones' in Malaysia, these are revered like a national sport. On business cards the number is preceded by 'HP'. Most people have two or three hand phones, often ringing at the same time. There are telephone shops everywhere – you will see them plastered with flags and stickers of the companies they deal with. Major service providers are **Celcom**, **Maxis** and **DiGi**, which have expansive chains of stores and dominate roadside billboards. If you want to put a Malaysian SIM card in your phone (much cheaper for internal calls), it will cost 10–30MYR depending on the provider. Celcom and DiGi offer pre-paid starter packs with SIM cards for 8.50MYR, which includes 5MYR credit. Code-induced top-ups for whatever provider you are with can be purchased in shops or by phone. It is compulsory to register the SIM number with a name, so take your passport along. **Hot Link Maxis** pre-paid mobile phonecards are very popular and their rates are better than Celcom for overseas calls, providing '20 sen/min to 20 countries' (around US6 cents per minute to many countries including the UK, US, France and Australia). However, it is not the best option for making domestic calls. If you are travelling in Malaysia, top up with 100MYR before leaving, your account stays active for up to eight months.

INTERNET AND WI-FI Borneo has started to embrace the rest of Malaysia's enthusiasm for high-tech and internet communications, though the service is slower than on the peninsula. The two major Malaysian internet service providers are TMNet and Jaring, the latter being more prevalent in East Malaysia. In large and small cities and towns it is usually very easy to find internet cafés, charging from 2 to 4MYR per hour; some offer decreased rates for the second or third hour, and a free drink. There are also quite a few cafés that offer free Wi-Fi internet for customers. See *Accommodation*, page 103, for information on internet in hotels.

BUSINESS

In Brunei Darussalam, contact the **Ministry of Industry and Primary Resources** (*One-Stop Agency, Ministry of Industry & Primary Resources, Bandar Seri Begawan;* ☎ *+673 2380026; www.brunei.gov.bn/about_brunei/business.htm*) about all business opportunities.

In Sabah, contact the **Department of Industrial Development and Research** (*7th & 8th Floors, Block C, Wisma Tun Fuad Stephens, Karamunsing Centre, Kota Kinabalu;* ☎ *+60 088 215035; www.sabah.gov.my/didr/english/WhySabah.htm*). Their website has a good section on doing business in Sabah.

LIVING IN BORNEO

Not all tropical destinations offer the combination of natural and cultural riches that Borneo does. The sunshine, islands, jungle, food and outdoor adventure are enough to tempt anyone to live there on a more permanent basis. But is it actually viable to realise such an exotic dream? There are many factors to consider and all are fairly personal decisions. A practical issue might be the climate – how well do you fare when humidity is high? Though I can survive happily in such conditions I do find that my sportier habits become somewhat subdued – sport should generally be done indoors to escape the heat. The isolation of living in more remote areas, and of living in such a different culture, may be a blessing or a curse for you.

There are sizeable expat communities in Brunei and Miri in Sarawak, working in the oil industry (oilfields and research). There may be scientific jobs available at forest research institutes and centres, and universities in both Brunei and Malaysian Borneo, as well as primary and secondary schoolteaching in foreign and Malaysian schools.

The attractions of living in Borneo include the simplicity of life, warmth of the people, rich culture and religious and cultural tolerance. Many colonially inherited English customs, and the common use of spoken English, make settling in relatively easy.

You may experience quite a cultural shock, but this in itself is an adventure just as travelling is. Many of the obstacles of settling into daily Malaysian Borneo life are as relevant today as when Heidi Munan, a Swiss-born, New Zealand-educated author wrote *Culture Shock! A Guide to Customs and Etiquette, Borneo* in 1988 (revised 1992). It's a great book – personal and straight-talking. There will be some administrative frustrations: transport, roads and communication may not be up to the standard to which you are accustomed, but not to such an extent that life is impossible. You will soon enjoy the easier-going pace. It can be enriching to be surrounded by other languages and cultures, and English is widely spoken in the circles where you need it most: health, education and commerce.

MALAYSIA MY SECOND HOME (*23rd Floor, Menara Datuk Onn, Putra World Trade Centre, Kuala Lumpur; www.mm2h.gov.my*) Increasing numbers of people are being wooed to Borneo for the lifestyle. The 'Malaysia My Second Home' programme is a government initiative aimed at attracting foreigners to invest in Malaysia by buying a second house there. As well as the cheaper house prices, the programme promotes the low crime rates, political stability, favourable climate, low risk of natural disasters and access to quality education as tempting reasons to sign up.

The programme is open to foreigners of all races and religions. Those aged below 50 are required to make a minimum deposit of 300,000MYR; over-50s must put up 150,000MYR or provide proof of a monthly offshore income of 10,000MYR. After a year, money can be withdrawn from the account for house purchase, education, medical expenses, etc, as long as a minimum balance of 60,000MYR is maintained. You must also take out Malaysian medical insurance and provide a full medical report. If your application is accepted, the Immigration Department grants you a 'Social Visit Pass' and multiple-entry visa, which allow you to come and go as you please. These are initially valid for ten years but can be renewed thereafter. Since 2009, people have been able to apply to participate in the MM2H programme directly, without going through a third party. Alternatively they can use the services of licensed MM2H 'agents' – a list of which is available on the website. Over-50s wanting to live in Sabah or Sarawak can still apply directly to their immigration departments.

Immigration departments

Department of Immigration Sabah Tingkat 6, Bangunan Wisma Dang Bandang, Jln Tuanku Abdul Rahman, 88550, KK; \+60 088 80700

Department of Immigration Sarawak Tingkat 1&2, Bangunan Sultan Iskandar, Jln Simpang Tiga, 93550, Kuching; \+60 082 245661

Housing is available in both rural and urban areas and ranges from terraced and semi-detached houses and bungalows to chic flats and apartments. There are an increasing number of luxury apartment and condominium developments, especially in Kuching and Kota Kinabalu and nearby coastal areas, specifically aimed at foreign investors. Prices are therefore skyrocketing, but they are still relatively low. Look at the real-estate section of one of the online daily newspapers (see *Media and communications*, above) to get an idea.

STUDYING IN BORNEO

There are many opportunities in Sabah, Sarawak and Brunei for pre-tertiary and tertiary studies, through student-exchange programmes, years abroad and short-term student tourism programmes. There is both a state education system and private schools, including international schools, universities, private colleges and expatriate schools (British, American, French and German).

MALAYSIAN BORNEO In Sabah, the Yayasan Sabah Group (*Tun Mustapha Tower, Yayasan Sabah HQ, PO Box 11623;* \ *+60 088 326300;* e *ysinfo@ysnet.org.my; www. ysnet.org.my*) is a progressive education foundation with information on secondary- and tertiary-level scholarships under its education development programme.

A website that posts student exchanges, study options and participating schools and institutions in Malaysia is www.studymalaysia.com.

Useful national education contacts with links to East Malaysia are the **Ministry of Higher Education** (\ *+60 03 88835000; www.mohe.gov.my*), which has a focused Department of Private Education; the **National Accreditation Board** (\ *+60 03 79687002; www.lan.gov.my*); and the **Malaysian Association of Private Colleges and Universities** (MAPCU) (\ *+60 03 86569981; www.mapcu.com.my*).

Major universities include the **Universiti Malaysia in Sabah** (*Locked Bag 2073, 88999 Kota Kinabalu;* e *crd@ums.edu.my; www.ums.edu.my*) and the **Universiti Malaysia in Sarawak** (UNIMAS) (*Jln Datuk Mohd Musa, 94300 Kota Samarahan, Sarawak;* \ *+60 082 581388;* f *+60 082 665088; www.unimas.my*).

The **British Council** in Malaysia (*Wisma Selangor Dredging, 142C Jln Ampang, 50450 Kuala Lumpur; www.britishcouncil.org.my*) is a good point of contact for inquiries about secondary school cultural exchanges. Australia's **Curtin University of Technology** (*www.curtin.edu.my*) also has a campus in Miri, Sarawak.

BRUNEI English-medium degree subjects offered at the Universiti Brunei Darussalam (UBD) (*www.ubd.edu.bn*) include education, mathematics and computer science; electronics and electrical engineering; geography/economics major; management studies; and public policy and administration.

CULTURAL ETIQUETTE

NAMES AND TITLES Malay people will address you by your first name, so I immediately got baptised Miss Tamara. It's at once very respectful and warm. Most people would not be offended if you called them by just their first name instead of adding Encik (Mr/Sir) or Puan (Mrs/Lady). While there are many formalities in Malaysian society, the people are also personable by nature and fairly laid-back about such things. It is appropriate, however, to address people formally in written correspondence and on formal occasions.

Chinese people are addressed by their surnames – which appear before their given names. So a lady named Chia Wei Li would be addressed as 'Ms Chia'. Many Chinese people have English names though, such as a friend of mine Ivy Yap. Officially she would be 'Ms Yap', but everyone simply calls her Ivy. In my experience most people are not fussy about these things except in official circles where formalities must be observed.

DRESS Women who visit Muslim Brunei are requested to dress modestly in keeping with local customs. The same applies to Muslim-dominated parts of Sabah

3

and Sarawak. Elsewhere, many women wear a *tudung* (a hair scarf), whilst some bare arms and legs. It is best to avoid baring too much flesh. See also *Women travellers*, pages 91–2.

GREETINGS The customary Malay greeting is the *salam*: the person greeting you reaches out and grasps your hand gently whilst bringing their right hand to their chest. This graceful gesture means sweetly 'I greet you from my heart'. Hotel and restaurant staff and people in the streets and at marketplaces may greet you with an eclipsed version of this – just the hand to the heart bit. It is good manners, and greatly appreciated, to return the gesture. The reciprocated greeting is called *bersalaman*. Muslim members of the opposite sex do not generally touch in greetings. Chinese people tend to shake hands in the more traditional way. It is quite rare to see couples showing public displays of affection.

GESTURES It is deemed impolite to refuse food and drink (including rice wine!) by saying 'no' or shaking the head. If you can, accept a little; to refuse, touch the plate or glass lightly with the right hand. Use the right hand when giving and receiving objects or passing something, particularly food. The right hand is also used when eating with one's fingers. You should never point Western-style – instead curl the four fingers of your right hand inwards and point with the thumb.

BEHAVIOUR Malaysians are gracious, polite people that may be offended by boisterous behaviour; Chinese people are usually more outgoing. It is courteous to respect these cultures and behave appropriately. Avoid smoking in the streets.

ALCOHOL AND FOOD Muslims do not drink alcohol. It may be offensive to offer alcohol to a Muslim or drink it in their presence, though some restaurants and hotels openly encourage you to bring your own – but don't expect them to pull the cork for you! Discretion is the key.

During the Islamic fasting month of Ramadan, Muslims fast between sunrise and sunset (for about 12 hours); it is inconsiderate to blatantly eat and drink in their company during this time. If someone insists you do so, that's fine – this is Malaysian politeness. Muslims only eat halal food, and no pork.

MOSQUE DECORUM Mosques have strict non-Muslim visiting hours that avoid prayer times; these vary between places. Most mosques, temples and other places of worship ask all visitors to remove their shoes before entering. This also applies to Malaysian homes, homestays, guesthouses and public areas of some resorts. Some mosques provide robes and/or headscarves for female visitors. Remember to be respectful of rules and traditions. Avoid passing in front of a person who is praying, making lots of noise, or touching the Koran.

LONGHOUSE DECORUM Longhouse dos and don'ts vary between ethnic groups and even between individual communities. Remember that longhouses are people's homes rather than museums, and you are a guest. Enter a longhouse only when invited; don't enter or peep into sleeping quarters (*sirang*) or other private rooms unless invited to do so; do not enter a longhouse during times of mourning or as it is being built (this is considered to bring bad luck); never walk under a longhouse; upon your departure, say goodbye to everyone and thank them for their hospitality.

TRAVELLING POSITIVELY

The best way to 'give something back' can be done before you even arrive in Borneo, with your choice of holiday operators. As well as volunteer projects (outlined below), the tour operators you choose will dictate how 'responsible' your holiday can be, whether they are organising your entire trip or you are travelling independently. Using local tour operators does not guarantee local development, but several are committed to helping local communities. By choosing such responsible operators, you can directly help community development initiatives such as homestay programmes, or conservation efforts such as tree planting.

A good example of such responsible tourism is the work of **SI Tours** (see *Tour operators*, page 79) on Sabah's northeast coast. When you stay at their forest lodges or choose them as a day-trip host, they send 1MYR to a local village. The money is used to help families buy school uniforms and bags for their children and improve their homes. SI Tours also source food and other products locally, boosting the local economy.

TYK Adventure Tours (see *Tour operators*, page 79) aim to demonstrate to local people that long-term benefits of tourism outweigh the short-term gains of cash crops, thus helping to change the 'slash and burn mentality' of communities and protect the environment. By involving indigenous communities in local tourist ventures such as native rafting and survival camps, the safeguarded environment becomes the livelihood.

If you book your trip with an international operator, ensure that they are working with local communities, operators and NGOs. Those that bear the stamp of responsible travel are usually legitimate. **Intrepid Travel** (*www.intrepidtravel. com*) are a shining example.

For more information and links, try **Responsible Travel** (\ *+44 01273 600030; www.responsibletravel.com*), a Brighton-based ecotourism travel directory that includes adventure travel, orang-utan conservation tours and volunteer programmes.

CARBON OFFSETTING Carbon emissions generated from your trip can be offset at www.atmosfair.de, a legitimate company recommended by *BBC Wildlife* magazine. The travel industry is the fastest-growing contributor of CO_2 emissions – mostly due to air travel. **Conservation International** (*www.conservation.org*) offers lots of helpful advice about carbon emissions, calculating your eco-footprint and reducing your negative impacts on the environment. Al Gore's (2006) film *An Inconvenient Truth* offers more information on the negative repercussions of travel, and ways of limiting them, as does the book *The Weather Makers* by Tim Flannery.

VOLUNTEER VACATIONS There are many volunteer programmes to choose from in Malaysian Borneo, from conservation to teaching and village development. A good place to look for volunteer programmes in Sabah and Sarawak is Travel Tree (*www.traveltree.co.uk*). More student-oriented sites include www.realgap. co.uk and www.gapyearforgrownups.co.uk. In the US, I-to-I (*www.i-to-i.com*) runs Borneo summer camps and volunteer programmes for 16–19 year olds. Raleigh International (*Raleigh Hse, 3rd Floor, 2007 Waterloo Rd, London;* \ *+44 020 7371 8585;* e *info@raleigh.org.uk; www.raleighinternational.org*) calls itself an 'international development charity'. Its expeditions in Sabah call on volunteers from the UK, Malaysia and other countries, who get incredible life experience while working on community and environmental projects, as well as some real adventure.

3

NATURE CONSERVATION Enormous efforts are being made for conservation by a great number of organisations. Leading the way is WWF (*www.panda.org*), with teams of international and Malaysian scientists active in dozens of projects for fauna and flora conservation. See *Chapter 2*, pages 63–5, for more information on WWF's trailblazing 'Heart of Borneo' project. They publish many invaluable reports on Borneo's biodiversity and work alongside international universities and research institutes. They are in constant need of funds – see their website for details of how you can help.

There are also many small Malaysian local groups making a big difference. Some are in need of volunteer experts – **Wild Asia** (*www.wildasia.net*) has a 'Naturalist in the Lodge' programme that places volunteers in Borneo's wildlife lodges to boost their natural history knowledge base.

Other organisations, as well as general nature sites, post jobs on their websites. **Wildlife Extra** (*www.wildlifeextra.com*) is a British-based web wildlife magazine with links to wildlife volunteer and paid jobs, projects, wildlife holidays and lots of good causes and campaigns. The website www.greenvolunteers.com is a good guide and source of information on worldwide nature conservation volunteer programmes.

Sometimes the best way to help is with a donation to appeals such as the **Sepilok Orang-utan Appeal** (*Charbury, Orestan Lane, Effingham, Surrey;* \ *+44 0771 863 6022;* e *info@orangutan-appeal.org*) – you can adopt an orphaned orang-utan at Sabah's foremost orang-utan rehabilitation centre.

The **Malaysian Nature Society** *Persatuan Pencinta Alam Malaysia* (*www.mns. my mns@mns.my*) has many conservation and community projects in Sabah and Sarawak. Its website links to grassroots organisations and their upcoming events and activities. To support them you can volunteer, join or donate.

Friends of the Earth Malaysia (\ *+60 42 276930*) or Sahabat Alam Malaysia (SAM) carry out many grassroots, community activities in Borneo and are involved in environment and community issues. They have an office in Marudi, in the Baram river area in Sarawak, but their main office is in Penang.

Borneo is one of **Conservation International**'s biodiversity 'hotspots' (*1919 M Street, NW Suite 600 Washington, DC 20036;* \ *(202) 9121 000/1(800) 4062306;* e *hotspots@conservation.org; www.biodiversityhotspots.org; www.conservation.org*). There are plenty of suggestions about how you can help on their website.

Forests Monitor (*69a Lensfield Rd, Cambridge CB2 1EN; www.forestsmonitor. org*) is an NGO working with traditional communities of the world to lobby against activities destroying their habitats. You can donate to their appeals and volunteer with projects.

INDIGENOUS RIGHTS AND CULTURAL CONSERVATION The **Borneo Project**
(*1771 Alcatraz Av, Berkeley, California, CA 94703;* \ *510 547 4258; www. borneoproject.org*) is a major advocate for indigenous rights, rainforest protection and sustainable community development in Borneo. Established in 1991, they have helped indigenous people with native land claims, legal aid, reforestation and rural development primarily in Sarawak. A non-profit organisation sponsored by Earth Island Institute, it works closely with local groups who initiate and oversee various projects while a volunteer advisory board in the US gathers resources and educates audiences about the rainforests and people of Borneo. One recent reforestation scheme brought nine Penan, Kayan and Iban communities together: 'The villages share skills and strategies in reforestation of timber trees, coffee, pepper, rattans, medicinal plants, fruit trees, and vegetable gardening. Nine new nurseries have

been constructed and are well on their way to rejuvenating degraded rainforests.' Other programmes focus on legal aid, community mapping (for claims to ancestral lands) and indigenous pre-schools.

The **Borneo Research Council** (*www.borneoresearchcouncil.org*) draws together a worldwide network of humanitarian field academics with an expertise in the history, language, culture, performing arts, etc, and is keen to recruit volunteers. The Sabah Museum and Sarawak Museum have many different research projects and departments in cultural heritage. **Survival International** (*6 Charterhouse Bldgs, London EC1M 7ET;* \ *+44 020 7687 8700;* e *info@survival-international.org; www.survival-international.org*) do a lot of work protecting indigenous peoples of the world, including those in Borneo.

PACOS (Partners of Community Organisations) (\ *088 712518;* e *pacos@ tm.net.my*) is a community-based volunteer organisation in Sabah that supports indigenous communities.

Tropical Forest Research The following are research institutes and organisations dedicated to unravelling the mysteries of Borneo's nature as well as conserving it. Many areas of Borneo's natural wonders remain unstudied and not fully understood. There is a great need for this research, and there may be opportunities for you to contribute your own knowledge.

The **Royal Botanic Gardens, Kew** (England) (e *info@kew.org; www.kew.org*) is a world leader in botany and plant conservation. At least one of its research teams works in Borneo; it also relies on 500 affiliated researchers, students and volunteers, collaborating in the UK and overseas to build the knowledge base. Information is beautifully presented, for both children and adults on its website.

Local organisations Organisations working on a local level are always in need of extra help, through volunteers and donations. Check out the **Institute of Biodiversity and Environmental Conservation** at Universiti Malaysia Sarawak

MORF REFORESTATION PROJECT KUDAT PENINSULA

SEPILOK SUN BEAR CONSERVATION CENTRE The Borneo Sun Bear Conservation Centre was founded by researcher Wong Siew Ti, taking inspiration from the neighbouring Sepilok Orang-utan Sanctuary. 'Probably the most exciting new conservation initiative in Borneo, this is a truly unique project,' says the Raleigh team. 'The sun bear is the smallest of the nine bear species in the world. With little known about the animal and its numbers decreasing, something needs to be done to secure its future.' The development project is being overseen by LEAP (Land Empowerment Animals People), in close co-operation with the Sabah Departments of Forestry and Wildlife. The centre aims to raise awareness of the plight of the sun bear while allowing for the rehabilitation of sun bears that have been kept in captivity or orphaned. 'Those that can't be released back into the wild will have the best life possible. Through a visitor programme the centre will become self-funding with any profits used for further research of the species.'

Raleigh groups are helping with the construction of the centre – particulary fencing, enclosures and boardwalks. 'Bear necessities' to enable completion of the project include a whole lot more money. Read more about the project at http://sunbears.wildlifedirect.org.

(*www.ibec.unimas.my*), the **Institute for Tropical Biology** and the **Borneo Marine Research Institute** at the Universiti Malaysia Sabah (*www.ums.edu.my*); Sabah's **Wildlife Department** (*www.sabah.gov.my/jhl*) carries out conservation projects all over the state with the university and NGOs; **Sabah Forestry** (*www.forest.sabah.gov.my*) and **Sarawak Forestry** (*www.sarawawforestry.com*) have various national park activities and sustainable forest research programmes.

GIVING GIFTS Small gifts are a nice way of showing gratitude to hosts. These may be 'exotic' things from your own home country that are not available in Borneo. When visiting longhouses or other traditional communities, the custom is to present gifts to the village chief (*penghulu*) or longhouse chief (*tuai rumah*) so that they can be shared around.

BEGGING Giving money to children is not encouraged. Begging is uncommon in Sabah and Sarawak. The main exceptions are some coastal towns with a lot of poor Filipino and Indonesian migrants. Children might cheekily extend their hands for money when parents are not looking.

Part Two

BRUNEI

4

Brunei Darussalam

Being an inkblot of a nation has bruised neither Brunei's self-image nor its prosperity. The Islamic pride and sovereign swishness are embodied in the flag – regal, striking and strict all at once – the yellow banner with white and black diagonal stripes bears a red insignia of wings, umbrellas and masts signifying justice, peace and prosperity. A lofty sense of all three permeates the watery ambience of Brunei, along with the sounds of Muslim prayer time emanating from its golden-domed mosques. Brunei is the most strong-spirited Muslim place in Borneo – nearly two-thirds of its population is of Islamic faith, and the foundations of the national philosophy Melayu Islam Beraja ('Malay Islam Monarchy') are deeply entrenched.

While it describes itself as a moderate Muslim country, there are signs of severity: the death penalty for drug possession, imprisonment for drinking alcohol, fines for not fasting, corporal punishment with rattan canes, and less individual freedom than in Malaysia. Women are 'strongly encouraged' by state authorities to cover their hair with a *tudung* and men wear the traditional Malay cap, the *songkok*. However, this clothing is far more about cultural expression than it is a sign of oppression. The people of Brunei are smiling, warm people, washed over by gentle Malay-ness, albeit a little socially straight-jacketed and undeniably parched when it comes to full individual freedom.

In the aftermath of the first Arab country uprisings in 2011, CBS News highlighted Brunei and Sultan Hassanal Bolkiah in a World Watch series programme dedicated to 'The world's enduring dictators'. Listing its 'most despotic acts' it claimed: 'Bolkiah's government is accused of arbitrary detention; limits on freedom of speech, press, assembly, and association; restrictions on religious freedom; discrimination against women; restricted labour rights; and exploitation of foreign workers, according to the US State Department.' While voices of dissent are negligible, the media is largely state-owned or controlled.

For their reverence to the monarchy and Muslim ideology, there are many rewards: people get free education and health care, tax-free salaries, cheap housing loans and many other incentives. There's virtually no crime, unemployment is below 5% and inflation hovers at around 0.5%. Duty-free imports account for the majority of goods consumed, from food to electronics, and most people have two newly imported cars. Driving around is a breeze on the uncongested roads and a high quality of life is also accorded by the low-density population and plenitude of gardens and other urban spaces. Brunei is ten times the size of Singapore with one-tenth of the population; it is also a youthful nation – 90% of its population is under 50.

The modern face of Brunei is still in the making. The sultan-owned national carrier Royal Brunei Airlines only started to promote its realm to the world in the

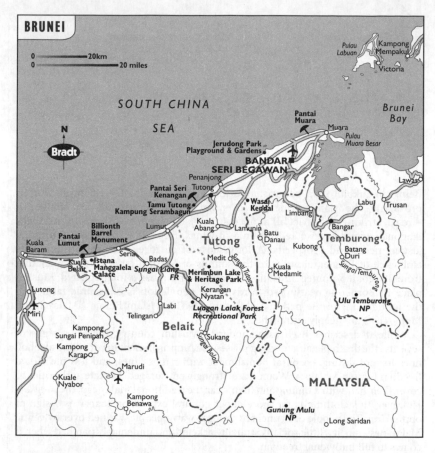

mid-1990s and markets Brunei as a 'stopover' to Sabah and Sarawak. The country is aware of its size limitations, yet Bruneians love their high quality of life and boast that they have jungle, sea, mosques and malls on their doorstep. As local DJ and television presenter, Jenny Malai Ali says, Brunei is 'a magical little place that offers the luxuries of the new world against a rich and beautiful historical backdrop'.

HISTORY

Sultan Bolkiah is the 29th ruler of a 650-year-old un-broken Muslim dynasty in Brunei. Prior to Islamic rule, ancient settlements were a mixed bag of Malay, Chinese and Hindu influence. Chinese historical texts tell of thriving 10th-century trade with a region variably referred to as Puni, Po-li, Po-lo, Poni and Bunlai. In Arabic records, the early settlement was known as Dzabaj or Randj. In the 14th century, a Malay–Hindu–Buddhist settlement developed on the banks of the Sungai Brunei River. Folklore dictates that on discovering the area the newcomers exclaimed '*barunah!*' – a Malay expression of satisfaction which roughly translates as 'this is it!' Barunah later became Barunai, derived from the Sanskrit word *varuna*: a nation of seafarers. In subsequent centuries, the name of the small trading post endured countless changes – merchants, explorers and passers-by cited it as Bornei, Borney, Borneo, Bruneo, Burne and Bruni. The Chinese called it Wen-lai and Bun-lai.

The first Malay king to seriously entertain Islam was Raja Awang Alak Betatar. He changed his name to Muhammad Shah and became the first sultan of Brunei, dramatically altering the course of history and Brunei's cultural identity. Ever since his reign from 1363 to 1402, the line-up of sultans has represented the longest-lasting – though colonially interrupted – dynasty in the world.

Subsequent sultans ruled through an era which is widely known as Brunei's 'golden age', from the 15th to 17th century, when Brunei's control extended over the entire island of Borneo and into the Philippines. The kingdom was particularly powerful under the fifth sultan, Bolkiah (1473–1521). According to the *Brunei Times*, his successor, Sultan Abdul Kahar, continued through sea expeditions to expand Brunei's territories, 'which included the whole of Borneo, Palawan, Sulu, Balayan, Mindoro, Bonbon, Balabak, Balambangan and Bangi and Luzon …With the Brunei traders, Islam spread far including to the southern Philippines islands and Brunei was recognised as a centre of Islamic propagation.'

Brunei's expansion in the region provoked a showdown between Islam and Christianity. From the late 16th century, the Spaniards used Manila as a trade centre and base from which to spread their religion, and were fed up with Brunei proselytising on what they considered their territory. In 1573, a Spanish delegation

POMP AND SULTANATES

Once the world's richest man, Hassanal Bolkiah has fallen a few rungs to become simply one of the world's richest monarchs. Forbes place the oil-rich sultan's US$20 billion fortune in second place to that of Thailand's King Bhumibol Adulyadej, who is worth US$30 billion.

Within his palace there are stables, a concert hall, helipads, several swimming pools, 200 bathrooms, a priceless art collection and many luxury 'toys' including Boeing airplanes and helicopters (the sultan is a licensed pilot and did his military training at Sandhurst in England). A keen equestrian and car collector, he has 200 ponies and an automobile empire of some 2,000 cars, including Rolls-Royces, Ferraris, McLaren F1s, Porsches and Bentleys.

The perennially handsome, polo-playing sultan is revered by his subjects, who call him Sultan Kitani (our sultan), and he is seen to share his riches around and have a genuine interest in the people. The seemingly down-to-earth manner with which he deals with the public contrasts with his own lavish lifestyle and privileged halo of friends. Honorary titles such as Dato and Pehin are handed out among this group on his birthday. While vast amounts of media space are given over to every detail of the royal family's official life, his private one is off-limits.

In 2005, the sultan's third marriage (Islam allows men to have up to four wives) was to a woman 32 years his junior – then 26-year-old Azrinaz Mazhar Hakim. The Queen, or Raja, of Brunei is his first wife (and first cousin), Anak Saleha, whom he married in 1965. Both the Queen and his young wife appear with him on all official occasions. The sultan's birthday is celebrated each July with three weeks of public partying, in which the palace dons a large shawl of fairy lights and big (booze-free) festivities take place.

was sent to Brunei seeking an audience with the 7th Sultan Saiful Rijal, in an attempt to bring Brunei under Spanish protection and spread Christianity in the country. The treaty was rejected, and five years later the Spaniards returned to Brunei with an armada of 40 warships, demanding the sultan in a letter 'to send no preachers of the sect of Mohama to any part of these islands'.

The Spaniards attacked and burnt down the Great Mosque. Though they succeeded in nipping Brunei's influence in the Philippines in the bud, they failed to bring it under Spanish sovereignty. They did however, according to Moshe Yegar in his book *Between Integration and Secession* on the Muslim communities of the southern Philippines, succeed in 'turning it into a small coastal state'. This marked the beginning of a period of decline for the Sultanate, caught between internal rifts over royal succession, and the rising influence of European colonial powers in the region.

From the 1830s, during the reign of the 22nd sultan, Muhammad Alam, (1828–52), and the 23rd sultan, Omar Ali Saifuddin II, (1852–85), the era of direct European involvement in Brunei began, starting with the arrival of James Brooke as the white Rajah of Sarawak. (See *Background Information*, pages 6–7.)

The signing of the 1906 Brunei Treaty paved the way for a strong period of British influence in Brunei that has left a permanent mark on its royalist Islamic make-up. Executive powers were handed over to Britain through a British Residential System, by which a Brunei-dwelling British diplomat advised the sultan on all state matters excluding Malay customs and religion. Throughout this period, the 25th sovereign, Sultan Hashim, had nominal powers. Honoured for his co-operation with British authorities, with awards including Knight Commander of the Order of Saint Michael and Saint George, he died from Malaria in 1924 at the age of 35.

In 1929 Brunei's fortunes took a positive turn when the only major onshore oilfield was discovered in the southern Seria District. Before the outbreak of World War II, British-administered Brunei was already enjoying many oil-export profits. At the end of Japanese occupation (1945), retreating British troops sabotaged all oil infrastructure in Brunei and Sarawak to prevent them falling into enemy hands. Brunei Town was also bombed when the allies repossessed it. After the war, the British era in Brunei began to wane, and in 1959 a constitutional agreement handed back more domestic rule to the sultanate. At around the same time, the Brunei Shell Petroleum Company started offshore drilling, striking oil for the first time in 1963, off the coast of Belait.

BUDGETING

If you visit Brunei after Sabah or Sarawak, you might start out feeling that 1BND for market produce, a bus fare or bottle of water is on a par with the Malaysian states. The dollar, however, is double the value of the Malaysian ringgit, and you actually pay almost twice the price for many food items, transport, and even accommodation. If you are on a tight budget, eat at food stalls and coffee shops, and walk or take buses instead of taxis. Though hostel accommodation choices are limited, good deals can be struck in budget hotels. In the words of one traveller: 'Brunei may be a wealthy country but it is certainly affordable.' The great exception is petrol, which drops in price by almost half to 53 cents a litre. Bottled water, everyone jokes, is more expensive – a litre costs 1BND.

The 28th sultan, Haji Omar Ali Saiffuddien III (the father of the current sultan), is widely regarded as the architect of modern Brunei. From his ascendancy in 1950 he used Brunei's oil revenues to finance a five-year development plan to bring some modernity and infrastructure to the town.

A DEMOCRATIC BRUNEI? The British Ghurkhas army of Nepalese troops are revered in Brunei today for helping bring to an end Brunei's last brush with democracy – a 1962 coup by the pro-democratic **Brunei People's Party** (PRB). The PRB and other political parties have been outlawed ever since. Brunei was the only Malay state to snub the Federation of Malaysia in 1963 through fear of losing the absolute monarchy's regal hold and oil wealth. It remained a British Protectorate until 1 January 1984, when it regained full independence.

In late 2007, the new 62 million BND Legislative Council was formed after being fast-tracked towards completion in two years. Alleged to be part of a slow move towards increasing democracy, this process is clearly in no hurry, despite the sultan's awareness that his kingdom is something of a relic. At a conference on royalty hosted by His Majesty in 2006, he himself predicted the eventual demise of absolute monarchies.

GETTING THERE AND AWAY

Brunei is divided into four administrative divisions: **Brunei Muara**, which includes the capital Bandar Seri Begawan, **Tutong**, **Belait** and **Temburong**. Brunei is an eighth of the size of Switzerland, and, therefore, the longest car trip in the country takes little more than three hours.

BY AIR
Brunei International Airport Some 11km from the capital, Bandar Seri Begawan, the airport is connected to worldwide destinations with Royal Brunei Airlines' direct services, and by Singapore Airlines, Thai Airways, Philippines Airlines, Malaysia Airlines and Dragonair through their hubs in Singapore, Bangkok, Kuala Lumpur and Hong Kong. Long-mooted plans for a new airport to cope with increasing traffic were on hold in 2011.

National carrier Royal Brunei Airlines (RBA) flies from Bandar Seri Begawan to 20 major cities in the Asian Pacific, the Middle East and Europe. RBA has direct flights several times weekly between Melbourne, Brisbane, Perth, Auckland and Bandar Seri Begawan and flies from London to Bandar Seri Begawan (via Dubai) three times a week. Connections in the Asia Pacific region are set to expand as Brunei's importance as both an economic hub and popular stopover destination grow.

Within Borneo, RBA have several daily flights between Bandar Seri Begawan and both Kota Kinabalu and Kuching.

Airline offices All are in Bandar Seri Begawan city centre. Most are open between 08.00–12.00 and 13.00–17.00.

✈ **Royal Brunei Airlines** RBA Plaza, Jln Sultan; ☏2212222/2240500
✈ **MAS** Mezzanine Floor, Bangunan Hj Ahmad building, Lot 38–39 Jln Sultan; ☏2223074/1 ticketing; 2224097 admin

✈ **Singapore Airlines** 5th Floor, Bangunan Hj Ahmad Bldg, 38–39 Jln Sultan, ☏2244901/2

Getting to/from the airport The **Central Line** buses stop at the airport every 15 minutes and make several stops in the city district before arriving at the city bus terminal. Some hotels have airport transfers. Average taxi fares to the city are 15BND. The website of Brunei Tourism (*www.tourismbrunei.com/info/ground. html*) has a useful list of metered fares to dozens of destinations – hotels, city landmarks and attractions – with the airport taxi service.

BY CAR Apart from its northwestern seaboard, Brunei is hemmed in on all sides by the Malaysian state of Sarawak. The 'Pan-Borneo' Highway – a network of federal roads – connects Brunei with Sarawak and Sabah. It takes about 12 hours to drive between Brunei's capital and Kuching, and half that to Kota Kinabalu. An immigration checkpoint is located at Sungai Tujoh in northern Brunei. From Limbang in Sarawak to Bandar Seri Begawan, the trip time is 45 minutes and the checkpoint is in Kuala Lurah.

BY BOAT
To and from Sarawak A once-daily ferry service from Brunei's Serasa Muara terminal for Utama Lawas in Sarawak departs at 09.30. It is prone to regular interruption so please check with Brunei Tourism (*www.tourismbrunei.com*) or the Marine department (*www.marine.gov.bn/boat_schedule_arrival.htm*) for updates.

A daily speedboat for Sundar in Lawas leaves the riverside ferry terminal on Jalan Residency at 10.30.

To and from Sabah A new car ferry service between Brunei's Serasa ferry terminal and Menumbok in Sabah has revolutionised international travel between Brunei and Sabah, principally in terms of ease and travel time, but also in terms of cost. The *Shuttle Hope* ferry travels once a day from Brunei to Menumbok and vice-versa. The journey takes 2½ hours and costs 70BND per vehicle, including driver, plus 25BND for each additional adult or 12.50BND for children. Foot passengers pay 25BND for a ticket, meaning budget travellers can make the journey from Bandar Seri Begawan to Kota Kinabalu, buses included, for under 35BND. The ferry cuts down the travel time from as much as 12 hours by bus to a total of five hours. Sailings are at 09.30 from the Serasa terminal, and 15.00 from Menumbok, though drivers are advised to arrive an hour in advance.

To and from Pulau Labuan Car and passenger ferry services link Brunei with the Malaysian island of Labuan. The ferries operate from the Serasa terminal in the Muara District, about 20km from the capital. Take the blue Eastern Line bus (No 33). Boats leave six times a day, at 07.30, 08.30, 09.00, 13.00, 15.30 and 16.40. From Labuan to Brunei, the departure times are 08.00, 11.00, 12.15, 14.00, 16.00 and 16.30. The journey takes around 45–60 minutes. Ferries to Lawas also leave here daily at 11.30, and to Menumbok at 09.30. Ferry schedules are subject to change and it is best to check the boat schedule online (*www.marine.gov.bn*) or by calling the **Shipping Office of the Marine Department** (❨*02 773071 for services to Labuan & Lawas;* ❨*02 244251 for services to Temburong & Limbang*). Brunei Tourism (*www. tourismbrunei.com*) also has updated ferry schedules on their website under Visitor Info, Getting Around.

BY BUS The bus journey between Sarawak and Brunei is far from straightforward: it takes five hours, three buses and a ferry to cover 120km. Nevertheless the quality and efficiency of operators are showing signs of improvement. The new PHLS Express bus service runs twice a day, in both directions (Bandar Seri Begawan–Miri and Miri–Bandar Seri Begawan). Departures are 07.00 and 13.00 from Brunei's capital, and 08.15 and 16.15 from Miri's long-distance bus station. The one-way journey costs 18BND. Prior to the introduction of this service, in 2010, Malaysian bus company Biaramas Express launched the first, near-seamless commercial transport service from Brunei to Miri. The 'Bus Asia' service operated twice daily but now seems to have disappeared from the company's services. It's high time the company got itself a decent website as a service to travellers, but they are not alone in falling short on providing such information. Currently their site is http://202.190.123.254/ and it's worth checking in for changes in the Sarawak–Brunei bus situation.

LOCAL TOUR OPERATORS

Continental Yachting Tours ☏2233200; e continentaltour@brunet.bn; www.onebrunei.com

Freme Travel Services ☏2234280; e fremeinb@brunet.bn; www.freme.com, www.brunei-tours.freme.com. An established company with its head office in Kuala Belait, an office in the capital, & a firm foothold nationwide. The company has its own fleet of premium coaches, & is said to be good with British clients.

Intrepid Tours Unit 105, 1st Floor, PGGMB Bldg,Jalan Sungai Kianggeh, BSB (opposite *tamu* market & above express coach stop for

Kota Kinabalu & Miri); ☏2221685/6; e tours@ bruneibay.net; www.bruneibay.net

Mega Borneo Marketing Services ☏2224026; e megaborneo@brunet.bn. Recommended. Familiar with British, Australian & continental clients.

Sunshine Borneo Tours & Travel No 2 Simpang 146, Jln Kiarong, Kampung Kiulap, BSB; ☏2446509, after hours ☏8715863; e sales@ exploreborneo.com; www.exploreborneo.com. Efficient choice for day trips & excursions. A 2nd branch is found in the lobby arcade of the Empire Hotel & Country Club in Jerudong (☏2610578).

BANDAR SERI BEGAWAN

Few people have heard of Brunei's capital city before visiting, and it's hardly the catchiest of names. Fortunately, everyone calls it BSB. Known as Brunei Town – Pekan Brunei – up until 1970, the idyllic-sounding replacement of Bandar Seri Begawan (roughly translated as 'city of the glorious retiree') honours the 28th sultan, who took this title when he abdicated in 1967. It is a fascinating city – on the one hand, you feel you are in a place entrenched in trading history and Islamic exoticism, while on the other, is the emerging face of a 'modernised capital'. The much-publicised 'lavish adornments, gold towers, sparkling fountains and colourful mosaic tiles' are scattered about the city, from the riverbank area to the new modern districts. There is no historic mass of buildings as the old town and its colonial edifices were bombed by the Allies during World War II.

The city spreads out over 16km from the downtown area, which is hemmed in by riverside recreational areas, state-owned land, museums and ministries.

When the lights go out, so does most of the action. At 18.00 all public transport stops, and locals head for their favourite evening spot as the sun sets over the river. With the Muslim chants and the drone of cicadas resonating through the city, the country's full name becomes very fitting – Brunei Darussalam, 'Brunei, abode of peace'.

Once you get past the logistical challenges and locate the most animated *tamu* (markets), the museums and mosques, the gorgeous green spaces and nearby

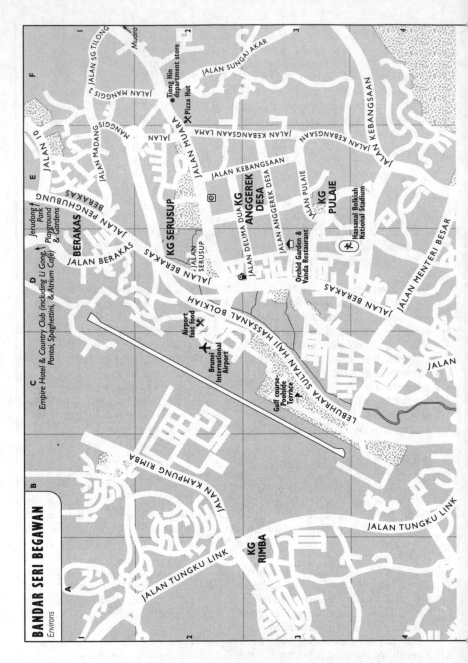

BANDAR SERI BEGAWAN
Environs

Map labels (clockwise/various):
JALAN SG TILONG · JALAN MANGGIS 2 · Muaro · Tiong Hin department store · Pizza Hut · JALAN SUNGAI AKAR · JALAN MANGGIS · JALAN MADANG · JALAN · JALAN KEBANGSAAN LAMA · JALAN KEBANGSAAN · JALAN KEBANGSAAN · JALAN KEBANGSAAN · JALAN 10 · BERAKAS · JALAN PENGHUBUNG · Jerudong Park · Playground & Gardens · JALAN BERAKAS · KG SERUSUP · JALAN MUARA · JALAN KEBANGSAAN · JALAN DELIMA DUA · KG ANGGEREK DESA · JALAN ANGGEREK DESA · JALAN PULAIE · KG PULAIE · Hassanal Bolkiah National Stadium · JALAN SERUSUP · Orchid Garden & Yanda Restaurant · JALAN BERAKAS · JALAN MENTERI BESAR · Empire Hotel & Country Club (including Li Gong, Pantai, Spaghettini, & Atrium Café) · Airport fast food · Brunei International Airport · LEBUHRAYA SULTAN HAJI HASSANAL BOLKIAH · Golf course- Poolside Terrace · JALAN · JALAN KAMPUNG RIMBA · KG RIMBA · JALAN TUNGKU LINK · JALAN TUNGKU LINK

beaches, you can join the locals and enjoy a high quality of life for a few days as well as some rich cultural experiences.

ORIENTATION Bandar Seri Begawan has three districts: **Bandar**, the city centre or central business district (CBD) hedged around the riverfront; and **Gadong** and **Kiulap**, two neighbouring commercial districts on the western side of the river.

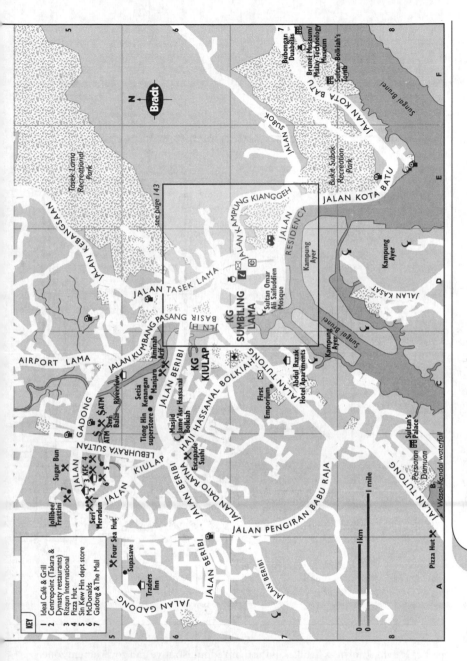

see page 143

Unless you intend to stay longer than the standard couple of stopover days, you will probably base yourself either in the CBD or in Gadong. Vibey Gadong is home to markets, malls, shop-lots, restaurants, cafés and a handful of hotels. Kiulap is an up-and-coming urban precinct, developing around an old village. The upmarket beachside suburb of Jerudong, 13km northwest of the city, is part of the Brunei Muara District (the Jerudong Playground theme park is located here). The northern

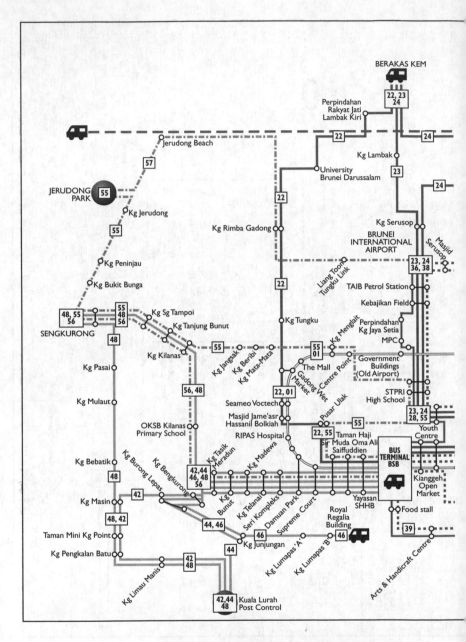

part of Muara, known as Berakas, is the main administrative and government zone, which also has many sports facilities (stadiums, swimming pools, sports complexes, etc) and a couple of hotels. Muara's beaches lie north of the capital on Brunei Bay.

GETTING AROUND

By car Brunei's capital is not an easy place to get around by public transport. The main problem is not infrastructure, but hours. The last buses run at 18.00, so if you

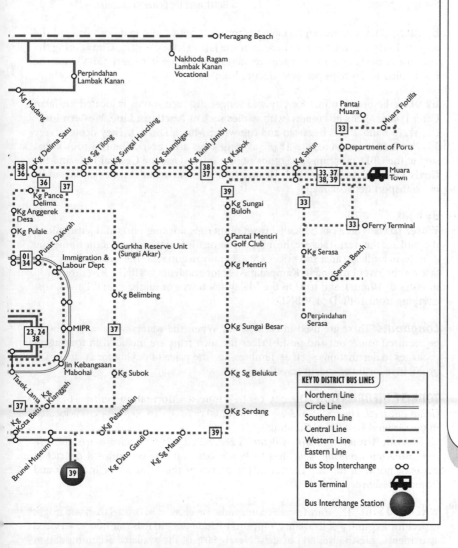

Meragang Beach

Nakhoda Ragam
Lambak Kanan
Vocational

Perpindahan
Lambak Kanan

Kg Madang

Pantai
Muara

Muara Flotilla

33

Kg Delima Satu

Kg Sg Tilong

Kg Sungai Hanching

Kg Salambigar

Kg Tanah Jambu

Kg Kapok

Kg Sabun

Department of Ports

38
36

38
37

33, 37
38, 39

Muara
Town

36

37

39

33

Kg Pance
Delima

Kg Anggerek
Desa

Kg Sungai
Buloh

33

Ferry Terminal

Kg Pulaie

Pantai Mentiri
Golf Club

Kg Serasa

Pusat Dakwah

Gurkha Reserve Unit
(Sungai Akar)

Kg Mentiri

Serasa Beach

01
34

Immigration &
Labour Dept

Kg Belimbing

23, 24
38

MIPR

37

Kg Sungai Besar

Perpindahan
Serasa

Jln Kebangsaan
Mabohai

Kg Subok

Kg Sg Belukut

Tasek Lama

Kg Kianggeh

37

Kg Pelambaian

Kg Serdang

Kg Kota Batu

39

Brunei Museum

Kg Dato Gandi

Kg Sg Matan

39

39

KEY TO DISTRICT BUS LINES

Northern Line	
Circle Line	
Southern Line	
Central Line	
Western Line	
Eastern Line	
Bus Stop Interchange	⚬⚬
Bus Terminal	
Bus Interchange Station	●

Brunei Darussalam   BANDAR SERI BEGAWAN

4

plan to be out after dark you have to rely on your feet, a taxi or a car. The key city sites are spread out over several kilometres, so the best option if you want to see as much as possible in a couple of days is to have your own car, or combine a day of car hire for the city sights with day or overnight tours to other places of interest. A litre of petrol costs around 53 cents – a tank is filled for around 20BND. Diesel is 31 cents a litre.

Car hire A list of car hire agencies can be found on Tourism Brunei's website: www.tourismbrunei.com/visitor-info/getting-around/ground/.

🚗 **Avis Rent A Car** ☎2426345. Avis have an airport counter & a branch at the Sheraton Utama Hotel (☎2227100).

🚗 **Azizah Car Rental** ☎2229388
🚗 **Budget-U-Drive** 5th Floor, D'Anggerek Hotel, near the Convention Centre; ☎2345573

By taxi Metered taxis can be hailed from most hotels, shopping centres and the airport. In the capital, taxis are located at the Jalan Cator car park. Considering the low cost of petrol, taxis are expensive, about 1BND per kilometre (3BND for the first kilometre, 20 cents per subsequent kilometre).

By bus The bus terminal for city and longer-distance routes is located on Jalan Cator [143 C3]. Six bus routes (with names such as **Northern Line**, **Western Line**, etc) serve Bandar Seri Begawan and the wider Muara District. They depart every 15–20 minutes from 06.30 to 18.00; average fares are 1BND. The two routes that stop at the CBD, museums and other sites of interest are the **Central Line** and the **Circle Line**. The widely available Brunei Tourism map includes the essential public bus transport network map.

By boat
Water taxis These can be hailed from numerous docking ports and jetties along the banks of the river. They are the most common form of transport for the Kampung Ayer (water village) area and prices are generally negotiable. The standard one-way fare for the river crossing to Kampung Ayer for residents is 1BND. River tours (30 minutes or 1 hour), and trips to the Malaysian towns of Limbang and Lawas, cost anything from 10BND to 30BND.

Longboats These are used in rural areas. When the waters are low, you might be required to get out and push! Prices for such trips are included in tour agent packages to destinations such as Temburong. The price of paying for such trips is prohibitive for independent travellers.

TOURIST INFORMATION The city centre's **tourist information centre** [143 C3] (*Jalan Elizabeth Dua;* ☎2223734; ⊕ *08.00–12.00 & 14.30–16.30 Mon–Sat*) is located in the General Post Office Building.

   Tourism Brunei (*Jln Menteri Besar;* ☎2382822/2382832; e *info@tourismbrunei. com; www.tourismbrunei.com*) has its headquarters in the government district of Berakas, north of the city centre, in the offices of the Ministry of Industry and Primary Resources.

🏠 **WHERE TO STAY** There are fewer accommodation choices in Brunei than you might expect for a country of its stature. Options include one- to five-star hotels, serviced apartments, guesthouses and hostels. Nearly 90% of the available accommodation is in the capital. Given the dispersed nature of the city, and generally poor public transport, be sure to pick your accommodation according to your priorities: CBD, retail and riverfront; nightlife and markets in Gadong; or groomed greenery, golfing and beaches in Jerudong. All of the hostels are in Bandar. Keep in mind it is sometimes possible to get better value for money by staying in a suburban hotel. The **Brunei Association of Hotels** website (*www.hotelsofbrunei.com*) provides links to its members, bringing together two-thirds of the country's hotels.

Map labels:

The Mall, Jaya CentrePoint
Masjid Jame'Asr Hassanal
Tasek Recreational Park
JALAN KUMBANG
JALAN BERIBI
JLN H BASIR
JALAN TASEK LAMA
500m
500yds
Taman Selera
JALAN TUTONG
JLN ISTANA DARUSSALAM
JLN SUMBILING
Taman Selera
Radisson & Tasek Brasserie
JLN KG BERANGAN
Royal Regalia Museum
JALAN SUNGAI KIANGGEH
JALAN STONEY
JALAN SULTAN
N
Bradt
Popular
Hospital
Pusat Belia Youth Hostel
JALAN KAMPUNG KIANGGEH
KG SUMBILING LAMA
Public library
Historical Centre
JALAN ELIZABETH DUA
Istana Darussalam
Chinese temple
RBA Plaza
Sultan Omar Ali Saifuddien Mosque
JLN PEMANCHA
ATM
JALAN MCARTHUR
Yayasan Shopping Complex, Padian Food Court, Fratini's Restaurant, Zaika & RMS Portview
Pizza Hut
Brunei
Tamu Kianggeh
Kampung Ayer
JL CATOR
JL ROBERTS
France
Canadian High Commission
Buhongan Duabelas Arts & Crafts Centre
Germany Embassy & British High Commission
USA Embassy & Australian High Commission
JALAN RESIDENCY
Season's
The Arts and Handicrafts Centre
Temburong Ferry Terminal
Sungai Brunei
Kampung Ayer
Kampung Ayer

BANDAR SERI BEGAWAN
City centre

Luxury

🏠 **Empire Hotel & Country Club** [138 D1] (423 rooms) Muara Tutong Highway, Jerudong (13km north of town); ☏2418888; e sales@ theempirehotel.com; www.theempirehotel.com. Fit for a sultan (or sultaness), the 6-winged hotel has swirled marble floors, stairway railings plated in 21-karat gold & wool carpets interwoven with gold thread. The stunning open-tiered lobby is actually on the 5th floor overlooking the sea; most rooms have ocean-facing balconies & the smallest suites are 30m². The swimming pools are Olympic-sized, fluid-formed & sand based. Within the majestic grounds of the Country Club there are amazing sport & spa facilities. The dining alternatives rival those of a luxury shopping galleria & entertainment includes 3 cinemas. **$$$$$**

🏠 **Rizqun International Hotel** [139 B5] (168 rooms, inc non-smoking floor) Abdul Razak

Complex Gadong; ☏2423000; e info@rizquninternational.com; www.rizquninternational.com. An uplifting Muslim-Malay feel to this hotel, with its touch of palatial, huge marble & granite lobby, classical comfort & gracious staff. De luxe rooms come with luxurious marble bathrooms, high-tech touches, ample lounge furnishings & work spaces. Excellent location close to city centre but in the heart of Gadong. Good Chinese/Malay/Indian/Western b/fast. Premier Club floor benefits include a club lounge (⊕ 06.30–23.00), complimentary b/fast & free 24hr internet access in rooms. Terrace swimming pool & fitness centre. **$$$$$**

Upmarket

🏠 **The Centrepoint** [139 B5] (216 rooms) Abdul Razak Complex, Km4 Jln Gadong; ☏2430430; e centrepoint@arhbrunei.com; www.arhbrunei.com. Comfortable with good facilities

(AC, writing desk, minibar, satellite TV, kettle, swimming pool, gym). Very service oriented & well staffed. De luxe rooms, junior/executive/ business suites & non-smoking floor. Dining choices in the hotel are plentiful & frequented by locals, especially Dynasty Restaurant (see *Where to eat*, page 145). **$$$$**

🏠 **Radisson Hotel** [143 B2] (142 rooms) Jln Tasek; ☎ 2244272; e reservations.brunei@ radisson.com; www.radisson.com. After 29 years in Brunei, the former Sheraton Utama closed in May 2010 & re-emerged as a Radisson, which I am yet to test drive since its subsequent facelift. The new hotel brand immediately embarked on a 2-year room refurbishment (due for completion in mid-2012). The most centrally located upmarket hotel, 10mins' walk from the CBD has a pleasant lobby, good dining choices, 2 meeting rooms & free high-speed Wi-Fi throughout. The spacious well-furnished, superior & executive de luxe rooms have high-tech features; ask for pool-facing if you don't want traffic noise. **$$$$**

Mid range

🏠 **Orchid Garden Hotel** [138 D3] (155 rooms) Lot 31954, Simpang 9, Kampung Anggerek Desa (3km from CBD), Jln Berakas; ☎ 2335544; e ogh@brunet.bn; www. orchidgardenbrunei.com. Chinese pagoda-style cream building in Berakas District. Swimming pool, fitness centre & restaurants, rather floral

but quality décor & furnishings, spacious rooms & nice lobby. Western & Chinese restaurants with dim sum Sun buffet. **$$$**

🏠 **Riverview Hotel** [139 C6] (130 rooms) Km1, Jln Gadong (1km from CBD); ☎ 2238238; e rivview@brunet.bn. Halfway between Bandar & Gadong on an estuary of the Sungai, big 3-star leisure hotel, not for peace-seekers but family fun, poolside BBQ & steamboats, business centre, jacuzzi & gym, kids' playground, 24hr café. Shuttle service to both Gadong & CBD. **$$$**

Budget

🏠 **Brunei Hotel** [143 C3] (63 rooms) 95 Jln Pemancha; ☎ 2244828; e info@thebruneihotel. com; www.bruneihotel.com. The best budget hotel in the city centre for standard rooms, with some mid-range (more spacious) de luxe rooms. AC, satellite TV, tea & coffee making & safe in rooms. 10–15min walk to riverfront & Jln Residency. **$$**

🏠 **Traders Inn** [139 A6] (84 rooms) Block D, Lot 11620 Jln Gadong (3km from CBD); ☎ 2442828; e traders@brunet.bn; www. tradersinn-bn.com. Budget business hotel, very pleasant atmosphere & management, on industrial edges of Gadong area with market & coffee shops close by. Spacious, simple, freshly decorated & well-appointed rooms, business centre, free Wi-Fi, in-house coffee lounge (⊕ *06.30–23.00*) plus foot reflexology centre; great value. Best value of the budget hotels. **$$**

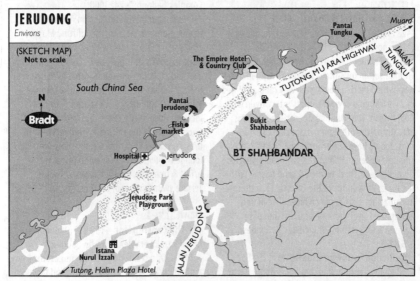

Shoestring

⌂ **Pusat Belia Youth Hostel** [143 C2] Jln Sungai Kianggeh; ☎ 2223936; e jbsbelia@brunet. bn. The best & only place to stay on a very strict budget in Brunei. It has also beaten a couple of formerly listed budget accommodations in passing the necessary cleanliness tests. AC, 4-bed dorms with comfortable beds, good showers & access to a pool. Approx 10BND/US$6. **$**

Serviced apartments

⌂ **Abdul Razak Hotel Apartments** [139 C7] (96 rooms & suites) Jln Laksamana

Abdul Razak, Km2, Jln Tutong (5km from CBD, 7km from airport near Supreme Court); ☎ 2241536; e dmarp@arhbrunei.com; www. arhbrunei.com. 24 rooms, 56 1-bed suites & 16 2-bed suites all with fully equipped kitchenettes, central AC, daily room-cleaning services, writing desk, fridge & minibar, satellite TV & room service until 21.30. A good choice if you have your own car, though buses do run this way. Described by one friend as 'apartments for the flashpacker'. **$$**

✕ **WHERE TO EAT** Street food in Brunei is among the most delicious and immaculately presented in Borneo. Indoors, there are many good coffee shops and casual restaurants; more sophisticated dining and international restaurants are chiefly found in four- and five-star hotels, though Brunei's modern dining scene is embryonic. Gadong is the best place for multi-ethnic, well-priced food at small, family-run businesses. New-wave cafés in the Kiulap District are home to East-meets-West flavours, trendy décor and a young, affluent crowd. Restaurants are not open as late as they are in Malaysian Borneo, with last orders from 21.00–22.00. (A number of 24-hour cafés and food stalls cater for night owls.) Given the lack of chic eateries, and the growing demand, it pays to make a reservation at hotel restaurants on weekends.

Malay/Bruneian

✕ **Aminah Arif** [139 C6] Unit 2–3, Block B, Bangunan Haji Abdul Rahman; ☎ 2236198. An institution among locals for the *ambuyat* (see box, page 146). In the Kiulap District. **$$$**

✕ **Restoran Seri Balai** [139 C5] Unit 3, Bangunan Haji Menudin, Block A, Kampung Pengkalan Gadong; ☎ 2456447. *Ambuyat*, but with quality Malay dishes, snacks & cakes also on the menu, this is a place for the adventurous. Found in the village of Kampung Pengkalan Gadong opposite the Gadong commercial centre. **$$**

✕ **Seri Kiantan Restaurant** 5 Bangunan Menglait, Gadong; ☎ 2444848; ⊕ Mon–Sat. Casual place for Malay staples such as *nasi lemak*, *cucur udang* (prawn fritters) *kelupis* (glutinous rice rolls) & lots of Malay *kueh* (cakes). **$–$$**

Chinese

✕ **Li Gong Chinese Restaurant** [138 D1] Empire Hotel & Country Club, Tutong Muara Highway, Jerudong; ☎ 2418888; ⊕ 11.00–14.00 & 18.00–22.00 daily. Favourite local haunt for Sun brunches of dim sum & Cantonese roast duck. The interior is chic, with a semblance of a

modern Chinese temple in its glass-walled form. **$$$–$$$$**

✕ **Dynasty Restaurant** [139 B5] Ground Floor, Centrepoint Hotel, Abdul Razak Complex, Gadong; ☎ 2430430; ⊕ 08.30–14.00 &18.00– 22.00 daily. The most popular & established Chinese eatery in Brunei, famed for introducing halal dim sum & more recently for its rock melon *sago* dessert. Alongside the Centrepoint shopping mall in Gadong. **$$–$$$**

✕ **Four Sea Hut or Shikai** [139 A5] Unit 1, Block E, Sempurna Complex, Jln Batu Bersurat, Gadong; ☎ 2456222; ⊕ lunch/dinner. High on rustic ambience, décor & food quality, this little place among suburban shop-lots serves Hong Kong-style roast duck & chicken dishes, plus a mix of Malay & Chinese noodle & soup staples. **$$–$$$**

✕ **Vanda Restaurant** [138 D3] See above for details. A popular suburban Chinese at the Orchid Garden Hotel, 3km from CBD. **$$–$$$**

Seafood

✕ **The Pantai** [138 D1] Empire Hotel & Country Club, Muara Tutong Highway, Jerudong; ☎ 2418888; ⊕ evenings only. Very popular, breezy beachside seafood buffet & BBQ, 20mins from the city. $$$–$$$$

✗ **RMS Portview** [143 B3] Block H, Yayasan Shopping Complex; ✆231465. Mix of Western (burgers) & seafood, River-lapping location. $$$

Indian

✗ **Zaika** [143 B3] G24 Block C, Yayasan Complex; ✆2231155; ⊕ 11.00–14.00 & 18.00–22.00 daily. For Indian delicacies in the city centre, reputedly excellent, stylishly antiquated décor. $$–$$$

✗ **Popular Restaurant** [143 A2] Ground Floor, Seri Complex, Mile 1, Jln Tutong; ✆2221375; ⊕ 08.00–22.00 daily. Quality Indian savouries & sweets, samosa, *vadai* & many vegetarian dishes. Finish with the Indian twist on Malaysia's favourite tea, *the-tarek halia* (ginger-pulled tea). Cash only. $$

Japanese

✗ **Takara** [139 B5] Ground Floor, Centrepoint, Gadong; ✆2450180; ⊕ 11.00–14.00 & 18.00–22.00 daily. Established Japanese restaurant with a Teppanyaki kitchen – seafood, meat & vegetables grilled by the chef on large steel hotplate before you. $$$

✗ **Escapade Sushi** [139 B6] Ground Floor, Block A, Q-lap Complex, Kiulap; ✆2234012;

⊕ 11.00–22.00 daily. Sushi-train restaurant – fast but high-quality Japanese food. $$

Italian

✗ **Fratini's Restaurant** [143 B3] Yayasan Complex, BSB; ✆2232555; ⊕ 10.30–22.30 daily. Brunei does very average Italian food, but the upper balcony of this franchise Italian restaurant overlooks the Sungai Brunei, offering river-soaked ambience. Another branch is located at Centrepoint, Gadong (✆*2451200*). $$$

✗ **Spaghettini** [138 D1] Empire Hotel & Country Club, 6th Floor, Lobby Building, Jerudong; ✆2418888; ⊕ 18.00–22.00 daily. A tiny place serving Italian food. $$$

Western

✗ **Deals** [143 B2] Radisson Hotel (see above); ⊕ 12.00–14.00 & 19.30–21.30 daily, 19.30–21.30 public holidays. Fine dining restaurant with soft lights, nice décor, business lunch or formal dinner. $$$$

✗ **Atrium Café** Empire Hotel & Country Club, Tutong Muara Highway, Jerudong; ✆2418858; ⊕ 06.30–22.30 daily. An impressive buffet spread & sublime location with floor-to-ceiling glass windows looking over the sea from up high. Alongside the

BRUNEIAN FEAST

Some Malay specialities are still sold from people's homes – you knock on the door to place your order, which is how *nasi katok*, 'knock rice', gets its name. Served in a cone of waxed brown paper and topped with a bit of fried chicken, beef or egg, and spicy sauce, it is the snack specialty à la Brunei. The famous *ambuyat* is a bowl of sago paste served with a variety of foods including beef jerky strips, fried fish, vegetable pickles, bamboo shoots, mango and chilli preserves. You can also eat these side dishes with rice if you prefer. For dessert, *kueh wajid* (pounded Temburong hill rice) is slow-cooked in palm sugar and coconut cream then wrapped in banana leaves and steamed until the sugar caramelises. Bruneians love their biscuits and cakes, collectively known as *kueh* or *kuih*. Green pandan-flavoured crêpes (*kueh gulung*) are filled with coconut and palm sugar. Every morning at Jing Chew, Bandar's oldest coffee shop, they serve fresh-baked egg buns, toasted and spread with coconut jam (*kaya*).

Each district of Brunei has its specialities, closely linked with agriculture. Tutong's savoury signature, *pulut panggang*, is grilled rolls of glutinous rice filled with shrimp or beef. *Chendol Temburong*, is a dessert-drink made from droplets of green bean flour mixed with palm sugar, with or without coconut milk.

rotating buffet of international, Malay & Indian specialities, there is a menu with local & Western dishes. $$$–$$$$

✗ Manjaro [139 C6] B1, Shakirin Complex, Kiulap; ✆ 2236493. A chic, banqueted restaurant with an eclectic lounge-lit atmosphere. Western & fusion food of the likes of 'Jumbo Combo's' with buffalo wings, fish fillets & coconut prawn fritters, deep-fried chicken wantons, & aromatic peppered tenderloins. Late-evening crowd move towards the boudoir-style upstairs salon for house music. $$$–$$$$

✗ Tasek Brasserie [143 B2] Radisson Hotel (see above); ✆ 2244272; ⏱ 18.30–22.00 daily. Warm, woody setting & poolside eating. Excellent range of seafood & meats. BBQ evenings & good salad buffet. $$$

Market and street food Two of the most animated food markets are the Kianggeh market (pasar Kianggeh) and the Gadong night market (pasar Gadong). Held near the riverside along Jalan Residency, the **Kianggeh market** [143 D2] is a vestige of rural life in the city centre. Many of the *gerai makan* (food stalls) here are family-run, opening from around 15.30 and running through until late; a couple remain open all night. They serve satays and soups, noodle and rice dishes, fresh coconut juice and *ketupat* – origami-like pouches of rice wrapped in coconut palm or *padan* leaves, served with peanut satay sauce.

The renowned **Gadong market** [139 B5] is a food-only, night-time affair – an outdoor eating theatre with the best range of food stalls in the city. The several dozen stalls fire up from 17.00 until midnight. Held in a vast parking lot near the 'wet market' in the Gadong District, it is one of the best *pasar malam* (night markets) in the whole of Sarawak, Sabah and Brunei. Meticulously packaged portions of rice wrapped in banana leaves are a market mainstay; the trays of pyramid and finger-shaped *nasi lemak* contain rice filled with chicken, beef or anchovies and topped with spicy *sambal* sauce. *Nasi katok* is another popular rice dish (see box opposite).

For those staying in the city centre, the **Taman Selera** [143 B2] (⏱ *17.00–as late as 02.00*) is an excellent night-time, food stall area. Set in a large car park zone between Jalan Tasek Lama and Jalan Kumbang Pasang, opposite the Radisson Hotel, the name literally means 'appetite park'. While it lacks the overall ambience of Gadong, some of the food is still very good, and the market is a godsend in this rather uneventful and dining-deprived zone. The **Bob U Me** stall [143 B2] is recommended for fresh seafood, cooked before your eyes, whichever way you like it.

As far as shopping-centre food courts go, the **Padian Food Court** [143 B3] in the city centre area – in the riverfront Yayasan complex – serves chicken, rice, *laksa*, Indian and Western food. In Gadong, there are two food courts – one on the ground-floor **Centrepoint Food Court** [139 B5], the other on the top floor of the more upmarket shopping centre, **The Mall** [139 B5]. Fast food is on the rise and the big international and domestic names – KFC, Pizza Hut, McDonald's, Sugar Bun and Jollibee – all have outlets in the city and at Jerudong Park. But why eat foreign fast food, when you can have *nasi katok* around the clock from the many coffee shops and stalls?

Cafés There are **Coffee Bean & Tea Leaf** outlets on the ground floor of the Bangunan Maya Puri Building on Jalan Sultan (corner of Jln Permancha) [143 B2], downtown Bandar Seri Begawan [143 B2] and at Centrepoint, Gadong [139 B5]. A 24-hour meeting place, **De Royalle Café** [143 B2] (*ground floor of the Bangunan Haji Ahmad Bldg, 38 Jalan Sultan*), is run by a veteran journalist and serves Illy espresso. In Gadong, **Chill Cafe** [139 B5] is at The Mall, while the **Coffee Zone** [139 B5], near Centrepoint, serves espresso drinks and decent light food.

ENTERTAINMENT AND NIGHTLIFE In a place where there are no bars, where alcohol is banned and public transport ends at 18.00, you could be forgiven for assuming the nightlife is non-existent. Though not exactly the life and soul of the party, Brunei's capital has plenty to offer, especially in the way of family fun and theme-park entertainment.

The **Jerudong Park Playground and Gardens** [138 E1] (*Muara-Tutong Highway, 20mins from the city;* ⊕ *17.00–24.00 Wed–Fri, 17.00–02.00 Sat, 16.00–24.00 Sun & pub hols; 1BND, day ticket 15BND adults, 5BND children; bus No 55*) is the Sultanate's take on Disney, with 57 acres of gilt-lined roller coasters and marbled fun for everyone – 'including members of the Royal Family!' states the brochure. Despite the marble excess, the playground is reportedly a bit lacklustre (like many other faded urban theme parks of the world), but the night-time atmosphere is still lots of fun.

FESTIVALS Food plays the leading role in Brunei's festivals. Celebrated festivals include the **Chinese Lunar New Year** in late January and the month-long **Ramadan** (mid-September to mid-October) when government offices close for the day at 14.00 and food markets spring into action all over the city (See *Chapter 3*, page 112).

SHOPPING It may not be obvious that you are in a tax-free country, as the savings are pretty much offset by higher living costs compared with most of Asia. Still, there are savings to be had, with zero tax on clothes, food and (non-alcoholic) beverages; 5% tax on watches, jewellery, cosmetics, cameras, electrical equipment, furniture, photographic materials and electronics; and 20% tax on vehicles and car accessories.

Cultural buys Brunei's riches are revealed in its 'handicrafts' – not just beads and basketry, but silverware, brass artefacts (such as cannons), and most famously, the intricately designed brocades called *kain tenunan*, hand-woven with silver and gold threads. The gold thread is imported from Japan but the fabric is woven in Brunei: costing 500–600BND a yard it makes for quite an expensive sarong!

The riverside **Arts and Handicrafts Centre** on Jalan Residency may be an expensive place to purchase artefacts and fine handicraft items, but it is well worth a visit. For more affordable handicrafts and traditional souvenirs, head to the markets. At the **Tamu Kianggeh** [143 D3] (*in the city centre*), you can buy a keepsake *tudung dulang* – the decorative rattan food covers – or take home machete-like *pemarang* (though you may have trouble getting this through customs, depending on your country's particular rules). Many traditional handicrafts are made from bamboo, rattan and leaves, and are woven, waved and plaited. The best place to buy them is at city and rural *tamu*. For fabrics, head to Gadong – there are a couple of shops selling batiks, silk and sarongs near the Mall Shopping Arcades. Plant lovers shouldn't miss the **Horticulture Centre** in Kampung Rimba, in the Gadong District. In the further-flung area of Serusop, 'Little India's' shops (*Jln Muara, in the Berakas District*), sell *songkets* in multi-gilded tones and bolts of bright silks. **Serusop** is an off-the-beaten-track shopping hub, and a favourite among foreign workers.

Markets The open-air market, **Kianggeh Tamu** [143 D3], is held every day in the village of Kampung Kianggeh, adjacent to the city centre. The stalls unfurl for half a kilometre along the banks of the Sungai Kianggeh (*off Jln Residency*). Water taxis ply the river waiting for a catch (to take tourists to the Kampung Ayer and around). From morning to evening, you can buy fresh and cooked food, handicrafts and baskets – all the typical things of a rural *tamu*. A 24-hour weekend market is held along Jalan Sultan [143 B2] (⏺ *18.00 Sat–18.00 Sun*). On Friday and Sunday mornings, the Gadong marketplace blooms into a **flower market**, the *pasar bunga* [139 B5] (⏺ *07.00–12.00*).

Shopping centres
The largest shopping complex in Bandar Seri Begawan is the **Yayasan** [143 B3] (*CBD, riverfront*), another sultan-owned business, billed as an 'upmarket array of shops and boutiques'. More serious retail activity is found in the Gadong and the Kiulap commercial districts. **The Mall** [139 B5] in Gadong (*bus Nos 55 & 01*) has a tad more ritz than glitz; it houses over 150 shops, including some international brands and boutiques. The neighbouring **Jaya Centrepoint Hypermarket** [139 B5] is lacklustre in presentation but has lots of cheap buys in jewellery, clothing and food.

Food/supermarkets
The **Utama Grand** [139 B5] superstore on the ground floor of the Gadong Mall is the best supermarket for variety with a smattering of cool international products (Californian teas, Italian coffee, French cheese). **SupaSave** in Gadong has a huge range. The supermarket of the **Hua Ho** [139 B5/143 B3] department store has branches in the Yayasan complex and in Gadong and Kiulap, with fewer imports than the Utama Grand but loads of local and Asian produce. A chain store for food and other goods around Brunei is the **Milimewah.**

OTHER PRACTICALITIES
Post office The General Post Office is located in the CBD on Jalan Elizabeth Dua [143 B2] (⏺ *07.45–16.30 Mon–Thu & Sat, 08.00–11.00 & 14.00–16.00 Fri*). There is also a post office in Muara town.

Internet Internet cafés are not as common in Brunei as they are in Malaysian Borneo. There are a couple of cafés in the city centre (see map, page 143), at the Yayasan complex [143 A3] and the RBA Plaza [143 A3]. There are more around the main shops of the Gadong District, and one in Muara town centre.

Money There are many licensed money exchanges in Bandar Seri Begawan city centre (see map, page 143), one at the airport and one in Gadong, but there are very few elsewhere so make sure you have enough money on you for excursions. The same goes for ATM machines – you will find them in towns, but they are few and far between in rural areas.

Hospital The Raja Isteri Pengiran Anak Saleha (RIPAS) Hospital [139 C7] (☎ *2242424*) is on the corner of Jln Tutong and Haji Hassanal Boliah.

BANDAR SERI BEGAWAN MUST-SEES

Sandra Bloodworth, Area Manager, Royal Brunei Airlines UK

Have you seen the proboscis monkey, been for an early morning walk up the hill behind the Radisson Hotel, sat by the water fountain in the Yayasan shopping mall at 18.00 and watched the sun go down behind the mosque, or had a dinner cruise on the Brunei River? Another great place to watch the sun set is at the Empire Hotel – looking out over the South China Sea.

WHAT TO SEE AND DO A full-day (six-hour) city tour, offered by many tour companies, usually takes in three or four sites, including museums, mosques and markets, plus a river trip to the water village, Kampung Ayer. Brunei Tourism's website (see page 130) has a list of all reputable tour operators, while Freme Holidays (*www.freme.com*) gives a clear idea of overall tour possibilities.

Palaces and parliaments
Built in 1984 at a cost of US$400 million, the **Istana Nurul Iman** [139 B8] – the sultan's home – has 1,788 rooms and stretches over 0.5km along the riverbank, making it the largest residential palace in the world. The Istana (meaning palace) opens once a year to the public at the end of Ramadan, during the Hari Raya Aidilfitri celebrations. Thousand of Bruneians and foreigners queue for hours at its gates to get a peek inside. The open-house times are published in local newspapers, including the *Borneo Bulletin* (English-language) and *Media Permata* (Malay). At other times, the best exterior view of the palace and its 300-acre grounds is from a boat on the Sungai Brunei. On a night cruise, you will see it lit up like a true fairy-tale palace, thanks to some 55,000 light bulbs (the electricity is apparently very cheap, powered by gas turbines). Failing that, you can gaze at it from the public parking lot on Jalan Tutong, or from the adjacent park **Persiaran Damuan** [139 B8] (*Jln Tutong; ⊕ daily; free*). This 1km-long riverbank jogging haven has paved walkways and a series of sculptures by artists from the original six members of the Association of Southeast Asian Nations. The 'ASEAN-6' includes Indonesia, Malaysia, the Philippines, Thailand, Singapore and Brunei Darrusalam.

On a river tour, you also get to see a rather different kind of palace. The **Istana Darussalam** [143 A3] is a modest, mint-coloured wooden home in Kampung Sumbiling – one of the many individual water villages that make up Kampung Ayer. It is here that the sultan's father, the 28th sultan, was born – and where he returned to die.

If Brunei does one day become a democracy, the doors of the **Lapau** (Royal Ceremonial Hall) will probably be thrown open as a monarchical museum piece. For the time being, official permission is required to enter the gold-lined chamber where his majesty was crowned on 1 August 1968. In the same neighbourhood, on Jalan Sungai Kianggeh, is the old **Dewan Majilis** (Legislative Council). The new legislative home is located well away from these city centre landmarks, on Jalan Mabohai in the Berakas governmental district.

Mosques
The most beautiful night-time views in Brunei come from the lights and bulbous forms thrown from its two very distinct mosques. The cream and gold **Sultan Omar Ali Saifuddien Mosque** [143 A2] (*in the CBD, near the Central Bus Station; ⊕ 08.00–12.00, 14.00–15.00 & 17.00–18.00 Sun–Wed*) is the older city mosque, built in 1958. It is a magical apparition of stained glass, Shanghai granite, chandeliers and Italian marble, surrounded by a lagoon on which a replica of the royal barge floats. The mesmerising gold dome contains 3.3 million fragments of Venetian mosaic, over a surface of 520m².

Despite it lacking any historic awe-factor, you will be struck by the opulence and strong sense of Islamic faith at the **Masjid Jame'Asr Hassanal Bolkiah Mosque** [139 B6] (*⊕ 08.00–12.00, 14.00–15.00 & 17.00–18.00 Sun–Wed, & Sat if no official ceremonies; bus No 1 & 22*). Gloriously ornamental, the edifice is a solid statement of the place of Islam in Bruneian life: architectural elements come in 29s. There are 29 golden domes, 29 steps and 29 pillars – the magic number represents the number of sultans that have ruled to date. Built to commemorate the 25th year of the current sultan's reign, it is known as the Kiarong Mosque.

Kampung Ayer (water village) [143 D3] With 30,000 residents, this watery suburbia is actually composed of 28 individual villages, linked up by 8km of stilted walkways. One of the largest floating communities in the world, it has mosques, schools, markets and a fire station. The government has been trying to relocate the people onto land, but they refuse to abandon their spiritual home. Though it has burnt down several times, the origins of the water village pre-date the 16th century, when Italian historian Antonio Pigafetta described it as the 'Venice of the East'. The latest village addition, Kampung Bolkiah, is a high-tech set-up built from fireproof materials, with an eco-sewage system and houses spaced nearly 10m apart. In other words, the exact opposite of its predecessor!

Residents of 'KA' commute to work on a flotilla of water taxis, leaving their cars parked along Jalan Residency in town. To visit Kampung Ayer, you can take a water taxi from several points along Jalan McArthur and Jalan Residency to any location in the village, then walk about; the one-way fare is 1–2BND. Alternatively, you can take a guided tour. For me, the water village is at its most mesmerising at night, viewed from the riverfront, as water taxis whizz past in trails of coloured lights ferrying people home.

River cruises Most local operators (see page 137) offer half-day trips, taking in the main city sights and the water village. Prices start from 50–70BND depending on the market they work with. There are also night-time cruises on the river.

Museums All the leading museums are located in the Muara District, outside the CBD. During Ramadan, museum opening hours are usually shorter, closing at around 15.00 rather than 17.00.

The most interesting from a historical point of view is the **Brunei Museum** [139 F7] (*Jln Kota Batu;* ✆ *2244545; www.museums.gov.bn/bangunan.htm;* ⊕ *09.30–17.00 Sat–Thu, 09.00–11.30 & 14.30–17.00 Fri; free; bus No 39*) with its bronze and brass artefacts, Chinese ceramics, jewellery and natural history displays, and chronicle of the oil industry. A real highlight is the Islamic art gallery, which contains exquisite jewellery and tapestries from around the world from the sultan's private collection, dating from the 10th and 11th centuries. In a lovely, leafy riverside location just out of town, the museum is situated on an archaeological site in **Kota Batu** where Brunei's former settlements are still being unearthed. Ceramics and coins from the Tang dynasty have been found here. Nearby is the tomb of Brunei's fifth Islamic monarch, Sultan Bolkiah, who ruled from 1473–1521.

KAMPUNG OR KAMPONG?

Between Brunei and Malaysian Borneo, expect constant variations in the spelling of *kampung* and *kampong*, both of which mean 'village'.

It's one of the maddeningly erratic things about Borneo – spelling discrepancies boil down to more than different dialects; they even occur within the same states and regions. Moreover, the spelling of an administrative entity, food or cultural dance can vary three times within as many pages of the same brochure and it is impossible to tell which instance is the correct version. Is it *kueh* (cakes) or *kuih*? *Chendol* or *chendul*? Once you get used to the frequent discrepancies, you can start ignoring them and appreciate the charm of such a fluid language.

The **Malay Technology Museum** [139 F7] (*Jln Kota Batu, opposite the Brunei Museum;* ✆ *2244545;* ⏱ *09.30–17.00 Sat–Thu, 09.00–11.30 & 14.30–17.00 Fri; free; bus No 39*) uses rather unrealistic dummies in its exhibits – natives in their primitive Kampung Ayer stilt houses and Iban tribespeople in their longhouses. Nevertheless, it provides a fascinating insight into ancient housing and water-village cottage industries, including boatmaking technology, goldsmithing and fishing.

Celebrity attracts, and the **Royal Regalia Museum** [143 B2] (*Jln Sultan;* ✆ *2238358;* ⏱ *09.30–16.30 Sat–Thu, 09.00–11.30 & 14.30–16.30 Fri; free*) is Bandar Seri Begawan's most visited museum. It puts on show the insignia, pomp and privileges relating to the stronghold sultanate, with a particular focus on the coronation of the present sultan in 1968. The large collection of artefacts includes royal family photographs, a replica of the throne from the royal palace, ceremonial armoury, the crown jewels, costumes and gold and silver chariots.

The oldest surviving colonial building in Brunei, **Bubongan Duabelas** [139 F7] (*Jln Residency;* ✆ *2244181;* ⏱ *09.00–16.30 Mon–Thu, 09.00–11.30 & 14.30–16.30 Fri*) is a timber house with a dozen peaked canopies (it's name literally means the 'house of 12 roofs'), balustraded porches and wide roof overhangs. Built in 1906, it was once home to the British Resident and British High Commissioner of Brunei.

Back closer to town is the **Arts and Handicrafts Centre** [143 D4] (*Jln Residency;* ✆ *2240676;* ⏱ *08.00–17.00 daily; free*), which conducts classes in making *songkoks* (traditional caps), weaving, woodwork, basketry and other age-old local skills, whilst revealing some of the cultural history of Brunei.

Urban reserves The major inner-city nature reserve is the **Tasek Lama Recreational Park** [143 C1] (*Jln Tasek Lama, about 2km north of the riverfront; Bus Circle Line*), a protected pocket of urban rainforest with waterfall and lakes. On Jalan Residency, the hilly **Bukit Subok Recreational Park** [139 E7] (⏱ *07.45–18.00 daily; free*) is a more centrally located green oasis with views of the river and Kampung Ayer.

EXCURSIONS FROM BANDAR SERI BEGAWAN

Most other destinations in Brunei (and there are only two or three) are best done as day trips from the capital, or at a stretch with an overnight stay. Outside of the capital, the number of quality accommodations can be counted on one hand. Thankfully, the short distances involved make day trips possible, but this does not mean you should rule out immersing yourself in beautiful Ulu Temburong National Park, or the oil district, for a night or two.

ISLANDS AND RESERVES If you want to go green for a day, morning or afternoon, several reserves within an hour's drive or boat trip of the capital offer nature trails for hiking and biking and picnicking spots.

Bukit Shahbandar (*15km from Bandar, along the Muara–Tutong Highway;* ⏱ *07.45–18.00 daily; free*) A 70ha hilly recreational park with a network of well-signed trekking paths, a mountain-bike trail, an observation tower with views over the capital and the Jerudong area, and resident long-tailed macaque monkeys. This is where the Brunei Marathon is held every December.

Wasai Kendal (*off Jln Tutong, the road running by the palace*) Thanks to its waterfall, this is a favourite forest retreat for family outings with its picnic facilities,

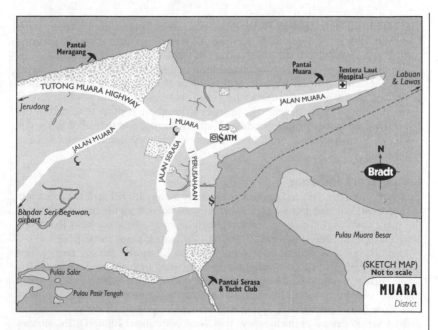

Map labels:
Pantai Meragang
Pantai Muara
Tentera Laut Hospital
Labuan & Lawas
TUTONG MUARA HIGHWAY
JALAN MUARA
Jerudong
J MUARA
$ATM
JALAN MUARA
JALAN SERASA
PERUSAHAAN
N
Bradt
Bandar Seri Begawan, airport
Pulau Muara Besar
Pulau Salar
Pulau Pasir Tengah
Pantai Serasa & Yacht Club
(SKETCH MAP) Not to scale
MUARA District

trails, tropical flora and easy trekking. It is within 20 minutes' drive south of the capital, in Brunei Muara.

Pulau Selirong (Mosquito Island) A small mangrove-forested island with a plankwalk through tropical forest (a half-day tour). It's a 45-minute boat ride away from Bandar Seri Begawan, off Brunei Bay.

LEISURE AND SPORTS CENTRE
Hassanal Bolkiah National Stadium (*5km from city centre;* ⊕ *08.00–12.00 & 13.30–16.30 daily*) The Hassanal Bolkiah sports stadium in Berakas was built in 1999 for the SEA Games. It includes a high-tech sports medicine and research centre, indoor and outdoor stadium, an international swimming complex and track-and-field training facilities. A swimming pool and squash and tennis courts are open to the public.

BEACHES AND WATERSPORTS Situated to the north of Bandar Seri Begawan, the Muara District is the most popular urban beach escape.

Pantai Serasa Beach (*off Jln Serasa; bus No 33, Eastern Line*) A ten-minute drive from the CBD, Pantai Serasa is home to the Royal Brunei Yacht Club, the Royal Brunei National Windsurfing Association and the Serasa Water Sports Complex, so you can come here to sail, windsurf, kayak and water-ski, or just hang out. It's also frequented by those who like fishing – not just men, but women too.

Pantai Muara Beach (*off Jln Serasa; bus No 33, Eastern Line*) Some 27km from the city, the beach has a long waterfront esplanade with picnic, playground and toilet facilities. Of a weekend, plenty of food and drink stalls set up around the headland. Bus No 57 heads northwest to Pantai Jerudong Beach, where there are watersports, as well as seafood and other food stalls.

ULU TEMBURONG NATIONAL PARK Referred to as the 'green jewel', the 50,000ha rainforest within the huge Batu Apoi Forest Reserve is Brunei's only national park. The park spills into the 'Heart of Borneo' conservation area, which sweeps in central forests of Sabah, Sarawak and Kalimantan (see *Natural History*, pages 63–5). The Temburong District, in northern Brunei, is a major rice-growing area, producing nearly half the country's harvest. It is home to a multi-ethnic mix of Iban, Murut and Malay people. The journey to get there is more than half of the fun – the boat speeds through wide bays and mangrove forests full of proboscis monkeys, then trespasses briefly on Malaysian territory before swinging back into Brunei.

Getting there and away

By boat From Bandar Seri Begawan, the journey to the national park requires a mix of speedboat, longboat and road transport. Express boats from the capital to Bangar, the main town in Temburong, leave regularly from the jetty on Jalan Residency between approximately 07.00 and 17.00. The 45-minute journey costs 7MYR.

From Bangar a vehicle transfer is necessary to **Kampung Batang Duri** where local Ibans navigate the 30–40-minute trip to the park in a *temuai* (longboat). The whole trip can be completed within a couple of hours, depending on water levels in the river, and the smoothness (or not) of negotiating more than a dozen rapids. A cost-efficient and comfortable option is to book the trip through a tour operator in Bandar Seri Begawan, as the longboat trip alone costs about 100BND. The various tours offered range from day trips to overnight stays, with park accommodation.

By car If you opt for self-drive, you can continue as far as Batang Duri, then proceed upriver to the park.

Tours to Temburong A day tour from Bandar Seri Begawan to the park, including all transport, a longhouse visit and lunch (adult 170BND, child 128BND), is available with **Sunshine Borneo Tours and Travel** and with **Freme**. Count on double that price for an overnight stay at a park chalet. **Intrepid Travel** are good for groups and adventure tours; they do specialised rafting trips to Temburong, and say the Grade I–II rapids are ideal for beginners. Some of the operators offer student discounts.

See *Local tour operators*, page 137, for contact details for the companies listed above.

🏠 **Where to stay and eat** The big news in Temburong has been the 2010 opening of the **Ulu Ulu Resort** (❨ *2441791/2446812*, e *sales@uluuluresort.com; www. uluuluresort.com*). Some 45 minutes by boat from Temburong town, the 17 villas and suites of the Malay-style wooden eco-lodge have bright contemporary touches, air conditioning and fans, and there is a restaurant. Contact them direct to organise day and overnight tours (starting at 270BND for the latter), or go through one of the main Brunei tour agencies.

The traditional national park lodgings and the information centre are operated by the Forestry Department, and consist of a 'hostel' (a few bunk rooms), some self-contained chalets (sleeping 2–4, with basic cooking facilities & shower), and a campsite. Connected by a boardwalk through the forest, and along the riverbank, some rooms are over 500m from the arrival jetty. Lights (generator-powered) go off at 22.00. There is a canteen but it is not always open, so pack some food. The insect sounds and isolation at night are an incredible experience. There is no online booking system in place; it is best to either go through a tour operator in Bandar Seri Begawan or contact Temburong Tourist Information Centre (*13/14 Kedai Rakyat Jati;* ✆ *5221439*) for further information on how to get to the park, general lodgings and touring.

Outward Bound Brunei Darussalam (OBBD) (*www.outward-bound.org*) operate in the Temburong National Park rainforest and there are opportunities for education groups and activities. Several *kedai* along the main street of Bangar serve Chinese, Malay and Indian food. If you are heading for the park, stock up here as it's your last chance.

What to see and do Bangar consists of the river jetty area and two or three streets. There is a daily market with fruit and other fresh produce, from wild ferns and bamboo shoots to handicrafts. There are some Iban longhouses in the area – if you want to visit for a traditional dance show, book through the Temburong Tourist Information Centre or request it as part of a day tour from Bandar Seri Bagawan.

The **Bukit Patoi Recreational Park** is 15km from Bangar in Kampung Labu. A 2½-hour trek takes in rainforest and waterfalls and every September the hilly area is the site of an International Challenge Run (15km).

Only reached by a river trip, the park headquarters are situated in a big rainforest buffer zone at the confluence of the Sungai Temburong and Sungai Belalong rivers. The deep forest of the 'Heart of Borneo' is an extremely peaceful place where the evening conversation of cicadas and insects will drill through your hut walls. The variety of life is incredible; one entomologist discovered over 400 species of beetle on a single tree here.

By day you can bathe in the river, kayak and hike. The park has 7km of well-marked elevated boardwalks, with in-depth, intelligent and finely illustrated botanical interpretation. The Temburong **canopy walk** is an out-of-this-world, 250m-high stainless-steel pathway in the sky, built with funds from the sultan-owned Shell oil company. Reached after a 2km upwards trek from park HQ, the structure has five ladders, interconnected by metal bridges, which take you to progressively greater, king-and-queen-of-the-jungle heights. Don't let minor panic stop you from enjoying the breathtaking views, and forest-top immersion. Best experienced early morning, possible wildlife encounters along the way include Bornean gibbons, macaques, civets, sun bears, pit vipers, hornbills and Rajah Brooke's birdwing butterflies. On the return journey, take the standard jungle trail for an off-boardwalk real forest experience.

The Kuala Belalong Field Studies Centre On the way up the river to park HQ, you will pass an attractive building set into the rainforest – a series of dark timber houses with pike roofs and swerving balustrades; at night it glows like a beetle on stilts. The rainforest research base, run by the Universiti Brunei Darussalam, is an important centre for rainforest studies and it is not uncommon to bump into visiting scientists at night at park HQ further upstream. Researchers and students can enquire about studying here via the university's biology department (✆ *2463001;* e *kbfsc@ubd.edu.bn*).

TUTONG AND BELAIT DISTRICTS The Tutong District is largely rural with hillier rainforest and lake reserves inland, with some longhouse territory bringing together people from the Dusun, Iban, Kedayan and Tutong tribes. Further south is the Belait District and Brunei's oil coast, centring on the towns of Seria and Kuala Belait.

4

Getting there and away

By car There are two roads heading to the Tutong and Belait districts – the coastal Muara–Tutong Highway and an inland route along the old road Jalan Tutong. From Seria to Kuala Belait (17km), the fast route is via the Seria bypass. The longer coastal road passes the Istana Manggelela, the sultan's residence during his visits to town. The road leads to the Sungai Belait River, where there is a ferry to the village of Kampung Sungai Teraban. Coming from Sarawak you can arrive in Kuala Belait via the Sungai Tujuh checkpoint. Kuala Belait is about 90km from the capital, and 30km from Miri in Sarawak.

By bus There are hourly bus services between the main bus terminal in Bandar Seri Begawan (Jln Cator) and Seria – tickets are about 6BND. Local buses travel between Seria and Kuala Belait – the 30km journey costs 1BND. The Miri-Belait Bus Company runs five daily services between Miri's Jln Padang bus terminal in Sarawak and Kuala Belait, with a change of bus at the Sungai Tujuh border checkpoint.

🏠 Where to stay

🏠 **Plaza Sutera Biru** (21 rooms) Lot 73, Jln Sungai, Kuala Belait; ✆3347268; e info@psb. com.bn; www.psb.com.bn. The upmarket niche on the oil coast was filled in 2007 with this non-smoking hotel by the Belait River, 16km from Seria & 50km from Miri. High-tech, aesthetic rooms & kitchenette-equipped suites spread over 6 floors, with slim TVs, smart keys & AC. Sports Café specialises in northern Chinese cuisine. **$$$$–$$$$$**

🏠 **Riviera Hotel** (30 rooms) Lot 106, Jln Sungai, Kuala Belait; ✆3335252. Well-fitted standard & de luxe rooms, AC, satellite TV, Shahryza Restaurant (⏰ 07.00–23.00), 3–4-star. Both this & the following hotel send clients on to nearby Harun's Gym for a workout (in DBB Bank). **$$$**

🏠 **Sentosa Hotel** (36 rooms) 92–93 Jln McKerron, Kuala Belait; ✆3334341/2; e enquiry@bruneisentosahotel.com; www. bruneisentosahotel.com. AC, satellite TV, broadband internet, non-smoking rooms, mini fridge & safety-deposit box. The Syazana Café has good Malay & Indian food (⏰ 06.00–23.00). Recommended. **$$$**

🏠 **Halim Plaza Hotel** Lot 9003, Kampung Petani, Mukim Pekan Tutong; ✆4260688; e halim_plaza_hotel@hotmail.com; www. onebrunei.com. Located 30mins from Bandar Seri Begawan, a riverside plaza hotel dealing in weddings & banquets. Well furnished though frilly decorated rooms & suites. Serviced apartments, café, restaurant & shops. **$$**

✗ Where to eat

For a district population of just 60,000, there is a good selection of restaurants in Kuala Belait. There are daily fish, fruit and vegetable markets with many food stalls set up along the riverbanks and around town, as well as the usual Malay and Chinese dishes – noodles, *laksa* and spicy prawns – served in several coffee shops. The **Buccaneer Steakhouse** (*Lot 94 Jln McKerron;* ✆ *3334553*) is recommended by Western meat-eaters and **Jolene Restaurant** (*Lot 83, 1st Floor, Jln Bunga Raya*) has good, though relatively expensive, Chinese food – clay-pot dishes, prawns and noodles. **Zaika Restaurant** (*Lot 308, Bangunan Maju, Jalan Bunga Raya;* ✆ *3347340*) has good northern Indian food such as chicken tikka masala in a wooden-tabled, warmly lit, restful setting. Some locals refer to the **Orchid Room** (*83 Jalan Pretty, corner Jln Bunga Raya;* ✆ *3334650*) as the 'grand dame' of town, because the family-run restaurant has been open since 1967. With rather gaudy décor and walls of photos, it serves a mix of Thai, Chinese and Western dishes at mid- to upper-range prices, though there is a very good value three-course set lunch Monday–Friday for under 10BND.

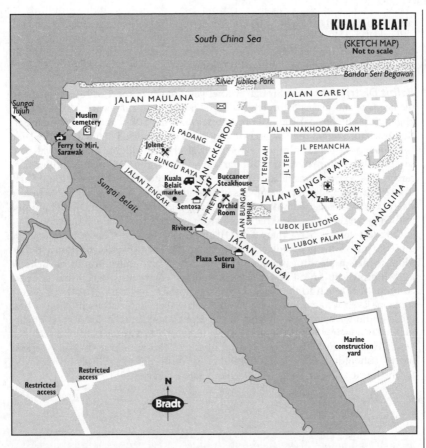

South China Sea

Bandar Seri Begawan

Silver Jubilee Park

JALAN MAULANA

JALAN CAREY

Sungai Tujuh

Muslim cemetery

Ferry to Miri, Sarawak

JL PADADG

JALAN NAKHODA BUGAM

JALAN McKERRON

JL PEMANCHA

JALAN TENGAH

JL TENGAH

JL TEPI

Sungai Belait

JL BUNGU RAYA

Jolene

Kuala Belait market

Buccaneer Steakhouse

JALAN BUNGA RAYA

Sentosa

JL PRETTY

Orchid Room

JALAN BUNGAR SIMPUR

Zaika

Riviera

LUBOK JELUTONG

JALAN PANGLIMA

JALAN SUNGAI

JL LUBOK PALAM

Plaza Sutera Biru

Marine construction yard

Restricted access

Restricted access

N

Bradt

What to see and do The following interesting locations are listed in approximate ascending order if you were driving from Bandar Seri Begawan to Kuala Belait.

Tutong District Barely 40km from the capital, the town of Tutong (also known as Kuala Tutong) lies among coconut palms near the Tutong River. *Kuala*, by the way, means 'river mouth' and has nothing to do with Australian marsupials. There are several *kampung* named Kuala along Brunei's estuary-specked coast. The **Tamu Tutong Kampung Serambagun** is a daily open-air market held 1km from the town centre, selling lots of local fruits, vegetables and handicrafts. Many vendors come from the rural hinterland to buy and sell their produce.

Pantai Seri Kenangan – 'the unforgettable beach' – is a popular recreation spot (fishing, swimming, picnics) five minutes' drive from Kuala Tutong town. Located on a narrow spit of land between the South China Sea and the Tutong River, it has beach chalets, picnic pavilions, restaurant and food stalls. From here, you can also take a trip on the Sungai Tutong.

Situated 27km inland, **Tasek Merimbun**, a serpentine, freshwater lake surrounded by peat swamp and grass marsh, is a wildlife sanctuary, research station and recreational centre. Proclaimed an ASEAN (Association of Southeast Asian Nations) Heritage Park in 1984, some say it is the de facto first national park, though it is not a gazetted one. There is an island in the centre of the lake for picnics, and a trail through the forest. Resident fauna includes the clouded leopard, white-collared fruit bat, Bornean gibbon, giant squirrel, silver leaf monkey, pig-tailed macaque, sambar deer, honey bear, western tarsier, argus pheasant, hornbill, purple heron, pangolin and reticulated python.

Belait District Driving through Brunei you are never short of recreational and picnic spots and places to stretch the legs. On the coast side of the Muara Tutong Highway is the **Sungai Liang Forest Reserve**, some 70km south of Bandar Seri Begawan (turn left at the Sungai Liang junction and proceed 450m along the Jalan Labi road to the park's entrance on the right). Here you will find a canopy walk and several other well-marked trails of varying grades through lowland rainforest. A further 25km or so along Jalan Labi is the **Luagan Lalak Forest Recreational Park**, whose alluvial freshwater swamp fills up like a lake in the wet season. From here, a steep 2km trek leads to the **Wasai Wong Kadir** waterfall. The Labi District is home to Iban people and there are chances to visit their longhouses along the way.

Oil coast starts in Seria: there is an **Oil and Gas Discovery Centre**, an interactive museum of oil history and technology, and the hard-to-miss **Billionth Barrel Monument** – a blend of Islamic tiles with industrial architecture. Kuala Belait is a town grown up on oil and a foreign workers' community, which has added a cosmopolitan touch to the place. Loved by expats, it has a bit of an R&B edge – someone even wrote a love song about Kuala Belait. Entertainment choices beat those found anywhere else outside of the capital, and locals enjoy a good quality of life. For jogging and family recreation, they head to **Pantai Lumut**, a secluded beach 10km from Seria off the coastal highway. Those looking for some serious partying should do as the locals do, and cross the border to the lively town of Miri for the weekend (see *Chapter 12, Northern Sarawak*, page 295).

Part Three

SABAH

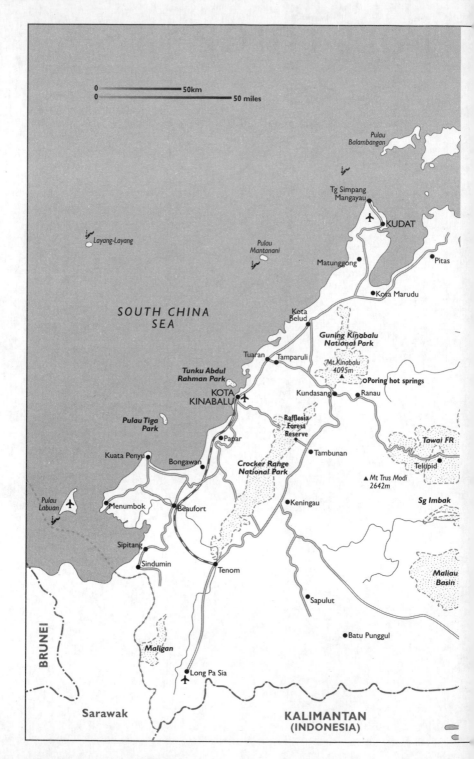

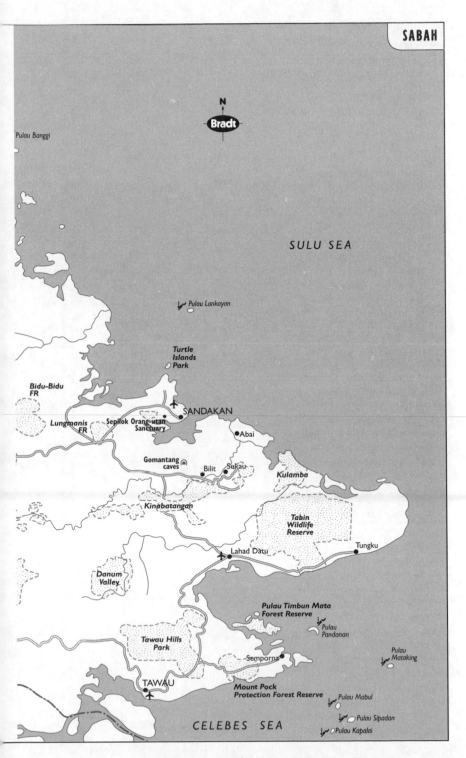

SABAH

N

Bradt

Pulau Banggi

SULU SEA

Pulau Lankayan

Turtle
Islands
Park

Bidu-Bidu
FR

Lungmanis
FR

Sepilok Orang-utan
Sanctuary

SANDAKAN

Abai

Gomantang
caves

Bilit   Sakau

Kulamba

Kinabatangan

Tabin
Wildlife
Reserve

Tungku

Lahad Datu

Danum
Valley

Pulau Timbun Mata
Forest Reserve

Pulau
Pandanan

Tawau Hills
Park

Pulau
Mataking

Semporna

TAWAU

Mount Pock
Protection Forest Reserve

Pulau Mabul

Pulau Sipadan

Pulau Kapalai

CELEBES   SEA

SABAH AT A GLANCE

Telephone area code +608

Currency Malaysian ringgit (MYR)

Exchange rate US$1 = 3MYR, €1 = 4MYR, £1 = 4.8MYR (May 2012)

Climate Humid; average daily temperature lowlands 30°C, highlands 22°C

Geography 76115 km^2, northern Borneo

Population 3.2million; approximately 17.5% Kadazan Dusun, 13% Bajau, 12% Malay, 9.5% Chinese, 14% from other indigenous tribes, 5% Indian & others. One-quarter of the population foreigners (non-citizens).

Capital Kota Kinabalu (KK)

Visa requirements Visa-free 3-month stay for most nationalities; see details *Chapter 3*, pages 79–80

Language Official language Malay (*Bahasa Melayu*); Chinese and Kadazan common community languages. English widely spoken.

Emergency numbers 999 for police, fire and ambulance

Banking hours 09.30–15.00 Mon–Fri

Business hours 08.00–13.00 & 14.00–17.00 Mon–Fri, 08.00–13.00 Sat

Shopping centre hours 10.00–22.00 daily

Government website www.sabah.gov.my

Tourist board 51 Gaya Street, Kota Kinabalu; +6088 21212; e info@sabahtourism.com; www.sabahtourism.com

5

Kota Kinabalu

Emerald bays, islands and a backdrop of lush, low-lying hills … the coastal city of Kota ('fort') Kinabalu may be an architectural hotchpotch, but the sea setting is sublime. Among the ramshackle shop-lots and piecemeal development sites, it has a palpable resort atmosphere – many locals take to the water after work and on weekends, enjoying the beach location to the full.

Levelled during World War II, some of its shabbier buildings are gradually being revamped, as mangrove swamps cede to shopping centres. From up on Signal Hill, you can see how 70% of the town centre lies on a narrow belt of land reclaimed from the sea in the 1920s. The Waterfront Esplanade – an animated strip of markets, hotels, seafood eateries, cafés and bars – hugs the city shoreline. Off the coast, colourful cargo vessels fill the bay.

Of the 350,000 residents, 60% are Malay, Kadazandusun and Bajau, 35% are Chinese, 3% are Murut and 1% are Indian; Filipino and Indonesian immigrants make up the remainder. Kota Kinabalu seems to be striving for a futuristic image, akin to that of Kuala Lumpur, though on a much smaller scale. It will never be able to match the Malaysian capital's modernistic superstructures, however, thanks to a seven-storey limit on new constructions, due to low-flying air traffic.

HISTORY

Like the stilted water villages found on the fringes of Kota Kinabalu today, the earliest coastal settlements were those of indigenous people. The first British presence came when the British North Borneo Chartered Company (BNBCC) set up a trading settlement in 1882 on Pulau Gaya, the largest of the five islands across the bay from Kota Kinabalu. Before Europeans arrived, the island was inhabited by the Bajau people. Approval of the foreign administration was far from unanimous – the BNBCC was deemed insensitive to local customs and heavy-handed with taxes. Indigenous rebel, Muhammad Salleh (popularised as Mat Salleh), was a Bajau trader who virulently opposed a controversial tax on rice. In 1897, he and his supporters raided the British settlement on Pulau Gaya and burnt it to the ground. Salleh and some 1,000 followers were killed in a gun battle with the British police a few years later. By then, the BNBCC had restored its headquarters, with a small mainland settlement named Jesselton, in honour of the company's vice chairman Sir Charles Jessel. The town was known to locals as *Api-Api* – 'fire-fire' – apparently because of the frequent fires that blazed in water villages during firecracker-filled celebrations. A less politically correct version says it came from the sight of the BNBCC trading base on Pulau Gaya going up in flames. As is the case with many questions on the history of Malaysian Borneo, answers are few and far between and shed little light on the plausibility of either side of the story. Jesselton was renamed Kota Kinabalu in 1968.

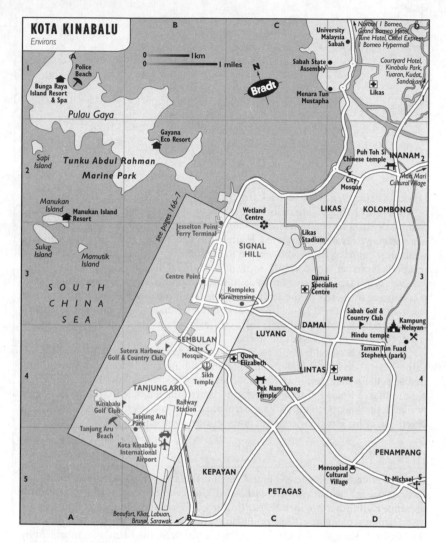

KOTA KINABALU
Environs

0 ———— 1km
0 ———— 1 miles

N

Bradt

Pulau Gaya

Police
Beach

Bunga Raya
Island Resort
& Spa

Sapi
Island

Tunku Abdul Rahman
Marine Park

Gayana
Eco Resort

Manukan
Island   Manukan Island
            Resort

Sulug
Island   Mamutik
            Island

S O U T H

C H I N A

S E A

University
Malaysia
Sabah

Novotel 1 Borneo,
Grand Borneo Hotel,
Tune Hotel, Cittel Express,
1 Borneo Hypermall

Sabah State
Assembly

Courtyard Hotel,
Kinabalu Park,
Tuaran, Kudat,
Sandakan

Menara Tun
Mustapha

Likas

Puh Toh Si
Chinese temple   INANAM

City
Mosque

Mari Mari
Cultural Village

Wetland
Centre

Jesselton Point
Ferry Terminal

Likas
Stadium

LIKAS   **KOLOMBONG**

SIGNAL
HILL

Centre Point

Kompleks
Karamunsing

Damai
Specialist
Centre

Sabah Golf &
Country Club

Kampung
Nelayan

DAMAI   Hindu temple

SEMBULAN   State
               Mosque

LUYANG   Taman Tun Fuad
               Stephens (park)

Sutera Harbour
Golf & Country Club

Sikh
Temple

Queen
Elizabeth

LINTAS   Luyang

TANJUNG ARU

Kinabalu
Golf Club

Tanjung Aru
Park

Pek Nam Thong
Temple

Railway
Station

Tanjung Aru
Beach

Kota Kinabalu
International
Airport

KEPAYAN

Monsopiad
Cultural
Village

PENAMPANG

St Michael

PETAGAS

Beaufort, Klias, Labuan,
Brunei, Sarawak

see pages 166–7

GETTING THERE AND AWAY

BY AIR Kota Kinabalu International Airport (KKIA) (\ *088 238555*) is the major hub for international and domestic flights to Sabah. Perched by the South China Sea, 8km from the city centre, KKIA commands a stunning view over a blue horizon dotted with green islands. A five-year 1 billion MYR renovation project completed in 2009 enhanced floor space, parking, interior design, check-in counters and banking machines, as well as adding a dedicated low-cost terminal. Terminal 1 serves international flights as well as **Malaysia Airlines** domestic flights, while Terminal 2 is home to **AirAsia** and **Fly Asian Express** (FAX). The heavy investments saw little improvement to public services – though there are decent duty-free shops and food outlets, the airport is lacking internet stations, baggage lockers, transport shuttles and a decent individual website, all of which you might expect from Malaysia's second-busiest airport.

Royal Brunei Airlines connects Bandar Seri Begawan and Kota Kinabalu. **Cebu Pacific** operates direct flights between Kota Kinabalu and Manila. **Malaysian Airlines** operates direct international flights between Kota Kinabalu and Perth, Singapore, Seoul, Osaka, Tokyo, Hong Kong, Guangzhou, Taipei and Kaohsiung (Taiwan), as well as domestic flights to Kuala Lumpur. It also flies from Kota Kinabalu to other Borneo destinations, including Sandakan and Tawau and Sibu, Miri and Kuching in Sarawak, as well as to the island of Labuan. **AirAsia** flies direct between Kota Kinabalu and Singapore, Ho Chi Minh City, Jakarta and Clark in the Philippines, and domestically to Kuala Lumpur, Penang and Johor Bahru (the nearest Malaysian city to Singapore). The airline also connects Kota Kinabalu with Sandkan and Tawau and Miri and Kuching.

Many of the hotels have their own transport; if you've booked a package, ensure transits are included. For taxis, buy a coupon in the arrival hall (around 30MYR) before heading out front to catch a cab. You can also catch a minibus to the city from the main road. The taxi fare from a hotel to the airport is generally 30–40MYR.

For information on **visas**, see pages 79–80.

Airlines Many of the airlines have an office in both Kota Kinabalu International Airport (most on Level 2) and in the city. Several of the city offices are located in the Kompleks Kuwasa (*Jln Karamunsing*) and Kompleks Karamunsing commercial centres, in the southern zone.

✈ **AirAsia** Ground Floor, KKIA, Terminal 2, & sales office in Wisma Sabah shopping centre; ✆088 538756/341; www.airasia.com. Book online for the best fares.

✈ **Malaysia Airlines** T1 KKIA (ticketing office); ✆088 260106; first-class check-in ✆088 243617. Also in Kompleks Karamunsing; ✆088 213555

✈ **Royal Brunei Airlines** Ground Floor, Kompleks Kuwasa; ✆088 242193

✈ **Singapore Airlines** Level 2, KKIA; ✆088 219940. Also Ground Floor, Block C, Lot GC 12–13, Kompleks Kuwasa; ✆088 255444

BY CAR There are four main highways in Kota Kinabalu. The Kota Kinabalu–Sandakan Highway (A4) connects the capital to the east coast cities of Sandakan, Lahad Datu, Semporna and Tawau (via Tuaran, Tamparuli, Kundasang, Ranau and Telupid); although it is only 335km, the cross-state trip takes six or seven hours. The Kota Kinabalu–Kudat Highway (A1) heads north up the west coast to the Kudat Peninsula, via Tuaran, Tamparuli, Kota Belud, Kota Marudu and Pitas. The Kota Kinabalu–Sindumin Highway (A2) leads south towards the Brunei border, and on to Sarawak, via Penampang, Papar, Beaufort and Sipitang. The Kota

KOTA KINABALU – REVERED PLACE OF THE CHINESE WIDOW?

Named after the mountain that looms over the city, folklore holds that *Kinabalu* means 'Chinese widow' – *kina* being the Dusunic word for Chinese and *balu* Malay for widow. The story tells of a Chinese prince who came to the mountain in search of a pearl guarded by a dragon at its summit. During his quest, he married a local, but returned to China, leaving her heartbroken.

The Kadazandusun people provide a more spiritual explanation. For them the name means 'revered place of the dead', derived from the term *Aki Nabalu* – *Aki* meaning ancestors or grandfather, and *Nabalu* the mountain's name in Dusun language.

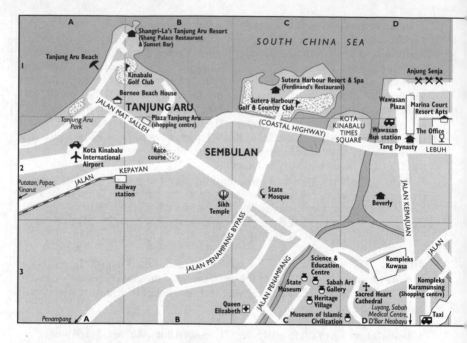

Kinabalu–Nabawan Highway (A3) steers southeast into west coast hinterland, via Penampang, Tambunan, Keningau and Tenom.

Inter-city distances Kota Kinabalu to Mount Gunung Kinabalu National Park 88km; Kota Kinabalu to Kota Belud 75km; Kota Kinabalu to Kota Marudu 131km; Kota Kinabalu to Kudat 190km; Kota Kinabalu to Sandakan approximately 350km; Kota Kinabalu to Semporna 565km; Kota Kinabalu to Sindumin 158km.

BY BOAT There are daily ferry services between Kota Kinabalu and Labuan, and on to Brunei – see *Chapter 4, Getting there and away*, page 136.

GETTING AROUND

ON FOOT The city centre is reasonably compact, though not particularly pedestrian-friendly. The traffic is chaotic; watch out at crossings, as cars tend to fly through them. Poorly lit, lowly frequented areas behind the waterfront are best avoided at night.

BY CAR It is not convenient to have a car in the city centre; the layout is confusing and congested and parking is not easy. For sightseeing further afield, however, a car is very useful. Sabah Tourism (*www.sabahtourism.com*) provides links to all **car-rental** companies state-wide on their website.

🚗 **Adaras Rent-A-Car** Counter at the airport (KKIA); ☏088 211866. Also in the city's Wisma Merdeka shopping centre, Jln Tun Fuad Stephens, Lot G03 Ground Floor; ☏088 222137
🚗 **Extra Rent A Car** Beverly Hotel, Lrg Kemajuan, 2nd Floor; ☏088 218160;

e admin@e-erac-online.com; www.e-erac-online.com
🚗 **Kinabalu Rent A Car** 1st Floor, Kompleks Karamunsing; ☏088 232602; e jose_loh@kinabalurac.com.my; www.kinabalurac.com.my

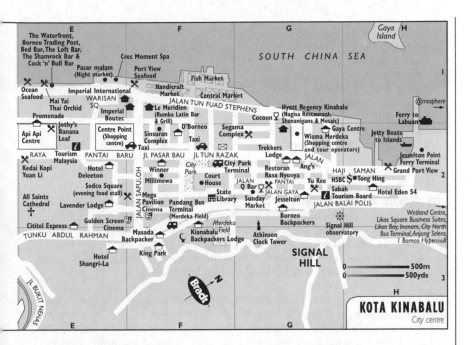

🚗 **KMT Global Rent A Car** Wisma Merdeka, Lot G02 Ground Floor; ☎ 088 223022; e info@ kmtglobalrentacar.com; www.kmtglobalrentacar. com

🚗 **Mayflower Car Rental** Unit D3-3A, 3rd Floor, Block D, Plaza Tanjung Aru, Jln Mat Salleh; ☎ 088 221244; e mcr-kk@mayflower.com.my; www.mayflowrecarrental.com.my. Email & arrange for airport car pick-up.

BY TAXI Taxis are generally cheap and plentiful, though fares vary. Some fares are set, such as the journey from the airport to the city. Expect to pay around 5–10MYR for inner-city trips, and double that at night. Fares can be shared by up to four people in a cab. There are several ranks in the city: opposite the Hyatt Hotel on Jalan Datuk Salleh Sulong [167 G1]; at the post office on Jalan Tun Razak [167 F2]; and outside Centre Point shopping centre on Lebuh Raya Pantai Baru [166 E2]. A long-distance taxi station for trips to places such as Mount Kinabalu is located alongside the long-distance bus station at Padang Merdeka (Merdeka Field) [167 F2].

BY BUS With four different bus terminals, it's not always clear which one you should be using. Drop by Sabah Tourism (see page 168) for an updated list of departure terminals and destinations, schedules and prices.

Wawasan Bus Terminal [166 D2] (*corner Jln Tun Fuad Stephens & Jln Kemajuan*). The main minibus depot is at Wawasan Plaza, at the south end of the waterfront. Buses from here serve the city and outskirts and cost 2–4MYR. This is also where minibuses serving the airport depart and arrive. They leave when all seats are taken, and are marked with a route number, corresponding to destinations listed at the station.

City Park Terminal [167 F2] (*in front of City Hall, on Jalan Pantai*) Buses to and from Wawasan Plaza stop along the waterfront stretch of Jalan Tun Razak, and past the city hall, court house and post office. Mid-distance buses for mostly south-of-the-city destinations such as Beaufort, Kuala Penyu, Sipitang and Menumbok (for Labauan island ferries) also leave from here, as do long-distance coaches for Lawas, Limbang, Brunei and Miri.

Pandang Bus Terminal [167 F2] Also known as the Merdeka Field bus terminal, this chaotic station near the Merdeka sports field (Padang Merdeka), serves Gunung Kinabalu National Park, and southern and northern Sabah. Air-conditioned express buses, minibuses and vans head to Kundasang and Ranau via Gunung Kinabalu National Park, as well as to Papar, Beaufort, Tenom, Keningau and Tambunan. Northern destinations include Tamparuli, Tuaran, Kota Belud, Kota Marudu, Kudat and Pitas.

City North Bus Terminal [167 H3] Located in the northern suburb of Inanam, the city's biggest bus terminal is the hub for long-distance express buses, predominantly to the east coast. Destinations include Sandakan, Lahad Datu, Kunak, Tawau and Semporna. The journey to Sandakan takes about eight hours, passing by Gunung Kinabalu National Park and Ranau. Minibuses link the city with Inanam. Be prepared for ticket hustlers outside this station.

BY RAIL Sabah State Railway operates the only railway in Borneo, a 134km line from Tanjung Aru (just south of Kota Kinabalu) to Tenom. Known by locals as 'the slowest train in the world', it takes four hours to cover 93km. The journey via Papar and Beaufort is more a scenic tourist attraction than a viable means of public transport. Schedules plus a distance/fare grid are available online (*www.sabah.gov. my/railway*). The station is near the airport on Jalan Kepayan [166 A2] and there are four trains each day.

BY BOAT The jetty and ferry terminals lie on the northern edge of the waterfront at Jesselton Point [167 H1]. Boats leave here to the islands of the Tunku Abdul Rahman Marine Park, as well as to Labuan (see page 210). There is a terminal fee for all passengers of 7.20MYR for adults and 3.60MYR for children under 12. Various tickets for one, two, three or four islands cost from 20MYR to 50MYR; about 50% less for children. The trip takes 15–20 minutes, weather dependent – the boarding passes warn passengers to be prepared to get wet 'without complaining'!

TOURIST INFORMATION

i **Sabah Tourism Board & Tourism Information Office** [167 G2] 51 Jln Gaya; ☎088 212121
i **Sabah Tourist Guide Association** [167 G2] (STGA) Lot 128, 1st Floor, Wisma Sabah; ☎088 242990; e sabah_stga@hotmail.com; www.stga.com.my

i **Tourism Malaysia** [167 E2] Sabah office, Lot 107, Ground Floor, Block 1, Lorong Api-Api 1 (in the Api-Api Centre); ☎088 248698; e enquiries@ tourism.gov.my; www.tourism.gov.my

WHERE TO STAY

Jalan Tun Fuad Stephens, which faces the waterfront promenade, is traditionally home to luxury and upmarket hotels, but lately a flourish of very competitively priced boutique budget to mid-range hotels have sprung up here. Shoestring hotels and hostels are concentrated around Jalan Pantai and Jalan Haji Saman. For those who prefer not to stay in the city, but still within easy reach, see the accommodation listings under *Excursions from Kota Kinabalu*, page 181.

HOTELS Kota Kinabalu has many **budget-priced hotels** (see pages 172–3), usually classified locally as one-star. There is so much variation in the price and the quality it is very hard to classify them. Some quite ordinary places have suites at budget prices, and very ordinary rooms at shoestring prices. Other overall better establishments have de luxe rooms at budget prices even though they are more mid range in services and facilities, with coffee shops and restaurants.

Often cheaper still, the **shoestring hotels** are locally classed as no-star 'budget hotels' (see pages 172–3). The best you can hope for in this category will be clean, modern and security-wise, with friendly staff, air conditioning, satellite television, hot showers and fridges. The worst will have cramped, windowless rooms, tepid showers, a fan rather than air conditioning, and be either borderline clean or just plain shabby. Price-wise these rooms mostly cost under 100MYR, though fall as low as 50MYR for a single/double. Some will offer family rooms for 100–150MYR and there is usually the choice of 'upgrading' to a superior room, which may just mean the addition of a bathtub, and a piece of furniture or two. A newcomer is AirAsia's Tune Hotel in the new 1 Borneo commercial zone northeast of the city.

A whole new field of forward-thinking **hostels** has arrived in recent years, edging others out, or to the back of the pack (see page 172). I have included only those I know either first hand or those that come recommended by other travellers. The website www.hostelworld.com provides information on many other hostels; which vary in price from around 20–30MYR for a dorm bed, 60–80MYR for a twin share and 100–150MYR for family quarters. The tariff often includes breakfast, and free Wi-Fi abounds. A hive of hostels is located in the streets between Jalan Gaya, where the Sunday *tamu* market is held, and the base of Signal Hill. One new hostel here worth checking out is **Kinabalu Backpackers** [167 F2] (*Lot 4, Lorong dewan,* \ 088 253385; www.kinabalubackpackers.com).

Luxury

🏠 **Le Meridien** [167 F1] (306 rooms) Sinsuran Complex, Jln Tun Fuad Stephens; \ 088 322222; e reservations.kk@lemeridien.com; www.starwoodhotels.com/lemeridien. Smart, black-uniformed staff, though service can swing from personal to poor. A happening & central location, some rooms have views over the bay & market. There are great deals to be had on the Club Floor; high-speed internet access & Wi-Fi in public areas, if you don't mind the cigarette smoke. $$$$$

🏠 **Shangri-La's Tanjung Aru Resort & Spa** [166 B1] (492 rooms) 20 Jln Aru, Tanjung Aru (3km south of city centre); \ 088 327888; e tah@ shangri-la.com; www.shangri-la.com. Expansive coastal resort with beach, island & mountain views, flourishing gardens, a golf course & sunset bar. A hotel's consistency of quality is largely determined by its general manager, & for several years Australian Andrew Steele has ensured the

sublime location is matched by top-notch facilities, food & service (which frequently rake in *Condé Nast Traveller* & Smarttravelasia.com awards for top Asian resorts). Major room renovations since 2009 have capped off the Kinabalu Wing with an executive lounge for guests in the superior & business-oriented Kinabalu Club rooms, while the sumptuous suites have separate sitting rooms, bedrooms & private, wraparound balconies. Breakfast is a smorgasbord of Malay, Indian, Chinese & European dishes. Lovely breezy lobby area & bar, excellent spa, gym & entertainment facilities. See details of the highly commendable Shang Palace Restaurant in *Where to eat*, below. $$$$$

🏠 **Sutera Harbour** [166 C1] (956 rooms) 1 Sutera Harbour Bd; \ 088 318888; e sutera@ suteraharbour.com.my; www.suteraharbour. com.my. Resort facilities here are second to none, with a private marina, Olympic-size swimming pool, golf course, several restaurants, live entertainment & suites with marble-lined bathrooms & balconies. However, if you don't think size matched with sizzle & style is everything, this might not be your cup of tea. Spread over 150ha, adjacent to the city, the resort has 2 distinct sections – the Pacific Sutera & Magellan Sutera – the first is more business-oriented, the second dedicated to luxury leisure. Between them, there is a plethora of dining choices, from dressy Chinese & Italian restaurants to bright, breezy family-oriented brasseries, pool bars, DJ clubs & lobby lounges. $$$$$

⌂ **Hyatt Regency Kinabalu** [167 G1] (288 rooms) Jln Datuk Salleh Sulong; ☎088 221234; e reservation.hrkinabalu@hyattintl. com; www.kinabalu.regency.hyatt.com. Best location on waterfront, next door to Wisma Merdeka. The large, luxurious rooms have been urbanely renovated. The sea view & club rooms are over 45m², are decked in artwork & beige furnishings & offer access to a private lounge. Good business & meeting facilities, gym & pool, & well-frequented entertainment outlets. Both the Chinese & Japanese restaurants are excellent, see page 174. Great-value deals on booking.com (for example) can result in mid-range prices on upmarket double & club rooms. $$$–$$$$$

Mid range

⌂ **Gaya Centre Hotel** [167 G2] (260 rooms) Jalan Tun Fuad Stephens; ☎088 245567; e reservations@gayacentre.com; www.gayacentre. com. New 3-star hotel with good reviews & in a prime waterfront city location, between banks & shopping centres. Rooms & pricey suites have satellite TV, tea- & coffee-making facilities & complimentary Wi-Fi. $$–$$$$$

⌂ **Novotel 1 Borneo** [164 D1] (263 rooms) 1 Borneo Hypermall, Jalan Sulaman Highway (7km north of Kota Kinabalu); ☎088 529888; e info@novotel1borneo.com; www.novotel. com. Located in Sabah's largest shopping centre, within a 20min drive of the airport, this hotel has spacious rooms starting at budget price deals through to top-dollar luxury suites. Restaurant & bar, high-speed paying internet, spa & meeting facilities for up to 1,200. $$–$$$$$

⌂ **Hotel Shangri-La** [167 E3] (121 rooms) 75 Bandaran Berjaya; ☎088 212800; e enquiries@kkshang.com; www.kkshang.com. my. Nothing to do with the famous Shangri-

La brand, this hotel is upper mid range, with presentation & services to match. Spacious, well-furnished, bright AC rooms, satellite TV, fridge & minibar. Away from the waterfront location, close to shopping kompleks, banks, long-distance bus terminal & restaurants of the SEDCO Square area. Good-value deals include B&B for 2. Round-trip airport transfer for 20MYR (07.00–17.00) to 40MYR pp (17.00–07.00) $$$–$$$$

⌂ **Imperial International Hotel** [167 E1] (208 rooms) Block D, Warisan Sq; ☎088 522888; e info@imperialkk.com or reservation@ imperialkk.com; www.imperialkk.com. In the chic Warisan Square shopping zone I am yet to try this new 4-star, which has finally emerged out of the former Mercure Waterfront. The rooms appear stylish & high-tech (only the super de luxe at 35m² pass the mid-range price bar). There's a swimming pool, 'Sun' & 'Moon' bars, rooftop restaurant, fitness centre & meeting rooms. $$–$$$$

⌂ **Promenade Hotel** [167 E1] (451 rooms) Lorong Api-Api 3, Api-Api Centre; ☎088 265555; e enquiry@promenade.com.my; www. promenade.com.my. Right in the thick of things, this is considered the best 4-star hotel in town centre, with good service & dining. The slightly small rooms can come at budget prices. Larger superior rooms or de luxe suites have city or sea views. Internet specials regularly available. Gym & pool. $$–$$$$

⌂ **Beverly Hotel** [166 D2] (200 rooms) Lorong Kemajuan; ☎088 258998; e khkkmal@ po.jaring.my; www.vhhotels.com. South of the CBD, close to business district. An amicable 3-star run by the excellent VH (Value Hospitality) group, this is a predominantly business hotel with some leisure tour groups attracted to its great value. Spacious, well-appointed rooms, roof-terrace pool, excellent gym, spa, good dining, live bands & babysitting. $$–$$$

⌂ **Cititel Express** [167 E2] (275 rooms) Jalan Singgah Mata 1; ☎088 521188 (hotel), 088 521 311 (restaurant); e resvnbki@cititelexpress.com, infobki@cititelexpress.com; www.cititelexpress. com. 10min walk from downtown. Brightly coloured, warm-toned new hotel. Wi-Fi in public areas & rooms. Key cards, satellite TV & safes in standard & superior rooms & 40m² studios. Complaints of exceedingly small room size on standard rooms. $$–$$$

🏠 **Grand Borneo Hotel** [164 D1] (325 rooms) 1 Borneo Hypermall, Jalan Sulaman Highway, (7km north of Kota Kinabalu); ✆088 526888; e info@grandborneohotel.com; www.grandborneohotel.com. Within 1 Borneo's 'shopping paradise'. Standard rooms are small, but superior club rooms through to executive suites all come at mid-range prices with lounge access privileges & complimentary breakfast. **$$–$$$**

🏠 **Jesselton Hotel** [167 G2] (32 rooms) 69 Jln Gaya; ✆088 223333; e jesshtl@po.jaring.my; www.jaring.my/jess. Opened in 1954 when Sabah was still British North Borneo, this old-world hotel promises its guests will receive 'the personalised service & impeccable attention to detail that delighted such illustrious colonial-era guests as Lady Mountbatten'. Held in high esteem among business clientele, it has good service & a good location in the heart of the banking & financial district of Kota Kinabalu. Rates include breakfast & airport transfer. **$$–$$$**

🏠 **Tang Dynasty Hotel** [166 D2] (203 rooms) 1–1 Lorong Plaza Wawasan, Coastal Highway; ✆088 263389; e tdhhotel@tm.net.my; www.hoteltangdynasty.com. Near southern side of waterfront area in the Wawasan Plaza shopping centre, a big 3-star buzzing & bright business hotel, with banquet halls, business centre, swimming pool, & Taipan coffee house. Good rates include breakfast. **$$–$$$**

Budget

🏠 **D'Borneo Hotel** [167 F2] (24 rooms) Lot 6 Blk L Sinsuran Complex; ✆088 266999; e info@dborneohotel.com; www.dborneohotel.com. Bright & business oriented budget hotel on waterfront. Very personal presentation & welcome for such a small, no-frills hotel. Good services, non-smoking floor. The budget-priced suite rooms are spacious. Café serves Malay & Western food. Despite being flagged by Sabah Tourism, the website is continually out of order. **$$**

🏠 **Hotel Deleeton** [167 E2] (47 rooms) Lot 45–45 Block E Asia City, Jln Coastal (just off Lebuh Raya Pantai Baru); ✆088 252222. Good CBD location for Centre Point & Sedco Square area, 5min walk from waterfront. Small, smart hotel for 1-star category, with AC, minibar, air transfers, non-smoking floor. **$$**

🏠 **Imperial Boutec Hotel** [167 F2] (93 rooms) 7th Floor, Block D, Warisan Sq, Jln Tun Fuad Stephens; ✆088 525969; e reservation@imperialboutec.com; www.imperialboutec.com. The short-lived Radius International has morphed with new management into a minimalist-sleek hotel, describing itself as 'boutech' rather than boutique. In a happening, commercial district, rooms are bright & furnishings fun. AC, satellite TV, de luxe & non-smoking rooms & suites. The switched-on 3-star has a business centre, complimentary broadband internet, bar, rooftop restaurant & budget-priced promotional rates, yet it is low on other facilities (no pool, gym, etc). **$$**

🏠 **King Park Hotel** [167 F3] (112 rooms) Jln Masjid Lama, Bandaran Berjaya; ✆088 270500. www.kk.kingparkhotel.com.my. A 10min walk from the waterfront, close to Padang Merdeka bus station & shopping centres. Comfortable standard, family & executive rooms have workstations, internet, satellite TV & tea/coffee-making facilities. An efficient, budget-priced business with all the mod cons & 24-hour reception. **$$**

🏠 **Courtyard Hotel** [164 C1] 1 Borneo Hypermall, Jalan Sulaman; ✆088 528222; e info@courtyardhotel1borneo.com; www.courtyardhotel1borneo.com. Is the rate of hotel openings at 1 Borneo a sign of the hyper-mall shopping future? In a shiny new building, the standard rooms are small, & sometimes window-less, yet well-furnished with LCD TV, free cable internet, AC & nice beds (funnily described by the hotel as 'used in Sydney Olympic'). Other more spacious rooms include premier, 'jumbo family' & 'Balinese'. All room prices include breakfast & service comes with a smile. The lack of other hotel facilities (gym etc) is in line with the 3-star rating, which in many aspects this hotel surpasses, bar the bargain basement prices. **$–$$**

🏠 **Hotel Eden54** [167 H2] (23 rooms) 54 Jalan Gaya; ✆088 266054; e stay@eden54.com; www.eden54.com. Described by one traveller as big 'bang for buck', I have not had the chance to test out this new centrally located hotel. Certainly the all-inclusive free Wi-Fi, satellite TV, AC, complimentary water, guest lounge, kitchenette & common fridges topped off with stylish guestroom & studio interiors & astute guest service mentality make strong first (though virtual) impressions. **$–$$**

🏠 **Winner Hotel** [167 F2] (36 rooms) 9–10 Jln Pasar Baru; ✆088 243222; www.winnerhotel.com. Prides itself on budget

x

Kota Kinabalu **WHERE TO STAY**

5

brilliance. Though rooms look very boxy, they are clean & cheap. The suite rooms are not much more stylish but are bigger, with sofa beds, kitchenettes & lots of furniture. All rooms have AC, Wi-Fi, TV & phone. Standard rooms not much bigger than the king-sized bed, but cheap. Option to add a table to superior rooms, or coffee table & chairs to de luxe rooms, all still at very low prices. **$–$$** (suites)

Shoestring
🏠 **Ang's Hotel** [167 G2] (35 rooms) 28 Lorong Bakau (off Jln Pantai); ☎ 088 234999; e angshotel@asi.com.my. A clean, partly windowless box with AC & (non satellite) TV, double bed & toilet/shower. Falls into the no-star budget category & value for this price. Complaints of bed bugs have to be balanced against comments by other travellers, such as: 'A bargain with clean sheets'. Good location & many coffee shops in the area, including at the hotel itself. **$**

🏠 **Tune Hotel** [164 C1] (165 rooms) 1 Borneo Hypermall, Jalan Sulaman; ☎ 03 7962 5888; e enquiry@tunehotels.com; www.tunehotels. com. Like a white & red Meccano block, AirAsia's minimalist budget hotel concept has arrived in Kota Kinabalu at Malaysia's largest hyper-mall – which has become a destination in itself for many travellers. Check-in is after 14.00, check-out at 10.00. The hotel offers a free shuttle service to the city centre. **$**

Hostels
🏠 **Borneo Backpackers** [167 G2] Jln Balai Polis; ☎ 088 234009; www.borneobackpackers. com. Run by Borneo Eco Tours (of Sukau Rainforest Lodge fame), former accolades of being clean, cosy, friendly & well run have lessened of late. 4/6/10-bed dorms, plus private rooms, free Wi-Fi, laundry, lounge & roof garden deck, fan & AC. The hostel's basement café-cum-wartime museum has become a bit of a landmark, loved for its yesteryear ambience. Styled as a traditional post-war coffee shop, the Borneo 1945 Museum Kopitiam is decked with copies of war memorial plaques, photos of 'unsung' wartime heroes – Australian & British – & antique furniture. **$**

🏠 **Borneo Beach House** [166 A1] House No 122, Lorong Ikan Lais, Jalan Mat Salleh, Tanjung Aru; ☎ 088 218331; e borneo.beachouse@gmail.

com; www.borneobeachouse.com. In a side lane, off a busy road in the Tanjung Aru area between the airport & the city, this backpacker's lodge enjoys a beachy, casual location. My fan-cooled room was exceedingly hot – the dorms seem to be the best place to be as they have AC. Budget beach house says it all; it's a place to hang out, & I was surprised at how peaceful my quarters were, back from the road & away from the buzzing reception-bar area. Very friendly but no-frills place. Sleeps 45 in dorms, double & family rooms. **$**

🏠 **Lavender Lodge** [167 E2] No 6, Jalan Laiman Diki, Kg Air; ☎ 088 217 119; e lavend07@ streamyx.com; www.lavenderlodge.com.my. Located in the Kampung Air zone, a 10min walk from the waterfront, the clean, comfortable hostel has AC dorm rooms, doubles, twin sharing & family rooms with bathrooms, free Wi-Fi & 24hr reception. **$**

🏠 **Masada Backpacker** [167 F3] 9, 1st Floor, Jalan Masjid Lama, ☎ 088 234 954; e masadabackpacker@gmail.com; www. masadabackpacker.com. 10mins' walk from the Gaya Street market, Padang Merdeka bus terminal & the waterfront, the single, double & family rooms are topped off by common lounge & dining areas, free Wi-Fi & tea/coffee. The hostel, which sleeps 33, gets its name from an interesting play on the Malaysian expression *emas ada*, 'there is gold'. **$**

🏠 **Trekkers Lodge** [167 G2] 30 Jln Haji Saman; ☎ 088 252263; e sales@trekkerslodge. com; www.trekkerslodge.com. A central, reputable, B&B hostel with an age-varied clientele. Dorm, twin & family rooms with shared bathroom facilities, & homely common room facilities, plus a balcony, & Wi-Fi. Breakfast included. **$**

Serviced apartments
🏠 **Penthouse KK** [166 D1] Marina Court; e noel@penthousekk.com; www.penthousekk. com. A New Zealand couple lease this fully equipped, 2-level, 5-bed penthouse with views over the bay, for 500MYR/night. **$$$$**

🏠 **Marina Court Resort Condominium** [166 D1] Lorong Api-Api 3, Api-Api Centre; ☎ 088 260003; e mcrc@promenade.com.my. 3-bedroom luxury condominium apartments managed by the Promenade Hotel group. **$$$–$$$$**

🏠 **Likas Square Condotel** [167 H2] 1 Lorong Likas Sq, Jln Istiadat Likas (2km north of city); 📞088 252233; e info@likassquare.com.my; www.likassquare.com.my. 1 to 3-bedroom suites for day & night/weekly/monthly lease, overlooking Likas Bay or Mount Kinabalu. Living & dining rooms, fully equipped kitchens, AC, satellite TV, phone, fridge, etc. Within Likas shopping & business centre, many restaurants & its own De Square Café. Internet deals can slash the published rates in half. **$$–$$$$**

🏠 **Promenade Apartments** [167 E1] Api-Api Centre; 📞088 260888; e apartments@ promenade.com.my. More budget to mid-range apartments for weekly/monthly leases. **$$–$$$**

✖ WHERE TO EAT

While there are many food highlights to discover in Kota Kinabalu, there are also some things to watch out for. Flashy décor doesn't always mean good food, so don't look for shiny counters and dozens of Western faces as signs of a good place to eat. It is often the less polished places that serve the best food, at the best value. You can get a good meal of noodles with meat or seafood for as little as 6MYR.

STREET FOOD/FOOD COURTS For quality food on the go, there are food stalls at several places in the city.

Night markets (*pasar malam*) The city's most accessible *pasar malam* is located on the waterfront, near the handicraft centre [167 F1]. *Gerai makan* food stalls set up here from late afternoon until midnight, serving grilled fish, satays, Malay and Indo-Malay fast (but good!) food. Try the Murtabak. Alongside them are traders selling fresh fruit, fish and vegetables. Another night market with a big choice of food can be found on Jalan Kampung Air, near City Park [167 F2]. Right at the back of town, towards the museum district, the **Kompleks Karamunsing** commercial zone [166 D3] has outdoor evening food stalls serving Malay and Indonesian food.

On the southern end of the waterfront, near the Promenade Hotel, the **Anjung Senja** [166 D1] – 'sunset deck' – is an outdoor feasting area with mostly Malay and Indonesian halal food. The **Anjung Selera** [167 H2], in Likas Bay, has food stalls and tables set up on a headland overlooking the sea.

Tanjung Aru Beach [166 A1] 3km south of the city (in the direction of the airport). Head here for a beachy night atmosphere. **First Beach**, Tanjung Aru, holds a nightly barbecue where you can select a platter of seafood or meat and have it cooked and served with different sauces. **Anjung Perdana** is a waterfront area of under-roof, open-air food stalls with plastic tables and chairs; aside from the food being tasty, cheap and authentic, it is a fun and vibey place to visit at night.

Wisma Merdeka Food Court [167 G2] On the second floor of the landmark Wisma shopping centre, there are at least a dozen different stalls. The fantastic range of food includes Malay, Chinese and Indian dishes, noodles, curries and *laksas*, and one vegetarian stall (**Healthy Vegetarian**). Count on as much as you can eat and drink for under 12MYR. For ready-made dishes served from bains-marie, it is best to arrive between 11.00 and 14.00, when the food is fresh and hot (anytime in shopping centre hours is fine for stalls that cook on the spot).

The **Tea Time Express** cake shop, located by the entrance, has pork-free pastries and sweets including English-style cakes, Chinese buns, avocado cake and mango puddings.

5

Segama Complex [167 G2] Opposite Wisma Merdeka and crammed with ordinary shop-lots, retailers here also include coffee shops and fast-food chains such as KFC.

Warisan Square [167 E1] Less authentic than Malaysian food court grub, but this centre caters to cosmopolitan tastes with its cafés and restaurants spread over several floors. On ground level, you will find **Fish & Co** for 'Seafood in a Pan', while **Starbucks, San Francisco Coffee** and **Yoshima Japanese Restaurant** are all on the first floor

'COFFEE-SHOP' RESTAURANTS (Kedai Kopi or Kopi Tiam) Scattered all around the city's streets, and squeezed between shop-lots, coffee shops serve from breakfast through to dinner. At many of them you can down good-quality food and drink for 5–10MYR. I have eaten excellent *kway teow* noodle dishes with prawns for 3–4MYR from no-name coffee shops in the Kampung Air zone.

✗ **Kedai Kopi Yuan Li** [167 E2] 28 Jln Pantai; ✆088 255864; ⊕ 06.00–15.30. Cheap curry noodles, noodles with seafood & plenty of other noodle dishes.

✗ **Yu Kee** [167 G2] 74 Jln Gaya; ⊕ 16.30–23.00. Famous for its *bak kut,* the herb & meat hotpot soup (about 5MYR a bowl), which has a variety of meats in it. Apparently this dish 'attracts lots of ex-Hong Kong film stars' to the place!

RESTAURANTS Formerly known as **Sedco Square** food court, **Sri Selera** [167 E2], Jln Haji Saman, Kampung Air (*next door to Golden Screen Cinemas*), is a large courtyard in which you can dine al fresco (with a rolling roof in case of wet weather) at a few seafood restaurants or kitchens. **Suang Tain Seafood**, **Sri Mutiara** and others display an array of seafood in tanks, so you can choose by weight from the lobster, elephant tusk clams, squid, crab and fish. There's also an à la carte menu and plenty of vegetables – jungle ferns, spinach, cauliflower, broccoli. Seating up to 1,200 people, the place has plenty of atmosphere and can be noisy. Prices average around 30MYR per person (nearby *gerai* food stalls provide cheaper options).

✗ **The Chinese Restaurant** [167 G2] Hyatt Regency, Jln Datuk Salleh Sulong; ✆088 221234; www.kinabalu.regency.hyatt.com. The English name might not seem very original, but the Chinese calligraphy version rhymes with Hyatt! A favourite with local & visiting VIPs & business milieu, most dishes on the 9-page menu are Canton & Szechuan served in a classical Chinese Empire setting of miniature teapots & hand paintings. Steamboats Wed & Sat nights. Meat, seafood, vegetable & noodle dishes served sizzling, spicy or wok fried; signature dish Peking Duck; delicious vegetarian silken tofu, wok & claypot choices. $$$$–$$$$$

✗ **Ferdinand's Restaurant** [166 C1] Level 2, Magellan Sutera Resort, Sutera Harbour Bd; ✆088 318 888; www.suteraharbour.com. my; ⊕ 18.00–23.00 daily. The 'Italian' food, granted, is cooked by an Italian chef, but is often undermined by a lack of proper Mediterranean ingredients. When in Rome do as the Romans do … if you are going to splurge, it's best to do so on local cuisine. Malaysians & foreigners however appreciate the chance to eat international food, in a fine dining atmosphere. The over-the-top formality would work better if the restaurant was animated, but my experience, & that of others, is to dine alone. Main course fish dishes & lamb racks cost 60MYR+. The restaurant should shake off a few of the pretensions & the price-tags to gain a few clients. $$$$–$$$$$

✗ **Nagisa Restaurant** [167 G1] Hyatt Regency, Jln Datuk Salleh Sulong; ✆088 221234; www.kinabalu.regency.hyatt.com. Best Japanese food in Borneo. Served from open kitchen in traditional turned modern décor of dark wooden tables, lattice screens, weaving baskets, traditional costume & other artefacts. 'Set Dinner Menus' 56–80MYR specials & à la carte dishes; new world wines. Must tries include gindara (cod fish) teriyaki & black sesame custard. Dining views of sun setting over the South China Sea explain the restaurant's name: 'waterside'. The VIP rooms & sushi counter are perfect for solo diners. $$$$

✗ **Shang Palace** [166 A1] Ground Floor, Shangri-La Resort, 20 Jln Aru, Tanjung Aru; \088 327888; www.shangri-la.com. Traditional food & elegant atmosphere. You can breakfast, lunch or dine on the renowned dim sum & sample other menu specials, from fried minced seafood salad to Shenzhen crispy roasted goose & deep-fried tempura mango ice cream. $$$$

✗ **Grand Port View** Jln Tun Fuad Stephens (between the Customs Department & Marine Police, by Jesselton Point ferry terminal); \088 538178; ⊕ lunch & dinner. Along the redeveloping Jesselton Point Waterfront area. An AC, more upmarket version of Ocean Seafood. with more of a business clientele. $$$

✗ **Kampung Nelayan Restaurant** Taman Tun Fuad (15mins' drive east of town); \088 231003/5; ⊕ 11.30–14.00/18.30–23.00; dance performance 19.45–20.45. It may well be a tour-group magnet, but a special evening can be had at this antiquated floating 'seafood market restaurant' which opens onto the sea. Diners are treated to a cultural dance performance, seafood, & Chinese & Malay dishes (including many vegetarian options). Private VIP rooms have AC, karaoke, couch & washroom, though a less watery atmosphere. $$$

✗ **Ocean Seafood** [167 E1] Jln Tun Fuad Stephens, waterfront (next to Promenade Hotel); \088 264701; ⊕ lunch & dinner. Like a theme park of seafood dining, this place is famous countrywide & some see it as a destination in itself. If you don't mind the tour buses rolling into its car park, the food experience is excellent. Crabs, prawns, scallops, oyster & lobster are cooked by the kilo (min 300g) in whatever style you choose. You can pick your preferred catch straight from the eel-filled aquarium at the entrance & eat it in the part open-air (no AC), water-facing dining room. $$$

✗ **Port View Seafood Restaurant** [167 F1] Jln Tun Fuad Stephens (opposite Warisan Sq

shopping mall); \088 221753; www.portview. com.my; ⊕ 11.00–23.00 daily. This gaudy Chinese pergola on the waterfront serves many Chinese halal fish dishes: steamed fish & lobster in lemon butter sauce, crabs with black pepper, prawns 'Cantonese fisherman style', mussels with green pepper & soybean sauce. While many reviews criticise the over-the-top prices & label this restaurant a 'tourist trap', other regular customers cannot fault its exceptionally fresh seafood, huge variety of dishes & AC environs (which can be icicle cold). The prices *are* high, but at least half what they would be in London for such a top meal. The outdoor dining area has overtly touristy cultural performances that won't be to everyone's tastes. $$$

✗ **@mosphere Restaurant** [167 H1] 18th Floor, Menara Tun Mustapha; \088 425100. A fun, pastel-toned eatery with the best views in town from its revolving restaurant & cocktail bar. The menu is modern, with a mix of fish, meat & pasta dishes. $$

✗ **Restoran Rasa Nyonya** [167 G2] 50 Jln Gaya; \088 218092 ⊕ lunch through to late. Tasty, budget-priced & authentic Nyonya food – spicy chicken & fish, Penang *laksa*, noodles. Halal. $$

✗ **Restoran Sir Melaka** 9 Jln Laiman Diki (Kampung Air); \088 224777; www.srimelaka. com; ⊕ 10.00–21.30 daily. Another inexpensive place for very good Nyonya & Malay dishes, such as the famous Malaysian fish-head curry. $$

✗ **Jothy's Fish Head Curry & Banana Leaf Restaurant** [167 E2] Ground Floor, Api Api Centre; \088 261595; ⊕ 11.00–22.00 daily; www.jothyscurry.com. Cheap but good southern Indian grub, in what the owner describes as a 'Karma Sutra setting' (though the place is famously child-friendly)! The restaurant's namesake, fiery hot fish-head curry, is served with a homemade blend of herbs & spices, & with *brinjals*, tomatoes & lady's fingers. Another popular dish is biryani fragrant rice served on banana leaf. $

✗ **Mai Yai Thai Orchid** [167 E1] The Waterfront zone; \088 234841; ⊕ daily 12.00–22.00. Traditional Thai favourites, lots of veggie choices & a pork-free menu in this simple, open-fronted hut restaurant. $

5

WESTERN-STYLE CAFÉS AND ASIAN BAKERIES For local baked goods sniff out the **Southern Cake Shop** – there's one on Jalan Pantai, near the Sunday market area. The **Coffee Bean & Tea Leaf** have four outlets about town: in Wisma Merdeka [167 G2], along the Waterfront Esplanade [167 E1], in Kompleks Damai shopping centre and in Kompleks Karamunsing [167 D3]. Despite the Westernised style and standardised sandwiches, salads and sweets, these cafés will quell your cravings for Arabica bean espressos and lattes or waffles and scones. Here you can sit and sip peacefully, with free Wi-Fi, then stock up on freshly ground coffee and speciality teas. Prices on the vast drinks menu average 7–10MYR, while snacks, sandwiches and pastas range from 10 to 15MYR.

ENTERTAINMENT AND NIGHTLIFE

Most of the action, from bars to nightclubs, exists along the waterfront stretch from south to north. For a medium-sized city, Kota Kinabalu has a lively nightlife and thriving gay and lesbian scene. If you prefer musical and cultural events to clubbing, the best thing is to check with Sabah Tourism Board (\ *088 212121; www.sabahtourism.com*) for current shows and festivities. During major cultural celebrations, better hotels organise music and dance performances on a daily basis. Drink prices vary between venues (as does the quality of mixed drinks and cocktails), from 13–18MYR for a beer, 12–24MYR for a single shot of spirits and 14–29 MYR for a glass of wine. Many bars have happy hours and even 'ladies' nights', serving free drinks to female customers.

♀**Cocoon Bar & Restaurant** [167 G1] Jln Tun Fuad Stephens; \088 0211252; ⊕ 11.00–01.00/02.00; bar from 17.00. Though far from cosy, the name aptly describes the low lights & modern décor. It's a big place – primarily a lounge club – with live bands, inexpensive bar food & a garden restaurant. The last serves light food by day (from *laksa* to Western) & more substantial dishes at night, when the main bar is crowded & bands are noisy.

♀**Mosaic** [167 G1] Jln Datuk Salleh Sulong; ⊕ 10.00–23.00 daily. The Hyatt's sleek glass-walled café & wine bar is good for people-watching, with AC & modern dining.

♀**Q Bar** [167 G2] 50 Jln Gaya. Many gay clubbers rave about the décor & friendly staff here.

♀**Rumba Latin Bar & Grill** [167 F1] Ground Floor, Le Meridien hotel, Jln Tun Fuad Stephens; ⊕ 17.00–01.00 Sun–Thu & until 02.00 Fri–Sat. Latino touch complete with Filipino male dancers happy to give ladies free salsa lessons. The bouncers here woo passing clients in through the back door.

♀**Sunset Bar** [166 B1] 20 Shangri-La, 20 Jln Aru, Tanjung Aru (3km south of city centre); ⊕ 17.00–20.00 daily. For the perfect sundowner cocktail or glass of wine, this is the most select &

serene outdoor bar location in the city, with prices to match. Sunset falls between 17.30 & 18.30 depending on the time of year – onlookers are often treated to a natural, techno-coloured light show of sublime reds, purples, crimson & blue.

♀**Shenanigans** [167 G1] Fun Pub Jln Datuk Salleh Sulong; ⊕ 17.00–01.00 Mon–Thu & until 02.00 Fri–Sat. The Hyatt's bar/disco is the highest-profile watering pot in the city & an established party place. Locals come here to spend their savings on extravagantly priced drinks. 'Sheni's', as they call it, pulls a mixed crowd, & is popular with the gay crowd.

♀**Shenanigans Terrace** [167 G1] Jln Datuk Salleh Sulong; ⊕ 17.00–01.00 Mon–Thu & until 02.00 Fri–Sat. The calmer face to the fun pub, the seaside & poolside terrace is a great sunset-watching spot over a long, cool drink, if you are not bothered by the live sports screen. BBQ on the last Sat of every month.

♀**The Office** [166 D2] Api-Api Commercial Centre, Lorong Api-Api; ⊕ 16.00–01.00 Sun–Thu & until 02.00 Fri–Sat. With its big range of beers (Tiger, Heineken, Guinness, San Miguel, etc), raging happy hours, sporting screen & lower than average prices, this is a popular place with an old 'public house' allure.

The Waterfront Esplanade is a work in progress. The southern end in particular has a raffish mix of souvenir shops, bars and cafés, but also hot clubbing spots for the in-crowd. At twilight, the temporary shop-lot look fades into the watery setting and often-resplendent Kota Kinabalu sunsets. **Bed** [167 E1] (I believe it stands for 'Best Entertainment Destination') is good for live bands, live dance and international DJs. If you make it out before 23.00 you can head next door to the waterfront food stalls before going back to the other places on the waterfront. European beers flow freely at **The Loft** [167 E1], and trendy crowds frequently stay to see the sunrise. Drinks average 15MYR. The lobby wine bar **Blue Note** [166 B1] at Shangri La's Tanjung Aru is far more low-key and low-light, and one of the few places with a range of wines by the glass. Things can liven up here too – it is also the dance floor and venue for live band and DJ nights.

For a traditional Irish or British bar **The Shamrock** [167 E1] and the **Cock 'n' Bull** [167 E1] have beer, pool tables and live music on tap (if a Filipino band doing Phil Collins renditions is your thing!).

FESTIVALS AND EVENTS

For further details on the following or other cultural celebrations and events, contact Sabah Tourism (e *info@sabahtourism.com*). Also pick up a copy of the bi-monthly *Discover Sabah* magazine.

TADAU KA'AMATAN (HARVEST FESTIVAL) Celebrations of the Kadazandusun and Murut communities happen during the month of May so look out for dance and other cultural performances at your hotel, or in the streets.

SABAH ART GALLERY During the month of May, watch out for the Patterns and Colours of Sabah, an annual month-long exhibition where craftspeople from Sabah's multi-ethnic communities show new samples of their intricate combinations of pattern and colours in their designs.

THE SABAH DRAGON BOAT RACE A traditional Chinese festival that attracts dragon boat teams from China, Japan, Brunei and Australia during the month of June. It is held at Likas Bay (also the site of Merdeka Month – a month-long celebration to celebrate Malaysian independence, from mid-August).

MOONCAKE FESTIVAL Usually held in late September, and known as the mid-autumn festival, it marks the rebellion against the Mongols in 14th-century China and is celebrated with the eating of many moon cakes and with lantern parades.

RAMADAN BAZAAR (spelt Ramadhan in Malay, as opposed to Ramadan in other societies) Sometime around mid-September to mid-October, Muslims fast for a month from sunrise to sunset. Amazing food is served at the sundown Ramadan bazaars held at various locations in Kota Kinabalu and organised by the Kota Kinabalu City Hall.

SHOPPING

Handicrafts Sri Pelancongan [167 F2] (*Lot 4, Ground Floor, Block L, Sinsuran Complex, off Jln Chong Thian Vun; e kadaiku@sabathtourism.com*) is a handicraft shop, owned by Sabah Tourism, that sells woven items, tapestries, paintings, books, musical instruments, T-shirts, beads, baskets, bookmarks, souvenirs and locally produced products such as Sabah tea and Tenom coffee.

The **Borneo Trading Post** [167 E1] (*Waterfront precinct, Jln Tun Fuad Stephens, www.borneotradingpost.com*) is an upmarket, online distributor of ethnic goods, with a Monsopiad warrior called 'Borneo Bob' as its mascot.

SHOPPING CENTRES Kota Kinabalu is not yet major high-street territory, but with new developments, the way is being cleared for luxury flagship stores. **Warisan Square** [167 E1] on Jalan Tun Fuad Stephens has more upmarket brands – international, casual couture labels and Asian natural cosmetic brands. Overall, it's a chic shopping mall in a partly glass-roofed pavilion, with arcades of shops to each side (rather than the predominant wall-to-wall, sometimes unattractive and cramped, style of other shopping centres). The **Wisma Merdeka** [167 G2] on Jalan Tun Razak is more down to earth – the second-biggest shopping centre in Sabah has plenty of shops, restaurants and a food court. It is good for electronics and clothes, and many 'buy-one-free-one' offers. **Centre Point** [167 E2] on Lorong Centre Point is the choice for entertainment, electronics and photographic stores. **KK Plaza** on Jalan Lapan Belas is quite stuffy and dowdy, but it has a good hypermarket on the basement level, cheap phone/electronic and clothing stores, and is open late.

The best supermarket if you want imports, foreign wines and liquor, or if you are pining for Lindt, McVitie's or Walkers Highland Oatcakes, is the **Tong Hing Supermarket** [167 H2] (*55 Jln Gaya; ⊕ 08.00–22.00*). It also has a nice little Chinese bakery. Nearby, is **Milimewa** [167 F2] (*1 Jalan Pantai*), the oldest supermarket chain in the state.

Hypermalls The largest mall in Sabah, **1 Borneo**, lies 7km north of the city [164 C1] (*Jalan Sulaman Highway; www.1borneo.net*). Its 400 businesses include Malaysian department store Parkson, international- and Asian-brand leisure, food and entertainment outlets, and hotels (see *Where to stay*, above).

MARKETS The CBD's main foreshore area along Jalan Tun Fuad Stephens is market row. Stretching over half a kilometre, side by side, are the handicraft market, the central market (*pasar besar*) and the fish market. A fresh fruit and fish market, interspersed with tables and chairs, is set up on the water's edge each afternoon opposite Le Meridien Hotel. By evening it transforms into a *pasar malam* (night market), full of food stalls. The main night market is held around the streets south of City Park. The 'handicraft market' seems to have been renamed as such to obscure the real name, *pasar Filipino*. With its flood of cheap Filipino produce, the large under-cover market has few genuine Sabahan crafts, but is still a vivid place to mingle. The **Sunday market** (also referred to as **Pesta Jalan Gaya** or the **Gaya Street Fair**), is held along Jalan Gaya every Sunday [167 G2] (⊕ *06.00–13.00*). Kota Kinabalu's take on the rural *tamu* sells remedial herbs, aquarium fish, baskets, bric-a-brac, crafts and potted plants. Refreshments include *nasi lemak*, all kinds of *kuih* cakes and coconut juice.

OTHER PRACTICALITIES

Ambulance/Police ☏999
Police hotline ☏088 221191. There are police stations on Jln Dewan (near the Atkinson Clock Tower) & at the southern end of town, along Jln Kemajuan.

Queen Elizabeth Hospital [166 C3] South, direction of airport; ☎088 218166. Public hospital.
Sabah Medical Centre Lorong Bersatu, off Jln Damai; ☎088 211333; www.sabahmedicalcentre. com. Private clinic.

Sabah State Library [167 F2] Jln Tasik, off Jln Maktab Gaya; ☎088 214828; www.ssl.sabah.gov. my; ⊕ 09.00–18.00 Mon-Fri, 09.00–14.00 Sat/ Sun. Closed public holidays.

WHAT TO SEE AND DO

Crammed between the ocean and hills, the city is concentrated around three main streets, which run parallel and span just a few hundred metres.

Along the waterfront, Jalan Tun Fuad Stephens is the hub of mid- to high-range hotels, shopping plaza and markets. It stretches from the Sutera Harbour area in the south to the Jesselton Point ferry terminal in the north. One block in, Jalan Tun Razak, runs by shop-lots and shopping centres, and changes name several times along its course. Hugging closer to the foothills of Signal Hill, Jalan Gaya is a neighbourhood as much as it is a street, encompassing smaller boutique and budget hotels, hostels, banks, restaurants and the Sunday *tamu* market.

LOOKOUTS AND LANDMARKS

Signal Hill [167 G3] This is the green belt that swathes Kota Kinabalu, and forms a leafy backdrop to the city. The view from the Signal Hill observatory takes in the entire city, coast and islands. Below, at Jalan Gaya 51, you can see the **Sabah Tourism building** [167 G2], dating to 1916, which is one of just three buildings to withstand World War II bombings. After minor restoration work, it was gazetted as a heritage structure and held many hallowed roles, including Government Printing Office, Treasury, Audit Office, District Office and Attorney General's Office, before the Sabah Tourism Board set up office there in 1991. At the other end of Signal Hill Road on Bukit Brace (Brace Hill) is another wartime survivor, the **Atkinson Clock Tower** [167 G2], a quaint, white, wooden structure. It was built in 1905 by Englishwoman, Mary Edith Atkinson, in memory of her son, Francis George Atkinson, the first District Officer of Jesselton, who died of malaria aged 28.

Sabah's State Mosque (Masjid Negeri Sabah) [166 C2] (*visiting hours change according to prayer times, but generally are mornings & afternoons, never around midday & after 16.00, with shorter hours Fri*) Lying south of the city centre in Sembulan, its towering minaret and pewter-coloured bulbous dome bear striking gold inlay motifs. Visitors must report to the information officer on duty prior to entering, and are asked to dress appropriately.

Likas Bay [164 C2] The coast road from the city around Likas Bay offers a strip of the best edge-of-city nature and leisure, passing through parklands and mangroves – a favourite area for picnics and evening jogs. On one side is the ocean, with the Crocker Range foothills in the background, capped by Mount Kinabalu.

Wetland Centre [164 C3] (☎ 088 246955; ⊕ 08.00–18.00 Tue–Sun, closed Mon; adult 10MYR, student 5MYR, under 6s free) Set within a rare patch of mangrove forest, the former Kota Kinabalu City Bird Sanctuary morphed into this more educational and recreational centre, with 24ha of parklands, tree planting and other activities. Binoculars can be rented for 5MYR to view the 80 different types of birds. To reach it by public transport, take bus No 1 (direction Likas), from City Hall or Wawasan Plaza stations, and alight at Likas Square.

5

Menara Tun Mustapah [164 C1] The modernistic tower looms over the foreshore of Likas Bay, 3km north of the city. The 30-storey building looks like a glass-windowed kaleidoscope – its walls are composed of 2,160 special reflective panels, which help it withstand winds of up to 272km/h. Despite its cylindrical appearance, the structure is actually a 72-sided polygon. The avant-garde landmark, built in the 1970s, stunningly reflects the silhouettes of surrounding mountains, mosques and sea. Though the building is mostly occupied by offices, the public can enjoy the views from the top-floor revolving restaurant and cocktail bar.

City Mosque [164 D2] (*same visiting hours as Sabah's State Mosque, see page 179*) Perched by a small lake near the water village of Kampung Likas, the mosque's white walls and blue bulbous dome shimmer in the sunlight. A fine example of contemporary Islamic architecture, built in 1997, the prayer floor can accommodate 10,000–12,000 people, and houses three *madrasahs* (Islamic religious schools). Take bus No 5A or a taxi for around 12–15MYR.

MUSEUMS
Sabah Museum Complex [166 C3] (*Jln Bukit Istana Lama;* \ *088 253199;* e *muzium.sabah@sabah.gov.my; www.mzm.sabah.gov.my;* ⊕ *09.00–17.00 daily; 15MYR*) It is refreshing to find most of the city's museums located together. The cultural complex is located 4km from the city, on Bukit Istana Lama (Old Palace Hill), where British North Borneo's colonial governor once resided. It brings together the **State Museum**, a **Science and Education Centre**, **Sabah Art Gallery**, the **Museum of Islamic Civilisation** and a reconstructed 'heritage village' with traditional tribal houses and ethno-botanical gardens. Transport alternatives are bus No 13 (direction Penampang) – get off at the bottom of the hill and walk up – or a taxi for 12–15MYR. Photos can only be taken outside, not within the museum buildings.

The State Museum [166 C3] This has an exhibition hall on its ground floor with changing expos and six permanent galleries: the Islamic Civilisation Gallery, the Archaeology and History Gallery, Natural History Gallery, Art Gallery, Ceramic and Brassware Gallery, and Traditional Costumes Gallery.

The Science and Education Centre [166 C3] The centre houses the Geology Gallery, permanent exhibitions on the petroleum industry and copper mining in Sabah and other, temporary exhibitions.

BEACHES Some 3km south of the city centre, **Tanjung (Cape) Aru** [166 A1] gets its name from the rows of casuarina trees (*aru*) along the shoreline of its long, beach-rimmed headland. It's a peaceful, sand-lovers escape from the city centre, yet with quite enough nightlife, shopping and dining (see *Where to eat*, page 173) of its own. Most upmarket resorts here offer bus-shuttle services to and from Kota Kinabalu city centre. Alternatively, take the bus marked Tanjung Aru Beach from City Hall terminal. Ahead of the most spectacular sunsets, join locals running or walking along the shoreline, through Tanjung Aru Park. The previously named Prince Philip Park, has a children's playground.

WELL-BEING
Cres Moment [167 E1] (*Warisan Sq, Block A*) A relatively upmarket southeast Asian chain, offering foot reflexology, shiatsu back massage, body massages, milk baths and steam baths. Treatments cost 48–128MYR.

D'Bor Neobayu Spa (*Wisma HCS, Jln Kolam, Luyang;* ☎ *088 216648;* e *neobayu1@ streamyx.com*) For a more traditional treatment, take a taxi to Luyang. Situated 15km from the CBD, this family-run business of traditional Kadazandusun healers has been operating under the guidance of 'Auntie Rosie' for almost three decades. The Kadazandusuns use lemon grass (*sogumau*) in healing as well as cooking. It's one of the main detox ingredients used here in massages, scrubs, steams, compresses and exfoliations. The two-hour Neobayu Sirih Pinang treatment won an award as Best Traditional Treatment during the 2006 Malaysia Spa & Wellness Awards in Kota Kinabalu. If you have children, they are taken good care of while you have a treatment – they may even come away having learnt the *sumazu*, the Kadazandusun traditional dance.

Jari Jari (*Lot 2.1, Block B, 2nd Floor, Tanjung Aru Plaza;* ☎ *088 272606;* e *sales@ jarijari.com.my; www.jarijari.com.my*) Traditional Dusun massage.

EXCURSIONS FROM KOTA KINABALU

Some of the places included in the following chapter, *West Coast Sabah*, see page 187, are also possible day trips from Kota Kinabalu. The following destinations are much closer to the capital (30–35km), and can either be enjoyed as half-day trips or used as an alternative accommodation base.

SOUTHEAST OF KOTA KINABALU – PENAMPANG The Penampang District is the nerve centre of Kadazandusun culture. Fringed by rice paddies and the Sungai Babujong/Penampang River, the region was once deep hinterland, but is now virtually Kota Kinabalu city limits. **Kampung Dongonggon** is the heart of the district and the place to be every Thursday and Friday morning for the *tamu*. Starting from about 06.00 and continuing through to early afternoon, you will find everything from *lihing* (rice wine) to *butod* (sago worms) – the witchetty grubs of Borneo. There are a couple of places in town serving typical Kadazandusun food.

For a taste of mythical Kadazandusun culture, tribal warriors and headhunting, visit **Monsopiad Cultural Village** (MCV) (☎ *088 774337;* e *info@monsopiad.com; www.monsopiad.com;* ⊕ *09.00–17.00 daily; adult 75MYR, teenager/student 50MYR, children free*). This major cultural tourist attraction is run by the artist-grandson of Sabah's most famous headhunter, Monsopiad. The crowd-pullers are cultural dances and the ghoulish House of Skulls (Siou Do Mohoing), where 42 'trophy' heads of the Dusun warrior hang from the rafters. The village comprises other traditional houses, including the *tangkob*, or granary, where the *padi* is housed, and a small museum with artefacts such as ceramic jars, *padi* grinders, bamboo items and *bobohizan* (high priestess) costumes. Admission includes welcome drink, performance (three daily) and guided tour (three daily).

A more staged, gee-whiz experience comes at the new **Mari Mari Cultural Village** in Kionsom, Inanam, which can only be visited on organised, half-day tours from Kota Kinabalu (☎ *088 260501;* e *sales@traversetours.com; www.traversetours.com; adult 130MYR, children 5–11 100MYR, inc transfers, guide, meal & cultural performance; from various pick-up locations, expect a 4–5hr total trip to link in with 10.00, 15.00 & 17.00 tours*). You will be greeted by theatrically threatening headhunter types, in various states of dress, who will guide you around the different housing of the Bajau, Murut, Rungus and Dusun tribes. They'll encourage you to taste traditional food cooked on the spot, and to try out your skills with a blowpipe. They'll demonstrate fire-starting and tattoo-making, before treating you to a dance performance.

5

Getting there and away

By car Take Jalan Penampang from near the State Mosque just south of downtown Kota Kinabalu (in Sembulan), and head about 13km southeast to Donggongon. MCV is another 2km from here.

By taxi The cost is 35MYR one-way from Kota Kinabalu.

By bus Take the No 13 bus to Donggongon town in Penampang from either the City Hall or Wawasan Plaza station. From here, board a minibus bound for Terawi and ask the driver to let you off at the MCV. The entire journey will cost less than 3MYR.

NORTH OF KOTA KINABALU – TUARAN Rivers and rural markets meet headland silhouettes and wispy beaches in the Tuaran District. While the coast is being built up, it is still far from a riviera – to reach it you will pass roadside food stalls selling *kelapa* (coconut pudding), mangrove swamps, lagoons and water buffalo in rice *padi*. The sprinkling of luxury and mid-range resorts in the area offer an alternative to the rush of Kota Kinabalu for families, beach and nature lovers, with the city still in close reach. From the Karumbunai Peninsula in Meggatal the beach continues 6km through to Pantai Dalit Beach in Tuaran interrupted by a few lagoons.

Getting there and away

By car Approximately 35km north of Kota Kinabalu, and 42km from Kota Kinabalu airport. The journey takes about 40 minutes along the north-heading Kota Kinabalu–Kudat highway.

By bus From Wawasan Plaza, buses leave frequently for Tuaran between 07.30 and 17.00. Make sure to indicate to the driver where you want to get off. The trip takes about an hour and costs 3MYR.

Where to stay

 Nexus Resort & Spa Karambunai (485 rooms) Off Jln Sepangar Bay (28km from Kota Kinabalu), Meggatal; ☎088 411222; e info@ nexusresort.com; www.nexusresort.com. One of 10 Malaysian recipients of the ASEAN Green Hotel award in 2010, this luxury resort describes its ocean-fronting lawns as 'manicured', which is spot-on. The big news here is the new, exclusive wing of modern 2-bed pool villas & 1–2-bed spa suites, 2km from the main resort (with free shuttle service). The duplex villas are self-contained with kitchen & dining area, master & twin rooms, private garden & lap pool. Traditional de luxe garden & ocean rooms occupy 2-storey garden villas; spacious at 42.5m^2, they have private balconies, local carved wood & Borneo rattan. Public areas include a lovely lobby-lounge, pool bars & dining choices galore. The resort's 18-hole golf course & Borneo Spa are topped off by several pools, a swimming beach (with jellyfish alerts), & dedicated kids' care & activities. **$$$$–$$$$$**

 Rasa Ria Resort (420 rooms) Jln Pantai Dalit, Tuaran; ☎088 792888; e rrr@shangri-la. com; www.shangri-la.com. Set in 400 acres of ocean-facing gardens, bordering a 64-acre nature reserve & orang-utan sanctuary. The sublime new Ocean Wing, with its heavenly landscaping & artefacts, offers club-like intimacy, 90m^2 rooms with balcony tubs & an exclusive swimming pool & breakfast restaurant. A major renovation of the Garden Wing's rooms & suites, lobby & lounge was completed in early 2012. Ground-floor rooms have gardened patios; upper floor rooms have a 2-level layout with daybed & balconies with rainforest or garden & sea views. Leisure facilities include fitness centre, spa, golf, watersports, horseriding, children's activities & nature walks. Western, Malay, Indian & Asian dining, traditional dance shows & resident musicians.

Shuttle service into Kota Kinabalu for about 28MYR return. **$$$$-$$$$$**

🏠 **Tuaran Beach Resort** Off Jln Pantai Dalit, Jln Sabandar; 📞088 788271/793593; e info@tuaranbeachresort.com; www.tuaranbeachresort.com. Despite its lovely location on 5km of beach & an extensive makeover in 2007, there is still much work to do here to bring overall service

standards & facilities in line with the prices. Most of the gym equipment was out of order on my 2010 trip, staff attitudes were slack & food was average. Many of its chalet-style rooms & suites (25m² upwards) have sea-facing balconies. Coffee house, nice pool area, massage rooms & shuttle service to & from Kota Kinabalu. **$$$-$$$$**

✖ Where to eat

✖ **Coast Restaurant & Bar** Pantai Dalit, at the Rasa Ria Resort; ⊕ 17.30–24.00, last order 22.30. If you're craving Mediterranean food, this stunning, glass-walled place through which the sun sets has décor extravagance, lights like neon octopus tentacles hanging over tables, Italian cooking, & a chef from Norwich. Average 80MYR main course. **$$$$**

✖ **Gayang** Jln Sulaman Tuaran; 📞088 229066. A seafood restaurant in a mesmerising setting among mangrove forest & inlets, with fish straight from the aquariums if you wish. **$$$**

✖ **Salut Seafood Restaurant** Jln Sulaman Tuaran; 📞088 301300. Just next door to Gayang & said to be good for its fresh seafood, crab & grilled fish. **$$$**

What to see and do The district township of **Pekan Tuaran** has a wistful river setting where you'll see people fishing from longboats. Smoke from the daytime *gerai makan* food stalls billows around its banks and you can get excellent cheap Malay food – grilled fish and meats and *murtabak* – and try the local noodle dish, *Tuaran mee* in the village coffee shops. Home of the Lotud tribe – part of the Kadazandusun – there is also a lively Sunday *tamu* market here (⊕ 06.00–14.00). There's also a *tamu* in neighbouring **Tamparuli**, about 5km further north, on Wednesdays. The *bambangan* condiment, made from a sour mango-like fruit, is delicious.

Dalit Bay Golf Club & Spa (e *sales@karambunaigolf.com*; ⊕ *07.00–20.00 daily*) Situated in Tuaran, the club has an 18-hole course, designed by golf architect Ronald Fream, sculpted from a former mangrove swamp. There is also whitewater rafting on the Kiulu River, and there are equestrian centres for horseriding.

Kampung Mengkabong (*4km from Tuaran*) This is a satellite-dish-decked, yet dilapidated, Bajau village perched on the river that is perhaps a little overrated as a tourist attraction. Some locals welcome tourists and have crafts ready, others do not. The Mengkabong River estuary has many mangroves, and there are river cruises to go on. For watersports enthusiasts, the beach resorts offer them all, while **Lagoon Park** near Karambunai has skiing, jet-skiing, kayaking and windsurfing (and river cruises start from here too).

Rasa Ria Nature Reserve Established by Shangri-La's Rasa Ria Resort in collaboration with the Sabah Wildlife Department in 1996 as an orang-utan sanctuary, the babies proceed to Sepilok when they reach a certain age. The reserve runs nature activities, birdwatching and nocturnal animal trips. Treks range from 20 minutes to two hours; the latter 'climb' reaches a 95m-high observation tower with good views over the Tuaran District.

WEST OF KOTA KINABALU – TUNKU ABDUL RAHMAN (TAR) PARK Off the coast of Kota Kinabalu, the five islands of the TAR will accompany you through your journey in Kota Kinabalu and in coastal areas north and south of the capital. Pulau

Gaya, Pulau Manukan, Pulau Sapi, Pulau Mamutik and Pulau Sulug make up a marine park, created in 1974 and named after Malaysia's first prime minister, the fiercely pro-independence (*merdeka, merdeka!*) Tunku Abdul.

Overseen by Sabah Parks, TAR takes in about 50km² of islands, coral reefs and ocean. The largest and most handsome, **Pulau Gaya**, is home to several *kampong ayer*, or water villages, with hundreds of houses precariously perched on stilts over the water looking back over to the shores of Kota Kinabalu. The Bajau people were allowed to remain living in the park under native customary land rights. The original trading settlement of the British North Borneo Chartered Company was established here. The tiny (10ha) outcrop of **Pulau Sapi** was once connected to Pulau Gaya and you can still cross between the two by foot at low tide.

Water conditions in this marine park are not always in keeping with those of a marine reserve. Tourism is part of the problem, while educational campaigns are tackling the serious problem of rubbish in the water villages. The islands are contained by a fringe of reefs, particularly on the sheltered southern and eastern fronts facing the mainland. The beaches of **Pulau Manukan** and **Pulau Sapi** descend gradually into the reef drop-off, which can be seen quite clearly unless the winds are up. The ocean-facing western and northern coasts of the islands are more remote and marked by rocky cliffs and coral debris.

A shattered chain of lumps of sandstone and sedimentary rock, the islands broke off from the mainland during the last Ice Age. They are marked by honeycombed cliffs, caves, and a mix of coastal and strand flora including screw pines (*Pandanus dubius*), casuarinas and coconuts; big (really big!) monitor lizards and long-tailed macaque monkeys are among the terrestrial animals most commonly encountered. Along the trails, you may sight the weird, scaly anteater, or pangolin, or even a bearded pig.

Getting there and away Speedboats leave from Jesselton Point wharf in town about every half-hour from early morning until late evening. Local tour companies will arrange transfers, lunch, park entry fees, etc. If you are staying at one of the resorts on the islands, transfers are included. The trip takes 10–20 minutes. The conservation fees to Sabah Parks are 10MYR for adults or 6MYR for visitors below 18 years. Divers pay 50MYR per person per day.

🏠 Where to stay and eat

🏠 **Bunga Raya Island Resort & Spa** (47 villas) Gaya Raya Island; ☎088 271000; e info@bungarayaresort.com; www.bungarayaresort.com. A newcomer sister resort to Gayana Eco Resort, the timbered villas are immersed in Gaya Island's jungle setting, built into a hillside over a croissant-shaped beach & bay. The villas range from rustic chic to opulent 3-bed with wraparound decks, plunge pools & private beach access. The secluded resort offers activities such as diving, jungle treks & the indulgences of a spa, which pairs traditional Asian treatments with indigenous plants. Ferries run to & from the island & Jesselton Point in Kota Kinabalu 3 times a day. **$$$$$**

🏠 **Gayana Eco Resort** (52 villas) Malohom Bay, Gaya Island; ☎088 380390; e reservations@gayana-eco-resort.com; www.gayana-eco-resort.com. Standing like cormorants over the sea, the jetty, main pavilion, villas, bars & restaurants are all built on water stilts & connected by duckboards. Set between jungle & coral reef, the design features natural materials with some swish & exotic details. The lagoon & forest-facing villas have private balconies, AC & high-tech fittings, from DVD players to power showers & free Wi-Fi. With its own marine ecology research centre, vast 'Nature Pool', private 162ft luxury motor yacht for cruising, & extravagant prices, the new resort management is aiming for the luxury eco market. The open-air bar-lounges & restaurants offer Chinese-Malay seafood & Western-Malay fusion. **$$$$$**

right   Top nature watching spot at the Danum Valley Conservation area, Sabah (FL/FLPA) page 239

below   Mudskippers bask in mangrove mud at Bako National Park (DA)

bottom   Mangrove in Bako National Park, Sarawak — a favourite habitat of proboscis monkeys (SS) page 267

left   Typical pom-pommed and woven costume of Iban in Brunei and Sarawak (BT) page 16

below   Iban tribeswoman raking through drying rice crop on the Lemanak River, Sarawak (SS) page 17

bottom A traditional Iban longhouse (GB/DT) page 17

right   **Traditional Orang Ulu warrior and Kenyah woman in Sarawak** (SS) page 17

below left   **Bajau Laut boys eating papaya, Kampung Mengkabong** (TT) page 19

below right   **Iban woman weaving, Sarawak** (SS) page 29

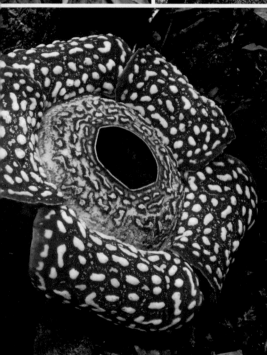

There are around 30 species of pitcher plant in Borneo of which half occur on Mount Kinabalu; see page 43.

The impressive *Nepenthes bicalcarata* is endemic to Bornean peat swamp forests. Unique among pitcher plants, it lives in close association with an ant species that helps to defend the plant against pest insects *(above left)*.

N muluensis growing in a thick carpet of moss on Mount Mulu, Sarawak *(above centre)*.

The large, vase-shaped pitchers of *N lowii* are not purely for trapping insects but attract tree shrews that use them as a toilet! *(above right)* (all UB)

There are 17 different species of the rafflesia or 'corpse flower' — so called for the whiff of rotting flesh they give off when in bloom — all of them endemic to Borneo. Indigenous tribes believe the species have aphrodisiac powers; see page 42. Here a *Rafflesia pricei* *(left, SB)*, a *Rafflesia keithi* *(below left, kk/Sh)* and the bud of a *Rafflesia tuan-mudae* *(below right, DA)*.

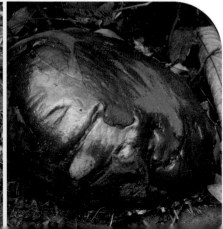

Aerial view of Semporna Peninsula and the Celebes
Sea. Boats leave Semporna town for day and
overnight visits to several islands including Mabul,
Sipadan and Kapalai. Pictured below, Sipadan Island
(main image: GAR/TIPS, *below:* SP/C) page 234

above left   Fish drying in the sun, Semporna Island (NG)

above right   The fishing village of Teluk Melano, in the Tanjung Datu Peninsula, Sarawak (SS) page 270

right   Fishermen attend their nets on the Sematan Peninsula, Sarawak (SS)

below   Stilted water village of the Bajau people, Pulau Gaya, Tunku Abdul Rahman Marine Park in Sabah (AY/C) page 184

above   Illegal logging is devastating Borneo's rainforests. In the 1980s; 75% of Malaysian Borneo was covered in primary forest; today that has been reduced to **50%** (GAR/TIPS) page 60

left   NGOs and passionate locals do what they can to replace cleared areas (TT) page 62

below   In recent years, forests have also been cleared for palm oil plantations resulting in huge losses in biodiversity and indigenous people's homes (SS) page 60

🏠 **Manukan Island Resort** (20 chalets) Pulau Manukan; ☎ 088 302399; e info@suterasanctuarylodges.com; www.suterasanctuarylodges.com. The hilltop & beachfront chalets & lodges all have a back-to-nature feel, built from chunky wood, with big windows soaking up the forest green & ocean blue, & nice aesthetic touches. As the island gets invaded by day-tripping hordes it is still easy to escape the crowds & go trekking, boating or make your way to a private cove & beach. By night it is bliss, as the crowds retreat to the mainland by early afternoon. The cosy yet spacious single- & double-storey chalets feature traditional building materials & decorations, have AC, a living area, TV & 1–2 bedrooms. Food-wise there are a couple of resort restaurants, but you'll be a captive audience to higher resort prices – don't expect street food & markets. All-inclusive prices for chalets, transfers, breakfast, park fees are quite expensive for the accommodation style. **$$$–$$$$**

Å Camping Sabah Parks (*www.sabahparks.org*) runs campsites on Mamutik, Sapi & Gaya islands. 5MYR pp per night (2MYR under 18s).

What to see and do
Many tourists don't see beyond the somewhat cattle-herded barbecue buffet lunches offered by Sutera Sanctuary Lodge on **Pulau Manukan**. This is fine for a packaged taste of the islands, but there are many other marvellous things to do. In peak season, dozens of people descend on these islands every day, but you can escape the crowds by planning a less prescribed activity: sailing the park waters to a secluded cove; hiking to one of the island interiors; or staying out on one of the islands overnight with just a handful of people.

Trekking Pulau Gaya This is the largest island, covered in primary rainforest that rolls its way voluptuously through creases and indents in the landscape. The forest is said to be one of the few undisturbed coastal dipterocarp forests left in Sabah. There are several trekking paths you can follow that criss-cross the island, ranging from 20 minutes' duration to several hours. One plankwalk leads inland to a mangrove forest. Pulau Manukan also has several treks and there is a nice trail on Pulau Mamutik with cliff views over the sea.

Yachting and private boat charter There are numerous secluded beaches and bays that are reachable only by boat, including **Police Beach** on the northern end of Gaya. This is the place for snorkelling, diving and swimming in clear 15m-deep waters of the bay. Its western cove is a popular resting point for sailboats. For island or cove hopping, charter boats from the **Sutera Harbour Marina** in Kota Kinabalu.

Diving and snorkelling
The fish are almost as numerous and even more colourful than the corals, spotted, striped and patterned in a variety of rainbow colours. Pink-and-green parrot fish, the turquoise moon wrasse, clown fish, sea cucumbers and star fish are all common. If you are very lucky, you might spot an ever-friendly whale shark!

Sabah Travel Guide.com

Pulau Mamutik The smallest island (just 6ha across) has the best reefs and coral, with clear deep waters. It is Borneo Divers' dive station and frequently used for both novice and advanced PADI courses. It is also an access point to the more vibrant corals of the TAR marine park. The beaches, white sand and reefs start almost immediately in the shallows. The waters descend quickly on the eastern side facing Tanjung Aru on the mainland. Basic facilities include toilets, picnic shelters, tables and barbecue pits. Contact **Borneo Divers** to arrange diving trips (*9th Floor, Menara Jubili, 53 Jln Gaya;* ☎ *088 222226;* e *information@borneodivers.info*).

Pulau Sapi ('Cow Island') The deep crystal aquamarine channel between Pulau Gaya and Pulau Sapi has many reef patches for snorkelling and diving. Pulau Sapi has far more facilities than Pulau Mamutik, and far more tourists. It has a watersports centre and is also a big barbecue day spot, indented with gorgeous deep blue pool coves. Its marine life is said to be good, towards the reef drop-off, on its sheltered eastern and southern sides.

Pulau Manukan I was very disappointed with the snorkelling off the main beach in Pulau Manukan. The waters are seriously stirred up by the day-tripping crowds and the island is also subject to strong currents and winds, though not as strong as the exposed north and western sides of the park. With a longer stay, you can discover Manukan's other long sandy strips and isolated bays.

Pulau Sulug At 8ha, Pulau Sulug is an island-beach, formed from a large sandbar and rimmed by coral reefs. It is the most remote and least-visited of the islands. The rocky northwestern side of the island provides interesting diving with many sightings of sea turtles and rays, and there is watersports equipment for hire on the island as well as decent facilities.

SOUTH OF KOTA KINABALU – KINARUT The rural Papar District begins around Kinarut, and this area is another option for coastal accommodation, about 20km from Kota Kinabalu. A car or taxi from the airport will have you at your lodging within 15 minutes. The taxi fare will be about 40MYR. Between visits to Kota Kinabalu you can take catamaran trips to nearby islands, go fishing or picnicking or head further south into Papar's *padi* fields, sago palms and Kadazan culture.

⌂ Where to stay

⌂ **Beringgis Beach Resort** (76 rooms, 2 chalets) Km 26 Jln Papar, Kampung Beringgis (26km from Kota Kinabalu); ☏ 088 752333; e maxcarry@yahoo.com, maxcarry@tm.net. my; www.borneoresorts.com. Next to a fishing village on a 3km stretch of beach. Clean, spacious AC rooms & units with garden/sea views & Wi-Fi. Rates quoted on website include breakfast. Facilities include 3 restaurants & business centre. **$$–$$$**

⌂ **Langkah Syabas' Beach Resort** (18 chalets) ☏ 088 752000; e langkahsyabas@ myjaring.net. 100m from the beach, the resort chalets with swimming pool appease budget travellers & families who want it leisurely & laid-back. Food mostly Western. Australian managed, leafy surrounds. **$**

⌂ **Seaside Travellers Inn** (24 rooms) Km 20 Jln Papar (Papar–KK Highway); ☏ 088 750555; e stinnjo@tm.net.my; www.seasidetravellersinn. com. Friendly, family-run beach-house accommodation sipping up the Kinarut seashore & South China Sea. Basic bungalows, 'de luxe' rooms with bathroom & family chalets dot the leafy cat-filled gardens, around a swimming pool. The sea-balcony café serves breakfast, & simple Malay & Western dishes through the day. **$**

6

West Coast Sabah

Between Kota Kinabalu, hilly coastal plains and a range of mountains separating the coast from the interior is Gunung (Mount) Kinabalu. The mountain reaches nearly all of the west coast, with the exceptions of its northern and southern tips – the rocky coastline of the Kudat Peninsula and the wetlands environment of Kota Klias. The Kudat Peninsula – the traditional territory of the Bajau and Rungus tribes – is a blend of forested and agricultural landscapes. It culminates on the headland, Tanjung Simpang Mengayau, the Tip of Borneo. South of Kota Kinabalu, inland roads wind their way through the Crocker Range, lined with tapioca plants, rubber trees, rice paddy fields and water buffalo, which are commonly given as dowry by the Kadazandusun.

KOTA BELUD AND KUDAT PENINSULA

Flagrantly promoted by Sabah Tourism as a day trip to 'Cowboy of the East' country, Kota Belud is the stronghold of the Bajau, who have a reputation for being expert horsemen and women. A predominantly Muslim town, the rural surrounds of Pekan Kota Belud are river-ribbed and picturesque, plaited with well-irrigated wet rice *padi*. Further north, the Kudat Peninsula is inhabited by the Rungus people and some of their *kampung* are involved in tourism through homestays and cottage industries. The woven fabrics, beadwork and basket-ware are being sustained partly for tourists. Minority races, including the Irranun and Suluk, originally from the Philippines, dwell on the coast.

It is possible to continue travelling as far as Sandakan on the northeast coast, via Kota Marudu, the Bengkoka Peninsula and Pitas. Be warned that both the roads and visitor facilities are poor – though this may add to the attraction of such a trip.

GETTING THERE AND AWAY

By car Kota Belud is 75km north of Kota Kinabalu, reached along the Kota Kinabalu–Kudat Highway; Kudat is 175km from Kota Kinabalu, the Tip of Borneo is 215km. If you are continuing around the coast of Sabah, it takes another 1½ hours to Kota Marudu from Kudat and about seven hours to Sandakan.

Car hire Sabah Tourism says 4x4s and saloon cars for self-drive trips are stationed near the Indian restaurant opposite the health clinic in Kampung Air, Kota Kinabalu. The 4x4s take seven or eight passengers at 20–25MYR per person return; the cars take up to four passengers and cost 240MYR for a return trip to the Tip of Borneo.

By bus Air-conditioned buses destined for Kudat, via Kota Belud, leave from Padang Merdeka at 06.30, 07.30, 12.00 and 13.00. Buses leave from the City Bus

6

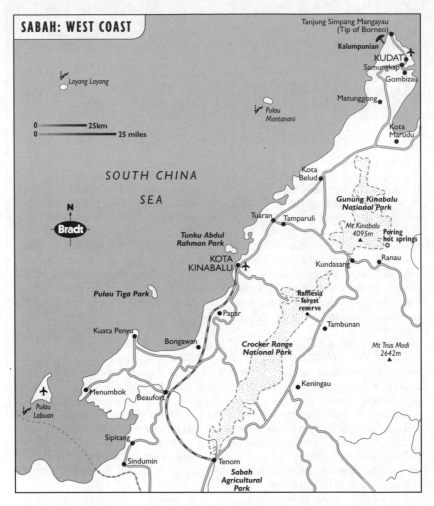

Tanjung Simpang Mangayau
(Tip of Borneo)
Kalumpunian
KUDAT
Samungkap
Gombizau
Matunggong
Kota Marudu
Layang Layang
Pulau Mantanani

0 _____ 25km
0 _____ 25 miles

SOUTH CHINA

SEA

Bradt
N

Kota Belud
Gunung Kinabalu National Park
Tuaran
Tamparuli
Mt Kinabalu 4095m
Poring hot springs
Tunku Abdul Rahman Park
KOTA KINABALU
Kundasang
Ranau
Pulau Tiga Park
Rafflesia forest reserve
Papar
Tambunan
Kuata Penyu
Bongawan
Crocker Range National Park
Mt Trus Modi 2642m
Menumbok
Beaufort
Keningau
Pulau Labuan
Sipitang
Sindumin
Tenom
Sabah Agricultural Park

Terminal North (Inanam) between 07.30 and 17.00. The trip takes three hours and costs approximately 18MYR.

By air MASWings (*www.maswings.com.my*) have three-weekly services (Mon, Wed & Sat) to Kudat from Kota Kinabalu in 19-seater Twin Otters. The 40-minute trip from Kota Kinabalu International Airport is quite bumpy. One-way fares start at 70MYR.

 WHERE TO STAY The only three-star hotels are in Kudat town, which also has over a dozen small hotels and guesthouses for under 60MYR a double. Few of them are recommended on the basis of their cleanliness and safety standards.

Kudat town

⌂ Kudat Golf & Marina Resort (88 rooms) Jln Abdul Rahim; ☎ 088 611211; www. kudatgolfmarinaresort.com. In a commanding position over Marudu Bay, this is a welcoming hotel with a small fitness centre, swimming pool, tennis court, sauna, 18-hole golf course, Wi-Fi in lobby & a good Chinese coffee house/restaurant.

Poolside rooms can be noisy during holiday periods. Rooms are spartan but bright, with kettle, fridge & TV. Spacious suites at mid-range prices. **$$–$$$**

🏠 **Kudat Rest House** (20 rooms) Jln Abdul Rahim (adjacent to the town sports field), Padang; ☎ 088 622708. Former government resthouse overlooking Kudat golf course. AC, TV, bathroom & balcony, VIP suites. Some reports of cleanliness not being up to scratch. **$–$$**

🏠 **Ria Hotel** (24 rooms) Jln Marudu, Ground Floor, Lot No 3, Kudat; ☎ 088 622794. In a bright tangerine & yellow, cube-shaped building, this is the best budget hotel in town. With AC, TV, phone, minibar & kettle. The suites are even better value for money, spacious & with a kitchenette. Next door there is a restaurant & 'Hawaii Internet Centre'. **$–$$**

🏠 **Upper Deck Hotel** (26 rooms) Jln Lintas, Kudat; ☎ 088 622272. On the top floor of a modern, but bland, city-centre building, above the Milimewa supermarket, some with views over Kudat Bay. Best shoestring option, AC, attached bathroom, phone, satellite TV, kettle. There are 2 suites with a few more fittings. **$–$$**

Tip of Borneo

🏠 **Kampung Bavangazo Rungus Longhouse** (10 rooms) ☎ 088 621971. Also known as Meranjak Longhouse. Located in a valley a few kilometres off the main road to Kudat, signposted at the turn-off along Jln Tinangol. Family-run venture consisting of 2 purpose-built longhouses made traditionally with split bamboo, beaten bark & rough-hewn wood. As well as rustic twin bedrooms (with mosquito-netted mattresses, an oil lamp & plenty of natural ventilation), there are double bedroom chalets. Approx 80MYR pp for dinner, bed, cultural dances & breakfast. Can be arranged through Sabah Tourism. **$**

🏠 **Misompuru Homestay** Kampung Minyak, 26km south of Kudat; ☎ 013 8721765 or 016 8155056; www.sabah-homestay. com. Co-ordinator Jeffry Yahya. A homestay network in the Kudat region, involving some 35 families who live in modern housing rather than longhouses, yet claim to offer a taste of traditional life through Rungus lifestyle & daily activities such as boat trips through mangrove forest, cultural dances, gathering wild food & fishing. **$**

✕ WHERE TO EAT

Kota Belud Day and night food stalls animate the riverbank. In town, amid the main block of shop-lots, **Kota Raya Restoran** is clean, bright and open-fronted with an excellent low-priced buffet.

Kudat Kudat seafood is excellent – shellfish, fish, squid, prawns. A Hakka (northern Chinese) speciality is stuffed tofu with minced pork, *yong tau foo*. Adjacent to the *pasar Ikan* fish market are a couple of shoebox-sized permanent food and drink stalls, opening onto a tree-lined car park used as extra seating space in the evenings. **Gerai Makan Dan Minum** (food and drink stall No 2899) is very good. Just 5–6MYR will get you a generous seafood noodle or rice dish and a drink – seaweed, coconut or sugar-cane juice. Its neighbour, **Gerai Makan Sing Wang**, is also good. In the new part of town, **Sungai Wang Restaurant** is a popular Chinese restaurant with air conditioning and outdoor dining, standard Chinese food choices but seafood-heavy, with beer and soft drinks. **Ah Foo Coffee Shop** at the Kudat Golf Club, is a Chinese seafood restaurant, good and open to the public.

A night market of Malay (halal) food stalls is held on Jalan Data near the Lembaga Bandaran, the open-air *gerai makan* stalls serve grilled meats and fish. No alcohol is served here. **Kedai Kopi Yu Hing** (*ground floor at the rear of the Ria Hotel*) has good, cheap breakfasts and lunch of *pau* (steamed buns), dim sum and noodles; also good for local coffee or Chinese tea. Famous for its *yong tofu* is a small unnamed shop in a group of old shops along the main road (it's right beside the Siew Lan tailor shop and Jaja Trading).

WHAT TO SEE AND DO

Kota Belud Acclaimed home of the *tamu* tradition, Kota Belud ('hill fort') grew up around the site of the original market, held every 20 days as a meeting place for people from all over the region. It still has that essential social flavour; the market is held every Sunday (⊕ *06.00–14.00*) at Jalan Hasbollah near the town *padam* (sports field). Lots of handicrafts and food can be found among the rather jumble-sale produce. At the major **Tamu Besar** held every October, the market turns into a showground complete with beauty pageant, water buffalo races and traditional dress parades.

Rungus Kampung (Kampung Gombizau) (*5min drive from main Kudat road along Jln Kampung Gombizau, 43km from Kudat town*) The village, with its communal longhouse and local honey production, has come to be known as Kampung Madu or 'honeybee village'. The Rungus also gather wild plants for use in traditional herbal medicines, and make many useful and decorative items, including brooms, bowls and wooden poles from coconut husks and fibre. At neighbouring **Kampung Sumangkap** the cottage industry is gong-making. There are 'nominal entry fees' to some of these villages and many tour operators in Kota Kinabalu will organise day visits to these longhouses. A visit to **Kampung Bavanggazo** costs 35–40MYR for a welcome drink, cultural dance and handicraft item.

Tip of Borneo The Kudat Peninsula and Borneo itself end at **Tanjung Simpang Mengayau** or 'lingering junction'. On one side is the South China Sea, on the other the Sulu Sea, separated by Marudu Bay. Off the coast are the islands **Pulau Banggi** and **Pulau Balambangan**. The first-ever British settlement in southeast Asia was a quickly thwarted effort to establish a trading post on the latter in 1773 to further the

LAYANG LAYANG – A DIVER'S PARADISE

Situated 300km northwest of Kota Kinabalu, Layang Layang is a manmade atoll, built as a Malaysian navy base and later developed into a dive resort – the **Layang-Layang Island Resort** (e *res@avillionlayanglayang.com; www.avillionlayanglayang.com*). Dive writer William Moss says:

Layang Layang is the summit of a huge seamount rising 2,000m from the ocean's abyssal depths. The submerged atoll spans over seven kilometres, encircling a vast lagoon. Its steep walls are a magnet for pelagics. The most famous residents are the scalloped hammerhead sharks. Usually making an appearance from April to July, they gather in their dozens or even hundreds. Other frequent visitors include manta rays, schools of barracuda, dogtooth tuna, grey reef sharks, and leopard sharks. Spinner and bottlenose dolphins frequently follow the dive boats. Rarer sightings include whale sharks, orcas and melon headed whales. Isolation from the mainland keeps the reef pristine, and the small inhabitants are equally splendid. Dives at Layang Layang are often drifts and tend to be deep, so are best for experienced divers. There are sheltered waters in the lagoon, but divers with at least an advanced qualification will get the best of the atoll's pelagic majesty and 35–40m visibility. The resort is comfortable and has a great swimming pool. Layang Layang is reached by Twin Otters from Kota Kinabalu. The small aircraft have limited carrying capacity, so photographers or others carrying excess baggage should plan well ahead.

empire's developing trade with China. An 11km road leads to the Tip of Borneo, past Chinese plantation houses and coconut palms – a long-overdue project to resurface the road was still incomplete in 2011, leaving sealed parts alongside sections with many pot-holes. The rocky headland, with its stone-scaped pathways and giant pewter globe, is skirted by glorious long beaches, such as **Pantai Kalampunian**. The lighthouse here came too late for the numerous ships that lie wrecked under this sometimes treacherous stretch. Tour operators do day trips from Kota Kinabalu to the Kudat Peninsula, taking in some of the longhouse cottage industries, lunch and Tip of Borneo, from 250–300MYR.

Kudat The town is named after the coarse *lalang* grass that grows between coconut and sago palms. Until the 1970s, the only way in was by boat along the river from Sikuati, 20km west – and it still feels marvellously isolated today. Despite its isolated location, Kudat was British North Borneo's 'capital' from 1882 until 1884. In 1882, the chartered company wooed Christian Hakka families to Kudat from southern provinces of China to fill a labour shortage on farms and coconut plantations. Those immigrants – and the coconuts – have had a long-lasting impact on the town. The **Pesta Kelapa** coconut festival is held here every September. Declared the cleanest district in Sabah in 2003, Kudat is seaside relaxed with a 2km waterfront esplanade connecting the old and new towns. The former lies along Jalan Lo Thien Chok, with its fan-cooled *kedai kopi* and mixed businesses, temples and mosques. The *tamu Kudat* is held here on Tuesdays and Wednesdays (⊕ *06.00–14.00*). The market is a great spot to mingle with local traders who sell Rungus handicrafts, such as beadwork and handwoven Tinohian cloth, vegetables, dried fish, tropical fruits and edible seaweed. This is a prime angling destination, and you can negotiate with local boat owners to hire fishing or cruising vessels down at the marina. From here, an air-conditioned ferry leaves every day at 09.00 for **Pulau Banggi** (its main township is Kerakit) and returns mid-afternoon. The **Kudat Golf Club** – Sabah's first – boasts of its historic links with St Andrews in Scotland.

Beaches The beaches in Kudat District are much cleaner than anywhere else in Sabah, largely because of low population density. On the peninsula's west coast, the deeply indented, funnel-shaped bay of **Teluk Agal** – accessed via Kampung Bingolon – has a beach bookended by two rivers. Past Kampung Minyak – oil village – **Pantai Terongkongan** features a narrow cave carved into the rocky headland to the north. **Pantai Kelambu**, near the Tip of Borneo, has a sand spit leading to two small islands, with bays on either side – it's pleasant for picnics and swimming. The closest beach to Kudat is **Pantai Bak Bak**, 7km north. It's rocky rather than sandy, but rimmed with a picnic area. A few kilometres north is **Pasir Putih**, a good swimming beach with fine white sand true to its name.

Diving Kampung Kuala Abai, a fishing village 20km west of Kota Belud, is the departure point for the coconut-palm-covered **Mantanani Islands**, about a 40-minute speedboat ride from the mainland. Accommodations here have come and gone. Current options include diving and snorkelling day trips from Kota Kinabalu, operated by Traverse Tours, with the possibility of staying overnight at the **Mari Mari Backpackers Lodge** (℄ *088 260501/2; www.traversetours.com; AC cabins*). On the largest of Mantani's three islands, **Mantani Kechil**, the dormitory, twin-share and private *kulap* huts provide no-frills, back-to-nature lodgings suited to shoestring or budget economies. Traverse Tours organise day trips from Kota Kinabalu and from Kuala Abai jetty for 120–150MYR per person.

Many boats went down on the northwest coast before the lighthouse went up on Pulau Kalampunian, so the region is popular for wreck-diving. Traverse Tours says the 2.5km beach, shipwrecks and visibility up to 40m, offer a great diving experience: 'Blue spotted ray and marbled stingray flutter around amid large schools of fish. Muck diving is excellent, with imperial shrimps, jaw fish ribbon eels, seahorses, pink-eyed gobbles, the jaw-dropping blue ringed octopus and nudibranch of all sorts.'

Whether these new forays on Mantanani signal a flourishing of dive ventures here remains to be seen.

GUNUNG KINABALU NATIONAL PARK

Mount Kinabalu was sacred to local indigenous communities long before Gunung Kinabalu National Park gained World Heritage UNESCO status in 2000. For the Kadazandusun the mountain is the resting place of their ancestral souls, so climbers have always made an offering to avoid being cursed. Lower zones of Gunung Kinabalu National Park have been scarred by forestry, mining and slash-and-burn agriculture; UNESCO's decision did not come too soon – and some would argue, not soon enough.

Spread over 754km², an area larger than Singapore, the park encompasses several distinct mountain environments and climate zones. The coolest place in Borneo, it is a botanical and ornithological paradise, with over 300 bird species, 5,000 flowering plants and a multitude of mosses, ferns and fungi. The floral inventory includes 26 rhododendrons, nine pitcher plants, over 80 fig tree species and more than 60 species of oak and chestnut tree. The 1,200 orchid species range in size from being as small as a pinhead to having 2m-long stems.

Ascending from 600m to 4,095 above sea level, Gunung Kinabalu passes through 12 climate zones. With this variety comes a wealth of biodiversity, and flora and fauna adapted to the varying local conditions; from conifers and lowland rainforest to alpine meadows. The massif is marked by 16 granite peaks of various heights, culminating at the 4,095m summit. The highest is called Low's Peak, after Sir Hugh Low who led the first official expedition to the summit on 7 March 1851, when he was colonial secretary of Labuan.

At Panar Laban hut – 6km up the 8.5km trail – Low and his local guides performed the ritual sacrifice of a chicken to appease the ancestral spirits and seek safe passage. Two expeditions to explore the mountain's flora and fauna led by Professor John Corner on behalf of the Royal Society of London in 1961 and 1964 were also important steps to the creation of the national park in 1964. According to the UNESCO World Heritage Centre, a World War II prisoner of war also played an instrumental role. One of six survivors of the Sandakan to Ranau death march, he formed the Kinabalu Memorial Committee hoping to 'preserve the Kinabalu area for the decency of man and a facility for the enjoyment of all of Sabah'.

The pride of Sabah, the park gets about 400,000 visitors a year. Most do not climb to the top, preferring to soak up the sublime surroundings on the mountain's lower slopes. It is hoped that gradually this tourism will provide more jobs to locals, so they can rely less on agriculture.

GETTING THERE AND AWAY

By car About 88km from Kota Kinabalu, the journey to the park takes about two hours. The last hour's climb passes vegetable markets, food stalls and craft stalls. At Kampung Nabalu, a few kilometres before the park, there is a *tamu* market every Thursday.

By taxi If you leave from the long-distance taxi rank near Merdeka Field, taxis charge around 160MYR for up to four passengers, while the standard taxi fare from a hotel is 300MYR. You can reserve taxis at the park reception counter for the return journey.

By bus Take minibuses and vans heading to Kundasang-Ranau from the Merdeka Field station. Buses leave from 07.30 to 17.00, and a one-way fare will cost around 18MYR. Get off on the main road opposite the park entrance. Air-conditioned express buses between Kota Kinabalu's city north terminal and Ranau or Sandakan also pass the turn-off 100m from park HQ. Fares are around 15MYR.

WHERE TO STAY Accommodation in the park consists of the lodges and chalets around park HQ, those at Mesilau Nature Resort and the mid-climb accommodation at Laban Rata. All are operated by **Sutera Sanctuary Lodges**, who have a contract

PARK INS AND OUTS

Whether you are planning to visit Gunung Kinabalu National Park for a day trip, stay for a few days or plan to climb the mountain, the following information is essential. More climbing-specific information is outlined in the *Climber's essentials* box, pages 196–7.

CLIMATE Do not underestimate the cooler temperatures you will encounter in the Gunung Kinabalu National Park area, not only compared with the coast, but also with towns only half an hour away. Daytime averages around park HQ (1,563m altitude) are 21°C, but can drop to 8°C overnight. Have a thermal layer ready and trousers instead of shorts. There are dense downpours rather than prolonged rain. From Poring Hot Springs on the southern edges of the park to the summit, temperatures shift from a humid 25–28°C to 4–8°C and colder.

ARRIVAL Gunung Kinabalu National Park HQ is the nerve centre for all people arriving in the park. Just off the main road, and engulfed in a swirling mass of clouds, there can be too many coaches and coach fumes to really feel the wonder of the place here, but you don't have to venture far to see the beauty of the area.

ADMINISTRATION The park is very efficiently run. Well-informed Sabah Park naturalists staff the park, most of them locals with a passion for their culture and nature.

OPENING HOURS Offices, shops and restaurants are open for a minimum of 12 hours, restaurants up to 16 hours. The reception office is open 07.00–12.00, as most visitors have arrived in the park by then for day or overnight visits. Sabah Parks operation counter is open 07.00–19.00, but it can be very hard to get assistance here, and you really have to insist on obtaining one of the scanty maps they provide. The Sutera Sanctuary reception has helpful staff, dressed in jungle greens. The souvenir shop is open 07.00–22.00.

PARK ENTRY (CONSERVATION FEES) Adult 15MYR, under 18 years 10MYR. NB: If you plan to visit Poring Hot Springs, hold on to your ticket stub as it entitles you to entry at the springs as well.

from Sabah Parks to manage accommodation and eateries in the park. The main office is in Kota Kinabalu (*G15, Ground Floor, Wisma Sabah;* 088 303915/16/17; e info@ suteraharbour.com.my; www.suterasanctuarylodges.com.my, www.suteraharbour. com). It is always best to book ahead, especially in high season – around June–September and school holidays. Major mountain-climbing events and festivities such as the Chinese New Year are also very busy times (see *Chapter 3, Public holidays and festivals,* pages 111–12, for important dates). Consider staying outside of the park (see listings on page 200 for Kundasang and Ranau), where there are a few budget to mid-range hotels and guesthouses and more expensive resorts.

Park accommodation consists of lodges including both hostel accommodation and chalet units of one to three bedrooms, heated showers and fireplaces (the first lot of firewood is included in the price), and in some cases television, kitchen and living room. The omnipresence of fireplaces gives an idea of the temperature drop you might experience from the coast region – especially at night (and still 2,500m from the summit of Mount Kinabalu).

Sutera Sanctuary Lodges, Gunung Kinabalu National Park 088 889086; www.suteraharbour.com) There are two hostels and eight lodges scattered through the forest near park HQ. Lodges include those consisting of individual suites around common areas, as well as single-standing, self-contained chalets with one to three bedrooms. The key difference among these 'premier chalets' is size, and thus suitability for individuals, couples or families.

🏠 **Liwagu Suite** (4 units) Split-level units plunging into the forest, 1 double bedroom upstairs, living room & balcony downstairs. Tea/coffee-making facilities, AC, TV. At busy times the beauty of this place can be marred by noise through thin walls & communal TV – the units are in the exhibition centre for the park, so there is quite a lot of traffic. **$$$**

🏠 **Nepenthes Lodge** (8 units) 2 bedrooms with 4 single beds, 1 queen, dining & living rooms. **$$$**

🏠 **Rajah Lodge** (3 bedrooms: 2 twin, 1 dbl) Dining & living areas, TV, kitchen, attached bathrooms. **$$$**

🏠 **The Hill Lodge** (10 units) Twin bedroom chalets. Pleasant rooms, with rattan furnishings, lamps, desk, sofa & armchair. **$$**

🏠 **Menggilan, The Rock Hostel** (28 beds in dorms) & **Medang, Grace Hostel** (20 beds in dorms) have 48 beds between them in 4/6/8-bed dormitories. They provide a basic & clean place to sleep, in misty forested settings, with a communal lounge with TV, common bathroom & toilet facilities. **$**

Mesilau Nature Resort 088 871519; **$$–$$$**) In the eastern part of Gunung Kinabalu National Park on the Mesilau Plateau, this resort is the best bet for climbers taking the alternative Meislau Trail to the summit and those who prefer a less crowded, more secluded forest environment. Situated 17km from park HQ (11km from the Kundasang turn-off), the venue is popular for scientific seminars and meditation retreats. Accommodation includes the 96-bed Bishop's Head Resthouse and nine other split-level lodges with names such as Donkey's Ear Peak

THE GROWING MOUNTAIN

The official figure of the summit height of Gunung Kinabalu varies between 4,095.2m and 4,102m, perhaps explained by the fact that the massif is still growing – some clearly haven't caught up with the latest growth spurts!

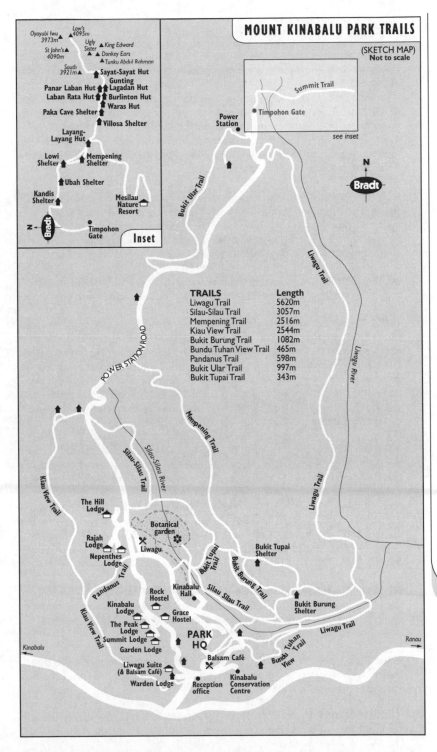

MOUNT KINABALU PARK TRAILS

(SKETCH MAP)
Not to scale

Inset

Oyayubi Iwu 3973m
Low's 4095m
St John's 4090m
Ugly Sister ▲ King Edward
South 3921m ▲ Donkey Ears
▲ Tunku Abdul Rahman
Sayat-Sayat Hut
Gunting Lagadan Hut
Panar Laban Hut
Laban Rata Hut
Burlinton Hut
Waras Hut
Paka Cave Shelter
Villosa Shelter
Layang-Layang Hut
Lowi Shelter
Mempening Shelter
Ubah Shelter
Kandis Shelter
Mesilau Nature Resort
Timpohon Gate

Summit Trail
Timpohon Gate
Power Station
see inset

Bradt

N

Bukit Ular Trail

Liwagu Trail

Liwagu River

TRAILS

TRAILS	Length
Liwagu Trail	5620m
Silau-Silau Trail	3057m
Mempening Trail	2516m
Kiau View Trail	2544m
Bukit Burung Trail	1082m
Bundu Tuhan View Trail	465m
Pandanus Trail	598m
Bukit Ular Trail	997m
Bukit Tupai Trail	343m

POWER STATION ROAD

Mempening Trail

Kiau View Trail

Silau-Silau Trail
Silau-Silau River

The Hill Lodge
Botanical garden
Rajah Lodge
Liwagu
Nepenthes Lodge
Pandanus Trail
Rock Hostel
Kinabalu Lodge
Kinabalu Hall
The Peak Lodge
Grace Hostel
Summit Lodge
Garden Lodge
PARK HQ
Liwagu Suite (& Balsam Café)
Warden Lodge
Balsam Café
Reception office
Kinabalu Conservation Centre

Bukit Tupai Trail
Bukit Tupai Shelter
Bukit Burung Trail
Silau Silau Trail
Bukit Burung Shelter
Liwagu Trail
Bundu Tuhan View Trail

Kinabalu
Ranau

6

PERMITS All climbers are legally bound to obtain and pay for a climbing permit, mountain guide and insurance. Permits are available from the Sabah Parks counter at park HQ.

In high season (May–September), it is generally necessary to book ahead to climb Mount Kinabalu, otherwise you will arrive and be put on a waiting list, without any guarantee of making the ascent. Book through **Sabah Parks** (☏ *088 889098;* e *info@ sabahparks.org.my; www.sabahparks.org.my*). First- and second-class certificates include transport to and from Timpohon Gate (Power Station) or Mesilau Nature Resort. See box, page 198, for a guide to prices.

MOUNTAIN GUIDES If you plan to climb the mountain, a guide is mandatory rather than optional, not only for the safety considerations and expertise of local guides on the hiking routes, but also because of the sacredness of the park to indigenous peoples and the need to oversee climbers in both their hiking practice and general comportment. See box, page 198, for prices.

ACCOMMODATION For any accommodation in the park pre-, post- or mid-climb, you must book well ahead through Sutera Sanctuary Lodges, see *Where to stay*, above.

TRAILS There are two trails to the summit, the **Summit Trail** (8.5km) and **Mesilau Route** (10.2km). They intersect at Layang Layang, at 2,740m, 4km from the start of the Summit Trail (Timpohon Gate), and 5.5km from the Mesilau Nature Resort. There are shelters along the way of both trails. The Meislau Trail started out in 1998 being used mostly by scientists and researchers. It is considered richer in plant and wildlife, not just altitude gain. It is tougher in parts, with 2km of unrelenting steps leading to the Tikalod Shelter. If you want to taste both trails, pay the fees to ascend the Summit Trail and descend the Mesilau or vice versa.

DURATION Though the hike can be done in a day, it is not advisable – many people have ended up with altitude sickness as a result. The best approach is a two-day overnight climb. On the Summit Trail, it takes four to five hours to reach Laban Rata (at 6km mark); add an hour or two for the Mesilau Trail. The next morning the final stretch to the summit, (2.5km) takes two to three hours. There are ladders, hand railings and ropes to help you on your way. After taking in the scenery at the top, climbers return to Laban Rata or Panar Laban for breakfast, before the final four- or five-hour descent to the park (the record slowest is 12 hours!).

ETIQUETTE This is a deeply sacred and special place. You should show the highest respect to the nature and to the local tribes who value it more than most. Shouting, fooling around and damaging the mountain environment should be avoided.

Lodge and Ugly Sister's Peak Lodge. The latter lodges comprise a total of 16 three-bed chalets with heating, living areas but no kitchen, and six two- to three-bed free-standing chalets with kitchens.

Mid-climb lodgings (☏ *088 872907*) At 3,273m, **Laban Rata** is the acclimatisation spot for climbers that have started out from the Gunung Kinabalu National Park

PEAK TO PEAK Other peaks on the mountain include Donkey's Ear Peak (4,054m), St John's Peak (4,091m) and Victoria's Peak (4,090m) on the western plateau and King Edward Peak (4,086m) and King George Peak (4,062m) on the eastern plateau. Special permits are required from Sabah Parks to experience these more challenging climbs.

CLIMATE Be prepared for the cold. Temperatures at the top can drop to 0°C but average around 4–8°C in the morning. At Laban Rata and the other mountain resthouses (around 3,300m/10,800ft) the early-morning temperature hovers around 10°C (50°F). Wind, cloud and frequent rain (even when the weather is mild) must be expected, so waterproofs are essential to avoid a miserable ascent.

THINGS TO BRING

Clothing Suitable walking shoes, warm clothing, windbreaker, long-sleeved shirts, change of clothes, extra socks, hat, gloves.

Trail munchies Don't forget to bring some food. The canteens and lodges in the park organise packed lunches but they are pretty basic cheese sandwiches in a polystyrene container. It is best to bring your own trekking eats and drinks. Include drinking water and high-energy food (chocolates, nuts, raisins, glucose).

First-aid kit Headache tablets, sun block, lip balm, deep-heat lotion, plasters, insect repellent, mosquito oil.

Equipment Binoculars, camera, waterproof bag for camera, torchlight, towel/tissue paper, toilet roll.

Items available for rent Jackets, torchlights, blankets, sleeping bags and towels can be rented.

MEDICAL NOTE It is recommended that all climbers should have themselves medically checked before attempting any mountain climb. Sabah Parks advise people not to climb if you suffer any of the following ailments: heart disease, hypertension, diabetes, palpitations, arthritis, severe anaemia, peptic ulcers, epileptic fits, obesity, chronic asthma, muscular cramps, hepatitis (jaundice); or any other sickness which may either hamper your climb, or be triggered by severe cold, exertion and high altitude.

DEPARTURE For safety reasons all climbers must depart from the Kinabalu National Park HQ by or before noon. There is also a horrific 03.00 start from the Laban Ratu hut the following morning, to avoid the cloud that quickly gathers at the peak.

6

or Mesilau Nature Resort that morning. There are several rustic accommodations where climbers and guides spend a few hours resting before resuming the climb to the peak the following morning at 03.00.

🏠 **Laban Rata Resthouse** (76 bunk beds, 2 units) At 3,274m, dorm accommodation, heated shower, room heater, restaurant area, & a common bathroom. Within the same building there is a heated unit, Laban Rata Buttercup 1, a twin-share room & bathroom, & the Laban Rata Buttercup 2, which has 2 twin-share rooms. There is also a restaurant. **$**

🏠 **Panar Laban Hut** (12 beds) at 3,314m, Waras Hut (12 beds) at 3,244m & the Gunting Lagadan Hut (60 beds) at 3,324m. All have basic cooking facilities, common bathroom & heated shower, though no room heater. **$**

✗ **WHERE TO EAT** Whether you arrive at 07.00 or 17.00, getting quality food within the park is no trouble at several venues. The **Balsam Café** (⊕ *06.00–22.00 daily*), down among the ferns near park HQ, serves buffet breakfasts and à la carte lunches with plenty of Asian, Western and vegetarian options. The daily climbers' briefing is held here at 18.00. At the **Liwagu Restaurant** a few hundred metres along from park HQ there is an à la carte menu and a set menu with higher (but still reasonable) prices. On the same site, there is a second **Balsam Café** (⊕ *06.00–22.00*) which has a menu-breakfast, buffet lunch and à la carte options.

The **Kedamaian Restaurant**, at the Mesilau Nature Resort, is much the same style as the Liwagu.

WHAT TO SEE AND DO

Mountaineering The summit peaks of the mountain are divided between western and eastern plateaux along a 16km-long chasm, which plunges over a kilometre into Low's Gully. Most people who attempt the 17km-return **Summit Trail** do so overnight, and with an average trekking duration of some 15 hours. The record return time is two hours and 37 minutes, set in 2003 by an Italian during the annual (October) Climbathon up the mountain. Some tour operators tackle the mountain along different routes to avoid the crowds.

HIKES Other than the summit climb, there are relatively few trails around the park. If you want a good hike, consider paying for a guide for the first leg of the mountain-walk return in a day. There are nine walks of varying lengths near park HQ (see *Mount Kinabalu Park Trails* map, page 195) for which you do not require a guide, though you can hire the services of a resident naturalist if you wish. The **Bukit Tupai Trail** is the shortest at just 343m; the **Silau Silau** is a very pretty trail of just over 3km through the nearby forest and back to the botanical garden. The longest is the **Liwagu Trail**, over 5.5km. A daily guided walk also sets out from park HQ at 11.00.

Nature appreciation The parks run an **Interpretative Education Programme** – ask for a sheet with the current range of educational activities on offer (for both children and adults) at the Sabah Park Operation Counter or Sutera Sanctuaries desk. Activities include a Mount Kinabalau **Botanical Garden Tour** (*09.00, 12.00 & 15.00 daily; 4MYR*), daily screenings of the documentary *Kinabalu Park – A Beacon of Biodiversity* (2MYR) and the **Mount Kinabalu Natural History Gallery** at Liwagu (⊕ *09.00–15.00 daily; 2MYR*). Flora from all over the park has been planted at the **Mount Kinabalu Botanical Garden** or **Mountain Garden** (⊕ *09.00–13.00, 14.30–16.00 daily*), not only beautiful ones, but those esteemed for their medicinal value by the local Dusun community.

The Liwagu conference and exhibition centre houses another small display on the park history and conservation, and there is a slide-show presentation held here (*14.00 & 19.00 daily except Wed & Sat; days & times are subject to change, however, so it is always best to check*) that introduces you to the park and its splendour.

In the vicinity of the **Mesilau Nature Resort**, wild orchids and the world's largest pitcher plant – the *Nepenthes rajah*, or Emperor – grow in abundance and there are guided nature walks (*09.30, 11.00 & 14.00 Mon–Fri, 07.30, 10.30 & 14.00 Sat & Sun*). Whether you are staying in the area or not, try to do some strolling or trekking around the **Mesilau Plateau** as it provides a very different picture of mountain ecology from park HQ, due to the higher altitudes. At the Mesilau Gate, you will be welcomed by a rather loud sign: *GRANITY MESILAU: YOU ARE NOW STANDING 2,000m AND INHALE 100% FRESH AIR FROM OUR HIGHLAND TROPICAL RAINFOREST*. In the vicinity are conifers, climbing bamboos, Agathis trees, orchids and orange rhododendrons. Near the ridge crest, the forest becomes more stunted with rocks, tangled tree roots, spongy mosses and liverworts.

KUNDASANG AND RANAU

The first settlement after Gunung Kinabalu National Park is Kundasang, a village surrounded by conical hills like Chinese hats, dropping into a knife-cut in the valley.

Crops cover the hills from head to toe. Kundasang is famous for its cool-climate vegetables – asparagus, spinach, broccoli, cauliflower, cabbage and mushrooms – and people come from Brunei and Sarawak to bulk-buy. The loss of forest habitat to intense cultivation has been high. There is still apparently no firm buffer zone between these communities and Gunung Kinabalu National Park – private land continues right up to its borders. The slippery-slide Kundasang road is lined every morning with wooden market stalls, selling local produce, *lihing* (rice wine) and honey. Ranau, an industrious yet relaxed town, is the commercial centre of the district – its population of 50,000 is bloated every day by those who come to market to buy and sell. Sitting prettily in a surround of hills tipped with mountain mist, it's a nice place to absorb some atmosphere, eat and stock up at the market.

GETTING THERE AND AWAY Kundasang is 7km along the road from the Gunung Kinabalu National Park HQ, Ranau another 15km. From Ranau there is a road through to Tambunan, the Crocker Range and Tenom.

WHERE TO STAY

Perkasa Hotel Mount Kinabalu
Kampung Kundasang Ranau; ☎ 088 889511; f 088 889101; e hpmk@tm.net.my; www. perkasahotel.com.my. This red & white structure is up on the highest of Kundasang's conical hilltops with a commanding view from 1,500m over the valley. The décor is a bit dated, but this 3-star hotel is efficient & comfortable with well-furnished AC rooms. The hotel's Tinompok Restaurant (**$$$**) is considered among the best in the district (Chinese, Malaysian & Western menu). There's also a cocktail & karaoke lounge, Kouvangha. The Perkasa offers a lot of golfing packages including accommodation, meals, golf fees & transfers. **$$$**

Zen Garden Resort (7 chalets, 120 rooms) Km2 Jln Mohimboyon (2km from Ranau); ☎ 088 889242; e info@zengardenresort.com; www. zengardenresort.com. Sprawling hillside resort, units with kitchenettes & living rooms, TV, coffee house, big restaurant, BBQ dinners, steamboats, Malaysian & Western food. **$$–$$$**

Kinabalu Pine Resort Kampung Kundasang (along Kundasang–Ranau rd); ☎ 088 889388; e k_pine2002@yahoo.com.sg; www. kinabalupineresort.com. The Dallas homestead-like entry is just on the right after the Kundasang market. Gorgeous nature-lodge setting in the forest, attractive hardwood cabins. A Malaysian Tourism Award for excellence (2-star winner in 2006), the site includes children's playground & BBQs. The Pines Restaurant has Western & local food & steamboats, & there's the ubiquitous karaoke lounge (⏲ 21.00–23.30). **$$**

Sabah Tea plantation (17km from Ranau, see details below) There is some purpose-built Rungus longhouse accommodation here. The longhouse sleeps about 25 & can be group booked. There are also twin-share bungalows (12 rooms) with ceiling fans. There's an on-site restaurant & tea garden serving Western & Asian dishes from pancakes to butter prawns. **$$**

D'Villa Rina Ria Lodge Km53 Jln Tinompok (500m from Gunung Kinabalu National Park); ☎ 088 889282; e info@dvillalodge.com; www.dvillalodge.com. Family, twin & bunk rooms, unadorned but spotless, with bathroom, heating, TV; lodge has a leisure corner & restaurant. **$–$$**

Kinabalu Rose Cabins Km18 Jln Ranau-Tamparuli (4km from Park HQ); ☎ 088 889233; e maxcarry@tm.net.my; www.mtkinabaluhotels. com. Family & de luxe rooms & chalets & a 10-bed budget room. Plain but clean lodge with big hostel-like restaurant (⏲ 07.30–21.40 daily) with home-cooked, Western, local & vegetarian dishes. **$–$$**

Slagon Homestay (15 rooms) Kampung Silou, Ranau; ☎ 088 878187; e cruzellyn@ yahoo.com; www.slagonhomestay.com. Guests at the Minudin family's home are told they can fruit-hunt & do mini jungle treks on this forest property. Twin/double bedrooms with & without bathroom & AC, chalets with kitchenettes. Meals served. Strangely enough, peak visitor season here is during the northeast monsoon, when Japanese people come & live for weeks to escape the cold at home. **$–$$**

✗ WHERE TO EAT Ranau's dearth of accommodations is countered by a smorgasbord of food outlets, all crammed within a couple of streets. There are dozens of *restoran* and *kedai makan dan minum* (food and drink shops), serving Islamic, Malay and Chinese food. At the bottom of Jalan Persiaran there is a market every evening. Nearly all the Chinese shops are good (even if some toilets are best avoided) such as **Sung Fun Tong** (*Jln Kibarambang*), which serves great food. Next door is a good cake shop, **Kedai Kek Delicious**. Opposite there is a **food corner** with some open-fronted *kedai kopi* serving noodle and rice dishes. **Selan Kembera** near the market has Malay food.

WHAT TO SEE AND DO

The Other Mountain Obscured by its big sister, **Gunung Tambuyukon** (2,579m) also lies within the Kinabalu National Park. It's about a two-hour drive from Ranau by 4x4 to Kampung Manggis, a vegetable-, chilli- and pepper-farming area and the closest village to the mountain's base. You will still need a climbing permit and insurance from the Sabah Park Office at park HQ, though a guide is not compulsory. Local tour guides put the summit trek at three days and two nights, with two camps on the way up. There is a government-established homestay programme at Kampung Manggis, with a population of about 150. Some locals can be hired as porters for the trip. **TYK Adventure Tours** are experts on this climb, which takes in lowland dipterocarp and lower montane of oaks, laurels up to 30m tall, mossy forest, pitcher plants, bright rhododendrons and orchids.

Kundasang War Memorial (⊕ *09.00–17.00 daily*) At the Ranau end of the atrocious World War II 'death march' from Sandakan (see page 8), this memorial in landscaped gardens with ponds and pools and water features might look like a fort but is a stone-walled peace haven on the hilltop. The dichotomy of war and peace, horror and beauty couldn't be greater. There are four interlinking gardens representing the homelands of soldiers: an Australian garden, an English rose garden, a Borneo garden with wild flowers of the Gunung Kinabalu National Park, and a Contemplation garden with a reflection pool and pergola. Having fallen into a state of degeneration as a hangout for local youths, the memorial and gardens were restored in 2005 – on the 60th anniversary of the end of World War II. Memorial services are often held here. Just a few metres from the memorial is the **Agro T Nursery** with flowers, fruit and vegetable plants – roses, orchids, hibiscus, tomatoes.

Nepenthes Garden The garden is within the Mesilau Nature Resort, on the eastern slopes of the Gunung Kinabalu National Park, a mountain slope covered with pitcher plants, including the giant *Nepenthes rajah*.

Mount Kinabalu Golf Course If you want to go golfing with your head in the swirling mists and massifs, this 18-hole course is nearby, at 1,500m above sea level in the Kundasang–Ranau area.

Pekan Ranau The undercover *pasar pekan* (town market) is at the bottom of Jalan Persiaran. This is a wet market with fish and meats. Alongside is the rainbow-coloured cultural and produce market, the **Pasar Terbuka Pekan Ranau**, an open-air market where Dusun and Murut people from the region sell myriad items, all fresh and fascinating. If you need supplies for the onward journey (or electrical items and car repairs), Ranau is the place. As well as fresh market produce, there is a Milimewa supermarket on Jalan Kibarambang, and a 'Superstore' 2km past the town on the right-hand side of the road.

Roadside rafflesia There are several private plots of rafflesia on the lower slopes of Mount Kinabalu, near Ranau and Poring Hot Springs. Look out for roadside signs in English announcing 'rafflesias blooming'. One such plot is found at Kokob Baru, 5km east of Ranau along the Ranau–Sandakan road.

Sabah Tea (*Km17, Jln Ranau-Sandakan Kampung Nalapak;* \ *088 889330;* e *info@sabahtea.net; www.sabahtea.net*) Situated 17km east of Ranau on the Ranau–Sandkan road is the plantation and factory behind the prominent Sabah Tea label (which you will find in just about every hotel room and guesthouse in Sabah). In a blanket of 800m-high hills, the plantations produce both standard and organic (certified by a Dutch association) tea. Following a factory visit, you can sit at the tea house/restaurant with its wonderful views. The venture won the Malaysia Tourism Award's 2004 Best Tour Programme for Educational Tourism. **TYK Adventure Tours** (see page 79) organise a Sabah Tea Adventure – a strange brew of tea education with jungle survival skills, night treks and traditional longhouse immersion. The tour (including transfers, accommodation, etc) costs about 550–650MYR per person for the package. They also run day tours to the plantation.

Hiking and biking The 2,500ha tea plantation is buffered by forest, and the trails through the tea bushels and surrounds of the Sapon Recreational Area are terrific terrain for mountain biking and hiking. Sabah Tea organise an annual mountain-bike competition in August. There is an easy two- to three-hour return trek to the top of the picturesque hill Bukit Kamunsu, through a condensed marvel of rivers, rafflesia, waterfalls and wild ginger.

Jungle survival camps Brothers Sadib and Maik Miki run **Miki Survival Camp** near the foothill of Mount Kinabalu in Kampung Kiau. Both are highly experienced Bornean trekkers, licensed mountain and cycling guides. During the camp they pass on skills from their Dusun ancestors. It's a three-day, two-night adventure in tents, about two hours' walk from Kiau. Others choose to visit Kampung Kiau for a big rice-wine party, held every Sunday. Contact **Maik Miki** directly (\ *019 8072814*) or via **TYK** (\ *088 720826; www.thamyaukong.com/miki*). **Intrepid Tours** do a homestay in the Kinabalu foothills area, sleeping in hammocks and staying with locals.

PORING HOT SPRINGS

Many climbers end their walk and ease their tired limbs and muscles with a near-direct descent into the hot springs. *Poring* is a Kadazandusun word for the bamboo that grows here. The lowland forests of Poring are part of Gunung Kinabalu National Park, located on its southern fringes at about 550m altitude in prime rafflesia territory – the park posts a notice if there is a rafflesia in bloom. Butterfly and birdwatchers are also in for a treat – both thrive amid the mixed dipterocarp forest of Menggaris 'bee trees' (*Koompasia excelsa*) and durians, mangos and figs, adorned with epiphytic lianas, ferns and orchids. The eastern flank of Mount Kinabalu bears the scars of the Mamut copper mine, which was mined for decades after the creation of the national park, up until 1997. The health of local communities is still affected by pollution from the mine and its heavy metal run-offs. Plans have been mooted to convert the huge mining lease into an ecotourism resort, as the state tries, if a little tardily, to rectify errors of the past.

GETTING THERE AND AWAY The springs are 126km from Kota Kinabalu, 38km northeast of Gunung Kinabalu National Park HQ. Coming or going from Kota Kinabalu's city bus terminal north (Inanam), you must change in Ranau. (The terminal is near the market, and the springs are a further 15km from Ranau along the Ranau–Sandakan road).

The buses operate between 07.30 and 17.00, and cost 15MYR for the first leg of the journey, 6MYR for the second. All long-distance buses plying the route between Kota Kinabalu and Sandakan also pass the springs, and there are several minibuses each day between Gunung Kinabalu National Park HQ and Poring.

WHERE TO STAY AND EAT

Sutera Sanctuary Lodges ℡088 878801. Camping, hostel, lodges & chalets. Sutera Sanctuary again makes its mark in the park, though there are other choices beyond the springs' gates. The camping ground accommodates 100 people. There are 2 hostels, the Serindit Hostel 1 (24 beds) & the Serindit Hostel 2 (48 beds), with common bathrooms & a sitting room & pantry (**$**). The Tempua Cabin has a double bedroom, lounge, TV, kettle, lovely big bathroom, outdoor bath & harem-like bed. The cabin is great by night, but not ideal by day if you value your privacy & peace, as it's wedged between 2 car parks & the entry to the springs (**$$**). Enggang Cabin has 3 bedrooms, a ceiling fan, dining & living rooms, bathroom &

kitchen (**$$**). The Rajawali Lodges (2 units) have 3-bedroom chalets with AC, a dining & living area, bathroom & kitchen (**$$**).

Round Ine (10 rooms) Main road at entry to the springs. Family-run, basic twin share, AC, cold showers, borderline clean rooms. There is an adjoining Chinese coffee shop with noodles & Western breakfasts, fish & chips & steak. **$**

Sungai Biru Guesthouse A few kilometres before Poring Hot Springs, on Jln Ranau-Sandakan. **$**

✗ Rainforest Restaurant ⏰ 07.00–22.00 daily. An undercover wood pavilion by the springs. Serves Malaysian & Western dishes & drinks. **$–$$**

WHAT TO SEE AND DO

Poring Hot Springs & Nature Reserve (*40km northeast of Gunung Kinabalu National Park in Ranau;* ℡ *088 878801;* ⏰ *07.00–18.30 daily; adult 15MYR, children under 18 10MYR*) Operated by Sabah Parks, this sulphuric wonder-world by the banks of the Sungai Mamut River combines a series of hot sulphur baths with the park's other natural attractions. Once used by Japanese troops, the baths are five minutes' walk from the entrance down a gully and over a suspension bridge. The surrounding gardens brim with hibiscus, palms and ferns. As well as hot and cold pools (temperature controlled from different sources), there are individual tubs and four indoor sulphur bathtubs (15–20MYR per hour) complete with living room, showers and toilet, and one with a jacuzzi. The conservation (entrance) fee should be paid at the visitor centre and park administration building, and includes access to an open-air bath, a slide pool, rock pool and Gunung Kinabalu National Park. However, there are several add-on costs for activities around the springs, including camera and video fees. The springs are very busy during holidays and festivities.

Walks There are several treks starting from the springs. The jungle-walk attraction is the 150m-long **canopy walkway** (⏰ *09.00–16.00; adult 5MYR, children under 18 2.50MYR*). Strung above the forest floor in 40m-high Menggaris trees, it provides an adrenalin-rushing view of the forest floor. A 1km hike leads to the small **Kipungit Waterfall**, a pretty picnic spot. The 3.3km Lanangan Trail leads to the highest waterfall in the Poring area, 120m-high **Langanan Waterfall**. Along the way, about 30 minutes from the entrance, is **Bat Cave** and a boon for botanists

6

Over 70% of the local populations in the Crocker Range districts harvest wild plants and vegetables, mostly for their own consumption. The rest gather wild vegetables to sell at the marketplace. Studies have shown that the rate of harvest of these plants is not an environmental threat, with the exception of wild palms (many are used to make crafts for tourists). The Kadazandusun people here use over 50 plant species for treating minor wounds, skin diseases, diarrhoea, fever, coughs, malaria, hypertension and rheumatism.

with frequent sightings of *Rhizanthes* – a parasitic flower and cousin of the rafflesia. The grounds also include a **butterfly farm** and **tropical garden** (2–10MYR). The **Orchid Conservation Centre** has the largest collection of endemic wild orchids with all 1,200 species found in Gunung Kinabalu National Park represented.

TAMBUNAN TO TENOM

The Crocker Range – the backbone of Sabah – runs south from Gunung Kinabalu National Park *en route* for Tenom, skirting Tambunan and its large bamboo plantations, the small industrial town of Keningau, the Padas River, and the swamp forests on the Sarawak border. The journey is a wonderful one, through changing landscapes of lowlands and highlands, mossy forests and mountain mist, gorged river valleys, Kadazandusun communities and coffee crops. Taman Banjaran Crocker – the **Crocker Range National Park** – is the biggest park in Sabah. The mountain has been an integral part of the ethnographic history of the interior. Today, native land titles and conservation values are both weighed up seriously. Many locals are still hunter-gatherers, collecting forest vegetables and plants for food and medicine.

GETTING THERE AND AWAY

By car Tambunan is 65km southeast of Kota Kinabalu in the direction of Penampang. The Crocker Range National Park is 144km from Kota Kinabalu, and 13km from Keningau on the Keningau–Papar Highway (Jalan Raya Keningau-Papar); Tenom is 200km from Kota Kinabalu. This circuit can make a pleasant round trip from the capital, up over the Sinsuran Pass at 1,670m and back, with a slight detour to Tenom. If you are coming from Gunung Kinabalu National Park, there is a road from Ranau.

By bus Take the Keningau bus from the long-distance bus station, Padang Merdeka (Merdeka Field). Buses offered by various operators leave at 07.00, 08.00, 10.00, 12.00, 13.00, 16.00 and 17.00; the fare is 16MYR. One of the operators, Tungma Express, also runs buses from Merdeka Field to Tenom, via Keningau, departing at 07.00, 08.00, 10.00 and 16.00. The three-hour journey costs approximately 17MYR and stops briefly in Keningau.

By train The Kota Kinabalu–Beaufort train (*07.45 departure Mon–Sun Tanjung Aru; Station Master Tanjung Aru* ✆ *088 262536; Sabah State Rail* ✆ *088 254611*) is particularly scenic as it passes the Padas Gorge between Tenom and Beaufort.

WHERE TO STAY AND EAT Food is always available at coffee shops in the small centres of Keningau and Tenom (such as **Storkbill Kingfisher** café in the latter), but accommodation is thinner on the ground. There are a couple of decent two- to three-star hotels with very competitive rates and internet promotions offering a 40% discount, including breakfast.

🏠 **Pesona Hotel Tenom** (63 rooms) Tenom; ☎ 087 735881; e pesona_tm@hotmail.com. Chinese hotel on top of a forested hill above the town, with rafflesia jungle & jogging tracks adjacent. The rooms are comfortable, though not highly fashionable. TV & AC. The hotel has 2 good eateries, the Kemabong Garden Terrace (coffee house) & Sapong Restaurant (Malaysian/Chinese/Western). Standard rooms a bit gloomy, best to opt for a spacious de luxe suite with views. Even executive suites are affordable. (Formerly Perkasa Hotel.) **$–$$$**

🏠 **Hotel Juta Keningau** (91 rooms) Peti Surat 25; ☎ 087 337888; e hjuta@tm.net.my; www.sabah.com.my/juta. A flashy tower for this part of the woods, marble lobby, heavy tropical wood panelling in rooms, AC, TV, safe deposit, internet, room service. Restaurant & bar. **$$**

🏠 **Perkasa Hotel Keningau** (63 rooms) Jln Kampong Keningau; ☎ 087 331045; e phkgau@tm.net.my; www.perkasahotel.com.my. Established 3-star on the edge of town, with coffee house (Top Corner), Full Moon Restaurant, Peppermint karaoke lounge & a health centre. **$$**

🏠 **Hillview Gardens Resort** (20 rooms) 1 Jln Menawo, Keningau; ☎ 087 338500; e hillview@alfons.com; www.hillviewgardens.com. A 3-Orchid homestay in a pretty tropical garden setting, the resort is run by a family, their friends & some amateur radio enthusiasts. Very good at local tours (& massages) & there are mountain bikes, Wi-Fi, cultural shows & karaoke by the pool-bar. All flower-named rooms have TV, AC & phones & include a couple of de luxe rooms & a family room. **$–$$**

TAMAN BANJARAN CROCKER

The Crocker Range extends over more than 120km, separating Sabah's coastal region from the interior. Often nestled in rain cloud, its peaks undulate between 800–1,800m, covered in mixed lowland and hill dipterocarp, montane forest, primary and secondary forest. Indraneil Das from the Institute of Biodiversity and Environmental Conservation at the Universiti Malaysia in Sarawak says the Crocker Range is 'geologically and floristically' part of the same range as Mount Kinabalu. 'The altitudinal variation of this park is remarkable, in rising from near sea level to 1,670m and extending from the base of Gunung Alab to the town of Tenom. The higher slopes are dominated by moss forests and by a profusion of rhododendrons and orchids.' The largest protected area in East Malaysia, the 139,919ha national park was established in 1984, taking its name from William Maunder Crocker, a British administrator in the late 1800s under Rajah Brooke's Sarawak Civil Service.

The Crocker Range is bisected by the Padas Gorge and the rapids of the Padas River. Dozens of different studies are being carried out on the biodiversity of this large remaining slice of montane forest: on the many species of fish fauna in its upper rivers and mountain streams; its bats, birds, insects and small mammals; and its amphibian and reptile fauna. Over 200 kinds of vascular plants, 30 birds, 250 moths, 15 cicadas and 40 bat species have been found here, and high levels of deforestation of surrounding regions, particularly lowland rainforests, have sharpened the urgency to protect its primary forests. On its eastern side, the range cedes to the most densely mountainous parts of Borneo – from Gunung Trusmadi mountain (2,642m) and thickets of highland montane forest to the peaks of the 'Heart of Borneo' (see *Chapter 2, Natural History*, page 64). Many rivers have their source in this area, including the mighty Kinabatangan.

🏠 **Tambunan Village Resort Centre** **(TVRC)** Jln Tvrc, Kampung Keranaan, Pegalan Riverside, Tambunan; ☎ 087 774076. Split bamboo chalets & longhouse hostel. A hostel for activities – rafting, hiking, kayaking, mountain biking & buffalo riding, though not held in high esteem by the travel industry. **$**

Shoestring inns A few (un-tested) hotels in Keningau where rooms will cost 50–100MYR include **Tai Wah Hotel** (*Jln Besar;* ☎ *087 332092*) and **Paramount Hotel** (*Lot 1 Jln Masak Spur;* ☎ *087 333084*). In Tenom, recommended by the nearby Sabah Agricultural Park, are the **Orchid Hotel** (*Blok K Jln Mustapha;* ☎ *087 737600; 50–80MYR*) and **Sri Jaya Hotel** (*Lot 78, Blok L, Jln Datuk Hj Yassin;* ☎ *087 736000; 40–50MYR*). The Agricultural Park itself has an 88-bed **Hostel & Camping Ground** (*hostel 25MYR, tent 10MYR*).

WHAT TO SEE AND DO

Matt Salleh Memorial (*Kampung Tibabar, Tambunan;* ☎ *088 253199;* ⊕ *09.00–17.00 daily; free*) Opened in 1999, this concrete igloo-like structure is a tribute to Sabah's rebel son and freedom fighter on the place where he lived and died. The bronze inscription outside the government-funded memorial to this local hero reads 'This plaque marks the site of Mat Salleh's Fort which was captured by the North Borneo Armed Constabulary on the 1st February 1900. During this engagement, Mat Salleh, who for six years led a rebellion against the British Charted Company administration, met his death'. Under the umbrella of the Sabah Museum, which provides tour guides to this area on request, the memorial contains some photographs, weapons and other paraphernalia.

Rafflesia Information Centre (*KK–Tambunan road;* ☎ *087 774691;* ⊕ *08.00–15.00 daily*) This education and conservation centre is set up in a forest reserve along the main road. Rafflesia plots are planted all over the reserve between 1,000m and 2,500m altitude and can be reached within a 15–90-minute walk. Mandatory ranger-guides charge 30MYR for a maximum of six people. Phone ahead to check if you have your hopes pinned on blooming buds.

Crocker Range National Park (*Taman Banjaran Crocker Park HQ, Keningau–Papar road;* ⊕ *08.00–07.00; adult 10MYR, under 18 6MYR*) This is a very peaceful park to visit, especially after the masses of Gunung Kinabalu National Park. There are just a couple of short walking trails, including the 2km Crocker Trail, some rafflesia sites and educational facilities. Accommodation comprises a camping ground (*5MYR pp*), a 16-bed hostel (*adult 20MYR, under 18 10MYR*) and a hut with two double rooms (*50MYR each*). Book through Sabah Parks Kota Kinabalu office, or online.

Trekking, cycling, rafting The 40km **Salt Trail** traversing the Crocker Range has been used by locals for decades, originally to get to the *tamu* markets on the coast where salt was among the prized produce. The walk can be done in either direction, between Inobong in the Penampang District to Tikolod in Tambunan, in two to three days. The Sabah Parks **trail permit** (*adult 80MYR, under 18 40MYR*) is compulsory, guides and porters are optional. TYK Adventure Tours and Borneo Eco Tours are both old hands at organising this trek, as well as trips to Gunung (Mount) Trusmadi. They and other specialists listed in *Chapter 3* (see pages 78–9) do cycling, hiking, camping and whitewater rafting trips throughout the Crocker Range, Tenom and Padas region.

As Joseph Binkasan and Paskalis Alban Akim wrote in the *New Straits Times* after the opening of the Mat Salleh Memorial in 1999:

> The locals were unhappy due to alleged exploitation, and one man that stood up and led a rebellion against British rule was Datu Paduka Muhammad Salleh better known as Mat Salleh. To the British, he was a rebel but to locals, he was a warrior. He was killed in a gun battle with the British police on Feb 1, 1900 … Also killed in the gun battle were about 1,000 of Mat Salleh's followers who fought from the neighbouring villages of Lotud, Tondulu, Piasau, Timbou, Kitutud, Kepayan and Sunsuron.

Mat Salleh and his followers were fed up with the British North Borneo Company's meddling in local law, especially the imposition of taxes on rice. Salleh was a voice for many angry people, but contrary to misconceptions, he was neither a lone crusader, nor the sole voice of dissent. Many others tried to throw off foreign rule in Sabah – each district seemed to have its warriors – and there is a spattering of memorials to them around the state including the Ontoros Antanom statue of a Murut hero killed in a battle with the British in the Tenom District in 1915.

LOCAL HERO, LOCAL HISTORY In the heavily British-tainted history of North Borneo, it's not very often you get to read what you feel are truly unbiased and non-British versions of Sabah's history. Other than accounts written by outsiders, in English, there appears to be a dearth of local records. It is therefore refreshing to discover a fresh slant to the rather top-heavy pro-colonial viewpoint. In a story about the new Mat Salleh memorial, published in the *New Straits Times* (9 March 2000), Sabah Museum director and Tambunan local, Joseph Pounis Guntavid, suggested the British had long bragged of downing Mat Salleh's rebellion to their rule. 'But a search and study on Mat Salleh's actions strongly indicated that he was not a rebel but a warrior who went against foreign rule, fighting for North Borneo's self-government,' he said. 'Mat Salleh initiated patriotism that led the people to fight for self-rule until Sabah gained her independence through Malaysia on 16 September 1963.'

Keningau Some 13km from the Crocker Range Park HQ, squatted down among the timber factories, this is the largest town in Sabah's hinterland and home of the Murut peoples. The surrounding mountains and cultural colours of the region are the attraction rather than the town itself. The owners of Hillview Gardens resort say the area was built up on the timber industry – high-quality plywood and sawn timber – which is now being replaced by oil palm plantations as well as 'more sustainable agriculture and economic activities'.

Tenom This is a pretty area, interlaid with gorges, rivers, mountains and coffee crops. The so-called 'local coffee' you will drink in hotels and coffee shops throughout Sabah is from Tenom. Some of the factories are open for visits; most are Chinese run. At the **Fatt Choi Coffee Factory** (*Jln Tenom-Kemabong*) you can sample the coffee, and also try iced coffee with durian ice cream (hold your nose as you drink). Tenom Kopi is mostly made from lower-altitude Robusta beans and is powder-fine, with a dark and muddy taste. The factories sell it for about 10MYR per kilogram. Other than caffeine kicks, Tenom has several short forest trails passing streams and waterfalls.

Markets Keningau's *tamu* on Sundays is a great place to see Kadazandusun traders from the region selling fresh produce and handicrafts.

Sabah Agricultural Park (*Taman Pertanian Sabah, 15km from Tenom;* ☏ *087 737952;* e *agripark@sabah.net.my*) Set among vast gardens and lakes, this is an agri-world with permanent living crop museums, bee centres, a native orchid centre, ornamental garden, agro-forestry and ethno-botany displays, as well as temporary expositions and events. A good family attraction, the grounds also contain forest trails, an animal park, picnic areas and a restaurant.

BEAUFORT – KLIAS PENINSULA

The **Klias Wetlands** region has recently become a top destination for nature lovers thanks to its large population of proboscis monkeys. Relatively secluded on a table-shaped cape and intersected by the Sungai Klias, the area is one of just a few remaining dabs of mangrove forest on the peninsula – most of it has been swallowed up by forestry, agriculture and coastal development. The wetlands are made up of a mix of habitats – tidal areas, rivers, swamps, mangrove and nipah forest. On the way to Klias through Papar and Beaufort, you will see a lot of sago palm (*Matroxylon sagus* or *M. rumphii*). Known locally as *rumbia*, the Kadazandusun and Bisayas use it for roofing, floor mats and baskets, and also produce the starchy food *ambuyut* from it (as Bruneians do). On the tip of the peninsula, Kuala Penyu is the launching point for the **Pulau Tiga Park**, a marine-and-reef park of more than 15,000ha, taking in three small islands about 10km offshore.

GETTING THERE
By car Beaufort is 95km from Kota Kinabalu, the Klias Peninsula around 110km.

By bus Take a minibus to Beaufort, then a connecting bus to Kuala Penyu. Contact the lodges below to arrange transport. Alternatively, book the whole thing through a Kota Kinabalu-based tour company (see page 168) that also offers the wetlands as a day trip.

By train Kota Kinabalu to Beaufort.

By boat Pulau Tiga Island is a 30-minute trip from the Kuala Penyu jetty. Boats leave at 10.00 and 15.00 and return 09.00 and 16.00.

 WHERE TO STAY AND EAT
Klias Wetlands/Kuala Penyu
🏠 **Borneo Proboscis River Lodge** Kota Klias (1km from the bridge over Klias River); ☏087 209221; e lyndatang@pd.jaring.my; www.borneowildlife.org. Beautiful riverbank & traditional village setting, the nicest place to stay in Klias & very professional, friendly operators in Tang & Lynda Yeu. Rungus longhouses on stilts with bamboo walls & thatched-palm roofs & AC terrace-house room with attached bathroom. Also has good food & riverside dining. Excellent value. Overnight package with 5 meals, accommodation & 3 river cruises for 300MYR. **$$–$$$**

🏠 Tempurung Seaside Lodge (11 rooms) Putatan Point (off JKR Rd), Kuala Penyu; ☎088 773066; e info@borneo-authentic.com; www. borneo-authentic.com. Stunning, remote seaside location, on a forested hill above a beach. The wooden walkway-connected rooms, snuggled into lush native gardens, are simple & peaceful with bathrooms & AC. Good, inexpensive food (& free Wi-Fi) at the open-air chalet-like restaurant. **$$–$$$**

🏠 Naga Puri Putatan Point Kuala Penyu; ☎087 884929; m 016 8802357; e mail@ nagapuri.com; www.nagapuri.com. A 'private hideout', this guesthouse looks out over the sea from the hillside opposite the above accommodation, & takes its name from that hill – Bukit Bukit Naga Aman Puri, or 'dragon's hill peaceful place'. For 100MYR a night including breakfast, lunch & dinner, 'freeflow' tea, coffee & water, this is hospitality incarnated, with a personal, but chilled touch. The 2- & 3-night packages are just as good value & it would be a shame to stay here only a rushed night. **$–$$**

🏠 Bukit Naga Aman Puri Beach Retreat (8 rooms) 1 Jln Bukit Naga, Kampun, Tempurung, Kuala Penyu; ☎087 884929; e mail@nagapuri. com; www.nagapuri.com. A hip & homely place but shared bathrooms & no AC. Just bed & beach. Owner-operated, above the beach with volleyball, archery & a small library. **$**

Pulau Tiga Island

🏠 Pulau Tiga Resort 11th Floor, Wisma Shopping Centre, KK; ☎088 240584; www.pulau-tiga.com. Operated by Sipadan Divers, with PADI diving centre, 12 standard & superior chalets with balcony, double or twin bed, fan or AC, as well as budget priced longhouse (triple share). Good buffet meals & casual friendly atmosphere, games room & watersports. Overnight packages from Kota Kinabalu or Kuala Penyu include transfers, accommodation, meals & park entrance fees. **$$–$$$**

🏠 Sabah Parks ☎088 243629. Accommodation on the island includes hostel rooms, 2-person cabins & a campsite. **$**

A few no-star, no-frills hotels in Beaufort about 20km away are the **Mandarin Inn** (*Lot 38 Jln Beaufort Jaya*; ☎ *087 212800*), the **Beaufort Inn** (*Lot 21–22 Lochung Park*; ☎ *087 211232*) and the **Beaufort Hotel** (*Lot 19–21*; ☎ *087 211911*).

WHAT TO SEE AND DO For visits to the Klias Wetlands, boats leave the Kota Klias jetty late afternoon on river wildlife safaris. Other residents that may be spotted are macaques, crocodiles, monitor lizards, tree snakes and eagles. The night-time spectacle comes with a glowing performance by thousands of fireflies having a good feed out on the mangrove tree enzymes to impress their female friends.

Pulau Tiga (*adult 10MYR, under 18 6MYR*) The crêpe-shaped island is 4.5km long and 1.5km wide, upholstered in old-growth rainforests, some palms and volcanic outcrops. It shot to minor fame as a location for the US television series *Survivor*.

In Kuala Penyu, there is a **Rumbia Information Centre** (*Kampung Kasugira*; ☎ *087 897078*; ⊕ *Mon–Fri (but closed lunchtimes) & Sat am*) with handicraft displays on things made with sago palm, and sago cooking demonstrations. Padas River whitewater rafting trips set out from Panggi station near Beaufort.

6

RESPONSIBLE TOURISM

Whilst visiting the park in 2003, youth volunteers from the aid organisation Raleigh International upgraded several trails in the Crocker Range, including the Salt Trail. They also helped local communities in the region repair water piping and paint buildings, while experiencing true village life; a good example of responsible tourism.

PULAU LABUAN (*www.labuantourism.com.my*) Situated 10km off the coast of Sabah at the entrance to Brunei Bay, Labuan is a Federal Territory of Malaysia, a duty-free island and Brunei's main import–export hub. Its capital, Victoria, lies in a deep-sheltered harbour and is a centuries-old maritime crossroad. Part of British North Borneo, the township suffered grievous damage in World War II. In 1990, it was declared a tax haven to boost its development as an offshore finance centre. Historic landmarks include the War Memorial Cemetery and Surrender Point where the Japanese surrendered to Australia in 1945. The 98km² isle has a population of 55,000, made up mostly of Malay and Kadazandusun. An increasing pack of international retirees are also settling here, attracted by its relaxed lifestyle and safe-haven environment, with Brunei and Malaysia both in easy reach. With all those flunked ocean passages beneath it, Labuan has become one of Malaysia's wreck-diving hubs, and Borneo Divers have a PADI dive centre here.

Getting there and away
By air Malaysia Airlines has four flights daily each way between Kota Kinabalu and Labuan, and two between Kuala Lumpur and Labuan. AirAsia has a daily flight between Kuala Lumpur and Labuan. MASWings operates Twin Otter flights between Kota Kinabalu and Labuan and Miri in Sarawak.

By boat High-speed, air-conditioned ferries ply daily between Kota Kinabalu and Labuan. There is also a passenger and vehicle ferry wharf at Menumbok – just across from Labuan on the south coast of Sabah. Express Labuan services leave from Kota Kinabalu at 08.00 and 13.30, and from Labuan to Kota Kinablau at 08.30 and 13.00; the journey takes approximately three hours and costs 21MYR for a child, 34MYR for an economy adult, and 39MYR for a first-class adult ticket. Check the Labuan tourism website for the latest fares and timetables: www.labuantourism.com.my.

 Where to stay There are many hotels; the top for service and facilities is the **Grand Dorsett Labuan Hotel** (*462 Jln Merdeka;* \ *+60 87 422000;* e *reservation.labuan@granddorsett.com; www.dorsethotels.com/labuan*), which has three restaurants, a fitness centre and a pool. Online specials start at 290MYR for a double with buffet breakfast.

7

Northeast Sabah

SANDAKAN

Overlooking a huge belly of water, dotted with islands, rickety fishing vessels and cargo boats, Sandakan has an old-world trading flavour. The beautiful harbour carries winds of other lands and people: the sea border with the Philippines, just 28km away, is visible across the water, and hundreds of Filipino migrants are just the latest in many exotic waves of immigration to have populated the town. From the port area up, there is a very Chinese flavour to Sandakan. Known as 'Little Hong Kong', its charm lies in the creaky water villages that throw rich hues and reflections over Sandakan Bay. Capital of British North Borneo from 1883 until 1899, Sandakan was nearly flattened by bombings at the end of World War II. Now Sabah's second-largest city, with a population of around 350,000, its economy is increasingly being bolstered up by the palm oil industry, taking over from the export in tropical woods, which dominated its port from the 1930s.

Crowned by a swathe of lush – though secondary forested – hills, the name *Sandakan* means 'the land that was pawned' in Suluk tongue (Suluk are Filipino people who settled in the area). The town's foundations were set in the 1870s when the Sultan of Sulu forfeited some land on adjacent Pulau Timbang Island to Scottish adventurer and engineer William Clarke-Cowie, in return for ammunition and protection from Spanish conquerors. The area was subsequently leased by the BNBCC. Curious colonial dregs include Edinburgh-style streets, English tea houses, Anglican churches and an Old Rex Theatre. The modern sobriquet is 'nature city' because of Sandakan's strategic position as a gateway to many of Sabah's natural wonders: the Kinabatangan River, the Gomantong Caves and Sepilok's Forest Reserve and Orang-utan Rehabilitation Centre. It's a slogan that will soon ring hollow, if that nature continues to be swallowed up by expanding industrial crops. While most people come to Sandakan to see the orang-utans and the Kinabatangan, try to spend at least one night in this fascinating anchorage of maritime and migratory history.

GETTING THERE AND AWAY

By air **Malaysia Airlines (MAS)** and **AirAsia** operate daily flights between Sandakan and both Kota Kinabalu and Kuala Lumpur. MAS flies from Kota Kinabalu to Sandakan seven times a day, with connecting flights from Sandakan to Lahad Datu and Tawau. The MAS office is between Jalan Lima and Jalan Pelabuhan.

Relative newcomer **Firefly** (*www.fireflyz.com.my*) also connects Kuala Lumpur and Sandakan. The airport is 12km from the central business district (CBD), a 20–30-minute taxi ride (around 20MYR). There are no buses to town.

By car By road, Sandakan is 227km from Kota Kinabalu (a five- to six-hour drive), 91km from Lahad Datu. Tawau and Semporna are 177km away.

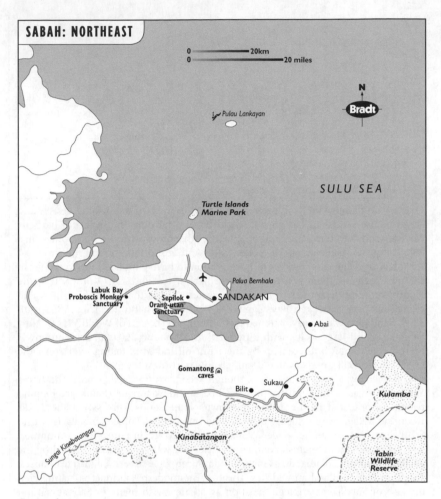

0 ————————20km
0 ————————20 miles

N

Bradt

Pulau Lankayan

SULU SEA

**Turtle Islands
Marine Park**

Palua Bernhala

**Labuk Bay
Proboscis Monkey
Sanctuary**

**Sepilok
Orang-utan
Sanctuary**

● **SANDAKAN**

● Abai

Gomantong
caves

Bilit ● Sukau ●

Kulamba

Kinabatangan

Sungai Kinabatangan

**Tabin
Wildlife
Reserve**

By taxi Taxis are relied upon a lot in Sandakan. The **Sandakan Taxi Association** (*Jln Leila, Hsiang Garden;* ✎ *089 222439*) charges about 6MYR for around-town trips, 20MYR to the airport, 35MYR to Sepilok and 80MYR to Labuk Bay.

By bus Air-conditioned long-distance buses run to and from Kota Kinabalu, Tawau and Lahad Datu. The buses from Kota Kinabalu leave several times a day, the journey is seven hours and costs 43MYR. From Tawau, the journey takes six hours and costs 19.5MYR. All buses arrive and leave from Sandakan's long-distance express bus station terminal, 5km north of town in the commercial zone known as Taman Fajar (a 10MYR taxi fare). There are also minibuses from the local bus station on Coastal Road near Centre Point Mall. Further along on Jalan Pryer, towards the Central Market, buses come and go all day, to Sepilok and Labuk Bay.

By boat Various companies operate boat trips from the jetty on Sandakan Bay to the islands and the lower Kinabatangan area. Outside the established tours, there are limited boat services, but that does not stop the adventurous chartering a speedboat (or even a fishing boat) as a water taxi and heading off to an island in the bay. The **Sandakan Yacht Club** is on the marina.

TOUR OPERATORS Established operators for excursions in the region are **SI Tours**, **Borneo Eco Tours** and **Wildlife Expeditions** (see *Tour operators, Chapter 3,*

MONOCULTURE?

Travelling around the east coast of Sabah, you will be struck by huge expanses of oil palm crops along the coast, inland, down hillsides, and deep into areas once covered by forest or jungle. Soaring global demand for palm oil products has seen Malaysia and Indonesia become the world's two leading producers, supplying over 80% of the market – using their Bornean states for large-scale monocultures of the high-yielding, thick-fronded palms *Elaeis guineensis*.

The reddish-brown oil, extracted from crushed fruit of the palm, is riding high on the international commodities charts after coming into demand for being cheap and quickly produced. You will see 'palm oil' as an ingredient in a range of products from foodstuffs to cosmetics, including chocolate, biscuits, ice cream, bread, toothpaste, soap and body lotions. It's also being investigated as a source of biofuel. Intended as a green fuel, critics knock biofuel as 'deforestation diesel' because of the widespread forest clearing carried out by the industry.

Oil palm plantations contribute about 5% of Malaysia's national GDP, and provide nearly 1.5 million jobs. Sabah is the biggest producer, though Sarawak is quickly catching up. Since the end of the 1990s, production in Sabah has multiplied and the amount of land under plantation has doubled from 700,000 to 1.4 million hectares – that's a staggering 20% of the total state area.

Sabah's favourable climate yields the highest palm oil crops per hectare, attracting a swarm of potential investors. The majority of palm oil plantations are found in the east of the state where, according to the Sabah Institute of Development Studies, 'suitable agricultural land is available'. However, much of what is claimed to be 'suitable agricultural land' is actually destroyed forest, ruined by logging or oil palm practices.

In precious natural areas such as the Kinabatangan River, it is deeply troubling to see just how much of the habitat of endangered species has been swallowed up by the industry. Orang-utans who once lived in the jungle now live in plantations, where they are considered pests. The Palm Oil Council says these environmental encroachments are errors of the past, and that it is now seeking greater yields through seed technology rather than through land clearing. But as the voracious appetite for palm oil and plantation space continues, they are accused of 'the genocide of the orang-utan' – many animals are killed during forest clearing and many more lose their habitat – doomed to nibble away at plantations for the rest of their life instead of living freely in their once-dense forest home.

The increasingly common large-scale plantations in Sarawak are also said to be encroaching on the land of indigenous people, who repeatedly find themselves in confrontation with police called in by contractors. Instead of palm oil production being an answer to rural poverty, as the government claims it to be, critics see it as a gateway to misery, as indigenous people are forced to abandon their homes and work for a pittance on plantations.

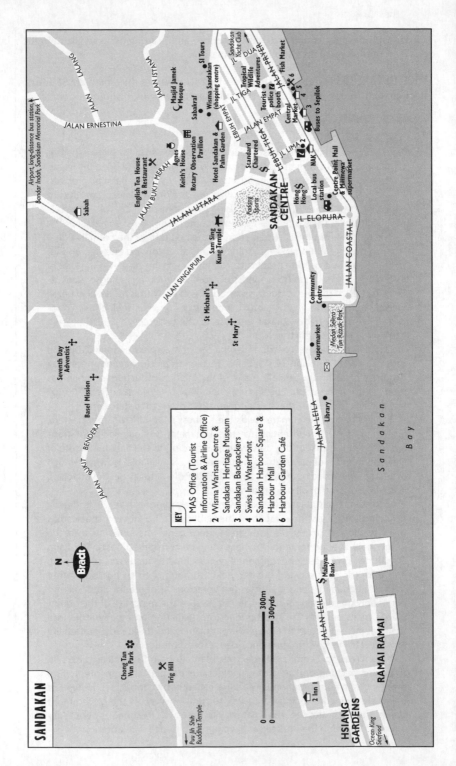

SANDAKAN

KEY
1 MAS Office (Tourist Information & Airline Office)
2 Wisma Warisan Centre & Sandakan Heritage Museum
3 Sandakan Backpackers
4 Swiss Inn Waterfront
5 Sandakan Harbour Square & Harbour Mall
6 Harbour Garden Café

Airport, long-distance bus station,
Bandar Indah, Sandakan Memorial Park

JALAN LANG

JALAN ISTANA

Masjid Jamek Mosque
SI Tours
Wisma Sandakan (shopping centre)
Sabakraf

JALAN ERNESTINA

English Tea House & Restaurant
Keith's House
Agnes
Rotary Observation Pavilion
Hotel Sandakan & Palm Garden

JALAN BUKIT MERAH

Sabah

JALAN UTARA

JALAN SINGAPURA

Sam Sing Kung Temple

Padang Sports

Standard Chartered $

JL TIGA
LEBUH EMPAT
JALAN EMPAT
LEBUH TIGA

Sandakan Yacht Club
JL DUA
Tropical Wildlife Adventures
JALAN PRYER
Fish Market
Tourist police
Central Market
Buses to Sepilok

SANDAKAN CENTRE

JL LIM
Hong $ Hong
NAK
Local bus station
Centre Point Mall & Milimewa supermarket

JL ELOPURA

St Michael's

St Mary

Seventh Day Adventist

Basel Mission

JALAN BUKIT BENDERA

Chong Tan Vun Park

Trig Hill

Puu Jih Shih Buddhist Temple

N
Bradt

JALAN LEILA

Community Centre
Supermarket
Medan Selera Tun Razak Park

Library

Sandakan Bay

0 ___ 300m
0 ___ 300yds

2 Inn 1

Malayan Bank $

JALAN LEILA

RAMAI RAMAI

HSIANG GARDENS

Ocean King Starfood

214

pages 78–9, for details). All three can facilitate the excursions outlined in *What to see and do* below, including day and overnight trips to the Kinabatangan River and the Turtle Islands. Other lodges organise their own transport and tours, including **Uncle Tan Wildlife Adventures** (see page 222). A newcomer is **Tropical Wildlife Adventures** (*Jln Tiga*; 𝄞 *089 271077*; *www.stwadventure.com*), which offers tours of Sandakan town, Sepilok's Orang-utan Rehabilitation and Rainforest Discovery Centres and the Gomantong Caves.

🏠 WHERE TO STAY

A new mid-market Malaysian chain has made its way onto the Harbour Square precinct in what should be a welcome widening of the city's offerings, though it is yet to prove its worth. Similarly, a new boutique property has joined the budget and shoestring hotels located about 1.5km along the coast in the Ramai Ramai commercial centre and Hsiang Garden districts.

🏠 **Sabah Hotel** (120 rooms) Km1, Jln Utara (1km from city centre); 𝄞 089 213299; www. sabahhotel.com.my. Sandakan's top leisure hotel in 5ha of garden overflowing into the rainforest (with jogging trail), big & bright de luxe rooms, business centre, swimming pool fed by a waterfall, fitness club & spa. Great buffet breakfasts & lunches, fun dining themes, warm layout, ambience & staff. **$$–$$$$**

🏠 **Hotel Sandakan** (105 rooms) Block 83, 4th Av; 𝄞 089 221122; e info@hotelsandakan. com.my; www.hotelsandakan.com.my. Excellent range of rooms & suites, switched-on service & technology. It has more of a business beat about it than the Sabah. Save 30–40% on internet bookings. **$$–$$$**

🏠 **Swiss-Inn Waterfront Sandakan** (138 rooms) HS12, Sandakan Harbour Sq; 𝄞 089 240888; e resvns_siwsdk@swissgarden.com; www.swissgarden.com. Malaysian budget to mid-range hotel chain. While I haven't tried it out myself yet, I have heard many complaints about bed & bathroom linen & service standards. Some rooms & suites with views over Sulu Sea. LCD TV, rain showers, business centre, car park, Swiss-Deli & Waterfront Seafood Bar & Grill. **$$–$$$**

🏠 **Sanbay Hotel** (58 rooms) Mile 1¼, Jln Leila; 𝄞 089 275000; e sean@sanbay.com.my; www.sanbay.com.my. A couple of miles out of town, 3-star with views over the bay, good service & well-furnished rooms; in-house Raja's café. Spacious rooms with satellite TV/CNN, en-suite bathrooms, AC throughout & generator-backed power. **$$**

🏠 **2Inn1** (50 rooms) 𝄞 089 202121; Lot 1–7, Block B, Bandar Fajar, Jalan Leila; e hotel2inn1@ yahoo.com; www.2inn1.com.my. Between the airport & the city, in the Fajar retail area, is this catchy boutique budget hotel in a swirling mango & cream low-rise building. The hotel name plays on one of Malaysia's favorite jingles – the '2-' & '3-in-one' drinks that invariably include instant coffee, milk & sugar. Rooms named 'Superior Nature Green' & 'Family Yellow Sweet Lemonade' have funky furnishings & colours. Wi-Fi internet, business facilities & restaurant with open-kitchen serving international food. If you do stay here, there's a new vegetarian restaurant in the vicinity, which is getting good reports from locals: Vegetarian Restaurant, Lot 6, Block 1, Bandar Pasaraya. **$–$$**

🏠 **Nak Hotel** (35 rooms) Jln Pelabuhan; 𝄞 089 272988; e info@nakhotel.com; www.nakhotel. com. This shoestring boutique is a characterful, family-run hotel, named after a former MP. Great value for money, but noisy. Pleasant roof garden-bar, clean comfortable rooms & old Chinese trading world aesthetic of reds & blacks. Standard singles & doubles, de luxe family rooms & upper-price range 'suites'. **$–$$**

Sandakan Backpackers (11 rooms) Lot 108, Block SH-11, Sandakan Harbour Sq; 𝄞 089 221104; e enquiries@sandakanbackpackers. com; www.sandakanbackpackers.com. Dorm, single/double rooms & 1 family room. No curfew; lounge & sundeck, internet, complimentary breakfast. Good for backpacker tours in the area. **$**

🍴 WHERE TO EAT

Sandakan has fantastic fresh seafood which can be enjoyed at food stalls and coffee shops selling it at a fraction of the price of seafood restaurants.

Some good Malay, Chinese and Western eateries are found in hotels of all price brackets, usually with the choice of sitting outdoors or inside with air conditioning.

✖ English Tea House & Restaurant 2002 Jln Istana, adjacent to Agnes Keith Hse Museum; ☎089 222544; e info@englishteahouse.com. Very British, with its Bermuda grass & croquet lawns. The food is a rather bland fusion of Western & Asian, of sandwiches & *laksa*, but the gorgeous breezy hilltop location & viewpoint over the sea & city merit a cup of tea at least. Relatively expensive. $$$–$$$$

✖ Ming Restaurant In Sabah Hotel, Km1, Jln Utara; ☎089 213299. Large menu of Cantonese & Szechuan dishes including some interesting vegetarian 'chicken' & 'pork' meals (ie: sweet & sour tofu or honeyed soy). In the same hotel, the poolside Plantation Café has excellent lunch & dinner buffets, including steamboats & BBQs. In-house breads (Chinese & European, white & sourdough) & pastries are sold in the lobby delicatessen. $$$–$$$$

✖ Ocean King Seafood Parlour Pasir Putih (White Sand). A 20min drive from town centre on the coast, but worth the trip for the fresh seafood platter menu at very reasonable prices. Recommended by locals. $$$

✖ Palm Garden In Hotel Sandakan, Block 83, 4th Av; ☎089 221122; ⊕ food served 6.30–23.00. Chinese restaurant specialises in Cantonese & dim sum delicacies. There is also a halal coffee shop – the Palm Café. $$$

✖ Harbour Garden Café Ground Floor, Sandakan Harbour Sq. New Chinese café getting rave reviews for the views & food. Johhny Lim from the Sepilok Jungle Resort says this: 'Came to the café because it was recommended by some tourists. Did not regret. Thoroughly enjoyed the great food (try the chicken pau & dim sum). Best part was the friendly staff & the amazing waterfront view.' $$

Street food Head to the Central Market, and then to the adjacent Open Market, where you will find dozens of stalls with fresh and cooked food as well as coffee shops. Malay eateries are always set up between the waterfront Jalan Coastal and the Sandakan Community Centre.

ENTERTAINMENT AND NIGHTLIFE At Mile 4, about 5km from town towards Sepilok, **Bandar Indah** is a young, nouveau-riche suburb – a happening place with lots of bars, pubs and happy hours from 17.00 to 18.00. Live performances often follow, and things really start heating up at around 22.00 with karaoke and disco action. There is also some local nightlife for those staying in the **Ramai-Ramai** area, in the form of discos, bars and hotel entertainment.

SHOPPING The newcomer is the five-storey **Harbour Mall**, a retail hub in the Harbour Square development (*www.shsquare.com.my*). The established city shopping centre, **Wisma Sandakan**, is a multi-levelled mall at the back of town. Here you will find plenty of fast food, electronics, clothing and internet cafés in an uninspiring environment. The state-owned souvenir and crafts-shop chain, **Sabakraf**, is just behind this plaza. For books, the **South East Asia Bookstore** is located off Jalan Empat in the CBD. The **Centre Point Mall** off the waterfront's Jalan Coastal has a department store, supermarket and various shops and eateries.

OTHER PRACTICALITIES The **banks** district revolves around the visitor information centre – HSBC, Bumiputera Commerce and Standard Chartered. The **post office** and **library** are on the southwest edge of town, near Medan SeleraTun Razak Park.

WHAT TO SEE AND DO
Waterfront Sandakan is a port city and can be enjoyably explored on foot. The new shoreline development of **Sandakan Harbour Square** links with the 1.5km-long

Esplanade to form a pleasant strolling stretch. In the middle of Harbour Square, the **Fish Market** and **Central Market** are situated in a modern three-storey complex, with the 'wet' and 'dry' markets on the ground level and clothing stores and shop-lots on the upper levels. The more rural *tamu* held here on Sundays is a cultural bouillabaisse of all the flavours ocean migrations have brought to Sandakan. Around the harbour, water villages are strung out on stilts; residents of the creaky, colourful, flower-potted Kampung Buli Sim Sim simply throw the fishing line out their window to catch their dinner and enjoy views of Sandakan's cargo boats and islands.

Temples and mosques Sandakan's velvety hills are covered with places of worship. **Sam Sing Kung** ('Three Saints Temple') is the city's oldest building, completed in 1887 – its three deities uphold righteousness, safety of fishermen and success in exams. A high spiritual, architectural and panoramic experience is the **Puu Jih Shih Buddhist Temple**, a red-shingled, white-walled spectacle of writhing dragons and gilded Buddhas. Perched on a hilltop a few kilometres north of the town centre, the temple was built in 1987 at a cost of 7 million MYR. Other holy places lie along the **Sandakan Heritage Trail**, including the **Masjid Jamek Mosque** and **St Michael's & All Angels' Church**. One of the only pre-war buildings to survive, St Michael's was built in 1893 from local granite. Pick up a map of this trail from the **visitor information centre** (*between Lebuh Empat & Lebuh Tiga avs*) – it lists 14 places linked together over a 90-minute to two-hour loop from waterfront to hilltop. The walk also takes in the **Chinese World War II Memorial** and some more temples, up to the **English Tea House** via forested parkland and the **Stairs with a Hundred Steps** (warning: there have been reports of muggings in this area despite it being alongside a police station).

Museums Agnes Keith's book on life in pre-war Sandakan popularised the use of the old seafarer's name for Sabah - 'Land Below the Wind'. The American writer lived in a colonial wooden bungalow overlooking Sandakan Bay with her husband Henry Keith, the first forestry chief of British North Borneo. **Agnes Keith's House** (*Jln Istana;* ✆ *089 222679;* ⊕ *09.00–17.00 daily; 15MYR*) is along the heritage trail, as is the more interesting local history depot, the **Sandakan Heritage Museum** (*Wisma Warisan Centre;* ✆ *089 222679;* ⊕ *09.00–17.00 daily*).

Memorials Within the Sibuga Forest Reserve, 12km north of the city, is the **Sandakan Memorial Park** (*Mile 7 Jln Labuk Utara;* ✆ *016 8221616;* ⊕ *09.00–17.00 daily*), just opposite the site of the original Sandakan prisoners of war camp. The 2,700 Australian and British POWs brought here in 1942 were used as labour force to build a military airstrip – later destroyed by the Japanese. This is also where the dreadful Sandakan to Ranau 'death marches' set out from (see *History, Chapter 1*, page 8). The memorial park's Commemorative Pavilion has a graphic display with an excellent, though heart-rending, interpretation of this appalling period. See also the **Chinese World War II Memorial.**

EXCURSIONS FROM SANDAKAN

ISLANDS For diving and turtle-watching (or just playing Robinson Crusoe), there are several islands within and beyond Sandakan's beautiful harbour.

Pulau Berhala (reached by charter boat or tour) Right in Sandakan Bay, the soaring red cliffs and dark forested clusters of Berhala Island are stunning. It was used as a POW camp during the war – and prior to that, a leper colony. Some

Australian POWs used the old leper settlement as an escape route, swimming to the cliffs where they were helped by natives to freedom.

Turtle Islands Marine Park Situated 40km north of Sandakan in the Sulu Sea, the Turtle Islands Marine Park lies within a major nesting ground for green and hawksbill turtles. The turtle sanctuary, established in 1977 to protect the two species, encompasses three small islands: Pulau Selingan, Pulau Bakungan Kecil and Pulau Gulisan. Pulau Selingan is the main nesting area for hundreds of green turtles, while the hawksbills are more attracted to the shores of Pulau Gulisan. Shaped like a musical note with a sandy rim and green core, it is less than 9ha in size.

Green turtles usually spend their time in shallow seagrass beds, but come ashore to lay their eggs. Each night during the nesting season, hordes of turtles drag themselves up the beach to deposit their unhatched offspring. An individual may spend hours choosing the right spot, before she commences digging a hole in the sand with her flippers. The best time to visit is between March and September (peak laying season and calm seas). Personally, I found the overcrowded spectacle quite upsetting. Rangers spotlight the scene with torches, revealing not only the egg-laying but also the newly hatched youngsters making their way to the sea, for their first fragile hours in the big world. One can't help but feel that these creatures deserve the dignity of living out these moments in private.

Getting there A boat leaves Sabah Parks' jetty on Jalan Buli Buli daily at 09.30. The trip to Selingan takes an hour. Sabah Parks has enlisted **Crystal Quest** (\ *089 212711;* e *cquest@tm.net.my*) to manage the park visits, trips and accommodation (**$$–$$$**). For overnight visits (the only way to witness the egg-laying exhibition), there are simple but clean rooms with bathrooms in several wooden **chalets** spread across the island. Expect sudden power cuts as electricity is provided by a generator. The rest of your time can be spent swimming in the crystal clear waters.

Pulau Lankayan The 80-minute speedboat trip out to Lankayan, through Sandakan Bay and into the Sulu Sea, is thrilling. Boats will not go if the weather is too bad. The 14 dive sites offer an ocean cocktail of reef, wreck and macro-pelagic diving. With increased protection (relying on observation by Malaysian and Filipino fishing vessels), large marine life to the surrounding reefs is said to be making a comeback – leopard sharks, marbled stingray, mimic octopus and giant grouper. 'Jawfish Lair' is home to yellow camouflaged jawfish. 'Lankayan Wreck' – a fish-poaching vessel put out of business – lies very close to shore. The visibility here was poor when I dived, but I still saw stingrays, painted frogfish, harlequin ghost pipefish and schools of parrotfish.

Where to stay and eat It's another one-island, one-resort set-up, operated by **Pulau Sipadan Resorts & Tours** (\ *089 230782;* e *psrt@po.jaring.my; www. lankayan-island.com;* **$$$–$$$$**). There are 16 chalets, nestled prettily at the water's edge or near the trees; the food served up in the main lodge is simple but fresh. Take any extras you may require, as there are no shops. You don't have to be a diver to stay here – the seclusion and simple wooden chalets make a heavenly Robinson Crusoe-style break.

SEPILOK AND LABUK BAY Sandakan would surely receive only a fraction of the visitors it does if it wasn't for Sepilok's famous orang-utan sanctuary to the west. Further along, Labuk Bay is a proboscis monkey sanctuary, hedged in by plantations.

Getting there and away Sepilok is 22km west of Sandakan, 11km from the airport, along Jalan Lintas Labuk. Labuk Bay is a further 25km in this direction. There are signs for both. **Minibuses** for both destinations depart from near the Central Market, Jalan Pryer. From Sandakan town centre bus station, take bus No 14 to the Sepilok Rehabilitation Centre (MYR3), which is 25km from Sandakan. Expect to pay MYR35 for a 45-minute journey by **taxi**.

MIGHTY OR BLIGHTED KINABATANGAN RIVER?

Flowing 560km from its source near the Crocker Range of Sabah through to the Sulu Sea in the east, the Sungai Kinabatangan – Kinabatangan River – is Sabah's longest (and Malaysia's second-longest) waterway. The watery journey deep into jungled hinterland, home to proboscis monkeys and river people, is one of my most memorable experiences in Borneo.

The boat journey starts from Sandakan Bay, heading out into the Sulu Sea before swerving back up the estuary, through gaping floodplains and narrow straits. Much of the deeper river area is protected as the Lower Kinabatangan Sanctuary – a 28,000ha reserve created in 1999. In this zone, the serpentine bends of the river meander through the floodplain and swell to bursting during the rainy season. The sanctuary provides a variety of habitats for flora and fauna – freshwater swamp, mangrove, palms and bamboo; it is one of only two places in the world inhabited by ten species of primates. Four are endemic to Borneo – silvered, maroon and Hose's langurs, and the distinctive proboscis monkey. The Kinabatangan conservation area boasts the highest concentration of proboscis monkeys, as well as orang-utans, in Malaysian Borneo.

Other wildlife encounters may include long-tailed and pig-tailed macaques, Bornean gibbons, the rare slow loris, pygmy elephants and Sumatran rhinoceros. Over 200 species of birds are found here, including eight types of hornbill (among them the rare wrinkled hornbill), lesser fish eagles, stork-billed kingfishers, black and yellow broadbills, pitas and bulbuls.

The name Kinabatangan comes from a combination of the words *Kina* – China – and *Batang* – large river. Evidence suggests there was a Chinese settlement on the banks of the river as far back as the 7th century, trading in birds' nests, beeswax, rattan and ivory. The Orang Sungai Kinabatangan – river people who live along the riverbanks today – are of mixed ancestry including Dusun, Suluk, Bugis, Bajaus and Chinese. It was a Chinese princess from the Kinabatangan that married the first sultan of Brunei in the 15th century.

Worryingly, oil palm plantations are encroaching on this beautiful river environment at an alarming rate. Decades of logging have cleared the riverbanks, opening the zone up for more exploitation. Electric fences shock pygmy elephants that try to feed on the plantations, which have replaced the once-forested land they used to roam through freely. Local villages that once looked out onto forests and orang-utans now see only agricultural estates. Despite the state government dubbing it a 'Corridor of Life' in 2002, and gazetting it as a Wildlife Sanctuary, the Kinabatangan's continually shrinking and disturbed habitat will remain seriously vulnerable until it is declared a national park. Joining the river rush hour for dusk wildlife tours, you can't help but wonder whether the tourist traffic is also upsetting the balance of nature. See the section on responsible travel (page 125) for ways to minimise the negative impacts on the environment as you travel.

🏠 Where to stay

🏠 **Sepilok Forest Edge Resort** (16 rooms) Jln Rambutan (off Jln Sepilok, Mile 14); ✆089 533190; e sepilok@sepilokforestedge.com; www.sepilokforestedge.com. 9 standard & luxury chalets, plus 7-room backpacker longhouse. 'In farm environment' on edge of jungle, 10min walk from Sepilok. $–$$$$

🏠 **Sepilok Nature Resort** (17 twin rooms) Off Jln Sepilok, near the organg-utan sanctuary; ✆089 673999; e sepilok@po.jaring. my; www.sepilok.com. A 10min walk from the orang-utan viewings, the twin-bed chalets overhang a lake, festooned in rainforest species, orchids & ferns. This friendly, relaxed resort organises jungle treks & wildlife-spotting trips. Its rattan-roofed lodgings have AC, ample hot water & forest-viewing balconies. $$

🏠 **Paganakan Dii Tropical Retreat** (6 rooms, 36 longhouse beds) Taman Hiburan Jalil Alip (Recreation Park); ✆089 532005; e info@ paganakandii.com; www.paganakandii.com. Nuts & bolts forest accommodation, calling itself a 'truly tropical retreat'. Loved by those wanting

a bargain-basement jungle experience, yet with a tropical dream location. You get what you pay for lodgings wise, but fans would say you also get much more in the form of the Kadazan-Dusun family friendliness & budget-jungle cool.Taxi from the airport 35MYR. $

🏠 **Sepilok Jungle Resort** (60 rooms) Km22 Jln Labuk; ✆089 533031; e info@sepilokjungleresort.com; www. sepilokjungleresort.com. In beautiful jungled gardens, Johnny Lim's resort is far from reaching its potential, due to sometimes uninterested staff & all-round tired décor. Despite ongoing upgrades (& the warning of possibly noisy stays) since late 2008, the 'accommodation blocks' (which are a bit cell-like rather than cosy), are still in a state of being dolled-up. The upside is the forest location, wild animals (orang-utans & tarsiers are often seen in the gardens), & cheap prices for fan-cooled rooms. 'We are pampering you with the natural surrounding & the beautiful garden around the lodge,' says Lim. $

What to see and do

Rainforest Discovery Centre (*Jln Labuk, Sepilok;* ✆ *089 533780;* e *rdcsepilok@ yahoo.com; www.forest.sabah.gov.my/rdc;* ⊕ *08.00–17.00 daily; adult 10MYR, children 5MYR*) The exciting newcomer in Sepilok, adding to the long-established and at times over-visited orang-utan rehabilitation centre, is this Sabah Forestry-run centre with its 147m-long canopy walk through Menggaris and other dipterocarp trees, 28m above the forest floor. The steel walk is punctuated by viewing towers – great for stealing a glimpse of the 250 resident birds, including the rare Bornean bristle heads, as well as hornbills, pittas, kingfishers and broadbills. The 800m rainforest discovery trail is a well-interpreted suspension-bridge stretch with possible sightings of flying squirrels, and, on night walks, tarsiers, mouse deer, large geckoes, stick insects and civets. While welcoming visitors, the centre's main role is as an environmental education centre for students, teachers and 'junior ranges'.

Sepilok Orang-utan Rehabilitation Centre (*Jln Labuk, Sepilok;* ✆ *089 531180;* e *soutan@po.jaring.my; www.sabah.gov.my/jhl;* ⊕ *08.30-17.00 daily; adult 30MYR, children 18 & under 15MYR; video/photo fees extra*) One of Borneo's orang-utan-viewing hotspots, entry prices have soared here in recent years. 'SOURC' was set up in 1964 to rehabilitate orphaned orang-utans who had lost their parents and their habitat through logging. The apes were brought here to be taught the necessary survival skills before returning to the wild. Operated by Sabah's Wildlife Department, it has now branched out into tourism and education, as well as conservation of other species.

A boardwalk leads to the feeding platform, perched up in the trees about 25m from the viewing area. The number of orang-utans to be viewed depends on luck – and whether orang-utan females' favourite 'Mr B' is there. Once the huge apes are full of bananas and vitamin shakes, they set off to have a swing and a play. Macaques and gibbons also come for a bite to eat. This is a great way to get a close-up view of the 'Man of the Jungle' and his primate cohorts.

Feeding times are at 10.00 and 15.00 – the latter is generally quieter.

Kabili-Sepilok Forest Reserve Sabah's number-one tourist attraction – Sepilok's orang-utans – actually lies within an often-overlooked rainforest reserve. Most visitors watch the feasting frenzy and leave, but there is plenty to see in the reserve too. The 43km² of lowland rainforest contains 350 different tree species and almost 40% of the known Dipterocarpaceae flora in Sabah. There is also a 5km trekking trail to Sepilok Laut, through mangrove forest – for which you need to get a Forestry Department permit.

Labuk Bay Proboscis Monkey Sanctuary (*Mile 8, Bandar Sibuga Jaya, off Jln Lintas Labuk;* ℅ *089 672133;* e *labukbay@proboscis.cc; www.proboscis.cc; feeding times 09.30, 11.30, 14.30 & 16.30 daily; adult 60MYR, children 12 & under 30MYR*) This sanctuary offers an opportunity for proboscis monkey sighting and birdwatching for those who don't have time to travel up the Kinabatangan River for an overnight stay. Located in mangrove forest along the coast near Kampung Samawang, Labuk Bay, it's about an hour's drive from Sandakan (48km) – the last 15km is along a gravel road through the centre of oil palm plantations. The best viewing times are said to be 10.30 and 16.30.

Deathly Trek While some might find this too upsetting, TYK Adventure Tours (℅*088 720826;* e *www.sandakantrack.com*) trace the steps of the chilling Sandakan–Ranau death march of World War II POWs, on a five- to seven-day trek. The trip is usually organised from Kota Kinabalu, and involves a flight to Sandakan and transfer to Tolupid (about three hours away) to begin the walk there, in order to avoid palm oil plantations. You could join the group in Sandakan rather than Kota Kinabalu if you prefer.

KINABATANGAN RIVER

Sukau A small settlement on the banks of the lower Kinabatangan River, Sukau is the jungle hub for those who want to dwell within the wildlife habitat of the Sungai Kinabatangan conservation area. Be prepared to go back to basics.

GETTING THERE AND AWAY Travelling **by car** Sukau is 80km from Sandakan and around 120km from Lahad Datu. The recent sealing of the last 42km of road from Sukau Junction has taken the bumps out of the ride (hopefully not with funding from the oil palm plantations, which dominate 90% of the scenery along this road). **Buses** operate from Sandakan market to Sukau. Local tour operators and river lodges use **speedboats** for transfers from Sandakan's jetty and the Sepilok area to the lower Kinabatangan. A few of these operators also run lodges, but will provide transport to a different lodge. **Seagull Sea Transport** (℅ *089 215841*) in Sandakan is another port of call for independent travel transfers to Sukau and Abi.

Where to stay and eat A handful of new lodges have recently sprung up in this area. Accommodation options now range from budget eco-lodges and jungle camps to more upmarket lodges with bungalow-style wood-panelled rooms, modern bathrooms and some individual chalets. Most offer packages that include accommodation, meals, transfers and excursions. The area is run on generator electricity, and offers an enriching back-to-nature experience. Tapping in on the growing demand for more comfortable quarters and surrounds, Sukau Rainforest Lodge got the ball rolling with a major overhaul in 2010. Other lodges have also recognised shortfalls in accommodation standards and food, and have made significant upgrades in recent years. **Food at the budget lodges** can still be ordinary, so take some snacks and drinks and any special dietary foods you may require.

Luxury
🏠 **Sukau Rainforest Lodge** (20 rooms) 📞088 438300; e info@borneoecotours.com; www.sukau.com. Run by Borneo Eco Tours, this part solar-powered lodge has won various international prizes for its eco-approach & has been a pioneer in ecotourism since it opened in 1995. A renovation programme completed in 2011 has brought new-look rooms, a lounge, a reception area, a restaurant, a jetty & sunset deck. It is an intimate stay alongside nature, with 4 bird- & wildlife-viewing decks & a 450m-long 'hornbill boardwalk' complete with 2 'elephant passes' to accommodate regular migrations of the animals through the lodge grounds. The river-facing restaurant & sunset deck is a scenic & savoury highlight. The lodge uses electric boats for the river cruises to minimise wildlife disturbance. **$$$$$**

Mid range
🏠 **Abai Jungle Lodge & Restaurant** (24 twin rooms) 📞089 213502; e info@sitoursborneo.com; www.sitoursborneo.com. Set in mangroves with a 300m boardwalk through the forest, the lodge is run by SI Tours as a rustic ecotourism experience with biodegradable products, rainwater & minimal electricity. The river-facing lodge is eco-rustic & beautiful. Twin rooms are spacious, with powerful fans, modern bathrooms & furnishings. An incredible wildlife immersion, there are 500–800m-long jungle trails made from hardwood or 'belian' & a bird-viewing tower. Silver langur, maroon langur, hose langur & orang-utan are regularly spotted here – I slept with a snoring orang-utan very nearby! Clouded leopard & sun bear have been seen on the trails behind the lodge. Food is served from a simple but dedicated restaurant, with locally sourced produce. Get your hands dirty with tree planting & other local development activities. Prices have risen by about 25–30% in the past few years. **$$$$**
🏠 **Kinabatangan Riverside Lodge** (33 rooms) 📞089 213502; e info@sitoursborneo.

com; www.sitoursborneo.com. On the banks of the Kinabatangan in a lush setting, also run by SI Tours. A new wing here has introduced more spacious & comfortable double/twin & family rooms, 12 semi-detached units & 3 3-room chalets. The 2009 makeover also improved the jetty & added a lovely river-facing sun deck. I am yet to experience for myself the upgrades to the food, though second-hand reports say it has improved considerably. Elephants visit frequently & macaques, proboscis, hornbills, crocodiles & monitor lizards all hover close by. Staff are lovely & atmosphere around the main lodge is fun. River excursions are a highlight, with knowledgeable guides. Packages approx 500MYR for 2 days/1 night/pp, including transfers, meals, accommodation & excursions. **$$$$**
🏠 **Proboscis Lodges** (21 bungalows) Sukau; 📞088 240584; e proboscislodge@sipadandivers.com; www.sdclodges.com. Accommodation at this new, community-connected Sukau lodge, run by Kota Kinabalu-based Sipadan Dive Centre, includes twin, double & family rooms. AC or fan, wooden furnishings & a balcony with full-length glass door. Packages include 3 buffet meals, cruises & transfers from Sandakan. **$$$**

Budget
🏠 **Abi Village Homestays** (approx 30 houses) Tour operators can arrange for you to stay in the Abi village in people's homes, instead of a lodge. **$$–$$$**
🏠 **Uncle Tan Wildlife Adventures** Mile 16, Jln Gum Gum, Sepilok; 📞089 531639; e eugene@uncletan.com; www.uncletan.com. If you don't mind sleeping with several people (& perhaps a monkey or 2), this operation is basic but with its heart in the right nature-loving place. On the edge of an oxbow lake of the lower Kinabatangan, the quasi-bush camp is remote & offers greater chances of seeing wildlife in the 'back garden' than many other river lodges. The founder, 'Uncle Tan', has passed away, but his family still run the business & the guides are

passionate about their work. Lodgings are open-fronted with just a mosquito net for protection. All-inclusive packages of 3 days/2 nights with transfers, 6 river & jungle excursions, start at around 350MYR pp. Bring wellies, raincoat & torch. Pick-up & transfers start from Uncle Tan's shoestring B&B on Jln Gum Gum. **$$**

Bilit

Bilit Since 2009, the Kampung Bilit area has emerged as an alternative Kinabatangan River base to Sukau. Most of the new lodges around Kampung Bilit village have a very strong emphasis on conservation, and community. The accommodation is an interesting mix of eco-rustic and quality, eco-chic, sometimes with both options available within the same walls.

Getting there and away For **self-drive travellers** it's straightforward, though most lodges offer budget to mid-range packages, including transfers from Sandakan. For shoestring (dormitory accommodation) travellers, where transfers are not part of the deal, the lodge will arrange a pick-up in Sandakan or at bus stops, for a fee. It's 122km from Sandkan to Kampung Bilit (roughly a 2½-hour drive), then a quick cross-river trip to the lodges. The Nature Lodge Kinabatangan's advice for **bus travellers** is: 'For those coming by bus from Lahad Datu, Tawau or Kota Kinabalu, get off at Medan Selera, a coffee shop at Bukit Garam Kota Kinabatangan. We will arrange a pick-up from this point at 13.30.'

Where to stay and eat

Nature Lodge Kinabatangan Kampung Bilit; \088 230534; e sales@ nasalislarvatustours.com; www. naturelodgekinabatangan.com. An eco-lodge that's proud to have almost no frills other than recently introduced electricity. 'Not so basic after all' says the website, with news of washroom upgrades & the extra creature comforts of the Agamid wing chalets: attached bathrooms, hot water, anti-mosquito mattress & windows with jungle view. The Civet Wing is more basic cabin or dorm accommodation. Widely reported as a budget & eco-friendly jungle-drenched lodge, this group clearly has its conservation heart in the right place. 3-day/2-night packages range from 370MYR for dorm only, to a surprisingly steep 1,250MYR for chalet accommodation with transfers from Sandakan included. The lodge also runs pick-up vans 'for a minimum charge' from Sandakan, \013 863 6263 to book. **$$–$$$$**

Bilit Adventure Lodge (24 rooms) Kampung Bilit; \089 271077; e info@ stwadventure.com; www.stwadventure.

com. Sandakan-based Sepilok Tropical Wildlife Adventure put a strong focus on local staff & conservation at their lodge. Travellers' expenditure on things such as snacks & leech socks, it says, go to staff earnings & their families. A friendly, homely place, albeit rustic with AC & fan-cooled rooms. 2-day/1-night packages including meals & transfers from Sandakan from 630MYR. **$$$**

Myne Resort (14 chalets) Kampung Bilit; \089 278288/90; e inquiryresort@myne. com.my; www.myne.com.my. Since its recent opening, good reviews have flooded in about this top-scoring lodge, which appears to be especially popular among continental Europeans & the British. The stay in a rich natural milieu, river cruises, amicable staff & excellent guides are being loudly applauded. The lodge offers various packages & is pitching itself as a boutique, back-to-nature & leisure experience. Facilities & activities include lounge grill & riverbank restaurant, mountain biking & jungle trekking. Friend & top-qualified Borneo nature guide, Chris Lo is working with the resort. **$$$**

WHAT TO SEE AND DO

River excursions All of the lodges and tour operators sail out on the Kinabatangan and its tributaries to see the wildlife from fibreglass boats. The Menanggol, a 26km offshoot heading towards the Gomantong Caves, is considered one of the best wildlife-spotting areas, taking in fig, orchid and rattan-entwined riverine environments and freshwater swamp forest. Boats leave most lodges at around 16.30 daily for 90-minute proboscis monkey-viewing trips. Other common sightings on these river excursions are pit vipers, macaques and gibbons. Orang-utans are more commonly seen on the trip to and from Sandakan. SI Tours offer a day-long 'Kinabatangan River Safari' from Sandakan, setting out to Sukau by road, to hook up with a dusk-departing boat.

For quieter early-morning trips, try bird- and wildlife-watching on the **oxbow lakes**, starting out before 05.00. These tranquil, disconnected river bends are teeming with bird life and afloat with water hyacinths.

Firefly spotting At night, float out on a boat for some tranquil firefly spotting. The 'bioluminescence' of the fireflies is produced to attract a mate, created in their abdomens by chemical reactions that emit light. The riverbanks are lit up like Christmas trees strung with garlands of fireflies, a beautiful sight to behold.

Local kampung On a U-turn bend in the Kinabatangan River, **Abi village** lies on the other side of the water from the Abai lodge. It's about equidistant between Sukau and Sandkan, and can only be reached by a one-hour boat journey from either direction. On a visit here you might see the 60 village children studying in their longhouse school, or time your visit with the local Hari Guru festivity – a day of paying tribute to the village teachers. To celebrate, a day of fun, sport and music is held – such as a banana-eating competition, *makan pisang* – skin and all!

Tree planting Roll up your sleeves and get involved in local tree planting, with initiatives such as **Bandok Abai Jungle Tree Planting Kinabatangan Project**, a joint project between WWF, a local NGO and Sabah Tourism. I planted a mango tree, and will go back to check on it in a year's time.

Gomantong Caves The Gomantong Caves are the largest limestone outcrop in Sabah. Set within limestone forest in the lower Kinabatangan, the cave is home to some two million bats as well as two million swiftlets, which produce edible mossy nests from their saliva. Locals use rattan and bamboo ladders to collect the nests, which hang from the cave roofs. The dusk performance is a delight for bird enthusiasts, as bat hawks and peregrine falcons pursue the bats. Some 27 species of bat roost here, predominantly wrinkled-lipped bats. The nests sell for about 2,000MYR per kilogram, though a top-grade white nest can fetch more than six times that – as much as US$4,000 per kilogram in Hong Kong.

Getting there and away The caves are 95km from Sandakan along the sealed Sandakan–Sukau **road**, and 26km from Sukau. **By boat** you can visit from Sandakan or Sukau and the Kinabatangan area. Coming from the south, the caves are about a two-hour drive from Lahad Datu.

8

Southeast Sabah

Between the islands, lagoons and straits off the coast of southeast Sabah lurks a treasure chest of marine biodiversity. On its drier parts, hilly hinterlands are interspersed with some of Borneo's biggest tracts of enduring rainforest. Cocoa, rubber and coconut crops thrive in the fertile volcanic soils – though the landscape is increasingly dominated by large oil palm plantations. The coast is inhabited by the Bajau Laut – maritime nomads whose ancestors set out from the Filipino island of Mindanao over 1,000 years ago. Many have now settled in stilt villages along the shores of the mainland as well as offshore islands and reefs. Others are still closely connected to the sea, living on the coast and making a living from fishing and seaweed cultivation. Local and international initiatives are under way to save the eco-region of the Sulu–Sulawesi seas. *National Geographic* magazine named it as one of the most diverse marine communities on earth – with nine times as many stony corals as the Caribbean Sea, and over twice the number found in the Indian Ocean. Six of the world's seven species of sea turtles can be found here, along with whale sharks, massive manta rays, and an incredible abundance of fish species. Bordered by three densely inhabited nations, it is a region of socio-political volatility, where ocean piracy and territorial tugs of war persist, and the population is forecast to double within three decades.

TAWAU

Spread around Sebuku Bay, the commercial port of Tawau claims a strategic sea and land location on the southeast frontier of Sabah, edging out towards Indonesia, whose border towns can be seen some 30km across the bay. Since the 1990s, the population of Sabah's third-largest town has doubled to about 250,000 due to the influx of illegal immigrants from the Philippines and Indonesia. With the fastest rate of development in the state, the hilly region is upheld by the government as an agricultural beacon; Tawau is Malaysia's leader in cocoa production, research and development, as well as a centre for oil palm plantations. The port still does a lively trade in timber, though the significant logging imports from poorer Kalimantan into Malaysia, and the manner in which that logging is carried out, raises serious questions.

A small coastal fishing village in the 19th century under the Sultan of Sulu, Tawau was ceded to the British North Borneo Company in 1878, which set up a rudimentary local government. In the 1890s its population of 200 was made up largely of immigrants from Balungan and Tawi-Tawi, who had fled Dutch rule in Kalimantan. By the end of the 1930s some 60 timber shop-houses, mostly Chinese-owned, lined the main street of Tawau. During Japanese occupation in World War II, many locals were killed. British military administration continued until July 1946, when North Borneo became a Crown Colony and civil government was resumed. The noticeable religious diversity is an indication of mixed roots and colourful history:

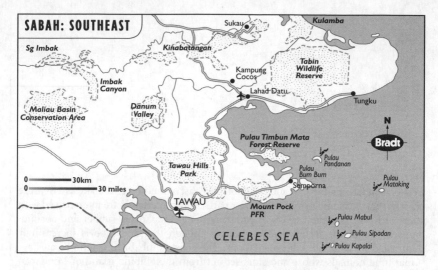

SABAH: SOUTHEAST

Sg Imbak

Imbak Canyon

Maliau Basin Conservation Area

Kinabatangan

Sukau

Kulamba

Kampung Cocos

Tabin Wildlife Reserve

Lahad Datu

Tungku

Danum Valley

N

Bradt

Pulau Timbun Mata Forest Reserve

Tawau Hills Park

0   30km
0   30 miles

TAWAU

Pulau Bum Bum

Pulau Pandanan

Semporna

Pulau Mataking

Mount Pock PFR

Pulau Mabul

CELEBES SEA

Pulau Sipadan

Pulau Kapalai

there is a rather gaudy green-roofed, salmon-sided Buddhist lodge, a new mosque, the Basel Christian church and Anglican church. Chinese make up about 15% of the population; Bajau and Malay peoples around the same; Indonesians comprise nearly a quarter; and there are minorities of Kadazan, Dusun and Murut. One Malay minority are the Bugis, an exuberant seafaring people who have been migrating to Sabah for centuries, from Sulawesi Island in Indonesia. As the main entry point for Indonesian traders and migrant workers, there is a thriving barter-trade economy with products from across the border. Overlooking an immense stretch of sea, the Tawau tip alone has 82km of coastline, 210 islands and 186 lagoons.

GETTING THERE AND AWAY

By air The Tawau International Airport is located at Apas Balung, about 35km from town and 70km from Semporna. As the transport hub for the southeast, most travellers to the nearby islands or Danum Valley area will pass by here, though there are plans for an airport in Semporna to handle island traffic. Daily flights link Tawau with Kota Kinabalu, Sandakan, Lahad Datu and Tarakan in Kalimantan. Malaysia Airlines have five flights every day to Tawau from Kota Kinabalu, a 45-minute flight. AirAsia have two direct daily flights daily from Kuala Lumpur to Tawau – a three-hour trip. MASWings operate a Fokker 50 flight from Sandakan to Tawau.

There are some buses from the airport to Tawau, operated by Kasah Transport. Some hotels operate shuttle services from the airport, charging around 18MYR for a return journey. A taxi will cost 40–60MYR. If you are visiting the areas for diving, organise transfers with the dive package.

By car From Kota Kinabalu, take the east–west highway to Sandakan, then the east coast highway to Semporna and Tawau. Tawau is also connected by major roads, such as the Tawau–Lahad Datu Highway and the Tawau–Kunak Highway.

By bus From Kota Kinabalu and Sandakan, express buses take eight hours and cost about 60MYR. From Lahad Datu the trip is 2½ hours. The long-distance bus station in Tawau is around Sabindo Square on the waterfront, between Jalan Dunlop and Jalan Chen Fook, adjacent to the mosque. Buses bound for Kota Kinabalu leave every evening at 19.45.

By ferry For travels to or from East Kalimantan in Indonesia, there are several daily ferry services between Tawau and the cities of Nunukan (one hour away) and Tarakan (a three-hour journey). Tawindo Express departs Tawau for Nunukan at 10.00 and 15.00, and from Nunukan to Tawau at 09.00 and 14.00. Tickets cost approximately 40MYR. The Tawindo Express sails between Tawau and Tarakan, Monday, Wednesday and Friday at 11.30, while the Indomaya express ferry departs Tuesday, Thursday, and Saturday at 10.30. Tickets costs 140MYR. Note that for travels to Indonesia you must obtain a visa beforehand, as none are issued at the border. The visa-obtaining process in Tawau is famously fast; however, the Indonesian Consulate relocated in 2010 to an inconvenient location about 4km north of town (*Konsulat Republik Indonesia Tawau, Bangunan Yunwah, Mile 2.5, Jalan Sin On, 91000 Tawau;* ℡ *089 772052/752969*). Take a taxi to Jalan Sin Onn, and alight at the glass-towered Wisma Fuj building. The consulate lies to the right of this office/shopping building, a couple of hundred metres off the main street. Within an average two-hour wait a 60-day tourist visa is issued, costing 160MYR. Make sure you have two passport photos with you and proof of onward travel.

GETTING AROUND Due to the spread-out nature of Tawau, the best way to see its coast and hills is by car. The minibus station for local (and airport) buses is near the mosque. Taxis are easier and cost 6–10MYR for most inner-town trips.

The main town centre and wharf lies between Jalan Dunlop, Jalan Chen Fook, Jalan Stephen Tan and Jalan Chester. Kompleks Fajar commercial centre is the hub of many hotels, supermarkets, banks, ATMs and food outlets, near to the waterfront area around the Sabindo Complex.

🏠 **WHERE TO STAY** There is a mini hotel boom under way in Tawau in the budget through to upper-mid-range categories, and hotel service overall is discernibly on the rise. To meet increasing demand from hikes in visitor numbers, new two- and three-star hotels (including La Hotel) were forecast to open in late 2011 and early 2012, in the city centre around Jalan Haji Karim. Up to ten openings are forecast by 2020, concentrated here and around the Fajar shopping complex. One wonders whether such rapid room number rises are being absorbed however, when spanking new hotels offer internet deals with prices on standard rooms and suites slashed by half.

Mid range/upmarket

🏠 **Belmont Marco Polo Hotel** (150 rooms) 3 Jln Clinic; ℡089 777988; e bmph@tm.net.my; www.sabahhotels.net. Large, centrally located in red-roofed pagoda-style. Deals range from standard rooms at budget prices to spacious mid-range executive-floor rooms & more expensive suites. Breakfast & Wi-Fi included. **$$–$$$$**

🏠 **Promenade Hotel** (180 rooms) 2nd Floor, Eastern Plaza, Jln Kuhara Mile 1; ℡089 982888; e comm_tawau@promenade.com.my; www. promenade.com.my. This 4-star newcomer, with its established sibling hotel in Kota Kinabalu, has shot to the top of the pile, with its large, excellently fitted rooms, good leisure & meetings facilities, modern décor & lighting, & fine array of coffee shops, bars, nightclubs & restaurants.

Prices are equally diverse, from the budget Internet deals for standard rooms with breakfast, to top-notch executive suites. **$$–$$$$**

🏠 **Heritage Hotel** (88 rooms) 210–213 Jln Bunga, Fajar Kompleks; ℡089 766222; e info@ heritagehotel.com.my; www.heritagehotel.com.my. Inside the main shopping & commercial centre, a soberly stylish hotel with de luxe & superior rooms & suites, Wi-Fi, satellite TV, kettle. Overall good value & promotional rates online. **$$–$$$**

🏠 **Hotel Emas** (126 rooms) 2103 Jln Utara (North Rd); ℡089 762000; e emas@teckguan. com. A 3-star business hotel about 0.5km from town centre, owned by a cocoa company. Room for improvement in service, but de luxe rooms are good value with modern bathrooms, tea/ coffee making, AC, TV & breakfast. Premier floor

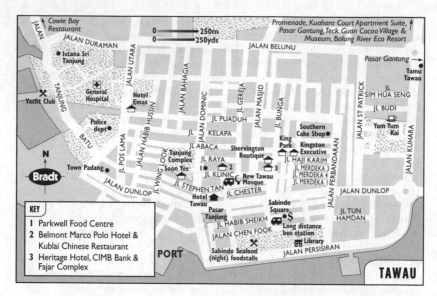

Map labels:

Cowie Bay Restaurant
JALAN DURAMAN
JALAN UTARA
JALAN BELUNU
Promenade, Kuahara Court Apartment Suite, Pasar Gantung, Teck Guan Cocoa Village & Museum, Balung River Eco Resort
Istana Sri Tanjung
Pasar Gantung
Tamu Tawau
JALAN BAHAGIA
JL GEREJA
JL BUNGA
JALAN ST PATRICK
JL SIM HUA SENG
JL BUDI
General Hospital
Hotel Emas
JL DOMINIC
JL MASJID
JALAN HABIB HUSSIN
Yacht Club
TANJUNG
Police dept
BATU
JL PUADUH
JL KELAPA
Southern Cake Shop
Yum Yum Kai
King Park
Kingston Executive
JALAN KUHARA
JL POS LAMA
JL ABACA
Shervington Boutique
JL HAJI KARIM
JALAN PERBANDARAN
N
JL WING OOK
Tanjung Complex
JL RAYA
JL MERDEKA 4
JL MERDEKA 3
Town Padang
Soon Yee
JL KLINIC
New Tawau Mosque
JL MERDEKA I
Bradt
JALAN DUNLOP
JL STEPHEN TAN
JL CHESTER
JALAN DUNLOP
Hotel Tawau
Pasar Tanjung
Sabindo Square
JL TUN HAMDAN
JL HABIB SHEIKH
Long distance bus station
JALAN CHEN FOOK
Library
PORT
Sabindo Seafood (night) foodstalls
JALAN PERSISIRAN

KEY
1 Parkwell Food Centre
2 Belmont Marco Polo Hotel & Kublai Chinese Restaurant
3 Heritage Hotel, CIMB Bank & Fajar Complex

TAWAU

---

single/twin with breakfast still border on budget rates. Shuttle-bus service to airport 15MYR 1-way/18MYR round trip. **$$–$$$**

Budget/shoestring

🏠 **Kingston Executive Hotel** Lot 3, Ground Floor, Jln Haji Karim; ✆089 769996; book via www.etawau.com. Great location amid cafés, shops & 24hr convenience stores, this is the newest of Tawau's budget hotels. Double & twin rooms are bright & comfortable & the service is friendly & helpful. **$–$$**

🏠 **King Park Hotel** (100 rooms) 30 Jln Haji Karim; ✆089 766699/767700; e kingpark@ streamyx.com; http://tawau.kingparkhotel.com. my. Reviews for this 3-star hotel have improved since a 2010 makeover of its rooms & suites & the introduction of new management. Health centre, shuttle service, satelitte TV, Wi-Fi & non-smoking floors. **$–$$$**

🏠 **Kuahara Court Apartment Suite** 4550, Mile 1, Jln Kuhara, Block C, Ground Floor; ✆089 768778. About 1.3km from town, next to huge new Eastern Plaza shopping centre. The condominium development has de luxe rooms & 2- or 3-bedroom units. Available for day & monthly leases in a complex with a pool, poolside café & catering. **$–$$**

🏠 **Hotel Soon Yee** (16 rooms) 1362 Jln Stephens Tan; ✆089 772447. Friendly. Sub-shoestring. **$**

🏠 **Hotel Tawau** (21 rooms) 72–73 Jln Chester; ✆089 771100; e tawauhtl@tm.net.my. Reports of the rooms being 'spartan but spacious'. Satellite TV, AC, phones, bathrooms, centrally located, with affable owner. **$**

🏠 **Shervinton Boutique Hotel** Lot 1–4, Fajar Complex, Jln Bunga; ✆089 770000; e info@ shervintonhotel.com; www.shervintonhotel. com. The new budget–mid-range hotel which enthusiastically calls itself an 'executive boutique hotel', opened in late 2011. Standard, de luxe, family, twin rooms & expansive suites all have modern furnishings, LCD TV, rain showers & fee Wi-Fi. The friendly reception & great value are quickly winning fans, despite some complaints of structural shortfalls (most apparent in smaller rooms), regarding soundproofing & thin walls. **$–$$$**

Out of town

🏠 **Roach Reefs Resort** (11 chalets) Office: Fajar Commercial Complex, Jln Merdeka 2, Tawau; ✆resort: 089 761140, ✆office: 089 779332; e info@roachreefsresort.com; www. roachreefsresort.com. Upmarket resort on manmade reef, 25mins' speedboat journey from Tawau, 50mins from Sipadan, on the edge of the Borneo shelf. A Hong Kong travel agent told me the rustic chalets are so close to the water that his airing trousers were carried away by a breeze into the ocean (but recovered by accommodating staff). PADI dive centre, restaurant with Asian & European dishes. Packages for divers & non-divers include airport & boat transfers from Tawau, accommodation, food, boat dives & unlimited reef diving from 06.00–18.00. **$$$–$$$$**

🏠 **Balung River Eco Resort** Mile 33, Apas Balung; ☎ 089 761339; e seavent@po.jaring. my; www.balungplantation.com. In the Tawau Hills Park (55km from Tawau) on a gloriously

lush & serene mixed agricultural plantation with 32 species, including cocoa, coffee, spices, medicinal plants & fruit trees. Camping, dorm accommodation, standard rooms & 3–4-bedroom 'eco-chalets' built with river stones & local timber. Surrounded by rainforest & rivers where you can fish your own dinner. Coffee house, karaoke lounge, swimming pool, river spa & guided tours of plantation. **$–$$$$**

✖ WHERE TO EAT

Street food and markets Many people claim the best seafood in Malaysia is found in Tawau, and it's from here that Kota Kinabalu gets much of its fresh catch. You can sample this from small open-fronted *kedai kopi*, in under-cover markets and open-air food stalls all over town. The nightly food park **Sabindo Seafood** (*opposite the Sabindo Shopping Complex, Jln Chen Fook*) is a large open-air set-up with many food stalls, tables and chairs. At **Kam Ling Seafood**, a good dinner for two will cost under 50MYR. The larger **Good View Seafood** gets mixed reports. The whole area bustles with people from 18.00 to 23.00. There is also a seaside strip of evening food stalls selling fast Malay, Indian and Indonesian food – barbecued skewers and satays, *murtabak* and *nasi ayam*, *roti cani* – some serve *sulawesi soto makassar*, a Bugis buffalo soup dish.

Sabindo has plenty of casual eateries by day. Food courts are located in marketplaces and shopping centres, from the **pasar Tanjung** central market to the Malay-oriented **Parkwell Food Centre** in the Parkwell supermarket (⊕ *06.00–18.00*).

Coffee shops and restaurants The **Kompleks Fajar** has cheap eateries but also some air-conditioned restaurants, including **Maxim's Seafood Restoran** (*Jln Baru, Block 30 Fajar Complex;* ☎ *089 771800*). Locals refer to the area of Jalan Budi (east of the Fajar centre) as 'Yum Cha Kai' – Yum Cha Street. All the coffee shops here serve good food and drink; try **Kedai Kopi Kim Kim**, **Mui Lok** and **Sin Hing**.

Nearby is a great place for vegetarian, rice and noodle dishes and soups: **Kedai Kopi Bunga** (*TB1722 Hotel Kuhara, Jln Kuahara*). Some hotel restaurants are good, with the added bonus of being off-street and air conditioned: **Kublai Chinese Restaurant** (*3 Jln Klinik;* ⊕ *11.30–14.00 & 18.00–22.00 Mon–Sat, 07.00–14.00 & 18.00–22.00 Sun & public holidays*) in the Marco Polo Hotel has a buffet lunch on weekdays for 12.99MYR, and Cantonese cuisine and dim sum in a mandarin court, and its **Venice Coffee House** (⊕ *06.00–13.00 Sun–Fri, 06.00–14.00 Sat & public holidays*) serves international and Asian dishes and is a good place for breakfast. **Cacao Palace Restaurant & Bar** in Hotel Emas goes a bit overboard on chocolate (including fish, soup and more!), but there is a good nightly steamboat buffet as well as à la carte. **Cowie Bay Restaurant** (*Rich Park, port area*) also gets good reports.

Cake shops Tawau makes excellent *kedai kek*. For all sweet and savoury bakes and cakes, head to the area around the Fajar complex; the **Southern Cake Shop** is on Jalan Merdeka next door to the more average chain **Multi Bake**, and just opposite is a coffee shop-style branch of the **Sugar Bun** (*2 Jln Merdeka*) fast-food chain.

OTHER PRACTICALITIES There are several **banks and ATMs** in Tawau, concentrated around the main city blocks, including a CIMB Bank in the Fajar Kompleks commercial centre on Jalan Haji Karim, an Ambank ATM at 13 Jalan

Southeast Sabah TAWAU 8

Dunlop and Bank Simpanan Nasional at Sabindo Square. A Milimewa superstore is found in the Complex Cahaya Baru, Lot 257–261, Jalan Bunga. For **medical issues** (other than emergencies in which case dial ☎ 999), there is a major public hospital in Tawau, barely 1km west of the town centre on the coastal road (*Peti Surat 67, Jln Tanjung Batu;* ☎ *089 773533*).

WHAT TO SEE AND DO

Mosques Al-Kauthar, or New Tawau Mosque (*Jln Stephen Tan*), is the biggest mosque in Sabah. Completed in 2004, it cost 31 million MYR to build, can hold 17,000 people and has a library, seminar hall and offices.

Markets Tawau's markets are marvellous. The pastel-pink-winged **pasar Tanjung** – the central market – on Jalan Dunlop is said to be largest in Borneo, with 6,000 stalls selling fresh food and fish, salted dried fish (*ikan masin*), clothes, baskets and much more. The old central market is known as **pasar Gantung** or 'hanging market', because all the items for sale (from clothing, handicrafts and handbags to house decorations) are suspended from the stalls. Most of the produce is Indonesian and Filipino. Colourful and relaxed, traders of all races mingle at the rural style *tamu* **Tawau** every Sunday morning on the corner of Jalan Apas and Jalan Kuhara. It has over 200 stalls laden with fruit, vegetables, handicrafts and clothing, as well as dried local specialities such as shark fins and seaweed. Running from 06.00 until early afternoon, it also has food stalls and a temporary eating area of tables and chairs.

Cocoa tours Tawau is trying to get people to taste its wares with its slogan of 'Asia Cocoa City'. The **Teck Guan Cocoa Village** (*Quoin Hill;* ☎ *089 772277 ext 2254 to organise tours*) dubs itself 'Cocoa Kingdom' – a cocoa plantation up in the hills near Tawau. During a two-hour tour, cocoa breakfasts and lunches can be enjoyed – with cocoa-flavoured noodles, porridge, prawn and banana rolls and fresh cocoa juice on the menu. A few minutes' drive away is a hiking trail that leads to a 9m-high waterfall, the **Culture Spring**. The same factory has a museum just out of Tawau – **Teck Guan Cocoa Museum** (*Mile 2, Tanjung Batu Laut;* ☎ *089 775566 ext 2601;* ⊕ *08.00–11.30 & 13.30–16.30 Mon–Fri; reservations necessary for guided visits*). Inside the Majulah Cocoa Factory, the one-hour visit is guided by factory staff and includes a quality multi-media presentation of the history of cocoa, topped off by tastings of cocoa drinks and sweets. It's a very personable, small-scale affair.

Festivals About a fifth of Tawau's population is Chinese, and February's **Chinese New Year Festival** is said to paint the town red with fireworks, festivities and fun. A **Cocoa Festival** is also held, featuring colourful cocoa-inspired cultural dances.

EXCURSIONS FROM TAWAU

TAWAU HILLS PARK (TAMAN BUKIT TAWAU) (*50km from Tawau; adult 10MYR, child under 18 6MYR*) This rainforest and lower montane park of about 28,000ha was gazetted in 1979 to preserve the Sungai Merotai, Ulung Sungai Tawau and Sungai Balung rivers and their unique ecosystems. Over 150 flowering plants have been recorded in the park, a small island of biodiversity within a region of limestone outcrops, rich alluvial volcanic soils, cocoa and oil palm crops. The reserve is managed by Sabah Parks and boasts waterfalls (including the 30m-high Banjir Kilat) and hot springs. It also contains mountain-bike trails and jungle treks to the tops of Gunung Magdalena and Gunung Maria, on which you can encounter monkeys, hornbills and orchids. In 2010, the world's tallest tropical rainforest tree and Malaysia's tallest tree was found here. The park has constructed a special nature trail leading to the 88.32m Seraya Kuning Siput (*Shorea faquetiana*).

The park rangers are very helpful. The nearest lodgings are on the adjacent **Balung Plantation**, also intersected by the Sungai Balung river; a nice place for swimming, trekking, birdwatching and mountain biking.

ASIA COCOA CITY TOUR (📞 *019 8830173; adult 550MYR, child 450MYR*) Ivy Yap, local livewire and special project manager at Teck Guan Cocoa company, organises four-day/three-night packages, taking in Tawau, the Balung Eco Resort, trekking, snorkelling and Semporna's Singamata Water Chalet.

LIVEABOARD *CELEBES EXPLORER* (📞 *088 224918/248331;* e *jworld@po.jaring.my, reservation1@myjaring.net; www.borneo.org*) Adventure Journey World Travel organises packages from Kota Kinabalu or Semporna on this luxury liveaboard. The custom-built vessel has eight en-suite air-conditioned cabins fitted out with five-star hotel equipment, a sundeck and salon. UK specialist tour group Dive Worldwide (e *sales@diveworldwide.com; www.diveworldwide.com/*holiday/celebes_explorer_liveaboard.html) offer three- to seven-night packages from London.

MALIAU BASIN CONSERVATION AREA A 'protected forest reserve' once open to logging, Sabah's so-called 'Lost World' lies in south-central Sabah, about 40km north of the Indonesian border – an enclosed 390km² basin up to 25km across. The area is drained by tributaries of the Maliau River, one of which forms a stunning series of waterfalls, the seven-tiered **Maliau Falls**. It is a remarkable block of tropical forest – virtually the entire catchment of the Maliau River – almost encircled by a dramatic escarpment rising over 1,600m in height, insurmountable from most

---

THE MALIAU EXPERIENCE   *Sir Peter Crane*

A few days in the Maliau Basin provides a truly authentic tropical rainforest experience. All year round, day or night, the temperature rarely deviates more than a few degrees from its average of about 30°C. The humidity is always high, so dripping with sweat becomes a way of life. Torrential downpours are a regular occurrence – the region receives more than 3m of rainfall annually, which is about a metre more than the English Lake District receives in a typical year. Clothes and camera gear – and anything else – never dry out, and even the shortest journey involves slithering up or down precipitous slopes that always seem to end in sandstone cliffs or whitewater torrents. The ubiquitous leeches take every opportunity to gorge themselves on any passing mammal; leech socks are a must.

The exuberance and diversity of plant and animal life in Maliau more than compensate for the challenging conditions. In the valleys, dipterocarp trees dominate small patches of lowland rainforest containing incredible plants – such as the rafflesia with its enormous, malodorous flowers, and giant strangling figs. This is also the habitat of the greatly prized ironwood – one of the most dense and resistant of all tropical hardwoods.

Sir Peter Crane is a former Director of the Royal Botanic Gardens, Kew, England. See page 65 for more information..

directions. The area was originally set aside by the Sabah Foundation and then formally upgraded to a Class 1 Reserve.

The basin has 12 different forest types, mostly Agathis tree-dominated lower montane, dry heath forest and lowland and hill dipterocarp forest. It is a faunal haven with over 1,800 species of plants and lots of wildlife including barking deer, banteng, sun bears, proboscis monkeys, clouded leopards, pythons and many species of birds including the rare Bulwer's pheasant, crimson-headed partridge and peregrine falcon. Only a couple of operators are allowed to visit this area – it is under tight wraps, and is very expensive – about 4,000–6,000MYR for five days and four nights excluding airfares, less with a bigger group. It's also a tough trip – camping in tents, with lots of leeches around (including tiger leeches) and 06.00 starts. With long walking days in humid conditions, participants must be physically fit, and mentally prepared. There are about 12 licensed tour operators, both local and international, who can visit the area. **Borneo Nature Tours** (*Block 3, Ground Floor, MDLD 3285 Fajar Centre, on edge of town near airport;* \ *089 880207; www.borneonaturetours.com*) is one. Maliau treks start with pick-up at Tawau Airport, followed by a five-hour drive in a 4x4 to the Maliau Basin Security Gate 180km away. The trip can also be done from Keningau on the west coast, with a six-hour drive in.

Those wanting to visit Maliau Basin independently must get permits and written permission from the **Conservation and Environmental Management Division of the Sabah Foundation** (*Yayasan Sabah*) (*12th Floor, Menara Tun Mustapha Tower, Kota Kinabalu;* \ *088 326300;* e *mbca_kk@icsb-sabah.com.my*) or the **Maliau Basin Conservation Area** Tawau office (\ *089 759214;* e *maliau@icsb-sabah.com.my*).

The new **Maliau Basin Studies Centre** (MBSC) (\ *087 745100/101/103*) has a hostel, camping ground, exhibition hall, mini theatre, conference room and library.

IMBAK CANYON Just north of the Maliau Basin, this 300km² valley has only recently been set aside as a conservation area and looks set to become another magnet for rugged treks. It's a sweeping area of one of the largest contiguous lowland dipterocarp forests left in Sabah, enclosed by high sandstone ridges and canyon waterfalls. A vital link in the biodiversity corridor linking Maliau Basin to the Danum Valley further east, it is also an important area for research and a botanical gene bank for forest rehabilitation projects. Visiting conditions are the same as for Maliau.

SEMPORNA

Semporna means 'perfect' in Bajau language, and that describes the seaside of Semporna far more than it does the town itself, though it is not lacking in cultural colour. At the end of the Semporna Peninsula, its feet bathing in the waters of the Celebes Sea, Semporna is a watery world: the bay is a whirr of engines, masts and boats of all forms. Bajau Laut, the indigenous population of the Bajau Sea, live along the coast in houses perched on stilts over shallow reefs. The high rate of conversion to Islam among the Bajau people explains the large proportion of Muslims – 90% of the 100,000-strong population in the Semporna area. Stone Age tools found in the hills above Semporna show the area was a prehistoric pottery hub.

GETTING THERE AND AWAY Semporna is a 90-minute **drive** from Tawau town, and an hour from Tawau Airport. A **taxi ride** from Tawau will cost 100MYR. **Express buses** from Kota Kinabalu leave daily at 07.30 and 19.30. It's a seven- or eight-hour trip and costs about 60MYR with a meal included. Minibuses between Tawau and Semporna take close to two hours, with tickets costing 15–20MYR. Buses from

Tawau arrive at the minibus station; those from Kota Kinabalu and Sandakan at the long-distance bus station. Both are in the town centre, though the latter is further back from the waterfront, to the side of the mosque.

🏠 WHERE TO STAY

🏠 **Seafest Hotel** (63 rooms) Jln Kastam; ☎089 782333; e info@seafesthotel.com; www.seafesthotel.com. Efficient, calm location a few blocks from town centre. Standard/de luxe rooms & suites, majority overlooking the all-surrounding water. Health centre at extra charge; kettle, AC, ceiling fan, & buffet breakfast included (though very ordinary). 3-star excellence; by far the best hotel in town comfort-wise; also lovely location at end of pier. **$$–$$$**

🏠 **Dragon Inn Floating Hotel** (65 rooms) 1 Jln Custom; ☎089 781088; e info@dragoninnfloating.com.my; www.dragoninnfloating.com.my. The atmosphere at this rickety inn on duckboarded stilts, extending into Sandakan Bay, is nothing less than magical. However, while you expect it in the longhouse lodgings, the standard double rooms of the wall-to-wall thatched roof chalets can also be very noisy (neighbour-dependent). The location can be enjoyed to the full from one of the 'VIP' rooms – the stand-alone chalets are a mix of greater comfort (AC, cable TV, heated showers) & rustic charm – the windows from the basic bathrooms open out to view passing boats heading to the local market. **$–$$$**

🏠 **Sipadan Inn** (32 rooms) Block D, Lot No 19–24; ☎089 782766; e booking@sipdadan-inn.com; www.sipadan-inn.com. Lives up to its slogan ('luxury budget accommodation') in many respects; modern rooms of rich furnishings, all with AC, satellite TV & free internet, & extra spacious superior rooms & ocean suites. Boutique-style at budget prices. **$–$$**

🍴 WHERE TO EAT

Anjung Lepa (*Seafest Hotel, Jln Kastarn;* ☎6089 7823333) is a small open-air hut with plastic chairs, jutting over the water. Charcoal-grilled fish (*ikan panggang*), satay, and prawns and octopus by weight (*2–4MYR per 100g, min 300g*) are barbecued and served with rice and fresh melon juices – no alcohol is served. At the Seafest Hotel opposite, the **Lepa Café** serves buffet lunches and a lunch and dinner menu of Western and Eastern dishes. Day and night food stalls are dotted about town, near the market and in the area along Jalan Kastarn. The more pricey **Pearl City Restaurant** (*1 Jln Custom;* ☎089 781 099) is part of the floating Dragon Inn complex. The casual **Seafest Café** is on Jalan Kastarn, near Seafest Inn.

OTHER PRACTICALITIES

Within a couple of streets, the town centre crams in accommodations, the wet (fish) and dry markets, a mosque and banks, but don't count on more than one or two ATMs. The Milimewa supermarket lies within the shop-lots of Jalan Datu Panglima Abdullah, along with coffee shops and a bakery.

WHAT TO SEE AND DO

Semporna is small, and easily navigated on foot. In a matter of minutes you can journey from the pier to the bus station, markets, banks and hotels.

Semporna Ocean Tourism Centre

(*1 Jln Custom;* ☎089 781077) Locally called 'the floating', this is a source of local tourist information. It is built in Bajau water-village style on the pier, with a few bungalows, a hotel (the Dragon Inn), restaurant, bar and souvenir shops, all connected by duckboards.

Pasar Ikan

The Fish Market is held in the beige pyramid-shaped structure right on the waterfront.

Semporna Islands

The largest in view is **Pulau Bum Bum** (pronounced 'Bom Bom'), and is bigger than Singapore – 1,000 families cultivate seaweed here.

Semporna is the springboard to Sabah's famous dive islands: Pulau Sipadan, Mabul, Kapalai and Mataking. In all, there are about 20 main dive sites: over half around Sipadan, and half a dozen around Mabul. All the resorts offer beginners and advanced diving opportunities around Sipadan, Mabul and Kapalai.

SIPADAN One hour by speedboat from Semporna, Pulau Sipadan looks like little more than a cluster of trees from above the water's surface. Formed by living corals growing on top of an extinct volcanic cone, it took thousands of years to develop and drops off 600m to the ocean floor. 'Sipadan's oceanic location keeps visibility at 30m or more, ar:d marine life has thrived thanks to limits on the number of divers,' says dive journalist William Moss. 'Barracuda Point' is so called due to the incredible vortices of thousands of chevron barracuda that swirl through it. Close encounters with turtles and sharks (grey reef sharks, leopard sharks, scalloped hammerheads…) are common here and at the 'Pinnacle'. The drop-off is popular for shore and night diving. A Sabah Parks permit for Sipadan is 40MYR per day.

For environmental and **security** reasons, there are no longer resorts on Sipadan. Dive operators visit there from the mainland and the other three islands, with enforced limits of 120 people per day. Since the kidnapping of divers on Sipadan in 2000, and with 'continuing threats', the British Foreign & Commonwealth Office (*www.fco.gov.uk*) and the Australian Department of Foreign Affairs (*www.smartraveller.gov.au*) have issued warnings against travelling to these islands (see *Diving in Borneo* box in *Chapter 3*, page 117). The islands and surrounding waters are under constant military surveillance.

MABUL AND KAPALAI Sitting on the edge of the continental shelf, 45 minutes from Semporna, these islands have very different ecosystems, and visibility can be low – as little as 10m – because of the sandy bottoms, especially at Kapalai. However, their reefs 'host a dazzling array of odd and photogenic creatures including frogfish and leaf fish, ghost pipefish, anemone and cleaner shrimps, lionfish, octopi, venomous catfish, elusive mandarin fish, and a rainbow of nudibranches,' says William Moss. Mabul is a beach-fringed atoll, part of a 200ha reef, and is popular for muck-diving. Kapalai sits further out to sea on the same reef, separated by a sand bar – the 'Jetty' dive has five wrecks, while the sloping 15m reefs of Kapalai are a highly photogenic place to dive.

MATAKING Mataking is a 40-minute boat ride from Semporna, for macro and pelagic diving with a 100m reef drop-off on the eastern shore.

RESORTS AND OPERATORS Most resorts offer two-, four- or six-night packages, including boat transfers from Tawau Airport to Mabul, three meals a day, accommodation, three boat dives a day, and most dive gear.

Mabul

⌂ **Sipadan Water Village** (45 chalets) ☎089 751777; e info@swvresort.com; www.swvresort.com. This gloriously located new water resort spreads its stilted tentacles over the waters of Mabul Island, its standard to de luxe bungalows built in Bajau style, barely 1m above the water, with sliding doors & sun decks. The resort has a 5-star PADI dive centre, dining hall &

lounge-bar. Packages from Tawau include road & boat transfers, twin share accommodation & buffet breakfast, lunch & dinner. **$$$$$**

🏠 **Mabul Water Bungalow** (15 chalets) ☎088 486389; e mabul@streamyx.com or mabul@ po.jaring.my; www.mabulwaterbungalows.com. The water bungalows have AC, fans & balconies. Though not as upmarket as SWV above, the resort demands similar prices, & there are frequent complaints about service. With restaurant, shop, business centre, & dive centre, Sipadan Island is a 15min boat ride. Dive the World (*www.dive-the-world.com*) offer 7-night packages with 20 dives & many other packages. Closer to the source, are the trips organised by Sipadan.com, a Mabul-based dive centre with a Semporna office: ☎089 782334; e info@sipadan.com. **$$$$–$$$$$**

🏠 **Sipadan-Mabul Resort** (45 chalets) ☎088 255514; e borneoicons@gmail.com; www.mabulresort.com. SMART, as it is known by divers, is a long-established name, though now under the new management of Borneo Icons Tours & Travel. The detached & semi-detached bungalows are homely, & have balconies, AC & tea- & coffee-making facilities. The resort has a restaurant, PADI TEC dive centre, Wi-Fi, swimming pool & jacuzzi. It organises packages, including land transfers from Tawau, accommodation, buffet meals, 3 boat dives daily, unlimited house reef & night dives, & diving equipment. **$$$$–$$$$$**

🏠 **Mabul Dive Resort** (Borneo Divers) ☎088 222226; www.borneodivers.info. Pretty wooden chalets with many simple comforts & ethnic furnishings, AC & bathrooms, in tropical gardens with pool. Good buffet meals & very friendly, helpful staff. PADI dive centre. Promotional deals & good negotiating skills can result in 2-night packages of around 1,000MYR pp, at least 100MYR less for a non-diver. **$$$–$$$$**

🏠 **Scuba Junkie** Block B Lot 36, Semporna; e info@scuba-junkie.com; www.scuba-junkie.com. Can arrange longhouse stays on Mabul Island for 50MYR pp including meals. Free transfers if you are diving with them, otherwise there is a small fee. **$**

🏠 **Uncle Chang's Sipadan Mabul Dive Lodge** (Borneo Jungle River Island Tours) ☎089 781002; e info@sipadanbackpackers.com, mabulbackpackerslodge@yahoo.com; www.sipadanbackpackers. A backpacker option on Mabul. 50MYR/night including meals. **$**

Kapalai

🏠 **Pulau Sipadan Resort & Tours** ☎089 765200; e rooney@sipadan-kapalai.com; www.sipadan-kapalai.com, www.dive-malaysia.com. Run by the same professional (Tawau-based) set-up that operates Sepilok Nature Resort & Lankayan Island stays. Staying at this stilted sea resort (the only accommodation on Kapalai) is like staying in an aquarium. Built above the shallow sandbanks of the Ligitan Reefs, its boardwalks extend over coral beds, punctuated by thatch-roofed bungalows with private balconies & sea-facing bathtubs. The buffet restaurant has 360° sea views & a fish-gazing window at its centre. 2-night packages, starting at around US$500 & US$650 respectively for non-divers & divers, include 3 boat dives daily & unlimited home reef diving. **$$$$–$$$$$**

Mataking Island

🏠 **Mataking Reef Dive Resort** ☎089 770022; e sales@mataking.com; www.mataking.com. The thousands of coral reefs in the Celebes–Sulawesi ecoregion are like paint splashes on the sea. The WWF describes the 600,000m^2 marine zone as a 'coral triangle' & 'hyper diverse underwater world', & it is this spectacular environment you will experience first hand while staying at Mataking's magical resort. Individual chalets, new high-end beach villas & a spa are nestled in the trees off a forest boardwalk, while the main restaurant is a focal point for good food & dining. This upmarket resort is popular with diving honeymooners & families, & its PADI dive centre is run by proficient, friendly staff. **$$$$–$$$$$**

Speedboats (20MYR) leave from the pier near the Seafest Hotel. **Sulawesi Sea Safari** (*Seafest Hotel, Jln Kastam;* ✆ *089 782318; www.sulawesiseasafari.com*) has an office here. Backed by local knowledge, it offers day and multi-day dive packages and Semporna–Sulawesi area touring, with accommodation at the Seafest. Personally I would opt for a tailor-made tour for a day of immersion into the culture of the Bajau Laut and Semporna Bay's remarkable sea world.

Bukit Tengkorak Archaeological Site Museum (*Kampung Tampi Tampi, 5km from Semporna;* ✆ *088 253199;* ⊕ *09.00–17.00 daily*)

The Department of Natural Heritage at Sabah Museum and university researchers found thousands of pottery residues here, with some specimens dating as far back as 8,000BC. This suggests the area was one of the largest Neolithic craft centres in southeast Asia and a major stop-off point on early Pacific trade routes.

Culture and festivities The *lepa*, a traditional wooden sailing boat with intricately carved embellishments, is an integral part of the life of the Bajau Laut people. Usually made of hardwoods, the *lepa* are decorated with a flotilla of red and yellow frilly sails (*sambulayang*) and small triangular flags (*tapis-tapis*). The **Regatta Lepa** is held in April with other traditional watersports including a rowing competition (*Lumba dayung*), in which rivals tug at the ropes of other boats, and races in small dugout boats (*kelleh-kelleh*). Traditional dances including the *daling daling* – an upbeat courting dance – accompany the festivities.

Diving The major 'dive islands' and their resorts are run by one operator or another (see box, pages 234–5). Some people stay in Semporna and go diving from there by day, finding it cheaper and/or more interesting. If you have arrived without a pre-booked package and want to go diving, beware of dodgy operations – there are at least a couple in town. Check blogs and reviews on major dive sites (such as www.scubatravel.co.uk and www.scubadiving-malaysia.com) – this is also an excellent way of getting feedback about different dive resorts and accommodation. Day diving is possible to many places, including Tampi Tampi, a dive resort ten minutes along the coast from Semporna.

People often ask how to get to the dozens of other small Semporna islands to dive. One answer is to eschew the dive operator/island resort packages; then you are free to cherry-pick. Some more budget-oriented Semporna-based operators visit such islands for day diving. Reputable operators for day dives include **Scuba Junkie** (*Block B, Lot 36 Semporna seafront;* ✆ *089 785372/019 584657;* e *info@scuba-junkie. com; www.scuba-junkie.com; 1-day PADI Discover Scuba 250MYR, 3-day Open Water 750MYR, 3-day Advanced Open Water 700MYR*) who also organise outings to some 25 islands in the area. They are a young, business-driven operation, and take groups of 12 as a maximum. **North Borneo Dive and Sea Sports** (*Semporna Ocean Tourism Centre, Dragon Inn, Jln Kastam;* ✆ *089 942788/769950;* e *borneo_ tours@hotmail.com*) also arranges diving in the area.

LAHAD DATU

Lahad Datu in Bajau language means 'a place of royals' – bestowed on the town by noble-blooded Bajau peoples who migrated from the Sulu Islands in the late 19th century. Facing over the Sulawesi Sea from the large inlet of Darvel Bay, palms and casuarinas line 'The Corso', which runs along the waterfront to the grubby old town centre. Here, the streets are packed with itinerant vendors, small shops, department stores, Islamic restaurants and food stalls. The large fish market, though a bit overbearing on the senses, is a captivating communal commotion.

The population of Bajau, Sulu islanders, illegal Filipino immigrants and minorities of 'river people' – the *orang sungai sagama* who live near the Sagama River – form an intriguing ethnic pool. Lahad Datu is trying to clean up its 'cowboy' image with a campaign driven by the local mayor. Results of the sprucing-up effort can already be seen around the 'new town', where more hotels and shopping centres are earmarked. Situated on the edge of town is a large immigrant *kampung* of 4,000, made up of Filipino and Indonesian migrants (the people underpinning the palm oil and construction industries with cheap labour).

GETTING THERE AND AWAY

By air MASWings fly to Lahad Datu direct from Kota Kinabalu and from Miri via Kota Kinabalu. One-way tickets from Kota Kinabalu cost as little as 30MYR if you are flexible with dates, and rise to an average 140MYR.

By bus With all the cheap flight options it's best to avoid the lengthy bus journey from Kota Kinabalu to Lahad Datu. Between Sandakan and Lahad Datu, **Syarikat Chin** buses (\ *019 8834962*) leave from Sandakan's open-air bus terminal at Batu (2.5km from town) at around 07.30 – the 179km journey takes four to five hours and costs about 20MYR. **Sida Bus Express** (\ *019 8737808*) runs the same trip at 07.15. Pay for tickets on board for first-in-first-served seating. There is a single daily return from Lahad Datu to Sandakan departing at 12.30.

By van/4x4 taxi Vans and 4x4 taxis run trips between Lahad Datu and Sandakan bus terminals, early morning (*about 07.00, 20–25MYR pp*), leaving only when they are full – with about six passengers. If not, they may postpone the trip until the next day. Regular services also go between Lahad Datu and Semporna.

 WHERE TO STAY For a few years now there has been talk of new mid-market and five-star hotels coming to the town, but the gap remains unfilled.

Asia Hotel (60 rooms) 639 Jln Teratai; \ 089 881771; e reservations@asiahotel. com.my; www.asiahotel.com.my. A 10-storey, recently renovated hotel with a competitive 3-star edge & constantly improving services. Secure parking & 24hr hotel security, business centre, boardrooms & free Wi-Fi. Rooms are light & well furnished, with AC, satellite TV, tea/coffee-making facilities & safe. Incredible online deals of 128MYR/288MYR for rooms/suites with breakfast & lunch included. **$$–$$$**

Grace Hotel (58 rooms) Levels 4/5, Centre Point, Jln Kastam Lama; \ 089 866649; e grchotel@streamyx.com, grchotel@streamyx. com. A 2-star, salmon-pink building block. Comfortable rooms, restaurant & business

centre, suites with breakfast in budget bracket **$–$$**

Perdana Hotel (23 rooms) Block 31 Jln Seroja; \ 089 881166; e ino@hotelperdana.com; www.hotel-perdana.com. The best of the basics by a country mile, with a pervading, out-to-please-all-tastes-attitude. Even its executive rooms are budget friendly. With its efficient, personable management, the hotel is constantly aspiring to offer even better value for money – key card room security, shiny & clean presentation, brightly furnished restaurant bar & free Wi-Fi. Standard rooms are small, but have good beds, DVD players & TV. Prices include breakfast & local newspapers, while laundry & 'butler service' are on offer! How could one ask for more at this price? **$**

There are two other shoestring hotels where you should be able to count on a clean room, air conditioning and bathrooms for under 100MYR for a double:

🏠 **Mido Hotel** (61 rooms) Jln Teratai; ✆089 881800. Restaurant, slightly more expensive than the Jagokota & Perdana.

🏠 **Hotel Jagokota** (55 rooms) Jln Kampung Panji; ✆089 882000

✖️ **WHERE TO EAT** Lahad Datu's split personality brings both new- and old-town eating. In the old town, a *pasar malam* is held along a paved strip in the middle of Jalan Mawar (directly opposite Emporium Ramai Ramai) – smoking, steamy stalls of skewers and satays, whole grilled fish (*ikan panggang*), chicken wings, roasted meats and sweets, among some tables and chairs. The other side of the street is full of late-night clothes shops and Restoran Islam. There are also some stalls on Jalan Kastam Lama. In the 'new town', the pedestrian-only Jalan Panji leading up to the waterfront 'Corso' has food stalls day and night, plus coffee shops and restaurants.

At **Sakura Seafood Restaurant**, a variety of fish and shellfish can be sampled for 2–8MYR per 100g. There are also many Chinese dishes: noodles, dumplings and roasted duck, priced at about 4MYR. **Choi Kee** has good noodles, clay-pot dishes, roasted pork and duck; **Ah Seng** offers chicken rice; and opposite the Kedai Kopi, **San Hoi Pow** serves homemade noodles. For vegetarian food, try **Kedai Kopi Jeet Lee** (*Block 48, Lorong 1, off Jln Teratai opposite the Executive Hotel*). The Executive Hotel's **Spring Palace Chinese Restaurant** is frequented by locals for its Cantonese and Szechuan cuisines and dim sum. There is an international menu of snacks and dinners in the **Plantation Coffee House**. In the Kompleks Fajar, near the airport, the **Unicorn Vegetarian Restaurant** (*Jln Segama*), has a Chinese buffet and menu. Also here are two Malay-Chinese eateries, **Restaurant Dovist** (*Lot 73, Fajar Centre*) and **Restoran Serai Wangi** (its name comes from the citronella plant).

WHAT TO SEE AND DO Most people come to Lahad Datu to go diving, or to visit the Danum Valley and surrounding region's natural attractions. The town appears grotty in places, but it still has a certain charm. A Sunday market is held in the town centre. A curiosity is **Kampung Cocos**, a village about 8km from town, populated by a large community of immigrants from the Cocos (Keeling) Islands in Australia. The 'Orang Cocos', as they are called in Malaysia, came here in the 1950s to work on the coconut plantations. With close to 4,000 residents, the population is six times bigger than that of their homeland (621 according to the Australian government census)!

SHOPPING The **Emporium Ramai Ramai** (*Jln Bunga Raya;* ✆ *089 880151; www. ramairamai.com*) is a bustling supermarket on the main street near the fish market. It has a mix of Chinese and Asian produce, health and beauty products, and a good range of international brands of biscuits, confectionery, jams and alcohol. It is part of the multi-level **Wisma Ramai Ramai** shopping centre. The 128 million MYR Darvel Bay Plaza, touted for completion in 2010 but pushed back for at least a year, will be the district's biggest shopping mall. As part of the overall Darvel Bay commercial centre development, it will include hundreds of retail shop-lots, a supermarket, food court, house wares, IT, fashion stores and cafés.

OTHER PRACTICALITIES Intra Travel Service (✆ *089 274988;* e *enquiry@intra-travel.com.my; www.intra-travel.com.my*) offers budget to mid-range tours in the region, including Tabin. An excellent **pharmacy** is the well-stocked Guardian Chemist (*Hotel Mido, Ground Floor, Jln Teratai;* ✆ *089 880137*), which has many international brands (UK, US and Australian). A good **air-freight and transport company** with a Lahad Datu office is Kangaroo Worldwide Express (*Block A, Lot A4, Jln Kastam Lama;* e *www.kangaroo.com.my*).

EXCURSIONS FROM LAHAD DATU

DANUM VALLEY It is a bitter irony that one of the greatest 'protected areas' of Sabah, the Danum Valley Conservation Area (DVCA), exists alongside some of the most severe over-logging. The 438km² reserve is promoted as 'the largest remaining area of undisturbed virgin lowland rainforest in Malaysia', which has been set aside for research and education. However, as you drive into the 'untouched' area you will undoubtedly come across well-laden log trucks on the road, which can be upsetting. As Sabah Tourism declare candidly 'a vast timber concession area borders all around Danum Valley'. The road into the reserve passes through logged and regenerating forest areas – the DVCA is touched on every side by 3–100km of commercial forest, and beyond are oil palm plantations. Guides here express their heartbreak at what is happening, and what has already happened. Together with the Maliau Basin, Danum Valley is part of the huge 10,000km² timber concession of Yayasan Sabah (the Sabah Foundation). Since the 1980s, it has been a Class 1 Protected Forest Reserve and part of the foundation's long-term Forest Management Plan, to remain un-logged for the purpose of wildlife conservation, education and research.

Getting there and away It's about 85km from Lahad Datu, a two-hour journey first along the Lahad–Tawau road, then on unsealed forestry roads.

 Where to stay

 Borneo Rainforest Lodge (24 chalets) www.borneorainforestlodge.com. Simple but beautifully built eco-cabins elevated through the forest, with a daily symphony of birds. Fan-cooled, bathrooms & forest balconies. Restaurant, good buffet food, lovely main lodge. Also a tent camp for 2–6 people. Prices of their 2–3-night packages are prohibitive for many & heavily penalise singles. Run by Borneo Nature Tours (details in Maliau Basin Conservation Area, page 232) **$$$–$$$$**

 Danum Valley Field Centre (DVFC) Block 3, Fajar Centre, Jln Segama, Lahad Datu; 📞089 881688/880441. Mostly for official researchers, but overseas students & scientists can visit with written approval from centre. 'Keen naturalists' can apply for a stay with written approval from the Danum Valley Management Committee (see www.ysnet.org for more info). VIP rooms, resthouse rooms, male & female hostels & campsite.

What to see and do Lying on the upper reaches of the Sungai Segama (Sabah's second-longest river) and its tributaries, the area is one of undulating lowland tropical rainforest – hilly but not mountainous. Gunung Danum forms its apex at 1,090m. The 438km² conservation area is home to 120 mammal species including the rarest – Sumatran rhino, pygmy elephant, sun bear, clouded leopard and banteng (wild cattle), ten of eastern Sabah's primates and over 340 recorded species of bird. There are amphibians and reptiles galore too – from the rare Wallace's flying frog and Bornean horned frog, to turtles, geckos, pythons, vipers, cobras and coral snakes. Activities include guided jungle treks, night wildlife excursions, canopy walks, birdwatching and guided visits to the Danum Valley Field Centre.

Trekking There are many marked trails in the Danum Valley including self-guided trails, but most longer (especially overnight) treks require a guide. One such trek is to the highest mountain in the DVCA – Gunung Danum, at 1,090m. Starting from the Danum Valley Field Centre (see below), four hours into this possible day walk are the Sungai Purut river's seven-tiered waterfalls.

Danum Valley Field Centre The DVFC paints itself as 'probably the leading rainforest research centre in the Old World tropics'. Scientists come from all over the world to conduct research here – including work on the impacts of logging. All visitors must get a **permit** from the Sabah Foundation sales office in Lahad Datu (*Block 3, MDLD 3286, Ground Floor, Fajar Centre, Lahad Datu*), unless you are on an arranged tour, in which case that is likely to be taken care of. Self-drivers must get a vehicle pass from the office. Viewing-spot highlights include a suspension bridge over the Sungai Segama river and 40m-high canopy observation platform.

TABIN WILDLIFE RESERVE

The reserve lies on the Dent Peninsula, northeast of Lahad Datu, wedged between the lower reaches of the Segama River and the Silabukan Forest Reserve. The endangered trio – Asian elephant, Sumatran rhinoceros and clouded leopard – make another of their rare appearances in this 122,539ha reserve of primarily logged lowland rainforest reserve, which has been put aside to protect 75 mammals, including orang-utan, proboscis monkeys, three wild cats, 220 birds and 45 reptiles. Contact the Wildlife Department Office in Lahad Datu (☏ *089 884416*) to check the current situation with permits.

Getting there and away It's 50km on a sealed **road** at first but then a very bumpy gravel road from Lahad Datu town. A daily **bus** from Lahad Datu (destination Tomanggong) passes the entry to Tabin, a one-hour trip.

Where to stay and eat

🏠 **Tabin Wildlife Resort** (26 rooms) ☏ 088 267266: e enquiry@tabinwildlife.com. my; www.tabinwildlife.com.my. Even if the hope of an elephant sighting is unfulfilled, the nature immersion in this resort's jungle environment (with local leaf monkey & hornbill populations) is thrilling. By night, the eco-chic cabins with cathedral ceilings glow like insects in the forest & on the hillside. The bungalows, which are linked by boardwalk to a restaurant & games room, have warm woody furnishings, AC, private balconies & homely fittings. The birdlife here makes it one of the most popular itineraries for expert guides such as C K Leong (see the Tabin blog on his website: borneobirds.com). The Sunbird Café (⏱ *07.00–19.00*) is a timber restaurant perched in the forest, with Western & local food. The website gives an idea of the nature-loving ethos of the excellent, award-winning operator, Tabin Wildlife Holidays, & the enthusiastic staff. Packages – including the 2-day/1-night Tabin Wildlife Encounter, & special interest & educational tours – include transfers to & from Lahad Datu, meals & lodgings. **$$$$**

What to see and do Selected from the exploited areas of the Silabukan Forest Reserve, and protected as a Wildlife Reserve, a core of old-growth rainforest remains in Tabin though most of it is disturbed – selectively logged and surrounded by oil palm plantations. There is also a wetland area to the northeast side, around the Segama River. Neighbouring Kulamba Wildlife Reserve, an area of 20,682ha on the east coast, is quite a different ecosystem of freshwater swamp forest, mangrove and beach vegetation. Access to it is by boat and there are no visitor facilities here at all. The chances of seeing wildlife such as rhinos and elephants in Tabin Wildlife Reserve may be just as good as in the Danum Valley, with an estimated 300 elephants, 100 banteng and 20 rhino. These animals are attracted to Tabin's mud volcanoes – mounds of mud and clay – for their salt fix, and there is an observation tower above one of the muddy mounds, about 700m from the chalet. Tabin is a special place for birdwatching – with eight species of hornbills, hawk-eagles and pink-necked green pigeons, attracted by the abundance of fruit trees. The giant flying squirrel glides around at night – up to 70m between trees. Some animals are more likely to look for you – leeches are particularly abundant in the wet season.

Part Four

SARAWAK

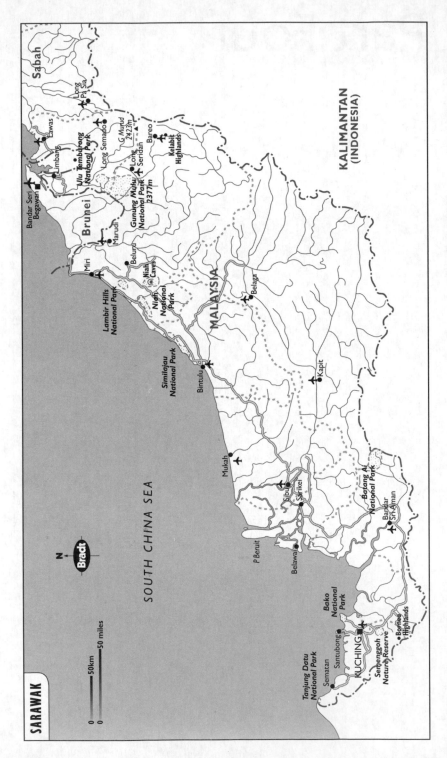

SARAWAK

Sabah

KALIMANTAN
(INDONESIA)

Long
Pa Sia

Lawas

Limbang

Bandar Seri
Begawan

Brunei

Ulu Temburong
National Park

Long Semado

Long
Seridan

G Murud
2423m

Bareo

Kelabit
Highlands

Gunung Mulu
National Park
2377m

Marudi

Beluru

Miri

Niah
Caves

Niah
National
Park

MALAYSIA

Belaga

Lambir Hills
National Park

Similajau
National Park

Bintulu

Kapit

SOUTH CHINA SEA

Mukah

Sibu

Sarikei

P Beruit

Batang Ai
National Park

Belawai

Bandar
Sri Aman

N

Bradt

Bako
National
Park

Tanjung Datu
National Park

Santubong

Sematan

KUCHING

Semenggoh
Nature Reserve

Borneo
Highlands

0   50km
0   50 miles

9

Kuching

The magic of Kuching, like much of Sarawak, emanates from the water that runs through it – the glorious, 120km Sungai Sarawak divides it in two. Across the water, the chants of Muslim prayer from the *kampung Melayu* (Malay villages) meet with the hustle and bustle of the old Chinese trading bazaar of the south. Under the weight of soaring urbanisation, the river has been battling pollution, mostly from untreated sewage and accumulating rubbish. Things are improving however, and Kuching has been awarded a gold star from the World Health Organisation for its efforts to become cleaner and greener. It's actually a very liveable city, rich in urban parks and surrounded by nature reserves and wetlands.

The name *Kuching* is said to derive from the Malay word for cat, *kucing*. One version of history says it came from the abundance of *mata kucing* ('cat's eyes') – a lychee-like fruit – growing on the riverbanks of the Sungai Sarawak. Though flagrantly promoted as 'Cat City' with cat statues and museums, others say the city was baptised by early Indian and Chinese traders as *Cochin* – 'port' in Indo-Malay.

A backdrop to the city skyline is provided by the Gunung Santubong. The limestone massif of the indigo mountain rises up on the shores of the South China Sea 32km away.

SARAWAK AT A GLANCE

International telephone code +608
Currency Malaysian ringgit (MYR)
Exchange rate US$1 = 3MYR, €1 = 4MYR, £1 = 4.8MYR (May 2012)
Climate Equatorial, humid; average daily temperature 28°C
Geography Largest Malaysian state, 124,450km²; northwest Borneo
Population 2.4 million; 31% Iban, 28% Chinese, 20% Malay, 8% Bidayuh, 6% Melanau, 5% Orang Ulu, 2% Indian Eurasian & minor ethnic groups
Capital Kuching
Visa requirements Visa-free 3-month stay for most; see pages 79–80
Language Official language Malay (*Bahasa Melayu*); Iban and Chinese main community languages. English widely spoken.
Emergency numbers 999 for police, fire and ambulance
Banking hours 09.30–15.00 Mon–Fri
Business hours 08.00–13.00 & 14.00–17.00 Mon–Fri, 08.00–13.00 Sat
Shopping centre hours 10.00–22.00 daily
Government website www.sarawak.gov.my
Tourist board +6088 21212; e info@sarawaktourism.com; www.sarawaktourism.com

Partly saved from World War II bombing, many early buildings were destroyed in fires and uprisings in the 19th century, and later by developers' bulldozers. With a generous sprinkling of colonial buildings and century-old Chinese remnants, Kuching serves up an evocative brew of the past with its watery character and multi-racial tones. The odd neo-classical building and Corinthian columns add a weird and wonderful touch to the potpourri of Chinese shop-houses, mosques and Buddhist temples. Curiously, the city has two mayors – one on either side of the river. The Majilis Bandaraya Kuching Selatan (Kuching South City Council) administers on the south side and the Dewan Bandaraya Kuching Utara (Kuching North City Hall) on the northern banks. Between the vibrant city centre, old villages and modern structures of its suburbs, the 580,000 residents represent a quarter of Sarawak's population.

HISTORY

Kuching's foundations were set in silt and on stilts, like so many of Borneo's river cities today. Before James Brooke sailed up the Sungai Sarawak in *The Royalist* (see *History*, page 6) in 1839, inklings of a water village (*kampung ayer*) existed in the same area as modern Kuching, with some 600 houses built from Nipah palm thatch on the banks of the river. Kuching was the epicentre of control for the century of white rule in Sarawak – a period once described as an era of 'benign despots'. After Brooke had been bestowed the title of Governor and Rajah of Sarawak in 1841, roots of a colonial settlement were embedded and the town grew up on the southern banks of the river. In 1868, Brooke's nephew Charles took the helm. More an administrator than an adventurer, under his rule a government was established and Kuching's streetscape took form with forts, courthouses and museums springing up. From 1917, the third White Rajah, James's grandson Charles Vyner Brooke, expanded infrastructure and development. In 1941 he steered Sarawak towards democracy, ceding state legislative and budget issues to the Sarawak General Council. However, the empowerment of the Council, composed of native chiefs and Chinese and Malay representatives, was to be short-lived. The democracy gains were crushed within a few months with the onset of World War II and Japanese invasion, during which Charles Vyner Brooke took refuge in Australia.

GETTING THERE AND AWAY

BY AIR
Kuching International Airport [250 7A] Modernised and attractive, Kuching airport is 11km from Bandaraya Kuching (Kuching City). There is a **Sarawak Tourism Board** information counter at the airport (⊕ *09.00–18.00 daily, closed 13.00–14.00*). A taxi to the city costs approximately 18MYR – buy a coupon at the taxi counter inside. The **Sarawak Transport Company** bus No 12A leaves every 45–50 minutes.

International flights Half a dozen airlines link Kuching directly with international destinations, including Brunei, Singapore and Indonesia. Malaysia Airlines (MAS), Silk Air, Tiger Airways and AirAsia all fly to/from Singapore; Batavia Air flies to Pontianak in neighbouring Kalimantan; MAS has twice-weekly direct flights from Perth and Sydney; and Royal Brunei Airlines operate flights from Bandar Seri Bagawan in Brunei.

One-stop international routes include MAS and China Southern Airlines flights from Guangzhou and Hong Kong; MAS and Lufthansa from Frankfurt; and the new MAS routes linking Kuching to Tokyo Haneda Airport and to Osaka Kanei.

Good websites for seeing all ticketing and price options are Expedia (*www.expedia. co.uk*) and FareCompare (*www.farecompare.com*).

Domestic flights Malaysia Airlines and AirAsia have direct flights between Kuala Lumpur and Kuching, Miri, Sibu and Bintulu, and from Kota Kinabalu in Sabah, and Labuan Island. Within Sarawak, both airlines fly from Kuching to Miri, Sibu and Bintulu.

Rural air services (RAS) From Kuching via Miri, MASWings operate flights to rural airstrips including Ba'Kelalan and Bario (Kelabit Highlands), Lawas, Limbang, Marudi, Mulu, Mukah, Long Akah and Long Lelang. Helicopter services are possible to other towns and more inaccessible areas in the Sarawak interior.

Airlines
✈ **AirAsia** No 291, Sub Lot 4, Ground Floor, Wisma Ho Ho Lim (shopping centre), Jalan Abell; ☎082 251491
✈ **Malaysia Airlines (MAS)** Lot 215, KCLD Block 47, Jln Song Thian Cheok; ☎082 246622. Located in the KCLD commercial centre.

✈ **Sarawak Convention Bureau** Lot 31, Jln Masjid; ☎082 242516; e info@sarawakcb.com; www.sarawakcb.com

BY CAR The smooth-sailing Pan-Borneo Highway connects Sarawak with Brunei and Sabah. It is 842km from Kuching to Miri in the north, via Sibu (462km) and Bintulu (644km). The road system within the state is being upgraded constantly as traffic volume increases. There are excellent English-language interactive digital road maps for Kuching, Sibu, Miri, Mukah and Bintulu at http://sidra.sarawaknet. gov.my with free login.

BY BUS For decades, the long-distance bus hub, the **Regional Bus Terminal** [250 7A] (☎ *082 461227/456261*) has been located about 5km south of the city, on Jalan Penrissen – explaining references to it as the 'Third Mile Bus Terminal'. All this is set to change with the opening of the new **Kuching Sentral** [250 7A] (forecast for 2012) along the same stretch of Penrissen Road, only at mile 6.5, just a couple of minutes from Kuching International Airport. The 55 million MYR project, which is invariably being called 'Kuching Sentral' or 'Kuching Regional Integrated Bus Terminal' (no doubt the former will stick as the more commuter-friendly label), began in 2007. The developers (*www.nationlinkgroup.com*) are calling the three-storey complex 'a one-stop of travel and shopping under one roof'. A shopping centre cum bus terminal, Kuching Sentral aims to become a major transport and retail hub for airport-bound or arriving air passengers, as well as for hundreds of thousands of long-distance and city bus travellers. In the former case, it will be a hub for buses arriving from and leaving for Indonesia, Brunei, Sabah, Sarikei, Mukah, Bintulu, Sibu, Miri Limbang, Bakong, Batu Niah, Betong, Sri Aman, Simunjan, Engkilili, Lubok Antu and Saratok. The terminal will help alleviate the increasing traffic problems in Kuching by streamlining city bus services and better integrating them with regional services. The following companies, which are currently operating out of the express bus terminal, will move to Kuching Sentral on its completion. The taxi fare between the express bus terminal and the city is 15–20MYR.

Biramas Bus Express (☎ *082 610111; Kuching booking office on Jln Khoo Hun Yeang, near Electra House;* ☎ *082 429418*) This company links Kuching with

Sibu, Sarikei, Miri and Bintulu, as well as Bandar Seri Begawan in Brunei and Pontianak in Indonesia. Timetables and fares can be found on the website. Child fares are mostly 40–50% cheaper, except for international trips. While services for most of the above destinations are several times a day, there is just one daily bus to Pontianak via the Tebedu–Entikong border crossing, leaving at 07.45. (From Pontianak the bus leaves at 09.00.) The fare for the eight- to ten-hour journey is 45RM (or 140,00IDR).

Borneo Highway Express (✆ *082 453190*) Tickets can be purchased at **Borneo Interland Travel** (*1st Floor, 63 Jln Bazaar;* ✆ *082 413595; www.bitravel.com.my*).

EVA Express (✆ *082 576761*) Operate buses between Kuching and Pontianak in Kalimantan, Indonesia.

PB Express Another long-distance bus company with business-class seats available; the Kuching sales counter is inconveniently located at 3.5 Mile, Jalan Kuching-Serian. There is however a ticket counter at the Saujana car park complex in Jalan Masjid, in downtown Kuching (✆ *082 244349*). Note that some buses north to Sibu, Bintulu and Miri involve a change of bus or stopover in Sarikei, so make sure you are booked direct, if that is what you want.

SJS Super Executive (✆ *082 456999*) This more upmarket coach service serves Pontianak from Kuching, with a daily coach at 11.00 costing 70MYR.

Tebakang Express Kuching (✆ *082 456999*) A subsidiary of Biaramas, they operate the journey between Kuching and Pontianak in Indonesia.

BY BOAT A company called **Express Bahagia** ('express boat services') (✆ *082 410076*) connects Kuching with other coastal cities and towns: Kuching–Sibu departs daily at 08.30. The 4½-hour journey costs 40MYR (45MYR first class) and stops at Sarikei and Tanjung Manis. Tickets are sold at the wharf in Pending. A taxi fare to the jetty is approximately 10MYR. From Sibu, boats to Kuching leave daily at 11.30, stopping at Sarikei and Tanjung Manis. Tickets are sold at the passenger terminal at Sibu's **Express Wharf** (✆ *084 319228; 40MYR/45MYR 1st class*).

GETTING AROUND

ON FOOT The city centre and waterfront areas are quite compact and easy enough to walk around. You will need to rely on other transport beyond that.

BY BOAT The traditional-roofed wooden boats, *tambang* (the local version of a *sampan*), are used for Kuching river crossings around the clock. A vital means of public transport around the waterfront area, they charge 30sen per person one-way, increasing to 1MYR after 22.00. The journey takes less than five minutes. You can also charter one from any of the small jetties where they pull in, for about 30MYR an hour. Ask them to take you anywhere you like, and to use either the motor or just to gently row the boat along the Sungai Sarawak.

BY BUS Buses are the main form of public transport in and around Kuching and offer plenty of character for money, as well as reasonable efficiency and safety. A big step away from the chaotic past has come with the gradual launch of the new Kuching City Bus Service. The consortium pulling together all the various transport companies is accompanied by a redesigned bus routing system (City Area Transit) and spanking new buses. Though departure points in Kuching still depend on destination and company used, there is far less duplication.

Under the system, **City Public Link** has been assigned all city and suburban routes from its terminal on Jalan Masjid [250 B3] (*No 2, 1st floor*). The buses will eventually serve over 40 city routes and 250 bus stops in Kuching.

The government is aiming to improve transport infrastructure, reduce carbon emissions and integrate modern technologies such as electronic tickets and GPS. The CAT transport system (perhaps intentionally playing on Kuching's city symbol) uses route corridors and loops instead of the old point-to-point bus services. In addition, the government announced in 2010 that the transport network would be decentralised through a series of suburban hubs to be built in key residential areas.

Aside from City Public Link, there are several other major bus companies. **Sarawak Transport Company** (*STC; Jln Leboh Jawa*) [250 B2] (↳ *242967/ 451573/242579*) serves the Kuching area and southwest Sarawak. Their green-and- yellow buses depart from Leboh Jawa, with major bus stops at Jalan Mosque, the post office and Gambier Street. Bus No 3A goes to the long-distance bus terminal. **Petra Jaya City Bus** [250 B3] (↳ *429418*) serves Bako, Buntal, Damai and Santubong; their white-and-yellow buses depart bus stop No 1 on Jalan Leboh Jawa from the open-air market near Electra House. **Matang Transport Company's** [250 B3] yellow-and-orange buses depart from outside the Saujana car park and go to Matang and Kubah. **Bau Transport Company** (↳ *763160*) buses depart from the same place for Bau Town. It would not be surprising to see these extra-urban routes relocated in coming years to the new Kuching Sentral, due for completion in 2012 (see *Getting there*, page 245). **Chin Lian Long** (*Jln Gambier*) operates services to the city and suburbs with major bus stops on Jalan Gambier, as well as Jalan Masjid and outside the post office. Bus No 1 goes to the express boat jetty in Pending (see page 246).

A kind of bus-hub area lies at the western end of the waterfront near the open-air market and Electra House, between Jalan Gambier and Jalan Mosque. Several bus companies operate in this area, each with their own station, serving distinct areas and marked with a bus symbol on the *Kuching Tourist Map* (available from most hotels and the tourism office in Kuching). You must have the correct fare on you as drivers generally do not give change. Trips within the city rarely exceed 2MYR.

BY BIKE There are some good mountain-bike trails close to Kuching, but the city itself does not lend itself to cycling. Bike rental can be arranged through many hostels and a couple of out-of-the-city-centre bike shops, such as **Thong Sen Cycle** (*5871B, Ground Floor Kuching Garden, Jln Tun Razak; www.thongsencycle.com*), though the hostels are the best bet.

BY TAXI Taxi drivers in Kuching, like much of Sarawak, do not use the meters their taxis are installed with, so before you get into a cab, it is best to negotiate and agree on a price. Expect to pay about 20MYR for the airport–city trip and 5–10MYR for inner-city journeys.

TOURIST INFORMATION

Kuching Visitor information centre [250 B3] Sarawak Tourism Complex, Lot 31, Jln Masjid; ↳ 082 410944/410942; e stb@ sarawaktourism.com; ⏰ 08.00–18.00 Mon–Fri,

09.00–15.00 Sat/Sun & public holidays. The best port of call for maps, hotel rates & bus routes. The office – along with the whole Sarawak Tourism Board – moved in 2011 from its offices in the Old Courthouse to this street near the mosque.

i **The National Parks & Wildlife Office** [250 B3] As for the visitor information centre above; 082 248088; http://ebooking. com.my. The place to obtain permits & book accommodation in the Bako, Gunung Gading & Kubah national parks & the Matang Wildlife Centre. Online booking service for parks state-wide available on the website. Park entry/ conservation fees vary from park to park but mostly 10MYR adult/5MYR children.

i **Sarawak Tourism Board** [250 B3] 6th & 7th Floors, Bangunan Yayasan Sarawak, Jln Masjid; 082 423600; e stb@sarawaktourism.com

i **Sarawak Tourist Association (STA)** [250 C2] Main Bazaar, Kuching waterfront near the Square Tower; 082 240620. Another very helpful outlet for recommending & organising tour guides in Kuching & for general visitor information. They prefer you to book weeks ahead for this service, directly or through a tour agent, but last-minute arrangements are not out of the question.

i **Tourism Malaysia** [251 E3] Kuching office, 2nd Floor Bangunan Rugayah, Jln Song Thian Cheok; 082 246575; e mtpbkch@tourism.gov.my

TOUR OPERATORS

Borneo Adventure [250 D3] 55 Main Bazaar, Kuching; 082 245175; e info@ borneoadventure.com; www.borneoadventure. com. One of the most notable tour companies in Borneo, Borneo Adventure targets an upmarket eco-trekking & cultural niche, with its innovative, personalised & insightful tours. It focuses on tapping into the ethnic communities & cultures, using the staff's local knowledge. They'll take you right to the source, in a sustainable manner, on set theme & special interest tours.

Borneo Transverse [250 D3] No 15, Ground Floor, Jln Green Hill; 082 257784; e bntv@ po.jaring.my; www.borneotransverse.com.

my. Knowledgeable local people, friendly & professional. At more mid-range prices, this is a good company to call even at shorter notice, if you want to do a trip from Kuching – whether you just require the transport or want the transfers & company of a guide.

Borneo Exploration Tours & Travel [250 D4] 76 Wayang St; 082 252137; e chris@ borneoexplorer.com.my; www.borneoexplorer. com.my. Recommended budget & independent travel group, can also help cut the costs incurred (ie: penalties & room price bias) for travelling alone.

🏠 WHERE TO STAY

There have been been plenty of changes to Kuching's lodgings in recent years; in fact, the city is undergoing a bed boom, with an overall raising of the bar on standards and modernisation. The 'Golden Triangle' riverfront area around Jalan Tunku Abdul Rahman (which locals shorten to TAR) is still five-star forte, with a prime location matched by high prices (though these are still much cheaper than in Europe or the US). In the streets of adjacent China Town, you can get some excellent deals on mid-grade business and leisure hotels. Many budget hotels and bead and breakfasts can be found in this area, while further north, in the residential area around Reservoir Park, new hostels have emerged. The vicinity of Jalan Ban Hock, known as 'new town', within a 1km walk of the waterfront attractions, is a neighbourly hub of eating, nightlife and commerce, including several budget to mid-range hotels. Bar a couple of pioneering new examples, there is still surprisingly little enforcement of total non-smoking bans in hotels, even in international chains with a strong American clientele.

HOTELS There are many **budget to mid-range hotels** (see pages 252–3) in the 'new town' area between Jalan Padungan, Jalan Tabuan and Jalan Ban Hock. Some

left   Curious looking, the western tarsier is a nocturnal primate species and is among the smallest in the world at around 1kg (FL/FLPA) page 52

below left   The slow loris creeps and clambers through the forests at night and can cling to branches for hours on end with its powerful grip (w/ShS) page 51

below right   Borneo is home to two gibbon species both of which inhabit dipterocarp forests, including the Mueller's gibbon pictured here (TA/FLPA) page 48

bottom   The long-tailed macaque (*Macaca fascicularis*) is also commonly known as the crab-eating macaque. This one at Bako National Park is seen living up to its name by eating a horseshoe crab (DA) page 51

above   The Malayan civet is one of several species found in Borneo (FL/FLPA) page 55

right   Fruit bats in Gunung Gading National Park (DA)

below left   A greater tree shrew eating katydid (FL/FLPA)

below right   Bornean mountain ground squirrels (*Dremomys everetti*) are easily seen at Mount Kinabalu (DA)

right The bearded pig is quite a shy creature despite its formidable size (SS) page 55

below The lesser mouse deer is the world's smallest hoofed animal – weighing in at just 2kg (SS/NV)

bottom *Pangolin* is the Malay word for 'something that rolls up' – it is a nocturnal scaly anteater (CL/FLPA)

There are eight species of hornbill in Borneo including: rhinoceros (*above, BT*), oriental pied (*below right, SS*), wreathed (*below left, T&PG/FLPA*) and yellow-billed hornbills (*left, MN/IS*). See page 56.

above   **Orange-bellied flowerpecker**
           (JH/FLPA) page 56

right   **Black-collared starling**
           (oa/Sh) page 56

below right **Temminck's sunbird** (NR/FLPA)

below   **Golden-naped barbet** (JH/FLPA)

above **Eastern grass-owl** (NB/FLPA)

below left **Crested serpent-eagle** (JH/FLPA)

below right **Oriental bay owl** (JH/FLPA)

above left	**Blue-eared kingfisher** (DA)
above right	**Striated heron** (HL/iS)
below left	**Storm's stork** (JH/FLPA)
below right	**Chinese pond heron** (NB/FLPA)

above   Chevron barracuda and big-eye jacks collide at Sipadan Island (SB)

The endangered green turtle (below left, AN/NV) and critically endangered hawksbill turtle (left, JC/NV) are both found in the pristine waters off Sabah's east coast (page 59)

below   The dugong is a protected species found in seagrass beds (I/FLPA) page 44

bottom   A resting whitetip shark casts a cautious eye over Sipadan Island (SB) page 59

above The tiny mandarin fish is one of the coral reef's most colourful residents (SB) page 59

right A compliant black-tip grouper poses near Mabul Island, eastern Sabah (SB)

below left A painted frogfish sits amid a cluster of tunicates at Kapalai (SB)

below right A purple-gilled hypselodoris, one of the many species of sea slugs found at Mabul Island (SB)

bottom left No bigger than a baby's fingernail, a pygmy seahorse is barely perceptible in its fan coral home near Mabul Island (SB)

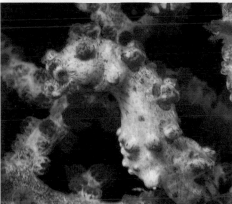

above The water monitor is a powerful lizard ranging from 20cm to nearly 3m in length (DA) page 57

left A juvenile Wagler's pit viper (SB) page 57

below left A crested agamid lizard perches astride a tree trunk at the Danum Valley (SB)

below The five-banded flying lizard (*Draco quinquefasciatus*) has large skin flaps that allow it to glide from tree to tree (DA)

bottom Though rare behaviour for crocodiles, the false gharial does not care for its young after birth (W) page 57

above **Asian horned frog** (SS) page 57
below left **Wallace's flying frog** (SS) page 57
below right **Harlequin flying tree frog** (B/DT) page 57

above   A stunning species, the Rajah Brooke's birdwing butterfly is one of more than 50 endemics found in Borneo (FL/FLPA) page 58

left   A long-legged centipede waits for passing prey in the Danum Valley (SB)

below left Tractor millipede (DA)

below   Atlas beetle (CL/FLPA)

bottom   Tiger leeches take great care to nurture their young — a trait which is rare among invertebrates (JH/Sh)

above	**Hermit crab** (DA) page 58
top right	**The horseshoe crab isn't actually a crab, but rather a descendant of the extinct marine arthropod lineage** (HA/NV) page 59
above right	**Male fiddler crabs are equipped with one over-sized claw to help attract the ladies** (BR/NV) page 58
right	**A blue mangrove crab** (DA) page 58
bottom	**Asian forest scorpion** (CL/FLPA)

above left **Forest canopy walk, Ulu Temburong National Park, Brunei** (TT) page 154

above **Gomantong Caves are the largest limestone outcrop in Sabah** (NG) page 224

left **The ascent of Mount Kinabalu, just above the tree line** (DA) page 192

bottom **A group of tourists search for wild orang-utans along the Kinabatangan River in Sabah** (DA) page 223

are cell-like with no windows. Better ones have air conditioning, phone, satellite television, fridge and bathrooms. Upgrade by moving away from the waterfront.

Hostels and guesthouses are your best bet if you want to be among fellow travellers or want cheap family rooms. If not, then some of the small, mostly Chinese, hotels can offer better value, with air-conditioned rooms and attached bathroom, television and phone.

Several hotels and inns in the area of Jalan Green Hill, Jalan Padungan and Jalan Nanas near the Sunday Market will provide you with a fan-cooled room, for 40–100MYR for a family room.

The Ascott group has traded in the Somerset Gateway and is preparing for the opening of a Citadines service apartment property (Citadines Upland Kuching, www.citadines.com) by mid-2012 in the government district of Jalan Simpang Tiga.

Luxury

Hilton Kuching [251 E3] (315 rooms) Jln Tunku Abdul Rahman; 082 223888; e kuching@hilton.com or sales_kuching@hilton. com; www1.hilton.com. Overlooking the river in Golden Triangle area (ask for river-view room), spacious rooms & suites, including non-smoking floors, pool with faux waterfall setting, fitness & business centres, several top-notch eateries & entertainment outlets. This hotel consistently receives glowing reports (more so than any of the other luxury hotels). Mid range prices possible on double rooms with internet specials & hotel promotions. Executive-floor rooms & suites include breakfast, Wi-Fi & access to executive lounge (US$120 dbl). **$$$–$$$$$**

Merdeka Palace Hotel & Suites [250 C4] (214 rooms) Jln Tun Abang Haji Openg; 082 258000; e info@merdekapalace.com; www.merdekapalace.com. Lots of character, though dated in parts (in both structure & service). Some standard rooms are a bit dowdy & cramped – best to opt for a de luxe room or even a huge apartment suite – the Wi-Fi is chargeable & there are a couple of non-smoking floors. Well located for museums & greenery, but less so for waterfront attractions. Fitness-centre facilities, including gym & steam bath. **$$$–$$$$$**

Pullman Kuching [251 E4] (389 rooms) 1A Jln Mathies; 082 222888; e H6332@accor. com; www.pullmankuching.com. Accor has arrived in Borneo & plunged into the luxury market with their top-end brand. Brand new in late 2011, with a stunning design inside & out, this hotel's hilltop views open out over the city & the Sarawak River. There's a 'check-in, chill-out' ethos, which is reflected in the high-tech rooms,

with fitness gear & espresso machines, & the groovy bars & restaurants, fitness & business centres & spa. Surrounded by shopping malls & restaurants, 10mins' walk from waterfront. **$$–$$$$$**

Upmarket

Riverside Majestic [251 E3] (241 rooms) Jln Tunku Abdul Rahman; 082 247777; e contact@rmh.my; www.riversidemajestic. com. (Formerly Crowne Plaza Riverside Kuching.) Now under new management & modernising, this prime location hotel (by the riverside) lies between main shopping centres, China Town & the old city. Good value & views, spacious rooms with work desk & free internet, non-smoking floor & rooms/facilities for disabled guests. Service here comes with a smile & the excellent facilities include a roof pool, squash, tennis courts, gym, Malay, European & Thai restaurants, meeting rooms, business centre & executive lounge. **$$$–$$$$**

Four Points by Sheraton [250 A7] (435 rooms) Lot 3186-3187, Block 16 KCLD, Jln Lapangan Terbang Baru; 082 280888; e reservations.kuching@fourpoints.com; www. starwoodhotels.com. In the 'BDC' retail hub, 2km north of the airport, 5km from the city. Bright, contemporary rooms with the brand's signature 'comfort' bed, lounge furniture & writing desk. Junior suites are 62m², while premier suites (with kitchenette) are geared to families. Lobby lounges, café, cheerfully decked eateries, business centre, 24hr gym & 100% smoke-free. Plenty of online deals for double & family rooms available, with rates starting from 270MYR breakfast included. **$$–$$$$**

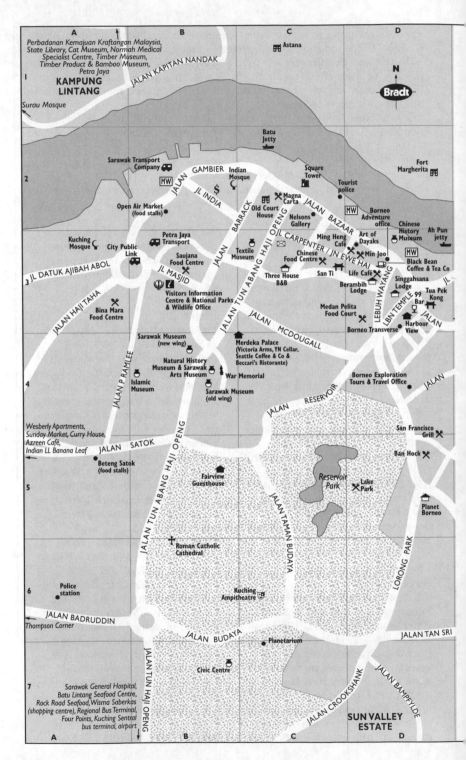

A

Perbadanan Kemajuan Kraftangan Malaysia,
State Library, Cat Museum, Normah Medical
Specialist Centre, Timber Museum,
Timber Product & Bamboo Museum,
Petra Jaya

1 KAMPUNG
LINTANG

Surau Mosque

B

Astana

JALAN KAPITAN NANDAK

C

D

N

Bradt

Batu
Jetty

Fort
Margherita

2 Sarawak Transport
Company

JALAN GAMBIER

Indian
Mosque

MW

JL INDIA

Open Air Market
(food stalls)

Square
Tower

Tourist
police

MW

Magna
Carta

Old Court
House

JALAN BAZAAR

Nelsons
Gallery

Borneo
Adventure
office

Chinese
History
Museum

Ah Pun
jetty

Kuching
Mosque

City Public
Link

Petra Jaya
Transport

Saujana
Food Centre

JL MASJID

Textile
Museum

JALAN

BARRACK

JL CARPENTER / JN EWE HAI

Ming Heng
Café

Art of
Dayaks

Min Joo

MW

3 JL DATUK AJIBAH ABOL

Visitors Information
Centre & National Parks
& Wildlife Office

Chinese
Food Centre

Three House
B&B

San Ti

Berambih
Lodge

Life Café

Black Bean
Coffee & Tea Co

Singgahsana
Lodge

LBN TEMPLE

LEBUH WAYANG

Tua Pek
Kong

99
Bar

JALAN

JALAN HAJI TAHA

Bina Mara
Food Centre

Medan Pelita
Food Court

Borneo Transverse

Harbour
View

Sarawak Museum
(new wing)

JALAN P RAMLEE

JALAN TUN ABANG HAJI OPENG

Merdeka Palace
(Victoria Arms, YN Cellar,
Seattle Coffee & Co &
Beccari's Ristorante)

JALAN MCDOUGALL

4 Islamic
Museum

Natural History
Museum & Sarawak
Arts Museum

War Memorial

Sarawak Museum
(old wing)

JALAN RESERVOIR

Borneo Exploration
Tours & Travel Office

JALAN

Wesberly Apartments,
Sunday Market, Curry House,
Azreen Café,
Indian LL Banana Leaf

JALAN SATOK

Beteng Satok
(food stalls)

San Francisco
Grill

Ban Hock

5 Fairview
Guesthouse

JALAN TUN ABANG HAJI OPENG

JALAN TAMAN BUDAYA

Reservoir
Park

Lake
Park

Planet
Borneo

LORONG PARK

Roman Catholic
Cathedral

6 Police
station

JALAN BADRUDDIN

Thompson Corner

Kuching
Ampitheatre

JALAN BUDAYA

Planetarium

JALAN TAN SRI

JALAN BAMPFYLDE

JALAN CROOKSHANK

7 Sarawak General Hospital,
Batu Lintang Seafood Centre,
Rock Road Seafood, Wisma Saberkas
(shopping centre), Regional Bus Terminal,
Four Points, Kuching Sentral
bus terminal, airport

JALAN TUN ABANG HAJI OPENG

Civic Centre

SUN VALLEY
ESTATE

A **B** **C** **D**

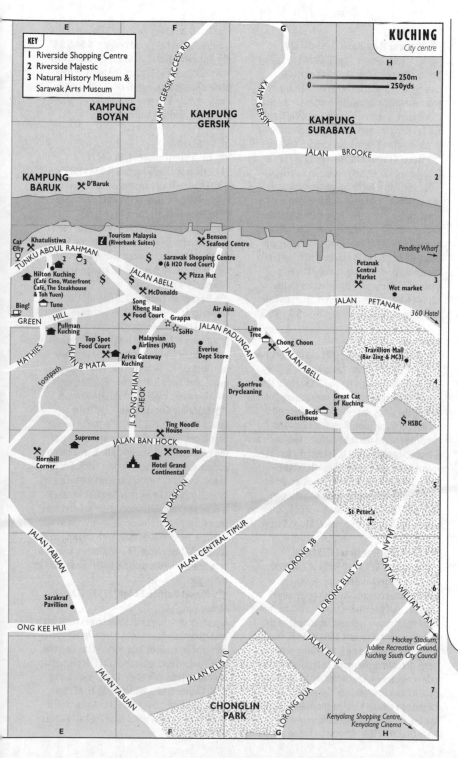

KEY
1 Riverside Shopping Centre
2 Riverside Majestic
3 Natural History Museum &
  Sarawak Arts Museum

KAMPUNG
BOYAN

KAMPUNG
GERSIK

KAMPUNG
SURABAYA

KAMP GERSIK ACCESS RD

KAMP GERSIK

JALAN   BROOKE

KAMPUNG
BARUK

D'Baruk

Cat
City
Khatulistiwa

Tourism Malaysia
(Riverbank Suites)

Benson
Seafood Centre

Pending Wharf

TUNKU ABDUL RAHMAN

2 3

Sarawak Shopping Centre
(& H2O Food Court)

Petanak
Central
Market

Hilton Kuching
(Café Cino, Waterfront
Café, The Steakhouse
& Toh Yuen)

JALAN ABELL

Pizza Hut

Wet market

McDonalds

Bing!

Tune

Song
Kheng Hai
Food Court

Air Asia

JALAN   PETANAK

360 Hotel

GREEN HILL

Grappa

SoHo

JALAN PADUNGAN

Lime
Tree

Pullman
Kuching

MATHIES

Top Spot
Food Court

Malaysian
Airlines (MAS)

Chong Choon

JALAN ABELL

Travillion Mall
(Bar Zing & MC3)

JALAN B MATA

Ariva Gateway
Kuching

Everise
Dept Store

footpath

Spotfree
Drycleaning

Great Cat
of Kuching

JL SONG THIAN CHEOK

Beds
Guesthouse

HSBC

Ting Noodle
House

Supreme

JALAN BAN HOCK

Choon Hui

Hornbill
Corner

Hotel Grand
Continental

JALAN DASHON

St Peter's

JALAN TABUAN

JALAN CENTRAL TIMUR

LORONG 3B

LORONG ELLIS 7C

JALAN DATUK WILLIAM TAN

Sarakraf
Pavillion

ONG KEE HUI

JALAN ELLIS

Hockey Stadium,
Jubilee Recreation Ground,
Kuching South City Council

JALAN TABUAN

JALAN ELLIS 0

LORONG DUA

JALAN ELLIS

Kenyalang Shopping Centre,
Kenyalang Cinema

CHONGLIN
PARK

Mid-range

⌂ **Harbour View Hotel** [250 D3] (245 rooms) Lorong Temple; ✆082 274666; e sales@ harbourview.com.my; www.harbourview. com.my. This 3-star, Chinese-run hotel is very popular with Malay people. Business feel, relaxed atmosphere & central location (opposite the Tua Pek Kong Temple). Free Wi-Fi & breakfast included with all rooms. **$$** (**$$$$** suites)

⌂ **Hotel Grand Continental** [251 F5] (192 rooms) Lot 42, Section 46, Jln Ban Hock; ✆082 230399; e kuching@ghihotels.com.my or reservation_kuching@ghihotels.com.my; www.ghihotels.com.my. In new town business district. Spacious attractive rooms (including non-smoking & facilities for disabled), bargain-priced de luxe & family rooms, & nice rooftop swimming pool, spa & gym make this very good value. Executive Lounge rooms on the 12th–14th 'Continental Comfort' floors include complimentary daily paper & Wi-Fi. **$$–$$$**

Budget

⌂ **360 Hotel** [251 H3] (273 rooms) Hock Lee Centre, Jln Datuk Abang Abdul Rahim; ✆082 484888; e reservation@360kuching.com; www.360kuching.com. A new, dazzlingly lit hotel among the shops, supermarkets, restaurants & banks of China Town. Rooms & suites are divided between the newly refurbished Tower A & less up-to-date Tower B. Colourfully furnished rooms with high-tech touches – LCD, Wi-Fi – tea-/coffee-making & ironing facilities. Views from some rooms over the city & Santubong Mountain. The very reasonably priced apartments include kitchenette, microwave, fridge & stove. **$$–$$$**

⌂ **The Lime Tree Hotel** [251 G4] (50 rooms) Lot 317, Abell Rd; ✆082 414600; e info@limetreehotel.com.my; www. limetreehotel.com.my. As fresh as its name suggests, this boutique-style leisure & business hotel has pleasing touches throughout, with in-built universal sockets, LCD TV, Wi-Fi, rain showers, cushy bedding & zesty lime, white & beige décor from the rooms to restaurants. The café serves lime-inspired healthy foods (fresh from its own lime garden). The rooftop lounge is targeting a hip but easy-on-the-wallet meetings market. Great internet specials such as the 'Sweet Suite Deal' for 250MYR/night including airport

transfers & breakfast for 2. The 58m² executive & Limetree suites have a kitchenette. **$$–$$$**

⌂ **Supreme Hotel** [251 E5] (94 rooms) Jln Ban Hock; ✆082 255155. In the heart of the Golden Triangle business & retail district, the single, double & de luxe rooms have AC, phone, satellite TV, fridge & bathrooms. **$$**

Shoestring

⌂ **Beds Guesthouse** [251 G4] 229, Lot 91, Section 50, Jln Padungan; ✆082 424229; e reservation@bedsguesthouse.com; www. bedsguesthouse.com. In the vibey Padungan China Town zone, this new, bright pink guesthouse has not yet been tested, but comes recommended by individuals & families. Single, double, twin, quad rooms & lofts, plus male/ female dorms. Kitchen, bar, TV lounge, reading corners, 24hr reception. **$**

⌂ **Berambih Lodge** [250 D3] 104 Ewe Hai/ Carpenter St; ✆082 238589; e berambih_lodge@ hotmail.com; www.budgetlodgekuching.com. In old town hub, a Dayak longhouse-style hostel, beyond basic & often borderline clean, where rates include AC. Dorm/double/twin/family rooms with breakfast, bed linen, coffee/tea/ drinking water, Wi-Fi & individual lockers. **$**

⌂ **Fairview Guesthouse** [250 B5] 6 Jln Taman Budaya; ✆082 240017 e thefairview@ gmail.com; www.thefairview.com.my. One of the most charming, idiosyncratic & welcoming budget accommodations Borneo-wide. Eric & Annie's family-run guesthouse sits within a leafy tropical garden setting near Sarawak Museum & Reservoir Park. Accommodation includes fan-cooled dorm beds, plus single, twin & triple AC rooms, a 3-bed 'master suite' with dressing room & a 5-bed family room. Shared kitchen, lounge & computers. Eric runs group & tailor-made tours in the region. **$**

⌂ **Planet Borneo Lodge** [250 D5] No 10 Lorong Park; ✆082 412100; e reservationkch@planetborneotours.com; www. planetborneolodge.com. In a leafy residential & parkland area, about 3km north of the city, this lodge (which opened in mid-2011) is promoting itself as a clean, safe place. Exotic garden, dip pool, kitchen & BBQ. With free Wi-Fi, AC, 3- to 11-person rooms & light breakfast included, it really appears to be great value for backpackers & families. **$**

⌂ **Singgahsana Lodge** [250 D3] Jln Temple 1; ✆ 082 429277; f 082 429267; e info@singgahsana.com; www.singgahsana.com. An ethnic-hip budget boutique somewhere between backpacker & guesthouse, in city centre. Low-lit dorms & single/twin/double rooms decked out in tribal prints cater to a maximum of 30 travellers. The lodge oozes the friendliness & local knowledge of its team of youthful staff & owners. Access cards, AC, bed linen (for dorms too, but not towels), continental breakfast included, non-smoking premises. Recommended. **$**

⌂ **Three House B&B** [250 C3] 51 Upper China St; ✆ 082 423499, 0198853998; e info@threehousebnb.com; www.threehousebnb.com. Absolutely bijou, newly opened in 2011; a bargain for its décor, location, friendliness & style, run by a Swedish woman. Modern Chinese tones of red & orange, silk & wooden furniture meet LCD TVs & Wi-Fi. There are cooking facilities, free lockers & storage, & no curfews. Dorm beds, twin 'private dorms' & doubles. **$**

⌂ **Tune Hotel** [251 E3] (135 rooms) Jln Borneo (off Jln Tunku Abdul Rahman); e enquiry@tunehotels.com; www.tunehotels.com. Rare for AirAsia's formula hotels to have such a great inner-city location, but its one of the charms of a smaller city. Rooms include singles & doubles; AC, towels & toiletries & Wi-Fi are all 'chargeable add-ons. Check-in 14.00, check-out 11.00 'sharp'; non-smoking building, CCTV, 24hr reception. **$**

Serviced apartments

⌂ **Ariva Gateway** [251 E4] (70 apts) No 9, Jln Bukit Mata; ✆ 082 250958; e Kuching.Enquiry@stayariva.com; www.stayariva.com. (Formerly Somerset Gateway.) Little seems to have changed with the switch in ownership, other than a warmer reception, obvious even on the website. Smartly furnished serviced studios & 2- or 3-bed apartments, with fully equipped kitchens, high-tech fittings & free Wi-Fi. Stunning rooftop swimming pool, gym, meeting & business rooms, 24hr reception & security, babysitting service. Breakfast served in 4th-floor residents' lounge. Located near shopping centres, airline offices & food courts, ideal corporate-stay bolt-hole for short term & extended stays. **$$$–$$$$**

⌂ **Wesberly Apartments** [250 A4] (5 apts) Lot 2812, Block 195, Jln Rubber (West); ✆ 082 246197; e enquiries@wesberly.com.my; www.wesberly.com.my. Spacious & light 2- or 3-bedroom apartments with open kitchen-lounges, quality furnishings & fittings, washing machines & parking. Near the Sunday Market, north of the city centre, the 110m^2 apartments with botanically inspired names are located above an art gallery & next door to Wisma Sandhu shopping centre. 300–400MYR per day. **$$$**

✖ WHERE TO EAT AND DRINK

FOOD COURTS AND STREET FOOD These are some of the best places for on-the-go eating — easy on the pocket, but with high-quality food and a bustling atmosphere. The indoor food courts are good if you want air conditioning. If the place serves predominantly Malay food, it will be halal. **Top Spot Food Court** [251 E4] (*6th Floor, Taman Kerata, Jln Bukit Mata Kuching; ⊕ 17.00–22.00 daily*), is one of the best places in Kuching for cheap, quality seafood and is found on the top of a multi-level car park. The 36 food stalls here offer a bevy of grilled fish, satays, chilli crab, clay-pot dishes, oyster omelette and curries. **Song Kheng Hai Food Court** [251 F3] (*off Jln Padungan, near cat statue*) has good, noodle-heavy food stalls operating day and night. Further east along the river on Jalan Petanak (continue on from Sarawak Plaza) there is a lively food centre in the **Petanak Central Market** [251 H3]. In the old town centre the daytime **Chinese Food Centre** [250 C3] (*opposite San Ti Temple on Leboh Ewe Hai*) has several stalls with fish balls, fish soups and noodles. **Medan Pelita Food Court** [250 D3] (*corner Wayang St & Temple St; ⊕ 11.00–17.00*) is a centrally located air-conditioned set-up. Near the mosque, *gerai makan* serve Malay, Chinese and seafood dishes, both day and night. The **Saujana Food Centre** [250 B3] (*5th Floor, Sajuana car park complex, Jln Masjid*) has stalls serving mostly Malay curry and rice dishes. **Benteng Satok** [250 A5] (*Jln Satok, left-hand side heading out of town;* ⊕ *18.00–24.00*) has many Malay food stalls along the roadside. **Thompson Corner** [250 A6] (*corner Jln Nanas & Jln Palm*) is loved by locals for its stalls of clay-pot noodle (*mee*) dishes and *mee sua*.

FAST FOOD This can be found everywhere, but for sushi, burgers or KFC on the run, several fast-food chains are found at the **H20 Food Court** [251 F3] (*Jln Tunku Abdul Rahman;* ⊕ *10.00–21.30*) basement level of Sarawak Plaza shopping centre.

COFFEE SHOPS For cheap breakfasts or lunches, head to traditional coffee shops.

✕ **Chong Choon** [251 G4] Lot 121, Section 3, Jln Abell. An old-style breakfast institution where people read newspapers while eating bowls of steaming *kolo mee* & *laksa*. **$–$$**

✕ **Choon Hui** [251 F4] Jln Ban Hock, near the Hindu temple. A breakfast hit for its *laksa* & *kolo mee* in unadorned surrounds. **$–$$**

✕ **Min Joo** [250 D3] Corner of Bishopsgate & Ewe Hai/Carpenter St. They still make their own noodles here. Very popular at breakfast – you may struggle to get through the door! **$–$$**

✕ **Ming Heng Café** [250 D3] 6 Ewe Hai. Serves *laksa, kolo mee,* other noodle dishes & satay. Count on paying 4–10MYR for a Sarawak *laksa* – more according to the serving size & the size of the prawns. **$–$$**

✕ **Ting Noodle House** [251 F4/5] 17B, Lot 132, Jln Ban Hock. More a lunchtime noodle joint with a menu of dumplings & many rice & noodle dishes including tangy Taiwanese beef noodles. **$–$$**

CHINESE RESTAURANTS

✕ **Toh Yuen** [251 E4] Jln Tunku Abdul Rahman; ☎082 248200. In the Hilton Hotel. Sophisticated (& relatively pricey), with Chinese food & atmosphere. The dim sum luncheon buffet is highly recommended; the menu is a mix of Cantonese & Szechuan. **$$–$$$$**

✕ **Café Harapan** [250 D3] Lorong Temple. The coffee shop at the Harbour View Hotel, is down to earth in décor but with good noodle dishes. **$$–$$$**

✕ **Hornbill Corner** [251 E4] 85 Jln Ban Hock; ☎082 252670; ⊕ 17.00–12.30. Perhaps the best downtown steamboat restaurant for all-you-can-eat buffet value. **$$–$$$**

✕ **Hong Kong Noodle House** [250 A7] Wisma Saberkas shopping centre, Jln Tun Abang Haji Openg (3km out of town). Chinese locals & Westerners 'in the know' flock here for a cheap, quality lunch. Sweet barbecued *char siew* is their speciality. **$–$$**

VEGETARIAN While many of the above are vegetarian-friendly, the following are particularly good. There are also daytime vegetarian food stalls in Jalan Green Hill, off Jalan Padungan.

✕ **Life Café** [250 D3] 108 Ewe Hai St; ☎082 411754; ⊕ 11.00–22.00 Mon–Sat. This paper-lantern-lit café serves many dedicated vegetarian dishes among its simple but spicy Szechuan fare, clay-pot dishes, spicy noodles, pork/vegetarian

dumplings. Dozens of different speciality coffees & teas are served charmingly – the teas with traditional tea service – & there are iced & fruit teas such as mango, lychee & passion fruit in tumbler glasses. **$–$$**

MALAY The best Malay food is in the several *kampung* on the northern side of the river just near Fort Margherita – reached by a two-minute *tambang* ride from Ah Pun jetty to Encik Oman jetty. With bamboo ceilings, *nibong* (spiky palm) pillars and rattan blinds, the traditional Bidayuh atmosphere at **D'Baruk** [251 E2] (*Kampung Boyan;* ☎082 375470; ⊕ 17.00–01.00) goes beyond the décor. The Malay-Bidayuh menu has many noodle dishes, rice and soup. They don't serve alcohol.

Kampung Boyan [251 E1] is the first of four Malay villages along the riverbank, and there are several eating choices here at night including a few simple food kitchens and tables. These places are on temporary licences under a government programme to promote jobs for the Melayu (Malay) locals. Clean and simple, and you couldn't ask for a better dining location for such cheap food. Opposite, there are a few more established Malay *kedai* with under-cover areas. Given that all of these restaurants are strictly halal, this is not the place for partygoers or beer drinkers, but more for those who want to feel the romance of water-crossings and views in an inky black setting at night. Have an aperitif first before heading here.

About a kilometre from the waterfront, in the vicinity of the Sunday Market, cheap southern Indian food is served beautifully on a banana-leaf 'plate' at **Indian LL Banana Leaf** [250 A5] (*7G, Lorong Rubber 1, Jln Rubber;* ✆ *082 239404;* ⏰ *07.30–21.00*) with its very basic décor, indoor and outdoor tables. It's also good for take-aways and vegetarian food. The area around Jalan Rubber is Indian stamping ground – try the **Curry House** [250 A5] (*Lot 409, Section 10, Lorong 3A, Jln Rubber*) and the **Azreen Cafe** [250 A5] (*351 Lorong 12, off Jln Rubber*).

SEAFOOD

✘ **Benson Seafood Centre** [251 F3] Jln Abell; ✆082 255262; ⏰ 18.00–22.00. On the eastern side of the riverfront, past the major hotel strip. Highly recommended. Very popular so best to book, especially on weekends. $$–$$$

✘ **Rock Road Seafood** [250 A7] 2nd Mile, Jln Rock; ✆082 241575. A bit further along from Batu Lintang Seafood Centre (below). You can select your catch here – fish or crustaceans – from tanks. $$–$$$

✘ **Batu Lintang Seafood Centre** [250 A7] Off Jl Batu Lintang (3km out of town along Jln Tun Abang Haji Openg & into Jln Rock). Excellent cheap outdoor seafood, the *kedai* & stalls are open evenings only. $–$$

INTERNATIONAL AND FUSION

✘ **Magna Carta** [250 C2] The Old Courthouse Kuching; ✆0128 773500; ⏰ 17.00–24.00 (last orders) Tue–Sun. Award-winning Magenta Restaurant has morphed from its antique Malay home just out of town, into an equally high-on-historic-ambience city location. The café interior with its mix of dark wooden tables, culinary artefacts & menu blackboards almost has a retro-classroom feel. On the menu are carbonara, beef stroganoff, steak & mash, burgers, pepperoni pizza – & free Wi-Fi. $$$$

✘ **Beccari's Ristorante** [250 B/C4] Merdeka Palace Hotel, Jln Tun Abang Hj; ✆082 258000; ⏰ 12.00–23.00. Good Italian trattoria atmosphere, dark & woody, with lots of choices, including wood-fired pizza. $$$

✘ **Khatulistiwa Restaurant** [251 E3] Jln Tunku Abdul Rahman. Perched over the river, this 24hr restaurant has a certain people-watching attraction to it. The architecture is traditional Bidayuh baruk warrior style with a belian (ironwood) roof. The Bidayuh name means Equator. The food is a mix of Malay & Western. $$$

✘ **Waterfront Café** [251 E3] The Hilton's turn on a coffee house is a good lunch place with daily themed buffets & both Western & local food, lots of fresh salads, good breads. Loved for its family-friendly all-day Sun buffet & high teas during the week. $$$

A good steak The **San Francisco Grill** [250 D/E4] (*Jalan Ban Hock*) has been recommended and, more upmarket, **The Steakhouse** in the Hilton Hotel [251 E3] (*Jln Tun Abdul Rahman,* ⏰ *dinner only*). The **Victoria Arms** ($$$–$$$$) in the Merdeka Palace Hotel [250 B/C4] (*Jln Tun Abang Haji Openg*) has lots of meat and other pub grub.

CAFÉS AND CAKES

✗ **Caffe Cino** [251 E3] Hilton Hotel; ⊕ late. The best Western breads (sourdoughs, baguettes, wholemeal) in Kuching. $$$

✗ **Seattle Coffee Co** [250 B/C4] Merdeka Palace Hotel, Jln Tun Abang Haji Openg; ⊕ 12.00–23.00. It's a rather chilly (excessive AC) environment, but spic & span, & offers a late-night coffee kick. $$–$$$

✗ **Bing! Coffee Company** [251 E3] 84 Jln Padungan; ⊕ late. The only café in town that serves seriously European coffee & Illy is the bean. Young, lively, laptop-loving crowd. Wi-Fi. $–$$

✗ **Black Bean Coffee & Tea Company** [250 D3] 87 Ewe Hai St: ✆ 082 420290; ⊕ daytime only. An exquisite little boutique coffee roaster, ancient-Chinese infused with wooden pigeonholes. Inside this shoebox of a shop, you can sample or purchase freshly roasted pure Borneo coffee (Sarawak Liberica, Ararbica & Robusta) & teas, including Chinese Green & Taiwan Oolong, among the vintage & contemporary accessories. The minimalist environment has just 1 table & a bow-sized counter. $–$$

✗ **Coffee Bean & Tea Leaf** [251 F3] Sarawak Plaza, street level, 291 Jln Tunku Abdul Rahman; ⊕ late. A popular place for espresso with free Wi-Fi connection. $–$$

ENTERTAINMENT AND NIGHTLIFE

Kuching is not exactly a pulse-point of nightlife, but there is a burgeoning scene of late-night café-bars and clubbing between the waterfront hotel strip along Jalan Tunku Abdul Rahman and around Jalan Padungan and Jalan Bukit Mata. Increasing urbanity seems to be accompanied by a decline of the once-prevalent karaoke culture and a greater crossover between day/night venues.

One of the key hubs for youthful clubbing and drinking is the **Travillion Mall** [251 H4], on Jalan Petanak, which consists of several bars and lounges; these include **BarZing**, a stylish chill-out bar with lounge and house music and reasonable prices, and **M3C**, a bar with dance floor and DJ, trance and techno music, and where you need to be under 30 to not feel out of place.

Another evening hotspot for unwinding and having a few drinks is along Jalan Padungan. According to Gustino Basuan from the Sarawak Tourism Board 'They are Kuching's most fashionable entertainment outlets, playing dance-oriented music and catering to a more mixed crowd'. **SoHo** [251 F3/4] (*64 Jln Padungan*) has a very à la mode pub atmosphere, with Latin and jazz music, à la carte menu in the restaurant area and snacks in the bar. **Grappa** [251 F3] (*58 Jln Padungan*) plays house, R&B and '80s music and hosts a very young crowd.

Other than bars, a number of cafés and restaurants have sprung up from old shop-house buildings and become popular evening hang-outs for those wanting to combine socialising with work. Many of these places also offer free Wi-Fi.

For sophisticated martinis and acid jazz, **Senso** [251 E3] at the Hilton Kuching has a mood-lit lounge-bar with a mix of live music and resident DJ, plus a good cocktail list. **The Club** [251 E3] (⊕ *17.00–01.00*) lounge-bar at the Riverside Majestic offers a cosy spot minus the loud music, and also has a poolside terrace bar.

The **Victoria Arms** [250 B/C4] at Merdeka Palace is more the boisterous pub, with imported beers and live bands (⊕ *22.00 onwards Mon–Sat*) and ladies-only sessions on Fridays (⊕ *19.00–21.00*).

The **YN Cellar** [250 B/C4], also at the Merdeka, is a bit of an old boys' establishment, with a long wine list, but you must like cigar smoke. Other busy corner pubs, include **99** [250 D3] on Jln Green Hill, and **Cat City** [251 E3] (*Taman Sri Sarawak, opposite the Hilton*), which has an open-air bar, karaoke lounge and music bar for live bands and DJ.

FESTIVALS

GAWAI DAYAK This important Iban festival venerates rice, and is held every June at the end of harvest and has developed into a state-wide celebration among the Dayak community with many dance and cultural performances.

THE INTER-CULTURAL MOON CAKE FESTIVAL (*30 Sep–6 Oct*) This is more of a friendship festival between the Malay and Chinese cultures of Kuching.

GERAI RAMADAN If you are in Kuching during mid-September–October don't miss the atmosphere at one of the Ramadan bazaars such as Gerai Ramadan, held for the breaking of the month-long dawn-to-dusk fast. Around 400 stalls are held around the city serving curries, barbecued meats and satays. The most easily accessible bazaar unfurls on Jalan Satok, with another across the river in Jalan Semarak, Petra Jaya. Stalls are open 13.00–19.00.

SHOPPING

MARKETS The **Sunday Market**, Pasar Satok [250 A5] (which strangely enough starts on Saturday), is held along Jalan Santok, north of the city centre (*stalls ⊕ 13.00–01.00/02.00 Sat, 06.00–12.00 Sun*). Take bus No 4A/4B from outside the post office, catch a taxi, or walk – it takes around 20 minutes. Some 1,500 traders gather here to sell food and fruit, Dayak handicrafts, forest produce such as wild honey, clothing, pets and plants. Saturday evening is a good time to go to eat, otherwise Sunday morning to see it in full swing. Be on the alert for pickpockets.

HANDICRAFTS Among the copious souvenirs and carbon-copy handicrafts found along Jalan Bazaar, there is some good and inexpensive basketry, some carved objects and textiles, and some more expensive, but authentic, *objets d'art*. The area is a treasure chest to be explored, with hidden gems to be discovered upstairs and in back rooms. Some places cater more to collectors and foreign dealers, pushing prices higher, though not necessarily out of reach. **Nelsons Gallery** [250 C2] (*84 Jln Bazaar*) is a floor-to-ceiling clutter of charm – tribal art, antiques, jewellery – run by members of a prominent family of Kuching art dealers, as is **Art of Dayaks** [250 D3] (*68 Jln Bazaar*). As well as handicraft demonstrations, the **Sarawak Handicraft Centre & Craft Council** [250 C2] (*Courthouse complex;* ☏ *082 425652; www.sarawakhandicraft. com; ⊕ 08.30–12.30 & 14.00–17.00 Mon–Fri, 08.30–12.00 weekends & public holidays*) offers a 'mini-bazaar' of Sarawak handicrafts, with different ethnic groups represented each month, and a resource centre with library and handicraft videos. More handicrafts and textiles are on sale at the **Sarakraf Pavilion** [251 E6] (*78 Jln Tabuan, near Reservoir Park; ⊕ 09.00–17.00 daily*); as well as crafts for sale there are demonstrations, and workshops in handicraft and dance. **Perbadanan Kemajuan Kraftangan Malaysia** [250 A1] (*Lot 3057 Blok 18, Daerah Salak, Jln Stadium, Petra Jaya;* ☏ *082 444205*) sells indigenous crafts gathered and commissioned at the source.

BOOKS A good range of English-language books and maps are sold at **Bell Books** [000000] (*Sarawak Plaza*).

GENERAL Of the many shopping centres, **Riverside shopping centre** [251 E3] has a department store but also lots of electronic stores etc, plus a supermarket. **Sarawak Plaza** [251 F3] also has a supermarket at basement level.

Kuching SHOPPING

9

257

OTHER PRACTICALITIES

BANKS AND MONEY CHANGERS Banks are generally open 09.30–15.00 Monday–Friday. Money changers are open much longer, including weekends.

$ **Bank Bumiputra-Commerce & Standard Chartered Banks** Inside the Wisma Bukit Mata shopping centre on Jln Tunku Abdul Rahman
$ **Everrise Money Changer** [251 F4] Everrise department store, Jln Padungan; ⊕ 10.00–21.00 Mon–Fri, 10.00–18.00 Sat/Sun

$ **HSBC Bank** [251 F3] Jln Padungan
$ **Majid & Sons** [250 B2] 45 Jln India; ⊕ 09.00–19.30 Mon–Sat, 09.00–15.00 Sun. Reputable money changers.
$ **Mohamad Yahia & Sons** [251 F3] Lower Ground Floor, Sarawak Plaza; ⊕ 10.00–21.00, closed Fri afternoons. Reputable money changers.

COMMUNICATIONS AND MEDIA
✉ **Post office** [250 C3] Jalan Tunku Haji Openg; ⊕ 08.00–18.00 Mon–Sat, 10.00–13.00 Sun

Internet There are many cyber cafés in Kuching, charging about 3–4MYR, decreasing in price by the hour. Some offer free coffee and tea.

🄴 **Cyber City** Opposite Hilton, Taman Sri Sarawak; ⊕ 09.00–23.00 daily. 4MYR per hr for 1st hr, 3MYR thereafter, with free tea & coffee; also printing & scanning.

🄴 **Deli Café** Jln Bazaar. Wi-Fi.
🄴 **Lunch & Such** Jln Bazaar. Wi-Fi.

Tourist press The annual publication *Kuching Guide* is very handy while the quarterly *Kuching Talk* has nice cultural background and human interest stories.

HEALTH AND EMERGENCY
Central Police Station Opposite Padang Merdeka (sports field); ☎082 241222; emergency calls 999.

Tourist Police Unit Kuching waterfront; ☎082 250522; ⊕ 08.00–12.00 daily
Fire ☎994

Hospitals
✚ **Sarawak General Hospital** [250 A7] Jln Ong Kee Hui, about 2.5km from city centre; ☎082 276666. Public accident & emergency dept. Foreign visitors charged 50MYR for consultation, payable by cash or credit card.
✚ **Timberland Medical Centre** Jln Rock; ☎082 234466. Private hospital with 24hr emergency facilities.
✚ **Normah Medical Specialist Centre** [250 A1] Jln Tun Abdul Rahman, Petra Jaya; ☎082 440055; e inquiry@normah.com; www.normah.com.my. Private hospital in northern Kuching.

Doctors
✚ **The Clinic** [250 D3] Jln Bazaar, opposite Chinese History Museum. Highly reputable & purportedly very experienced in dealing with tourists' complaints.

Pharmacies
✚ **Apex Pharmacy** [251 F3] 1st Floor, Sarawak Plaza; (⊕ 10.00–21.00 daily
✚ **UMH Pharmacy** [251 F4] Jln Song Thian Cheok (opposite Malaysia Airlines office); ⊕ 09.00–18.00 Mon–Sat. Helpful staff.

MISCELLANEOUS
Sarawak State Library [250 A1] ☎082 442000; ⊕ 14.00–21.00 Mon, 10.00–21.00 Tue–Sat. Petra Jaya bus No 6.

Spotfree Dry Cleaning [251 E4] 105 Jalan Padungan

While the greater city spreads out over 50km², the centre accounts for less than 4% of that (2km²). Being compact, it is easily seen on foot. Kuching feels like a very safe city but there are warnings about pickpockets on the waterfront and in the market area. There is a police booth along here in case of any problems.

KUCHING CENTRAL

The Waterfront Life ebbs and flows along the banks of the Sungai Sarawak. On one side there are the old Chinese coffee shops, with antique stores in the old town along **Jalan Bazaar** [250 C2–D3] ('Main Bazaar' in English, and the oldest street in Kuching). On the other riverbank is the stroller's esplanade, known as The Waterfront. Official lines say it grew from the pyres of a drab warehouse area in the early 1990s under a programme of 'urban renewal'; critics say some old gems were cleared in the process. From the marketplaces in the west on Jalan Gambier through to the **Golden Triangle** [251 E3] on Jalan Tunku Abdul Rahman, the riverside esplanade is one of the most atmospheric places to stroll, as dozens of *tambang* slip into the night shadows of the 200m-wide river.

Little India Here, in the pedestrianised area around Jalan India (adjacent to the Open Air Market) and along Jalan Gambier, you can buy spices and textiles while absorbing the atmosphere; ideal for people-watching. Nearby is the 1850s **Masjid India**, the city's oldest Indian mosque.

China Town Some places here have historic monumental walls, others have giant modern cat statues. The monument of Kitty Kitschery, the **Great Cat of Kuching** [251 H4], sits at the end of the street that forms the heart of China Town, Jalan Padungan. Most of the buildings here date to the rule of the Third Rajah, Charles Vyner Brooke, around 1910–30; a few even date back to the 1850s. Running parallel to the riverbank it's a hub of hip in the evenings, and a good street for eating.

Malay kampungs [251 E–H1–2] Crossing the river to these four villages (*kampungs*) is like a trip out of the city, without actually leaving. Reached from Batu jetty or Ah Pun jetty, land at Encik Omar jetty in Kampung Boyan.

Petra Jaya [250 A1] This northern side of the river is developing into a visionary hub of high tech and glistening new government buildings, state libraries and sports centres.

LANDMARKS

Mosques At the western end of the waterfront, **Kuching Mosque** [250 A3] (*Masjid*) sits like a piece of perfect Arabia on the Kuching skyline; its golden domes and minarets, and milky walled, aqua-pillared façade are most impressive when viewed from the river. The sound of evening prayer flowing from it through the marketplace and over the river adds to the spiritual high of Kuching's watery sunsets. From 1968 it was the state mosque, until a new mega-mosque with an Italian marble interior was built in Petra Jaya on the northern bank of the river.

The lime green façade announcing the Masjid Bandar Kuching – the **Indian Mosque** [250 B2] – looks like just another shop-house in the rather baubled Jalan Gambier – deceptive first impressions, as it is actually the oldest mosque in the whole of Sarawak. Built in 1837 by Indian Muslims who had migrated from southern India, for a long time it was called Masjid India. The original *nipah* palm roofs were gradually replaced by *belian* (ironwood), the floors were cemented and the mosque engulfed by new buildings so that you have to pass through a small laneway, Lorong Sempit, to reach the entrance. The sound of a *bedok* (drum) rings out at prayer times and hundreds of faithful descend upon the mosque. Tired travellers are welcome, in keeping with the mosque's tradition.

Temples At the other end of the Main Bazaar and the spiritual spectrum, the gaudy dragon-embossed pastiche of the **Tua Pek Kong Temple** [250 D3] (*corner of Jln Temple & Jln Padungan*) is, at heart, the city's oldest Chinese temple, dating back to 1843 but with several renovated layers, including the multi-coloured wooden and carved stone façade. The Sarawak Cultural Heritage Ordinance, which protects it, came too late for some other buildings. Many locals believe this temple protected the town from Japanese bombing and saved the whole row of old buildings along Jalan Bazaar from obliteration. The intersection of Jalan Bazaar and Jalan Tabuan opposite the temple has thus been named 'Corner of Good Hope'. Among the shop-houses of Ewe Hai, the small **San Ti Temple** [250 C3] fades into the shadow of the city's most famous Chinese worship house, yet is a picturesque mesh of mythical figurines, ruby-coloured lanterns and baubles. It also dates back to the 1860s and is the soul place of the Teochew Chinese population. As such it is frequently the nerve centre of celebrations and street festivals.

Colonial relics Among the older buildings in the city – all along Main Bazaar – are the English-castle-like **Square Tower** [250 C2], built in 1879 as the town's jail, a 1912 **Chinese Chamber of Commerce** [250 D3] (now the **Chinese History Museum**) and the colonial **Courthouse complex** [250 C2] – a stunning mix of building styles, New Orleans pavilions, white colonnades and *belian* roof tiles, it was built as the seat of Sarawak's government in 1871 and continued that way for just over a century. The colonial Baroque **Clock Tower** was added in 1883, and a 6m-high granite obelisk – the **Charles Brooke Memorial** – erected in front of the courthouse in 1924. The four decorative bronze plaques on the memorial signify the Malay, Iban, Chinese and European cultures of Sarawak. Since 2003 the restored building has housed the Sarawak Tourism Complex, Visitor Information Centre and National Park administration.

Two eminent buildings protrude from the dense slopes of greenery on the northern banks of the river. The **Astana** [250 C1] (a slight variation on *istana*, or palace, in Malay) was built in 1870 by Charles Brooke as a bridal gift to his wife Ranee Margaret. It was the seat of power for the White Rajahs and is now the official residence of the Governor of Sarawak and not open for visiting. The symmetrical cream-coloured citadel, **Fort Margherita** [250 D2], was built in 1879 to ward off pirates. Now on state-owned grounds of the police barracks, it houses the **Police Museum**, although this is frequently closed. Check with the visitors' centre before venturing that way, or just enjoy the view from the water. Alongside the fort is the stunning new spherical structure of the Sarawak State Legislative Assembly, the Dewan Undangan Negeri, which lights up like an origami spaceship at night. Opened in 2009, the nine-storey building with its Chinese pagoda-style *payung* or 'umbrella roof' also incorporates Malay architectural features in its steel and glass structure. The highest building in Kuching, its dome roof and pinnacle skylight rise 120m above ground level.

VIEWPOINTS The best 360° bird's-eye view of the whole of Kuching and outlying areas is from the lookout tower on top of the **Civic Centre** [250 B7]. From its rooftop you can see Mount Serapi and Mount Santubong, and on a clear day even the peaks rising up on the Kalimantan border.

SPORTS AND GREEN SPACES The green lung of Kuching is **Reservoir Park** [250 C5], which is good for jogging. The botanical gardens are in the grounds of the Sarawak Museum. With national parks on its back doorstep you can go hiking for a morning or afternoon (see *Chapter 10, Southern Sarawak*, for more on surrounding national parks). Most four- and five-star hotels have gyms and tennis courts. Crowne Plaza Riverside has a squash court. The public swimming pool and another recreational ground are off Jalan Padungan by the Kuching South City Council.

MUSEUMS AND GALLERIES Most Sarawak museums have free admission, though some have a small camera (photo and video) fee. Most that 'open daily' are closed on the first day of major festivals and public holidays. The first five museums here come under the umbrella of the **State Museums** (\ *082 244232; www.museum. sarawak.gov.my; ⊕ 09.00–17.30 daily; free*).

Sarawak Museum [250 B4] (*Old Building, Jln Tun Abang Haji Openg*) Built in the style of a Normandy townhouse, this museum was opened by Charles Brooke in 1891 and is the most interesting for its ethnographic collections, artefacts and historical documents and displays of indigenous arts and crafts. The foundations of the collection were put in place by Tom Harrisson, its curator from 1947 up until Sarawak's independence in 1963. Harrisson, distinguished naturalist, archaeologist and anthropologist, is also credited with 'discovering' the 39,000-year-old skull in the Niah Caves. On the other side of the overpass along the same avenue is the new wing of the museum in a former state parliament building, named after the second prime minister of Malaysia, Dewan Tun Abdul Razak. This houses special exhibitions and has a museum shop on the ground floor.

Natural History Museum and Sarawak Arts Museum [250 B4] (*opposite Sarawak Museum*) These are two relatively recent additions. The first has vast collections of flora and fauna (some gathered by Alfred Russel Wallace in the 19th century), mounted specimens of Sarawak reptiles, birds and mammals including the near-extinct *banteng* (*Bos javanicus*), or Asian wild cattle. The second houses historical paintings and photographs.

Sarawak Islamic Museum [250 B4] (*Jln P Ramlee*) Housed in the restored 1930s building Maderasah Melayu – Malay Islamic School – the Islamic Museum has seven galleries depicting the history and culture of Malay people in Sarawak and the entire Malay–Indonesia Archipelago, from weaponry and religion to literature, architecture and education.

Textile Museum [250 C3] (*Jln Tun Abang Haji Openg;* \ *082 246194*) This offers a fascinating look into the textile history of indigenous Borneans, from bark cloth to Iban *pua kumbu* weaving, raw materials, textile motifs and accessories.

Pua Kumbu Museum (*4th Floor, Tun Jugah Tower;* \ *082 239672; ⊕ 09.00–16.30 Mon–Fri, closed Sat, Sun & public holidays; free*) Another must for textile buffs, this museum goes a few steps further in the hands-on experience of Iban *pua kumbu* textiles – you can watch the weavers in action and take lessons, plus see antique and modern *pua kumbu*, Iban silverware and jewellery.

Cat Museum [250 A1] (*Lobby Floor, Kuching North City Hall;* ☏ *082 446688; www. dbku.gov.my/catmuseum;* ⊕ *09.00–17.00 Tue–Sun; free; RM4 photo fee*) Cat kitsch or kitty consecration, depending on your taste. The dedicated museum of meows plays on the rumour that Kuching's name comes from the Chinese word for cat (see page 243). It houses 2,000 cat-fetish exhibits, including a mummified cat said to have been discovered in Egypt sometime between 3000BC and 3500BC. The museum is on the hilltop Bukit Siol, a 15MYR taxi ride from the city centre, or take Petra Jaya bus No 2C and walk 15 minutes up the hill to the museum from the bus stop.

Chinese History Museum [250 D3] (*Kuching Waterfront, near Tua Pek Kong Temple;* ☏ *082 244232; www.museum.sarawak.gov.my;* ⊕ *09.00–17.30 daily; free*) In the old Chinese courthouse building, this museum shows the historical power of the Chinese as a trading people, from early trade routes and migration to modern times.

Timber Museum [250 A1] (*Wisma Sumber Alam, Petra Jaya;* ⊕ *08.00–13.00 & 14.00–17.00 Mon–Thu, 08.00–11.40 & 14.00–17.00 Fri; free*) A forest resources and timber industry showcase.

Timber Product and Bamboo Museum [250 A1] (☏ *082 368575; www. sarawakforestry.com;* ⊕ *on request 09.00–16.30 Mon–Fri; free*) Another forestry promotional point, displaying some 82 species of wood found in Sarawak and a collection of bamboo products. It's located in the Sama Jaya Nature Reserve in Stutong, 15 minutes from the city, along with the **Forest Biology Museum**.

EXCURSIONS FROM KUCHING

Easy day or half-day trips include Santubong Peninsula, the Sarawak Cultural Village and Damai Beach; Bako, Kubah and Gunung Gading national parks; and Semenggoh Wildlife Centre. All are detailed in the following chapter.

10

Southern Sarawak

From the Santubong Peninsula and Damai beach area on Kuching's doorstep, to the Borneo Highlands in the hinterland, and west towards Tanjung (Cape) Datu where Sarawak meets Indonesian territory, a lot of southern Sarawak is part of the huge Kuching Division. The district is one of 11 in Sarawak and encompasses six national parks. Stretching along the Indonesian border to the east, the Samarahan Division gives way to Sri Aman, the gateway to some of the deepest, most moving river journeys into Iban territory.

NORTH OF KUCHING

Heading north to the Semanjung Santubong (Santubong Peninsula), over the wide Sungai Santubong river, **Gunung Santubong** (810m) rises up through a swirl of clouds in the background. The peninsula is rimmed by beaches and bays: the resort area is **Pantai Damai** (Damai Beach) around which the majority of the peninsula's lodgings are located. As a popular beach getaway for Kuchingites it is still very *damai* – 'peaceful' – and one of Sarawak's special places. The big tourist beacon to the area is the Sarawak Cultural Village, but the jungle-thick landscape is a place to spend some time hiking, visiting the Malay fishing villages and nearby wetlands and mangrove environments. Some love it so much they do it in reverse – base themselves here and visit Kuching for the day.

In the past couple of years a new development has sprung up around the foreshore of Teluk Bandung Damai bay, opposite the Sarawak Cultural Village. The partially complete Damai Bay Bazaar extends along 658m of foreshore and includes parks and children's playgrounds, shops, restaurants, food stalls, bicycle rental and sea-sport centres as well as business centres, prayer halls and public toilets. By creating this new retail and leisure zone, the Sarawak Economic Development Corporation has really seized the need to liven up the Damai area and to make the South China Sea front more accessible to the public. Initially due to open in February 2011, many of the restaurants and retail outlets should be up and running by the time of publication. Located alongside the main hotels of the peninsula, one of the main aims of the project was to offer resort-weary tourists more cultural and evening activities. As well as seafood restaurants and convenience stores, an arts and crafts gallery and evening cultural performances are planned. Topping the whole thing off, amid the public squares and fountains, will be a centerpiece sculpture of the rhinoceros hornbill – Sarawak's state emblem. The 9m-wide, 7.4m-long and 6.8m-high bird, depicted 'in flight', is a tribute to the precious bird and largest of the hornbill species – so large that the Iban people believed it was a messenger of the gods.

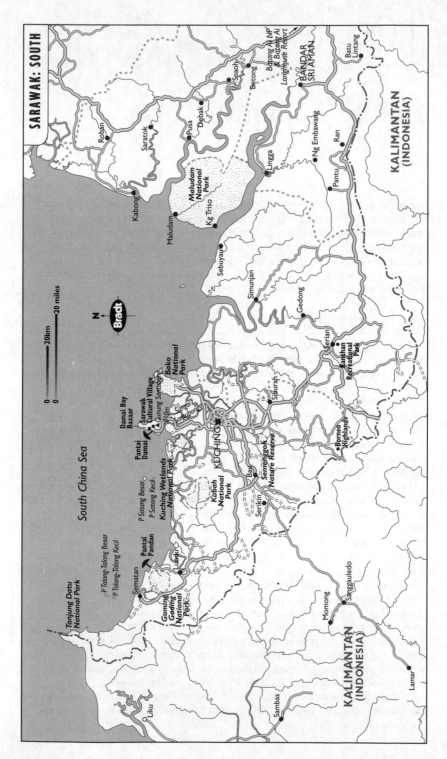

GETTING THERE AND AWAY

By car The village of Kampong Santubong is 32km north of Kuching; Pantai Damai (Damai Beach) is slightly further at 35km. The roads are quite bumpy over the mangroves.

By taxi A one-way fare from Kuching will cost around 40MYR, from the airport 50MYR.

By bus Take Petra Jaya Transport bus No 2d to Kampung Buntal, the first fishing village on the eastern side of the peninsula where there are beaches and seafood restaurants. The bus departs from Jalan Khoo Hun Yeang, not far from the Open Air Market, every hour between 07.00 and 18.00, returning every hour from 08.00 to 18.00. One-way fares are approximately 4MYR. A Kuching–Damai shuttle-bus service operates from outside the Holiday Inn and Crown Plaza in Kuching, with stops at the Damai Beach Holiday Inn Resort and Sarawak Cultural Village (SCV). The journey takes 1–1½ hours, and a one-way fare is 10MYR (for adults) or 5MYR (for children under 12). The first bus from Kuching is 07.30, the last bus back from Damai 21.00.

⌂ WHERE TO STAY

⌂ **Damai Beach Resort** (224 rooms) Teluk Bandung Santubong; 📞082 846999; e general@damaibeachresort.com; www.damaibeachresort.com. In a leafy beach location. Newish spa & 5-star wing of secluded hilltop rooms & suites, built in longhouse, Malay & 'Baruk' roundhouse style, private pool, water views & jacuzzi. Spacious standard rooms in sober, traditional style, good dining & entertainment – cocktail bars, pubs & cafés. Treez Café has good Malaysian cuisine at mid-range prices, though there are some complaints of slow service. **$$$–$$$$$**

⌂ **Damai Puri Resort & Spa** (207 rooms) Teluk Penyuk; 📞082 846900; e info@damaipurircsort.com; www.damaipuriresort.com. This beautifully located luxury resort lies on a cape with its own secluded beach on the bay of Teluk Penyuk. The hourglass-shaped swimming pool laps up the setting to the full. A US$10 million facelift in 2007 revamped all rooms & suites & added a spa village with yoga pavilion, speciality tea house & club floor. Tennis courts, state-of-the-art fitness centre, children's club, jungle & mountain trekking, Bako Park tours & meeting rooms. The 6 restaurants include Asian & international. All rooms have AC, satellite TV, kettle, safe, hairdryer, minibar. **$$$–$$$$$**

⌂ **Santubong Kuching Resort** (378 rooms) Jln Pantai Damai; 📞082 846888; e skresort@po.jaring.my. The biggest hotel, with big banquet & conference facilities & the Damai Golf Course

on its back doorstep. Well removed from the main road; café & restaurant, good-value rooms & suites & 2-bedroom chalets all with satellite TV, minibar, baths & showers. 4-star. **$$–$$$**

⌂ **Nanga Damai** (6 rooms) Jln Sultan Tengah; 📞019 8871017; e polseb@pc.jaring.my; www.nangadamai.com. Its name means 'home of peace' in Iban, & both the rainforest location & eco rustic design of this homestay are wonderfully peaceful. Run by Polycarp Teo Sebom, he makes his guests feel at home in this relaxed jungle house, whose wooden doors open onto a large deck. 4 double AC rooms on upper floors have phone, TV & jungle views. 2 cottage suites with small kitchen & forest-edge veranda. Breakfast is rye bread & freshly brewed coffee. Minimum 2 nights' stay for B&B. Considered unsuitable for children due to poolside sculptures, & best for peace-loving singles & couples. Polycarp is an expert 'freelance trekker' if you are ready for an off-track jungle adventure on Mt Santubong. **$$**

⌂ **Sarawak Cultural Village** 📞082 846411; e info@scv.com.my. Longhouse rooms with threadbare facilities – choose from Iban, Bidayuh, Orang Ulu or Melanau style. **$$**

⌂ **Permai Rainforest Resort** (39 cabins plus a longhouse) 📞082 846487; e reserve@permairainforest.com; www.permairainforest.com. (Formerly Camp Permai). Rustic back-to-jungle experience with some creature comforts, this rainforest resort has a jungle pool, Wi-Fi & Rainforest Café. Lodgings include 2-person, AC 'tree houses' (located at canopy level, not in the trees themselves), with breakfast included; cabins, sleeping 6–10, with fans & mosquito nets; & a 6-bed longhouse for a family/group. The Outdoor Activity Centre organises climbing & trekking. Be warned that this place attracts many school & team-building groups, so if leafy calm is important, avoid peak 'camp' periods. **$–$$**

✗ **WHERE TO EAT** There are many small seafood and other restaurants on the peninsula, along the main road and in the villages. The new hub of eating and nightlife – when completed – will be the Damai Bay Bazaar (see page 263). In Kampung Buntal (you will need to take a car or taxi from hotels) there are at least half a dozen inexpensive restaurants including **Lim Hock Ann** and **Teo Seafood**, all under 40MYR per person for a good feed. Many people point towards the **Palm Garden Seafood Restaurant** (*Jln Kampung Santubong*). Personally, I found the big metal structure lacking charm, and there was a strong smell of diesel; the food was average. In Kampung Santubong, **Dayang Seafood** is recommended. **Green Paradise Café** on the Jalan Santubong–Kuching road at the entrance to the Santubong mountain trek has simple but healthy rice and noodle dishes. At the Sarawak Cultural Village, the **Budaya Sarawak Restaurant** (☎ 082 846411) has a buffet lunch and menu, including ethnic specialities such as *manok pansoh* (chicken cooked in bamboo and served in banana stem). **Damai Lookout Point Seafood** restaurant has a good selection of dishes.

WHAT TO SEE AND DO

Trekking Gunung Santubong (Mount Santubong) is not a national park or reserve (though this may be in the pipeline), but its dense, lush beauty should not be underestimated. A mountain guide is not necessary, but can be arranged through hotel recreation desks. The trail head is on the main Kuching–Santubong road. The **Red Trail** to the summit is about a five-hour return trip. The **Blue Trail** is an easy 2km trek around the foothills of the mountain. On any of the walks caution should be taken: there are spiders, scorpions and snakes.

Birdwatching Buntal is an important wintering ground for migratory birds. Birdlife International has registered the whole area between Teluk Buntal and Teluk Bako bays as an 'Important Bird Area'. Between October and March many migratory birds can be sighted in the estuary of the Buntal River, including terns, egrets, sandpipers and godwits, as well as the resident white-bellied sea eagles and collared kingfishers. Pacific reef egrets frequently stop over on the rocky outcrop of Pulau Tokong Ara in Santubong Bay.

Kuching Wetlands National Park Damai is a good springboard for visiting the mangroves around the marine estuaries and tidal creeks that criss-cross between the Sungai Salak and Sungai Sibu rivers. Estuarine crocodiles, Irrawaddy dolphins (see box opposite), kingfishers, storks, silver leaf monkeys, proboscis monkeys, macaques and fireflies are some of the creatures to be sighted. Designated a 'wetlands of international importance' in 2002, the giant stretch of mangrove forest is a shadow of its former self, having been whittled down from 17,000ha to just 6,600ha through deforestation. The wetlands are 15km from Kuching and 5km from Damai Beach. Several tour operators offer coastal and river cruises; most boat trips start from either Damai Beach or the boat club in Kampung Santubong. 'Santubong Wildlife Cruises' operated by **CPH Travel** (☎ 082 243708; e *cphtrvl@streamyx.com; www.cphtravel.com.my*) leave from the Santubong jetty every day at around 16.00 and return at around 19.30. Transfers from Kuching can be included in a tour.

Sarawak Cultural Village (*Kampung Budaya Sarawak, Pantai Damai;* ✆ *082 8464111;* e *info@scv.com.my; www.scv.com.my;* ⊕ *09.00–16.45 daily; dance performances 11.30 & 16.00; adult 60MYR, children 30MYR, under 6 free*) The area's most popular tourist attraction allows a look into Sarawak's rich ethno-cultural history as well as being submerged in Santubong's impressive scenery. As you wander from the recreated Melanau tall-house to the Chinese pagoda and Orang Ulu longhouse, greater vitality is lent to the museum through its setting: nestled among trees, and between lakes reflecting the summit of Mount Santubong. The depth and breadth of the experience is even greater than the hyperbole surrounding it might suggest. As a living showcase of Sarawak's ethnicities, the traditional dwellings are decorated with artefacts but there are also real people from those tribes doing craftwork, cooking or chatting with visitors. The 45-minute dance show is really well done – Bidayuh, Malay, Orang Ulu, Iban and Chinese dances performed by the SCV staff. There is a very down-to-earth feel about this cultural extravaganza, yet it is impeccably presented. The SCV is also home to the **Rainforest Musical Festival** (*www.rainforestmusic-borneo.com*), held every July.

Sports and leisure The **Damai Golf Course** (*Jln Santabong;* ✆ *082 846088*) has a Mountain Nine below the foothills of Mount Santubong. The Damai Lagoon Resort and Holiday Inn Resort offer a range of **watersports** – snorkelling, sailing, windsurfing, canoeing – and the Permai Rainforest Resort rents **sea kayaks**. **Mountain bikes** can be hired to do a whirl of the 3.5km Damai Cross Country Track.

BAKO NATIONAL PARK

The oldest national park in Sarawak and second oldest in Malaysia, Taman Bako was established in 1957 and covers 27km² at the end of the Muara Tebas Peninsula – Santubong's neighbour. Bako has a spellbinding quality, perhaps due to its astounding diversity of landscapes. From Tanjung (Cape) Rhu to Tanjung Po, and all the beaches and bays in between, it sweeps through mangrove, heath, peat swamp and mixed dipterocarp forest, grasslands, sandstone cliffs and sea-eroded coastal formations. With a population of some 280 in the park, the chances

10

IRRAWADDY DOLPHINS

These shy cetaceans live in the coastal, brackish and fresh waters of the tropical and subtropical Indo-Pacific region. Their bulging forehead and snubbed beak give them a distinctive, friendly look, and they have been known for their friendliness towards people, helping Burmese fishermen by herding fish towards their boats. The fishermen tap their oars against the boat to attract the dolphins and share their catch with them. Not all Irrawaddy–fisherman relations are so good though – by-catch by fisheries is a major threat to the species, along with habitat degradation. With an estimated population of just 100 individuals they are critically endangered. The best time to see them in the Kuching Wetlands is from April to October, though their timid nature means they are not easily spotted, even by the guides.

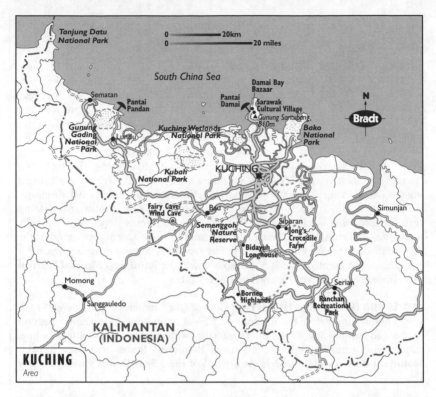

of seeing proboscis monkeys as you wander along the many well-marked trails are high, particularly early in the morning or towards dusk. Big-headed, bristly snouted pigs often wander right in front of the park HQ, scavenging for scrap food or wallowing in mangrove mud. The animals to be on alert for are the macaque monkeys – they are very audacious and have been known to raid many an unlocked room, as well as the canteen and dustbins, and even confront guests for food they might be carrying. 'Compulsive thieves' is how they are not-so-fondly described!

GETTING THERE AND AWAY Kampung Bako, the propeller-point for the boat trip to the park, is 37km northeast of Kuching along Jalan Bako. Petra Jaya Transport bus No 6 runs there every hour from 07.00 to 17.00. From the jetty you must charter a motorboat to take you to the park HQ. Organise this at the booth inside the boatmen's canteen. A one-way fare is roughly 50MYR, which can be shared by up to five people. The boat trip out of the estuary of the Sungai Bako into the bay is half of the fun.

OTHER PRACTICALITIES Park accommodation is extremely basic, consisting of two- and three-bedroom chalets with a fan and attached or shared bathrooms; four-bedroom hostels; and a camping ground. Cooking facilities amount to barbecue pits. There is a canteen at park HQ. The park registration desk and the Kampung Bako boat-ticketing counter are open daily (⏱ 08.00–16.15) including public holidays. A conservation fee must be paid (*adult 10MYR, children & students with international/ Malaysian student card 5MYR*). The information centre in the park shows films and slide shows on Bako's wildlife and has information on all the trails, and flora and fauna. The boatmen's canteen at Kampung Bako has cheap meals, snacks and refreshments. Bring all other necessary food and other items with you if you plan to stay.

WHAT TO SEE AND DO

Wildlife Bako is often tipped as the best park in Sarawak for wildlife experiences. Apart from the monkeys, there are otters, crabs, frogs and lots of lizards and snakes – lime green whip snakes, green spotted paradise snakes, and the only dangerous snake in Borneo, the triangular-headed pit viper. The wildlife experience starts right among the mangroves of Telok Assam, park HQ area, where many of the 150 listed birds can be sighted.

Treks Bako boasts one of the best networks of trails – 16 well-marked trails from hour-long forest strolls (1.6km return) to full-day treks (21km return). Pick up a map and flora-and-fauna guide at HQ, where you must also register for longer walks. You may find one or more of the trails closed for maintenance. It's amazing how many kinds of vegetation you will pass in an hour as you climb up a couple of cliffs, and circumnavigate the inland of a bay – Bako has 25 distinct kinds of plant life and seven ecosystems. The two supposed best trails for seeing the proboscis monkey – **Telok Delima** and **Telok Paku** – are both about 2km return from Telok Assam (park HQ), and sightings are also frequent in the mangroves around park HQ itself. Pitcher plants are found along the red-arrowed **Lintang Loop trail** (10.8km return).

Beach, bay and boat Telok Pandan Kecil, reached via the 2.5km yellow-arrowed trail, is one of the nicest beaches, nestled within a secluded bay and rocky headland. If you want to cut the journey down, or want to visit bays and coves further afield, you can charter a boat at park HQ and organise a pick-up time with a boatman for a return journey. On the way you will get to see the casuarina-topped limestone and sandstone cliffs and some of the coast's fascinating eroded rock features like the Sea Stack.

WEST OF KUCHING

West of Kuching there are three national parks: Kubah on its doorstep; further out, Gunung Gading; and out on the end of the peninsula, Tanjung Datu. As many in the Sarawak tourism industry declare quite openly, the coasts – and beaches – along this stretch are not on the same level, in beauty or infrastructure, as those of Santubong and Bako. Others love its relaxed, undeveloped nature. The main road passes some sleepy coastal and inland towns from Lundu to Sematan. Accommodation is threadbare, and that which does exist is mostly geared to the low end of the domestic market. On weekends it will be hard to avoid the karaoke and coastal exodus from Kuching; on weekdays you might get more of a chance to discover a relaxed beach atmosphere on the flat 'Gold Coast-like' beaches of Pantai Pandan and Patai Siar. The main attraction to the Lundu area – unless you are really into silkworms – might be an outdoor escape or rafflesia flower pursuit close to Kuching, in the form of Gunung Gading National Park.

GETTING THERE AND AWAY

By car The road heads west of Kuching to Lundu and Sematan, 100km from Kuching.

By bus Matang Transport buses go to Kubah Park from outside the Saujana car park in Kuching. STC buses go to Lundu four times daily from the long-distance bus terminal. From Lundu there is a connecting bus to Gunung Gading National Park or a taxi for under 10MYR. There are onward buses to Sematan from Lundu.

By boat There is no road access to the Tanjung Datu National Park. To reach it, you must first take a boat from Sematan to the village of Telok Melano, then, either take another boat to park HQ (a 15-minute trip), or make the 2½-hour walk along the Telok Melano–Telok Upas trail. The boats are infrequent, unscheduled and cater to local communities, so it is best to rely on your feet or on a tour operator departing from Kuching. The whole area is inaccessible by boat during monsoon season (October to February).

 WHERE TO STAY AND EAT Aside from national park accommodation, choices in this area are sparse and the 'resorts' rather downmarket and overpriced for the services they offer.

National park accommodation

Kubah Park HQ This has five bungalows that sleep six, a ten-bed resthouse and a 12-bed hostel, all with air conditioning, television, hot water, a veranda, full kitchen facilities and barbecue area. The nearby **Matang Wildlife Centre** has more basic chalets and a hostel 'Longhouse'. **$**

Gunung Gading National Park The infrastructure is not in the same league as Kubah Park: there are campsites, three-bedroom chalets and hostel accommodation, but neither a canteen nor cooking facilities – so stock up on ready-to-eat provisions, or come and go from Lundu 2km away. **$**

Tanjung Datu This has no accommodation in the park, but there is a community homestay in the fishing village of Teluk Melano. Call or visit the park office in Kuching for details (see page 248).

Other accommodation

Union Yes Retreat & Training Centre Siar Beach (15min drive from Lundu); 082 453027; e headoffice@sbeu.org. Seaside retreat in a beach-garden setting, hostel, de luxe rooms & penthouse family suites with AC, fridge & bathrooms, pool & BBQ. Café Rafflesia serves local & Western food. Attracts events such as weddings & conferences – can be overrun with 200 people with karaoke fever. **$$–$$$**

Ocean Resort 176 Siar Beach, Jln Pandan (10min drive from Lundu); 082 452245. 2-room AC chalets with basic self-catering facilities. **$$**

Sematan Palm Beach Resort No 12 Sematan Bazaar; 082 712388; www. sematanresort.com. Resort being revamped, chalets with AC, TV & en-suite bathroom. Individual & family rates include breakfast & dinner. Bikes, beach (often jellyfish) & possibly loud music in public places. **$$**

WHAT TO SEE AND DO

Kubah National Park Some 22km from Kuching, parts of the massive sandstone ridge in this park can be seen from Kuching – the 911m peak of Gunung Serapi stands out. Predominantly mixed dipterocarp, the limestone ridges of the Serapi range, rising between 150m and 450m, are punctuated by limestone-gouged waterfalls and over 100 different palm species. The park's six marked trails range from the 255m 'Palmetum' to a 5km summit trail. The 1,429m 'Belian' trail takes in lots of Bornean ironwoods and many fruit trees. The 3,830m 'Rayu' trail passes by several *bintangor* trees, which for nearly two decades have been tapped for their sap as a hopeful cure for AIDS (the chemical costatolide is extracted from the substance). The **Matang Wildlife Centre** is adjacent to the park; orphaned orang-utans are prepped up here before graduating to Semenggoh's more open jungle.

Lundu An hour's drive from Kuching, Lundu is a small, scenic, sleepy town with a thriving *ikan pusu* (anchovy) industry. Just a couple of rows of shop-houses, and a local market, it's spread out over the riverbank in the shadow of Gunung Gading mountain and close to the beaches of Patai Siah and Patai Pandan.

Gunung Gading National Park Another home to the rafflesia. Every park has its own signature rafflesia species; Gunung Gading hosts *Rafflesia tuanmudae*. There is a plankwalk leading to a common blooming ground of the rafflesia (guiding fees 20MYR per hour per group with ranger). For rafflesia-blooming checks, ring the national parks office in Kuching (✆ 082 248088) or park HQ (✆ 082 735714). There are three trails in the park – from a two-hour trip to the six- to eight-hour return 'Gunung Gading' summit walk.

Sematan Half an hour from Lundu on the South China Sea, Sematan is a hobby barramundi fishing area – the fish were introduced by the Agriculture Department. It also has a **Silk Farm** (✆ 082 320130; *www.sematansilk.com; 5MYR*) where you can purchase silk quilts. In the 14km² **Tanjung Datu National Park** on the Datu Peninsula, Sarawak meets Indonesia, land meets sea and rainforest meets coral reef – and turtle conservation territory. Lack of regular viable transport makes independent travel here difficult – the boats from Sematan to Telok Melano cater to local communities and are unscheduled, but that could be an adventure in itself. Tour operators in Kuching organise transport and guided tours to the park. The area is totally off-bounds during the October–February monsoon. Extreme mountain biker Hans Rey says the Sematan area is a **mountain-bike** paradise with 'an estimated 60–80km of all types of trails, with covered single-tracks, waterfalls, desert-heat, killer climbs and screaming downhills'. For tours contact **Outdoor Trek** (✆ 082 363344; e *best@bikcloud.com; www.bikcloud.com*).

SOUTH OF KUCHING

From the small market town of Serikin to the village of Anah Rais, the foothills of the Borneo Highlands area on the Indonesian border are Bidayuh homeland – fleeing the coast for the hinterland earned these timid people the name of the 'land Dayaks'. Here they built their longhouses and *baruk* warrior houses from bamboo. The border is punctuated by a series of peaks rippled between 400–1,400m, perfect for an off-the-beaten-track adventure. Sarawak's answer to the wildlife sanctuary of Sabah is in the neighbourhood, as are some lively Chinese market towns, caves and kayaking.

GETTING THERE AND AWAY
By car Take the Kuching–Serian road south from Kuching; for Bau (60km) veer right into Jalan Batu Kitang; for the Highlands, Jalan Penrissen.

By bus STC buses travel to Semenggoh from the city bus stand on Jalan Tun Abang Haji Openg. Take bus Nos 6, 6A, 6B or 6C and alight at the Forestry Department

Botanical Research Centre in Semengoh, from which there is a short stroll to the centre through the forest. Buses leave Kuching at 08.20, 10.30, 11.00 and 13.30. The last return bus leaves Semengoh at 17.00. The journey time is roughly 30 minutes and the fares are about 2MYR.

Buses to Bau leave from the Kuching Regional Bus Terminal (*Jalan Penrissen*). Operated by both STC and Bau Transport, buses leave every half-hour between 06.20 and 18.00; the journey costs 4.50–5MYR.

🏠 WHERE TO STAY AND EAT

🏠 **Borneo Highlands Resort** (62 rooms) 📞088 577930; e enquiry@borneohighlands. com.my; www.borneohighlands.com. A highland haven of ecotourism, organic agriculture, horticulture, rainforest & golf. Jungle spa, 18-hole golf course, rooms, suites & several secluded chalets, ethnically refined decor. The Annah Rais Café serves organic, vegetarian, local & international food. The Hornbill's Nest is a lounge-cum-tea parlour with highland organics. Requires a 4x4 to reach it – the resort does this for 40MYR return. Good 'Jungle Spa'

& other packages available online at www. sarawakresorts.com. **$$$–$$$$$**
🏠 **Annah Rais Longhouses** 71 Kampung Annah Rais, Jln Padawan, 60km from Kuching; 📞082 457941; www.longhouseadventure. com. In a traditional Bidayuh longhouse village, longhouse rooms, jungle treks, waterfalls & traditional food. 2-night packages include transfers, accommodation, meals & activities from 368MYR adult/198MYR child. Take any additional requirements – no major shops close by. Full itinerary on website. **$**

WHAT TO SEE AND DO

Semenggoh Wildlife Rehabilitation Centre (*20km from Kuching;* 📞 *082 618423;* ⊕ *08.00–12.30 & 14.00–16.00; adult 3MYR, child 1.50MYR*) Sarawak's first forest reserve, established in 1920, was converted into a rehabilitation centre for orang-utans, honey bears and hornbills in 1975. 'Semi-wild' orang-utan inhabit the sanctuary, having graduated up from the infant-oriented Matang Wildlife Centre. Visits revolve around feeding times (half an hour at 08.30 & 15.00). The viewing area is a 1km-long walk from the entrance, where a series of graphic images warn of the dangers of serious injury from inappropriate behaviour with the orang-utans. Such interaction most commonly includes goading and teasing the animals with food, and simply getting too close for comfort. Morning visits can be better, as the apes roam free until the afternoon feed and it is not uncommon to run into some on the reserve's pathways – but keep in mind the previous caution and do not wander alone. The rehabilitation centre is part of the **Semenggoh Nature Reserve**, whose arboretum and botanical research centre displays fernariums, ethnobotanic and other gardens. Visits to the latter must be booked in advance.

Bidayuh longhouses Tour operators visit longhouses as a day trip but you can also visit several independently, including those in Kampung Annah Rais: at Kampung Benuk (*off Jln Penrissen, 50km from Kuching*) there are about 80 families in a longhouse; Kampung Pelaman Dunuk is 62km from Kuching. Admission with or without a guide is 5MYR. If you are visiting in June, the Bidayuh villages celebrate the rice festival **Gawai Padi** (*Gawai Sawa'a* in Bidayuh dialect) in their own special way, with lots of shamanistic rituals, priestesses, trance dancers and music. Contact Mr Diweng Bakir (📞 *019 8565498;* e *diweng_bakir@yahoo.com*), director of a local indigenous NGO.

Borneo highlands trekking From Annah Rais, there is a three-hour trek into the Kalimantan border region, where a large community of some 200 Bidayuh families live traditionally in four longhouses, strung each side of a suspension bridge. Two- to three-day trekking excursions taking in Gunung Penrissen (1,329m), surrounding landscapes, longhouses and villages along small trails give views over Kalimantan, Kuching and the South China Sea.

Bau The Bau region bears scars from 19th-century mining – both on the land and in the memories of the people. Antimony was discovered here in the 1820s, and the area later became a hotspot of rebellion against oppressive Brunei rulers, who forced the Bidayuh to work in the mines for a pittance and sold the women and children as slaves. Local Malays and natives rebelled in 1836, proclaiming Sarawak's independence. The rebellion dragged on with James Brooke apparently playing the role of peacemaker when he arrived on the scene in 1839. In subsequent decades the gold rush began and migrants, mostly Hakka people, came from China and Dutch Kalimantan. In 1857 there was another uprising, this time by Chinese miners against Brooke – in a massacre that is not often talked about. Up to 2,000 Chinese men, women and children were killed by the rajah's forces, smothered in caves they had taken shelter in while their mining settlement was set alight. On the way to Bau is the small market town of **Siniawan**. Composed of 1920s double-storey wooden shop-houses, Siniawan was once the rebels' headquarters. Strong on local history is Borneo Adventure Tours guide Philip Yong (✆ 082 245175; e info@borneoadventure.com), also director of the Sarawak Tourist Association and son of the late Sarawak minister Stephen Yong. The opencast mine in Bau has created a small blue lake, **Tasik Biru**.

Caves and kayaking With lots of caves, rivers and limestone ridge features, the highlands area is popular for outdoor activity. The **Wind Cave** reserve towards the border is a pleasant picnic spot; **Fairy Cave** – which has some Chinese shrines at the entrance and interior – is also an **abseiling** destination. There are buses from Bau through to here.

Serikin At the left of the fork in the road towards the border is another (modern) Bidayuh town – there are no longhouses here. You can buy Indonesian crafts – bags, baskets and *kasah* floormats at the *gerai* stalls.

SOUTHEAST OF KUCHING

Southeast of Kuching, the sinewy Sri Aman Division skirts the Indonesian border. Over 90% of the population are Iban, and their rice paddy, rubber and pepper cash crops engrave the river-lined landscape. The longhouses that start appearing in fields after the town of Serian are a mix of traditional wooden ones with modern cement structures. Deeper inland, the rivers that run through national parks and longhouse communities can only be experienced by boat trip. Allow at least a two-night stay in this area whichever way you tackle it.

GETTING THERE AND AWAY
By car Head southeast along the Serian–Kuching road.

By bus From Kuching's Regional Bus Terminal on Jalan Penrissen, Sarawak Transport Company bus 3A leaves every hour for Serian and costs 6.60MYR. (From here there are local buses to Ranchan Pools.) STC buses make the three-hour journey to Sri Aman (tickets are 19MYR), with departures at 07.30, 09.45, 12.00, 15.15 and 19.45. Some of the Eva Express coaches that ply almost the entire length of Sarawak, between Kuching and Sibu and further onwards to Miri, also pass through Serian, Sri Aman and Betong.

By boat Longboats and speedboats are used for river journeys and to cross the Batang Ai.

SERIAN
Where to stay

KC Inn Jln Alamanda, Serian. Recommended if you need a room mid-journey. Very clean, spacious rooms, & hot showers. **$**

Ranchan Pools Chalets 082 876681. The district council hires out basic chalets & a 10-bed dorm room – used mostly by holidaying Malaysians & not promoted widely in tourist circles. **$**

Where to eat In the 200km between Kuching and Batang Ai, the food stops are at Serian (which has fantastic market and food-stall food), Lachau and Sri Aman. Lachau – a small car and coach rest-stop – is referred to as 'cowboy town', and there is still cross-border barter going on here with travelling traders who arrive in town from Indonesia. The Chinese coffee shops along its one street are a good place to have a drink and some noodles – **Lee Chong Café** is recommended.

What to see and do

In Serian Serian, 70km from Kuching, is a small but sparkling market town of 85,000 – nearly two-thirds of the population are Bidayuh, the rest a mix of Malay, Iban and Chinese. In the middle of the market square there is the **Big Durian** – a monument to the king of local fruits. The under-cover farmers' market is a maze of culinary forms: chillies, freshly picked peanuts, snake fruit and squirming sago worms. There are plenty of stalls for *pisang goreng* (fried banana) and savoury snacks. **Taman Danu** is a recreational park that's pretty at night with lights on the lake, a couple of restaurants and some food stalls. Near Serian is the **Ranchan Recreational Park**, a waterfall, picnic spot and pool in the rainforest. The park facilities and trails have been criticised for being run-down and seem set for an upgrade; on the other hand, the canteen and park chalets are relatively new and in a lovely setting.

In Siburan At Siburan, 30km from Kuching, is **Jong's Crocodile Farm** and minizoo (*off Serian Rd;* 082 863570; 09.00–17.00 daily, feeding times 11.00 & 15.00; adult 8MYR, child 4MYR).

BANDAR SRI AMAN Some 194km from Kuching, 9km from the turn-off on the main road, Bandar Sri Aman is on the banks of the Batang Lupar River. This is the trading hub of the district for the timber, oil palm, rubber and pepper industries, and the gateway to the Batang Ai National Park. The city's main claim to fame is its *benak* or 'tidal bore', which rolls in through the river mouth and fills the riverbed within minutes. The tidal bore is actually a daily occurrence but on such a small scale that it is not noticeable – however, a couple of times a year it reaches speeds of 7–18km/h and heights of up to 3m. The phenomenon was immortalised by Somerset Maugham in the short story 'The Yellow Streak'; he visited and was nearly drowned in 1921 while boating on the river with his companion. Sri Aman is trying to build up its tourism attraction with a **Pesta Benak** – tidal bore festival – with lots of merriment, food and dance. People even try surfing the bores. The only historical building of note, **Fort Alice**, was built out of *belian* wood in 1864, after Rajah Charles Brooke's claimed 'defeat' of the last of the great Iban chieftains, Rentap.

A few handy words to have up your sleeve for longhouse visits are:

Nama berita nuan?	How are you? (used as a general greeting instead of hello)
Berita akumana	I am well
Nyamai	It's delicious (a good one to comment on the rice wine)
Terima kasih	Thank you (the same as in Malay)

Batang Ai National Park A place for wildlife research more than orang-utan spotting, the national park is accessed after three to four hours of longboat journey. Mapped out with local Iban communities, the arduously challenging **Red Ape trail** has the endorsement of the Orang-utan Foundation. The full trek is 11 days, but shorter walks can be arranged. In November 2010, I felt I had come as close as possible to reliving a slice of Redmond O'Hanlon's classic adventure *Into the Heart of Borneo*, heading way upriver and into the jungle to tackle part of this trail, accompanied by Borneo Adventure's local Iban guides and foragers. To try it for yourself, contact **Borneo Adventure** (*55 Main Bazaar, Kuching;* \ *082 245175;* e *info@borneoadventure.com; www.borneoadventure.com*).

BATANG AI The water catchment of **Batang Ai Reservoir** was formed when the valley and some 30 longhouses in it were drowned in the 1980s – a controversial move in which hundreds of locals were relocated. The power station provides half of Sarawak's daily energy needs. The area is the starting point for excursions deep along the Sungai Batang Ai and Sungai Engkari rivers, leading to huge longhouses where Iban communities lead isolated lives somewhere between tradition and modernity.

Getting there Reaching Batang Ai Reservoir is remarkably inexpensive for the distance involved (275km), yet difficult, time-consuming and ill-advised. First take the express bus to Sri Aman from Kuching's regional bus terminal, a 3½-hour trip costing 15MYR, then catch a local bus to Lubock Antu (two hours). For the remaining 5km to the dam, the only option is to hitch a ride. If you get stuck in Lubok Antu, you will be faced with a private longboat charter to continue your journey, which is expensive unless pre-organised as part of a tour.

Where to stay and eat

Longhouse experiences Most longhouses that accept guests are in the Skrang and Lemanak river areas near Bandar Sri Aman, and the Batang Ai River and its tributaries. Most are in remote areas only reached by longboat. The easiest option is to go on a tour, but you can arrive in Betong and line up a journey directly with local Ibans for the Batang Skrang. Try:

Hilton Batang Ai Longhouse Resort (100 rooms) \ 083 584388, or via Kuching Hilton \ 082 248200. A 15min boat journey from the Batang Ai dam, the only hotel in the area is this 3-star longhouse construction on the banks of the reservoir. Wood-panelled rooms with rattan & belian furnishings are arranged in several inward-facing longhouses, while the veranda & outdoor dining areas face the water. Nice swimming pool, tennis court & ample buffet spread. The 31m² rooms are on the small side; the 71m² duplex suites have a separate living room & are very comfortable. Good base for excursions to longhouses, jungle treks, boating & fishing. **$$–$$$**

⌂ **Nanga Ukum Longhouse** www. borneoecotours.com. Borneo Eco Tours do a luxury safari, 3 days/2 nights from Kuching, stopping on the way at Semenggoh Orang-utan Centre & Serian town, staying at the Hilton Batang Ai & visiting Nanga Ukum longhouse by longboat. 1,800MYR.

⌂ **Nanga Sumpa Longhouse** Batang Ai. The community longhouse, shared by some 10 families, was modernised in 2009. An authentic stay in simple, clean rooms, participating in local life & subsisting on fresh fish & vegetables. Contact the visitor information centre in Kuching (see page 247) or one of the tour operators to organise this budget trip.

⌂ **Ulu Ai Jungle Lodge** Batang Ai; ☏082 245175; e info@borneoadventure.com; www. borneoadventure.com. Neighbouring the community longhouse, Nanga Sumpa, Borneo Adventure's ethically run lodge offers a rustic nature experience with mattresses & mosquito nets & excellent food prepared by village women. *2-night packages from 1,250MYR.*

Longhouse visits Reached either by self-chartered longboat trip or on a tour, some of the upriver longhouse communities still live a relatively isolated and traditional life that's fascinating to observe. At **Kampung Mengkak Longhouse** (*Rumah Burau, Mengkak;* ☏ *013 2867451*) on the Sungai Engkari, you can mingle with some of the 26 families who live in the 200m-long structure as they sit out in the *ruai* (communal veranda), drinking *tuak* (rice wine) and making handicrafts. The locals demonstrate their blowpipe skills, perform dances and play music in traditional dress on request, but with far more personality and passion than you could ever expect in a city cultural show. Indeed, the best visits can be those that just experience 'life as usual' rather than great shows. The key to making such a visit as enriching as possible is to be humble and respectful, learn a couple of Iban greetings and mingle gently with the people. Get acquainted with the chief (Tuai Rumah), and get ready to feel your face all smiled out as the whole community turns out to welcome you.

Central Sarawak

Central Sarawak is intersected by the mighty Batang Rejang and its tributaries, and the journey from the South China Sea through this vast region to remote inland areas is a compelling mix of tribal traditions, coastal modernity and mountainous isolation. River transport is a necessity for getting around the area as much as it is for getting to it. Long river journeys are rewardingly different, with the complex culture and landscape of the Rejang. Iban and Melenau riverbank settlements are found on its lower reaches, and way upstream is the territory of nomadic Penan hunter-gatherers and other upriver people, Orang Ulu.

SIBU

As Sibu lies at the confluence of the Rejang and the Igan, 130km from the South China Sea, river geography has played a major hand in its history. As a major transport hub for the whole Rejang Basin, parts of its harbour are over 1km in width. Sarawak's affluent second-biggest city – with a population of 180,000 – was pushed to modernity by a former mayor with the help of powerful Chinese community associations. About 60% of Sibuan are Chinese, the rest Malay, Melanau, Iban and Orang Ulu. Propelled by religious persecution and poverty, the Chinese started arriving in 1901, led by Methodist missionary Reverend Wong Nai Siong, who is heralded as the town's founder. He persuaded Charles Brooke to give land to the Chinese in the Lower Rejang region for farming paddy, pepper and rubber. Sibu rebounded in the post-World War II years as a centre of the timber industry, and boomed through the 1980s in timber trade, sawmilling and shipbuilding. The town's name comes from the Iban word for rambutan – *buah sibau*.

GETTING THERE AND AWAY
By air Malaysia Airlines has two daily flights in both directions between Sibu and Kuching and Sibu and Kuala Lumpur. AirAsia's bargain flights from Kuching to Sibu are renowned for delays. MASWings has Fokker 50 flights between Sibu, Kuching and Miri. The airport is a few kilometres from town and there is no bus service – a taxi costs 28MYR with a coupon purchased inside the airport.

Airlines
✈ **Air Asia** Jln Tuanku Osman; ✆ 084 307808
✈ **Malaysia Airlines** Jln Tuanku Osman; ✆ 084 321055. Town office.

By car Sibu is roughly midway between Kuching (462km) and Miri (380km).

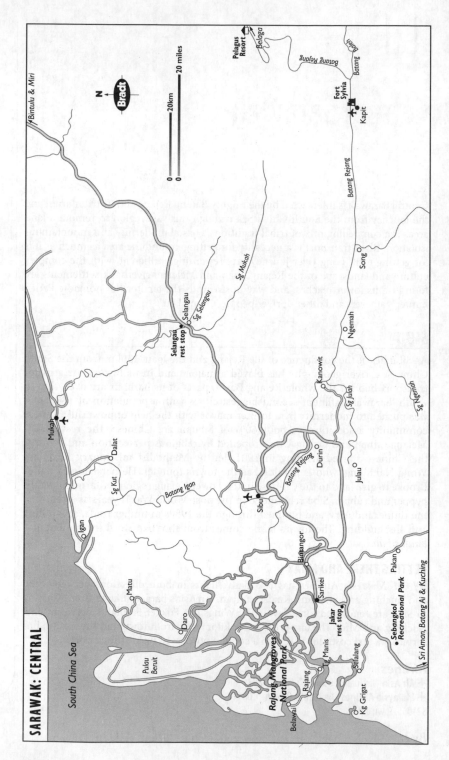

SARAWAK: CENTRAL

South China Sea

N

Bradt

20km
20 miles
0
0

/Bintulu & Miri

Pelagus Resort
Belaga

Batang Rejang
Batang
Balui

Fort Sylvia
Kapit

Batang Rejang

Song

Ngemah

Sg Ngemah

Kanowit

Sg Julah

Julau

Mukah

Dalat

Sg Kut

Sg Selangau

Selangau

Selangau rest stop

Sg Mukah

Igan

Batang Igan

Durin

Batang Rejang

Sibu

Matu

Daro

Binangor

Pakan

Sarikei

Jakar rest stop

Pulau Beruit

Rajang Mangroves National Park

Manis

Rajang

Selalang

Selang

Sebangkol Recreational Park

Belawai

Kg Grigat

/Sri Aman, Batang Ai & Kuching

278

By bus The long-distance bus hub, the Sibu New Bus Terminal, is on Jalan Pahlawan, 3km from the city centre. Several bus companies operate from here. **Biaramas Express** has daily buses to Kuching, Bintulu (20MYR) and Miri (40MYR) as well as Pontianak in Indonesia. **Borneo Amalgamated Transport** serves Bintulu, Kuching, Sarikei, Sri Aman and Kanowit. **Trans Borneo Resources** also goes to coastal and inland towns to the north in Mukah Division, including Mukah (16MYR), Oya and Dalat (17MYR). Bus 21 links the long-distance bus station to the city bus 'Transit Point' in about 20 minutes.

By boat Longer-distance express boats come and go from the Express Wharf for Kuching, Belaga, Dalat, Daro, Kapit, Kanowit, Sarikei and Song. Tickets are sold at the passenger terminal at the wharf. During peak holiday periods it's best to book in advance, otherwise arrive 30 minutes before departure. For up-to-date schedules, contact the **Sarawak Rivers Board** (↘ *084 339936*).

GETTING AROUND The city centre is small, and pleasant to walk around.

By car For car hire contact the visitor information centre (see below). They warn of unlicenced drivers and advise tourists to contact them for the latest details of recommended car hire companies.

By taxi Taxis do not use meters; shorter trips cost between 6MYR and 12MYR. Taxis are easily flagged outside the big hotels, at the taxi stand opposite the Express Wharf and on Jalan Lintang – or call the station (↘ *084 320773*). Official long-distance fares (one-way) are: Mukah 200MYR; Bawang Assan longhouse settlement 50MYR; Sarikei 100MYR; Kanowit 50MYR; and Bintangor 90MYR.

By bus The city Transit Point is opposite the Express Wharf on Jalan Khoo Peng Loong, with buses bound for the town area, Sibu region and neighbouring Sarikei. The destination is generally marked on the front of the bus. Prices for local trips range from 1MYR for city destinations to 10MYR to Sarikei.

TOURIST INFORMATION

🗷 Sibu Visitor Information Centre
32 Jln Tukang Besi; ↘ 084 340980; e vic-sibu@ sarawaktourism.com; ⊕ 08.00–17.00 Mon–Fri, closed Sat/Sun/public holidays. Brochures, guidebooks & maps available. The helpful staff can advise on travel plans & national park accommodation bookings in the district and whole Rejang river basin area, as well as car hire.

 WHERE TO STAY There are a handful of very good international-class **hotels** in Sibu, and some excellent medium-class hotels – usually lacking pools and gyms, but often with free Wi-Fi. Some three- to four-star establishments offer budget, mid-range and suite-level luxury options under one roof. There is a big crossover of **budget/ shoestring** prices in Sibu. In a three-star hotel it is possible to have a large double room for 100–150MYR; this will cost around 100MYR in a two-star hotel. Meanwhile standard rooms in some of the hotels listed below cost 60–100MYR and come with bathroom, television and fan or air conditioning; some also have a fridge and kettle.

Hotels
Upmarket to mid range
🏠 **Premier Hotel** (189 rooms) Sarawak House Complex, Jln Kampung Nyabor; ↘ 084 323222; e reservation@premierh.com.my; www. premierh.com.my. A business-oriented 4-star, with restaurant, music lounge, karaoke room,

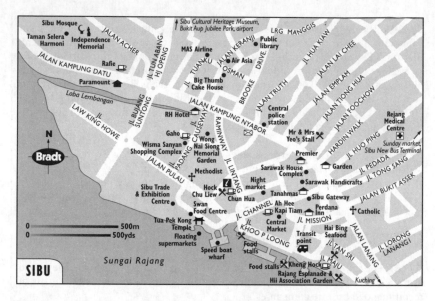

SIBU

Wi-Fi, 24hr business centre, near shopping malls & Cineplex. **$$**, suite **$$$$**

🏠 **RH Hotel** (226 rooms) Jln Kampung Nyabor; ☎084 365888; e reservationssibu@ rhhotels.com.my; www.rhhotels.com.my. The newest 4-star. Swimming pool, coffee shop, music lounge, fitness centre. **$$**, suite **$$$$**

🏠 **Tanahmas Hotel** (120 rooms) Lot 277, Block 5, Jln Kampung Nyabor; ☎084 333188; e enquiries@tanahmas.com.my; www. tanahmas.com.my. One of the best 3-stars in town, very centrally located near the market strip with swimming pool, karaoke & restaurant. **$$**, suite **$$$$**

Budget to shoestring

🏠 **Paramount Hotel** (95 rooms) 3 Lorong 9A, Jln Kampung Dato (1km from town); ☎084 331122; e paramount_hotel@yahoo. com www.paramountsibu.com. A 3-star hotel with great service & Malay courtesy, further out on town's edge in riverside area. Many Malay café & food stalls nearby. One of few hotels with non-smoking in lobby & some floors. Spacious

comfortable rooms & very good value suites with breakfast included. Only downfall is lack of sports & leisure facilities, though the riverside area outside is developing into a landscaped park, jogging & sports area. **$$–$$$**

🏠 **Garden Hotel** (40 rooms) 1 Jln Huo Ping; ☎084 317888; e enquiry@gardenhotelsibu.com. my; www.gardenhotelsibu.com.my. The updated website & seemingly glossy, new tangerine-toned rooms potentially demonstrate a new era for this hotel. Hopefully this is so, because during my last stay things went pretty much downhill from the reception, with smoky & shabby public areas & rooms. The coffee shop experience improved by ordering from the menu rather than sticking to the tired breakfast buffet. Today the revamped hotel promises: 'spacious & luxurious AC rooms complete with de luxe bathroom or shower, colour TV, satellite movies, minibar & IDD telephone'. **$–$$**

🏠 **Perdana Inn** 24 Jln Mission; ☎084 327007. Recommended as best 2-star, with budget prices for larger rooms. **$–$$**

Hostels There are a dozen very central hostels and lodging houses where you can pay under 50MYR (as low as 30MYR) for a room with fan, television and phone. Contact the tourism office for the latest recommendations on the best.

✕ **WHERE TO EAT** The food in Sibu is probably the best value in the whole of Sarawak. Food is of a high quality and most of the restaurants are as spotless as the rest of the town. Local specials include *kam pua mee* – noodles tossed in pork lard, chilli, onion and sliced pork; *mee sua* – longevity noodles in a tub of rich herbal soup with chunks of boiled chicken; *konpia* – the local 'bagel', yeast buns sandwiched together with spicy minced pork (or chicken in Muslim restaurants); and *mee udang* – river prawns with noodles in a bowl of spicy broth.

Coffee shops The streets are packed with coffee shops serving the above specialities from early morning onwards. For *mee udang* and other local specialities, head to **Min Kong Café** (*Jln Bank;* ⊕ *lunch & evenings daily; 5–20MYR*) and **Sin Chun Hua Café** (*next to the Sibu Visitor Information Centre*), both cheap, cheerful cafés. Moderately priced noodle dishes, steamed buns, dumplings, seafood, and barbecued pork and duck are all on the menu at **Kheng Hock Café** (*49 Jln Maju facing the Rejang Esplanade;* ⊕ *b/fast, lunch & dinner*). **Ah Hee Kopi Tiam** (⊕ *06.30–17.00*) on Leboh Market, has a very buzzy atmosphere, with a menu offering all the local dishes; try the fresh foaming green fruit drink *sour sop*. Two cheap, good-quality Malay coffee shops are **Gaho Café** (*opposite Wisma Sanyan*) and the Chinese (halal) **Rafie Café** (*opposite the Paramount Hotel*).

Restaurants More upmarket Chinese restaurants with mostly mid-range prices are found at leading hotels: **Golden Palace** (✆ *084 333188*) at Tanahmas Hotel and **Gold Hope Restaurant** (✆ *084 323222*) at Sarawak House, near the Premier Hotel. See *Where to stay*, opposite, for address details.

Seafood An open-air riverfront restaurant with some Western dishes and moderate prices, **Esplanade Seafood** (*Rejang Esplanade*) is open only in the evenings. **Hai Bing Seafood** (*31 Jln Maju*) offers the same, plus seafood and meat dishes, with indoor air conditioning and outdoor dining – a friendly, and recommended, place. **Sri Meranti** (*1 Jln Hardin;* ⊕ *evenings only*) is a Chinese Muslim (halal) seafood restaurant, bright and clean with air-conditioned section and outdoor tables. The famous fish-head curry (*tapah*) is made from fresh river fish.

Stalls and market food The first floor of the Sibu Central Market has around 30 (mostly Chinese) stalls, offering cheap, fresh food from 06.00–14.00. Some are open in the evening. There are stalls all along Jalan Market and at the **night market** (*pasar malam*) on Jalan Lebuh Tinggi. The **Swan Food Centre** (*Jln Temple, next to Sibu Trade & Exhibition Centre;* ⊕ *morning to evening*) has mostly Chinese food stalls with lots of chicken rice and roasted pork. For food on the go, there is a food court on the first floor of Express Boat Wharf, and Malay food to go from stalls next to the wharf. **Taman Selera Harmoni** (*near the Sibu mosque*) is a vast under-roof pavilion with several Malay *restoran*, each with its own allotment of tables and chairs, and multiple television screens. A *konpia* hotspot for breakfast is **Mr & Mrs Yeo's Stall** (*Lorong Tiong Hua 26, 15mins' walk or take a taxi*), where they serve pork buns in a pork broth with slices of stewed pork. A fantastic bakery is the **Big Thumb Cake House** (*71–73 Jln Tuanku Osman;* ✆ *084 339829*), a family business specialising in cakes, bread and Hong Kong *cha siew pau* (mini steamed bun).

ENTERTAINMENT AND NIGHTLIFE Sibu has several pubs and clubs, and even a few Iban karaoke pubs. For cocktails and sophistication, head to the international hotels – at the Tanahmas Hotel (*Lot 277, Block 5, Jalan Kampung Nyabor*) try **Club Emas** for cocktails and karaoke and the **Blowpipe Lounge** for music.

11

SHOPPING If you're travelling by car, the **Durin Handicraft Shop** (*35km southeast from Sibu, near the Rejang's Durin ferry terminal*) has handicrafts from all over the central region. Chinese potteries are produced at several workshops near Sibu. The narrow, crowded streets of the town centre are full of clothing and high-tech stores. The 28-storey **Wisma Sanyan** shopping complex – the tallest building in Sarawak – is Sibu's largest retail mall. On the fourth floor is a cyber café, **Forever Link**.

Markets With 1,200 stalls selling everything from fish, fruits, handicrafts and live ducks, Sibu's **Central Market** is one of the biggest trading markets in Malaysia, combining the former 'wet market' and indigenous Lembangan market. Good, moderately priced handcrafts can be bought at the Central Market and night market stalls, often from the source. The *tamu* is also held here on Sundays. The **night bazaar** (⊕ *17.00–22.00 daily*) on Leboh Market is a colourful melange of stalls selling household goods, fashion and footwear, and a variety of foods from steamed buns to satay.

OTHER PRACTICALITIES
Health and emergency There are several downtown clinics, a public hospital out of town and two modern and central private hospitals including the **Rejang Medical Centre** (*29 Jln Pedada;* ✆ *084 330733*).

Miscellaneous The website of **Sibu Municipal Council** (*www.smc.gov.my*) is a good source of local information.

WHAT TO SEE AND DO
Around town Sibu is a compact town easily explored on foot, with taxis or buses available for out-of-town locations. Climb to the top floor of the seven-storey **Kuan Yin** ('Goddess of Mercy') **Pagoda**, which towers above the 100-year-old **Tua Pek Kong Temple** – great for seeing the day-to-day activity on the water. A huddle of colourful 'floating supermarkets', wooden boats that service Rejang longhouse communities, are anchored in port. The **heritage walk** links several public places and memorial gardens. One of the prettiest is the Hokkien community's **Chiang Chung Immigration Garden** on the river in front of the temple. The **Rejang Esplanade** starts from the Express Boat passenger terminal and ends near the emblematic **Swan statue**. Sibu's swans symbolise its ugly-duckling transformation, drawing on Chinese folklore about a town saved from starvation by a sago-drinking swan. The vast **Town Square** – the largest urban square in Malaysia – is the venue for the **Borneo Cultural Festival** held every July, with performances from all of Sarawak's major ethnic groups as well as some from Sabah and Kalimantan. **Bukit Aup Jubilee Park** (*Tekub bus No 2/3;* ⊕ *08.00–18.00 daily; free*) is a great place for strolling, picnicking and jogging, with views from its 60m tower over the Igan River and nearby longhouses. The Iban bring offerings to the top of the hill for the benevolent spirit Naga Bari, believed to help people in need. Another workout-friendly place is the **Sungai Merah (Red River) Heritage Walk** (*Sungai Merah bus*), a landscaped river promenade area on the site of the original Chinese settlement in Sibu. True to its name, the water is rusty red in colour because of the tidal action on peat soils from upriver forests. The walk leads to the **Wong Nai Siong Memorial Garden**, which is graced by a dour statue of the town's revolutionary father.

Museums and galleries

Sibu Cultural Heritage Museum (*In the Civic Centre, Jln Tun Abang Haji Openg; 2km from city, take Sungai Merah bus No 1A; ⊕ 10.30–17.30 Tue–Sun; free*) Dull yet interesting presentation of antiques, artefacts and photos on the town's history, Chinese migration and the various ethnic groups of the Rejang river basin. The Foochow presence in Sibu is elucidated at the **World Fuzou Heritage Gallery** on Jalan Salim.

EXCURSIONS FROM SIBU

LONGHOUSES Day or overnight trips to **Kampung Bawang Assan**, a settlement of eight Iban longhouses both modern and old (*taxi 50MYR, vans from Central Market every 2hrs*), are available. Andy Austin, the son of one of the longhouse chiefs, acts as a guide and can be contacted via the visitors' centre (see page 279). Frankie Ting from **Sazhong Trading & Travel Service** (*4 Jln Central;* ✎ *084 336017;* e *sazhong@tm.net.my*) does tours to nearby longhouse settlements such as Bawang Assan, upriver trips and treks (for longer trips book at least one week in advance).

SARIKEI In 1856, Sarikei town was burnt down in an uprising against the Brooke administration – waged by Iban people from the Sungai Julau river area. Situated 122km southwest of Sibu (buses leave city station every 30 minutes), Sarikei is now an agro-industry hub and home of the *ananas* – curiously, they use the French name for pineapple. Various oranges, *pomelo* and avocado also thrive in the area's acidic soils, and Malaysia owes its ranking as the world's fifth-biggest pepper exporter to Sarikei Division, which produces more than 80% of Sarawak's crop. Tiger prawn farms and shrimp processing are being pushed with government subsidies to diversify from pepper. The town lies about 40km from the mouth of the Rejang; at the river's delta is the largest mangrove swamp in Sarawak. The coast is both a timber-processing zone and developing deep-sea port.

About 15km from Sarikei, **Bintangor** is a small market town at the heart of Sarikei's fruit production and is renowned for its green oranges. These *agrumes* infuse the Malay dish *rojak*, a spicy salad of fruits and vegetables. Situated 25km from Sarikei, the small (13ha) **Sebangkoi Forest Park** is a good mid-journey rest spot if you are travelling along the Pan-Borneo Highway.

🏠 **Where to stay and eat** If you're travelling independently, try **Sarakei's Dragon Inn** (*60 Jln Masjid Lama;* ✎ *084 651799;* **$–$$**). This plain, but clean, registered two-star hotel also has a coffee shop serving noodle- and rice-based meals. The prices suit shoestring to budget travellers, as they do at the **Oriental Hotel** (*48 Jln Repok;* ✎ *084 6555590;* **$**), which has a halal Chinese restaurant. Other inexpensive (budget-priced) Chinese eats in town include the **Golden Happiness Restaurant** (*Jln Masjid Lama;* **$$**) – one of the better coffee shops, serving seafood and venison specialities. The **Hung Kiew Kee Restaurant** (*Jln Masjid Lama;* **$$**) also serves up standard Malay and Chinese dishes. On the same street, there are two fast-food options: the **Sugar Bun bakery** (**$**) or **KFC** (**$**).

Tours For an organised tour of Sarikei and surrounding areas, contact Ling How Kang at **Greatown Travel** (✎ *084 211243;* m *019 8565041;* e *greatown@gmail. com*) – on regional knowledge he is second to none. The trip focuses on Sarikei's agricultural attractions: dragon fruit and orange orchards, pineapple farms and pepper gardens, as well as visits to Kampung Rejang to see *songket* weavers, and

11

Kampung Belawai – the heart of the smoked prawn (*sesar unjur*) processing industry. You can meet him in Sibu or in Sarikei.

MUKAH Originally from Mindano Island in the Philippines, the Melanau people have lived in Borneo since the 16th century – and Mukah is their heartland. The Melanau make a characteristically distinctive signature dish, *umai* – a spicy salad of raw shredded fish marinated with lime, ginger and chilli. Around 130,000 Melanau are spread along the coast from the Rejang Estuary to the city of Bintulu – with six distinct groups and 11 different dialects.

The Brooke dynasty rajahs and the Brunei sultans competed with each other to control the trade in *rumbia* (sago) in the late 1800s. Sago still underpins the economy and many local customs and cottage industries, but fishing and oil palm are zooming ahead. The region's façade on the South China Sea is seeing the beginnings of a riviera-effect, as the currently sparse stretch is slowly earmarked for coastal development. Many of the Melanau and Iban *kampungs* are built near rivers and above mangrove swamp around the coast.

Getting there and away

By air MASWings flies Twin Otters from Kuching to Mukah (1hr flight), Sibu to Mukah (30mins) and Miri to Mukah (30mins). One-way fares from 100MYR.

By car It's a 159km (about 2hrs) drive from Sibu, the last 40km along an unsealed and seriously pot-holed dirt road.

By bus Express buses from Sibu take about 3½ hours. See *Getting there and away*, page 279.

By boat The most engaging and enjoyable way to get to 'Melanau Heartland', if you have time on your hands, is by speedboat, from Sibu to Dalat, about 40km from Mukah township. The journey across the Batang Igan dam, down the tree-lined Sungai Kut river and into the Sungai Oya river at Dalat takes up to two hours depending on how many village-stops it makes *en route*. The boats leave from the jetty on Jln Khoo Peng Loong (at the junction with Jln Temple), roughly every hour from 07.00 to 14.30. Be sure to get there at least 15 minutes ahead of this time, as the boats leave when they are full. The journey costs approximately 20MYR. (Only two boats leave from Dalat to Sibu, at 06.30 and 12.30.) For the onward connection to Mukah, buses leave from the station behind the Hiap Leong Mini Market, and cost around 5MYR, compared to 30–40MYR for a taxi.

Getting around The best way to see to see the coastal and inland *kampung* is by car. A mixture of boat and bus travel is possible, if you are determined to see the area on a budget, but you must ensure that there are food options near your accommodation.

⌂ **Where to stay** Tourism in the region stands to benefit if the new road is completed by 2012, after five years of delays. It may bring more accommodation options to the area.

⌂ **Kingwood Resort** (99 rooms) Lot 96, Block 17, Mukah Land District; ☏ 084 873888; e kingwoodresort_mukah@yahoo.com. Located 12km from town & facing the South China Sea, the pillared, nouveau-Chinese structure stands pretty much on its own between the oil plantations & the ocean, with totally uninterrupted 180° views to the horizon. A vigorous promoter of the culture of the area. Friendly & incredible value for money, modern, spacious, light & bright, full of high-tech & leisure facilities. **$$**, suite **$$$$**

⌂ **King Ing** (19 rooms) 1–2 Jln Boyan, Mukah; ☏084 871400; e AcSG8@yahoo.com. Best choice if you want to be in Mukah town itself. AC, TV, bathroom, standard & superior rooms. **$–$$**

⌂ **Lamin Dana** (12 rooms) Kampung Tellian (4km from Mukah); ☏084 871543; e info@ lamindana.com; www.lamindana.com. Part riverside lodge, part cultural centre, Lamin Dana is built in Melanau style at the end of a village boardwalk through mangroves. Rustically alluring, it is much like a longhouse homestay but without the crowds. Earthy décor, with beautiful crafts on display. Twin & family rooms, fans, games/computer room. Melanau meals. Mangrove tours, boat trips, bike hire. **$–$$**

Homestays Sarawak Tourism describe homestays in the Mukah area as 'culture-based accommodation'. The following are best arranged through Sibu Tourism (*vicsibu@sarawaktourism.com*).

⌂ **Dalat Homestays** In the small Melanau township of Dalat, some 20km inland from Oya, on the Batang Oya. Express boats from Sibu to Mukah arrive in Dalat. Fishing, sago gathering, taking boat trips & trekking. **$$**

⌂ **Oya Homestay** Kampung Senau, Oya; ☏084 871416; e anail@yahoo.com. Homestay programme in 10 village houses run by the Malaysian Fisheries Development Board as a rural development initiative. Locals will cook

traditional Melanau food for you & perform *bermukun*, which involves playing drums, dancing & reciting poetry, & give healing Melanau massages. **$$**

⌂ **Pantai Harmoni Resort** Km4 Jln Mukah-Oya (4km south of Mukah on coast); ☏084 872566. Family-run, simple beach chalet, 2 bedrooms with double bed, sitting room & restaurant. **$–$$**

✗ Where to eat

Mukah's streets are packed with coffee shops for cheap and charming food. A row of basic kitchens serve Chinese and Malay food in a large open space. For more upmarket food (and mid-range prices) try **JS Seafood** and **River View Restaurant**, both situated near the Tua Pek Kong Temple and serving authentic Melanau food, including tasty *umai*, or **Nibong House** (*Jalan Orang Kaya Setia Raja, opposite the Civic Centre*). The (halal) **Palm Beach Restaurant** (⊕ 06.30–22.45 last order) in the Kingwood Resort (see above) serves Malaysian and Melanau specialities as well as Western food. In Dalat there are several Chinese coffee shops opposite the riverfront and a Melanau restaurant, **Taku Café**, serving local specialities.

What to see and do

There is a new town and an old town in Mukah – the fishing harbour is in the latter. The modern **mosque** and **civic centre** both have emblematic *terendak* (conical Melanau palm-leaf sun-hat) roofs. Melanau traditions are best seen on parade in the **Pesta Kaul**. Held at the beginning of the fishing season (usually April), to appease the spirits, a three-day taboo on leaving and entering the town precedes the festival and feasting. During the *seraheng* procession, food is carried up the Batang Mukah River by canoe – raised on bamboo poles by mask-wearing Melanau. **Fireflies** thrive in the mangroves of Mukah and one prime firefly territory is **Tanjung Pedada**, a cape in **Kampung Pedada**, just across the narrow stretch of river from Mukah town.

The award-winning **Lamin Dana Handicraft Centre** (*Kampung Tellian Tengah, 4km from Mukah town;* ☏ *084 871543*) sprang up from a Melanau performing-arts and youth development project in 1999, aimed at preserving Melanau heritage. In the first two years, 50 weavers were trained. The handicrafts are mostly woven

11

from sago fronds. The seven villages involved each focus on one craft industry, and receive 1,000–2,000MYR per month for their produce. The only original **Melanau longhouse**, dating to 1872, is in Kampung Sok, Matu. Vans go there from Daro wharf. Arrange visits through the Mukah Resident's office (☏ *084 872596*). **Kelidieng** are ornately carved wooden burial poles made out of hollowed ironwood (*belian*) tree trunks. One of the finest is in Dalat, opposite the wharf and Chinese temple.

KAPIT AND THE UPPER REJANG The Rejang flows through administrative borders into Kapit Division, a river-ribbed area the size of Switzerland and with a population density of fewer than three people per square kilometre. The Upper Rejang area, extending another 120km between Kapit and Belaga, is one of the last Bornean frontiers for remote, rugged adventure and deeper ethnographic encounters. Within a collection of peaks averaging 1,200m altitude are dozens of rivers – major tributaries of the Rejang flow through the region and provide the main means of transport. Thick carpets of forest are pockmarked from logging, mining and slash-and-burn agriculture – to make way for hill paddy, pepper, rubber, cocoa, fruit and vegetable crops, and increasingly for oil palm plantations.

Getting there and away
By boat Express boats run by various companies ply the Rejang daily between Kanowit, Sibu, Song and Kapit, starting as early as 05.30, through to mid-afternoon. The direct Sibu to Kapit boat takes two to three hours. The fare is 20MYR, or a first-class ticket – in a massage chair – is 25MYR. Other boats stop in Kanowit (40min trip, 6MYR) and Song (2½ hrs, 17/22MYR 1st class). One boat a day goes from Sibu to Belaga at 06.15 (leaving Kapit at 09.30). The journey takes eight hours and costs 35–40MYR.

Other practicalities Foreign visitors require a permit to travel beyond Kapit to Belaga or up the Baleh River, so an overnight stay in Kapit town is mandatory. One- and two-week permits are issued at the **Kapit Resident's Office** (*9th Floor, New State Office Complex, Beleteh Commercial Centre;* ⊕ *08.00–13.00 & 14.00–17.00 Mon–Thu, 08.00–11.45 & 14.15–17.00 Fri, closed Sat/Sun & public holidays*). Take a van from Jalan Airport to reach the office. You can view and request information via their website (*www.kapitro.sarawak.gov.my*). Belaga is not accessible by boat when water levels are low so services may not operate during the dry season from July to September. Air conditioning in the boats (as on many forms of Malaysian transport) can be icy-cold, so bring a long-sleeved top.

⌂ **Where to stay** The accommodation in Kapit is poor, with complaints even in the most flashy of hotels of cockroaches running over people's feet. The one out-of-town resort, the **Regency Pelagus**, was deathly deserted when I visited in 2009 (I was the only guest), and the hotel has now disappeared from the former hotel management company's website, with no new takers (thus the decision to exclude it in this new edition). There is very little incentive to stay in Kapit. Instead, think of visiting the Rejang River on a Pandaw river expedition.

⌂ **Meligai Hotel** (46 rooms) Lot 334, Jln Lapangan Terbang (Airport Rd); ☏084 796611; www.hotelmeligai.com. 2-star, AC, cable TV, bathroom. For a better room, pay for a suite. Restaurant & music lounge. **$–$$**

⌂ **New Rejang Inn** (18 beds) 28 Jln Temenggong Jugah; ☏084 796600. Considered the 'backpackers' of Kapit; rooms have fans. **$**

Longhouse stays The Kapit Resident's office can give you an up-to-date list of longhouses accepting visitors for day/overnight visits (it often changes). An overnight stay including longboat trip will cost around 320MYR per person, plus a minimum of 30MYR for meals. Those upstream from Kapit on the Sungai Tisa, Sungai Kain and Sungai Mujong require overnight stays. One of the guides, Joshua Muda Guna (\ *019 4676004;* e *joshuamuda@hotmail.com*) is a very capable and adventurous guide. As well as standard longhouse stays, he organises trips to places such as Long Singut, a remote Kenyah longhouse on the Sungai Baleh (7-day/6-night packages for 1,600MYR) and more arduous jungle treks and expeditions to the remote peak of Batu Tiban (12–14 days; physical fitness required), evoked in Redmond O'Hanlon's classic book *Into the Heart of Borneo* (see *Appendix 2*, page 316).

✗ **Where to eat** River prawns and fish dishes are big in Kapit. Try them at mid-priced **Hock Bing Seafood** (*off Jln Temenggong Jugah*) and air-conditioned **Jade Garden** (*Jln Lapangan Terbang, opposite the Meligai Hotel;* ⊕ *lunch & dinner*). **Orchard Restaurant** (*64 Jln Tlong Ung Hong;* ⊕ *09.00–23.00*), is also air conditioned, and has many pork dishes. Cheap coffee shops with good noodles and rice dishes are all over town. There are outdoor food stalls every evening in the **Taman Selera Empurau**, near the Eon Bank, and by day on the first floor of the **Pasar Teresang** town market – a good place to buy fresh food and fruits, sweets and cakes (*kuih*). It is possible to try the Iban cooking style *pansuh* at some local restaurants, though it's best to request ahead: chicken and fish are cooked in bamboo stems over an open fire.

What to see and do

Kapit Kapit is a lively trading centre and transport hub for the upper river regions. Express boats, longboats and steamboats converge on the wharf. Kapit was settled by Charles Brooke as a garrison town in the 1880s, using **Fort Sylvia** (⊕ *10.00–12.00 & 14.00–17.00 Tue–Sun*) to crack down on Iban warriors who were moving upriver to fight other tribes. A peacekeeping ceremony between the Iban and Orang Ulu was held at the fort in 1924. It was originally called Kapit Fort, but Brooke changed the name to honour his wife Ranee Sylvia. Once a district office and courthouse, the fort is now a small museum. More encompassing is the **Kapit Museum** (*Kapit Civic Centre;* ⊕ *09.00–13.00 & 14.00–16.15 Mon–Thu, closes 11.45 Fri; free*).

Belaga Beyond Kapit and up to Belaga, boat journeys on the Rejang and Balch rivers are a unique experience, with the greatest chance of traditional Kayan and Kenyah longhouse stays along the riverbanks. It's mandatory to do such trips with a licensed nature guide. Contact the Kapit Resident's office (see above) for details. Belaga is the last trading post on the Rejang – it sprang up in the early 1900s when some Chinese traders set up shop to supply goods such as kerosene, salt and cooking utensils to the Orang Ulu people upriver.

Warning There have been reports of alcoholism being rife among Belaga guides; do not use guides unless the operator can promise they will be sober. Women are advised not to travel alone.

Kanowit About 50km southeast of Sibu, Kanowit is the furthest point along the river accessible by road. A small riverside town of 1930s Chinese shop-houses, the main landmark is **Fort Emma**, a 19th-century Brooke-era wooden stockade. The area has one of the greatest concentrations of Iban longhouses in Sarawak, particularly along the Sungai Julau and the Sungai Katibas near Song.

11

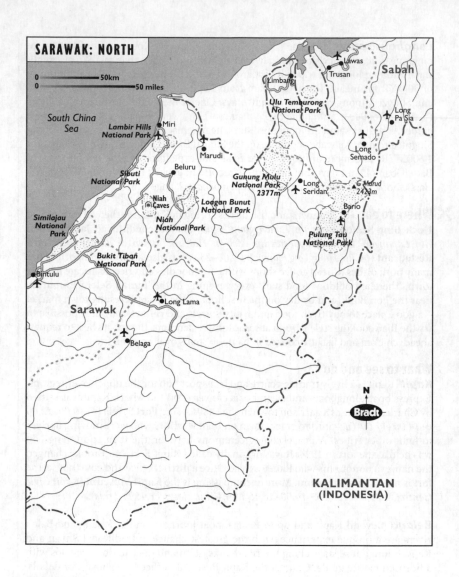

SARAWAK: NORTH

0 ————— 50km
0 ————————— 50 miles

South China
Sea

Sabah

Lawas
Trusan
Limbang
Ulu Temburong
National Park

Long
Pa Sia

Lambir Hills
National Park
Miri

Long
Semado

Marudi

Sibuti
National Park

Beluru

Gunung Mulu
National Park
2377m

Long
Seridan

G Murud
2423m

Niah
Caves

Loagan Bunut
National Park

Bario

Similajau
National
Park

Niah
National Park

Pulung Tau
National Park

Bukit Tiban
National Park

Bintulu

Long Lama

Sarawak

Belaga

N

Bradt

KALIMANTAN
(INDONESIA)

12

Northern Sarawak

The coastline stretching north from Bintulu to Miri is not known for its stunning beaches, but it does have some beautiful coastal geology and vegetation. As oil, petroleum and gas hubs, interest in Bintulu and Miri has traditionally been mostly from business travellers, foreign investors and workers. As such, Sarawak Tourism paints Bintulu as a 'transit point' for the Niah Caves and Miri as a 'gateway' to Gunung Mulu National Park. Sometimes disproportional interest is pinned on these two must-sees to the exclusion of nearly all else. But the often-overlooked coastal strip of northern Sarawak has other, quite lovely, national parks. Deep inland towards the Indonesian border, the temperate Kelabit Highlands are a haven for independent trekkers – subsisting on Bario rice and vegetables and living in basic accommodation.

BINTULU

'Boom-town Bintulu' got a real economic boost from the large natural gas and oil deposits found near its shores in the 1970s. Today, the city is a monument to the power of Petronas, the Malaysian government's oil corporation, whose subsidiary – the Malaysia Liquefied Natural Gas Corporation – owns Bintulu's natural gas processing plant, the largest in the world. Annexed as part of Sarawak by James Brooke in 1861, the town of Bintulu grew up along the banks of the Sungai Kemena river, which flows into the South China Sea. Until oil was discovered in the region, Bintulu's port was primarily a centre of the fishing and timber trades, with export wood sent downstream from the forests. Said to be the most wonderfully planned city in Sarawak, the city continues to prosper and grow in an independent fashion.

GETTING THERE AND AWAY

By air MASWings connects Bintulu to Kuching (from 189MYR; one-hour flight with five daily departures from Kuching, including one direct flight, and one daily departure from Bintulu at 12.25), Sibu (from 71MYR; two flights from Sibu, one from Bintulu) and Kota Kinabalu (from 189MYR; two flights daily from Bintulu, four daily from Kota Kinabalu including two direct ones). MAS also flies twice a day from Miri to Bintulu. AirAsia operate two flights daily from Kuala Lumpur to Bintulu at 10.00 and 16.20, and two flights every Tuesday from Bintulu to Kuala Lumpur (also at 10.00 and 16.20). The journey takes two hours and tickets start at 179MYR. The Bintulu Airport is about 20km from town.

By car Bintulu is about 644km north of Kuching, 192km north of Sibu, 214km south of Miri and 124km south of Niah National Park.

By bus There are express buses to Sibu (about 20MYR), Miri (20MYR) and Kuching (60MYR). Long-distance buses depart from the Medan Jaya express bus terminal on Jalan Tun Hussein Onn, 3km north of the civic centre, at the Medan Jaya shopping centre. The major bus companies operating from here include Biaramas, Borneo Highway and PB Express. A taxi to reach here will cost 10–15MYR.

GETTING AROUND Local buses leave from the town bus station near the markets off Main Bazaar.

TOURIST INFORMATION
Bintulu Information Centre Jln Keppel

WHERE TO STAY
The downtown area – along Jalan Keppel and Jalan Abang Galau – runs parallel to the riverbank for over 0.5km, where most budget hotels are found. A couple of three-star establishments are located a few hundred metres out of the CBD (Central Business District) towards the river's entrance and the landscaped area of Bintulu Park City. Contact Sarawak Tourism for help with arranging hotels.

Park City Everly (228 rooms) Lot 3062, Jln Tun Razak; ☎ 086 318888; e reservation.pehb@vhmis.com; www.vhhotels.com. On the newly landscaped waterfront esplanade that runs for a couple of kilometres along the shoreline. Top business hotel in town, AC, satellite TV, de luxe rooms & suites, swimming pool & gym, coffee shop, restaurant & pub. **$$$**, suite **$$$$**

Kemena Plaza Hotel (161 rooms) 116 Taman Sri Dagang, Jln Abang Galau; ☎ 086 335111. The former Regency Plaza Hotel still had no website or email address weeks after switching its ID in 2011. 3-star, satellite TV, AC, bath & fridge, swimming pool, sauna & coffee house. **$$**, suite **$$$$**

Li Hua 36 Berjaya Commercial Centre, Jln Sultan Iskandar (1km north of town, near civic centre & temple); ☎ 086 335000; e lihuab@po.jaring.my; www.ihuahotelbtu.com. Good value – standard but solid. AC, friendly 1-star with family rooms & suites, coffee house & restaurant, buffet meals 10–15MYR. **$$**

Regent Hotel (45 rooms) Kemena Commercial Centre (4km north); ☎ 086 335511. Edge of town budget hotel recommended in tourism circles, in green surrounds of Tanjung Batu. Coffee house. **$**

Å There is also a **campsite** at Tanjung Batu.

WHERE TO EAT
Restaurants/Coffee shops More chic and air-conditioned places with mid-range prices are found in the top hotels (see above for contact details). **M&D's Restaurant** (⊕ 06.00–24.00 daily) at the Park City Everly has an open kitchen and international food, while there are lighter snacks and drinks at its **Luconia Bay Coffee Terrace** (⊕ 10.00–01.00). The **Kemena Coffee House** (in the Regency Plaza) has good local as well as Western dishes.

Food to go Pantai Ria Food Centre (*2km from city, by the sea;* ⊕ *evenings only*) has stalls. A ten-minute walk from most hotels is the night market – *medan pasar malam*. There are many food stalls in the vicinity of the markets and Express Wharf on Main Bazaar.

SHOPPING City Point shopping mall on Jalan Keppel is the most central. The *pasar utama*, central market and *pasar tamu* handicrafts market are held by the riverside under a *terendak* (conical hat)-shaped roof.

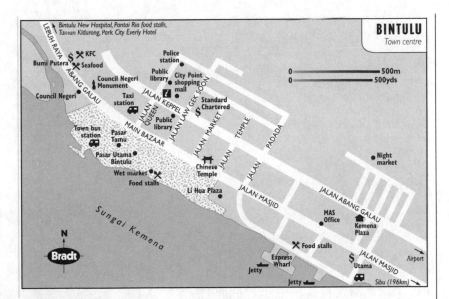

Bintulu New Hospital, Pantai Ria food stalls,
Taman Kidurong, Park City Everly Hotel

LEBUH RAYA

Bumi Putera

KFC

Seafood

JALAN ABANG GALAU

Council Negeri Monument

Council Negeri

Taxi station

Police station

Public library

City Point shopping mall

JALAN KEPPEL

JALAN QUEEN

Standard Chartered

JALAN LAW GEK SOON

Public library

MAIN BAZAAR

JALAN MARKET

JALAN TEMPLE

JALAN PADADA

Town bus station

Pasar Tamu

Pasar Utama Bintulu

Wet market

Food stalls

Li Hua Plaza

Chinese Temple

JALAN MASJID

Sungai Kemena

N

Bradt

Night market

JALAN ABANG GALAU

MAS Office

Kemena Plaza

Food stalls

Express Wharf

Jetty

Jetty

JALAN MASJID

Utama

Airport

Sibu (196km)

0 ——————— 500m
0 ——————— 500yds

OTHER PRACTICALITIES
Banks
$ **Standard Chartered Bank** Jln Keppel
$ **Utama Bank** Near the jetty area off Jln Masjid

Health and emergency
Police station Jalan Queen, off Jln Keppel

✚ **Bintulu New Hospital** On Jln Nyabau,
north of town

Miscellaneous
Public library Jalan Queen, off Jln Keppel

WHAT TO SEE AND DO Spiritual landmarks include the modern **Bintulu Mosque** Masjid Assyakirin, meaning 'gratefulness to God', set in landscaped surrounds on Tanjung Batu headland, and the **Kuan Yin Tong Temple** on Jalan Sultan Iskandar, 2km north of the CBD. **Kampung Jepak**, a traditional Melanau fishing village, is on the other side of Sungai Kemena near the river mouth – take a short ride over on a *bot tambang* riverboat to see fish-drying and sago-processing activities. The **Council Negeri** (State Council) **Monument** in the **civic centre** commemorates Sarawak's 1867 convened legislative assembly, and the oldest parliament in Malaysia, composed of five British officers and 18 Malay and Melanau chiefs. The best view is from the **Observation Tower** in Tanjung Kidurong, where you can gaze up the coast along the Bintulu Port area.

Two connecting coastal parks, **Taman Tumbina** and **Taman Kidurong,** start about 3km north of the town centre from the small headland of Tanjung Batu where there is a beach. Taman Tumbina has a wildlife park with a small zoo, botanical garden and butterfly world. The second-biggest port in Malaysia and an industrial port for agro-food, petrochemical and timber industries, the **Bintulu deep-sea port** and container terminal covers an area of 320 acres with a total quay length of nearly 0.5km.

Sports The sports complex in Taman Tumbina parklands has a swimming pool and tennis courts and the **Bintulu Golf Course** is located on the headland of Tanjung Kidurong.

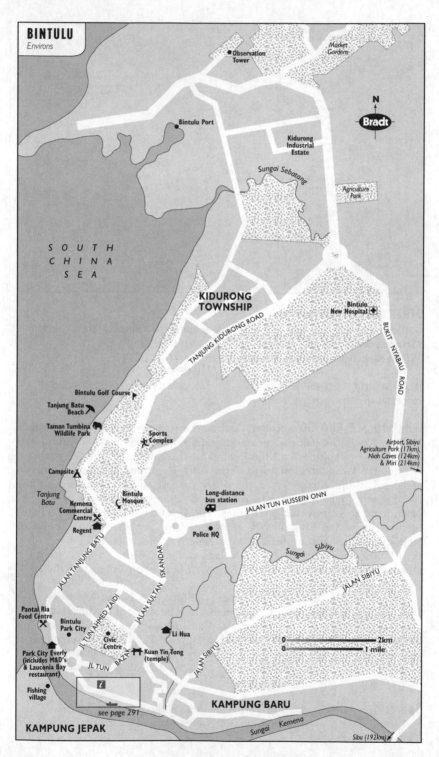

BINTULU
Environs

Observation Tower

Market Gardens

N

Bradt

Bintulu Port

Kidurong Industrial Estate

Sungai Sebatang

Agriculture Park

S O U T H
C H I N A
S E A

KIDURONG TOWNSHIP

Bintulu New Hospital ✚

TANJUNG KIDURONG ROAD

BUKIT NYABAU ROAD

Bintulu Golf Course

Tanjung Batu Beach

Taman Tumbina Wildlife Park

Sports Complex

Campsite

Tanjung Batu

Kemena Commercial Centre

Regent

Bintulu Mosque

Long-distance bus station

JALAN TUN HUSSEIN ONN

Airport, Sibiyu
Agriculture Park (17km),
Niah Caves (124km)
& Miri (214km)

Police HQ

Sungai Sibiyu

JALAN SIBIYU

JALAN TANJUNG BATU

JALAN SULTAN ISKANDAR

Pantai Ria Food Centre

Bintulu Park City

JL TUN AHMED ZAIDI

Civic Centre

BAZAR

Li Hua

Kuan Yin Tong (temple)

Park City Everly (includes M&D's & Lauconia Bay restaurant)

JL TUN

Fishing village

ℹ

see page 291

JALAN SIBIYU

0 _____ 2km
0 _____ 1 mile

KAMPUNG BARU

KAMPUNG JEPAK

Sungai Kemena

Sibu (192km)

332

EXCURSION FROM BINTULU

SIMILAJAU NATIONAL PARK Some 30km north of Bintulu on an unsealed road, with no regular bus service, this park lives largely in the shadow of the Niah Caves, but is really a great nature getaway, with lovely brackish water beaches, skirted in *kerangas* and rainforest. Stretching 32km up the coast in a 1.5km-wide strip, the park covers an area of over 9,000ha. There is just one main trail with a few possible deviations along the coast to various beaches – where turtles come ashore to lay eggs. You could easily spend a day here. The park is home to saltwater crocodiles and, though there have been no attacks reported, be alert and avoid swimming.

Where to stay Park accommodation is disappointing – the chalets (which sleep four) have electricity and running water but not much more. There is also a campsite and barbecue pits. That doesn't necessarily mean seclusion however, and holiday periods can be particularly busy. Accommodation can be booked at the park HQ registration and information desk (there is also a canteen here) (✆ *086 391284; www.forestry.sarawak.gov.my/forweb/homepage/contact.htm;* ⊕ *08.00–12.30 & 13.30–17.15 daily*), through the Miri office, online, or by calling the park direct.

NIAH NATIONAL PARK

Rising up dramatically behind the small township of Batu Niah, the 388m limestone massif of Gunung Subis dominates the Niah National Park, and hosts the famous archaeological site of the Niah Caves among its huge outcrops. First gazetted as a National Historic Monument in 1958 after the find of a 44,000-year-old skull at the entrance to the caves, 3,100ha of surrounding rainforest and limestone hills were swept into the park's realm when it was created in 1974. Most people visit for the day from either Miri or Bintulu, though the visitors' accommodation facilities are among the better maintained of Sarawak's parks. The discovery of coffins, urns, pottery, paintings, textiles, tools and ornaments in Niah show consistent habitation over thousands of years – the area within and around the caves is full of archaeological, cultural and natural history.

GETTING THERE AND AWAY

By car The Niah National Park HQ are located at Pengkalan Batu, 109km south of Miri and 131km north of Bintulu. The closest town to HQ is Batu Niah, which is also the public transport hub for the caves.

By bus Syarikat Bas Suria operates bus services from Miri's express bus terminal (at Pujut Corner), and from Bintulu to Batu Niah. The journey from Miri takes one hour 40 minutes to two hours; from Bintulu it's closer to three hours. The park office is 3km from Batu Niah. You can reach it either by foot – a 45-minute plankwalk along the riverbank – by motorised longboat or taxi. Tour buses go all the way to HQ. The above bus services have been known to be disrupted for long periods so check with Miri Tourism beforehand or telephone the bus company (✆ *085 424311/430417*). Another option is the unmarked 4x4s which leave from opposite the tourism information centre to various destinations, including Niah. It's a bit of a pot-luck situation as drivers only leave if and when there are six passengers. They generally charge 15–20MYR and take you right to the park entrance, though the tariff will rise if passenger numbers are low. Many express buses heading south to Bintulu, Sibu and Kuching can let you off along the highway, at the village of

Simpang Ngu, near the Batu Niah turn-off. The ticket costs about 10MYR. The taxi for the remaining 12–15km will cost about three times more.

OTHER PRACTICALITIES The park has a visitor centre and canteen and an extensive network of plankwalks to and throughout the caves. The caves are about a 3km walk from park HQ. A torch and good walking shoes are recommended as the caves are unlit and the plankwalk can be slippery. Conservation fee is 10MYR.

WHERE TO STAY AND EAT

🏠 **National Park accommodation** (9 chalets) 📞085 737450. Basic 2-room chalets (4-beds), with attached bathroom, some with AC, plus a 'Forest Hostel' sleeping 16 in 4 rooms,

---

THE GREAT CAVE OF NIAH – A BRIEF HISTORY   *Dr Huw Barton*

The Great Cave of Niah is enormous by any measure. The floor area of the cave has been calculated at almost 10ha, and in places the majestic cave roof rises 75m above the rubble-strewn floor. As well as being home to multitudes of bats, darting swiftlets (their nests are the famous ingredient of Chinese bird's nest soup) and the occasional snake, it is also the site of human occupation dating back at least 46,000 years. The richness of the deposits at Niah, and the great span of time they encompass, marks the site as one of the most important archaeological sites in southeast Asia.

The site was first excavated by the brilliant but cantankerous Tom Harrisson, a self-trained archaeologist, curator and ethnologist of the Sarawak Museum, who realised the enormous potential of the site and began excavation in 1954. In 1958 came the discovery of a 44,000-year-old human skull at the front of the West Mouth (an area affectionately referred to as 'Hell' – due to the working conditions in the heat of the day!) The skull has since been determined to belong to a 15–17 year old, probably female. Flaked stone and other evidence of human activity were found as well.

Food remains recovered more recently show people had a fairly broad diet, using a wide range of plant and animal foods from the forest and nearby freshwater streams. Recent analysis of bone fragments shows evidence that people were hunting arboreal primates, butchering them on-site, and manufacturing bone tools. A favoured food appears to have been the bearded pig, *sus barbatus* – still a popular food today. Fabulous preservation of plant remains at Niah has shed new light on ancient diet and foraging knowledge. Charred remains of edible but toxic tubers and nuts have been recovered, indicating a degree of sophistication in food processing not previously believed to occur this early. We have also found evidence that these early foragers knew how to make complex multi-component tools: some of these tools included jagged stingray spines and bone splinters finely worked to make spears or arrows.

Use of the cave changed over time. At one time used occasionally by roaming foragers, it later became a major repository of the dead around 4,000 years ago. At this time, there is evidence for the use of pottery as funerary gifts and burial jars, with later evidence of imported metals, ceramics and glass. Remarkably, even textiles were recovered from some graves. Some of the recovered material is on display at the site museum at Niah Cave, and also in the Sarawak Museum in Kuching.

& a 30-site campsite. All have 24hr electricity & piped water, but there are no cooking facilities.

Common park facilities include washrooms, a canteen, an AV room & information centre. **$**

If you choose to stay in Batu Niah, there are some basic lodging houses and coffee shops in this one-street township.

⌂ **Niah Cave Inn** Lot 621, Batu Niah Bazaar; ☎ 085 737333. TV, AC. **$**

WHAT TO SEE AND DO The **Great Cave** is just over 3km from HQ along a path buttressed with huge *tapang* trees, *pandanus* plants, orchids and fungi – sightings of monkeys, lizards, butterflies, hornbills and squirrels are likely. The cave's spectacular entrance (West Mouth) is over 60m high and 250m wide – inside, guano collectors gather bat excrement to sell as fertiliser. The walls of the nearby **Painted Cave** feature a set of etchings in red hematite depicting boat journeys of the dead into the afterlife. The wall paintings tie in with the discovery of a number of 'death ships' in the cave – boat-shaped coffins containing human remains and a selection of 'grave goods' considered useful in the afterlife, such as Chinese ceramics, ornaments and glass beads. The death ships date to sometime between AD1 and AD780, although local Penan folklore tells of death-ship burials as late as the 19th century. Some birdwatching enthusiasts come just to witness the sunset 'changing of the guard', which happens when up to half a million swiftlets return to their nests and the bats swarm out to forage in the forest.

From HQ there are two other well-marked but short trails of 2–3km: the Bukit **Kasut Trail** through rainforest and *Kerangas* forest to the top of a hill; and the **Madu Trail** along the Sungai Subis river through peat and alluvial swamp forest to the base of Bukit Kasut.

MIRI

Determined to shake its reputation as an industrial oil town, Miri has become an important leisure stretch for the local expat community, and a weekend playground for escaping Bruneians under the local government tag 'Miri Resort City'.

If you want a bit of a beach atmosphere before, in between or after backcountry trips, Miri is the best place for it, with its big choice of classy-to-budget hotels and relaxed social buzz. Evolving from the oil slick of its past, Miri's future as a self-made resort town is positively glowing with the rise of coastal condominiums and luxury hotels. Sarawak's second metropolis with a population of 300,000, locals live, eat, work and play hard. Chinese and Iban form the bulk of the rich cultural infusion, topped up with Malay and Orang Ulu .

GETTING THERE AND AWAY

By air Miri's modern airport is a major midway hub in northern Borneo. AirAsia and Malaysia Airlines have several direct daily flights between Miri and Kuala Lumpur (prices from 80MYR/159MYR respectively for the two airlines), Kuching (from 40MYR/100MYR) and Kota Kinabalu (from 40MYR/152MYR) as well as Johor Bahru in southern Malaysia and to Singapore (from 103MYR/227MYR). Royal Brunei Airlines fly between Miri and Bandar Seri Begawan. MASWings (*www.maswings.com.my*) operates rural air services on both Fokker 50s and Twin Otters from Miri to Gunung Mulu National Park, Ba'Kelalan and Bario (Kelabit Highlands), Marudi, Lawas, Limbang and Labuan, Sibu and Bintulu. Most of these

12

30–60-minute flights cost under 100MYR one-way. As of 2011, ATR 72-500 planes were being introduced for some journeys, with a carrying capacity of 68 passengers, compared with the Fokker's 50, and 19 on the Twin Otters. Luggage limits for the smaller planes are 10kg.

Airlines

🏠 **Malaysia Airlines** 1st Floor, Lot 239, Beautiful Jade Centre; 📞 085 417315, toll-free 1 300 88 3000; e info@maswings.com.my; www.malaysianailines.com.my

By car Miri lies 800km north of Sarawak's capital Kuching, along the Pan-Borneo Highway. The supposedly smooth stretch is far from that in places – in fact its notoriously pot-holed surface has, of late, earned it a very bad name. In 2011 there were cries of 'killer highway' after a spate of fatal accidents within a few months, some of them involving foreigners – *and* express bus services. Having driven the road in 2009, I encountered some very bumpy, narrow and poorly lit sections, between Sibu and Bintulu and between the Niah Caves area and Miri, which made night driving in particular rather unsettling.

Miri is 215km north of Bintulu, and 30km to Kuala Belait in Brunei via the Sungai Tujuh immigration checkpoint, a journey that can take over two hours depending on the queues. Make sure you have your passport and money for a visa – there are no ATMs or credit card facilities.

By bus Express air-conditioned buses connect Miri to Kuching (14 hours, 80MYR), Sibu (7¼ hours, 40MYR) and Bintulu (4½ hours, 20MYR). They arrive and leave from Miri's edge-of-town express bus terminal (Terminal Bas Pujut), at the location known as 'Pujut Corner'. Its precise location is opposite the Boulevard Commercial Centre, on Jalan Miri Pujut, near the intersection with Miri Bypass. To and from here there are connecting minibuses to/from the city's central bus station on Jalan Padang. The various companies operating from here include Biramas, Suria Bus Express, Borneo Highway Express and MTC Express (*www.mtcmiri.com*). MTC, for example, has six daily departures from Miri which pass through Bintulu, Sibu and Serian before arriving in Kuching. For Brunei, Miri-Belait bus company runs several daily services to Kuala Belait from the Jalan Padang bus station, switching buses at the Sungai Tujuh border checkpoint. Between here and Brunei's capital, there are another two changes of bus – allow for the best part of a day for the whole journey. (For more details on getting to Brunei see pages 136–7.)

GETTING AROUND Miri is a spread-out town and walking around can be tiring. Buses for the city area and surrounds leave from the central bus station on Jalan Padang, a couple of hundred metres from the visitor information centre on Jalan Melayu. Average prices for local journeys are 1MYR or less. The Taman Selera/Hawaii Beach buses Nos 11/13 go towards the marina, beach and luxury resort area.

TOURIST INFORMATION

ℹ **Visitor Information Centre** Lot 452 Jln Melayu (entry off Jln Padang); 📞 085 434181; e vic-miri@sarawaktourism.com. The national park booking office is at the same office.

Tour operators

Borneo Adventure Lot 1344, 1st Floor, Miri Waterfront Commercial Centre; 📞 085 424332; e info@borneoadventure.com; www. borneoadventure.com. The award-winning Kuching-based company has a Miri office, for launching its excellent, top-of-the-range but well-

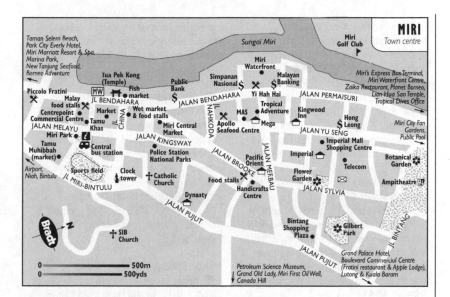

Taman Selera Beach,
Park City Everly Hotel,
Miri Marriott Resort & Spa,
Marina Park,
New Tanjung Seafood,
Borneo Adventure

Sungai Miri

Miri
Golf Club

Miri's Express Bus Terminal,
Miri Waterfront Centre,
Zaika Restaurant, Planet Borneo,
Lian-Hua San Temple,
Tropical Dives Office

Miri
Waterfront

Piccolo Fratini

Tua Pek Kong
(Temple)
Fish
market

Public
Bank

Simpanan
Nasional

Malayan
Banking

Yi Hah Hai

JALAN PERMAISURI

Malay
food stalls

MW

JL BENDAHARA

JALAN BENDAHARA

Tropical
Adventure

Kingwood
Inn

Hong
Leong

Miri City Fan
Gardens,
Public Pool

Centrepoint
Commercial Centre

Market

Wet market
& food stalls

CHINA

MAS

Mega

JALAN YU SENG

JALAN MELAYU
Miri Park

Tamu
Khas

Miri Central
Market

Apollo
Seafood Centre

NAHKODA

Imperial Mall
Shopping Centre

Botanical
Garden

Tamu
Muhibbah
(market)

Central
bus station

JALAN KINGSWAY

Police Station
National Parks

JALAN BROOKE

Pacific
Orient

Imperial

JALAN MERBAU

Telecom

Ampitheatre

Airport,
Niah, Bintulu

Sports field

JL MIRI-BINTULU

Clock
tower

Catholic
Church

Food stalls

Flower
Garden

JALAN SYLVIA

Dynasty

Handicrafts
Centre

JALAN PUJUT

Bradt

N

SIB
Church

Bintang
Shopping
Plaza

Gilbert
Park

JL BINTANG

JALAN PUJUT

Grand Palace Hotel,
Boulevard Commercial Centre
(Fratini restaurant & Apple Lodge),
Lutong & Kuala Baram

0   500m
0   500yds

Petroleum Science Museum,
Grand Old Lady, Miri First Oil Well,
Canada Hill

priced tours to the Niah & Mulu Caves (2 nights for 530MYR), northern Sarawak's Headhunters' trail (4 nights, 1,870MYR), for jungle trekking in the Bario Highlands & trips to Brunei. Tailor-made trips are also common ground.

Borneo LI-SU Tours 012 8509970; e andyson_sulang@yahoo.com.my. Andyson Sulang, ex-park ranger, leads nature conservation tours from Miri to Niah & the Kelabit Highlands, with mountaineering & trekking, birdwatching, rock climbing, whitewater rafting, fishing & diving excursions.

Planet Borneo Tours & Travels Lot 273, Ground Floor, Brighton Centre, Jln Temenggong Datuk Oyong Lawai; 085

415582; e info@planetborneotours.com; www. planetborneotours.com. For local city tours as well as trips outside of Miri (to Brunei & Sabah, as well as Sarawak-wide). Formerly known as Seridan Mulu, this is the parent company of Tropical Dives (see *Diving*, page 117).

Tropical Adventure Tours & Travel Mega Hotel, Lot 907, Jln Merbau; 085 419337; e info@borneotropicaladventures.com; www. borneotropicaladventures.com. Experienced in Mulu tours (overnight packages from 599MYR), Headhunters' trail (from 1,700MYR) & other adventures. Though their target market is more mid-budget, their prices often are not.

WHERE TO STAY Ever-tougher competition is pushing standards higher and higher, with prices still available across the board. The long-awaited new five-star hotel (Convention Hotel) in the Miri Marina Park has clearly been stalled along with the rest of the development, with no inkling available on completion dates.

Upmarket

Miri Marriott Resort & Spa (220 rooms) Lot 779, Jln Temenggong Datuk Oyong Lawai, 2km from city; 085 421121; e sales@mirimarriott. com; www.marriott.com. A comfortable luxury hotel. Spacious, well-furnished garden & sea-facing rooms, with balconies arranged in breezy wings, well away from lobby area. Possibly the best hotel breakfast in Borneo. Large pool, gym, spa, free parking. **$$$**, suite **$$$$$**

Mid range The suites of the following hotels cost 500–1,000MYR; standard rooms are at budget prices and de luxe rooms at mid range.

Park City Everly Hotel (168 rooms) Jln Temenggong Datuk Oyong Lawai; 085 440288; e reservation.pehm@vhms.com. More business-oriented than the Marriott, but bright, upbeat, & with beachside location near Miri Marina. Well-furnished rooms with balcony &

Executive Club floor. 4-star. Very affordable Malay & international food at Melinau Terrace Coffee House with in/outdoor dining & entertainment. Shuttle service to city. **$$–$$$$**

⌂ **Grand Palace Hotel** (125 rooms) KM2 (north of city centre) Pelita Commercial Centre, Jln Miri-Pujut; ✆ 085 428888; e gpalace@ po.jaring.my. A big pink hotel in popular shopping/entertainment complex. Family-run 4-star; large rooms with elegant Chinese-style furnishings, free broadband, satellite TV, coffee house & Han Palace Cantonese restaurant, pool terrace. **$$**, suite **$$$$**

⌂ **Imperial Hotel** (96 rooms/144 apts) Jln Pos; ✆ 085 431133; e enquiries@imperialhotel. com.my; www.imperialhotel.com.my. In Imperial Mall, stylish rooms & self-catering apartment suites, good online promotional rates of up to 40% off. Fitness centre, sauna & swimming pool. **$$**, suite **$$$$**

⌂ **Mega Hotel** (293 rooms) Lot 907, Jln Merbau; ✆ 085 432432; e info@megahotel. com.my; www.megahotel.com.my. Standard & de luxe rooms are budget price, large junior & executive suites mid range. Free Wi-Fi, AC, satellite TV, non-smoking floor, babysitting

service, business centre, fitness & sauna, plus its own bakery, coffee house (⊕ 05.00–24.00) Chinese restaurant & pub. **$$–$$$**

Budget

⌂ **Dynasty Hotel** (130 rooms) Lot 683, Town Centre, Block 9, Jln Pujut-Lutong; ✆ 085 421111; e dyhlmyy@streamyx.com; www. dynastyhotelmiri.com. 3-star, eastern edge of town, comfortable well-equipped rooms, satellite TV, AC, 2 non-smoking floors, coffee house & gym. **$$**

⌂ **Pacific Orient Hotel** (66 rooms) 49 Jln Brooke; ✆ 085 413333; e ynt@pd.jaring.my. AC, satellite TV, fridge, central location, big noisy street. **$–$$**

Shoestring

⌂ **Apple Lodge** (31 rooms) Lot 343–344, Block 7, MCLD, Jln Miri Pujut; ✆ 085 419696; e applelodge@borneojunglesafari.com; www. borneojunglesafari.com. Orang Ulu-owned. Clean; varying room standards. Owned by Borneo Jungle Safari tours that also run the Ba Kelalan Apple Lodge Homestay in the highlands. **$**

There are many Orchid-classified hotels for under 100MYR for a double (some less than 50MYR).

✖ **WHERE TO EAT** There are food stalls in roads and at markets everywhere, though the waterfront's messy streets can make it less appealing. Some riverfront restaurants do not display prices, so enquire ahead of eating.

Seafood In the city, the **Apollo Seafood Centre** (*4 Jln South Yu Seng*) is a hit among locals and foreigners alike for simple but excellent steamed fish, prawns and black pepper crabs, at budget prices in a popular setting. The open-air **Taman Selera** food park (*3km from city past Marina Park, Jln Temenggong Datuk; bus Taman Selera No 11; ⊕ about 17.00–late*) has about 12 stalls serving seafood (by weight) and Chinese and Malay dishes at cheap to mid-range prices; there's outside and under-cover seating overlooking Brighton Beach. On the same stretch (*opposite the Miri Marriott*) is a cluster of seafood restaurants, with indoor/outdoor seating, where you can pick your fish from the aquarium. The last restaurant is perhaps the best, **New Tanjung Seafood** (*Jln Temenggong Datuk;* ✆ *085 433401*); look out for its big lantern with Carlsberg sign. It serves cheap to mid-range Chinese seafood, game and noodle dishes. A good seafood restaurant in the Miri waterfront vicinity in town is **Yi Hah Hai** (*Jln Bendahara*), with indoor and outdoor seating.

Chinese The **Boulevard Restaurant** (*Boulevard Commercial Centre, not city centre;* ✆ *085 436936*) serves excellent, mid-priced Chinese, favourites with locals. **Dynasty Chinese Restaurant** at the Dynasty Hotel, and the **Han Palace** in the Grand Palace

Hotel (see above for details) are good for their air-conditioned environments, big choice and mid-range prices. The Chinese coffee shops on the street-level shop-lots of **Centrepoint commercial centre** have excellent cheap local dishes cooked on the spot – **Tian Tian Café** has lots of *laksa, mee sua, kolok mee* and other noodle dishes. **Lok Thian Restaurant** (*Jln Merbau*) is part of a chain, and makes great fresh buns.

Western and international Mediterranean food is served at **Piccolo Fratini** (*off Jln Kubu, heading towards Marina Park*; \ *085 430255*) in a new district, opposite Centrepoint commercial centre, and serves Mediterranean food. There is a bigger **Fratini** in the Boulevard shopping centre (⊕ *lunch & dinner*). The **Boulevard** and the **Bintang** shopping plaza are the places to head for pizza, burgers and other fast-food chains. The **Boulevard commercial centre** also has Japanese and Korean restaurants and a huge **food court** with Chinese, Malay, clay-pot dishes, Western meals, steaks and snacks.

San Francisco Coffee (with free Wi-Fi) is in the Miri Square shopping complex, and **Coffee Bean** is in the Bintang plaza. A good chain bakery is **Hot Cross Buns** (*Jln Kubu*).

Indian The mid-budget **Zaika** (*Lot 2512 & 2513, 1st Floor, Block 5 MCLD Boulevard Commercial Centre;* \ *418 155*) serves good northern Indian food in a sophisticated, serene atmosphere. Part of a small but growing Brunei-based hospitality group, there is a branch in Kuala Belait, and sister restaurants, Fratini's, from Kota Kinabalu to Miri.

ENTERTAINMENT AND SHOPPING Miri is set out between shopping centres. The most central are the **Imperial Mall** and **Wisma Pelita**; the **Boulevard** commercial centre is to the north of town – the latter two also have nightspots, bars and lounges. There is a **handicraft centre** (⊕ *09.00–18.00 daily*) on Jalan Merbau.

OTHER PRACTICALITIES
Emergency
Police Central Police Station, Balai Polis Sentral, Jln Kingsway; \ 085 433730/085 433222

Media and communications
✉ **Post office** Corner of Jln Post & Jln Syliva, towards Miri City Fan

WHAT TO SEE AND DO Miri is rather raffish and relaxed. A spread-out city, it stretches in a thin lip along the estuary of the Sungai Miri for over 2km. Some of the prettiest parts, such as gardens and recreational areas, lie at either end. Though it is billed as a 'resort town', the beach is out of sight from the city centre. The painfully procrastinated **Marina Park Project** (*www.mirimarina.com*) to the south of the city centre is clearly a work in progress. After re-channelling the river to create a 3km canal, the much promoted plans were for a world-class marina, a festival park, business and retail park, leisure strip and new luxury accommodation. So far the only real things to have emerged from the drawing board into reality are a new marina with 78 wet berths, connected by nicely designed pontoons and pathways, and a restaurant. The developers give no idea of how long they expect the work to complete the fancy-on-paper marina – the 'Marina Quay' retail site, the 'Marina Market', serviced apartments, clubhouse and walkways – to take.

Many attractions lie just out of town. The best 360° view of Miri is from Canada Hill, a ridge above town where Miri's '**Grand Old Lady**' – an endearing term for Malaysia's first oil well – struck good in 1910. There's also a **Petroleum Museum** here. On the way up you will see a couple of giant sea horses – Miri's mascot.

About 3km from the city, people stop to gaze and walk around a geological marvel – a cliff face of multi-dimensions and myriad colours known rather unromantically as the **Airport Road Outcrop**, as it was exposed during the road's construction. The large **public park** is near here. Modern Miri is park upon park – underpinning its vision to become a health-resort city. At the city's northern end, the **City Fan** is a 10.5ha green space with promenades, fountains, public pools, amphitheatres, Islamic and Chinese cultural gardens, botanical gardens and IT library. Even the temples are well out of town – the **Lian Hua San** (Lotus Hill) **Temple** is a strange apparition planted in the nouveau residential area of Krokop in 2000. Far more charming is the **Tua Pek Kong Temple** in the old town near the river (*Jln Bendahara*) – the central market, fish market and spice-laden Malay *tamu lama* are all in this area. Orang Ulu people bring all kinds of Bario rice, highland fruit and vegetables, wild ferns and fruit, rattan mats and baskets to the fascinating under-cover **Tamu Muhibbah** and **Tamu Khas** (*opposite the visitor information centre, Jln Padang*).

South of Miri, the **beach** area begins. Near the **Taman Selera** recreational park and children's playground is Brighton Beach. Some 9km further on is the **Luak Bay Esplanade** picnic spot.

Diving Miri Reef is a developing dive area – within the 150km² triangle offshore are drop-offs, reefs and shipwrecks. There is good beginner and advanced diving in the patch reefs: 7–22m depth, few currents and visibility of 10–30m. The further out you go, the better it gets.

The best local operation to contact is **Tropical Dives** (*Lot 273, Ground Floor, Brighton Centre, Jln Temenggong Datuk Oyong Lawai;* ✆ *085 414300;* e *info@tropical-dives.com; www.tropical-dives.com*). I finally got my PADI Open Water with this bunch in 2009. Being in such professional hands made it all the more worthwhile and comforting. The dive master, Voo, has dived with Cousteau (senior) and done thousands of dives in his 40-year-plus diving career.

EXCURSIONS FROM MIRI

You may not even pass through Miri to visit the mountainous area of Sarawak: the Kelabit Highlands, Bario region and the Gunung Mulu National Park. It is, however, the region's commercial and transport nexus, and the most common departure point for locals and tourists alike heading inland.

LAMBIR HILL NATIONAL PARK The waterfalls, rainforest and low-lying peaks of this park are the closest green lung to Miri, 30km south of the city along the Miri–Bintulu road. There are over a dozen trails, from 20-minute walks to the 7km Pancur Waterfall walk, and 6km Summit Trail to Bukit Lambir. The 25m **Latak Waterfalls** is a popular bathing spot, less than 200m from park HQ. There is basic park accommodation (✆ *085 491030*) here. Local buses run from the park to Batu Niah Caves and Bintulu.

LOAGAN BUNUT NATIONAL PARK Some 120km southeast of Miri via Beluru, the park centres on Sarawak's largest natural lake, which sometimes dries up into an expanse of cracked mud, surrounded by mixed peat swamp forest. There are many wading birds, reptiles and small mammals here. The lake is fished by Berawan people, with whom you can charter rides on the lake and Baram River (*60MYR per hour for 4 people*). There's a forest hostel with seven bunk beds, small canteen, and

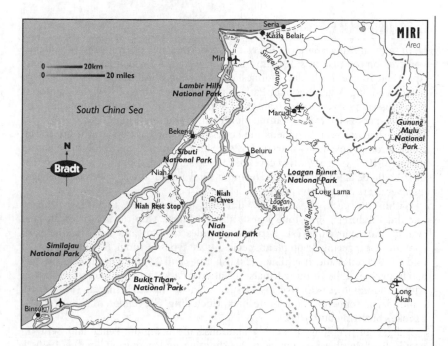

MIRI
Area

South China Sea

Seria
Kuala Belait
Miri
Lambir Hills National Park
Marudi
Gunung Mulu National Park
Bekenu
N
Bradt
Sibuti National Park
Niah
Beluru
Loagan Bunut National Park
Long Lama
Niah Caves
Loagan Bunut
Niah Rest Stop
Niah National Park
Similajau National Park
Bukit Tiban National Park
Long Akah
Bintulu

0 ———— 20km
0 ———— 20 miles

Sungai Baram

generator electricity from 06.00–24.00. A Berawan family run the **Mutiara Hostel**
(↘ *011 292164 or reserve via Miri's national park office*), with nine twin bedrooms,
simple cooking facilities, and floating grocery nearby. Buses from Miri go to Lapok
Bridge, 15km before the park HQ. Head to the coffee shops to arrange a lift, or
arrange with the Mutiara Hostel.

MARUDI Marudi is the commercial centre of the Sungai Baram river district.
Before there were planes to Gunung Mulu National Park and highland areas, it
was a major starting point for river trips to these areas, and is still a base for more
off-the-beaten-track adventures and longhouse safaris. Some people trek from
Marudi to the Kelabit Highlands over four days, or do the 'old-fashioned' river trip
starting from Kuala Baram (see *Getting there* details below). For all such trips you
are best to approach the Miri Tourism Office for information on the appropriate
tour operators, besides those listed in the *Tour operators* section on pages 296–7. If
you do stay in Marudi overnight, visit the Chinese Temple and belian-roofed Fort
Hose (now the Baram District Museum), which was home of 'Resident' (colonial
administrator) Charles Hose, from the late 1890s. For a workout, head to the hilltop
Taman Tasik Recreation Park with its suspended bridges, walkways and Baram
river views. At the end of September or early October the two-day **Baram Regatta**
is a tradition which has continued from 1899, when Charles Hose, organised the
annual race of war canoes in an effort to create a worthy diversion from headhunting and tribal warring. For overnight stays in Marudi, the **Mount Mulu Hotel**
(*60 rooms;* ↘*085 756671;* **$$**) is a one-star, with air conditioning and television; the
Mayland Hotel (↘*085 755106*) and Grand Hotel (↘*085 755711*) also have plain but
clean shoestring-to-budget-priced rooms. Many coffee shops for Chinese eats are
concentrated around the main street and Jalan Cinema, and there's food to go from
the stalls of the Pasar Rakyat food centre on Jln Merpati. The **Boon Kee Restaurant**
(*Jln Newshop*) gets good reports for a more substantial meal.

GUNUNG MULU NATIONAL PARK

Deep in the northern Sarawak interior is an isolated area of rivers and mountains, bordered on the eastern side by the Tama Abu Range – which faces Kalimantan's Apo Duat Range across the Indonesian–Malaysian border. The World Heritage Site of Gunung Mulu National Park is part of a corridor of lowland rainforest criss-crossed by rivers and streams and surrounded by peaks and pinnacles. The 53,000ha park is overseen by three mountains – Gunung Mulu, Gunung Api and Gunung Benarat – and contains the largest limestone cave system in the world, formed from thousands of years of erosion. Since a National Geographic expedition started in 1977, over 300km of caves have been surveyed, though it is believed that there could be at least twice as many more. Only four of the 25 caves and passages discovered are open to the public.

Within the park, there are 17 different habitat types, including primary lowland rainforest, limestone forest, alluvial forest, tropical heath forest, peat swamp and riparian forest. Between altitudes of 35m and 2,375m, the park contains a staggering 3,500 plant species, 4,000 types of fungi, 80 mammals, 270 birds, 130 reptiles and amphibians, 50 fish types and 2,000 different bugs, beetles and butterflies. Like Gunung Kinabalu National Park it's an entomologists dream, with hundreds of distinctive insect species including stick insects (*Phasmids*), camouflaged crawlies and butterflies (including *Trogonoptera brookiana* – Brooke's birdwing butterfly).

Indigenous people were the first naturalists of the region. Penan and Berawan people lived in the area for centuries, hunting and gathering. In the 1920s a Berawan rhino hunter, Tama Nilong, discovered the southwest ridge of Gunung Mulu and opened the way for its successful ascent. Nilong led South Pole explorer Lord Shackleton and an Oxford University expedition to the summit in 1932. The National Geographic Society subsequently lobbied for the creation of a national park there in 1976 – the 544km² area was opened to visitors in 1985. Listed as a World Heritage Site in December 2000, this is one UNESCO nature site where the negative effects are on show just as much as positive ones. Threats to the environment other than logging include pollution from locals, tourist hordes and slack tour companies.

GETTING THERE

By air MASWings operates a couple of flights daily, in both directions, between Miri and Mulu (30 minutes), and once-a-day flights between Kota Kinabalu and Mulu (50 minutes direct flight or 2¼ hours via Miri). The Miri–Mulu prices start at 79MYR, Kota Kinabalu to Mulu from 149MYR. Check schedules at www.maswings.com.my/flights.html.

By boat The adventurous and potentially tedious day-long trip starts with taking a bus or taxi to Kuala Baram (15km north of Miri, taxi 40MYR). Express boats leave here hourly from 07.30 to Marudi, along the Baram River. The boats operated by Tinjar Express take 2½–3 hours and tickets cost 30MYR. From Marudi, another boat will take you to Long Terawan – a four-hour journey costing 20MYR. From there you must charter a longboat to take you up the Sungai Tutoh river to the park. This journey is unreliable, with boats between Marudi and Long Terawan cancelled at short notice due to water levels or inadequate passenger numbers. The prohibitive cost of private longboat hire (as much as 400MYR for a 30–60-minute trip) excludes this option for most travellers.

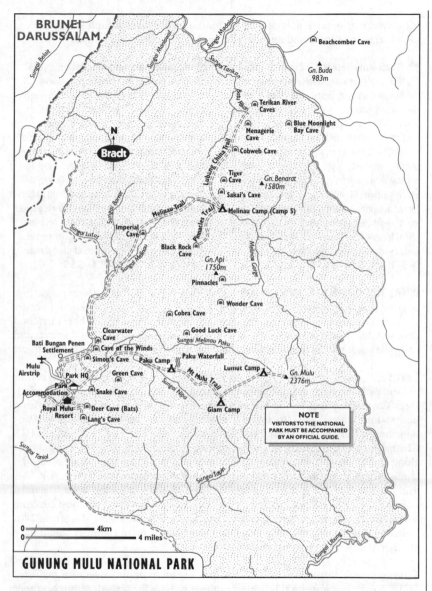

GUNUNG MULU NATIONAL PARK

Map labels:

BRUNEI DARUSSALAM

N
Bradt

Sungai Belait
Sungai Mandovai
Sungai Madalam
Sungai Tarikan
Batu Rikan

Beachcomber Cave
Gn. Buda 983m

Terikan River Caves
Menagerie Cave
Blue Moonlight Bay Cave
Cobweb Cave
Lubang China Trail
Tiger Cave
Gn. Benarat 1580m
Sakai's Cave
Melinau Camp (Camp 5)
Melinau Trail
Pinnacles Trail
Sungai Borar
Imperial Cave
Sungai Lutut
Sungai Melinau
Black Rock Cave
Gn. Api 1750m
Melinau Gorge
Pinnacles
Wonder Cave
Cobra Cave
Clearwater Cave
Good Luck Cave
Bati Bungan Penen Settlement
Cave of the Winds
Sungai Melinau Paku
Mulu Airstrip
Simon's Cave
Paku Camp
Paku Waterfall
Park HQ
Green Cave
Mt Mulu Trail
Lumut Camp
Gn. Mulu 2376m
Park Accommodation
Snake Cave
Sungai Npa
Royal Mulu Resort
Deer Cave (Bats)
Lang's Cave
Giam Camp
Sungai Taniol
Sungai Tayn
Sungai Ubung

NOTE
VISITORS TO THE NATIONAL PARK MUST BE ACCOMPANIED BY AN OFFICIAL GUIDE.

0 — 4km
0 — 4 miles

OTHER PRACTICALITIES On arrival, head to the National Park HQ (⊕ 08.00–17.00 daily) for visitor registration and payment of **entrance fees**. Single entry per adult is 10MYR. Students, senior citizens and disabled persons get 50% off and children aged six and under go free. The park has no ATM or credit card facilities so you must carry cash. Transport within the park is by longboat, van or foot, with all but the national park lodgings 3km from park HQ.

🏠 **WHERE TO STAY AND EAT** There are limited accommodation choices in the Gunung Mulu Park. This is good news for nature, but the higher end, privately run accommodation in particular falls short on standards relative to price. Take any extras you may require, as shopping for food or other items is limited and there is no self-catering accommodation, so you are captive to the food on offer.

🏠 **Royal Mulu Resort** (188 rooms) ☎085 790100; e sales@royalmuluresort.com; www. royalmuluresort.com. Despite the grand name, these wood-panelled chalets are rather dated & unstylish. Average buffet & menu food. Drink & food prices at the Wildlife Restaurant (⏰ 07.00–23.00) are relatively high, as are other costs (internet etc). If you don't like the sound of karaoke in the jungle, this might not be for you. It's a 3km (30–40min walk) to the park. Lots of activities & traditional treatments at the spa. 2-night packages include FB. A basic 'village' café is located 50m away – just over the entry bridge – offering noodles & Western breakfasts for 5–10MYR. **$$$–$$$$**

🏠 **National park accommodation** ☎085 792301; e enquiries@mulupark.com; www. mulupark.com. By far the best for location – at the entrance of the park. The proximity to trailheads eliminates extra costs for longboat transfers. Various longhouse & chalet rooms, double/single en-suite bathroom, AC or fans. The most upmarket choice is the 'Garden Bungalow Rooms', sleeping up to 3, with tasteful décor, & pleasant edge-of-the-forest setting. The 21-bed hostel dorm has fans & bed linen (but not towels) & lockers for luggage. It costs 40MYR pp including breakfast. Check-in at 14.00, check-out at 10.00. Reservation essential. Cheap basic local & Western food at the open-air Café Mulu (⏰ 07.30–21.00). **$–$$$**

WHAT TO DO AND SEE It's worth taking one cave trip as well as a longer jungle trek or river safari to experience the incredibly beautiful forest world. Freedom to enjoy the park in a more independent manner is difficult due to a highly bureaucratised park service. I found that the best way to enjoy the area was to see past the caves and enjoy the rainforest that houses them, and the traditional people who have lived there.

Caves All caves are reached along solid timber-plank walks, and have eco-lit cement paths through them. The 3km duckboard walk through rainforest to reach **Deer Cave** and neighbouring **Lang's Cave** is a lovely experience in itself, passing peat swamp, alluvial flats, streams and some spectacular limestone outcrops. Two-hour return treks led by park guides leave daily at 13.45 and 14.30 from park HQ. **Clearwater Cave** and **Cave of the Winds** are reached from park HQ by longboat along the Melinau River in about 15 minutes (27MYR pp return), or along the almost 4km Moonmilk Walk that hugs the riverbanks much of the way. Park guides lead tours to the Cave of the Winds at 09.45 and 10.30 from the entrance. The most impressive for stalactites and other formations is Lang's Cave, but the most amazing overall for its size and cavernous pit is Deer Cave, Gua Rusa. At a staggering 2km in length it is the largest cave passage in the world. Its main chamber would have enough room for five St Paul's cathedrals!

Caving Speak with the park HQ or a tour organiser about adventure caving at Mulu. A park brochure on this subject outlines eight cave escapades from beginner to advanced level, lasting from 45 minutes to ten hours. Some popular caves have been fitted with fixed ropes on the short descents and traverses, but you are advised to bring your own equipment for anything beyond that. The **Sarawak Chamber** – on the way to Gunung Api – is compared to an aircraft hanger that would house 40 Boeing 747s. The day trip starts at 07.30, following the Summit Trail for about three hours.

Trekking There's no doubt that trekking – away from the headquarters and hotels – is the best way to feel the wonder of the park's nature and to get up close to the wildlife. There are many treks in the park, some that require a guide and some that can be done independently. Inform park officers before you do an unguided walk as they are aware of weather conditions, including dangerously high water levels. Unguided treks include the four-hour **Paku Waterfall** through rainforest to a good swimming spot and the three-hour **Long Lansat River Walk** (180MYR for the longboat return transfer, 3 people minimum). The day walk to 'Camp 1' (guided) follows part of the **Mulu Summit Trail** and concludes at one of the camps used during the 1977 Royal Geographical Society expedition. The **summit** (guided) trek to the top of solitary-standing **Gunung Mulu** (2,376m) – Sarawak's second-highest peak – is a 24km climb, over two to three nights with lodgings in forest huts with basic cooking facilities (park guide costs 1,000MYR for 1–5 people). *En route* to Gunung Api (1,750m) the **Pinnacles** is a 50m-high series of razor-shaped limestone outcrops, pointing skyward and interlinked with several caves. This tough (and guided) climb requires at least one overnight stay at Melinau Camp ('Camp 5'). Most people will stay two nights; it depends on fitness levels. The first day's trekking takes in visits to a couple of Mulu's caves. Lodgings consist of sleeping mats in five open rooms, a self-catering kitchen (cooking equipment and utensils provided) and a dining room. You have to carry all of your own food, a sleeping bag and appropriate clothing. It costs 250–800MYR, depending on numbers. Accommodation costs 22MYR per person per night; park guide 400MYR for one to five people; longboat return 370MYR for a group of one to four.

The popular tour-operated **Headhunters' Trail** combines 15km of deep jungle trekking over two days with longboat journeys and an optional longhouse stay, along a route taken by Kayan headhunting parties who paddled up the Melinau River to Melinau Gorge before launching raids against the people of the Limbang area. This trip can also be done from Limbang to Mulu Park HQ. Another option is to add a night and include the Pinnacles climb (from Camp 5) in the trip.

Longboat safaris A couple of trips visit Penan settlements along the Sungai Tutoh and Sungai Melinau rivers. These are very prescriptive though, so if you prefer to explore more independently then take your own day trip on the rivers.

KELABIT HIGHLANDS

The isolation of the Kelabit Highlands did not save them from the snowballing appropriation of Sarawak territory by Rajah Brooke, and his corps claimed it in 1911. It was, however, one of the only Bornean regions that didn't fall into Japanese hands during World War II. Allied troops led by Tom Harrisson, the future curator of the Sarawak Museum in Kuching, had bases in the area. During the Konfrontasi with Indonesian militants in the 1960s, people from settlements near the Indonesian border fled further inland and **Bario** came into existence. Geographical isolation continued to play a big hand in shaping its culture – there was very little in the way of telecommunications or reliable power sources until early 2000. There are still no paved roads. All this means a great sense of remoteness and peace for the highland trekker or visitor. The rounded, velvet upholstered peaks fall off to valleys of temperate crops – Bario rice, oranges, pineapples, highland coffee and sugar cane – between villages and longhouse settlements of Kelabit, Kenyah, Kayan and Penan peoples. Hopefully the area will retain its secluded charm with the onset of tourism and technology.

GETTING THERE AND AWAY MASWings (*www.maswings.com.my/flights.html*) have near-daily flights both ways between Miri and Bario, and Miri and Ba'kelalan. The hours vary day by day; some Bario flights are via Marudi and some Ba'kelalan flights via Lawas. Approximate one-way fares for the one-hour flight are 100MYR. Check full updated schedules and fares on the website.

🏠 **WHERE TO STAY/EAT** A good website with listings and online booking for several lodges and homestays (and guides) is www.ebario.com; visit it for details and photos. All the lodgings are cheap: some offer packages of 50MYR a day for airport transfer, bed and three meals – 30–40MYR extra for a guide; others are rooms only for about 20MYR per person with lots of options for guided activities. The most recommended are **Nancy Harris Homestay** (*10 rooms*; e *nancyharrissy@yahoo.com*) and **De Plateau Lodge** (*8 rooms*; e, *munney_bala@kelabit.net*) with Munney and Mille Bala and their four children. **Leminan Lodge** (*7 rooms*; e *jtarawe@bario.com*) is in Bario town, with satellite television, back-up solar power and electricity from 18.00 to 23.00.

OTHER PRACTICALITIES

Climate At 1,000m above sea level, average day temperatures are usually between 21 and 26°C, whereas nights can be as cool as 15°C. Walking conditions can be muddy, with many leeches, and you need good shoes and protective clothing, including leech socks.

Electricity and communications The town runs on a diesel generator boosted by solar power. A UNESCO-backed engineering project has helped set up the **E-Bario Telecentre** – a cyber café – which is open about three days a week, with phones and internet provided via solar-powered VSAT.

Shops Bario's town centre has just a row of small bazaars, coffee shops and grocery stores. Sundries are more expensive because everything is flown in.

WHAT TO SEE AND DO

Treks and walks Most of the Bario highland treks follow the network of muddy trails and dirt roads that link the community longhouses and villages, so expect to share the trails with locals on foot and on bike, and the odd buffalo. The treks take in the Bario valley area, longhouse settlements, local markets, rice paddy and some primary and secondary rainforest. Organised trips of four to seven days from Miri stay in longhouses and jungle camps but you can also organise your guide and accommodation independently in either Bario or Ba'kelalan.

Note that women travellers are said to be in safe hands in Bario, where there is not the same problem with alcohol among guides as in Belaga region. Walks include Bario to Pa Ukat and Pa Lungan, four to five hours each way with a stay at the Pa Lungan longhouse. The hardy trek to the small settlement of Ba'Kelalan is two days – some trails go via Pa Rupai in Kalimantan.

Mountaineering The Kelabit Highlands make for some of the most challenging non-national park climbing in Borneo – the region is flanked by Sarawak's highest mountain, Gunung Murud (2,423m) – the five- to six-hour trail goes from Bario through a couple of longhouse settlements. Considered more tricky is Batu Lawi (2,043m).

LIMBANG AND LAWAS

Separated by a section of Brunei, Limbang Division's two main towns are typical border-town thoroughfares – both have track records as small-scale sin-city destinations, full of sleazy pubs, massage parlours and prostitution – at the centre of timber, agricultural and oil palm industries. It is rare to hear Sarawak Tourism allude to these two towns, other than as transit points. Lawas sits the prettier, bound by forest and river on one side and Brunei Bay to the northwest.

GETTING THERE

By air MASWings operates some three to four daily flights from both Limbang and Lawas to Miri as well as other weekly flights. There are flights a couple of times a week from Lawas to Kota Kinabalu and vice versa. Single journey prices start at 78MYR. Check prices and updates at www.maswings.com.my/flights.html.

By car Lawas and Limbang are near-border checkpoints with Brunei and Lawas about 20km to the Merapok-Sindumin checkpoint into Sabah. Limbang is two hours' drive from Miri.

By bus Express buses run to Brunei, Kota Kinabalu and Miri.

WHERE TO STAY If you're passing through Limbang, the most recommended lodging is the **Purnama Hotel** (*Jln Buangsiol;* \ *085 216700;* **$**) where a de luxe room costs just 3MYR more than a standard room. In Lawas, **Mega Inn** (*15 rooms; 1 Tingkat, Lot 152, Jln Muhibbah;* \ *085 283888*) has rooms with air conditioning, satellite television, fridge and bathroom.

Appendix 1

LANGUAGE

A good dictionary for reference is the *Periplus Pocket Malay Dictionary* (available online from www.peripluspublishinggroup.com for about €5). Berlian are another publisher (Malaysian) of good Bahasa Melayu–Bahasa Inggeris dictionaries.

Teach yourself CD kits are much harder to come by for Malay than for Indonesian language, but there is a noticeable bolstering under way of Malay learning tools for foreigners. Two courses I have used in the past are *Colloquial Malay: The Complete Course for Beginners* by Zaharah Othman and Sutanto Atnosumarto, and Hodder Education's *Complete Malay (Bahasa Malaysia)* by Christopher Byrnes and Tam Lye Suan with Eva Nyimas as narrator.

Routledge's original *Colloquial Malay* published in 1995 can still be found in many libraries. I am delighted to learn that it will finally re-emerge as a second edition in April 2012 – the 256-page textbook and two 60-minute CDs still accompanied by Zaharah Othman (*www.routledge.com*). The audio combines dialogues, readings and grammar points, using authentic Malay voices on top of the soft, international tones of Othman.

The meaty 400-page tome plus CDs of the 2010 edition of *Complete Malay* (*www. hoddereducation.co.uk*) is widely available. Eva Nyimas's accent-less English conceals her Indonesian nationality, but the audio relies on distinctive Malay accents to deliver language units clustered into themes from 'Eating Out' to 'Changing Money'. The interaction between the book and the audio dialogues is very useful, and a constant reminder that the two elements are there to be used together. At times, there appear to be large sections of dialogue with insufficient grammar and vocabulary explanations. That is because the effectiveness of the audio learning relies on you doing lots of textbook homework.

PRONUNCIATION Vowels differ from English pronunciation but words are relatively phonetic and consistent. All vowel sounds are short. Consonants are mostly the same as English, with a couple of exceptions.

a	*apa* (how, what) first a as in father; at the end of a word as in again
e	there are two e sounds, *empat* (four), a low sound like a in about and *mereka* (they/their), a high sound as in met
h	*apa kabah* (how are you?) the h, says Hodder's author, is a 'puff of air'
i	*nasi* (rice) 'ee' sound as in Bali
k	*tuak* (rice wine) at end of word, only just pronounced
o	*orang* (human being) as in not
u	*juga* (also) like oo in too but short
sy	sounds like sh as in shoot (also applies to English words used widely in Malaysia, eg: 'fashion' is spelt *fesyen* to bring it in line with standard Malay pronunciation)
c	ch as in chain/cheese

sy	sh as in shut
ng	sounds like ny – banyan/oignon
t	*selamat* (greeting) barely pronounced at end of word

BASIC GRAMMAR

- There is no verb 'to be' in Malaysian. The word saya means 'I', 'me' and 'my'.
- There is also no word for 'is' in Malay, so for example *apa nama anda* ('What is your name?') literally means 'What name you?'
- There are no gender pronouns – *dia* means both he and she
- Bahasa Malaysia – commonly referred to as BM – is an *agglutinative* language – a word can be changed simply by adding various prefixes and suffixes to root words, both nouns and verbs. Eg: makan is the verb to eat, and can become memakan – eating/is eating … dimakan (eaten), and the noun makanan – food.
- Plurals are formed by repetition though sometimes with slight variations: *rumah-rumah* (houses) from *rumah* (house) and *gunung-gunang* (mountains) from *gunung* (mountain)

VOCABULARY
Greetings

English	Malay	English	Malay
Hello	*hello*	Good evening	*selamat petang*
Goodbye	*selamat tinggal*	Welcome	*selamat dating*
Good morning	*selamat pagi*	See you again	*jumpa lagi*
Good afternoon	*selamat tengahari*	(literally 'meet again')	

Basic vocabulary

English	Malay	English	Malay
Please	*tolong*	I am from England	*saya datang dari England*
Thank you	*terima kasih*		
You are welcome	*sama sama*	How are you?	*apa khabar?*
I am fine	*khabar baik terima*	I am fine	*khabar baik terima kasih,* or simply *baik*
yes	*ya*		
no	*tidak* – also means 'not'	Do you understand?	*faham anda?*
	Tak is an informal abbreviation	I don't understand	*saya tidak faham*
		Excuse me	*maafkan saya*
What is your name?	*apa nama anda?*	you	*anda*
My name is (eg: Tamara)	*nama saya/ saya Tamara*	we/us/our	*kita*
		they/their	*mereka*
Where are you from?	*kamu datang dari mana?*	Where is the toilet?	*tandas di mana?*

Questions

English	Malay	English	Malay
How?	*bagaimana?*	Who?	*siapa?*
What?	*apa?*	How much?	*berapa?*
Where?	*di mana?*	How long?/	*berapa lama?*
What is it/this?	*apa ini?*	How long will it take?	*berapa lama?*
Which?	*yang mana?*		
When? (also 'if')	*bila?*	How far?	*berapa jauh?*
Why?	*mengapa?* or *apa sebab?*		

Numbers

English	Malay	English	Malay
one	*satu*	11	*sebelas*
two	*dua*	12	*dua belas*
three	*tiga*	13	*tiga belas* etc
four	*empat*	20	*dua puluh*
five	*lima*	21	*dua puluh satu* etc
six	*enam*	30	*tiga puluh* etc
seven	*tujuh*	99	*sembilan puluh*
eight	*lapan*		*sembilan*
nine	*sembilan*	100	*seratus*
ten	*sepuluh*	1,000	*seribu*

Time

English	Malay	English	Malay
What time is it?	*pukul berapa sekarang?*	tomorrow	*esok*
It is…am/pm	*Sekarang pukul… pagi/ malam*	yesterday	*semalam* or *kelmarin*
		morning	*pagi*
eg: it is 7am/7pm	*Sekarang pukul tujuh pagi/ tujuh malam*	evening	*waktu malam/petang*
		day	*hari*
today	*hari ini*	month	*bulan*
tonight	*malam ini*		

Days of the week

Monday	*Isnin*	Friday	*Jumaat*
Tuesday	*Selasa*	Saturday	*Sabtu*
Wednesday	*Rabu*	Sunday	*Ahad*
Thursday	*Khamis*		

Months

January	*Januari*	July	*Julai*
February	*Februari*	August	*Ogos*
March	*Mac*	September	*September*
April	*April*	October	*Oktober*
May	*Mei*	November	*November*
June	*Jun*	December	*Disember*

Public transport

English	Malay	English	Malay
in 30 minutes	*dalam masa 30 minit*	tour bus	*bas persiaran*
car	*kereta*	bus station	*stesen* or
taxi	*teksi*		*perhentian bas*
minibus	*bas mini*	airport	*lapangan terbang*
boat	*perahu*	fare	*tambang*

Directions

English	Malay	English	Malay
to	*ke*	to the left	*kiri*
from	*dari*	to the right	*kanan*
here	*sini*	north	*utara*
there	*sana*	south	*selatan*

English	Malay	English	Malay
Can you help me?	*bolehkah anda tolong saya?*	east	*timur*
Where is…?	*di manakah…?*	west	*barat*
Where would you like to go?	*anda hendak ke mana?*	behind	*di belakang*
		in front of you	*di hadapan anda*
I would like to go...	*saya hendak ke...*	straight	*ke hadapan*
Can you give me the address of…?	*bolehkah kamu beri saya alamat untuk...?*	near	*dekat*
		far	*jauh*
How far is it from here?	*berapakah jauhnya dari sini?*		

Road signs

English	Malay	English	Malay
stop	*berhenti*	exit	*keluar*
toll	*tol*	street	*jalan*
enter	*masuk*		

Other signs

English	Malay	English	Malay
open	*buka* or *terbuka*	level	*aras*
closed	*tutup*	toilets	*tandas*
floor	*tingkat*	danger	*bahaya*

Food

English	Malay	English	Malay
food	*makanan*	Do you have any vegetarian dishes?	*anda ada makanan vegetarian* or *anda ada makanan sayu sayuran?*
eat	*makan*		
drink	*minum* (v), *minuman* (n)		
menu	*menu*		
drinks price list	*harga minuman*	Please can I have…?	*boleh saya …?*
food price list	*harga makanan*	want	*mahu*
I am a vegetarian	*saya vegetarian*	Please bring the bill	*tolong bawa/ bawakan bil*
don't want	*tak mahu*		
a lot/plenty/many	*banyak*	hot (temperature)	*panas*
a little	*sedikit*	hot (spicy)	*pedas*
more	*lebih banyak labi*	cold	*sejuk*
less	*kurang*	sweet	*manis*
without	*tanpa*	sour	*masam*
What would you like to drink/eat?	*anda hendak minum apa/makan apa?*		

Basics

English	Malay	English	Malay
bread	*roti*	salt	*garam*
cheese	*keju*	pepper	*lada*
rice	*nasi*	sugar	*gula*
noodles	*mee*	cake	*kuih* or *kueh*
oil	*minyak*	curry	*kari*
sago	*sagu*		

Fruit

English	Malay	English	Malay
fruit	*buah*	mango	*buah mangga*
apples	*epal*	mangosteen	*buah manggis*

coconut	*kelapa*	oranges	*limau manis*
bananas	*pisang*	lime	*kapur limau nipis*
lemon	*limau* or *lemon*		

Vegetables

mixed vegetables	*sayur campur*	broccoli	*brokoli*
garlic	*bawang putih*	potato	*ubi kentang*
onion	*bawang*	yam	*ubi keladi*
carrot	*lobak merah*	eggplant	*terung*
cabbage	*kubis*		

Fish

fish	*ikan*	prawns/shrimp	*udang*

Meat

beef	*daging lembu*	pork	*daging babi*
chicken	*daging ayam*		

Condiments

chilli	*cabai*	chilli paste	*sambal*
shrimp paste	*sambal belacan*	sauce	*sos*

Drinks

water	*air*	alcohol	*minuman keras* or *alkohol*
fruit juice	*jus*		
coffee	*kopi*	wine	*wain*
tea	*teh*	rice wine	*tuak*
milk	*susu*	beer	*bir minuman*

Shopping

English	Malay	English	Malay
I'd like to buy...	*saya hendak beli...*	It's too expensive	*mahal*
How much is it?	*berapa harga ini?*	cheap	*murah*
Do you have...?	*anda ada...?*	more	*lebih lagi*
I'm just looking	*saya pandang*	less	*kurang*
Can you give it to me a bit cheaper?	*Boleh bagi saya murah sikit?*	rural market	*tamu*
		night market	*pasar malan*
Market	*pasar*		

Communications

English	Malay	English	Malay
I am looking for...	*saya ingin mencari...*	post office	*pos*
I wish to go to ...	*saya ingin pergi ke ...*	telephone	*telefon*
bank	*bank*	mobile phone	*hand phone* (HP)

Emergency

English	Malay	English	Malay
Help!	*tolong!*	police	*polis*
I'm lost	*saya hilang*	fire	*api*
Leave me alone	*tinggalkan saya sendirian*	ambulance	*ambulans*

NB If you are trying to get rid of peddlers, it suffices to say *tak mahu*, meaning 'I don't want it'.

English	Malay
hospital	*hospital*
doctor	*doktor*
I am ill/in pain	*saya sakit*
thief	*pencuri*

Health/Medical

English	Malay
prescription	*preskripsi*
medicine	*ubat*
pharmacy	*farmasi*
painkiller	*ubat sakit*
antibiotics	*antibiotik*
antiseptic	*antiseptik*
I am ill	*saya sakit*
I have ...	*sakit ...*
diarrhoea	*cirit* or *cirit-birit*
allergic	*alergi*

English	Malay
nausea	*rasa hendak muntah* or *rasa mual*
headache	*(sakit) kepala*
stomach ache	*(sakit) perut*
fever	*demam*
asthma	*asma*
epilepsy	*epilepsi*
diabetes	*diabetes* or *kencing manis*

Other useful words

English	Malay
my	*saya punya*
mine	*kepunyaan saya*
yours	*kepunyaanmu* or *kepunyaan tuan*
white person	*orang putih*
and/but	*dan/tetapi*

English	Malay
forest	*hutan* or *rimba*
beach	*pantai*
shop	*kedai*
room	*bilik*
island	*pulau*
great! beautiful, fine	*bagus!*

Appendix 2

FURTHER INFORMATION

BOOKS
General history/reference

Bellwood, P *Prehistory of the Indo-Malaysian Archipelago* Academic Press, 1986. 'Landmark work in southeast Asian archeology and prehistory'. Peter Bellwood is Professor of Archaeology at the School of Archaeology and Anthropology, Australian National University.

Payne, R *The White Rajahs of Sarawak* Oxford University Press, 1960.

Runciman, S *The White Rajahs: A History of Sarawak from 1841 to 1946* Cambridge University Press, 1960.

Saunders, G E *A History of Brunei* Routledge, 2002.

Turnbull, M C A *A History of Malaysia, Singapore and Brunei* Allen & Unwin, Australia, 1989. Revised sub-edition.

Wallace, A R *The Malay Archipelago: The Land of the Orang-Utan and the Bird of Paradise. A Narrative of Travel, with Studies of Man and Nature*. London, 1869. Newer editions by various publishers. The legendary Alfred Russell Wallace's defining work from his travels around the Malay Archipelago. Stanfords Books (*www.stanfords.co.uk*) have recently republished this as part of their Travel Classics series.

Historic memoirs/biographies

Brooke, C *Ten Years in Sarawak* London, 1866. Available online as a Google book (*http://books.google.com/books?id=61oLAAAAIAAJ&printsec=frontcover&dq=Charles+Brooke*).

Brooke, Ranee M *My Life in Sarawak* Oxford University Press, Singapore, 1913 (reprint 1986).

Brooke, Ranee S *Sylvia of Sarawak: An Autobiography* Hutchinson, 1936, and *Queen of the Headhunters* Oxford University Press, London 1970. The two-volume autobiography of the last Ranee of Sarawak.

Eade, P *Sylvia, Queen of the Headhunters: An Outrageous Woman and Her Lost Kingdom* Weidenfeld & Nicolson, 2007. A biography of Lady Sylvia Brooke.

Keith, A N *White Man Returns* Little Brown and Company, Boston, 1951.

Keith, A N *Three Came Home* Mermaid Books, London, 1955.

Keith, A N *Land Below the Wind* Michael Joseph, London, 1958.

Reece, R H W *The Name of Brooke: The End of White Rajah Rule in Sarawak* Oxford University Press, South East Asia, 1982.

Culture

Ave, J B and King, V T *People of the Weeping Forest: Tradition and Change in Borneo* Leiden, National Museum of Ethnology, 1986. An informative introduction to the region's contemporary cultures.

Davis, W *Nomads of the Dawn: The Penan of the Borneo Rainforest* Pomegranate, 1995. Wade Davis is an anthropologist/ethnobotanist.

Geddes, W R *Nine Dayak Nights* Oxford University Press, 1985. Anthropologist Geddes spent two years in a remote inland village of Sarawak after World War II.

Hose, C and McDougall, W *The Pagan Tribes of Borneo* 1912 (reprinted Oxford University Press, USA 1993). Charles Hose spent 24 years as a civil officer under James Brooke's rajah-ship – mostly in Baram but also in Rejang District – and McDougall was part of the Cambridge anthropological expedition, in Baram area, in 1898. The magnum opus of ethnology can be read as an e-book.

Jones, L V *The Population of Borneo: A Study of the Peoples of Sarawak, Sabah and Brunei;* Athlone Press, 1966.

King, V T *The Peoples of Borneo* Blackwell, 1993. A pace-setting anthropological history.

Lasimbang, R and Moo-Tan, S (eds) *An Introduction to the Traditional Costumes of Sabah* Natural History Publications in association with Department of Sabah Museum, 1997

Munan, H *Beads of Borneo* Editions Didier Millet, Singapore, 2005

Sather, C *The Bajau Laut: Adaptation, History and Fate in a Maritime Fishing Society of South-eastern Sabah* (South-East Asian Social Science Monographs) Oxford University Press, 1997. Interesting cultural and historic portrait of the Bajau Laut peoples.

Travel literature

Hansen, E *Stranger in the Forest: On Foot Across Borneo* 1988, reprinted in 2001 by Methuen, London/Vintage Books, USA. The best classic travel literature on Borneo – an account of Hansen's 4,000km of tripping by foot across Borneo, in the company of Penan hunter-gatherers in 1976.

Hansen, E *Orchid Fever: A Horticultural Tale of Love, Lust and Lunacy* Vintage Books, 2001. Hansen brings his wit to our fascination with orchids, with some of the action set in Borneo.

Hatt, J *The Tropical Traveller: An Essential Guide to Travel in Hot Climates* Penguin Travel Library, London, 1982. Good background on travel in sticky places.

Maugham, S *Borneo Stories* Heinemann Educational Books, Kuala Lumpur, 1976. A collection of stories about expatriate Englishmen and women in exotic settings. Also included in his *Collected Short Stories.*

Munan, H *Culture Shock! A Guide to Customs and Etiquette, Borneo* Times Books International, Singapore, 1988 (revised 1992, reprinted 1996). A personal, engaging account of expat life in Borneo, social etiquette, customs and insider views on subjects as varied as 'Do You Speak Bahasa?', 'Bornean Social Circles' and 'Lo! The Cute Native'. The author was born in Switzerland, brought up in New Zealand and moved to Sarawak in 1965 where she continues to work as a journalist and cultural historian.

O'Hanlon, R *Into the Heart of Borneo* Salamander Press, Edinburgh, 1984. An account of a journey made in 1983 into the mountains of Batu Tiban on the Sarawak–West Kalimantan border, with James Fenton.

St John, S *Life in the Forests of the Far East* Elder Smith, London, 1862.

St John, S *Thirteen Years of Spencer St John's Travels in North and Western Borneo* Elder Smith, London, 1862.

Wassner, J *Espresso with the Headhunters: A Journey Through the Jungles of Borneo* Summersdale, Australia, 2001. A light but personal account of travels in Sarawak, by a Sydney advertising executive turned writer.

Natural history If your interests lie in flora and the fauna, it's worth checking the list of titles published by Sabah-based **Natural History Publications.** The **Sabah Society** (*Kota Kinabalu;* ✆ *088 250443; www.sabahsociety.com*), responsible for the establishment of the Sabah Museum and Sabah Parks, is an NGO with natural heritage at its heart, and brings together a very interesting circle of local experts – a good source of information.

ARBEC *ASEAN Review of Biodiversity and Environmental Conservation* Available online at www.arbec.com.my. Web journal published by MIMCED in conjunction with the Malaysian University of Science and Technology.

Beaman, J H, Anderson, C and Beaman, R S *The Plants of Mount Kinabalu* Natural History Publications, Borneo, 2001. Fourth volume in a series with sections on the history of plant collecting on Mount Kinabalu and a biographical sketch of two of the most important collectors, Mary Strong and Joseph Clemens. Analysis and indexes of collections, and list of plants. Information on each species on habitat, elevation range, literature and specimens upon which the study is based.

Cranbrook, Earl of (ed) *Wonders of Nature in Southeast Asia* Oxford University Press, 1997. Compilation of excerpts from famous and obscure works by the great explorers, with comments by Cranbrook.

Davidson, G *A Photographic Guide to the Birds of Borneo* New Holland, 4th edition, 2009. Illustrated pocket field guide of 250 species found in Borneo.

Francis, C M *Pocket Guide to the Birds of Borneo* Sabah Society, 1984. Very popular, easy-to-use pocket guide for field reference.

Garbutt, N and Prudente, C *Wild Borneo: The Wildlife and Scenery of Sabah, Sarawak, Brunei and Kalimantan* New Holland, 2006. Illustrated book with 250 colour photographs, preface by Sir David Attenborough and accompanying essays on Borneo's fauna and flora and conservation (including a chapter on the Heart of Borneo project). Published in association with WWF.

Inger, R F and Stuebing, R B *A Field Guide to the Frogs of Borneo* Natural History Publications, Malaysia, 1997.

Myers, S *Birds of Borneo: Brunei, Sabah, Sarawak, and Kalimantan* Princeton Field Guides, 2009 (published in UK by New Holland, 2009). Beautifully illustrated and painstakingly researched book with over 1,500 colour illustrations. A comprehensive field guide to 630 species accompanied by distribution maps, yet not overly cumbersome to carry on a birding trip.

Nais, J *Rafflesia of the World* Natural History Publications, 2001. By the assistant director of Sabah Parks. Can be ordered through Royal Botanic Gardens, Kew Books (*www.kewbooks.com*).

Payne, J and Cubitt, G; *Wild Malaysia: The Wildlife and Scenery of Peninsular Malaysia, Sarawak, and Sabah* 2nd edition, New Holland, 1999. Another coffee-table book with photographs of Malaysian wildlife and natural history.

Smythies, B E *The Birds of Borneo* 4th edition, Natural History Publications, Borneo, 2000. Essential reference on Borneo ornithology; still considered by many to be the most comprehensive guide.

Tweedie, M W F *Malayan Animal Life* (*and the Common Birds of the Malay Peninsula*) University of Chicago Press, 1954.

Whitehead, J *The Exploration of Mount Kina Balu, North Borneo* Graham Brash, 1993. Revised edition of the classic work published in 1893. Whitehead was the first European to reach the summit of Mount Kinabalu in 1888. The first edition included hand-coloured plates and is now rare and valuable.

Whitmore, T C *An Introduction to Tropical Rain Forests* 2nd edition, Oxford University Press, 1998. Tim Whitmore was a tropical botanist at the Geology Department of the University of Cambridge until his death in 2002. He produced several major reference works on tropical rainforests – see also *Tropical Rainforests of the Far East* Clarendon Press, 1984 and *Palms of Malaya: White Lotus* White Lotus Co Ltd, 2nd edition, 1998.

Conservation

Bevis, W *Borneo Log: The Struggle for Sarawak's Forests* University of Washington Press, 1995. An account of travels in Sarawak; travel narrative and environmental observation.

Harrison, B *Orang-utan* Collins, 1962.

Health

Wilson-Howarth, Dr J, and Ellis, Dr M *Your Child Abroad: A Travel Health Guide* Bradt Travel Guides, 2005

Wilson-Howarth, Dr J *Bugs, Bites & Bowels* Cadogan, 2006

WEBSITES

www.brunei.gov.bn Brunei government
www.gov.my Malaysian government
www.sabah.gov.my Sabah State government
www.sarawak.gov.my Sarawak State government

OTHER SOURCES OF INFORMATION

Institute of East Asian Studies (*Universiti Malaysia, Sarawak;* e *aroshima@ieas. unimas.my; www.ieas.unimas.my*) Publishes many books on historical and contemporary culture in Borneo, anthropology and Dayak society. Titles include: *Mapping the Peoples of Sarawak; The Malay Population of Sarawak; Suket: Penan Folk Stories; Changing Borders and Identities in the Kelabit Highlands;* and *Life in the Malay Kampongs of Kuching Fifty Years Ago.*

Natural History Publications (*9th Floor, Wisma Merdeka Kota Kinabalu, Sabah;* \ *088 233098;* e *chan@nhpborneo.com; www.nhpborneo.com*) A very active local publisher of nature titles by international experts in their field, headed by C L Chan. Titles include books on rafflesia and rhododendrons of Sabah, the ferns of Mount Kinabalu and the *Nepenthes* (pitcher plants) of Borneo. They have also published historical documents such as *A Botanist in Borneo: Hugh Low's Sarawak Journals from 1844–46.* Some books have been published in conjunction with the Royal Botanic Gardens, Kew, England.

WWF *Terrestrial Ecoregions of the Indo-Pacific: A Conservation Assessment.* WWF report, Island Press, December 2001. WWF reports are available online at www.panda.org. They include *Borneo's New World: Newly Discovered Species in the Heart of Borneo,* 2010.

WIN A FREE BRADT GUIDE

READER QUESTIONNAIRE

Send in your completed questionnaire and enter our monthly draw for the chance to win a Bradt guide of your choice.

To take up our special reader offer of 40% off, please visit our website at www.bradtguides.com/freeguide or answer the questions below and return to us with the order form overleaf.

(Forms may be posted or faxed to us.)

Have you used any other Bradt guides? If so, which titles? ....
....

What other publishers' travel guides do you use regularly? ....
....

Where did you buy this guidebook? ....

What was the main purpose of your trip to Borneo (or for what other reason did you read our guide)? eg: holiday/business/charity ....
....

How long did you travel for? (circle one)

weekend/long weekend   1–2 weeks   3–4 weeks   4 weeks plus

Which countries did you visit in connection with this trip?....................
....

Did you travel with a tour operator?' If so, which one? ....
....

What other destinations would you like to see covered by a Bradt guide?
....

If you could make one improvement to this guide, what would it be?
....

Age (circle relevant category) 16–25   26–45   46–60   60+

Male/Female (delete as appropriate)

Home country ....

Please send us any comments about this guide (or others on our list).
....
....
....

Bradt Travel Guides
IDC House, The Vale, Chalfont St Peter, Bucks SL9 9RZ, UK
☎ +44 (0)1753 893444 **f** +44 (0)1753 892333
e info@bradtguides.com
www.bradtguides.com

TAKE 40% OFF YOUR NEXT BRADT GUIDE!
Order Form

To take advantage of this special offer visit www.bradtguides.com/freeguide and enter our monthly giveaway, or fill in the order form below, complete the questionnaire overleaf and send it to Bradt Travel Guides by post or fax.

Please send me one copy of the following guide at 40% off the UK retail price

No	Title	Retail price	40% price
1	. . . .	. . . .	. . . .

Please send the following additional guides at full UK retail price

No	Title	Retail price	Total
. . .	. . . .	. . . .	. . . .
. . .	. . . .	. . . .	. . . .
. . .	. . . .	. . . .	. . . .

Sub total . . . .
Post & packing . . . .
(Free shipping UK, £1 per book Europe, £3 per book rest of world)
Total . . . .

Name . . . .

Address . . . .

Tel . . . .   Email . . . .

☐ I enclose a cheque for £. . . . . made payable to Bradt Travel Guides Ltd

☐ I would like to pay by credit card. Number: . . . .

    Expiry date: . . . / . . . . 3-digit security code (on reverse of card) . . . . .

    Issue no (debit cards only) . . . . .

☐ Please sign me up to Bradt's monthly enewsletter, Bradtpackers' News.

☐ I would be happy for you to use my name and comments in Bradt marketing material.

Send your order on this form, with the completed questionnaire, to:

Bradt Travel Guides
IDC House, The Vale, Chalfont St Peter, Bucks SL9 9RZ, UK
☎ +44 (0)1753 893444   f +44 (0)1753 892333
e info@bradtguides.com   www.bradtguides.com

Bradt Travel Guides
www.bradtguides.com

Africa

Access Africa: Safaris for People with Limited Mobility	£16.99
Africa Overland	£16.99
Algeria	£15.99
Angola	£17.99
Botswana	£16.99
Burkina Faso	£17.99
Cameroon	£15.99
Cape Verde	£15.99
Congo	£16.99
Eritrea	£15.99
Ethiopia	£17.99
Ethiopia Highlights	£15.99
Ghana	£15.99
Kenya Highlights	£15.99
Madagascar	£16.99
Madagascar Highlights	£15.99
Malawi	£15.99
Mali	£14.99
Mauritius, Rodrigues & Réunion	£15.99
Mozambique	£15.99
Namibia	£15.99
Niger	£14.99
Nigeria	£17.99
North Africa: Roman Coast	£15.99
Rwanda	£15.99
São Tomé & Príncipe	£14.99
Seychelles	£16.99
Sierra Leone	£16.99
Somaliland	£15.99
South Africa Highlights	£15.99
Sudan	£15.99
Tanzania, Northern	£14.99
Tanzania	£17.99
Uganda	£16.99
Zambia	£18.99
Zanzibar	£14.99
Zimbabwe	£15.99

The Americas and the Caribbean

Alaska	£15.99
Amazon Highlights	£15.99
Argentina	£16.99
Bahia	£14.99
Cayman Islands	£14.99
Chile Highlights	£15.99
Colombia	£17.99
Dominica	£15.99
Grenada, Carriacou & Petite Martinique	£15.99
Guyana	£15.99
Nova Scotia	£14.99
Panama	£14.99
Paraguay	£15.99
Turks & Caicos Islands	£14.99
Uruguay	£15.99
USA by Rail	£15.99
Venezuela	£16.99
Yukon	£14.99

British Isles

Britain from the Rails	£14.99
Bus-Pass Britain	£15.99
Eccentric Britain	£15.99
Eccentric Cambridge	£9.99
Eccentric London	£14.99
Eccentric Oxford	£9.99
Sacred Britain	£16.99
Slow: Cornwall	£14.99
Slow: Cotswolds	£14.99
Slow: Devon & Exmoor	£14.99
Slow: Dorset	£14.99
Slow: Norfolk & Suffolk	£14.99
Slow: Northumberland	£14.99
Slow: North Yorkshire	£14.99
Slow: Sussex & South Downs National Park	£14.99

Europe

Abruzzo	£14.99
Albania	£16.99
Armenia	£16.99
Azores	£14.99
Baltic Cities	£14.99
Belarus	£15.99
Bosnia & Herzegovina	£14.99
Bratislava	£9.99
Budapest	£9.99
Croatia	£13.99
Cross-Channel France: Nord-Pas de Calais	£13.99
Cyprus see North Cyprus	
Dresden	£7.99
Estonia	£14.99
Faroe Islands	£15.99
Flanders	£15.99
Georgia	£15.99
Greece: The Peloponnese	£14.99
Helsinki	£7.99
Hungary	£15.99
Iceland	£15.99
Kosovo	£15.99
Lapland	£15.99
Lille	£9.99
Lithuania	£14.99
Luxembourg	£14.99
Macedonia	£16.99
Malta & Gozo	£12.99
Montenegro	£14.99
North Cyprus	£13.99
Serbia	£15.99
Slovakia	£14.99
Slovenia	£13.99
Spitsbergen	£16.99
Switzerland Without a Car	£14.99
Transylvania	£14.99
Ukraine	£15.99

Middle East, Asia and Australasia

Bangladesh	£17.99
Borneo	£17.99
Eastern Turkey	£16.99
Iran	£15.99
Iraq: Then & Now	£15.99
Israel	£15.99
Jordan	£16.99
Kazakhstan	£16.99
Kyrgyzstan	£16.99
Lake Baikal	£15.99
Lebanon	£15.99
Maldives	£15.99
Mongolia	£16.99
North Korea	£14.99
Oman	£15.99
Palestine	£15.99
Shangri-La: A Travel Guide to the Himalayan Dream	£14.99
Sri Lanka	£15.99
Syria	£15.99
Taiwan	£16.99
Tibet	£17.99
Yemen	£14.99

Wildlife

Antarctica: A Guide to the Wildlife	£15.99
Arctic: A Guide to Coastal Wildlife	£16.99
Australian Wildlife	£14.99
Central & Eastern European Wildlife	£15.99
Chinese Wildlife	£16.99
East African Wildlife	£19.99
Galápagos Wildlife	£16.99
Madagascar Wildlife	£16.99
New Zealand Wildlife	£14.99
North Atlantic Wildlife	£16.99
Pantanal Wildlife	£16.99
Peruvian Wildlife	£15.99
Southern African Wildlife	£19.99
Sri Lankan Wildlife	£15.99

Pictorials and other guides

100 Alien Invaders	£16.99
100 Animals to See Before They Die	£16.99
100 Bizarre Animals	£16.99
Eccentric Australia	£12.99
Northern Lights	£6.99
Swimming with Dolphins, Tracking Gorillas	£15.99
Through the Northwest Passage	£17.99
Tips on Tipping	£6.99
Total Solar Eclipse 2012 & 2013	£6.99
Wildlife and Conservation Volunteering: The Complete Guide	£13.99
Your Child Abroad	£10.95

Travel literature

Fakirs, Feluccas and Femmes Fatales	£9.99
The Marsh Lions	£9.99
Two Year Mountain	£9.99
Up the Creek	£9.99

Index

Entries in **bold** indicate main entries; entries in *italics* indicate maps

327

INDEX OF ADVERTISERS